Adobe®

Photoshop® CS3
STUDIO TECHNIQUES

Ben Willmore

Adobe Photoshop CS3 Studio Techniques

Ben Willmore

Copyright © 2008 by Ben Willmore

This Adobe Press book is published by Peachpit Press.
For information on Adobe Press books, contact:

Peachpit Press
1249 Eighth Street
Berkeley, CA 94710
(510) 524-2178
Fax: (510) 524-2221
http://www.peachpit.com

To report errors, please send a note to errata@peachpit.com
Peachpit Press is a division of Pearson Education

For the latest on Adobe Press books, go to http://www.adobe.com/adobepress

Project Editor: Wendy Sharp
Contributing Editor: Regina Cleveland
Production Editor: Hilal Sala
Compositor: Danielle Foster
Indexer: Valerie Perry
Cover Design: Aren Howell
Cover Illustration: Regina Cleveland
Cover Images: ©2007 iStockphoto, www.istockphoto.com

Notice of Liability

The information in this book is distributed on an "As Is" basis, without warranty. While every precaution has been taken in the preparation of the book, neither the authors nor Peachpit Press shall have any liability to any person or entity with respect to any loss or damage caused or alleged to be caused directly or indirectly by the instructions contained in this book or by the computer software and hardware products described in it.

Trademarks

Throughout this book trademarked names are used. Rather than put a trademark symbol in every occurrence of a trademarked name, we state we are using the names only in an editorial fashion and to the benefit of the trademark owner, with no intention of infringement of the trademark. Photoshop, Illustrator, GoLive, ImageReady, Acrobat, Streamline, and After Effects are all trademarks of Adobe Systems, Inc.

ISBN: 0-321-51046-1

9 8 7 6 5 4 3 2 1

Printed and bound in the United States of America

Contents

About the Author

A senior engineer from NASA once said that this man gave the best technical seminar he ever attended. That same year a computer-phobic who had been struggling with Photoshop for years proclaimed that "He takes the Boogie Man out of Photoshop!" This seems to be **Ben Willmore's** special gift; he has an ability to connect with users of every level and mindset; whether it's first-timers taking their first sniff of Photoshop, or razor-sharp nerds and nerdettes who are on the fast track to technical illumination. The common echo that Ben leaves in his wake seems to be "Aha! I finally GET Photoshop!"

Known for revealing the simplicity that lies within Photoshop's complexity, Ben has personally taught over 60,000 Photoshop users on four continents. He is co-author (with Jack Davis) of another best-seller, *How to Wow: Photoshop for Photographers*, as well as *Up to Speed: Photoshop CS3*.

Ben speaks at publishing conferences and events worldwide, including Photoshop World, American Society of Media Photographers (ASMP), and Professional Photographers of America (PPA). He writes for numerous digital imaging and photography publications, including a monthly column for Photoshop User magazine. In 2004 he was inducted into the Photoshop Hall of Fame at Photoshop- World. His reputation as the "expert's expert" prompted NAPP's president, Scott Kelby, to say, "When we get stuck, we call Ben!" In 2006, Ben took his Photoshop adventures on the open road in a giant touring bus. His home/offfice-on-wheels has enabled him to rekindle his great passion for phtography and while many of us are hitting the snooze button, Ben is likely to be prowling around in the pre-dawn hours waiting for the perfect light. To see Bens' photos from the road, and to keep track of him while he is exploring America, visit www.WhereIsBen.com.

Much Obliged!

Even though my name appears on the cover of this book, as with all collaborative efforts, this would not have been possible without the help of the following people:

Regina Cleveland, who has helped me with this book through every version since 5.0; editing and writing into the wee hours of the morning, and now doing illustration work as well. Had she not been a part of this project, it would have been like piloting a ship across the ocean with part of its hull missing.

Wendy Sharp, our editor at Peachpit, who is the best mother a project could ever have, and can juggle so many details at once, we suspect that there's actually two of her.

Hilal Sala, our divine production coordinator, **Anne-Marie Walker**, our copy-editor, **Danielle Foster**, our compositor, and **Valerie Perry**, our indexer, for handling everything so gracefully, even when we turned everything in at the absolute last minute.

Dan Burkholder, who reviewed this edition with a fine eye for the latest info about all the technologies covered.

Chris Murphy for always being my wizard behind the curtain when it comes to color management issues.

Jay Nelson, who has helped me in more ways than I can imagine or remember. He's an amazing guy who always comes through in a pinch, and seems to be most happy whenever he's lending someone a hand.

Ben Long, author of *Complete Digital Photography* and *Getting Started with Camera Raw*, for the work he did in bringing this book to CS3 users.

Megan Ironside and all the good folks at iStockphoto, **Jerry Kennelly** (formerly of Stockbyte), and **Stephanie Robey** (formerly of PhotoSpin), whose generous contributions of stock imagery made it possible for us to produce this book, as well as include a bunch of great practice images on the CD at the back of the book.

Andy Katz, for keeping things lively with his maniacal laugh, and for his gorgeous imagery. (Congratulations, Andy and Ellen, for being featured in Sunset Magazine!)

My brother **Nik Willmore**, who was always at the ready with as much constructive criticism as I could handle, when others would simply say "Oh, that's nice."

Scott Kelby, **Kleber Stephenson**, **Dave Moser**, and the rest of the crazies at NAPP (National Association of Photoshop Professionals), who have made my life as a Photoshop hack more enjoyable than I thought possible.

To all the gifted artists who contributed images to this book. Your illuminating work transformed our bare pages into things of elegance, sparkle, and humor.

Howard Berman

Robert Bowen

Alicia Buelow

Tom Nick Cocotos

Conner Huff

Gary Isaacs

Andy Katz

Brian Kelsey

Nick Koudis

Emin Kuliyev

Bert Monroy

Michael Slack

Richard Tuschman

And finally, I thank all the people who have attended my seminars over the past decade. You've given me a limitless supply of inspiration and feedback and have allowed me to follow my passion for knowledge and understanding.

Foreword

Learning to use Adobe Photoshop is similar to learning to play an electric guitar—with a little instruction and a little practice, you can create some very pleasant art. Or, if you're really motivated, you can lock yourself in a closet with it for 12 years and emerge playing some amazing "licks." Most of us fall somewhere in between, and all of us have more to learn.

But the thing is, although few people are frightened by a guitar, many people find Photoshop intimidating. That's what is so great about Ben Willmore, the author of this book: He takes away your fear.

For the past decade, Ben has traveled across the United States, presenting his unique Photoshop seminar. Unique, because it focuses on real-world jobs done every day by Photoshop users, and unique because Ben explains concepts and techniques in a way that everyone in the room can understand. Ben's examples are based on his professional production experience, so everything he teaches helps you create images that successfully reproduce on paper or the web.

I attended his seminar and was especially impressed by his ability to avoid technical jargon and his uncanny knack for answering questions before they're asked. Ben is a rare teacher; even advanced users are satisfied, and rank beginners never feel lost. Like all great teachers, Ben uses metaphors, relating new ideas to concepts you're already comfortable with. In the pages of this book, you'll see Photoshop's most esoteric concepts clearly explained, while its major features are masterfully positioned into a framework of "How do I accomplish the task at hand?"

We each have different uses for Photoshop, and we each have different ways of learning. Fortunately for our increasingly overtaxed brains, less than half of Photoshop's features are used to accomplish most real-world tasks. And more fortunately for us, Ben Willmore has written this book.

Enjoy the time you share with Ben and Photoshop. I'm sure you'll find it a rare pleasure.

—Jay J. Nelson
Editor, *Design Tools Monthly*, www.design-tools.com

I

Introduction

Introduction

Ben Willmore
Founder: Digital Mastery

My mission is to help you graduate from "I'm just going through the motions," to "At last, I really understand Photoshop."

Why This Book?

I asked the same question when I set out on this project. I found myself at Barnes & Noble staring at a shelf full of Photoshop books, and I discovered that there were more special-effect "cookbooks" and technical tomes than I'd ever care to read. The problem was that none of the "cookbooks" gave enough detail to really let me feel like I understood the program (I just blindly followed the listed steps), and all of the technical books were deep into terms like rasters, vectors, and bit-depth settings. There was a void just begging to be filled and that is the primary reason that most people aren't truly comfortable with Photoshop. They either get the 1, 2, 3 steps (but no real understanding), or they get so many technical terms that it makes Photoshop impossible to grasp.

So how is this book different? My approach is to use the same language that you use in everyday life to explain everything from the simplest feature to the most advanced techniques. I acquired this approach as a result of teaching tens of thousands of people in hundreds of seminars and hands-on workshops. I'll still provide a fair share of step-by-step techniques, and we will delve into some rather advanced features, but through it all I'll use metaphors and stories that will make everything easy to understand and digest.

With that in mind, my mission is to help you graduate from "I'm just going through the motions" to "At last, I really understand Photoshop." Once you've made that leap, you will experience an incredible ripple effect. Your efficiency will skyrocket. Your costs will go down. Your creative genius will come out of the closet like gangbusters, and your clients (or boss) will be thrilled. But what's most important to me is that through learning how to master Photoshop, you'll find the passion and energy that come from knowing you're really good at something.

A New Voice in Studio Techniques

I've been writing this book since Photoshop 5.0 (almost a decade) and while it's been a rewarding experience, it's a mammoth undertaking and the time was right to bring someone on board to help with the updates. The CS3 revisions in this book were written by Ben Long, a fellow digital photography expert who knows his way around Photoshop and is an accomplished author in his own right.

Will I Understand It?

First and foremost, I hate technical mumbo jumbo! If words like raster, gamma, absolute colorimetric, bitmapped, algorithms, dither, and anti-aliasing drive you crazy, you better believe that they drive me even crazier. I see no reason that those terms can't be done away with and replaced by plain English. I'll do whatever it takes to communicate a concept to you, without relying on 10-syllable words or terms that sound like they came from the inside of an engineer's head.

Does It Start at My Level?

If you are generally comfortable with your computer, you should be able to fully comprehend the information, no matter how advanced the topic. I've made the assumption that you've either installed Photoshop or that you're using the *Photoshop User Guide* to figure out how to do that. And if you're an advanced user, don't worry. Just because this book is very understandable doesn't mean that we won't get into the real meat of Photoshop.

Mac or Windows?

From a functionality standpoint, Photoshop is pretty close to identical on Mac and Windows platforms. Anything you can do on one platform, you can do on the other. But those darn keyboards are different. You can put your worries aside, because *both* Mac and Windows keyboard commands are integrated right into the text. For screen shots, I had to picked one platform and run with it, and I went with Mac OS X for those.

What's on the CD?

To make it as easy as possible for you to follow along with my examples, I've provided a boatload of practice images for you to play with. You'll find these on the shiny disc that is hiding inside the back cover, in a folder called Practice Images. iStockphoto, Stockbyte, and PhotoSpin were kind enough to provide many of the images in this book and on the CD. If you like what you see, you can get more of their delicious imagery at their respective web sites, www.istock-photo. com, www.stockbyte.com, and www.photospin.com.

Photoshop is getting so robust (dare we say "fat!") that trying to pack everything onto the printed page has become pretty much impossible without bloating up the book to 20 pounds or more! Our solution was to put five chapters on the CD: Line Art Scanning, Channels, Shadows, Type & Background Effects, and Resolution Solutions. These chapters required no updating for CS3, which made them good candidates for the CD. Just because they're on the CD, doesn't make them less useful, just less weighty, so make sure to give them a look.

What's Missing?

There is now a hybrid version of Photoshop called Adobe Photoshop CS3 Extended. It has all the features of regular Photoshop, plus more. "More" includes a number of features designed for more technical users (engineers, scientists, medical professionals, architects, television/film folks, etc.). This book is intended for photographers and graphic designers, and because the extended features are beyond the scope of this book they will not be covered in any kind of detail.

Where's the New Stuff?

If you have a previous edition of this book or just want to jump right into the new features, this is the place to start. Here's a snapshot of the new features covered in this book.

Chapter 1 Tool and Palette Primer

Both Bridge and Photoshop's palette system changed dramatically in CS3. There is a new palette docking system and Bridge is now faster and smarter and comes with many improved interface changes, including a Photo Downloader.

Chapter 4 Optimizing Grayscale Images

The Brightness/Contrast adjustment tool has been completely rebuilt and is now surprisingly useful. There is also a new Black and White tool which makes converting your color images to black and white a breeze.

Chapter 5 Understanding Curves

The Curves dialog box got a radical makeover and is now one of the most useful tools in Photoshop.

Chapter 8 Using Camera Raw

Camera Raw has a significantly improved interface, a profusion of sophisticated new sliders and adjustments, including a Red Eye tool.

Chapter 14 Collage

CS3 gives us Smart Filters (which allow you to non-destructively apply filters to a layer or Smart Object), and the new Auto-Align and Auto-Blend layers command (which make creating panoramas easier than ever before).

Chapter 15 Retouching

The new Clone Source palette is home to a multitude of new features that make the Healing brush and Clone Stamp tools much more versatile.

Ready to Get Started?

So, enough blabbing, let's get on with your personal Photoshop "transformation." I'll make it as easy on you as I possibly can, but just remember the words of my favorite character, Miracle Max, from the movie *The Princess Bride*: "You rush a miracle man, you get rotten miracles."

PART I

Working Foundations

1

Tool and Palette Primer

Courtesy of Tom Nick Cocotos, cocotos.com

Out of clutter, find simplicity.

—Albert Einstein

Opening Photoshop for the first time and seeing all the tools and palettes competing for space on your screen can be a dizzying experience. You might find yourself thinking, "That's great, but they forgot to leave room in there for me to work!" Some of the more fortunate Photoshop users have a second monitor just to hold their palettes. The rest of us make do and find ways to keep our screens neat and tidy. You'll discover that finding places to put your tools and palettes is almost as important as knowing how to use them. This chapter is about effectively managing your workspace and getting acquainted with the oodles of gadgets and gizmos found in the tools and palettes.

Preparing Your Workspace

In previous versions of Photoshop, you had to do a lot of work to keep your monitor from being overwhelmed by palettes. Photoshop CS2 packed a huge number of palettes, and with CS3 Adobe has added even more. Fortunately, the way palettes work has changed in Photoshop, making it easier to hide and show palettes so that your screen is not filled with controls that you don't need. But a word of advice: No matter how many times you feel like nuking a palette when it's in your way, no matter how many times your screen turns into a blinding jumble of annoying little boxes, just remember that you can organize the clutter into an elegant arrangement in just a few seconds.

Palettes and Docks

To help you better control and manage your palettes, CS3 now provides palette docks, special interface elements that allow you to easily collapse and expand entire groups of palettes (**Figure 1.1**).

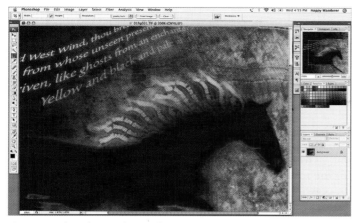

Figure 1.1 Photoshop's palettes take up a large portion of the screen. (©2007 Regina Cleveland)

By default, all palettes are docked. Those gray borders around the palettes are actually the docks, and they are permanently stuck to the sides of your screen. Clicking and dragging the gray boundaries does *not* allow you to move a palette dock (**Figure 1.2**), but it does allow you to expand it vertically or horizontally.

If you want to move a palette to a different part of the screen, you need to grab the title bar of the palette and drag it out of the dock (**Figure 1.3**).

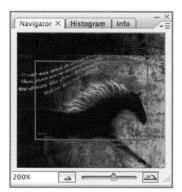

Figure 1.2 Palettes are now enclosed in docks—special constructs attached to the edge of your screen. You can't move a dock, but you can resize and collapse it.

Figure 1.3 You can move a palette out of the dock by clicking its title tab and dragging it. When a palette is undocked, you can place it wherever you want.

If pressing the Tab key doesn't toggle the visibility of your palettes, press Return or Enter on your keyboard and try again. If you happen to be working on a number in the options bar, instead of toggling the visibility of your palettes, the Tab key cycles through the different entry fields in the options bar. Pressing Return or Enter causes Photoshop to no longer focus on the numbers that appear in the options bar.

Figure 1.4 You can collapse a palette dock into a collection of buttons by clicking the bar at the top of the dock.

Figure 1.5 In a collapsed dock, you can click a palette icon to gain access to the collapsed palette's controls.

You can resize the width of any dock by clicking its edge and dragging. Within a dock, you can click the border between palettes to change the size of any palette. As you enlarge one palette, its neighbor will shrink.

Collapsing and Hiding Docks

The great advantage of palette docks is that you can easily collapse them to hide their contents. Simply click on the arrows in the upper-right corner of the dock to collapse it and show only the palette titles (**Figure 1.4**). This provides a simple way to free up some screen space.

An even better option is to completely hide the palette docks. If you press the Tab key, all docks disappear, but you can mouse to either edge of the screen, and the docks will reappear. This allows you to keep the palettes out of the way when you don't need them and serves to maximize screen space.

Shift-Tab also hides the palette docks but keeps the main Tools palette visible, letting you free up screen space but maintain access to the most common controls.

You can still select tools by keyboard shortcut when the docks are hidden, and the rollover dock behavior works in all Full Screen modes. (As in CS2, you can cycle between Full Screen modes by pressing F repeatedly, but now you can also select a Full Screen mode by choosing View > Screen Mode.)

When a dock is collapsed, you can still access any palette by clicking its icon in the collapsed dock (**Figure 1.5**).

To dismiss the palette, click its button again. Or if you prefer to have the palette recollapse automatically when you click in your document, choose Preferences > Interface and select Auto-Collapse Icon Palettes.

Collapsing Palettes

Within a dock, palettes are grouped together into collections. By default, the Navigator, Histogram, and Info palettes are at the top; Color, Swatches, and Styles are in the middle; and Layers, Channels, and Paths are at the bottom.

You can minimize any group of palettes so that only their title tabs show by clicking the – (minus) button at the top of each group; clicking the X will close the palette group (**Figure 1.6**). Clicking the – again will re-open the palette or you can re-open it by by selecting any palette in the group from the Window menu. Collapsing palettes frees up more space within the dock for other palettes.

Figure 1.6 At the top of each group of palettes in a dock is a – button. When you click it, the palette group minimizes so that only the title tabs show. Clicking the X removes the group from the dock.

Floating Palettes

While docks are a great way to ease your palette management pains, you can also drag palettes completely out of the dock. Click on the title bar of a palette within a dock and drag it somewhere else on the screen. The palette will be "torn" out of the dock and turn into a regular floating palette. Note that when you hide the docks using the Tab key, any floating palettes will also disappear.

The main advantage of creating floating palettes is that you can pull out the one or two palettes that you need, and then collapse the docks so that only your floating palettes are visible at full size.

Rearranging the Dock

As you've already seen, the palette dock is grouped into three sections. You can rearrange your palettes by dragging them from one place in the dock to another within the dock. You can also close a palette by clicking the X in the palette's title bar, and you can close one of the three groups of palettes in the dock by clicking the X in the upper-right corner of that group.

These controls allow you to easily refine the dock to contain only the palettes you need. For example, for a digital photo retouching workflow, you might eliminate the middle group (which by default contains Swatches, Styles, and Color) to afford more space for the Layers and Channels palettes.

Creating a New Palette Group

The main palette dock is divided into three sections, which each contain a collection of palettes. If you want to move a palette into its own section, drag it to a space between two existing sections. A blur bar appears to indicate that you'll create a new section.

NOTES

Unlike in CS2, holding down the Shift key when dragging a floating palette does not make it snap to the edges of the screen. With docks to contain your palettes, there's really no need for this behavior anymore.

History palette   Actions palette

Figure 1.7 By default, the second palette dock is collapsed. It sits next to the first dock.

The Second Palette Dock

If you're looking for the History and Actions palettes, which used to have their own palette group, they've been moved into a second palette dock, which sits right next to the main dock (**Figure 1.7**).

By default, the secondary dock is collapsed into icon mode. As with any other palette dock, you can expand the dock by clicking the bar at the top of the dock (**Figure 1.8**). You can also access individual palettes simply by clicking their icons.

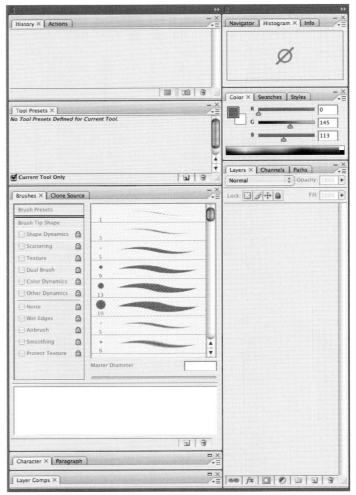

Figure 1.8 You can expand the second dock by clicking the double arrows in its title bar.

Photoshop CS2 stashed several palettes—by default, Brushes, Tool Presets, and Layer Comps—in a special well in the options bar that sat below the menu bar. Those palettes are now located in the second palette dock, along with the History and Actions, Character, Paragraph, and Layer Comps palettes. You'll also find a new Clone Source palette in the new palette dock. I discuss this feature in detail in Chapter 15, "Retouching."

The Tools Palette

Be default, Photoshop's Tools palette is now a single-column array of tools. This frees up a little bit of screen space, but if you prefer the traditional two-column Tools palette, just click the top of the Tools palette dock to toggle between the new single-column Tools palette and the old two-column one (**Figure 1.9**).

Another change from CS2: the Quick Mask control is now a single button that toggles between Quick Mask and Standard mode, and Adobe changed the Full Screen selector to a pop-up menu (**Figure 1.10**).

Workspace Presets

You might find that different palette layouts work better for different tasks. For instance, when retouching an image, you might find that you like to have the Brushes palette extend all the way down the right side of your screen and have most of the other palettes hidden away. Later, when you start to paint, you might prefer to have the Color, Swatches, and Brushes palettes along the right side of your screen. Well, that's when you'll want to save a workspace preset that will remember exactly where all your palettes were. To save a preset, choose Window > Workspace > Save Workspace, and give it a memorable name. To switch between saved workspaces, just choose the name of the desired workspace from the bottom of the Workspace (Window > Workspace) menu (**Figure 1.11**). This feature is great for people who have to share a computer with others, because each user can have a different arrangement of palettes saved as a workspace, so different users can quickly swap between those workspaces.

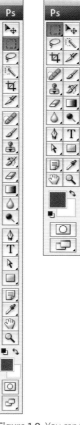

Figure 1.9 You can toggle the main Tools palette between a one-column and two-column layout by clicking its title bar.

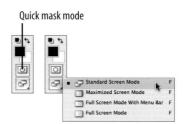

Quick mask mode

Figure 1.10 The Quick Mask toggle is now a single button at the bottom of the Tools palette, whereas the Full Screen selector is a pop-up menu.

NOTES

Photoshop CS3 no longer includes an ImageReady (the web graphics application that came bundled with Photoshop) launch button in the Tools palette, because ImageReady has been discontinued. Some of its functionality has been rolled into Photoshop, and the rest is now included in Adobe Fireworks.

By default, Photoshop provides a number of preconfigured workspaces. It's worth taking a look at these options to see if any of them are right for the way you like to work.

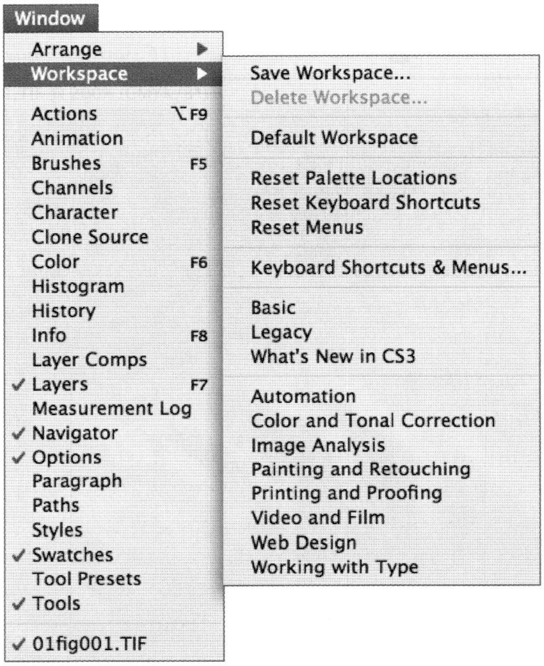

Figure 1.11 The Window > Workspace menu.

Working with Screen Modes

While palette docks make it simple to hide and show palettes, your image still doesn't use all of the screen space available. You can use the Screen Mode pop-up menu at the bottom of the Tools palette to easily solve this problem.

NOTES

Workspaces can also control which menu commands are visible, which keyboard commands are used to access them, and the color in which they are highlighted. We'll discuss how to make these changes later in this chapter.

Standard Screen Mode

By default, Photoshop uses Standard Screen Mode (**Figure 1.12**). You're probably used to working with this one. In this mode, the name of your document is at the top of the document window, and the scrollbars are on the side and bottom of that window.

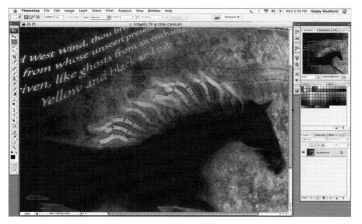

Figure 1.12 The first screen mode is Photoshop's default.

Maximized Screen Mode

If you click and hold on the Screen Mode pop-up menu, you'll see additional options for viewing your document. Maximized Screen mode expands the document window to the maximum possible size without overlapping any palettes or the option bar (**Figure 1.13**). As you hide and show the palette docks, your image will automatically expand and contract to fill the maximum space. Photoshop also places a gray background behind all windows and palettes to create a more color-neutral viewing environment.

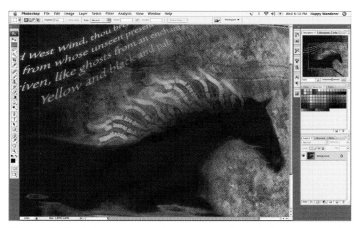

Figure 1.13 Maximized Screen mode gives you a window in front of a neutral gray background.

Full Screen Mode with Menu Bar

The third option, Full Screen Mode with Menu Bar, lets the image flow all the way across your screen and slip right under the palettes (**Figure 1.14**). If you choose this mode, the scrollbars will disappear, so you'll have to use the Hand tool to navigate around your document. But that's okay because you can hold down the spacebar at any time to temporarily use the Hand tool. If you zoom out of a document so that it doesn't take up the entire screen, Photoshop will fill the area around the image with gray.

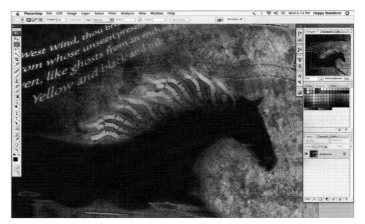

Figure 1.14 Full Screen Mode with Menu Bar allows you to use the entire screen.

Full Screen Mode

The fourth option, Full Screen Mode, is my favorite. In this mode, Photoshop even turns off the menu bar! Now your image can take over the entire screen (**Figure 1.15**). You can still use many of the menu commands, as long as you know their keyboard equivalents. If you zoom out while in this mode, Photoshop fills the area around your image with black. (You can right-click (Win), or Control-click (Mac) on the black to select a new color.) I use this mode whenever I show images to clients. If you don't let them know you're in Photoshop, they might think you are in a cheap little slide show program and won't ask you to make changes on the spot. However, you won't be able to fool anyone if all those palettes are still on your screen. Just press Tab and they'll all disappear (**Figure 1.16**). Don't worry: You can get them back just as quickly by pressing Tab again.

You can drag with the Hand tool to move your image within the gray or black surround that you get when viewing your image in the Full Screen modes.

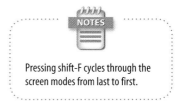

NOTES

Pressing shift-F cycles through the screen modes from last to first.

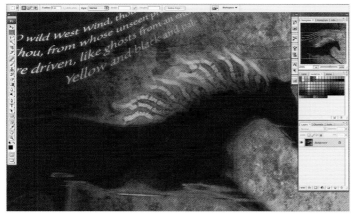

Figure 1.15 Full Screen Mode uses the full screen and hides the menu bar.

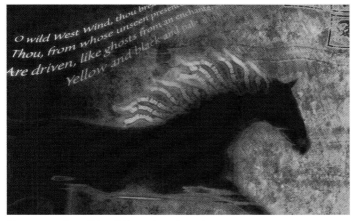

Figure 1.16 Press Tab to hide or show the palettes.

A Quick Tour of the Tools

The Tools palette provides you with 60 tools. Describing all of them in detail would take up a huge chunk of this chapter (which you probably don't have the patience for), so for now we'll take a look at the ones you absolutely can't live without. Don't worry about missing out on anything—as you work your way through the book, you'll get acquainted with the rest of the tools. In the meantime, I'll introduce you to some tool names so that when I mention one, you'll know what to look for (**Figures 1.17** and **1.18**).

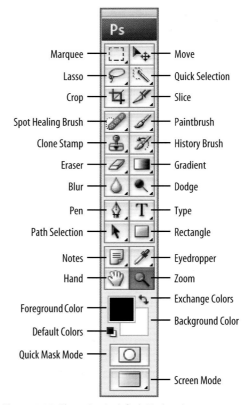

Figure 1.17 Photoshop's default Tools palette.

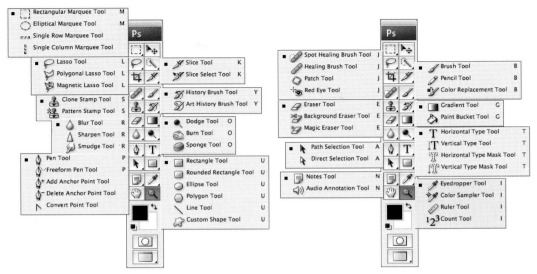

Figure 1.18 Photoshop's arsenal of tools.

The Options Bar

Most of the tools have settings associated with them. To access these settings, take a peek at the options bar that extends across the top of your screen.

You'll be able to change the various settings more quickly if you know exactly how to navigate the options bar. For example, each of the painting and retouching tools has a percentage setting near the right side of the bar. There are quite a few ways to change this number. One is to highlight the number and then type a new one. You can also click the number and then use the up arrow and down arrow keys on your keyboard. (Hold down the Shift key to change the number by increments of 10.) You can also click the arrow to the right of the number and drag across the slider that appears. And finally there's my favorite method; you can click on the name of the setting you'd like to change (such as Opacity) and then drag your mouse to the right or left to change the setting. All of these options will work with most numeric entries in a palette (not just the options bar), but there is a special method for changing the percentage setting for your painting tools. If none of the text fields in the options bar is active for editing, you can just type a number (not in a field, just type). If you type 1, you'll end up with 10%, 23 will give you 23%, 0 will give you 100%, and so forth (for smaller percentages, type 01 to get 1%, 02 to get 2%, and so on. You might need to type these numbers fairly quickly to get the whole number entered correctly.)

If there's more than one setting that lets you enter a number, press Return or Enter to highlight the first one, then Tab your way through the others. Once a number is highlighted, you can change it by pressing the up arrow and down arrow keys or by typing a new number.

If you've completely screwed up the settings that appear in the options bar, don't despair. You can Control-click (Mac) or right-click (Windows) on the Tool icon that appears on the far left of the options bar and choose Reset Tool to reset everything back to its default settings.

Navigating Your Document

Most of us struggle with monitors that are not large enough to view an entire document at 100% magnification (except, of course, the more privileged Photoshop users who have monitors that are practically as large as drive-in movie screens). To deal with this ever-present limitation, you must train yourself to be a quick and nimble navigator. Photoshop offers you a huge array of choices, and as usual, you'll need to weed through them to find your favorite method. In this section, we'll cover the palettes and tools you need to maximize the speed with which you get around your document.

The Navigator Palette

If you do a lot of detail work where you need to zoom in on your image as if you're wearing glasses as thick as Coke bottles, you should love the Navigator palette (**Figure 1.19**). The Navigator palette floats above your document and allows you to quickly move around and zoom in and out of your image. A little red box indicates which area of the image you're currently viewing. By dragging this box around the miniature image of your document that appears in the Navigator palette, you can change which

NOTES

If you don't like the color of the little red box or if there's so much red in your image that the box becomes difficult to see, you can change the box color by choosing Palette Options from the side menu of the palette.

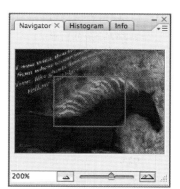
Figure 1.19 The Navigator palette.

area you're viewing in the main image window. You can also just click outside the red box and the box will center itself on your cursor.

There are a number of ways to zoom in on your document by using this palette. Use the Mountain icons to zoom in or out at preset increments (50%, 66.67%, 100%, 200%, and so on) or grab the slider between them to zoom to any level. You can change the number in the lower-left corner of the palette to zoom to an exact percentage. However, my favorite method is to drag across the image in the Navigator palette while holding down the Command key (Mac) or the Ctrl key (Windows) to zoom into a specific area.

Hand Tool

The Hand tool is definitely the most basic tool in Photoshop. By clicking and dragging with the Hand tool, you can scroll around the image. This tool is—excuse the pun—handy for scrolling around images that are too large to fit on your screen and for moving without the scrollbars. Because this tool is used so often, Adobe created a special way to get to it. While working with most of Photoshop's tools, if you press the spacebar, you will temporarily activate the Hand tool. When you release the spacebar, you'll be back to the tool you were using previously.

Zoom Tool

Whenever you click on your image by using the Zoom tool, you zoom in on the image to a preset level (just like the Mountain icons in the Navigator palette). I almost never use the tool in this way because it takes too long to get where I want to be. Instead, I usually click and drag across the area of my document that I want to enlarge, and Photoshop immediately zooms me into that specific area.

In addition to zooming in, you also have options for quickly zooming out. Double-click the Hand tool icon in the Tools palette to fit the entire image onscreen. You can also double-click the Zoom tool icon in the Tools palette to view your image at 100% magnification. (This will show you how large your image will appear when viewed in a Web browser or in any program designed for multimedia.

NOTES

When zooming in or out on your image via keyboard shortcuts in Standard Screen Mode, you can hold Option/Alt to control whether the window that contains your image will change size with your image. On a Mac, holding Option causes the window that contains your image to remain the same size as you zoom in or out of your image. In Windows, holding Alt does the opposite, causing the window to change size as you zoom. If you want to reverse the default behavior of these keyboard commands, choose Photoshop > Preferences > General and change the Zoom Resizes Windows setting.

Figure 1.20 Photoshop's Zoom In and Zoom Out icons.

To temporarily use the Zoom tool—that is, to use the Zoom tool without deselecting the active tool—hold down Command/ Ctrl-spacebar. Add the Option/ Alt key to this keyboard shortcut if you'd like to zoom out on your image.

It is not an indication of how large it will be when printed.) Option-clicking (Macintosh) or Alt-clicking (Windows) with the Zoom tool zooms you out at preset levels. Clicking on the Zoom Out icon in the options bar (**Figure 1.20**) allows you to zoom out without having to hold a key on your keyboard. When the Zoom Out icon is chosen, holding down Option (Mac) or Alt (Windows) will cause you to zoom in on the image.

View Menu

If you're going to be doing a bunch of detail work in which you need to zoom in really close on your image, you might want to create two views of the same document (**Figures 1.21** and **1.22**). You can then have one of the views at 100% magnification to give you an overall view of your image, and you can set the second one to 500% magnification, for instance, to see all the fine details. To create a second view, choose Window > Arrange > New Window. This creates a second window that looks like a separate document, but it's really just another view of the same document. You can make your edits in either window, and both of them will show you the result of your manipulations. Use the Tile commands (Window > Arrange > Tile) to automatically resize and tile the windows across your screen.

Figure 1.21 100% magnification. (© 2007 PhotoSpin, www.photospin.com)

Figure 1.22 500% magnification.

From the View menu, you can also select from the Zoom In, Zoom Out, Fit On Screen, and Actual Pixels options. As you'll probably notice, each of these actions can also be accomplished by using the Zoom and Hand tools. The reason they're also listed under the View menu is to allow you to quickly use them with keyboard commands. Here are the View menu options:

▶ **Zoom In/Zoom Out:** Same as clicking with the Zoom tool. Uses the easy-to-remember keyboard shortcut Command/Ctrl -+ to zoom in and Command/Ctrl — to zoom out. Those are plus signs and minus signs, in case that's not completely clear.

▶ **Fit On Screen:** Same as double-clicking the Hand tool. Uses the shortcut Command/Ctrl-0. That's a zero, not the letter O.

▶ **Actual Pixels:** Same as double-clicking the Zoom tool. Uses the shortcut Option-Command-0 (Mac) or Alt-Ctrl-0 (Windows). Again, that's a zero, not the letter O.

▶ **Print Size:** Allows you to preview how large or small your image will appear when it's printed.

> **NOTES**
>
> The Print Size option rarely reflects how large your image will print. To see if it's accurate, choose View > Show Rulers, then double-click on the ruler and set the measurement system to inches. Now create a new document that is one inch wide with a resolution of 100 pixels per inch, choose View > Print Size, and hold a physical ruler up to your screen to see if the document is actually one inch onscreen. If the document doesn't match the physical ruler, choose Window > Navigator, adjust the slider until the document is actually one inch onscreen and then note the percentage that appears in the lower left of the palette. Then double-click on the ruler that surrounds your image and set the Screen Resolution setting to the number you saw in the corner of the Navigator palette. Now choose Print Size to see if it's accurate.

Just when you thought there couldn't possibly be any more ways to zoom in and out of your document, Adobe threw in one more method for good measure. You can change the percentage that appears in the lower-left corner of your document window (CS2 and CS3) or at the bottom of the main Photoshop window when the status bar is visible (Windows CS); just drag across it and enter a new number.

There are indeed many ways to zoom around in Photoshop. Now all you have to do is test out all the options, decide which one you prefer, and ignore the rest.

Picking Colors

My father's Webster's dictionary—a 1940 model that's over half a foot thick—devoted four entire pages to describing one word: *color*. These pages are filled with lush descriptions of hue, tint, shade, saturation, vividness, brilliance, and much, much more. It's no wonder that choosing colors can be such a formidable task. Do you want Cobalt Blue or Persian Blue?

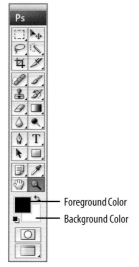

Foreground Color
Background Color

Figure 1.23 Foreground and background colors.

All painting tools use the current foreground color when you're painting on the image. So before you begin painting, make sure the active foreground color is the one you want.

Nile Green or Emerald? Carmine or Vermilion? Fortunately, Photoshop has done an excellent job of providing the tools you need to find the colors you want. Of course, each tool has advantages and disadvantages. You just have to play around with them and decide which one you prefer.

Foreground and Background Colors

The two square overlapping boxes that appear toward the bottom of your Tools palette are the foreground and background colors (**Figure 1.23**). The top box is the foreground color; it determines which color will be used when you use any of the painting tools. To change the foreground color, click it once. (This brings up a standard Color Picker.) The bottom box is the background color; it's used when you're erasing the background image or when you increase the size of your document by using Image > Canvas Size. When you use the Gradient tool with default settings, your gradient will start with the foreground color and end with the background color. You can swap the foreground and background colors by clicking the small curved arrows next to them in the Tools palette (or pressing the X key on your keyboard). You can also reset the colors to their default settings (black/white) by clicking the small squares in the lower-left corner of that same area. (Pressing D does the same thing.)

Color Picker Dialog Box

The Color Picker dialog box is available in many areas of Photoshop. The easiest way to get to it is to click your foreground or background color. There are many choices in this dialog box because there are many different ways to define a color. In this section, we'll cover all the various ways you can choose a color. I'll start off by showing you how to preview the color you're selecting.

Previewing a Color

While you're choosing a color, you can glance at the two color swatches to the right of the vertical gradient to compare the color you've chosen (the top swatch) to the color you had previously (the bottom swatch).

Be sure to watch for the out-of-gamut warning, which is indicated by a small triangle that appears next to these color swatches (**Figure 1.24**). This triangle warns you that the color you have chosen is not reproducible in CMYK mode, which means that it cannot be printed without shifting to a slightly different color. Fortunately, Photoshop provides you with a preview of what the color would have to shift to in order to be printable. You can find this preview in the small color swatch that appears directly below the triangle icon, and you can select this printable color by clicking the color swatch. Or, you can have Photoshop show you what all the colors would look like when printed by choosing View > Proof Colors while the Color Picker dialog box is open. That will change the look of every color that appears in the picker, but you will still have to click that little triangle symbol, because that's just a preview—it doesn't actually change the colors you're choosing.

Choosing Web-safe Colors

A set of special colors, known as Web-safe colors, are used for large areas of solid color on a Web site. By using a Web-safe color, you will prevent those areas from becoming dithered when viewed on a low-end computer (that is, simulated by using a pattern of two solid colors; for example, adding a pattern of red dots to a yellow area to create orange). So, if you are choosing a color that will be used in a large area on a Web page, look for the Color Cube symbol (Figure 1.24). Web-safe colors are also known as colors that are within the color cube—that's why Adobe used a cube symbol for this feature. When you click the cube symbol, the color you have chosen will shift a little to become a Web-safe color.

Selecting with the Color Field

Usually, the simplest method for choosing a color is to eyeball it. In the Color Picker dialog box, you can click in the vertical gradient to select the general color you want to use. Then click and drag around the large square area at the left to choose a shade of that color.

Figure 1.24 The warning triangle indicates a color that is not reproducible in CMYK mode. The cube symbol indicates that a color is not a Web-safe color and might appear dithered in a Web browser.

NOTES

CMYK colors are meant to be printed (which involves ink), whereas RGB colors (which involve light) are meant for multimedia. Due to impurities in CMYK inks, you can't accurately reproduce every color you see on your screen.

The Proof Colors command is accurate only when you have the proper settings specified in the Proof Setup menu (View > Proof Setup). The default setting indicates what your image will look like when converted to CMYK mode.

WARNING

If your method for picking white is to drag to the upper-left corner of the color field, be sure to drag beyond the edge of the square; otherwise, you might not end up with a true white. Instead, you'll get a muddy-looking white or a light shade of gray.

Selecting by Hue, Saturation, and Brightness

You can also change what appears in the vertical gradient by clicking any of the radio buttons on the right side of the dialog box (**Figures 1.25** to **1.27**). In this dialog box, H = Hue, S = Saturation, and B = Brightness. You can use the numbers at the right of the dialog box to describe the color you've chosen. (This can be a big help when you're describing a color to someone on the phone.) If you know the exact color you need, just type its exact numbers into that area.

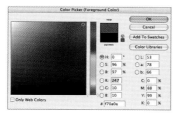

Figure 1.25 Hue.

Figure 1.26 Saturation.

Figure 1.27 Brightness.

Figure 1.28 The Color Libraries picker.

Selecting from a Color Library

If you want to pick your colors from a color library (PAN-TONE, TruMatch, and so on), click the Color Libraries button (Custom button in CS). This brings up the Color Libraries dialog box (**Figure 1.28**). Choose the color library you want to use from the pop-up menu at the top of the dialog box, then scroll through the list to find the color you desire. You can also type in numbers to select a specific color (I know, there isn't the usual text field to enter them in, but just start typing), but make sure you type really fast. I'm not sure why it works this way, but this part of Photoshop gets impatient with slow typists. For example, if you slowly type the number 356, Photoshop might jump to a color number starting with 3 and then go to one that starts with 5. This is sort of annoying, but it shouldn't pose a problem as long as you type the number quickly. (You can purchase various color library swatch books at an art supply store.)

WARNING

Although the Color Libraries are great for users printing with CMYK inks, it's not so hot for those using true spot colors (metallic, fluorescent, and other colors that cannot be reproduced using CMYK inks). If you're going to be using true spot colors, see Bonus Chapter, "Channels" on the CD.

Color Palette

You can think of the Color palette as a simplified version of the Color Picker dialog box. Just as with the Color Picker, you can pick colors by typing in numbers. However, you first need to choose the type of numbers you want to use from the side menu (**Figure 1.29**).

Two special options that are not available in the Color Picker dialog box can only be used in the Color palette. Web Color Sliders allow you to choose colors that are made from red, green, and blue light, but they will also force the sliders to snap to the tick marks that appear along the slider bars. Those tick marks indicate Web-safe colors, and they make this choice especially useful for creating Web graphics (**Figure 1.30**). You can turn on the Only Web Colors check box in the Color Picker dialog box if you'd like to make sure that you only select Web-safe colors. The second option that's only available in this palette is the Grayscale Slider. It's the quickest way to choose shades of gray (the Color Picker dialog box doesn't offer that option).

You can also pick colors by clicking the color bar at the bottom of the palette. (Use Option-click on the Macintosh or Alt-click in Windows to change your background color.) You can change the appearance of the color bar by choosing a color-range option near the bottom of the side menu of the palette (**Figure 1.31**).

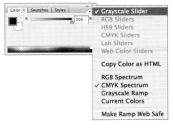

Figure 1.29 Choosing the slider type from the palette's menu.

Figure 1.30 When you choose Web Color Sliders, the sliders will snap to the tick marks on the slider bars that indicate where Web-safe colors are located.

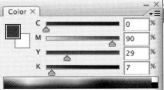

Figure 1.31 Changing the color bar's setting.

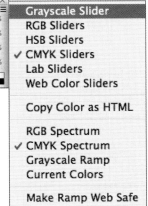

Here are the options:

▶ **RGB Spectrum:** Displays all the colors that are usable in RGB mode. Use this setting for multimedia and the Web.

▶ **CMYK Spectrum:** Shows all the colors that are usable in CMYK mode. Use this setting for images that will be reproduced on a printing press.

▶ **Grayscale Ramp:** Shows shades of gray from black to white. Use this setting any time you need shades of gray that do not contain a hint of color (also known as neutral grays).

▶ **Current Colors:** Displays a gradient using your foreground and background colors.

▶ **Make Ramp Web Safe:** Shows only the colors that are Web-safe from the previous choices.

Eyedropper Tool

In addition to using the Color Picker and Color palette to select colors, you can use the Eyedropper tool. One advantage to the Eyedropper is that you can grab colors from any open Photoshop file. After selecting the Eyedropper, you can click any part of your image and bingo!—you've got a new foreground color. You can also Option-click (Mac) or Alt-click (Windows) to change your background color. You don't have to click within the document you're currently editing; you can click any open image.

You can also change the Sample Size setting in the options bar to choose how it looks at, or samples, the area you click (**Figures 1.32** to **1.35**). Here are your options:

▶ **Point Sample:** Picks up the exact color of the pixel you click.

▶ **Averages:** The rest of the options average a square area of the given dimensions (3 x 3, 5x5, 11 x 11, 31 x 31, 51 x 51, and 101 x 101).

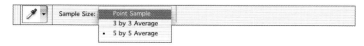

Figure 1.32 The Sample Size option determines the area the Eyedropper tool will average when you're choosing a color.

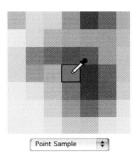

Figure 1.33 Point Sample.

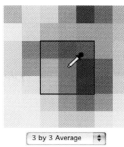

Figure 1.34 3 by 3 Average.

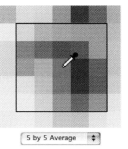

Figure 1.35 5 by 5 Average.

In many cases, you'll find it helpful to use one of the Average settings. They prevent you from accidentally picking up an odd-colored speck in the area from which you're grabbing, thereby ensuring that you don't select a color that isn't representative of the area you're choosing.

Swatches Palette

The Swatches palette is designed to store colors that you can use again and again. You can choose how you'd like to view the swatches by choosing either Small Thumbnail (**Figure 1.36**) or Small List (**Figure 1.37**) from the side menu of the Swatches palette. To paint with one of the colors stored in the Swatches palette, move your cursor over a swatch and click the mouse button. Your foreground color will change to the color you clicked. To change your background color, hold Command/Ctrl while clicking any swatch.

NOTES

With Photoshop's Eyedropper tool, you can click within a document and then drag to any area of your screen to choose a color. That means you can pick up a color from the menu bar or any other area of your screen, not just from within Photoshop but anything you can see on your monitor. I use this all the time to pick colors from my Web browser.

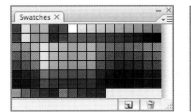

Figure 1.36 The Swatches palette using Small Thumbnail view.

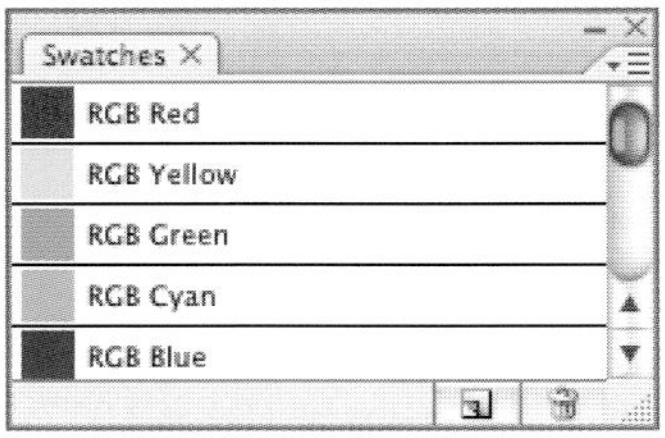

Figure 1.37 The Swatches palette using Small List view.

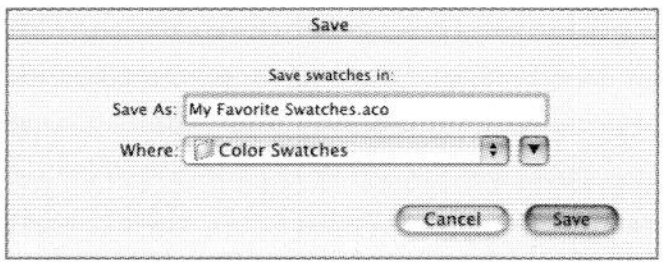

Figure 1.38 The dialog box for saving swatches.

Figure 1.39 Preset swatch files are listed at the bottom of the menu.

Figure 1.40 The Replace Swatches dialog box.

To store your current foreground color in this palette, just click in the open space below the swatches. Photoshop prompts you to name the color and then adds that color to the bottom of the palette. If there is no open space, resize the palette by dragging its lower-right corner. You can also click the New Swatch icon (it looks like a sheet of paper with the corner turned up) at the bottom of the Swatches palette to add a new swatch without being asked for a name. (Hold Option on the Macintosh or Alt in Windows to be prompted for a name.)

You can also remove a color from the Swatches palette by Option-clicking (Mac) or Alt-clicking (Windows) on the swatch. To reset the swatches to their default settings, choose Reset Swatches from the side menu of the palette.

If you'd like to change the order of the swatches, choose Edit > Preset Manager. Then choose Swatches from the pop-up menu at the top of the dialog box and click and drag to move the swatches around.

After you've stored the colors you want, you can choose Save Swatches from the Swatches palette's side menu. This brings up a standard Save dialog box to allow you to assign a name to your personal set of swatches (**Figure 1.38**). After saving a set of swatches, you can reload them again at any time by choosing Replace Swatches from the side menu.

Photoshop comes with a bunch of preset swatch files you can load into the Swatches palette. These files are stored in the Color Swatches folder in your Presets folder, which resides in your Photoshop application folder. If you save your swatches file into this folder, it will show up along with other preset swatch files at the bottom of the side menu in the Swatches palette (**Figure 1.39**). When you choose one of those presets, Photoshop prompts you with a dialog box that has three options (**Figure 1.40**). Append will add the swatches you are loading to the bottom of the swatches that are already there; OK will replace the current swatches with what you are loading; and Cancel will abort loading the swatches. If you'd like to avoid this dialog box altogether, you can hold the Option key (Mac) or Alt key (Windows) when you choose one of the presets from the side menu, and Photoshop will replace the swatches automatically.

Info Palette

The Info palette is a great resource for showing you color values, measurements, and other information that can be surprisingly useful if you know what to do with it. Although you can't actually choose a color by using the Info palette, you'll find it helpful for measuring the colors that already reside in your document. The top part of the Info palette measures the color that appears below your cursor.

You can change the measurement method used by the Info palette by clicking the tiny Eyedropper icons within the palette (**Figure 1.41**). RGB is usually used for desktop printing and multimedia purposes, and CMYK is usually reserved for images that will be printed on a printing press. Total Ink adds the C, M, Y, and K numbers to indicate how much ink coverage will be used to reproduce the area under your cursor.

Most images opened in Photoshop contain 256 shades of gray or 256 shades each of red, green, and blue (also known as 8-bits per channel). Many photographers are starting to use 16-bit images, which can contain up to 32,768 shades of gray or shades of red, green, and blue. If you're working on a 16-bit file, you can see 16-bit numbers (0–32,768) instead of the standard 8-bit numbers (0–255) in the Info palette. Do this by clicking on the tiny Eyedropper icon in the Info palette and choosing 16-bit (in CS, choose Palette Options from the side menu of the Info palette and turn on the Show 16-bit Values check box.) I don't find this to be all that useful, but you're welcome to try it if you're a bona fide numbers geek.

You can set up the Info palette to keep track of different areas of your image, so you can see what's happening when you make adjustments. You can do this by clicking your image using the Color Sampler tool (hidden under the Eyedropper tool). This deposits a little crosshair on the area you click and also adds another readout to the Info palette (**Figure 1.42**). You can add up to four of these "samples" to your image. Then when you are adjusting the image using any of the choices under the Adjustments menu (Image > Adjustments), the Info palette readouts will change into

NOTES

Photoshop CS3's Info palette can display extra information that is usually only found in the status bar that appears at the bottom edge of each document. To control which status readouts are visible, choose Palette Options from the side menu of the Info palette.

Figure 1.41 Changing how the Info palette measures color.

Figure 1.42 Color samples and Info palette readouts. (©2007 Stockbyte, www.stockbyte.com)

Figure 1.43 Info palette readouts while an adjustment dialog box is in use.

two readouts for each Color Sampler (**Figure 1.43**). The left number indicates what the color was before the adjustment; the right number indicates what the color will be after the adjustment. You can even add a color sample to your image while an adjustment dialog box is active by holding the Shift key and clicking on the image. (The Color Sampler tool does not need to be active to do this.)

To remove a sample, hold the Option key (Mac) or Alt key (Windows) and click on the sample, or just drag it off the screen. Or, if you'd like to remove all the color samples, click the Clear button in the options bar. (It's available only when the Color Sampler tool is active.) Occasionally, you may want to hide the sample points when you're working on your image; you can do this by choosing Color Samples from the side menu of the Info palette. We'll use these samples when you read about color correction in Chapter 7, "Color Correction."

Basic Editing Tools

You'll find, just as you've seen with the majority of Photoshop's features, that there's more than meets the eye with the editing tools. For now, we'll cover their most obvious applications, but as you make your way through the rest of the book, keep in mind that these deceivingly simple tools can perform some remarkable tricks. For example, the painting and gradient tools can be used for more than just painting and adding color—they can also be used for making intricate selections, compositing photos, and creating cool fadeouts. You can use them to create an infinite number of dazzling effects.

Painting

In Photoshop, you have two choices for painting: the Paintbrush (Brush) tool or the Pencil tool. The only difference between the two is that the Paintbrush always delivers a soft-edged stroke—even a seemingly hard-edged brush will produce a slightly blended edge—whereas the Pencil tool produces a truly crisp edge (**Figures 1.44** and **1.45**).

Figure 1.44 Paint stroke created with the Paintbrush tool.

Figure 1.45 Paint stroke created with the Pencil tool.

You can change the softness of the Paintbrush tool by choosing different brushes from the Brushes palette. When the Pencil tool is active, all brushes will have a hard edge.

Opacity

If you lower the Opacity setting of the Paintbrush tool, you can paint across the image without worrying about overlapping your paint strokes (**Figure 1.46**). As long as you don't release the mouse button, the areas that you paint over multiple times won't get a second coat of paint.

If you're not familiar with the concept of opaque versus transparent, take a look at **Figures 1.47** and **1.48**.

NOTES

To quickly change the Opacity setting of a painting tool, use the number keys on your keyboard (1 = 10%, 3 = 30%, 65 = 65%, and so on).

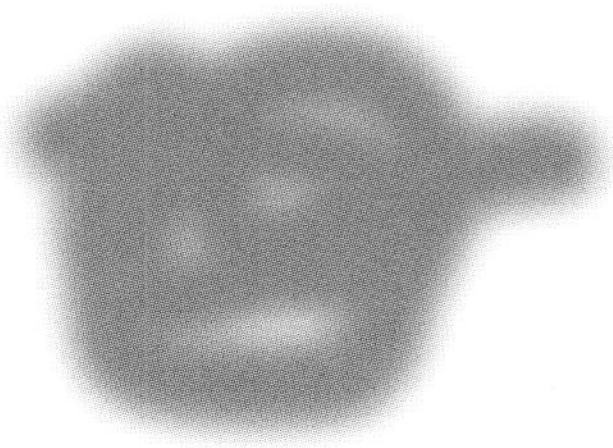

Figure 1.46 A continuous stroke using the Paintbrush tool.

Figure 1.47 Opaque (left) versus transparent (right). (©2007 Stockbyte, www.stockbyte.com)

Figure 1.48 Varying opacity. (©2007 Stockbyte, www.stockbyte.com)

Flow

The Flow setting determines how much of the opacity you've specified will show up on your first paint stroke. When the Flow setting is set to 20%, you'll get 20% of the opacity you've specified in the options bar each time you paint across an area (**Figure 1.49**). Each time you pass over the same area with that setting, you'll build up another coat of 20% of the opacity you've chosen. No matter how many times you paint across an area, you will not be able to achieve an opacity higher than what's specified in the options bar, unless you release the mouse button. If you set the Flow setting to 100%, it will effectively turn off this feature, so that you'll get the full opacity that you've requested each time you paint. The Pencil tool doesn't use the Flow setting, and therefore delivers the desired opacity setting in a single pass.

Figure 1.49 Paint stroke using the Flow setting.

Now let's take a look at the options available to you when using the painting tools.

Blending Mode

The Mode pop-up menu in the options bar is known as the Blending Mode menu. We'll be covering all the options under this menu in Chapter 12, "Enhancement," so right now I'll just explain a few basic uses (**Figures 1.50** to **1.52**). If you would like to change the basic color of an object, you can set the blending mode to Hue. If you're using a soft-edged brush, you can set the blending mode to Dissolve to force the edges of your brush to dissolve out. That's all for now; we'll explore the rest of this menu in Chapter 12, "Enhancement."

Figure 1.50 Normal.
(©2007 Stockbyte, www.stockbyte.com)

Figure 1.51 Hue.

Figure 1.52 Dissolve.

Eraser Tool

If you use the Eraser tool while you're working on a background image (we'll talk about the background in Chapter 3, "Layers Primer"), it acts like one of the normal painting tools—except that it paints with the background color instead of the foreground color. It even lets you choose which type of painting tool it should mimic by allowing you to select an option from the pop-up menu in the options bar (**Figure 1.54**).

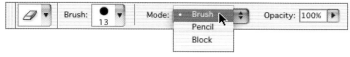

Figure 1.54 Choosing Eraser tool behavior.

However, when you use the Eraser tool on a nonbackground layer, it really erases the area. If you lower the Opacity setting, it makes an area appear partially transparent. Bear in mind that the same does not apply to the background image. You cannot "erase" the background.

Brush Presets Palette

Let's look at how Photoshop deals with brushes in general, and then we'll start to explore how to create your own custom brushes. When a painting or retouching tool is active, you'll see the currently active brush shown in the options bar. If you click on that preview, the Brush Presets drop-down

NOTES

To draw straight lines, Shift-click in multiple areas of your image; Photoshop will connect the dots (**Figure 1.53**). You can also hold down the Shift key when painting to constrain the angle to a 45-degree increment.

Figure 1.53 Shift-click to create straight lines.

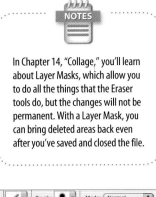

In Chapter 14, "Collage," you'll learn about Layer Masks, which allow you to do all the things that the Eraser tools do, but the changes will not be permanent. With a Layer Mask, you can bring deleted areas back even after you've saved and closed the file.

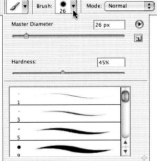

Figure 1.55 The Brush Presets palette.

Use the bracket keys ([ ]) to change the diameter of your brush, or hold Shift and use the brackets to change the hardness of your brush. If the Brush Presets palette is open, these keyboard shortcuts won't work.

palette will appear (**Figure 1.55**). All of the painting and retouching tools available in the Tools palette use the Brush Presets palette to determine their brush size. Each tool remembers the last brush size you used with it and will return to that same size the next time you select the tool. In other words, the brush size you choose doesn't stay consistent when you switch among the tools.

You can change the active brush by clicking once on any brush that's available in the Brush Presets palette. (Double-clicking will choose a brush and then hide the Brush Presets palette.) Each brush has a number below it, which indicates how many pixels wide the brush is.

For even more fun, keep an eye on the brush in the options bar and then press the < or > key on your keyboard (without holding Shift). You can use these keys to cycle through all the brushes shown in the Brush Presets palette.

Brushes Palette

Photoshop's Brushes palette has two versions; each is found in a different location in Photoshop. The one we've been talking about so far is the Brush Presets palette. When using that version (the "lite" edition), all you can do is switch between premade brushes. If you'd rather change the characteristics of a brush, you'll need to abandon that palette and work with the full Brushes palette by choosing Window > Brushes (**Figure 1.56**). In this version of the palette (the "I'll take that with everything" edition), you can still access the Brush Presets by clicking on the words *brush presets* in the upper left of the palette. But you can do a heck of a lot more if you click on the choices that appear across the left side of the palette. When you do that, be sure to click on the *words* that describe the feature you'd like to change, not the checkboxes. Clicking on the checkboxes just lets you turn a feature on or off, and you won't see the options for that feature within the palette. To do that, you must click on the *name*, not the checkbox. By clicking on each of those choices, you'll find that there are well over 30 settings that you can apply to a brush. When I first saw them, it felt like I was going to need to go back to college to learn how to use everything. But then I looked a little closer and noticed that the settings aren't that hard to deal with, and if you combine a bunch of the features, you can create some pretty awesome brush effects.

You'll need to think about one thing before you start experimenting with all of Photoshop's brush settings. You can work with two types of brushes: round brushes and sampled brushes. A round brush is just what you'd expect—it's round. The second type of brush you can use is based on a picture (known as a sampled brush) (**Figure 1.57**).

To work with a round brush, you must first select a round brush from the Brush Presets. To work with a sampled brush, either choose a nonround brush from the presets or select an area within any image that you'd like to convert into a brush from the active document and then choose Edit > Define Brush. Once you've chosen the type of brush you'd like to work with, you're ready to start experimenting with all the brush settings.

Brush Tip Shape

When you click on the Brush Tip Shape in the upper left of the palette, the central portion of the palette updates to show you the settings that determine the overall look of your brush. A paint stroke is made from multiple paint daubs; that is, Photoshop fills the shape of your brush with the current foreground color, moves over a distance, and then fills that shape again (**Figure 1.58**). The Brush Tip Shape settings determine what the paint daubs will look like and how much space there will be between them.

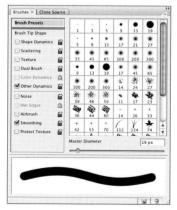

Figure 1.56 The full Brushes palette.

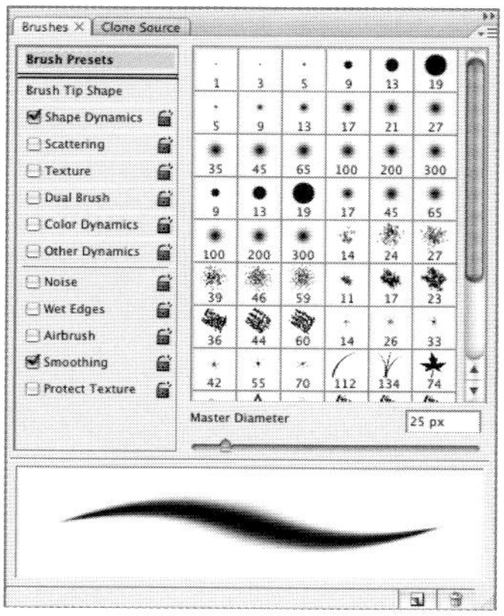

Figure 1.57 At the top of these brush palettes you'll find round brushes; these are followed by sampled brushes.

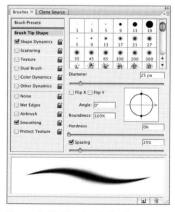

Figure 1.58 The Brush Tip Shape options.

Figure 1.59 Diameter from top to b ottom: 100 pixels, 50 pixels, 20 pixels.

Figure 1.60 Left: Sampled brush at actual size. Right: Sampled brush scaled to be much larger than sampled size.

▶ **Diameter:** Determines the size of the brush (**Figure 1.59**). You can use a setting between 1 and 2,500 pixels. The Use Sample Size button appears anytime you're using a sampled brush that has been made larger or smaller than its original size. When you click the Use Sample Size button, Photoshop resets the Diameter setting to the original size of the sampled brush, thereby delivering the highest quality. When you reduce the size of a sampled brush, it won't degrade the quality of the image much at all. Increasing the size of a sampled brush causes the brush shape to have a less crisp appearance (**Figure 1.60**).

▶ **Hardness:** Determines how quickly the edge fades out. Default brushes are either 100% hard or 0% hard (**Figure 1.61**). This option is only available with round brushes.

▶ **Roundness:** Compresses a brush in one dimension. When using round brushes, changes to the Roundness setting result in an oval-shaped brush (**Figure 1.62**). When working with a sampled brush, this setting compresses the brush vertically (**Figure 1.63**).

▶ **Angle:** Rotates oval and sampled brushes but has no effect on round ones (**Figure 1.64**).

▶ **Spacing:** Determines the distance between the paint daubs that make up a brush stroke (**Figure 1.65**). Turning Spacing off causes Photoshop to adjust the Spacing setting based on how fast you move the mouse while painting (**Figure 1.66**).

Figure 1.61 Hardness from top to bottom: 100, 50, 20.

Figure 1.62 Roundness from top to bottom: 100, 50, 20.

Figure 1.63 Roundness from top to bottom: 100, 50, 20.

Figure 1.64 Angle from top to bottom: 0, 45, 90.

Figure 1.65 Spacing settings from top to bottom: 25%, 75%, 120%.

Figure 1.66 Turning Spacing off varies the Spacing setting based on the speed at which you paint.

The rest of the choices available on the left side of the Brushes palette allow you to change how the brush tip shape is applied to your image. You'll find that three basic concepts are used over and over with the brush options. Let's first take a look at these three concepts, so you won't have to listen to me repeat myself when we get to the actual settings involved. Jitter settings allow a particular option (like size or opacity) to vary across a paint stroke (**Figure 1.67**). The higher the Jitter setting, the more the setting will vary. You will also find a setting called Minimum, which determines the range the Jitter setting can use to vary a setting (**Figure 1.68**). If the Minimum option is set to 10%, the Jitter control will be able to vary a setting between the amount specified in the Brush Tip Shape panel or options bar and the amount you specified in the Minimum setting (10% means 10% of the setting that's specified in the Brush Tip Shape panel or options bar.) The third setting you'll find is called Control, and it determines when Photoshop should vary a setting using Jitter. When it's set to Off, the Jitter command will apply all the time. Fade causes the variance to slowly fade out in a particular number of brush applications. If you set Fade to 20, Photoshop starts with whatever setting is specified in the Brush Tip Shape area or options bar, and then lowers the setting over the next 20 paint daubs, where it will end up with the amount specified in the Minimum setting (**Figure 1.69**). Setting the Control pop-up menu to any of the bottom three choices (Pen Pressure, Pen Tilt, and Stylus Wheel) causes the variance to be determined by the input of a graphics tablet.

NOTES

Instead of entering values for the Angle and Roundness settings, you can modify the diagram on the middle-right side of the dialog box. Drag one of the two small circles to change the Roundness setting; drag the tip of the arrow to change the Angle setting.

Lower the Spacing setting when using large, hard-edged brushes to prevent rough edges.

Figure 1.67 Size Jitter settings from top to bottom: 20, 50, 100.

Figure 1.68 Minimum settings from top to bottom: 1, 30, 75.

Figure 1.69 Fade settings from top to bottom: 20, 75, 130.

Shape Dynamics

The Shape Dynamics settings change the shape of the brush you have chosen. In essence, they allow you to vary the same settings that you specified in the Brush Tip Shape section of the Brushes palette (**Figures 1.70** to **1.72**).

Scattering

The Scattering setting causes Photoshop to vary the position of the paint daubs that make up a stroke (**Figure 1.73**). The Count setting allows you to vary how many paint daubs are applied within the spacing interval that you specified in the Brush Tip Shape area of the Brushes palette (**Figure 1.74**).

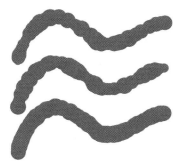

Figure 1.70 Size Jitter settings from top to bottom: 100, 50, 20. The higher the setting, the more variation in the blobs.

Figure 1.71 Angle Jitter settings from top to bottom: 100, 50, 20. The higher the setting, the more variation in the angle of the leaves.

Figure 1.72 Roundness Jitter settings from top to bottom: 100, 50, 20. This setting scales each brush tip vertically.

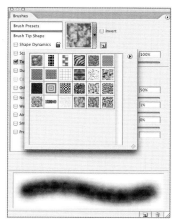

Figure 1.73 Scattering settings from top to bottom: 20, 100, 200.

Figure 1.74 Count settings from top to bottom: 1, 3, 7.

Figure 1.75 The Texture settings.

Texture

The Texture settings allow you to vary the opacity of your brush based on a texture that you specify (**Figure 1.75**). The Depth Jitter setting allows Photoshop to apply the texture in varying amounts. The Texture Each Tip setting must be turned on to use the Depth Jitter setting (**Figure 1.76**). If you find that the texture isn't changing the look of your brush, experiment with the Mode pop-up menu until you get the result you are looking for.

Dual Brush

The Dual Brush option allows you to create a brush stroke that's made with two brushes at once. Paint shows up only where the two brush shapes would overlap each other (**Figure 1.77**). This is a nice way to create sponge effects. You simply choose a normal, round brush in the Brush Tip Shape area of the Brushes palette, and then choose a textured brush in the Dual Brush area. If you find that the brushes aren't combining the way you'd like them to, experiment with the Mode pop-up menu and Spacing setting until you get the results you desire.

Figure 1.76 Depth Jitter settings from top to bottom: 100, 50, 20.

Figure 1.77 Three examples of dual brushes.

Color Dynamics

The Color Dynamics settings allow you to vary the color of your brush across the brush stroke. The Foreground/Background setting allows Photoshop to vary the brush color between the two colors being used as foreground and background colors (**Figure 1.78**). The Hue setting allows Photoshop to change the basic color of the brush to random colors. The higher the setting, the more it will deviate from your foreground color (**Figure 1.79**). The Saturation setting varies the vividness of the color that you are painting with (**Figure 1.80**). The Brightness setting allows Photoshop to randomly darken the color you are painting with (**Figure 1.81**). The Purity setting lets you change the saturation of the color you are painting with. A setting of zero makes no change; negative settings lower the saturation and positive settings increase it (**Figure 1.82**).

Figure 1.78 Foreground/Background using red and blue settings from top to bottom: 100, 50, 20.

Figure 1.79 Hue settings from top to bottom: 100, 50, 20.

Figure 1.80 Saturation settings from top to bottom: 100, 50, 20.

Figure 1.81 Brightness settings from top to bottom: 100, 50, 20.

Figure 1.82 Purity settings from top to bottom: +50, 0, −50.

Other Dynamics

The Opacity and Flow settings allow you to vary the settings that appear in the options bar for the painting tool that is currently in use (**Figures 1.83** and **1.84**). When you use these controls, Photoshop varies the Opacity and Flow settings across a brush stroke but will never exceed the settings specified in the options bar.

The Rest of the Brush Settings

Now let's look at the settings that are found at the bottom of the left side of the Brushes palette. The Noise setting adds a noisy look to soft-edged brushes (**Figure 1.85**). The Wet Edges setting causes the center of your brush to become 60% opaque and applies more and more paint as it gets toward the edge of your brush (**Figure 1.86**). The Airbrush setting just toggles the Airbrush icon that appears in the options bar on or off. It works in concert with the Opacity and Flow settings found in the options bar. The Opacity setting always determines the maximum amount that you'll be able to see through your brush stroke. The Flow setting determines how quickly you will end up with the opacity that you specified. When Flow is set to 100%, you will achieve the opacity amount specified in the options bar on each paint stroke. Lower flow settings cause Photoshop to apply a lower opacity while you paint but allows you to overlap your brush strokes to build up to the Opacity setting that's specified in the options bar. The Airbrush setting comes into play when the Flow setting is below 100%. It causes paint to build up when you stop moving your cursor, just as it would if you held a can of spray paint in one position (**Figure 1.87**).

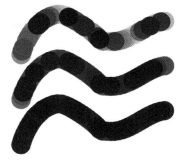

Figure 1.83 Opacity settings from top to bottom: 100, 50, 20.

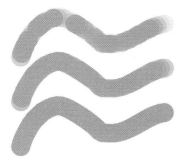

Figure 1.84 Flow settings from top to bottom: 100, 50, 20.

Figure 1.87 The Airbrush option causes more paint to apply wherever you pause when painting.

Figure 1.85 A brush stroke with Noise applied.

Figure 1.86 The effect of the Wet Edges setting.

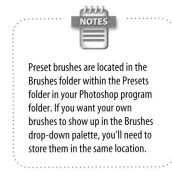

Saving Brushes

After you have changed the settings of a brush, you have in essence created a new brush that is no longer related to the original one that you chose in the Brushes palette. But the changed brush won't show up in the Brushes palette unless you save it by choosing New Brush from the side menu of the Brushes palette. When you have created a collection of brushes you like, you can choose Save Brushes from the side menu of the palette to save the currently loaded brushes into a file. If you ever need to get back to a saved set of brushes, choose Replace Brushes from the same menu. You can also choose Reset Brushes to get the brushes back to the default settings.

Preset Brushes

Photoshop comes with a variety of preset brushes. You can load these sets by choosing either Replace Brushes or a specific name that appears at the bottom of the Brushes palette side menu (**Figures 1.88** to **1.91**).

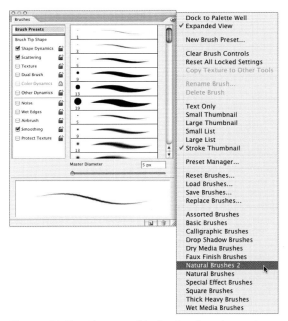

Figure 1.88 The side menu of the Brushes drop-down palette.

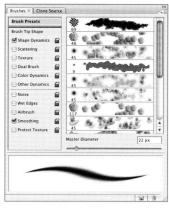

Figure 1.89 Special Effect brushes.

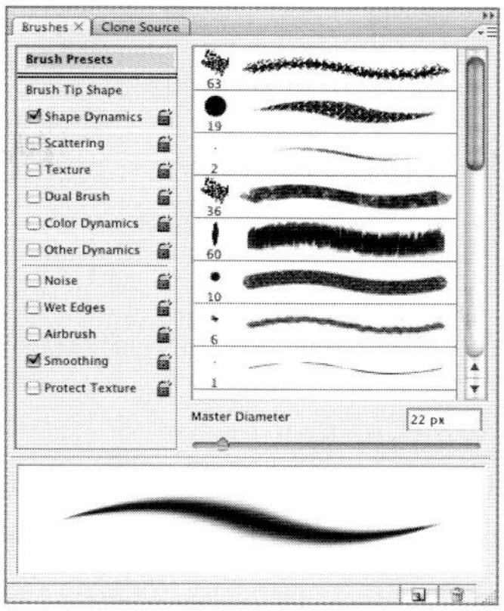

Figure 1.90 Dry Media brushes.

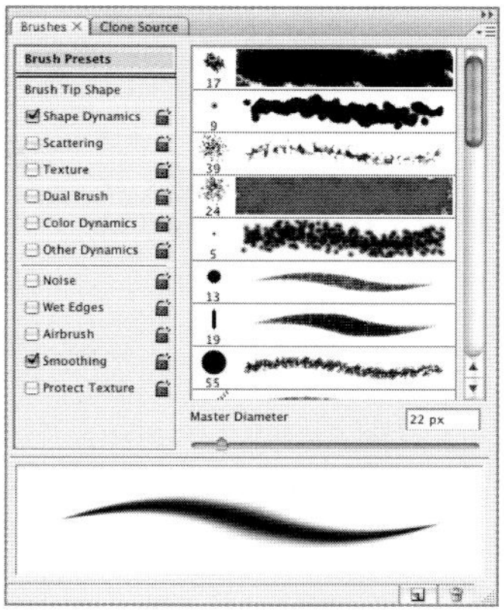

Figure 1.91 Wet Media brushes.

Paint Bucket Tool

Use the Paint Bucket tool to fill areas with the foreground color. Each time you click on the image, Photoshop will fill areas that contain colors similar to the one you clicked. You can specify how sensitive the tool should be by changing its Tolerance setting (**Figures 1.92** to **1.94**). Higher Tolerance settings will fill a wider range of colors.

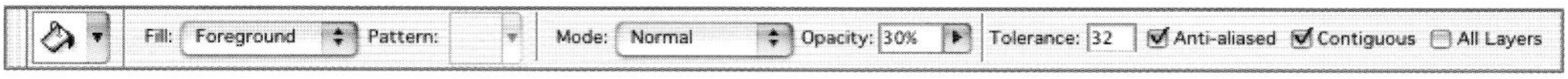

Figure 1.92 The Paint Bucket options bar.

Figure 1.93 Tolerance: 32.

Figure 1.94 Tolerance: 75.

Shape Tools

The Shape tools are great for creating simple geometric shapes (**Figure 1.95**). These tools are much more powerful than what you'd expect at first glance. We'll look at the basics here, and then expand on them in later chapters.

Before you dive into the Shape tools, you need to think about what kind of result you want to achieve, because you have three ways of using these tools, each of which leads

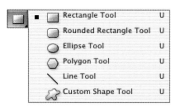

Figure 1.95 Press and hold one of the Shape tools to see a full list of the tools available.

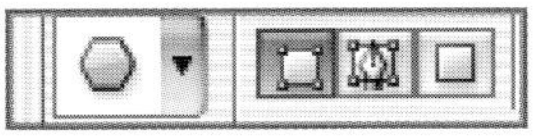

Figure 1.96 These three icons determine how the shape will be applied.

you to a different outcome. You'll find the trio of choices in the far left of the options bar (**Figure 1.96**). The first (leftmost) choice creates a special layer. It's known as a Shape layer, and it has some very special qualities:

▶ It will have crisp edges when printed on a PostScript printer (even if the pixels that make up the image are large enough to cause the rest of the image to appear jagged).

▶ You can scale it (up or down) without degrading its quality. This makes it ideal for creating button bars on Web sites where the client might decide to add more text to a button, which would require a larger button.

▶ You can add to or take away from it using the other Shape tools.

▶ It can be filled with a solid color, gradient, pattern, or adjustment.

The second choice in the options bar delivers a path that will show up in the Paths palette. This can be useful when creating a Vector Mask, as we'll discuss in Chapter 14, "Collage." The third choice in the options bar fills an area on the currently active layer using the current foreground color. I mainly use the Shape layer option (leftmost icon) because it seems to give me the most flexibility.

Once you've decided what type of result you want, you can click and drag across an image to create a shape. If you'd like to have a little more control over the end result, you can click on the small triangle that appears to the right of the Shape tools in the options bar. That presents you with options that are specific to the particular shape you are creating.

When using the Shape layer option, you can quickly create interesting effects by choosing a style from the drop-down menu (small triangle) next to the Layer Style preview image in the options bar. A layer style is a collection of settings that can radically transform the look of a layer by adding dimension, shadows, and other effects to the layer. You can also apply a layer style to any layer (it doesn't have to be one that was created using a Shape tool) by opening the Styles palette and clicking on one of the styles listed (**Figure 1.97**). We'll talk more about layer styles in the Bonus Chapter, "Type and Background Effects" on the CD.

Figure 1.97 The Styles palette.

Ruler Tool

The Ruler tool (previously called the Measure tool) allows you to measure the distance between two points or the angle of any area of the image, which can be helpful when you want to rotate or resize objects precisely. As you drag with the Ruler tool, the options bar at the top of your screen indicates the angle (A) and length (D, for Distance) of the line you're creating (**Figure 1.98**). The measurement system being used is the same as whatever your rulers are set to. After creating a line, you can click directly on the line and drag it to different positions. You can also click and drag one end of the line to change the angle or distance.

If you want to resize an image so that it fits perfectly between two objects, you can measure the distance between them with this tool and then choose Image > Image Size to scale the image to that exact width. Or, if you have a crooked image that you'd like to straighten, drag across an area that should be horizontal or vertical with the Ruler tool and then choose Image > Rotate Canvas > Arbitrary and click OK. Photoshop automatically enters the proper angle setting based on the measurement line that you drew.

You can also use the Ruler tool to determine the angle between two straight lines. If you Option-drag (Mac) or Alt-drag (Windows) the end of the line, you can pull out a second line and move it to any angle you desire. Now the angle (A) number in both the Info palette and options bar displays the angle between those two lines.

Gradient Tool

At first, you might not see any reasons to get excited about using the Gradient tool. However, after we cover layers (Chapter 3), Channels (Bonus Chapter on CD), and collage techniques (Chapter 14), you should find that the Gradient tool is not only worth getting excited about, but also downright indispensable. I want to make sure you know how to edit and apply gradients before we get to those chapters, so let's give it a shot.

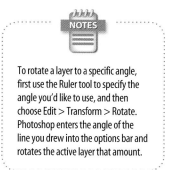

NOTES

To rotate a layer to a specific angle, first use the Ruler tool to specify the angle you'd like to use, and then choose Edit > Transform > Rotate. Photoshop enters the angle of the line you drew into the options bar and rotates the active layer that amount.

Figure 1.98 The Info palette indicates the angle of the Ruler tool.
(©2007 Stockbyte, www.stockbyte.com)

NOTES

If you're using the Extended version of Photoshop CS3, you can use the new Measurements Log palette to perform more advanced measurement operations. With the measurement log, you can measure areas defined not just with the Ruler tool but with any selection tool. You can also perform area calculations and track measurements across multiple images. See Photoshop's Help feature for more info (search for "measurement").

WARNING

Unless you select an area before applying a gradient, the gradient will fill the entire image.

Let's first look at how to apply gradients to an image. To apply a gradient, simply click and drag across an image using the Gradient tool. You'll get different results depending on which type of gradient you've chosen in the options bar (**Figure 1.99**).

Here's an explanation of the gradient settings:

▶ **Linear:** Applies the gradient across the length of the line you make (**Figures 1.100** to **1.102**). If the line does not extend all the way across the image, Photoshop fills the rest of the image with solid colors (the colors you started and ended the gradient with).

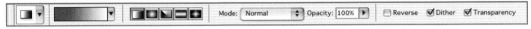

Figure 1.99 The Gradient options bar.

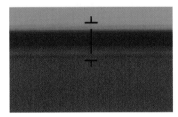

Figure 1.100 Linear gradient.

Figure 1.101 This book was created by transforming a PDF file so that it appears to be 3D.

Figure 1.102 Adding a linear gradient to the cover of the book effectively added subtle lighting to the cover.

▶ **Radial:** Creates a gradient that starts in the center of a circle and radiates to the outer edge (**Figures 1.103** to **1.105**). The point where you first click determines the center of the circle; where you let go of the mouse button determines the outer edge of the circle. All areas outside this circle will be filled with a solid color (the color that the gradient ends with).

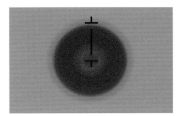

Figure 1.103 Radial gradient.

Figure 1.104 This brushed metal text appears rather flat and lifeless.

Figure 1.105 After adding a radial gradient, the text looks more interesting.

▶ **Angle:** Sweeps around a circle like a radar screen (**Figures 1.106** to **1.108**). Your first click determines the center of the sweep, and then you drag to determine the starting angle.

Figure 1.106 Angle gradient.

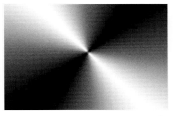

Figure 1.107 This angle gradient will be the base for an interesting trick.

Figure 1.108 By adding texture and layer styles, the simple angle gradient was transformed into a drill hole in metal.

▶ **Reflected:** Creates an effect similar to applying a linear gradient twice, back to back (**Figures 1.109** to **1.110**).

▶ **Diamond:** Similar to a radial gradient except that it radiates out from the center of a square (**Figure 1.111**).

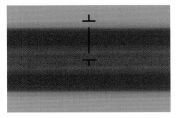

Figure 1.109 Reflected gradient.

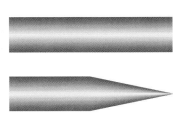

Figure 1.110 Top: A reflected gradient using metallic colors. Bottom: The end of the gradient was transformed to turn it into the tip of a pin.

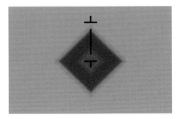

Figure 1.111 Diamond gradient.

Gradient Colors

You can choose from different preset color combinations by clicking on the small triangle that appears next to the gradient preview in the options bar (**Figure 1.112**). You can also reverse the direction of the gradient by turning on the Reverse check box in the options bar. Then, if you have a gradient that usually starts with blue and ends with red, it would instead start with red and end with blue (**Figures 1.113** and **1.114**). Some of the preset gradients contain transparent areas. To disable transparency in a gradient, turn off the Transparency check box.

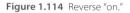

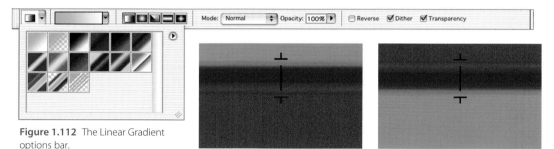

Figure 1.112 The Linear Gradient options bar.

Figure 1.113 Reverse "off."

Figure 1.114 Reverse "on."

You can press Return/Enter to show or hide the preset gradients without accessing the options bar.

Dithered Gradients

When you print an image that contains a gradient, you'll sometimes notice banding across the gradient (also known as stair-stepping or posterization). To minimize this, be sure to turn on the Dither check box in the options bar. This will add noise to the gradient in an attempt to prevent banding. You won't be able to see the effect of the Dither check box onscreen; it just makes the gradient look better when it's printed (**Figures 1.115** and **1.116**). If you find that you still see banding when you print the gradient, you can add some additional noise by choosing Filter > Noise > Add Noise. (Use a setting of 3 or less for most images.)

Figure 1.115 Dither "off."

Figure 1.116 Dither "on."

Custom Gradients

The Gradient Preset drop-down menu might not always contain the exact type of gradient you need. When that's the case, click directly on the gradient preview in the options bar to create your own custom gradient. The Gradient Editor dialog box that appears has so many options that it can sometimes feel overwhelming, but if you take it one step at a time, you shouldn't run into any problems (**Figure 1.117**).

The list at the top of the dialog box shows you all the gradients that usually appear in the options bar. Click any one of them, and you'll be able to preview it at the bottom of the dialog box. Once you have chosen the gradient you want to edit, you can modify it by changing the gradient bar (or you can click New to make a copy and proceed from there). To add colors (up to a maximum of 32), click just below any part of the bar. This adds a color swatch to the bar and changes the colors that appear in the gradient.

You have three choices of what to put into your new color swatches. You'll find these choices on the drop-down menu to the right of the color swatch at the bottom left of the dialog box. The Foreground and Background choices don't just grab your foreground or background colors at the time you create the gradient, as you might expect. Instead, they look at the foreground and background colors when you apply the gradient. Therefore, each time you apply the gradient, you can get a different result by changing the foreground and background colors. If you don't

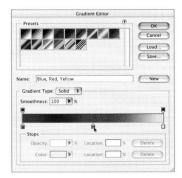

Figure 1.117 Click just below the gradient preview to add colors to the gradient.

NOTES

You can remove a color swatch or a transparency swatch by simply dragging it away from the gradient bar.

want the gradient to contain your foreground or background colors, choose User Color from the same menu and click on the color swatch to access the Color Picker.

After you have added a swatch of color to the gradient bar, you can reposition it by dragging it from left to right in the gradient bar or by changing the number in the Location box below. I like to click the Location number and then use the up arrow and down arrow keys on my keyboard to slide the color swatch around. A little diamond shape, known as the midpoint, appears between each of the color swatches; it indicates where the two colors will be mixed equally.

Transparent Gradients

You can also make areas of a gradient partially transparent by clicking just above the gradient bar. In this area, you cannot change the color of a gradient; you can only make the gradient more or less transparent. You can add and move the transparency swatches just as you would the color swatches below. Transparent areas are represented by the checkerboard pattern (**Figure 1.118**).

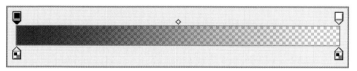

Figure 1.118 Editing the transparency of a gradient.

Figure 1.119 A text annotation. (© 2007 Stockbyte, www.stockbyte.com)

Notes Tool

When you use the Notes tool (which looks a bit like a Post-it Note), you can click and drag on your image to create a text box in which you can then type a note (**Figure 1.119**). When you're done typing, you can close the note by clicking the tiny box in its upper-left corner (Mac) or in its upper-right corner (Windows), and all you'll see is a tiny icon that indicates there is a note in that spot. Then, when you want to read the note, just double-click on that icon and the note will expand. Each note can have a different color and author, which you specify in the options bar. If you find the notes to be distracting, you are welcome to choose View > Show > Annotations to hide the notes.

Hidden under the Notes tool is another tool that allows you to record audio annotations. You'll have to have the proper hardware (such as a microphone) to get this feature to work. With the audio annotation, you simply click on your image and a Record dialog box appears (**Figure 1.120**). Click the Start button and then start talking. When you're done, click the Stop button and you're all set. Now anytime someone double-clicks that audio annotation, he or she will hear your notes. That's pretty slick, but be careful, because audio annotations will increase the file size of an image.

If you no longer need to keep the annotations you've created and you'd like to reduce your file size, you can click the Clear All button in the options bar. (The Annotations tool must be active for this button to be available.)

PDF Annotations

What's really special about annotations is that you can save them (along with the image, of course) in a PDF file. You can give that file to anyone; that person can read the annotations and see the image without having to use Photoshop. All he or she needs is a free program called Adobe Reader (available at www.adobe.com). Or, if the person has the full version of Acrobat, he or she can add his own annotations to the PDF file. Then you can import them into the original Photoshop file by choosing File > Import > Annotations. This allows you to save an image in a universal file format, send it out for review to as many people as you like, and get back comments that you can reimport into the original high-resolution Photoshop file. It's a great way to communicate with clients.

Tool Presets

Tool presets allow you to store and retrieve your favorite tool settings. You can access the presets in two ways: Click on the Tool icon that appears on the left side of the options bar, or choose Window > Tool Presets (**Figure 1.121**). To save a preset, click on the new Preset icon at the bottom of the Tool Presets palette. (It looks like a piece of paper with the corner turned down.) You'll also find the same icon in the upper-right area of the drop-down palette

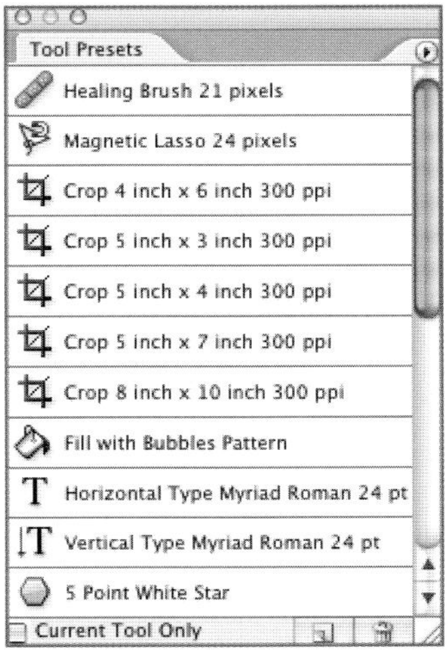

Figure 1.120 The Audio Annotation Record dialog box.

Figure 1.121 The Tool Presets palette.

that you can access from the options bar. When you save a preset, Photoshop remembers all the settings that were specified in the options bar and the Brushes palette (if you're using a painting or retouching tool). If you select the Include Color check box (**Figure 1.122**), it will even remember your foreground and background colors. Once you've saved a preset, you can get back to those settings at any time by clicking on the name of the preset from the Tool Presets palette.

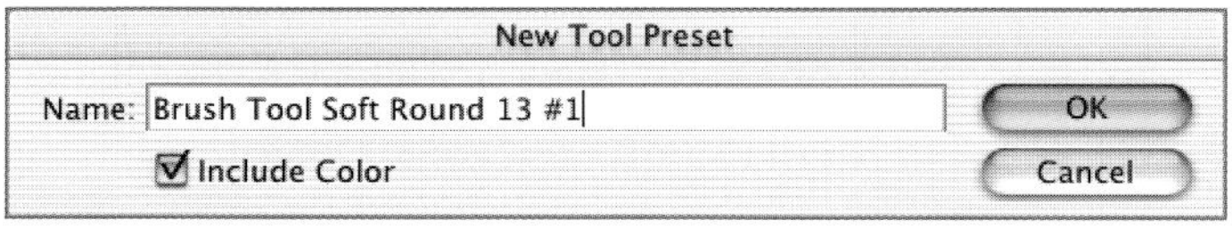

Figure 1.122 The Include Color checkbox.

You can work with the Tool Presets palette in two ways. The first is to use it as a replacement for Photoshop's main Tools palette. After all, when you click on a preset, Photoshop switches to the referenced tool and loads the setting you saved, so you could completely replace the main Tools palette with the presets. The only problem with that is it can get rather crowded once you have four or five settings saved for each tool. I prefer to select tools using the normal Tools palette, and then streamline the tool in the Tool Presets palette. I choose Show Current Tool Presets so that I see only presets that relate to the tool I have active. I also usually close the palette and access it by clicking the Tool icon that appears at the left end of the options bar. That way I reduce my screen clutter and can still quickly access the presets with a click or two of my mouse.

Adobe Bridge

Adobe Bridge is a file browsing and organizing tool bundled with Photoshop. Originally introduced with Photoshop CS2, Bridge CS3 has seen some major interface changes and now includes some important new features that will greatly streamline your workflow.

Bridge is a stand-alone application that you can access by choosing File > Browse in Photoshop, or you can launch it directly just like any other application (it installs into the same location as your Photoshop CS3 folder). With Bridge, you can view thumbnail-size previews of your images, sort and rotate them, compare images side by side, add and edit metadata, add ratings and keywords, and apply a variety of automated features. Bridge is so useful and offers so many options that I almost never use Photoshop's Open command (Image > Open) to access the files on my hard drive. Instead, I choose one of the following ways to open Bridge from within Photoshop:

▶ Select File > Browse.

▶ Press Option-Command-O (Mac) or Alt-Ctrl-O (Windows).

▶ Click the new Bridge icon on the far right of the options bar.

Bridge is organized into four panes, which, like Photoshop, can contain collections of tabbed palettes (**Figure 1.123**). You can drag the name of a tab onto another palette grouping to include that palette in the group. You can double-click on a tab to collapse that area so it takes up minimal space, and you can drag the dividing bar between palettes to control how much space one area uses compared to the others.

NOTES

Bridge is an independent application, which means it can be used by all the applications in the Adobe Creative Suite. It can also be used when Photoshop is busy batch processing multiple images.

To launch Bridge type Option-Command-O (Mac) or Alt-Ctrl-O (Windows). Type it again to quickly return to Photoshop without opening any images. This keyboard shortcut also launches Bridge in all Adobe Creative Suite applications (Illustrator, InDesign, etc.). The old shortcut—Shift-Command-O (Mac), or Shift-Ctrl-O (Windows)—still works for Photoshop and Bridge but is not universal to other Adobe applications.

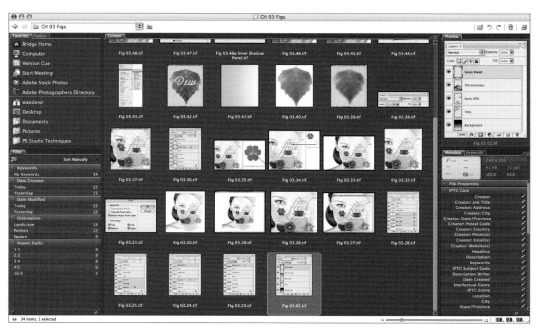

Figure 1.123 Adobe Bridge CS3 interface.

Navigating Your Hard Drive

You can navigate your hard drive in many ways. In Bridge's default configuration, the Folders palette appears in the upper left of the browser window. You can navigate your drive in the Folders pane by clicking on arrows next to each folder to view its contents. I prefer to use the arrow keys on my keyboard to quickly navigate the folder list. You can also navigate your hard drive using the thumbnail preview area on the right side of Bridge. Double-click on folders within the thumbnail view to open them and click the Up One Level icon (it looks like a folder with an up arrow on it) to move one level closer to your desktop. The menu next to the Up One Level icon indicates the folder you are currently viewing. Clicking on that menu presents you with a list of recently accessed folders as well as any favorites you added. If you've navigated to a folder that you'll want to access frequently, click on the Favorites tab and drag the folder to the bottom of the list (or choose Add Folder to Favorites from the File menu). Then, when you need to access that folder, click on it from within the Favorites pane or choose it from the pop-up menu that appears at the top of the Bridge window.

If you're not sure in which folder an image resides, choose Find from the Edit menu to search for it based on its filename, date modified, keywords, and many other criteria (**Figure 1.124**). One nice feature about Bridge's search capability is that it allows you to view the results even if they happen to be located in multiple folders. If you end up viewing another folder after performing a search, you can return to the search results by clicking the Back button that appears in the upper left of each Bridge window.

The fastest way to access files that reside on your desktop is to choose Desktop from the pop-up menu that appears at the top of the Bridge window.

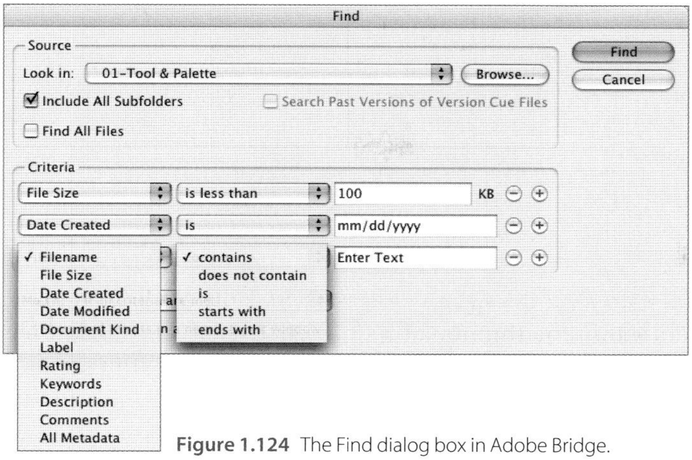

Figure 1.124 The Find dialog box in Adobe Bridge.

Working with Thumbnails

After you've navigated to the desired folder on your hard drive, the Content pane presents you with thumbnail images of the contents of that folder. Click any thumbnail to select a single image, then press either Command/Ctrl-click to select additional thumbnails, or Shift-click to select a range of thumbnails. When you have one or more thumbnails selected, you can do the following:

▶ Open the images in Photoshop by double-clicking on one of the selected thumbnail images or by pressing Command/Ctrl-O.

▶ Delete the selected images by pressing Delete (Mac) or Backspace (Windows).

▶ Rotate the thumbnails by clicking on one of the curved arrow icons that appear at the top of the Bridge window (although the thumbnail will rotate, the image will only be rotated after it has been opened in Photoshop).

▶ Move an image to a different location on your hard drive by dragging it to one of the folders in the Folders or Favorites tabs. You're not limited to dragging to folders shown in Bridge, you can also drag folders and files directly to your desktop or hard drive. To move a duplicate of the image, hold Option/Alt when dragging a thumbnail.

When you click on a thumbnail, a larger version of it appears in the Preview pane (assuming a Preview pane is visible). If you select multiple images, all of the images will be scaled and arranged to fit in the Preview pane. This allows you to easily compare images side by side. We'll look at more comparing options later in this chapter.

NOTES

The largest thumbnail you can view is 512 pixels on any side, even though behind the scenes Bridge is creating thumbnail images that are 1,024×768 pixels for each image.

You can control the size of the thumbnails by adjusting the slider that appears in the lower right of the Bridge window. Smaller thumbnails allow you to see more images at once, whereas larger thumbnails allow you to see more detail in each thumbnail image. You can control how much information appears below each thumbnail by choosing Preferences from the Bridge menu (Mac) or Edit menu (Windows) and changing the settings found in the Additional Lines of Thumbnail Metadata area of the Metadata preferences. That's where you can choose to add up to three additional lines of information below each thumbnail image (such as dimensions or keywords).

Sorting the Thumbnails

You can control the sorting order of the thumbnails by choosing from the options in the Sort menu (View > Sort). I really like that you can sort the files by file size and resolution. That makes it easy to find the images that can be used at a large size very quickly.

Alternately, you can choose a sort order from the Sort popup menu located at the top of the Filter pane.

You can also sort images by hand, rearranging them into whatever order you want. To manually sort images, just click and drag each image into the position in which you'd like it to appear. After you've done that, Bridge will indicate that your images have been manually sorted in the Sort menu.

Controlling Thumbnail Quality

When you opened a folder in Bridge CS2, Bridge displayed, as quickly as possible, the low-res thumbnails that are stored as part of most images. Then it immediately began processing new thumbnails and updating the display to show those higher-quality, exposure-adjusted images. In Bridge CS3, Adobe changed this behavior.

By default, Bridge now shows the stock low-res preview thumbnail and *doesn't* automatically begin generating higher-quality previews. This makes Bridge's overall performance a lot snappier and makes it easier to navigate quickly from folder to folder.

If you decide that you want to see a higher-quality thumbnail (and preview image in the Preview pane), you can choose Edit > Make High Quality Thumbnail. Bridge will generate a new thumbnail from your original image data.

You can change this behavior in the Preferences dialog box. In the Thumbnails section, you'll find three options (**Figure 1.125**):

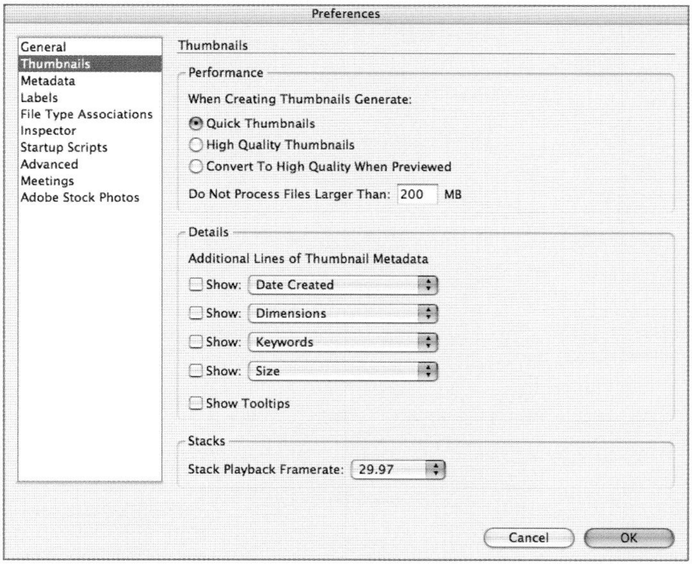

Figure 1.125 The Bridge Preferences dialog box.

▶ **Quick Thumbnails** is the default behavior. Low-res preview images are used for thumbnails and the Preview display.

▶ **High Quality Thumbnails** configures Bridge to generate high-quality thumbnails automatically for every image in a folder. This is the same as CS2's behavior.

▶ **Convert to High Quality When Previewed** displays a low-res thumbnail initially, but when you click an image, Bridge generates a high-quality thumbnail and preview image.

NOTES

Bridge no longer automatically adjusts the exposure of an image preview, as CS2 did. This functionality is not available with any of the thumbnail options.

Rating and Labeling Images

You can assign a rating of 0 to 5 stars to any image by selecting the image(s) you want to rate and then choosing a rating from the Label menu. Alternately, you can hold down the Command/Ctrl key and type a number from zero to 5. You can remove a rating by choosing No Rating or assign a Reject rating. Note that you can also make relative changes to ratings using the Increase and Decrease rating commands.

Bridge also lets you assign labels to images. Just as with ratings, all you have to do is select the images you want to label, and then choose the appropriate label from the Label menu.

Filtering Images

While "filters" in Photoshop refer to bits of plug-in code that perform image processing operations, "filtering" in Bridge refers to the process of filtering a selection of images to find only those that match some specified criteria. For example, you might filter a folder full of images to find only those with a 3-star rating, or a blue label, or both.

Filtering is very easy in Bridge CS3 thanks to the new Filter palette. Just click on the items that match the criteria for which you want to filter. Note that the Filter palette is updated on the fly to include only options relevant to the images you're currently browsing. So, for example, if none of the images you're browsing have ratings, there will be no ratings options listed in the Filter palette.

Rating and filtering are critical parts of a post-production photography workflow. Because you almost always shoot more images than you need, you can use Bridge to quickly winnow down the entire shoot to just the images that are worth editing. You can assign those images a rating or label, and then quickly filter your images to find only those that match that rating.

Additionally, in the lower right corner of the Filter palette you'll find a Clear Filter button, which lets you clear all filtering and return to view all of the images in the current folder.

Changing Layouts

By default, Bridge shows you a layout that displays all of the standard panes, including a large Preview pane. You can resize any of the panes by clicking and dragging on their borders. If you need to see more or fewer thumbnails, just resize the thumbnail pane.

Bridge also provides several predefined pane layouts that let you easily change to different window configurations, which allow for easier thumbnail viewing, or larger preview viewing, or better metadata editing.

Whereas Bridge CS2 let you change window layouts by clicking buttons in the bottom-right corner, Bridge CS3 has dispensed with these simple push buttons in favor of something a little more customizable. Now when you click and hold any of these buttons, you'll get a pop-up menu that lets you select one of the standard workspace configurations (**Figure 1.126**). The next time you click that button, the workspace you chose will be activated.

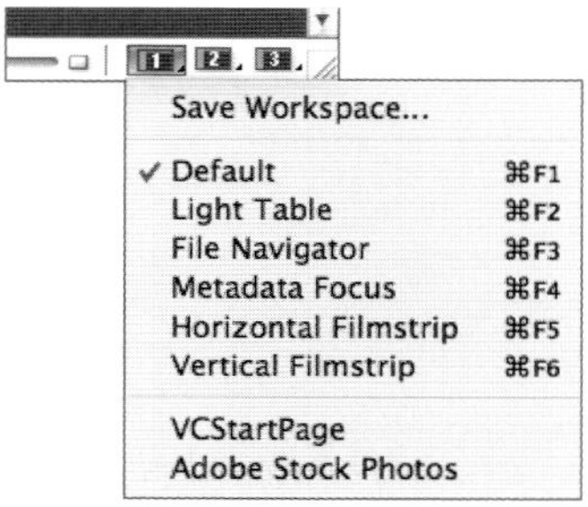

These customizable buttons allow you easy access to the three workflow configurations that you use most.

If you prefer your own custom workspace (that is, if you've resized the panes in a particular way), you can save that custom definition by opening the pop-up menu of any one of the buttons and choosing Save Workspace. The Save Workspace dialog box (**Figure 1.127**) lets you assign a keyboard shortcut as well as elect to save the Bridge window location and current sort order as part of the workspace definition.

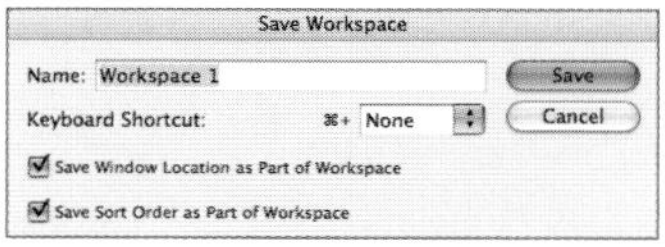

If you'd rather present your images full screen without the distraction of thumbnail images and the rest of the Bridge interface, choose View > Slide Show. In this mode, you can type H to access an onscreen guide that lists all the keyboard shortcuts necessary to control the slide show.

Renaming Files

You can quickly rename a file by clicking on its name in the Browser pane and then typing a new one. You can even press Tab to go to the next file in the list and rename it as well, making it very easy to rename an entire folder of

Figure 1.126 By clicking any of the three buttons in the bottom-right corner of the Bridge window, you can specify which workspace you want to activate when you click that button.

Figure 1.127 In the Save Workspace dialog box, you can specify how you want a customized workspace to be saved.

images. If you'd like to do that even faster, make sure you don't have any files highlighted in Bridge and choose Batch Rename from the Tools menu (**Figure 1.128**). This is where you can automatically rename an entire folder's worth of images. This is great for when you get images off a digital camera with odd filenames like 09864-01.JPG. Just use Batch Rename and specify the naming convention you'd like to use by changing the pop-up menus that appear in the Batch Rename dialog box. I usually set the first choice to Text and enter something like "Ben's Vacation." Next, I click the plus sign to the right of that to add a second choice, which I set to Sequence Number-Three Digits, and then add a third choice, which I set to Current File Name-Extension. Then all the images end up being named "Ben's Vacation 00X. jpg," where the X is a unique number for each image.

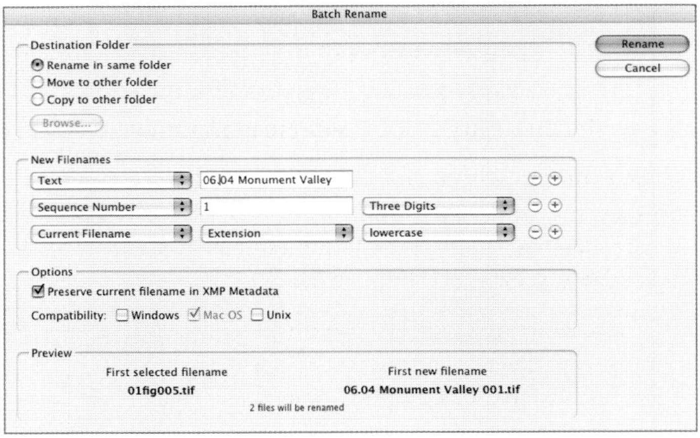

Figure 1.128 The Batch Rename dialog box.

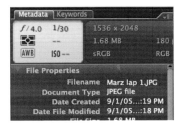

Figure 1.129 Bridge's Metadata palette makes it easy to read and edit the metadata attached to any image.

The Metadata Pane

Metadata is all of the data that's stored in your file along with the image. Your camera packs a lot of extra data into every image you take. All of your exposure settings, white balance settings, lens choice and focal length, date and time information, and more are stored in what's called EXIF metadata. This data is read-only, and you can view it using Bridge's Metadata Palette (**Figure 1.129**).

There's another type of metadata called IPTC metadata, which *is* editable. IPTC metadata is where you store your copyright information, name, byline, and more. You can edit all of these fields using the Metadata palette.

In most cases, these two panes contain all the metadata tags you'll need to see while browsing.

Comparing and Examining Images

One of the purposes of Bridge, of course, is to provide you with an easy way to compare images so that you can decide which ones you want to pass on to the rest of your workflow.

In CS2, the only way to compare images was to look at their thumbnails. Although Bridge's high-quality thumbnails can be viewed at a large size, they don't always afford the most efficient use of screen space. What's more, in thumbnail view, there's no way to view just a few images unless you move them into their own folder.

In CS3, you can use the Preview pane to compare images side by side in as large a view as your monitor allows.

To view images side by side, simply Command/Ctrl-click multiple images in the Content pane. Bridge will display those images in the Preview pane, arranging them so as to maximize screen space (**Figure 1.130**).

You can toggle an image on and off by Command/Ctrl-clicking it. As you select and deselect images, the Preview pane automatically changes their arrangement (**Figure 1.131**).

If the rating dots are visible, be careful when you're selecting an image in the Content pane. If you click the Rating portion of the thumbnail, you'll assign a rating to the image rather than select it. This is an easy way to incorrectly rate images by mistake.

The Loupe

No matter what size monitor you have, if you're working with high-res images Bridge won't be able to show you full resolution in the Preview pane when you have multiple images selected; there simply won't be enough room.

Figure 1.130 You can view multiple images simultaneously in the Preview pane by Command/Ctrl-clicking the images you want to view.

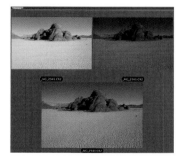

Figure 1.131 As you add and remove images, Bridge automatically rearranges them in the Preview pane.

NOTES

Though this functionality will work no matter what size the Preview pane is, you'll find comparing images far easier if you choose a layout with a large Preview pane, such as Horizontal Filmstrip or Vertical Filmstrip.

Figure 1.132 The new Loupe tool lets you see a 100 percent view of any image in the Preview pane.

Figure 1.133 When you group images into a stack, a special icon shows the number of images in the stack and the thumbnail of the first image.

When comparing images, you'll often want to check focus as you decide which image to use.

If you mouse over the image in the Preview pane, your cursor will change to the standard Photoshop Zoom In magnifying glass. Click your image, and Bridge's new Loupe will appear (**Figure 1.132**).

Click the Loupe and drag it around for a 100 percent view of your image. If you want to see higher magnification, press Command/Ctrl-+ (plus sign) to zoom in. You can zoom back out with Command/Ctrl- – (minus sign). These are, of course, the normal Photoshop zoom-in and zoom-out keyboard shortcuts.

To dismiss the Loupe, Command/Ctrl-click it in the Preview pane.

Stacks

Very often, many of the images that you shoot are related. If you shoot a bracketed sequence of images, for example, you probably think of those frames as being part of a related group. To keep those images organized together, Bridge now lets you group any images into a *stack*. A stack appears in the Content pane as shown in **Figure 1.133**.

The number in the top-left corner shows the number of images in the stack, and the thumbnail shows a view of the first image in the stack. If you click the number, the stack opens to reveal its contents (**Figure 1.134**).

Figure 1.134 When you click the stack number, the stack opens to reveal its contents.

You can preview and compare stacked images just as you would unstacked images. Stacking doesn't change the properties of any image or alter any of the operations you can perform on an image. A stack is simply a logical grouping that allows you to stay more organized and serves to free more space in the Content pane.

To create a stack, select the images you want to include in the stack and then choose Edit > Group As Stack or press Command/Ctrl-G.

You can rearrange the images in a stack simply by dragging them back and forth. A vertical bar appears to indicate where the new image will appear in the stack (**Figure 1.135**).

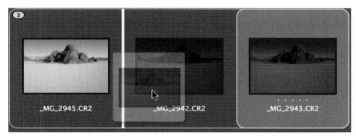

Figure 1.135 You can rearrange the images in a stack by dragging them to a new location. A vertical bar indicates where the image's new position will be.

To add images, just drag those images into the stack. You can add images whether the stack is opened or closed. To remove an image from a stack, drag it from the stack back into the Content pane.

To ungroup a stack, click any image in the stack. Choose Edit > Ungroup from Stack or press Command/Ctrl-Shift-G.

When a stack is closed, you only see the "pick" or "hero" image from the stacked group. In a bracketed set, for example, you usually decide to use one image from the set. Place that image in the leftmost position in the stack, and then close the stack. Now you'll see only the select image in the Content pane and won't have to hassle with all those additional frames. But if you ever need an alternative image, you'll be able to find it very easily.

NOTES

You cannot move a stack into another folder. If you drag a stack, only the first image will be moved.

As mentioned earlier in this section, stacks are handy for grouping bracketed sets of images, but you might also want to use them for any type of burst sequence, frames that you want to combine into a high dynamic range (HDR) image, frames that you want to stitch into a panorama, or any frames that are thematically related.

Importing Images

So far in this discussion of Bridge we've been assuming that you already have images on your computer. If you shoot with a digital camera, you'll need to go through a copying step to get the images from your camera's media card onto your computer's hard drive. Bridge now includes a special program called Photo Downloader, which can handle the image copying step for you.

To import images from an attached camera or reader, choose File > Get Photos from Camera.

Bridge opens an application called Photo Downloader, which is installed with CS3 (**Figure 1.136**). From the Get Photos from pop-up menu, choose your camera or device. If it doesn't appear, check your connections and then choose Refresh List from the menu. Configure the options in the Import Settings section and then click Get Photos.

Import Settings

The Import Settings in Photo Downloader include the following.

▶ **Location.** Click the Choose button next to Location to select the folder that you want to download into.

▶ **Create Subfolder(s).** Photo Downloader can automatically create subfolders within your chosen location. The Create Subfolder(s) pop-up menu lets you specify the metadata criteria you want to use as the basis for your subfolder structure (**Figure 1.137**).

▶ **Rename Files.** Your images are given initial filenames by your camera. If you want, Photo Downloader can rename the files upon import. Use the Rename Files pop-up menu to select a renaming scheme (**Figure 1.138**).

Figure 1.136 Photo Downloader lets you import images directly from a camera or media card.

Figure 1.137 The Create Subfolder(s) pop-up menu lets you specify how subfolders should be created within your destination folder.

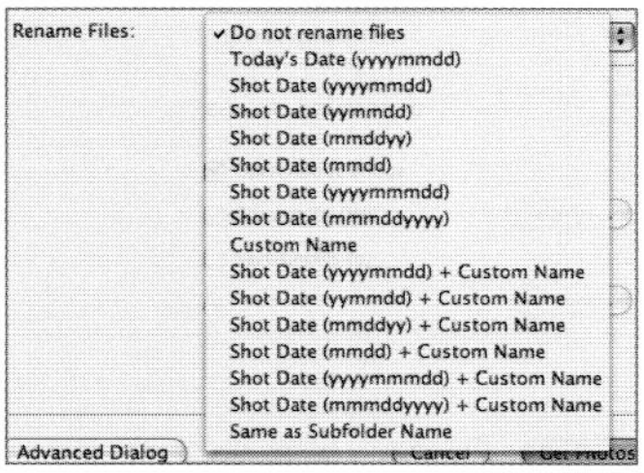

Figure 1.138 From the Rename Files pop-up menu, you can choose a renaming scheme for your imported images.

Renaming choices that include a "custom name" option require you to enter text in the field located below the menu. An example is displayed to show you what your resulting filename structure will look like.

- ▶ **Open Adobe Bridge.** When you first launch Photo Downloader, it will ask you whether you want to launch Photo Downloader automatically any time a camera or card reader is attached to your computer. If you choose this option, you won't always be launching Photo Downloader from within Bridge. If you want, you can select the Open Adobe Bridge check box to launch Bridge automatically after importing so that you can browse the imported folder immediately.

- ▶ **Convert To DNG.** If you shoot raw and use Adobe's Digital Negative (DNG) format for your images, you're already used to converting your raw files to DNG. The Convert To DNG option will perform this conversion for you.

- ▶ **Save Copies to.** If you want to save a second copy of the images you import, select the Save Copies to check box and then click the Choose button to select a destination. You can choose another folder or a different volume, which allows you to import and back up your files at the same time.

Advanced Importing

If you click the Advanced Dialog button at the bottom of Photo Downloader, you'll get additional importing controls (**Figure 1.139**).

In addition to all the features of Standard Dialog view, Advanced Dialog view provides a display of image thumbnails. You can deselect any images that you don't want to import, which allows you to make your first image culling during the import step.

The Apply Metadata section allows you to tag your images with metadata upon import. The default—the Basic Metadata template—lets you assign author and copyright metadata.

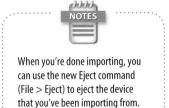

NOTES

When you're done importing, you can use the new Eject command (File > Eject) to eject the device that you've been importing from.

Figure 1.139 The Advanced Dialog button offers additional import controls including preview display and the ability to assign metadata.

Editing Menus

I find that the average Photoshop user (if there is such a thing) uses about 10 percent of Photoshop's features. That means that the vast majority of menu choices go unused, yet they still clutter the menus and make it more difficult to find the commands that you actually use. Adobe has come up with a nice way to clear away the clutter by allowing you to hide those commands you never use and color code those that you use most often.

Start by choosing Edit > Menus to access the Keyboard Shortcuts and Menus dialog box (**Figure 1.140**). Now choose the type of menu you want to edit from the Menu For pop-up menu. Next, click on the arrow next to the menu you'd like to work with to see the individual commands. Once you've located the command you want to work with (you might have to scroll quite a bit to find it), either toggle the eyeball icons to hide or show the menu command, or click in the color column and choose a color to assign to the menu command. It's that simple!

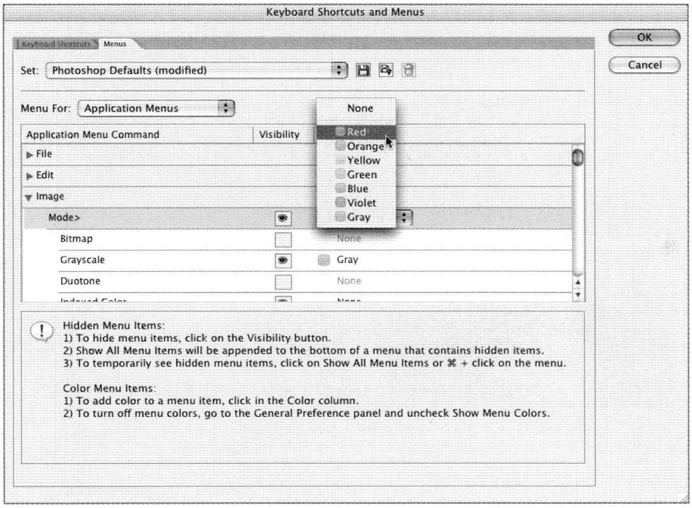

Figure 1.140 Editing menu commands.

You don't have to worry about hiding commands that you think you might need to use "some day" because you'll find a choice for Show All Menu Items at the bottom of each menu that contains hidden commands. You can also hold the Command/Ctrl key and then click on the menu to temporarily make all the commands visible (**Figure 1.141**).

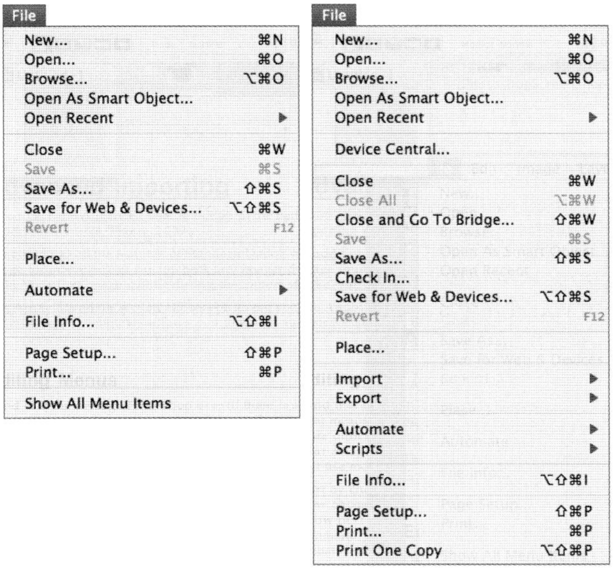

Figure 1.141 Left: Simplified menu; Right: Result of holding Command/Ctrl when accessing the same menu.

Editing Keyboard Shortcuts

Have you ever been annoyed to find that Command/Ctrl-I inverts your image instead of bringing up the Image Size dialog box? Well, you can bypass Adobe's logic and apply your own by editing the keyboard shortcuts you use to access tools and menus in Photoshop.

Start by choosing Keyboard Shortcuts from the Edit menu to access the Keyboard Shortcuts editor (**Figure 1.142**). This is just another section of the dialog box we used to hide and color code menu commands. You navigate in the same way and simply click on the name of a menu command and then type the key combination you'd like to assign to that command.

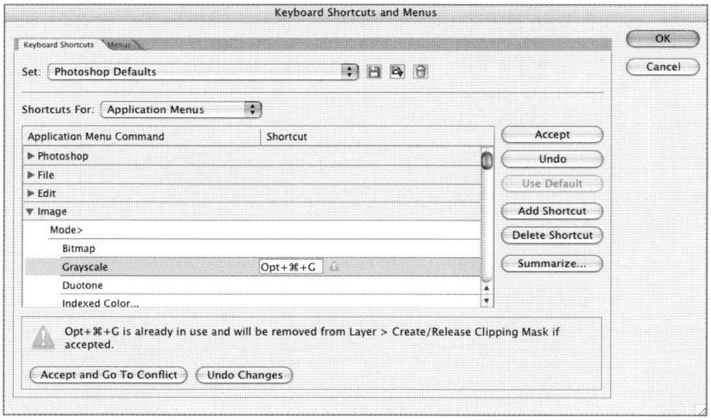

Figure 1.142 Editing keyboard shortcuts commands.

Every keyboard command must involve the Command key on the Mac or Ctrl key in Windows and a single letter, number, or symbol. The only exception is the F keys on the top of your keyboard, which can be used all by themselves. You can add any combination of Shift, Option, or Control (Mac) or Shift and Alt (Windows) to the keyboard shortcuts as well (although the Control key can't be used with F keys on the Mac). If the keyboard command you attempt to assign is already used by another command, Photoshop will warn you and ask if you'd like to undo or accept the change. If you choose to accept the change, Photoshop brings you to the command that was previously assigned that keyboard short-cut so you can assign it a new command or leave it without one. After you've changed all the keyboard shortcuts that you desire, click the Save Set icon (it looks like a floppy disk and is directly to the right of the Set pop-up menu) and give your newly assigned keyboard shortcuts a name (like "Ben's Favorites"). Then click the OK button to start using your reassigned keyboard shortcuts.

If you ever have to use someone else's computer and you find that person has edited their shortcuts in ways that just don't make sense to you, you have two methods for regaining your sanity. First, you could choose Edit > Keyboard Shortcuts and choose Photoshop Defaults from the Set pop-up menu. If Photoshop prompts you to save any unsaved shortcuts, click the Save button and give those settings a name so you can quickly get back to them when you're done using that computer. Second, if you'd rather use your own custom keyboard shortcuts, go back to your machine, choose Edit > Keyboard Shortcuts, click the Save Set icon (it's the middle of the three icons that appear to the right of the Set pop-up menu), and save your keyboard shortcuts on your desktop. Now copy the resulting file to a CD and bring it to the machine you're working on. Copy the file to the Keyboard Shortcuts folder (Photoshop > Pre-sets > Keyboard Shortcuts), which should appear in the Set pop-up menu in the Keyboard Shortcuts dialog box (Edit > Keyboard Shortcuts).

The Logic Behind the Keyboard Commands

Did you notice that Adobe limits the keyboard shortcuts you can assign to different commands? That's because there is a general logic to what different keys on your keyboard do within Photoshop. The Command key (Mac) or Ctrl key (Windows) does one of two things. If you press it by itself, it accesses the Move tool for however long that key is held. If you press it along with another key, it replaces a menu command. The only exceptions you'll find are those that involve an F key, which can also replace a menu command (like Shift-F5 to access the Fill dialog box [Edit > Fill]). Now let's look at what the other modifier keys do in Photoshop so you won't be surprised by the keyboard shortcuts that you run across as you progress through this book:

▶ **Shift:** Either constrains things or lets you work on more of something, depending on when you hold it down. For instance, if you grab the Paintbrush tool and hold Shift while you paint, Photoshop constrains your movement to either horizontal or vertical. If you have multiple images open, clicking the Full Screen Mode icons near the bottom of your tool palette will affect only the topmost image. When that's the case, typing Command/Ctrl-W to close the topmost image shows you that the underlying images are not in Full Screen mode. To affect all the open images, hold the Shift key when you click the Full Screen Mode icons, and all the images that are currently open will appear in Full Screen mode.

▶ **Option (Mac) or Alt (Windows):** Changes the behavior of something. If a button can perform two functions, you'll most likely have to hold Option or Alt to get to the second choice. For example, when you're in the Paintbrush tool, you can hold Option/Alt to temporarily access the Eyedropper tool, which allows you to click on your image to choose a color to paint with. Or, if you make an adjustment with any of the choices found under the Adjustments menu (Edit > Adjustments), you can hold Option/Alt to change the Cancel button to a Reset button, which allows you to return to the default settings of that dialog box.

▶ **Control (Mac) or right-click (Windows):** The Control key on a Mac isn't used very often. It's usually used with the mouse button to Control-click on something in Photoshop. That's the same as pressing the right mouse button in Windows, and it usually presents you with a menu full of choices that relate to the tool that you're currently using. For instance, Control-clicking (Mac) or right-clicking (Windows) on your image while the Paintbrush tool is active opens the Brush Presets palette as a temporary menu on your screen.

We've only explored a few examples of when these modifier keys are useful. I'll introduce you to additional uses for these keys as we progress through this book. The vast majority of the time, the keys I mentioned will conform to the logic we just went over. The only problem is that some icons, tools, and buttons can perform more than one function, so Adobe might have already used the key you're thinking of to do something else. For instance, when you click the New Layer icon (it looks like a sheet of paper with the corner turned over) at the bottom of the Layers palette, you create a new empty layer. (We'll talk about layers in Chapter 3.) If you add Option/Alt, you'll be prompted to name the layer when you create it. If you hold Command/Ctrl, it creates the layer below the one that is active. Not only that, but with so many chefs stirring the pot at Adobe, there were bound to be some who deviated from the standard logic. For instance, typing Command/Ctrl-W closes the frontmost image. You'd think that adding Shift to that would work on all of the images (as it does when working with the screen modes), but it doesn't. You have to instead hold down the Option/Alt key to close all the open documents.

Closing Thoughts

If you've made it through this entire chapter, you've just passed through Photoshop's welcoming committee of tools and palettes. By now your screen should look neat and tidy, and you should be able to zoom in and out and scroll around your image with ease. You should also have a nodding acquaintance with a good number of the tools and palettes—at least you should be familiar enough with them to know which ones you want to get more friendly with later.

Don't panic if some of this still seems like a blur. It will all begin to take shape once you spend some more time with the program. After a few intense Photoshop sessions, the information you learned in this chapter will become second nature to you. If any of the tools are completely new to you, you should probably play around with them before you move on to the next chapter.

Selection Primer

Courtesy of Tom Nick Cocotos, cocotos.com

*I choose a block of marble and chop off
whatever I don't need.*

—François-Auguste Rodin,
when asked how he managed to
make his remarkable statues

Whatever you do, don't skip this chapter, because the selection tools are central to your success in Photoshop. They allow you to isolate areas of your image and define precisely where a filter, painting tool, or adjustment will change the image. And, since selections can be saved and reused later, they allow you to easily go back and make alterations and changes at any time. After you've mastered the basics, try the more advanced selections in the bonus chapter, "Channels," which is on the CD at the back of the book.

What Is a Selection?

When you want to edit a portion of your image, you must first select the area with which you want to work. People who paint cars for a living make "selections" very much like the ones used in Photoshop. If you've ever seen a car being painted, you know that painters carefully place masking tape and paper over the areas they don't want to paint (such as the windows, tires, door handles, and so on). That way, they can freely spray paint the entire car, knowing that the taped areas are protected from "overspray." At its most basic level, a selection in Photoshop works much the same way but with a few additional advantages. In Photoshop, with one selection, you have a choice—you can paint the car and leave the masked areas untouched, or you can paint the masked areas and leave the car untouched. As you'll see later, you can also create areas that are only *partially* masked—as if you were painting part of a car that uses semi-opaque masking tape, which lets a fraction of the paint pass through to create a lighter shade.

When you select an area by using one of Photoshop's selection tools (Marquee, Lasso, Magic Wand, and so on), the border of the selection looks a lot like marching ants. Once you've made a selection, you can move, copy, paint, or apply numerous special effects to the selected area (**Figures 2.1** and **2.2**).

Figure 2.1 When no selection is present, you can edit the entire image. (©2007 iStockphoto.com/Lorado)

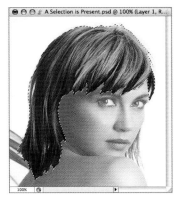

Figure 2.2 When a selection is present, you can change only the selected area.

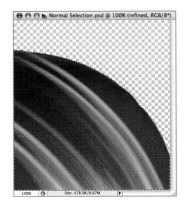

Figure 2.3 Normal selections have hard edges. (©2007 iStockphoto.com/MousePotato)

There are two types of selections in Photoshop: a normal selection and a feathered selection (**Figures 2.3** and **2.4**). A normal selection has a hard edge; that is, when you paint or apply a filter to an image, you can easily see where the effect stops and starts. A feathered selection slowly fades out at the edges. With a feathered selection, any painting or filters you apply will seamlessly blend into an image without producing noticeable edges. An accurate selection makes all the difference when you're enhancing an image in Photoshop. To see just how important it can be, take a look at **Figures 2.5** to **2.7**.

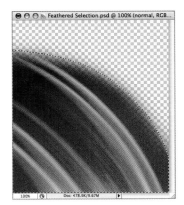

Figure 2.4 Feathered selections have soft edges.

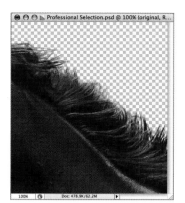

Figure 2.5 The original image. (©2007 iStockphoto.com/winhorse)

Figure 2.6 An unprofessional selection.

Figure 2.7 A professional selection.

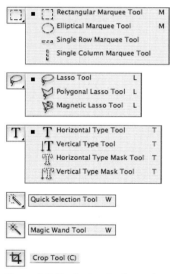

Figure 2.8 The basic selection tools.

WARNING

If you press any combination of the Option/Alt and Shift keys before you begin a selection, they might not perform as you expect, because these keys are also used to manipulate existing selections.

Basic Selection Tools

The Marquee, Lasso, Magic Wand, and Type Mask tools (**Figure 2.8**) are the essential implements in your selection toolkit, and they (as well as the new Quick Selection tool) are the tools you'll be using the most in your everyday work.

The Marquee tool is the most basic of all the selection tools, and we'll cover it first. However, don't let this tool's simplicity fool you—it can perform a surprising number of tasks. If you hold your mouse button down while your cursor is over the Marquee tool in the main Tools palette, you'll get a variety of choices in a pop-up menu. We'll cover these choices one at a time, and I'll throw in some tricks along the way.

Rectangular Marquee Tool

The Rectangular Marquee tool is the first choice listed in the Marquee pop-up menu in the Tools palette. It can select only rectangular shapes. With it, you create a rectangle by clicking and dragging across your document. The first click creates one corner, and the point at which you release the mouse button denotes the opposite corner (**Figure 2.9**). To start in the center and drag to an outer edge, instead of going corner to corner, press Option/Alt after you have started to drag (**Figure 2.10**). If you want to create a square, hold down the Shift key after you start to drag. You can even combine the Option/Alt and Shift keys to create a square selection by dragging from the center to an outer edge.

Figure 2.9 A corner-to-corner selection. (©2007 iStockphoto.com/blackred)

Figure 2.10 A center-to-edge selection.

Figure 2.11 Original selection is misaligned. (©2007 Stockbyte, www.stockbyte.com)

If you hold down the spacebar and drag around your screen while you're making a selection with the Marquee tool (but don't release the mouse button), you'll move the selection instead of changing its shape (**Figures 2.11** and **2.12**). This can be a real lifesaver. If you botch up the start of a selection, you can reposition it without having to start over. After you have moved the selection into the correct position, just let go of the spacebar to continue editing the selection. After you've finished making the selection, you no longer need to hold the spacebar to move it. To move a selection after it's created, select the Marquee tool and then click and drag from within the selection outline.

Elliptical Marquee Tool

The second choice under the Marquee pop-up menu is the Elliptical Marquee tool. This tool works in the same way as the rectangular version, except it creates an ellipse (**Figure 2.13**). And it's a little bit trickier to define its size because you have to work from the "corner" of the ellipse, which doesn't really exist. (What were they thinking when they came up with this idea?) Actually, you might find it easier to choose View > Show Rulers and then drag out a few guides (you can get them by dragging from the rulers) and let the "corners" snap to them. Either that or hold the spacebar to reposition the selection before you release the mouse button, just as I mentioned with the Rectangular Marquee tool.

Figure 2.12 Use the spacebar to reposition a selection while creating it.

NOTES

To discard the areas that appear outside a rectangular selection border, choose Image > Crop.

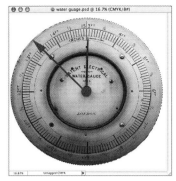

Figure 2.13 The Elliptical Marquee tool in action (from center to edge). (©2007 Stockbyte, www.stockbyte.com)

Now let's look at the choices in the Marquee options bar (**Figure 2.14**). When you click on any of the Marquee tools, their options will automatically be available in the options bar at the top of your screen. The following list describes the options you'll find in the Marquee options bar:

Figure 2.14 The Marquee options bar.

▶ **Feather:** Allows you to fade out the edge between selected and unselected areas. I usually leave this option turned off, because I might forget that a Feather setting had been typed in previously. This one little setting might mess up an otherwise great selection. Instead, I find it much easier to make a selection and then press Option-Command-D (Mac) or Alt-Ctrl-D (Windows), or just choose Select > Modify > Feather. An even better option is to use the Refine Edge command, which we'll examine in detail later in this chapter.

▶ **Anti-aliased:** Determines whether a one-pixel-wide border on the edge of a selection will blend with the image surrounding it. This provides nice, smooth transitions and helps prevent areas from looking jagged. I recommend that you leave this check box on at all times unless of course you have a great need for jaggies (sometimes they're preferred for multimedia applications).

▶ **Style menu:** Controls the shape and size of the next selection made. When the Style pop-up menu is set to Normal, your selections are not restricted in size or shape (other than their having to be rectangles or ellipses). After changing this menu to Fixed Ratio, you'll be confronted with Width and Height settings (**Figure 2.15**). By changing the numbers in these areas, you can constrain the shape of the next selection to the ratio between the Width and Height settings. For example, if you change Width to 2 and leave Height at 1, your selections will always be twice as wide as they are tall. This can be useful when you need to find out how much of an image needs to be cropped when printing it as an 8 by 10, for example.

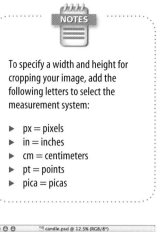

Figure 2.15 The Fixed Ratio option.

I use the Fixed Size option (**Figure 2.16**) much more often than the Fixed Ratio option. Fixed Size lets you type in an exact width and height; that way, anytime you click using either the Rectangular or Elliptical Marquee tool, you'll get a selection exactly that size. What's more, if you didn't get it in exactly the right spot, you can just drag the selection around the screen before releasing the mouse button. For instance, Macintosh OS 9 desktop icons are always 32 pixels wide and 32 pixels tall, so I use these numbers when selecting something I want to use as an icon. When entering a Width or Height setting, you can specify a measurement system by adding a few letters after the number you enter; otherwise, Photoshop will default to the measurement system used for the rulers.

Figure 2.16 The Fixed Size option.

Single Row and Single Column Marquee Tools

The third and fourth choices under the Marquee tool pop-up menu are the Single Row and Single Column Marquee tools. These tools are limited in that they select only a one-pixel-tall row or one-pixel-wide column. To be honest, I rarely use them (maybe once or twice a year). However, they have gotten me out of few tight spots, such as when I had to clean up a few stray pixels from in between palettes when taking screen shots for this book.

Crop Tool

Three spaces below the Marquee tool, you'll find the Crop tool. Although the Crop tool doesn't produce a selection, it does allow you to isolate a certain area of your image. Using this tool, you can crop an image, as well as resize and rotate it at the same time (**Figures 2.17** and **2.18**).

NOTES

To specify a width and height for cropping your image, add the following letters to select the measurement system:

- ▶ px = pixels
- ▶ in = inches
- ▶ cm = centimeters
- ▶ pt = points
- ▶ pica = picas

Figure 2.17 The original image. (©2007 Stockbyte, www.stockbyte.com)

Figure 2.18 The original image cropped and rotated.

Figure 2.19 The cropping rectangle.
(©2007 Stockbyte, www.stockbyte.com)

If the cropping rectangle extends beyond the edge of your screen, the extended areas will be filled with the current background color (if you have a background image) or will be transparent (filled with a checkerboard pattern) if you don't have a background image.

To match the size of another open document, click that document to make it active for editing and then click the Front Image button in the options bar. This will enter the Width, Height, and Resolution settings of that document into the options bar. Now you can use the Crop tool on any open document, and the result will match the size of the original document.

When you click and drag over an image with the Crop tool selected, a dashed rectangle appears. When the Shield Cropped Area check box is turned on, the area outside the cropping rectangle will be covered with the color indicated in the options bar and might appear to be partially transparent, depending on the Opacity setting (**Figure 2.19**). You can drag any one of the hollow squares on the edge of the rectangle to change its size. Also, you can hold down the Shift key while dragging a corner to maintain the width-to-height proportions of the rectangle. Anything beyond the edge of the rectangle is discarded when the image is cropped (if you haven't turned on the Hide option).

To rotate the image, you can move your cursor just beyond one of the corner points and drag (look for an icon that looks like a curve with arrows on each end). You can also drag the crosshair in the center of the rectangle to change the point from which the rectangle will be rotated. Press Esc to cancel, or press Return or Enter (or double-click within the cropping rectangle) to complete the cropping. If you're working on a layer (instead of the background) and the Delete option is chosen in the options bar, all information that appears outside the cropping rectangle will be discarded. If the Hide option is chosen, the area outside the cropping rectangle will not be discarded but will instead remain as image data that extends beyond the bounds of the visible image.

Occasionally, you'll need to crop and resize an image at the same time. Maybe you need three images to be the exact same size, or perhaps you need your image to be a specific width. You can do this by specifying the exact Width, Height, and Resolution settings you desire before you create a cropping rectangle. After you've created a cropping rectangle on your image, you'll notice that different options appear in the options bar (**Figure 2.20**). By typing in both a Width and a Height setting, you constrain the shape of the rectangle that you draw. I sometimes leave one of these values empty so that I can still create any rectangular shape.

Figure 2.20 The options bar after a cropping rectangle is added to the image.

When the Perspective choice in the options bar is turned on (it becomes available once you've created a cropping rectangle), you will be able to move each corner of the cropping rectangle independently. This allows you to align the four corners with lines that would be level in real life but may appear in perspective in a photograph (**Figure 2.21**). When you have all four corners in place, you can press Return or Enter to crop the image and correct the perspective of the image in one step (**Figure 2.22**).

> **NOTES**
>
> If you don't want to resize the image when you crop it, click the Clear button in the options bar to clear out the Width, Height, and Resolution fields before you create a cropping rectangle.

Figure 2.21 Getting the corners to line up with level lines.

Figure 2.22 Result of applying a perspective crop.

You don't have to crop the image while you are correcting its perspective. Once you have the corners in the correct location to establish the perspective of the image, move the side handles—or Option/Alt-drag the corner handles—until the area you'd like to keep is within the cropping rectangle, and then press Return/Enter (**Figures 2.23** and **2.24**).

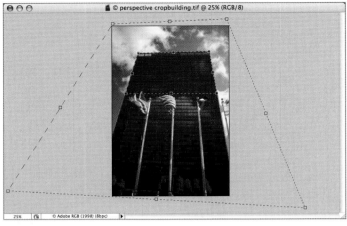

Figure 2.23 Establishing perspective and extending the cropping rectangle.

Figure 2.24 Result of correcting perspective.

Figure 2.25 Breaking a scan of multiple photos into individual images used to require a lot of cropping and straightening by hand. (©2007 Mark Clarkson)

Crop and Straighten Photos

If you shoot film and then scan your photos, the process of scanning in bunches of photographs has, up until now, required an annoying amount of rotation, cropping, copying, and pasting. Each scanned image must be individually selected, then cropped or copied and pasted to a new document. Despite your best efforts, the photos are rarely perfectly aligned; at least a few usually cant off to one side or the other a few degrees, requiring further rotation and cropping (**Figure 2.25**).

Photoshop's Crop and Straighten Photos can do most of this work for you, identifying the individual photographs within the scan, rotating them into perfect horizontal and vertical alignment, and then copying them into new documents. It leaves the original document untouched.

To use the command, place a handful of photos on your scanner and arrange them so that none of the images overlap. Make sure there is a good amount of space between each image, and that none of them are pressed up against the edges of the scanner glass. The more space you leave between each image, the better chance there is for Photoshop to successfully crop and straighten each image. After you've scanned them into Photoshop, make sure the layer containing the scan is active and then choose File > Automate > Crop and Straighten Photos. Photoshop will start chugging away at your document, creating one file for each image. It will also attempt to straighten each image (**Figure 2.26**). Crop and Straighten Photos does a pretty good job, but it can get confused. I find that it's always good to double-check its work because a few images might need to be fine-tuned by hand.

The Crop and Straighten Photos command doesn't do as well with very low-resolution scans; scan photos at 150 dpi or more for the best results. You can always scale down the images later.

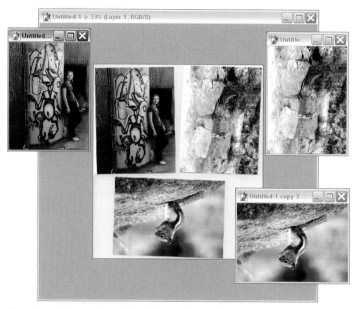

Figure 2.26 Crop and Straighten Photos automatically locates, crops, and straightens multiple photos from a single scan.

If Crop and Straighten Photos insists on breaking one of your photos in two or, conversely, treating two photos as one, you may have to give it a little help. Use the Marquee tool to draw a selection around the problem photo. Now, hold down Option/Alt when you choose the command. Holding down this key tells Photoshop that there is only one photo within the selection, making it easier for the program to locate the borders. Even if you have to select some photos

You can zoom in on your document to get a more precise view by typing Command/Ctrl-+. You don't even have to let go of the mouse button—just press this key combination as you're dragging.

I suggest you zoom in on your image to make sure you're creating an accurate selection. If you can't see the entire image, you can hold the spacebar to access the Hand tool. You can do this without ever releasing the mouse button, which means you can alternate between scrolling and selecting until you've got the whole object.

one at a time, the Crop and Straighten Photos command still saves you the work of rotating and cropping the photo, and then copying it to a new document.

Lasso Tool

The Lasso tool is the most versatile of the basic selection tools. By holding down the mouse button, you can use the Lasso to trace around the edge of an irregularly shaped object (**Figure 2.27**). When you release the button, the area will be selected. Be sure to create a closed shape by finishing the selection exactly where you started it; otherwise, Photoshop will complete the selection for you by adding a straight line between the beginning and end of the selection.

Sometimes you'll need to add a few straight segments in the middle of a freeform shape. You can do this by holding down Option/Alt and then releasing the mouse button (but not the Option/Alt key). Now, each time you click your mouse, Photoshop will connect the clicks with straight lines (**Figure 2.28**). To go back to creating a freeform shape, just start dragging and then release the Option/Alt key.

Figure 2.27 The Lasso tool in action. (©2007 iStockphoto.com/SilentWolf)

Figure 2.28 Using the Option/Alt key while clicking to create straight-line segments.

Polygonal Lasso Tool

You can use the Polygonal Lasso tool whenever you need to make a selection that consists mainly of straight lines. Using this tool, you click multiple areas of the image, and Photoshop connects the dots for you (**Figure 2.29**). If you need to create a freeform selection, hold down Option/Alt and drag. To finish a selection, you can either click where the selection began or double-click anywhere, which will create a straight line between where you double-clicked and where the selection started.

Magnetic Lasso Tool

Whereas the Lasso and Polygonal Lasso tools are relatively straightforward, the Magnetic Lasso tool has a bunch of neat tricks up its sleeve. This tool can be a huge time-saver in that it allows you to trace around the edge of an object without having to be overly precise. You don't have to break a sweat making all of those tiny, painstaking movements with your mouse. Instead, you can make big sloppy selections, and the Magnetic Lasso will do the fine-tuning for you (you don't even have to hold down the mouse button). What's more, if it doesn't do a great job in certain areas, you can hold down Option/Alt to temporarily access the freeform Lasso tool. However, before using the Magnetic Lasso tool, you'll want to experiment with its settings in the options bar (**Figures 2.30** to **2.32**). If you do nothing else, pay close attention to the Edge Contrast setting.

Figure 2.29 The Polygonal Lasso tool in action. (©2007 Stockbyte, www.stockbyte.com)

Figure 2.31 A Magnetic Lasso selection with a Frequency setting of 5. (©2007 iStockphoto.com/ Andrew_Howe)

Figure 2.32 A Frequency setting of 99.

Figure 2.30 The Magnetic Lasso options bar.

Edge Contrast

I think this setting is the most important of the bunch. It determines how much contrast there must be between the object and the background for Photoshop to select the object. If the object you're attempting to select has well-defined edges, you should use a high setting (**Figure 2.33**). You can also use a large Lasso tool width. On the other hand, if the edges are not well defined, you should use a low setting and try to be very precise when dragging (**Figure 2.34**).

Figure 2.33 High edge contrast (20%). (©2007 iStockphoto.com/JMSetzler)

Figure 2.34 Low edge contrast (7%).

If the Magnetic Lasso tool is not behaving itself, you can temporarily switch to the freeform Lasso tool by holding down Option/Alt as you drag (with the mouse button held down). You can also periodically click to manually add anchor points to the selection edge. If you want to use the Polygonal Lasso tool, hold down Option/Alt and click in multiple areas of the image (instead of dragging). If you don't like the shape of the selection, you can press the Delete key to remove the last anchor point. (Pressing Delete multiple times deletes multiple points.) When you have a satisfactory shape, finish the selection by pressing Return/Enter or by double-clicking. Remember, if you don't create a closed shape, Photoshop will finish it for you with a straight-line segment.

If you really get used to the features available with the Magnetic Lasso tool, you'll be able to create most of your basic selections with this tool alone. This will take some time, and you'll sometimes have to supplement its use by holding down Option/Alt to access the other Lasso tools for areas the magnetic one has trouble selecting. And if it ever gets completely out of hand, you can always press the Escape key to abort your selection and then start from scratch again.

Quick Selection Tool

If you've used previous versions of Photoshop, you've probably had a go with the Magic Wand tool. Photoshop CS3 still has a Magic Wand tool, and we'll get to it next, but most likely you'll find the new Quick Selection tool to be more versatile and powerful than Photoshop's Magic Wand.

The Quick Selection tool is like a really smart, interactive Magic Wand tool. It automatically makes selections for you, but it takes cues from where you point and paint to determine which pixels to select and which to leave alone.

Open an image that has something in it you'd like to select. It can be any object on any type of background. Choose the Quick Selection tool from the Tools palette by clicking on it or pressing W, click on the area you want to select, and begin dragging. As you drag, the selection automatically expands to add surrounding areas that are similar in color, contrast and texture to the area over which you are dragging (**Figure 2.35**).

Figure 2.35 As you paint over an area with the Quick Selection tool (left), the selection automatically expands intelligently to select the object you're painting on (right). (©2007 Ben Long)

If the Quick Selection tool selected an area that it shouldn't have, hold down the Option/Alt key and brush over the area to deselect it. The Quick Selection tool presents a number of options in the options bar (**Figure 2.36**).

Figure 2.36 The options bar holds a few Quick Selection options.

You can change the brush size using the brush pop-up menu. A larger brush simply means you don't have to work as hard to brush over the area you want to select, whereas a smaller brush lets you select a smaller area. As with any other brush tool, you can change the size of the brush using the bracket keys. Right bracket enlarges the brush, left bracket shrinks it.

If you select the Sample All Layers box, the Quick Selection tool analyzes all the layers in your image rather than just the current one to determine which pixels to select.

Auto Enhance yields a higher-quality edge on the selection. Without Auto Enhance, your edges will tend to be blockier. However, Auto Enhance will exact a slight performance penalty.

The Quick Selection tool does an amazing job of automatically figuring out what it is you want to select. However, it's not especially adept at selecting very refined detail such as blowing hair or transparency. In previous versions of Photoshop, you could use the Feather Selection command (Select > Feather Selection) to soften the edges of a selection, which often helped these and other difficult selection tasks. In CS3, the new Refine Selection command (Select > Refine Selection) offers far more edge correcting power. You'll find a button for it in the option bar of each selection tool.

Magic Wand Tool

Figure 2.37 A simple click of the Magic Wand tool can select a solid area of color with ease.
(©2007 Stockbyte, www.stockbyte.com)

Photoshop CS3 still includes a Magic Wand tool, which is now located in the same menu as the Quick Selection brush. Click and hold on the Quick Selection tool and then pick the Magic Wand. (Alternately, you can repeatedly press W until the Magic Wand is selected.) The Magic Wand tool is great for selecting solid (or almost solid) colored areas, because it selects areas based on color—or shades of gray in grayscale mode—as shown in **Figure 2.37**. This is helpful when you want to change the color of an area or remove a simple background.

You'll probably find it easier to understand how this works if you start by thinking about grayscale images, because they're less complex than color images. Grayscale images can contain up to 256 shades of gray. When you click one of these shades with the Magic Wand tool, it selects any shades that are within the Tolerance specified in the options bar. For instance, if you click shade 128 (Photoshop numbers the shades from 0 to 255) and the Tolerance is set to 10, you'll get a selection of shades that are 10 shades darker and 10 shades brighter than the one you clicked (**Figures 2.38** to **2.40**). When the Contiguous check box is turned on, the only shades that will be selected are those within an area that touches the spot you clicked—Photoshop won't jump across areas that are not within the tolerance.

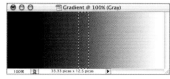

Figure 2.38 Tolerance: 10.

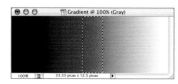

Figure 2.39 Tolerance: 20.

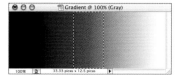

Figure 2.40 Tolerance: 30.

Just in case you're not comfortable thinking in the 0 to 255 numbering system and would rather think about percentages, I've included a conversion table (**Table 2.1**). Otherwise, you can make this conversion by multiplying any percentage by 2.55 (1% in the 0 to 255 numbering system). Remember, the Magic Wand tool selects twice as much as the number you type in.

Color images are a little more complex. They're made from three components: red, green, and blue (that is, when you're working in RGB mode). The Magic Wand tool analyzes all the components (known as channels) in your file to determine which areas to select. For example, if you click a color made up of the components 32 red, 120 green, 212 blue (these numbers can be found in the Info palette) and you use a Tolerance setting of 10, Photoshop will look for colors between 22 and 42 in the red channel, 110 and 130 in the green channel, and 202 and 222 in the blue channel. The only colors selected are those that fall within all three ranges.

TABLE 2.1 Percentage Conversions

PERCENTAGE	TOLERANCE SETTING
0%	0
10%	26
20%	51
30%	77
40%	102
50%	128
60%	153
70%	179
80%	204
90%	230
100%	255

To quickly change the Tolerance setting, press Enter and then type the desired number and press Enter again. I know it sounds weird, but try it—it works.

If you hold Shift while clicking with the Magic Wand tool, each click will add to the previous selection instead of completely replacing it.

Figure 2.41 The options for the Type Mask tool.

Figure 2.42 The selection will be previewed using a red overlay on the nonselected areas.

Figure 2.43 These four choices in the options bar allow you to create, add, subtract, or intersect a selection.

Fortunately, you don't really have to think about the numbers, because they're something of a pain. Instead, just experiment with the setting until you get a good result. If you really want to understand all about the color channels, take a look at the bonus chapter, "Channels," on the CD at the back of the book.

Type Tool

While Adobe includes a very powerful Type tool for superimposing text on an image, there might be times when you just want to make a selection in the shape of type—perhaps to fill it with a gradient or to apply a filter through it. You can do just that with Photoshop's Type Mask tool, which sits underneath the Type tool in the Tools palette (**Figure 2.41**). When you use that Type Mask, Photoshop shows you a preview of the selection (with a red overlay on the image, as shown in **Figure 2.42**) while you are editing the text, and then delivers a selection when you press Return/Enter. I'll cover the options of this tool in the bonus chapter, "Type and Background Effects," on the book's CD.

Refining a Selection

Selecting complex objects in Photoshop usually requires multiple selection tools. To combine these selection tools, you'll need to either use a few controls in the options bar (**Figure 2.43**) or learn a few keyboard commands that will allow you to add, subtract, or intersect a selection.

Adding to a Selection

To add to an existing selection, either click the second icon on the far left of the options bar (it looks like two little boxes overlapping each other) or hold down the Shift key when you start making the new selection. You must press the key before you start the selection; you can release it as soon as you've clicked the mouse button (**Figures 2.44 to 2.46**). If you press it too late, the original selection will be lost. Let's say, for example, you want to select multiple round objects. One way would be to use the Elliptical Marquee tool multiple times while holding down the Shift key.

But you might find it easier to use the choice available in the options bar because then you don't have to remember to hold down any keys.

Figure 2.44 The original selection. (©2007 Stockbyte, www.stockbyte.com)

Figure 2.45 Adding to the selection.

Figure 2.46 The end result.

Removing Part of a Selection

To remove areas from an existing selection, either click the third icon on the far left of the options bar (it looks like one little box stacked on top of another) or hold down Option/Alt when you begin making the selection. If, for example, you want to create a half circle, you could start with an Elliptical Marquee tool selection and then switch to the Rectangular Marquee tool and drag while holding down Option/Alt to remove half of the circle (**Figures 2.47** to **2.49**).

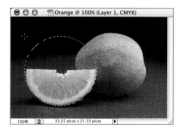

Figure 2.47 The original selection. (©2007 PhotoDisc)

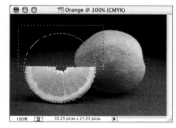

Figure 2.48 Subtracting a second selection.

Figure 2.49 The end result.

Clicking while holding down the Option/Alt key is particularly helpful when you're using the Magic Wand tool to remove areas of a selection (**Figures 2.50** and **2.51**). With each click of the Magic Wand tool, you can use a different Tolerance setting.

Figure 2.50 The original selection.

Figure 2.51 Option/Alt-clicking with the Magic Wand tool.

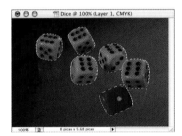

Figure 2.52 Applying the Magic Wand tool to the background and then choosing Select > Inverse. (©2007 Stockbyte, www.stockbyte.com)

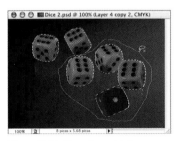

Figure 2.53 Dragging with the Lasso tool while holding down Shift-Option/Alt.

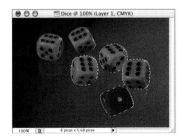

Figure 2.54 The end result.

Intersecting a Selection

To end up with only the overlapped portions of two selections, click the fourth icon on the far left of the options bar (it looks like two squares intersecting with the overlap area colored in) or hold down Shift-Option/Alt while editing an existing selection. Sometimes I use the Magic Wand tool to select the background of an image and then choose Select > Inverse to get the objects of the selected image (**Figure 2.52**). However, when there are multiple objects in the image, as there are in **Figures 2.53** and **2.54**, I often have to restrict the selection to a specific area by dragging with the Lasso tool while holding down Shift-Option/Alt.

The Select Menu

The Select menu offers you many choices that supplement the basic selection tools. Learning these features is well worth your time because they'll help you save heaps of it in your everyday work. We'll look at these features in the same order they appear in the menu; then, later in this chapter, I'll show you how to replace many of these commands with an alternative that allows you to think visually instead of numerically.

Select All

Select > All selects the entire document. This can be useful when you need to trim off any part of an image that extends beyond the edge of the document (**Figure 2.55**). You can crop out those areas by choosing Select > All and then Image > Crop (**Figure 2.56**). Also, if you need to copy an entire image, you'll need to select everything, because without a selection, the Copy command will be grayed out.

Figure 2.55 An example of areas that extend beyond the document's bounds (these areas are not usually visible). (©2007 Stockbyte, www.stockbyte.com)

Figure 2.56 When cropping the image, the information that used to extend beyond the document's bounds is discarded.

Deselect/Reselect

If you're done using a selection and want to work on the entire image, choose Select > Deselect. When you don't have a selection, you can work on the entire image. Now, if you need to use the last active selection (and there isn't a selection on your screen), you can choose Select > Reselect. This is great when you need to use the same selection over and over again. I use these two commands all the time.

Inverse

As you might expect, the Inverse command selects the exact opposite of what you originally selected. If, for example, you have the background of an image selected, after choosing Select > Inverse, you'll have the subject of the image selected instead (**Figures 2.57** and **2.58**). I use this command constantly, especially with the Magic Wand tool. Sometimes it's just easier to select the areas that you don't want and then choose Select > Inverse to select what you really want to isolate. Sound backward? It is, but it works great.

Color Range

You can think of the Color Range command (Select > Color Range) as the Magic Wand tool on steroids. With Color Range, you can click multiple areas and then change the Fuzziness setting to increase or reduce the range of colors that will be selected (**Figures 2.59** and **2.60**).

Figure 2.57 A Magic Wand tool selection. (©2007 Stockbyte, www.stockbyte.com)

Figure 2.58 The selection after using the Select > Inverse command.

Figure 2.59 The original image.
(©2007 Stockbyte, www.stockbyte.com)

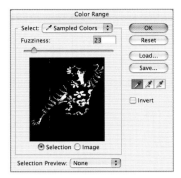

Figure 2.60 The same image in the Color Range dialog box after clicking on multiple areas within her blouse.

As you click and play with the Fuzziness control, you'll see a preview of the selection in the middle of the Color Range dialog box. Areas that appear white are the areas that will be selected. The Selection and Image radio buttons allow you to switch between the selection preview and the main image. (I never actually use these two controls because I find it easier to switch to the image view at any time by just holding down Command/Ctrl.) You can also see a preview of the selection within the main image window by changing the Selection Preview pop-up menu to Grayscale, Black Matte, White Matte, or Quick Mask (**Figures 2.61** to **2.63**).

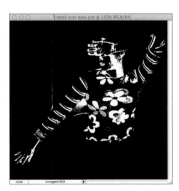

Figure 2.61 Choosing Grayscale will display the same preview that appears in the Color Range dialog box.

Figure 2.62 Choosing Black Matte or White Matte will fill the unselected areas with black or white.

Figure 2.63 Choosing Quick Mask uses the settings in the Quick Mask dialog box to create a preview of the image.

The Eyedropper tool on the right side of the dialog box allows you to add and subtract colors from the selection. Using the Eyedropper with the plus symbol next to it is really helpful, because it allows you to click the image multiple times. With each click, you tell Photoshop which colors you want it to search for. A low Fuzziness setting with many clicks usually produces the best results (**Figures 2.64** and **2.65**).

The selections you get from the Color Range command are not ordinary selections in that they usually contain areas that are not completely selected. For instance, if you're trying to select the red areas in an image and there happens to be a flesh tone in the same image, the fleshy areas will most likely become partially selected. If you then adjust the image, the red will be completely adjusted, and the flesh tones will shift a little bit.

If a selection is already present when you choose Select > Color Range, the command analyzes the colors only within the selected area. This means you can run the command multiple times to isolate smaller and smaller areas. If you want to add the Color Range command to the current selection, be sure to hold down the Shift key when choosing Select > Color Range.

Refine Selection

As you've already seen, feathering a selection is the process of blurring the selection edges to create a smoother transition between the selected and nonselected areas. Previous versions of Photoshop provided a Feather Selection command, which let you enter a value for the width of the blurring that you wanted added to your selection. However, there was no way of seeing the effect of this feathering until you applied some kind of effect through the selection. Determining the right amount of feathering often required a lot of trial and error—making a selection, applying an effect through it, then undoing and trying again.

CS3 offers a much improved way of adjusting the edge of your selection. After making a selection using any of Photoshop's selection tools (or a combination of selection tools), choose Select > Refine Edge to bring up the dialog box shown in **Figure 2.66**.

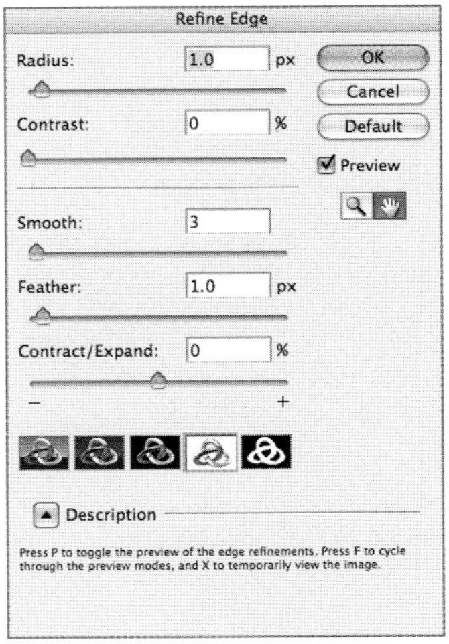

Figure 2.64 An example of a single click with a high Fuzziness setting.

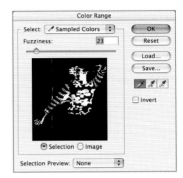

Figure 2.65 An example of five clicks with a low Fuzziness setting.

Figure 2.66 The new Refine Edge dialog box offers several tools for refining your selections.

The Refine Selection dialog box lets you interactively preview your selection on a number of different backgrounds and provides some important new controls that allow you to soften, resize, and improve the edges of your selection.

When you first open the Refine Selection dialog box, your selection is shown against a white background, allowing you to immediately see the quality of the edge. If you prefer, you can click the display buttons at the bottom of the dialog box to change the view to see your selection composited on different types of backgrounds or displayed as a regular selection of "marching ants" (**Figure 2.67**).

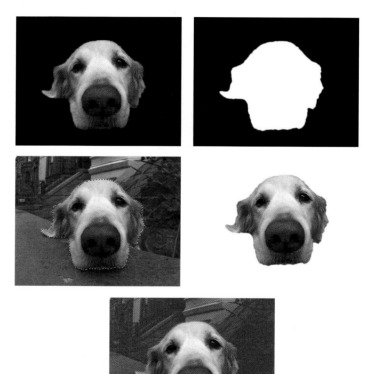

Figure 2.67 The Refine Edge dialog box lets you view your selection composited against different backgrounds. (©2007 Ben Long)

Radius creates a very slight falloff, or feathering effect, on the inside of your selection (**Figure 2.68**)—unlike Feather, which creates falloff on both sides of the edge. The falloff that Radius creates is very subtle and doesn't yield the blurred, transparent look of the Feather slider. In general, Radius does a good job of preserving the hue of the colors along the edge of your selection while screening those pixels back to make a more subtle transition along the edge.

Contrast has the opposite effect of the Radius slider. It serves to sharpen the edge by creating a more contrasty boundary along the selection's edge (**Figure 2.69**).

Smooth smears the pixels along the edge of the selection, just as if you had dragged along the boundary with the Smudge tool (you know, the "smeary finger" tool).

Feather applies the same effect as the old Feather command but with the added advantage that you can preview your feather and adjust it before committing to it.

Contract/Expand allows you to shrink or enlarge your selection by a given number of pixels. Drag the slider to the right to enlarge the selection—additional pixels will be added around the selection perimeter. Drag to the left to shrink the selection.

When you click OK, your selection will be modified.

Modify

The features in this little menu have helped get me out of many sticky situations. At first glance, it might not be obvious why you would ever use these commands, but I guarantee they'll come in very handy as you continue through the book. Here's a list of the commands found under the Modify menu (Select > Modify), as well as descriptions of what they do:

▶ **Border:** Selects a border of pixels centered on the current selection. If you use a setting of 10, the selection will be 5 pixels inside the selection and 5 pixels outside the selection. You can use this to remove pesky halos that appear when you copy an object from a light background and paste it onto a darker background (**Figures 2.70** and **2.71**).

Figure 2.68 Before (left) and after (right) a Radius adjustment of 18 pixels.

Figure 2.69 To harden the edge of a selection (left), adjust the Contrast slider (right).

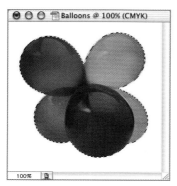

Figure 2.70 The original selection. (©2007 Stockbyte, www.stockbyte.com)

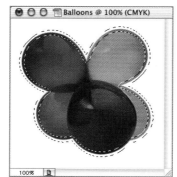

Figure 2.71 A 10-pixel border.

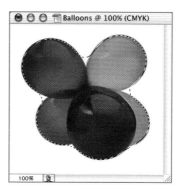

Figure 2.72 Smooth 16 pixels.

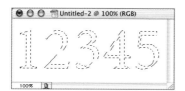

Figure 2.73 The original selection.

Figure 2.74 Smooth setting of 6.

▶ **Smooth:** Attempts to round off any sharp corners in a selection (**Figure 2.72**). This can be especially useful when you want to create a rounded-corner rectangle. It can also produce an interesting effect after you've used the Type Mask tool (**Figures 2.73** and **2.74**).

▶ **Expand:** Enlarges the current selection while attempting to maintain its shape (**Figure 2.75**). This command works well with smooth, freeform selections, but it's not my first choice for straight-edged selections because it usually slices off the corners.

▶ **Contract:** Reduces the size of the current selection while attempting to maintain its shape (**Figure 2.76**). The highest setting available is 16. If you need to use a higher setting, just use the command more than once.

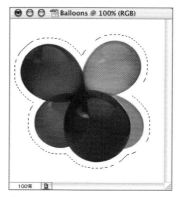

Figure 2.75 Expand 12 pixels.

Figure 2.76 Contract 12 pixels.

▶ **Feather:** Unlike the Feather option in the selection tools, this command affects only the selection that's currently active; it has no effect on future selections. You can't reduce the amount of feathering with this command once it's applied. Therefore, if you apply it once with a setting of 10 and then try it again on the same selection using a setting of 5, it will simply increase the amount again. It's just like blurring an image—each time you blur the image, it becomes more and more blurry.

I prefer using this command instead of entering Feather settings directly into the tool's options bar (where they affect all "new" selections). If you enter these values directly, you might not remember that the setting is turned on days later, when you spend hours trying to select an intricate object. By leaving the tools set at 0, you can quickly press Option-Command-D (Mac) or Alt-Ctrl-D (Windows) to bring up the Feather dialog box and enter a number to feather the selection. Because this affects only the current selection, it can't mess up any future ones (**Figures 2.77** and **2.78**).

The problem with the Feather command is that there is no way to tell if a selection is feathered by just looking at the marching ants. Not only that, but most people think the marching ants indicate where the edge of a selection is, and that's simply not the case with a feathered selection. If you take a look at **Figure 2.79**, you'll find that the marching ants actually indicate where a feathered selection is halfway faded out. So, these days, it's much better to use the new Refine Selection command.

Grow

The Grow command (Select > Grow) searches for colors that are similar to an area that has already been selected (**Figures 2.80** and **2.81**). In effect, it spreads your selection in every direction—but only into areas that are similar in color. It will not jump across areas that are not similar to the ones selected. The Grow command uses the Tolerance setting that's specified in the Magic Wand options bar to determine the range of colors for which it will look.

Figure 2.77 A flame pasted with a normal selection.
(©2007 iStockphoto.com/sdourado)

Figure 2.78 A flame copied using a feathered selection and then pasted into this document.

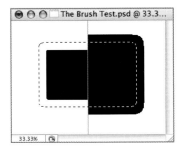

Figure 2.79 The left half of this split image shows where the selection would start to fade out and blend with the underlying image. The right half shows where the selection would stop affecting the image. Notice that the marching ants show up halfway between those two areas.

Figure 2.80 The original selection. (©2007 PhotoSpin, www.photospin.com)

Figure 2.81 The selection after choosing Select > Grow.

Figure 2.82 The original selection.

Figure 2.83 The selection after choosing Select > Similar.

Similar

The Similar command (Select > Similar) works just like the Grow command except that it looks over the entire document for similar colors (**Figures 2.82** and **2.83**). Unlike the Grow command, the colors that Similar selects don't have to touch the previous selection. This can be very useful when you've selected one object out of a group of same-colored objects. For example, if you have a herd of gray elephants standing in front of a lush green jungle, you can select the first elephant and then choose Select > Similar to get the rest of the herd (provided, of course, that they're all a similar shade of gray). The same works for a field of flowers, and so on.

Transform Selection

After making a selection, you can scale, rotate, or distort it by choosing Select > Transform Selection. This command places handles around the image. By pulling on the handles and using a series of keyboard commands, you can distort the selection as much as you like. Let's take a look at the neat stuff you can do with Transform Selection:

▸ **Scale:** To scale a selection, pull on any of the handles. Pulling on a corner handle changes both the width and height at the same time. (Hold the Shift key to retain the proportions of the original selection.) Pulling on the side handles changes either the width of the selection or its height, but not both. This can be a great help when working with elliptical selections because it lets you pull on the edges of the selection instead of its so-called corners (**Figures 2.84** and **2.85**).

Figure 2.84 The original selection.
(©2007 Stockbyte, www.stockbyte.com)

Figure 2.85 After choosing Select > Transform to scale the selection.

▶ **Rotate:** To rotate the selection, move your cursor a little bit beyond one of the corner points; the cursor should change into an arc with arrows on each end. You can control where the pivot point of the rotation will be by moving the crosshair that appears in the center of the selection (**Figures 2.86** to **2.88**).

Figure 2.86 The original selection.
(©2007 Stockbyte, www.stockbyte.com)

Figure 2.87 Rotating and scaling the selection.

Figure 2.88 The end result.

▶ **Distort:** To distort the shape of the selection, hold down the Command/Ctrl key and then drag one of the corner points. Using this technique, you can pull each corner independently (**Figures 2.89** to **2.91**).

Figure 2.89 The original selection. (©2007 Stockbyte, www.stockbyte.com)

Figure 2.90 Dragging the corner with Command/Ctrl.

Figure 2.91 The selection after all four corners have been dragged.

▶ You can also distort a selection so that it resembles the shape of a road vanishing into the distance. You do this by dragging one of the corners while holding down Shift-Option-Command on the Mac or Shift-Alt-Ctrl in Windows (**Figures 2.92** to **2.94**).

Figure 2.92 The original selection. (©2007 Stockbyte, www.stockbyte.com)

Figure 2.93 Dragging a corner while holding down Shift-Option-Command (Mac) or Shift-Alt-Ctrl (Windows).

Figure 2.94 The end result.

▶ To move two diagonal corners at the same time, hold down Option-Command on the Mac or Alt-Ctrl in Windows while dragging one of the corner handles (**Figures 2.95** and **2.96**).

▶ Finalize your distortions by pressing Enter (or by double-clicking inside the selection). Cancel them by pressing Esc.

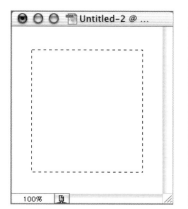

Figure 2.95 The original selection.

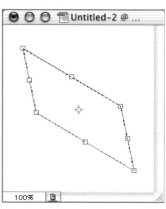

Figure 2.96 Dragging a corner handle while holding down Option-Command (Mac) or Alt-Ctrl (Windows).

You can Control-click/right-click while transforming a selection to choose the type of distortion you want to perform (**Figure 2.97**).

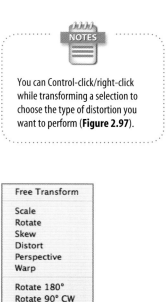

Free Transform
Scale
Rotate
Skew
Distort
Perspective
Warp
Rotate 180°
Rotate 90° CW
Rotate 90° CCW
Flip Horizontal
Flip Vertical

Figure 2.97 The menu that appears as a result of Control-clicking/right-clicking while you're transforming a selection.

Load Selection and Save Selection

If you've spent hours perfecting a selection and think you might need to use it again in the future, you can apply the Save Selection command (Select > Save Selection) (**Figure 2.98**). This stores the selection as an alpha channel. Don't worry, you don't need to know anything about channels to use these commands—all you have to do is supply a name for the selection. If you want to find out more about channels, you can check out the bonus chapter, "Channels," on the CD at the back of the book.

These saved selections remain in your document until you manually remove them using the Channels palette (see the bonus chapter, "Channels," on the CD to find out how to delete a channel). They won't be saved on your hard drive until you actually save the entire file. Only the Photoshop (.psd), Large Document Format (.psb), Photoshop PDF (.pdf), and TIFF (.tif) file formats support multiple saved selections.

When you want to retrieve the saved selection, choose Select > Load Selection and pick the name of the selection from the Channel pop-up menu (**Figure 2.99**). When you use this command, it's just like re-creating the selection with the original selection tool you used, only a whole lot faster.

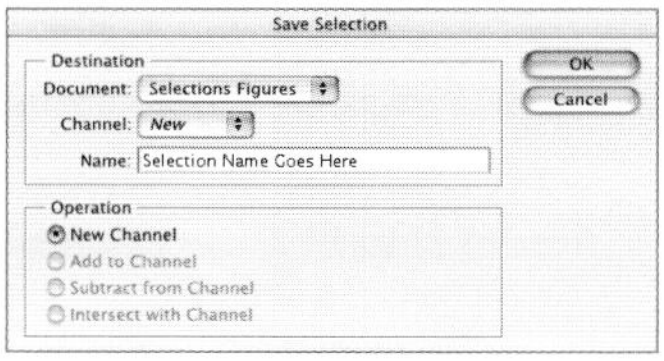

Figure 2.98 The Save Selection dialog box.

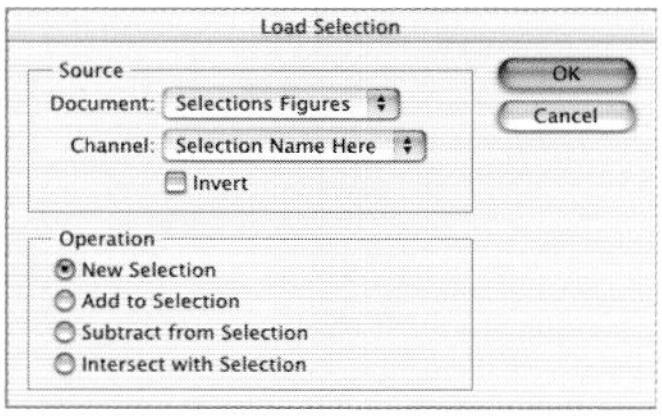

Figure 2.99 The Load Selection dialog box.

Figure 2.100 The quick mask icon.

Figure 2.101 A selection shown in Standard mode.
(©2007 Stockbyte, www.stockbyte.com)

Quick Mask Mode

Remember when we were talking about the marching ants and how they can't accurately show you what a feathered selection looks like? Well, Quick Mask mode can show you what a feathered selection really looks like and can also help create basic selections. The quick mask icon is located directly below the foreground and background colors in your Tools palette (**Figure 2.100**).

To see how it works, first make a selection using the Marquee tool, and then turn on Quick Mask mode by clicking on the Quick Mask icon under the foreground and background colors (or just type Q to do the same thing). In Quick Mask mode, the selected area should look normal and all the nonselected areas should be covered with a translucent color (**Figures 2.101** and **2.102**).

Now that you're in Quick Mask mode, you no longer need to use selection tools to modify a selection. Instead, you use standard painting tools and paint with black to take away from the selection or white to add to it. When you're done modifying the selection, switch back to Standard mode and you'll be back to marching ants (**Figures 2.103** and **2.104**).

Now let's see what feathered selections look like in Quick Mask mode. Make another selection using the Marquee tool. Next, choose Select > Modify > Feather with a setting of 10, and then switch to Quick Mask mode and take a look (**Figures 2.105** and **2.106**). Feathered selections appear with blurry edges in Quick Mask mode. This happens because partially transparent areas (that is, those that are more transparent than the rest of the mask) indicate areas that are partially selected (50% transparent means 50% selected).

The confusing part about this process is that when you look at the marching ants that appear after you switch back to Standard mode, they only show you where the selection is at least 50% selected. That isn't a very accurate picture of what it really looks like (**Figure 2.107**). But in Quick Mask mode, you can see exactly what is happening on the image's edge. So, if you want to create a feathered selection in Quick Mask mode, just choose a soft-edged brush to paint with. Or, if you already have a shape defined, choose Filter > Blur > Gaussian Blur, which will give you the same result as feathering and will show you a visual preview of the edge.

Figure 2.102 The same selection shown in Quick Mask mode.

Figure 2.103 A selection modified in Quick Mask mode.

Figure 2.104 End result after switching back to Standard mode.

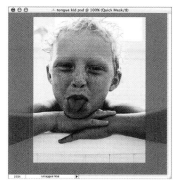

Figure 2.105 Normal. (©2007 Stockbyte www.stockbyte.com)

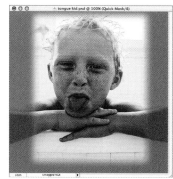

Figure 2.106 Feathered.

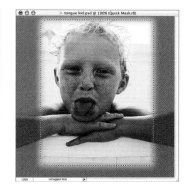

Figure 2.107 The marching ants show up where an area is at least 50% selected.

Shades of Gray

Try this out. Turn on Quick Mask mode—you don't need a selection to begin with. Type D to reset the foreground color to black, and then press Option-Delete (Mac) or Alt-Backspace (Windows) to fill the Quick Mask. Now paint within the Quick Mask with 20% gray (you can use the Color Picker palette to choose grays). Then turn off Quick Mask mode and paint in the selected area with bright red. Now choose Select > Deselect, lower the opacity of the painting tool to 80%, and paint with bright red. Your reds should look exactly the same. That's how Photoshop makes a selection fade out—by simply lowering the opacity of the tool you are using. This can sometimes be confusing, though, because the marching ants show up only where an

Figure 2.108 When painting in Quick Mask mode, only the areas that contain less than 50% gray will be visible when the selection is viewed as marching ants.

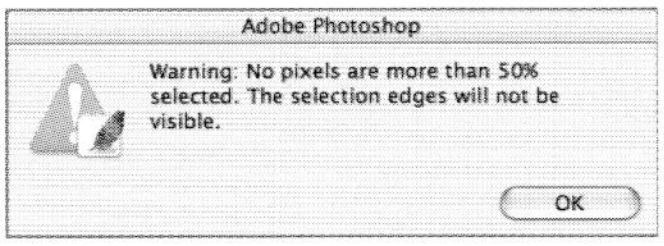

Figure 2.109 When you paint with shades brighter than 50% gray, a warning appears when you go back to Standard mode.

Figure 2.110 Applying the Ripple filter in Quick Mask mode. (©2007 Stockbyte, www.stockbyte.com)

image is at least 50% selected. So, try this one on for size. Turn on Quick Mask mode and paint with 49% gray, and then paint in another area with 51% gray. Then go back to Standard mode and paint across the area. Only the areas that are at least 50% gray show up as marching ants, but the other areas are still selected, even though the marching ants don't show up in those areas (**Figure 2.108**). Now turn on Quick Mask mode, reset the foreground color by typing D, press Option-Delete (Mac) or Alt-Backspace (Windows) to fill the Quick Mask, and then paint with 55% gray. Now go back to Standard mode, and you'll get a warning message (**Figure 2.109**).

We really haven't done anything fancy yet, so let's try something fun. To start with, you have to remember that when you work in Quick Mask mode, Photoshop treats the selection as if it is a grayscale image that you can paint on. That means you can use any tool that is available when working on grayscale images. So select an area using the Marquee tool, turn on Quick Mask mode, choose Filter > Distort > Ripple, and mess with the settings until you've created something that looks a little kooky (**Figure 2.110**). Finally, go back to Standard mode and see what you've got. You can create infinite varieties of fascinating selections with this simple technique.

You can also convert a logo or sketch into a selection using Quick Mask mode. All you need to do is copy the image, turn on Quick Mask mode, choose Edit > Paste, and then choose Image > Adjustments > Invert. If the logo was in color, you might end up with shades of gray (which will look like shades of red in Quick Mask mode). In that case, you'll need to choose Image > Adjustments > Levels and pull in the upper-right and upper-left sliders until the image is pure black and pure white (**Figure 2.111**). Once everything looks right, turn off Quick Mask mode and you'll have your selection.

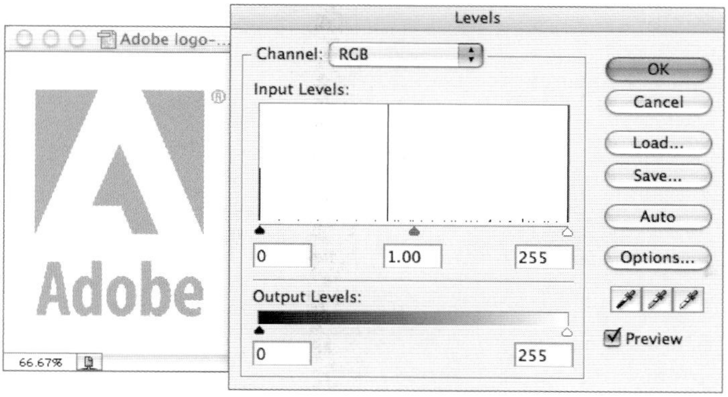

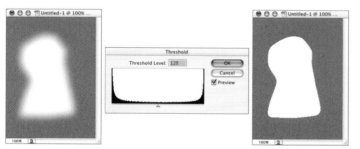

Figure 2.111 Adjusting a logo using the Levels dialog box.

Now let's figure out how to "unfeather" a selection using Quick Mask mode (**Figure 2.112**). Remember, a feathered edge looks like a blurry edge in Quick Mask mode. All you have to do to remove that blurry look is to then choose Image > Adjustments > Threshold. This will give the mask a very crisp, and therefore unfeathered, edge.

Figure 2.112 Unfeathering a selection using Threshold. Left: Original image. Center: Threshold setting used. Right: Result of applying Threshold.

Selections in Quick Mask Mode

You can even use a selection to isolate a particular area of the quick mask (**Figure 2.113**). A selection in Quick Mask mode can help you create a selection that is only feathered on one side. To accomplish this, turn on Quick Mask mode, type D to reset the foreground color, and then press Option-Delete (Mac) or Alt-Backspace (Windows) to fill the quick mask. Next, choose the Marquee tool and select an area. Now use the Gradient tool set to

Figure 2.113 Using a selection in Quick Mask mode to restrict which areas can be edited. (Original image ©2007 Stockbyte, www.stockbyte.com)

Black, White (the third choice from the left in the gradient presets drop-down menu) and create a gradient within the selected area. When you're done, switch off Quick Mask mode. Now, to see exactly how this selection will affect the image, choose Image > Adjustments > Levels and attempt to lighten that area by dragging the lower-left slider.

Color

Photoshop also allows you to switch where the color shows up. You can specify whether you want the selected or unselected areas to show up. To change this setting, double-click the quick mask icon and change the Color Indicates setting (**Figures 2.114** and **2.115**). Photoshop uses the term *Masked Areas* to describe areas that are not selected.

Figure 2.114 Changing the Color Indicates setting changes where the color overlay appears.

You can change the color that is overlaid on your image by clicking the color swatch in the Quick Mask Options dialog box. The Opacity setting determines how much you will be able to see through the Quick Mask.

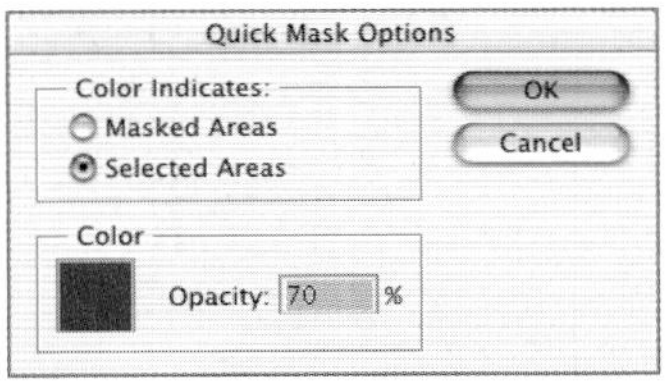

Closing Thoughts

After a few practice rounds with the various tools we covered in this chapter, you should be selecting like a pro. We'll go over more advanced methods of creating selections in Chapter 13, "Advanced Masking." Until then, it really is worth your while to build up your selection skills because you will be using them every day in Photoshop.

Figure 2.115 Quick Mask Options settings used.

3

Layers Primer

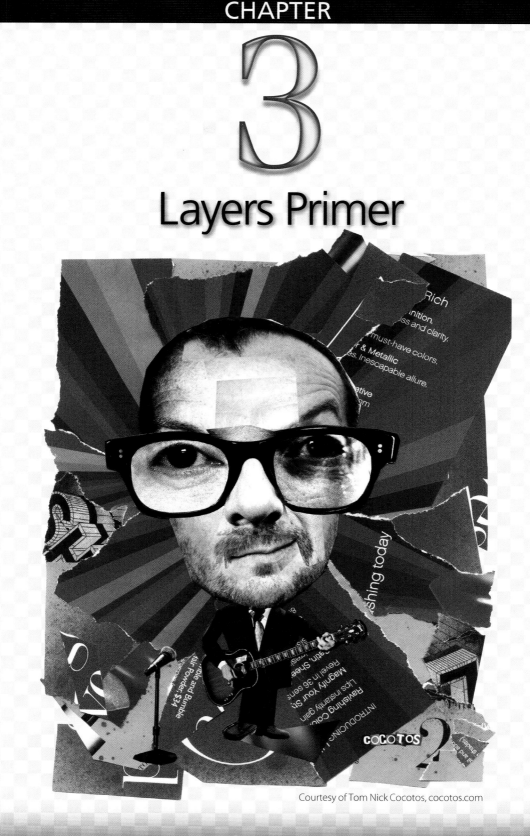

Courtesy of Tom Nick Cocotos, cocotos.com

The first rule to tinkering is to save all the parts.
—Paul Ehrlich

The Layers palette is like the mother everybody wanted as a teenager. Instead of yelling at you to clean your room, she patiently keeps track of all your stuff and she doesn't care if you are neat and tidy or an all-out slob. She is command central for everything you will ever do in Photoshop, and the better you get to know her, the more you will be rewarded for your efforts. Whether you have just a few elements in your document, or hundreds, the Layers palette keeps everything organized and gives you an amazing number of options for how to make the elements relate to each other. There's no getting around this one; learning all the nooks and crannies, and knowing how to use this palette effectively will dramatically ease your life in Photoshop. The good news is that an understanding of Layers—as opposed to some of Photoshop's more complex features—is relatively easy territory to conquer.

How Do Layers Work?

At first glance, layers might seem complex, but the idea behind them is rather simple: with layers, you isolate different parts of your image onto independent layers (**Figure 3.1**). These layers act as if they are separate documents stacked one on top of the other. By putting each image on its own layer, you can freely change your document's look and layout without committing to the changes. If you paint, apply a filter, or make an adjustment, it affects only the layer on which you're working. If you get into a snarl over a particularly troublesome layer, you can throw it away and start over. The rest of your document will remain untouched.

You can make the layers relate to each other in interesting ways, such as by poking holes in them to reveal an underlying image. I'll show you some great techniques using this concept in Chapter 12, "Enhancement," and Chapter 14 "Collage."

Figure 3.1 Layers isolate different parts of the image.
(©2007 Regina Cleveland)

But first, you need to pick up on the basics—the foundations—of layers. If you've used layers for a while, you might find some of this chapter a bit too basic. On the other hand, you might find some juicy new tidbits.

Meeting the Layers

Before we jump in and start creating a bunch of layers, you should get familiar with their place of residence: the Layers palette (**Figure 3.2**). You're going to be spending a lot of time with this palette, so take a moment now to get on friendly terms with it. It's not terribly complicated, and after you've used it a few times, you should know it like the back of your hand.

As you make your way through this chapter, you'll learn about the Layers palette and the fundamental tasks associated with it. Now, assuming that you've done your part and introduced yourself to the Layers palette, let's get on with the business of creating and manipulating layers in Photoshop.

Creating Layers

Photoshop automatically creates the majority of the layers you'll need. A new layer is added anytime you copy and paste an image or drag a layer between documents (we'll talk about this later in the chapter). If you're starting from scratch, however, you can click the New Layer icon at the bottom of the Layers palette to create a new, empty layer.

Give it a try: Choose File > New and create an RGB document that is around 200 x 200 pixels in size with a transparent background (the resolution doesn't matter at this point). Then, click the New Layer icon at the bottom of the Layers palette to create an empty layer. Next, click on your foreground color and pick out a bright color, choose the round Shape tool (it's called an Ellipse and is grouped with the Rectangle Shape tool found below the Type tool in the Tools palette) and click on the rightmost icon of the three available in the upper left of the options bar. Now, click and drag across your image to draw a big circle

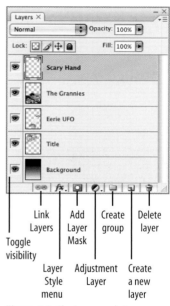

Figure 3.2 The Layers palette.

NOTES

If you hold the Command/Ctrl key when clicking the New Layer icon, the new layer will appear below the active layer instead of on top of it. The only time that won't work is when the Background is active—Photoshop can't add a new layer below the Background.

(**Figure 3.3**). When you're done with the first shape, create another layer and use the Rectangle Shape tool to draw a square on it, but with a different color (**Figure 3.4**). Finally, create a third layer and draw a triangle (**Figure 3.5**) with yet another color (create the triangle by using the Polygon Shape tool with the Sides setting to 3 in the options bar). You can use this simple document you've just created to try out the concepts in the following sections that describe the features of the Layers palette (**Figure 3.6**).

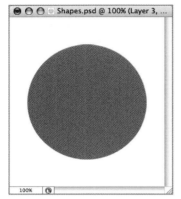

Figure 3.3 A new layer.

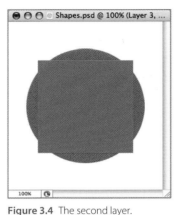

Figure 3.4 The second layer.

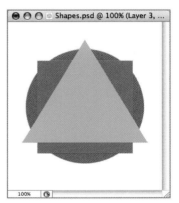

Figure 3.5 The third layer.

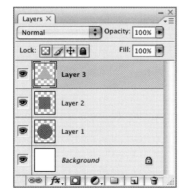

Figure 3.6 The Layers palette view.

Active Layer

The layer you're currently working on will be highlighted in the Layers palette. To change the active layer, just click the name of another layer. Or, if you'd rather not use the Layers palette, Command/Ctrl-click on your image while the Move tool is active. That causes the topmost layer that contains information under your cursor to become active. As you Command/Ctrl-click on different parts of your image (circle, square, triangle in this example), watch the Layers palette to see which layer becomes active. Photoshop CS2 and CS3 allow you to have more than one layer active at a time, but for now we'll stick to working with one layer to keep things simple.

Stacking Order

You can change the stacking order of the layers by dragging the name of one layer above or below the name of another layer in the Layers palette. The topmost layers can often obstruct your view of the underlying images. To change this, you can reorder the layers by dragging them up or down in the Layers palette (**Figures 3.7** to **3.10**).

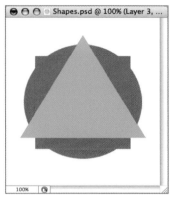

Figure 3.7 The original image.

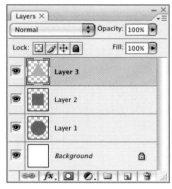

Figure 3.8 The original Layers palette.

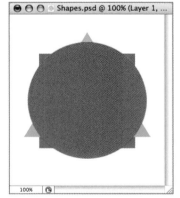

Figure 3.9 The changed stacking order.

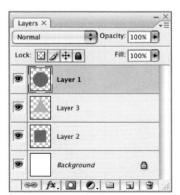

Figure 3.10 The revised Layers palette.

NOTES

If your document doesn't have a background (because you accidentally deleted or renamed the background), you can convert one of the existing layers into a background by choosing Layer > New > Background from Layer. Just changing the layer's name back to "Background" will not do the job.

To quickly turn off all the eyeballs in the Layers palette and view only the layer you're interested in, simply Option/Alt-click one of the eyeball icons. Option/Alt-clicking a second time will bring those same layers back into view. If you'd rather make all the layers visible, Control-click/right-click on the eyeball icon and choose Show/Hide All Other Layers.

You can change the checkerboard's appearance by choosing Edit > Preferences > Transparency & Gamut. You can even change it to solid white by changing the Grid Size setting to None.

Background Image

The Background image in Photoshop (which some people refer to as the Background layer) is a bit different than the other layers that make up your image. If you liken the layers to the individual pages in a pad of tracing paper, you could think of the pad's cardboard backing as the Background image. It might be the same size and it relates to the other pages in the pad, but it has some qualities that make it quite different.

The Background image has the same limitations as most of the common file formats in use today (such as JPEG and EPS): it's always 100% opaque, no part of the Background can extend beyond the document's bounds, and it's not actually considered a layer since most file formats don't support layers (with a few exceptions such as .PSD and .TIFF formats). In fact, that's the whole reason why the Background image exists. If all your document contains is the Background, you should be able to save the image in just about any file format without losing information. That's also why most images start life as a Background image—because they originated in a file format that didn't support layers or came from a program that doesn't support layers. When you save a layered document into a file format that doesn't support layers (like JPEG), Photoshop automatically combines all the layers that make up your image and turns the result into a Background image (known as flattening).

The Background image always displays a lock symbol to indicate that it cannot be repositioned with the Move tool, moved up or down in the layers stack, or be made transparent. For that reason, many tools will work differently when the Background image is active. For instance, the Eraser tool will paint with your Background color when the Background image is active since it is not able to make areas of the Background image transparent.

With all that said, you don't actually have to have a Background in your document. If you want to convert the Background into a normal layer, just change its name (the Background image must be named "Background"; otherwise, it becomes a normal, unlocked layer). To change the name of a layer, double-click the layer's name in the Layers palette and type a new name.

The Eyeballs: What They See Is What You Get

The eyeballs in the Layers palette determine which layers will be visible in your document as well as which ones will print. The eyeballs turn on and off in a toggle effect when you click them: Now you see them, now you don't.

If you turn off all the eyeballs in the Layers palette, Photoshop fills your screen with a checkerboard. This checkerboard indicates that there's nothing visible in the document. (If Photoshop filled your screen with white instead, you might assume that there was a layer visible that was filled with white.) You can think of the checkerboard as the areas of the document that are empty. When you view a single layer, the checkerboard indicates the empty areas of that layer. As you turn on the other layers in the document, the checkerboard is replaced with the information contained on those layers. When multiple layers are visible, the checkerboard indicates where the underlying image will not be obstructed by the elements on the visible layers (**Figures 3.11** to **3.14**).

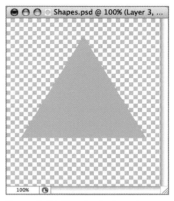

Figure 3.11 The checkerboard indicates a transparent area.

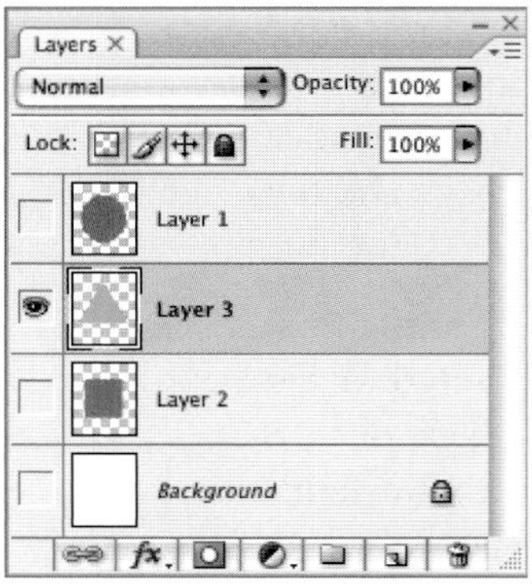

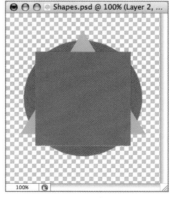

Figure 3.12 The Layers palette view.

Figure 3.13 As more layers become visible, the transparent areas become smaller.

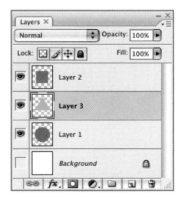

Figure 3.14 The Layers palette view.

To quickly change the opacity of a layer, switch to the Move tool (typing V will switch you to the Move tool) and use the number keys on your keyboard (1 = 10%, 3 = 30%, 56 = 56%, and so on).

You can figure out the exact opacity of an area by Option/Alt-clicking a layer's eyeball icon and then opening the Info palette. Click the eyedropper in the Info palette and choose Opacity; you'll get a separate readout that indicates how opaque the area is below your cursor.

When I need to precisely position a layer, I usually lower the Opacity setting just enough so I can see the underlying layers. After positioning the layer, just press 0 to bring the layer back to 100% opacity.

Opacity

The Opacity setting at the top of the Layers palette controls the opacity of the active layer. When this setting is lowered, the entire layer becomes partially transparent (transparent is the exact opposite of opaque). If you want to lower the opacity in a specific area instead of the entire layer, you can lower the opacity of the Eraser tool and then brush across the area of the layer you want to become more transparent—that is, unless the background is active. If you use the Eraser tool on the background, it will simply paint with your background color instead of truly deleting areas (remember, the background is always opaque).

Try this: Open the document you created earlier in this chapter. Create a new layer, and then use any painting tool to brush across the layer. Now, lower the Opacity setting in the Layers palette to 70% (**Figures 3.15** to **3.17**).

Now let's compare this effect with what happens when you lower the Opacity setting of the Paintbrush tool. Create another new layer; however, this time leave the layer's Opacity setting at 100%. Now choose the Paintbrush tool, change the tool's Opacity setting to 70% (in the options bar), and then brush across the layer (just don't overlap the paint you created earlier). The paint should look exactly the same as the paint that appears in the other layer (**Figures 3.18** and **3.19**).

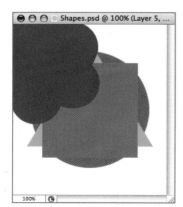

Figure 3.15 Layer at 100% opacity.

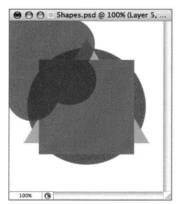

Figure 3.16 Layer at 70% opacity.

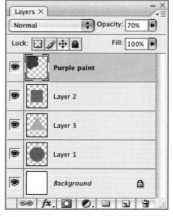

Figure 3.17 Lowering the opacity of a layer affects the entire layer.

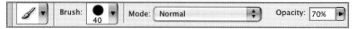

Figure 3.18 The Paintbrush options view.

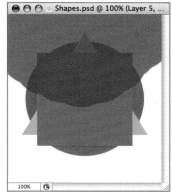

Finally, create one more new layer, and paint across it with the tool's Opacity setting at 100%. Now, brush across an area with the Eraser tool using an Opacity setting of 30% (**Figures 3.20** and **3.21**).

All of these options do the same thing to your image. You just have to think a bit: Do you want to apply the Opacity setting to the entire layer? If so, use the Layers palette's Opacity setting. Do you want to apply the Opacity setting to only part of the layer? If so, use the Opacity setting in the tool's options bar. Do you want to change the opacity of an area you've already painted across? If so, use the Eraser tool with an Opacity setting.

Photoshop always (well, almost always) offers you more than one way of doing things.

Figure 3.19 Painting with a 70% Opacity setting.

Figure 3.20 The Eraser options view.

Moving Layers

If you want to move everything that's on a particular layer, first make that layer active by clicking its name; then use the Move tool to drag it around the screen (**Figure 3.22**). If you drag the layer onto another document window, Photoshop copies the layer into that document. If you want to move just a small area of the layer, you can make a selection and then drag from within the selected area using the Move tool.

You can also use the arrow keys on your keyboard (when the Move tool is active) to nudge a layer one pixel at a time. Holding Shift while using the arrow keys will nudge the active layer 10 pixels at a time.

Figure 3.21 Using the Eraser tool with a low Opacity setting will also make areas of a layer transparent.

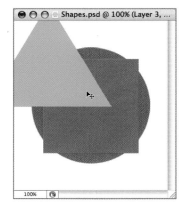

Figure 3.22 Using the Move tool to reposition a layer.

Selecting Multiple Layers

Starting with CS2, Adobe gave us the ability to make more than one layer active at a time. Clicking on individual layers with no keys held causes individual layers to become active (**Figure 3.23**). Command/Ctrl-clicking on a layer adds that layer to the other layers that are selected (**Figure 3.24**). Shift-clicking selects the range of layers that appears between the layer you Shift-clicked on and the one you clicked on previously (**Figure 3.25**). You can also Shift-Command-click (Mac) or Shift-Ctrl-click (Windows) within an image while the Move tool is active to add the layer that appears under your mouse to the layers that are currently selected. There is no limit to the number of layers that can be selected at one time.

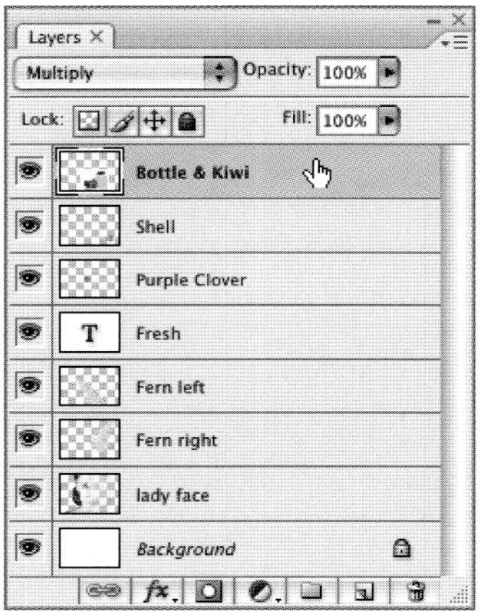

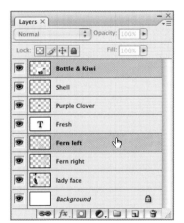

Figure 3.23 Clicking on individual layers activates a single layer.

Figure 3.24 Holding Command/Ctrl when clicking adds a layer to those already selected.

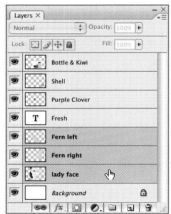

Figure 3.25 Shift-clicking a layer selects the layers between that layer and the last one you clicked on.

Many of Photoshop's features will be unavailable when multiple layers are selected (such as filters and adjustments) because they were designed to only work on one layer at a time. When multiple layers are selected, you can do the following:

▶ Reposition by clicking and dragging with the Move tool.

▶ Change the stacking order by dragging the selected layers up or down in the layers stack.

- ▶ Scale or rotate (but not warp) the layers by choosing an option from the Transform menu (Edit > Transform).

- ▶ Align or distribute the layers using commands found in the Layer menu.

- ▶ Duplicate, delete, link, or group the layers using commands found on the side menu of the Layers palette.

Linking Layers

When multiple layers are linked together, using the Move tool or choosing Edit > Transform causes the currently active layer and all the layers that are linked to it to change (as if all the linked layers were selected). The advantage to linking layers is that the linking behavior will be maintained regardless of which layer is active. So, if two layers should always relate in size and position, link them together so that relationship will remain consistent. To link multiple layers, select the layers and then click on the Link symbol at the bottom of the Layers palette (**Figure 3.26**). After linking the layers, moving or transforming the image while any one of the linked layers is selected causes all the linked layers to change. To unlink layers, select the layers you want to unlink and click the link symbol again.

Trimming the Fat

If you use the Move tool to reposition a layer, and a portion of the layer starts to extend beyond the edge of your document, Photoshop remembers the information beyond the edge (**Figure 3.27**). Therefore, if you move the layer away from the edge, Photoshop is able to bring back the information that was not visible. You can save a lot of memory by making Photoshop clip off all the information beyond the edge of the document (**Figure 3.28**). Here's a little trick for trimming off that fat. Just choose Select > All and then choose Image > Crop—no more wasted memory.

It also wastes memory when you leave extra white space around the edge of your image (**Figure 3.29**). Because the paper you print on is white to begin with, that extra white space just makes your file size larger and has no effect on how the image will look when it's printed. You can choose Image > Trim to have Photoshop remove any unnecessary

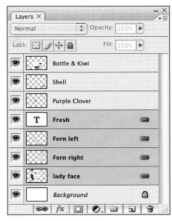

Figure 3.26 The Chain icon indicates linked layers.

Figure 3.27 The original image. (multiple images ©2007 iStockphoto.com)

Figure 3.28 After the image is cropped.

white space (**Figure 3.30**). Just adjust the Based On setting so that it will find white information in your image (depending on which corner of your image contains white), and then specify which edge of the document you'd like to trim away—I usually leave all four of the Trim Away check boxes turned on (**Figure 3.31**).

Figure 3.29 The white space around this image increases its file size.

Figure 3.30 Applying the Trim command removes the extra white space.

Figure 3.31 The Trim settings used on Figure 3.30.

Use the "trim the fat" technique only if you're absolutely sure you won't need the information beyond the edge of the document, because you cannot get it back once you've cropped it (that is, without resorting to the History palette).

The default setting in the Crop tool is to delete the areas that extend beyond the edge of your image. You can prevent it from deleting those areas by clicking the Hide setting in the Crop tool options bar (it will be available only in files that contain layers). That will cause Photoshop to reduce the size of the image based on the cropping rectangle you specify, but it will retain the information that extends beyond the edge of the image.

So far we've talked about how to make your images smaller to save memory and hard drive space, but now let's do the opposite with Photoshop's Reveal All command (Image > Reveal All). When you choose that command, Photoshop enlarges your document to include any information that extends beyond the bounds of your document (**Figures 3.32** and **3.33**). That means that all the layers that you've moved beyond the edge of your document will become visible once again.

Figure 3.32 Many of the layers in this document extend beyond the document's bounds.

Figure 3.33 After applying the Reveal All command, the elements that used to extend beyond the document's bounds are now completely visible.

Copying Between Documents

When you use the Move tool, you can do more than just drag a layer around the document on which you're working. You can also drag a layer from one image window to another (**Figure 3.34**). This copies the selected layers into the second document. The copied layers will be positioned directly above the layer that was active in the second document. This is similar to copying and pasting, but it takes up a lot less memory because Photoshop doesn't store the image on the clipboard. You can achieve the same result by dragging the name of a layer from the Layers palette onto another document window regardless of which tool is active.

NOTES

When dragging between documents, Photoshop positions the layer based on where your cursor was when you clicked the image and where you released the mouse button in the second document. Holding Shift when dragging between documents causes the layers to end up in the center of the destination document (if no selection is active) or centered on any active selection.

If the image you're dragging to another document is considerably larger than the destination document, you'll need to choose Edit > Transform > Scale to resize the image until it is an appropriate size for the destination document. If you can't see the transformation handles, just type Command/Ctrl-0 (zero) to zoom out until the handles become visible.

Figure 3.34 To copy between documents, use the Move tool to drag from the image window, or drag the name of the layer in the Layers palette.

When you drag layers between documents, occasionally an image will appear as if it has not only been copied, but also scaled at the same time. That's not what's really happening. Instead, you're viewing the two images at different magnifications (**Figure 3.35**). Look at the tops of the documents; if the percentages do not match, the image size will appear to change when you drag the image between the documents. If you view both images with the same magnification, this won't happen. It doesn't change how large the image is; it simply gives you a preview of how large it will look. It's just like putting your hand under a magnifying glass: Your hand looks larger, but when you pull your hand out, it looks normal again.

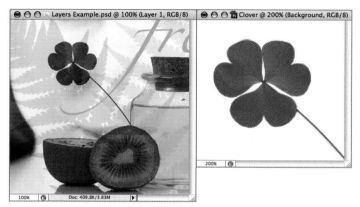

Figure 3.35 Images viewed at different magnifications.

Duplicating Layers

If you have a picture of Elvis and you want to make Elvis twins, just drag the layer onto the New Layer icon at the bottom of the Layers palette. This icon has two purposes: It duplicates a layer if you drag one on top of it, or it creates a new empty layer if you just click it. You can also hold Option/Alt when dragging a layer up or down within the layers stack, or type Command/Ctrl-J to duplicate the currently active layer. Just make sure you don't have a selection active; otherwise, this command will copy only the area that is selected instead of the whole layer.

Deleting Layers

If you've created a document that looks a little cluttered, you can delete a layer by dragging its name onto the Trash icon at the bottom of the Layers palette. Or, if you have a long distance to drag to get your layer in the trash, try Option/Alt-clicking the Trash icon instead (the Option/Alt key prevents a warning dialog box from appearing). However, this icon does not work like the trash on a Mac or the recycle bin in Windows. Once you put something in it, you can't get it back (that is, without resorting to the History palette).

Transforming Layers

To rotate, scale, or distort the active layers, choose one of the options in the Transform menu (Edit > Transform); then pull the handles to distort the image (**Figures 3.36** and **3.37**). When you like the way your image looks, press the Enter key to commit to the change (press Esc to abort). If you want to know more about the transformation controls, see Chapter 2, "Selection Primer" and Chapter 14 "Collage."

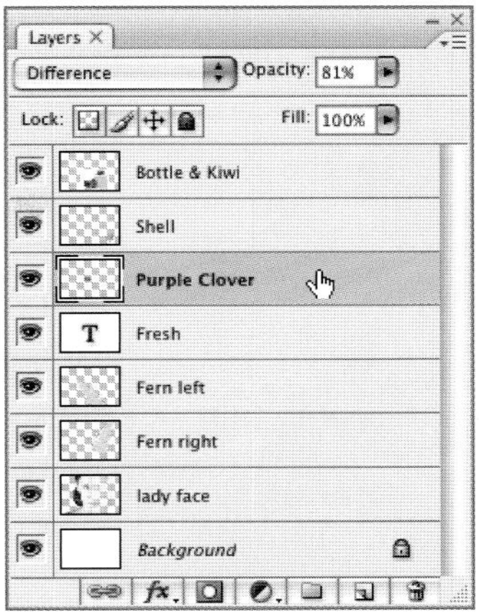

Locking Up

The icons at the top of the Layers palette allow you to lock the transparency, image, and position of an individual layer (**Figure 3.38**). Once a layer has been locked, changes that can be performed on that layer are limited.

Lock Transparency

The Lock Transparency icon (which looks like a checkerboard) at the top of the Layers palette gets in my way most often (because I forget it's turned on). Lock Transparency prevents you from changing the transparency of areas. Each layer has its own Lock Transparency setting. Therefore, if you turn on the Lock Transparency icon for one layer and then switch to another layer, the Layers palette displays the setting for the second layer, which might be different from the first one.

Try using the Eraser tool when Lock Transparency is turned on—it will mess with your mind! Because the Eraser tool usually makes areas transparent (by completely deleting them), it will start painting instead when Lock Transparency is turned on. It will fill any areas you drag over with the current background color. However, if you paint across an area that's transparent, it doesn't change the image at all (because the transparent areas are being preserved). You can see how it can get in your way if you forget you turned it on.

Try this: Open a photo, and delete areas around it using the Eraser tool. To accomplish this, you'll have to change the name of the background first (you can't poke a hole in the background, but you can on a layer); then make sure Lock Transparency is turned off. Otherwise, you can't make areas transparent. Now use the Eraser tool to remove

Figure 3.36 The Layers palette view.

Figure 3.37 Transforming a layer.

Figure 3.38 The Lock icons.

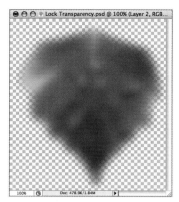

Figure 3.39 Lock Transparency is off.

Figure 3.40 Lock Transparency is on.

the areas that surround the subject of the photo, and then choose Filter > Blur > Gaussian Blur and use a really high setting. You'll notice that the edge of the image fades out and blends with the transparent areas surrounding it (**Figure 3.39**). Now, choose Edit > Undo and try doing the same thing with the Lock Transparency option turned on (**Figure 3.40**). Notice that the edge cannot fade out because Photoshop will not change the transparency with this option turned on.

Here is another example: Create a new layer, and scribble across it with any painting tool, making sure the Lock Transparency option is turned off. Next, drag across the image with the Gradient tool. The gradient should fill the entire screen (**Figure 3.41**). Now, choose Edit > Undo, and try doing the same thing with the Lock Transparency option turned on (**Figure 3.42**). Because Photoshop can't change the transparency of the layer, it cannot fill the transparent areas, and therefore is limited to changing the areas that are opaque to begin with.

Figure 3.41 Lock Transparency is off.   **Figure 3.42** Lock Transparency is on.

When you're trying to use any of the techniques in this book, be sure to keep an eye on that little Lock Transparency icon. If it's turned on when you don't want it to be, it might ruin the entire effect you're trying to achieve. Therefore, unless I specifically tell you to turn it on, you should assume that it should be left off (that's the default setting). If I ever tell you to turn it on, I'll let you know when to turn it back off again so that you don't get messed up when trying to reproduce a technique from this book. Now, turn off that pesky (but useful) setting, and let's continue exploring Photoshop.

Lock Image

The Lock Image icon (which looks like a paintbrush) at the top of the Layers palette prevents you from changing the pixels that make up a layer. That means you won't be able to paint, erase, apply an adjustment or filter, or do anything else that would change the look of that layer (although you can still move or transform the layer). Just as with Lock Transparency, each layer has its own Lock Image setting. I use this feature after I've finished color correcting and retouching a layer so I don't accidentally change it later on.

Lock Position

The Lock Position icon (which looks like the Move tool) at the top of the Layers palette prevents you from moving the active layer. I select this feature to prevent someone else from accidentally moving an element that I've taken great care to position correctly.

Lock All

The Lock All icon (which looks like a padlock) at the top of the Layers palette locks the transparency, image, and position of the current layer.

Layer Styles

A bunch of really neat options are available under the Layer Style menu (Layer > Layer Style) (**Figure 3.43**). You'll find some of the same options under the Layer Style pop-up menu at the bottom of the Layers palette (it's the leftmost icon). To experiment with these options, first create a new, empty layer, and paint on it with any of the painting tools. Then apply one of the effects found in the Layer Style menu: Drop Shadow, Inner Shadow, Inner Glow, Outer Glow, Bevel and Emboss, and so on (**Figures 3.44** to **3.46**). You can use the default settings for now. After applying an

You can press the forward slash key "/" at any time to toggle the last lock you changed on or off.

The Lock Image icon might prevent you from directly modifying the pixels that make up a layer, but it does not completely prevent you from changing the appearance of that layer. You can still add an Adjustment Layer directly above the layer in question to change its general appearance.

Figure 3.43 The Layer Style menu.

effect, use the Eraser tool to remove some of the paint on that layer. Did you notice that the layer effect updates to reflect the changes you make to the layer? Layer Styles create in one simple step the same results that would usually require multiple layers and a lot of memory.

Figure 3.44 The Layer Style dialog box with the Drop Shadow panel.

Figure 3.45 Left: The original image. Right: The image with Drop Shadow style applied to the text layer.

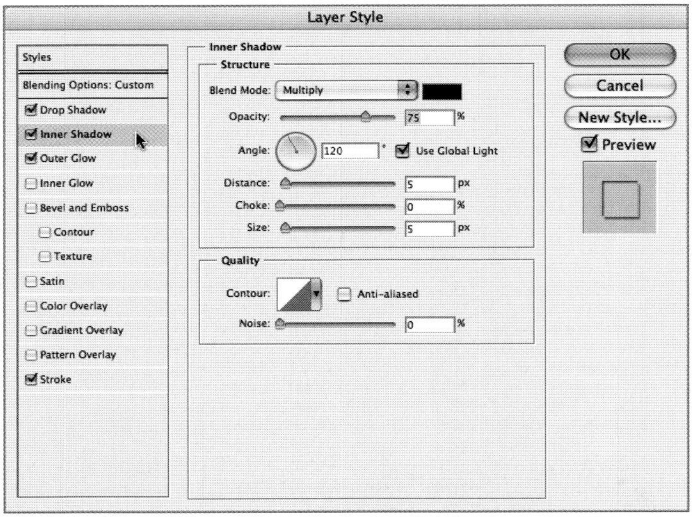

Figure 3.46 The Layer Style dialog box with the Inner Shadow panel.

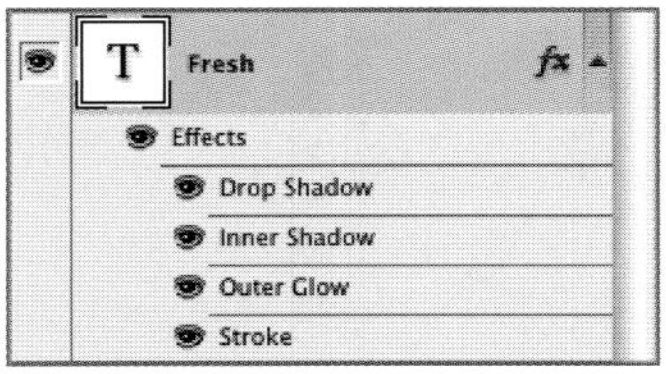

Figure 3.47 Click on the triangle that appears next to the "f" symbol to see a list of the Layer Styles that are applied to that layer.

When you have at least one Layer Style applied to a layer, you'll see a a small "fx" next to it in the Layers palette. That's the only indication that a layer has a Layer Style attached to it. You can click on the triangle that appears next to that symbol to see a list of the Layer Styles that are applied to that layer (**Figure 3.47**). If you drag one of the

Layer Styles from that list and release your mouse button when it's on top of another layer, you'll move that Layer Style to the second layer. Holding Option/Alt when dragging a style copies the style instead of moving it. Dragging the word "Effects" moves all of the Layer Styles that are attached to that layer. If you'd like to remove one of the Layer Styles, just click on its name in the list and drag it to the Trash icon at the bottom of the Layers palette.

You can even lower the Fill setting at the top of Photoshop's Layers palette to reduce the opacity of the layer contents (or hold Shift and type a number while the Move tool is active) while keeping the Layer Style at full strength (**Figure 3.48**). Not only that, you can choose Layer > Layer Style > Create Layer to have Photoshop create the layers that would usually be needed to create the effect. For example, you might want to choose Create Layer if you want to distort the effect separately from the layer it was attached to. Let's take a look at what a few of the Layer Styles do to your image (**Figures 3.49** to **3.51**).

Figure 3.48 A result of lowering the Fill opacity to 0.

Figure 3.49 Inner Shadow style is applied to the text layer.

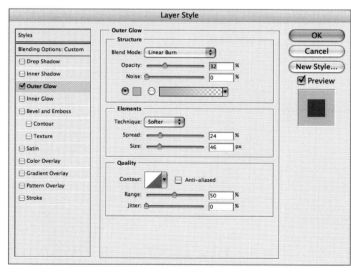

Figure 3.50 The Layer Style dialog box with the Outer Glow panel.

Figure 3.51 Outer Glow style is applied to the text layer.

Adjustment Layers

The Adjustment Layer pop-up menu at the bottom of the Layers palette (it's the half black and half white circle) allows you to apply adjustments that will affect multiple layers. This is the most versatile method for applying adjustments, and it is such a powerful feature that I've devoted an entire chapter to it (Chapter 10 "Adjustment Layers").

Fill Layers

The options in the New Fill Layer menu (Layer > New Fill Layer) allow you to add solid color, gradient, and pattern content to a layer. This is especially useful when combined with Vector Mask, as described in Chapter 14, "Collage." If you don't want a fill layer to fill your entire document, make a selection before creating one, which will create a layer mask. After a fill layer has been created, you can reset your foreground and background colors to black/white by pressing D. Then you can use the Eraser tool to hide the area and the Paintbrush tool to make areas visible again.

Solid Color Layer

Choosing Layer > New Fill Layer > Solid Color brings up a dialog box that asks you to name the layer you're creating. After you click OK, it opens the Color Picker, where you can specify the color that will be used for the solid color layer. When you've created one of these layers, you can double-click the leftmost thumbnail of the layer in the Layers palette to edit the color.

Gradient Layer

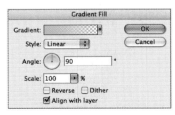

Figure 3.52 The Gradient Fill dialog box.

Choosing Layer > New Fill Layer > Gradient brings up a dialog box that asks you to name the layer; this creates a new layer that contains a gradient (**Figure 3.52**). The gradient is always editable by double-clicking the leftmost thumbnail in the Layers palette. If the Align with layer check box is turned on, the start and end points of the gradient are determined by the contents of the layer instead of the document's overall size.

Pattern Layer

Choosing Layer > New Fill Layer > Pattern allows you to create a new layer that contains a repeating pattern (**Figure 3.53**). I like to use this type of layer to add a brushed-aluminum look to a background. Then, if I ever decide to change the pattern, it's as simple as double-clicking the thumbnail in the Layers palette and choosing New Pattern from the drop-down menu.

Figure 3.53 The Pattern Fill dialog box.

The Blending Mode Menu

The Blending Mode menu at the top left of the Layers palette is immensely useful. It allows the information on one layer to blend with the underlying image in interesting and useful ways. Using this menu, you can quickly change the color of objects, colorize grayscale images, add reflections to metallic objects, and much more. This is an advanced feature, so you'll have to wait until you get to Chapter 12, "Enhancement," to find out more about it.

Automatic Selections

To select everything on a particular layer, just Command/Ctrl-click on the thumbnail image of the layer in the Layers palette. If the layer fills the entire screen, it will select all because this trick looks for transparent areas. You can hold down the Shift key to add to a selection that already exists or use the Option/Alt key to take away from the current selection (**Figures 3.54** to **3.57**).

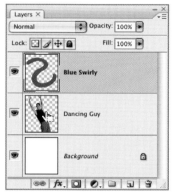

Figure 3.54 Command/Ctrl-click a layer to select all the objects on that layer.

Figure 3.55 The result of Command/Ctrl-clicking. (©2007 iStockphoto.com/joshblake)

Figure 3.56 Refining the selection with the Lasso tool while holding down Option/Alt to take away from the selection.

Figure 3.57 The result of copying the selected area of the guy and pasting it on a layer above the swirl (look at his chest and shoulder area).

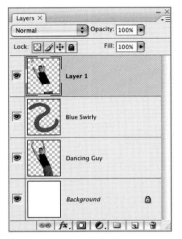

Figure 3.58 Result of using Layer > New > Layer Via Copy and moving the new layer over the swirly layer.

Via Copy

The Layers menu offers you a wide variety of options for copying, merging, and manipulating layers. Let's look at one of these choices. If you select an area of your image and then choose Layer > New > Layer Via Copy, the area you've selected will be copied from the layer you were working on and moved to a brand-new layer in the same position (**Figure 3.58**). This is particularly handy when you want to move just a portion of a layer so that you can place it on top of another layer.

Use All Layers

When you're editing on a layer, some of the editing tools might not work the way you expect them to. This happens because most of the tools act as if each layer is a separate document—they ignore all layers except the active one; that is, unless the tool has the Use All Layers check box (labeled All Layers in the Paint Bucket tool) turned on in the options bar of the tool you're using. This check box allows the tools to act as if all the layers have been combined into one layer (**Figures 3.59** to **3.61**).

Figure 3.59 Using the Paint Bucket tool to add color with the All Layers option turned off.

Figure 3.60 Using the Paint Bucket tool with All Layers turned on.

Figure 3.61 The All Layers check box in the Paint Bucket options bar.

Shortcuts

You'll be doing a lot of switching between layers, and this can get a bit tedious. Therefore, I'll show you some quick shortcuts. You can Command/Ctrl-click anywhere in the image window when using the Move tool to activate the layer directly below your cursor. Then you can find out which layer you're working on by glancing at the Layers palette.

You won't always need the layer below your cursor, so instead of Command/Ctrl-clicking, try Control-clicking/right-clicking. This brings up a menu of all the layers that contain pixels directly below your cursor; you just choose the name of the layer you want to work on and Photoshop switches to that layer.

Remember that you can get to the Move tool temporarily at any time by holding down the Command/Ctrl key. Therefore, if you hold down Command and Control (Mac) or Ctrl and right-click (Windows) at the same time, no matter what tool you are using, Photoshop presents you with the pop-up menu.

Grouping Layers

Have you ever had one of those mega-complicated images with dozens of layers? If so, you are probably familiar with the agony of having to fumble through an endless sea of layers, hoping you won't drown before you find the right one. If this describes you, you'll be ecstatic to know you can group a bunch of layers together. A group of layers looks like a folder in the Layers palette. You can view all the layers in the group or just the group name.

NOTES

To get rid of a group without throwing away the layers that are inside it, click on the group to make it active, click on the Trash icon at the bottom of the Layers palette, and then choose Group Only when prompted.

To group multiple layers, select the layers and then either Shift-click on the folder icon at the bottom of the Layers palette or choose Layer > Group Layers. You can also click the folder icon (without holding any keys) to create an empty folder. Then, you can move any number of layers into the folder by dragging and dropping them onto the folder you just created. The folder will have a small triangle just to its left that allows you to collapse the group down to its name or expand the group to show you all the layers it contains. You can even drag one folder onto another to

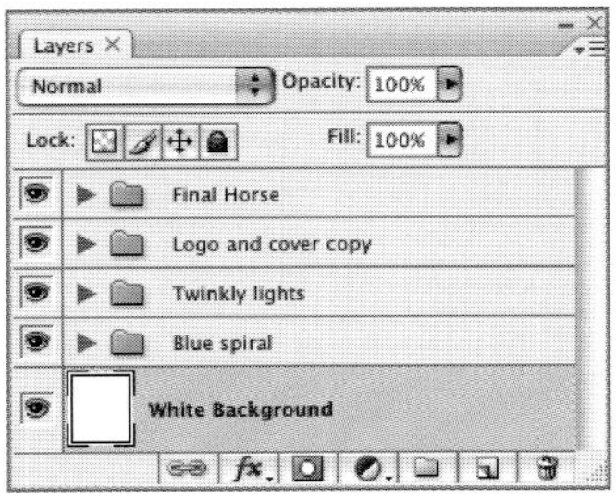

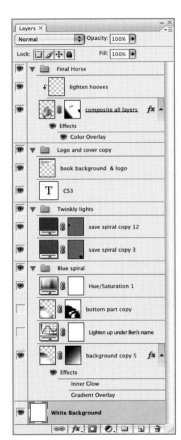

Figure 3.62 Collapsed layer sets.

Figure 3.63 Expanded layer sets.

create a hierarchy of up to five levels of folders (**Figures 3.62** and **3.63**). This can greatly simplify the Layers palette, making a document of 100-plus layers look as if it's made of only a few layers.

Option/Alt-clicking on the arrow next to a group expands or collapses all the groups and Layer Style lists within that group. Adding the Command/Ctrl key expands or collapses all the groups in the entire document.

Groups can also be useful when you want to reorganize the layers in your image. If one of the layers within a group is active, using the Move tool will affect only that layer (unless it's linked to other layers). If the group is active, using the Move tool will move all the layers within that group.

Smart Guides

When you choose View > Show > Smart Guides, Photoshop displays pink guides to indicate how the active layer aligns with the surrounding layers (**Figure 3.64**). Smart Guides pay attention to the top, bottom, left, right, and center of each layer, and extend the pink guides across all the layers that are aligned. The layers will also snap to these alignment points, making it especially easy to get your layers in alignment. You can toggle the snapping behavior off or on by choosing View > Snap To > Layers.

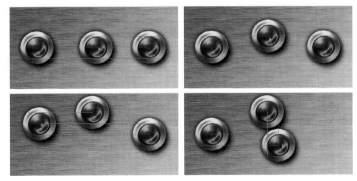

Figure 3.64 The pink guides indicate where the active layer aligns with the other layers in the document (you might have to get out your magnifying glass for this one, the pink lines are very fine and difficult to see on the printed page).

The Smart Guides ignore Layer Styles that are applied to a layer. In the example shown (**Figure 3.64**), the outer ring of each object was created using the Stroke and Bevel & Emboss Layer Styles, so it was not used when determining where the edge of the layer is located. The Smart Guides also ignore any areas that have an opacity of less than 50%, which will also affect any layers that have soft edges, causing the snapping behavior to treat the halfway point of the fadeout as the edge of the layer.

No Thumbnail View

If, after organizing your image into layer sets, you still find that the Layers palette is a mess, you might want to simplify the way Photoshop displays layers. If you choose Palette Options from the side menu of the Layers palette, you'll find the option that allows you to turn off the layer thumbnails. Once you've done that, you should find that the list of layers takes up a lot less space, but you still have the full functionality of all of Photoshop's features (**Figures 3.65** and **3.66**). This also speeds up the screen redraw of the Layers palette.

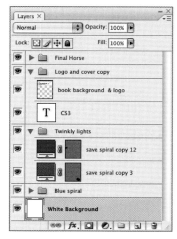

Figure 3.65 The Layers palette using the default thumbnail size.

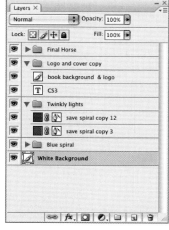

Figure 3.66 The Layers palette after setting the Thumbnails setting to None.

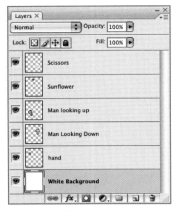

Figure 3.67 The Layers palette using the Entire Document setting.

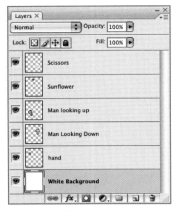

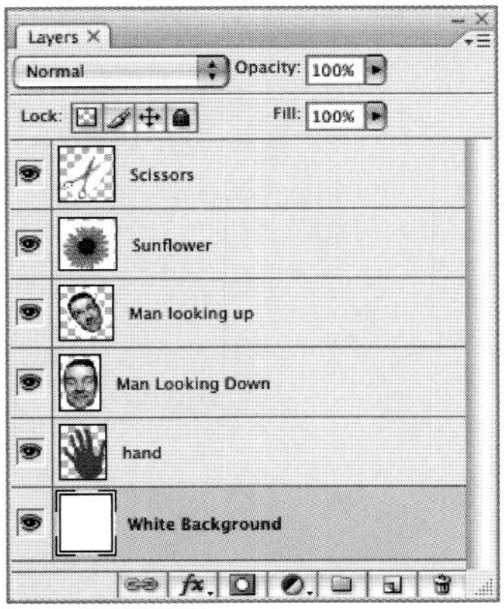

Figure 3.68 The Layers palette using the Layer Bounds setting.

Layer Bounds View

If you have many small elements on individual layers, the Layers palette might look like a sea of checkerboard. Photoshop CS2 and CS3 allow you to have Photoshop crop the layer thumbnails so that they show the contents of a layer while ignoring any empty area surrounding the content. To get to this view, choose Palette Options from the side menu of the Layers palette and turn on the Layer Bounds setting (**Figures 3.67** and **3.68**).

Color Coding

If you work within a large group of Photoshop users, it can be useful to assign colors to layers to indicate their current status. Maybe some text needs to be proofed, maybe the client approved a certain part of the image, or perhaps an area needs to be sent off for color correction. All you have to do is Control/right-click on the name of a layer and choose Layer Properties. That brings up a dialog box where you can color code a layer or a group (**Figures 3.69** and **3.70**). Even easier, Control/right-click on the Eyeball column to bring up color choices for that layer or group.

Figure 3.69 The Layer Properties dialog box.

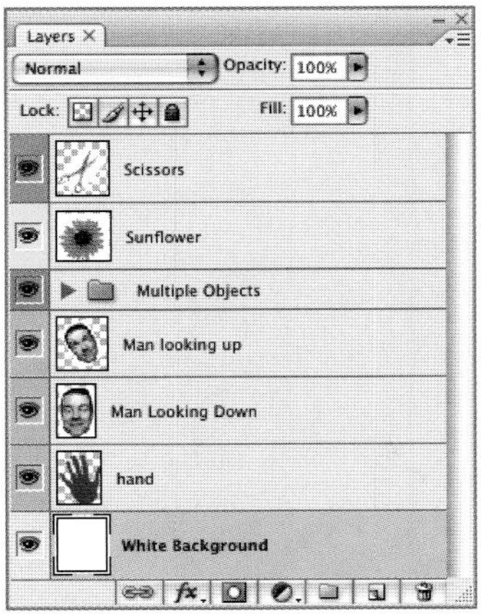

Figure 3.70 Each layer can be color coded using one of seven colors.

Merging Layers

When you create a complicated image that contains dozens of layers, your project can start hogging memory, which in turn makes it difficult to manage all the layers. Every time you create a new layer and add something to it, Photoshop gobbles up more memory. Photoshop not only has to think about what's on that layer, but also has to remember what's below the layer (even if that information is completely covered by the information on the layers above).

Whenever possible, I try to simplify my image by merging layers. This combines the layers into a single layer, and thus saves memory (because Photoshop no longer has to remember the parts of those layers that were previously being covered). The side menu on the Layers palette and the Layer menu itself give you several ways to do this:

▶ **Merge Down:** Merges the active layer into the layer directly below it.

▶ **Merge Visible:** Merges all the layers that are currently visible in the main image window.

▶ **Merge Layers:** Merges all the currently selected layers.

▶ **Merge Group:** Merges all the layers that are within the active group.

▶ **Flatten Image:** Merges all visible layers into the background, discards hidden layers, and fills empty areas with white.

If you want to know how much extra memory the layers take up as you're modifying your image, choose Document Sizes from the menu that appears at the bottom center of the document (**Figure 3.71**). The number on the left should stay relatively constant (unless you scale or crop the image); it indicates how much memory your image would use if all the layers were merged together. The number on the right indicates how much memory the image is using with all the layers included. This number changes as you add and modify your layers. Keep an eye on it so that you can see how memory-intensive the different layers are.

> **WARNING**
>
> Once you've merged two layers, it's awfully hard to get them apart—the only way to do so is to use the History palette. However, even with the History palette, you might lose all the changes you've made since you merged the layers.

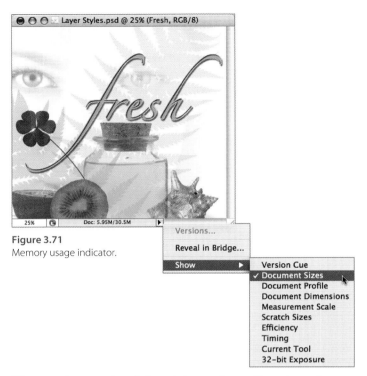

Figure 3.71
Memory usage indicator.

The number on the right might get huge if you're using a lot of layers; however, keep in mind that you'll know exactly how large the image will be when you flatten the layers by glancing at the left number.

Closing Thoughts

Layers play such a huge role in Photoshop that to deny yourself any crucial information about them is asking for trouble. With every new release, Adobe likes to pack more and more functions into the Layers palette. So as time goes on, understanding them will become even more essential. This is definitely a chapter you should feel comfortable with before you move on to the more advanced areas of Photoshop.

PART II

Production Essentials

Optimizing Grayscale Images

If you go through life convinced that your way is always best, all the new ideas in the world will pass you by.

—Akio Morita, founder of Sony

When you work with grayscale images, your adjustments and corrections are limited to only *tonal* adjustments—that is, changes to the brightness and contrast of the image. When you work with color images, you also have to worry about hue, saturation, and the other properties of color.

Photoshop provides several tools for making tonal adjustments, and we'll look at all of them. You can use these tools for correcting and adjusting both grayscale and color images.

Brightness/Contrast

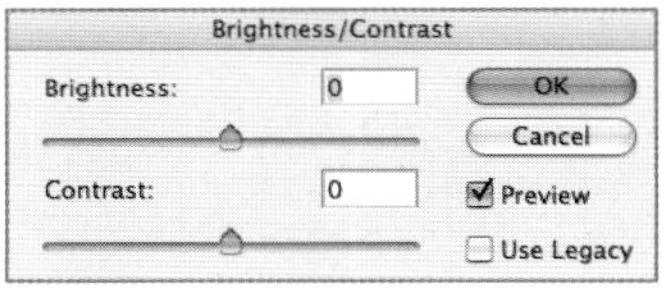

With all previous versions of Photoshop, it was safe to say that you should never use the Brightness/Contrast dialog box to make tonal adjustments. This was because Brightness/Contrast used to adjust the entire tonal range of the image by equal amounts, which made it difficult to adjust one part of the image—say, the shadows—without screwing up another part of the image, such as the highlights.

With CS3, Adobe has reengineered the Brightness/Contrast dialog box and turned it into a very useful, very powerful tonal adjustment tool.

You'll find the Brightness/Contrast adjustment by choosing Image > Adjustments > Brightness/Contrast. The dialog box is very straightforward (**Figure 4.1**). By sliding the Brightness slider back and forth, you can make your overall image brighter or darker. In general, the Brightness slider protects your shadow areas—it won't usually let you underexpose them too far. This means that you need to keep a very close eye on the highlights in your image. As you adjust the slider, be careful that you don't let the highlights overexpose and blow out to complete white (**Figure 4.2**).

Figure 4.1 The Brightness/Contrast dialog box.

Figure 4.2 As you slide the Brightness slider to the left or right, your image becomes darker or lighter. (©2007 Andy Katz)

The Contrast slider increases contrast in your image by brightening the light parts and darkening the darker areas (**Figure 4.3**). The overall effect is an image with more "pop" and better detail.

Moving the slider to the left lowers the contrast, resulting in a flatter image (**Figure 4.4**).

Brightness/Contrast is not the most refined tool, but it can be a great place to start if you're new to Photoshop.

Levels

Brightness/Contrast is especially useful if you've never performed tonal corrections before, and on many images, it's all the control you'll ever need. However, Photoshop's Levels adjustment provides a more sophisticated tool that offers a much finer degree of control (**Figure 4.5**).

Figure 4.3 With the Contrast slider you can add more punch to your images.

Figure 4.4 The Contrast slider can also be used to pull contrast *out* of an image.

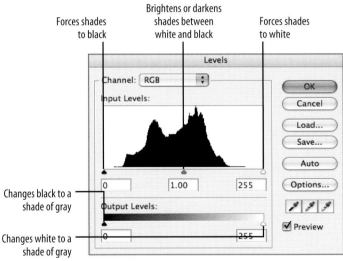

Figure 4.5 Understanding the Levels sliders.

With Levels you have five different sliders that you can adjust, as well as a histogram (sort of like a bar chart) (**Figure 4.6**) that indicates exactly what is happening to the image.

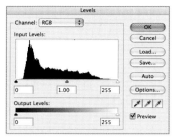

Figure 4.6 This histogram indicates that the shades between around 90% and 75% gray take up a lot of space (tall bars), and the shades between around 5% and 15% take up little space (short bars).

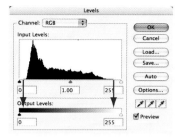

Figure 4.7 Look at the gradient bar directly below the ends of the histogram to determine the brightest and darkest shades present in the image.

The Histogram Is Your Guide

You can use the bar chart (also known as a histogram) at the top of the Levels dialog box to determine whether the adjustments you're making are going to harm the image or improve it. The histogram indicates which shades of gray your image uses and how prevalent those shades are within the image. If you find a gap in the histogram, you can look at the gradient directly below it to see which shade of gray is missing from your image.

By looking below the left side of the histogram, you can determine the darkest shade of gray in the image. By looking below the right end of the histogram, you can determine the brightest shade of gray in the image. If you look at **Figure 4.7**, you might notice the image contains no pure blacks or pure whites. The darkest shade of gray is about 95%, and the brightest shade is about 6%.

There is no ideal when it comes to a histogram; it's simply a representation of which shades of gray are most prevalent in your image (**Figure 4.8**). The peaks indicate a shade of gray that takes up a lot of space in the image, and the valleys indicate a shade that isn't very prevalent in the image. A histogram that extends all the way across the space available and does not have tall spikes on either end indicates an image that has the full range of shades available, and is usually a sign of a good scan or a well-adjusted image.

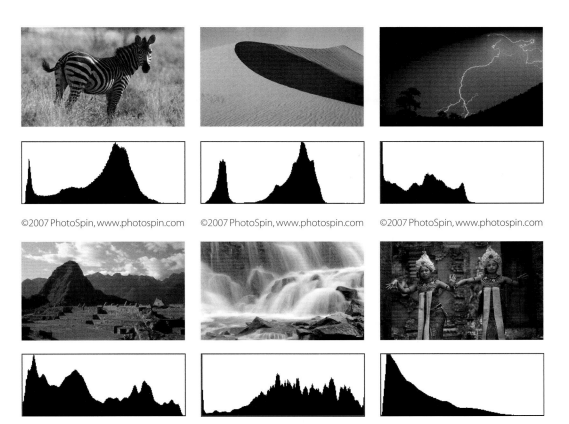

©2007 PhotoSpin, www.photospin.com ©2007 PhotoSpin, www.photospin.com ©2007 PhotoSpin, www.photospin.com

©2007 PhotoSpin, www.photospin.com ©2007 PhotoSpin, www.photospin.com ©2007 PhotoSpin, www.photospin.com

Figure 4.8 Each image will have its own unique histogram.

Evaluating and Adjusting Contrast

The brightest and darkest areas of your computer monitor are nowhere near as bright or dark as the objects you'll find in the real world. The difference is even more extreme when you look at the brightest and darkest areas of a printed brochure—the paper is actually pretty dull, and the ink isn't all that dark. Because of this, you'll need to use the full range of shades from black to white in order to make your photos look as close to reality as possible.

By adjusting the upper-right and upper-left sliders in the Levels dialog box, you can dramatically improve the contrast of an image and make it appear more lifelike. When you move the upper-left slider in the Levels dialog box,

The middle slider will move when you adjust the upper-right or upper-left slider. This happens because Photoshop is attempting to keep the middle slider in the same position relative to the other two sliders. So if the middle slider is centered between the other two, it will remain centered when you move one of the outer sliders.

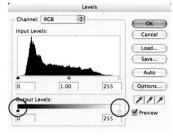

Figure 4.9 The shades that are beyond the upper-right and upper-left triangles become pure black and pure white.

If you're in the market for a new scanner, be sure to compare the D-max specifications for each scanner you are considering. Higher D-max specs indicate a scanner that is capable of capturing more shadow detail than a scanner with a lower D-max spec. If you can't find the D-max specification on the manufacturer's Web site, there's a good chance that it's too low to be proud of (for the same reason you don't find 0–60 ratings in brochures for economy cars). It's often worth the extra money to get a scanner that can deliver good shadow detail.

you force the shade of gray directly below it and any shade darker than it (see the gradient) to black. So moving that slider until it touches the first bar on the histogram forces the darkest shade of gray in the image to black, which should give you nice dark shadows.

When you move the upper-right slider, you force the shade that appears directly below the slider and any shade brighter than it to white. So, similar to dark colors, moving the right slider until it touches the last bar on the histogram forces the brightest shade of gray to white, which should give you nice white highlights.

By adjusting both sliders, your image will use the full range of shades available to a grayscale image (**Figure 4.9**). If you move the sliders past the beginning and end of the histogram, you will get even more contrast, but you risk losing important detail in the process.

Hidden Features to the Rescue

To achieve maximum contrast without sacrificing detail, Adobe created a hidden feature in the Levels dialog box. It's known as Threshold mode. This feature allows you to see exactly which areas are becoming black or white, and it's the key to ensuring that you don't sacrifice detail. To get to the hidden feature, hold down the Option/Alt key when you move the upper-right or upper-left sliders in the Levels dialog box.

When you move the upper-left slider with Threshold mode turned on, your image should turn white until the slider touches the first bar on the histogram; then small black areas should start to appear. These are the areas that will become pure black. With most images, you'll want to make sure you don't force a large concentrated area to black, so move the slider until only small areas appear. You also want to make sure the areas that are becoming black still contain detail. Detail will show up looking like noise (not the kind you hear—the kind you see on an old television when you don't have an antenna hooked up), so make sure those small areas also look noisy. You'll need to repeat this process with the upper-right slider to make sure you get optimal contrast (**Figures 4.10** to **4.14**).

Figure 4.10 Original. (©2007 Ben Willmore)

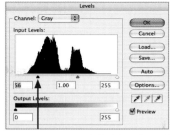

Figure 4.11 Upper-left slider adjusted way too far.

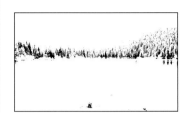

Figure 4.12 Large areas of the image are losing detail and becoming pure black.

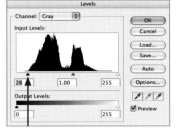

Figure 4.13 Upper-left slider adjusted correctly.

Figure 4.14 Small areas become black but still contain detail (noise).

Three things might cause an image to have large areas of black or white from the start:

1. Your scanner isn't capable of capturing good shadow detail.

2. The image simply didn't have any detail in the shadows to begin with.

3. The image has been adjusted without using Photoshop's Threshold mode.

The Histogram Gives You Feedback

After you have applied an adjustment to your image, you can see an updated histogram by choosing Image > Adjustments > Levels again. Notice that after adjusting the upper-right and upper-left sliders, the histogram stretches all the way across the area available. It's just like stretching out a Slinky—you remember, "It walks downstairs, alone or in pairs" (**Figure 4.15**). As you pull on the ends of the Slinky, the loops stretch out and start to create gaps. The

Figure 4.15 A Slinky.

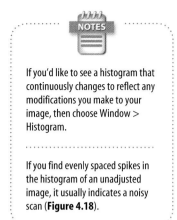

If you'd like to see a histogram that continuously changes to reflect any modifications you make to your image, then choose Window > Histogram.

If you find evenly spaced spikes in the histogram of an unadjusted image, it usually indicates a noisy scan (**Figure 4.18**).

same thing happens to a histogram—because Photoshop can't add more bars to the histogram, it can only spread out the ones that were already there. And remember, gaps in the histogram mean that certain shades of gray are missing from the image. So the more you adjust an image using Levels, the more you increase the possibility that you'll lose some of the smooth transitions between bright and dark areas (**Figure 4.16**).

If you see large spikes on either end of the histogram (**Figure 4.17**), it's an indication that you've lost detail. That's because you forced quite a bit of space to white or black using Levels. But you'd know you did that, because you used the hidden feature, right? Or maybe you couldn't control yourself and used that Brightness/Contrast dialog box, where you can't tell if you damaged the image! You might also get spikes on the ends of the histogram (**Figure 4.18**) if you scan an image with too high of a contrast setting or a brightness setting that is way too high or low, or if your scanner isn't capable of capturing enough shadow detail.

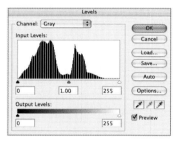

Figure 4.16 After adjusting the top two sliders, your image should use the full range of shades available.

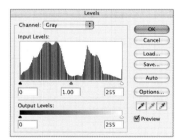

Figure 4.17 Spikes on the end of a histogram usually indicate lost detail.

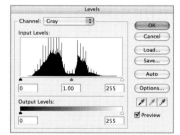

Figure 4.18 Noise.

Adjusting Brightness

After you have achieved good contrast, your image might look too bright or dark. The middle slider in the Levels dialog box can fix that. (Techies love to call this slider the Gamma setting, but we plain folks call it the midpoint.) If you move the middle slider to the left, the image becomes brighter without messing up the dark areas of your image. Black areas stay nice and black. Or you can move the middle slider to the right to darken the image without messing up the bright areas. White areas stay bright white (**Figure 4.19**). This is the one setting that is a personal choice. I can't tell you how bright or dark your image should be.

If you want to know what this adjustment is doing, just look directly below the middle slider; the shade of gray there will become 50% gray. Moving it to the left brightens your image because you'll be shifting what used to be a dark shade of gray to 50% gray. Moving the middle slider to the right darkens your image as you shift a bright shade to 50% gray. If you look at an updated histogram of the image, it will look like you stretched out a Slinky, then grabbed one side and pulled it to the middle (**Figure 4.20**. Some bars will get scrunched (is that a technical term?) together, whereas others get spread apart.

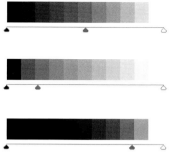

Figure 4.19 Effects of the middle slider.

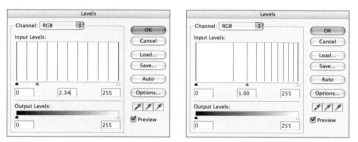

Figure 4.20 The adjustment shown on the left results in the histogram shown on the right.

Setting Up Your Images for Final Output

If your images are going to be printed on a commercial printing press, chances are that they will end up looking a lot darker than they did when you viewed them onscreen. This is known as dot gain. Fortunately, Photoshop allows you to compensate for it. You can tell Photoshop ahead of time how you intend to output your images, and it will adjust the onscreen appearance of your image to look as dark as it should be after it's printed.

To select or enter dot gain settings, choose Edit > Color Settings. In the Working Spaces area, you'll use the Gray pop-up menu (**Figure 4.21**). You'll definitely want to ask

NOTES

Spikes that show up after an image has been adjusted with Levels do not indicate noise. It's as if you took your trusty Slinky and tried to squish it down to a centimeter wide. Something would have to budge. The only way I can do it is to bend the Slinky into a V shape where the loops start piling up, one on top of the other. Otherwise, the loops just line up in a nice row and limit how much I can compress the Slinky. Well, the same thing happens with the histogram. Let's say you try to squish 20 bars into a space that is only 15 pixels wide on the histogram. Five of the bars have to disappear. They are going to just pile on top of the bars next to them and make those bars about twice as tall. When this happens, you get evenly spaced spikes across part of the histogram.

TABLE 4.1 Dot Gain Settings	
Newspapers	34%
Magazines and brochures	24%
High-end brochures	22%

your printing company about what settings to use; otherwise, you'll just be guessing and you might not like your end result. But just in case you don't have time to ask your printing company, you can use the settings that appear in **Table 4.1**. After you've specified the Dot Gain setting that is appropriate for your printing conditions, choose Image > Mode > Assign Profile, and select the Working Gray setting. That will set up Photoshop to properly preview what your image will look like under those conditions.

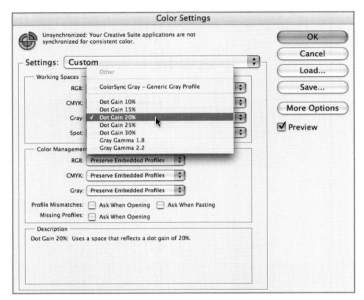

Figure 4.21   The Color Settings dialog box.

Preparing for a Printing Press

Take a close look at the black-and-white image in **Figure 4.22**, and imagine that you took that image to Kinko's and made a copy of it. Then you took the copy and copied it again at your local library. Then you took the library copy and ran it through the copy machine in your office. Then you held the version that had been copied three times next to the original. Would you expect them to look the same? Of course not. In fact, the tiny dots that are in the brightest part of the image would have begun to disappear and become pure white, because every time you make a copy,

Figure 4.22   Copy this image three times and you'll lose detail in the brightest part of the image.
(©2007 Ben Willmore)

you lose some quality. Well, the same thing happens when you hand over your image to a printing company. When you give your printing company your original output, it has to make three copies of it before it makes it to the end of the printing process. The company starts by converting the original into a piece of metal called a printing plate to make the first copy. Then the plate is put on a big, round roller on the printing press and flooded with water and ink. The oily ink sticks to the plate only where your images and text should be; the water makes sure it doesn't stick to the other areas (using the idea that oil and water don't mix). Next to that roller is another one known as a blanket; it's just covered with rubber. The plate comes into contact with the blanket so the ink on the plate will transfer over to the blanket—that's your second copy. Finally, the blanket transfers the ink onto a sheet of paper to create the last copy (**Figure 4.23**). Each time a copy is made, you lose some of the smallest dots in the image. Until you know how to compensate for this, you're likely to end up with pictures of people with big white spots in the middle of their foreheads.

> **NOTES**
>
> If the dot gain setting you need isn't listed in the Working Spaces area, you'll need a custom setting. Turn on the Advanced Mode check box at the top of the dialog box, and then choose Custom Dot Gain from the Gray pop-up menu. To get a traditional dot gain measurement (in which you measure only 50% gray), just add 50 to the dot gain setting you need, and enter the result in the 50% field.
>
> If your image will be displayed only onscreen or printed on a desktop printer (like an inkjet), change the Gray pop-up menu to the Gamma choice your monitor is set to. I'll show you how to set up your monitor in Chapter 6, "Color Management," but for now you should know that most Macs are set to 1.8 and most Windows machines are set to 2.2.

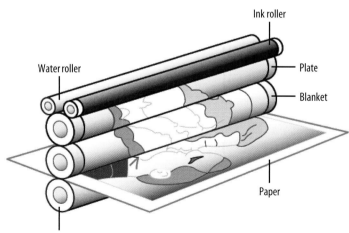

Figure 4.23 Three copies are made before your image turns into a printed page.

Before I show you how to compensate for the loss of detail in the bright areas of your image, let's look at what happens to the darkest areas, since we'll have to deal with

TABLE 4.2 Common Minimum Highlight Settings

Newspapers	5%
Magazines and brochures	3%
High-end brochures	3%

TABLE 4.3 Common Maximum Shadow Settings

Newspapers	75%
Magazines and brochures	90%
High-end brochures	95%

NOTES

If you'd like to measure the minimum highlight and maximum shadow settings for an output device that you own, be sure to try the highlight/shadow test that's available on my Web site at www.digitalmastery.com/test.

them as well. When you print with ink on paper, the ink always gets absorbed into the paper and spreads out—just like when you spill coffee on your morning newspaper. This causes the darkest areas of an image (97%, 98%, 99%) to become pure black. If you don't adjust for this, you will lose detail in the shadows of your image.

Most printing companies create a simple test strip that it prints on the edge of your job in the area that will be cropped after it's printed. This test strip contains shades of gray from 1% to about 5% to determine the lightest shade of gray that doesn't disappear on press and become pure white. Of course, the folks in the printing industry don't just use plain English to describe it; instead, they invented the term "minimum highlight dot reproducible on press." The test strip area also contains shades of gray from 99% to about 75% so they can see the darkest shade of gray that doesn't become pure black. For that one, they came up with the term "maximum shadow dot reproducible on press." If you ask your printing company, it can usually tell you exactly which settings to use. I know you don't always know who will print your images or don't have the time to ask, so I'll give you some generic numbers to use (**Tables 4.2** and **4.3**). But first, let's find out how we adjust for minimum highlight and maximum shadow dots.

By moving the lower-right slider in the Levels dialog box, you will change white to the shade of gray the slider is pointing to. You want to move this slider until it points to the minimum highlight dot—that is, the lightest shade of gray that will not disappear and become white on-press.

You don't want to eyeball this setting, so instead of just looking at the shades of gray, we'll use the Output Level numbers in the Levels dialog box. There is one problem with these numbers: They range from 0 to 255 instead of 0 to 100%! This is because you can have up to 256 shades of gray in a grayscale image, and Photoshop wants you to be able to control them all. When you're using this numbering system, think about light instead of ink. If you have no light (0), it would be pitch black; if you have as much light as possible (255), you could call that white. So that you won't need a calculator, I'll give you a conversion table (**Table 4.4**).

TABLE 4.4 Percentage Conversion Table

%	Value	%	Value	%	Value
100%	0	66%	87	32%	174
99%	3	65%	90	31%	177
98%	5	64%	92	30%	179
97%	8	63%	95	29%	182
96%	10	62%	97	28%	184
95%	13	61%	100	27%	187
94%	15	60%	102	26%	189
93%	18	59%	105	25%	192
92%	20	58%	108	24%	195
91%	23	57%	110	23%	197
90%	26	56%	113	22%	200
89%	28	55%	115	21%	202
88%	31	54%	118	20%	205
87%	33	53%	120	19%	207
86%	36	52%	123	18%	210
85%	38	51%	125	17%	212
84%	41	50%	128	16%	215
83%	44	49%	131	15%	218
82%	46	48%	133	14%	220
81%	49	47%	136	13%	223
80%	51	46%	138	12%	225
79%	54	45%	141	11%	228
78%	56	44%	143	10%	230
77%	59	43%	146	9%	233
76%	61	42%	148	8%	236
75%	64	41%	151	7%	238
74%	67	40%	154	6%	241
73%	69	39%	156	5%	243
72%	72	38%	159	4%	246
71%	74	37%	161	3%	248
70%	77	36%	164	2%	251
69%	79	35%	166	1%	253
68%	82	34%	169	0%	255
67%	84	33%	172		

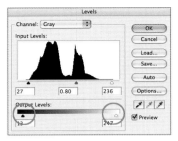

Figure 4.24 The bottom sliders reduce image contrast to compensate for the limitations of the printing press.

If you own a 30-bit or higher scanner and your scanning software contains a histogram and has the same adjustment controls available, you can make adjustments within your scanning software. Most scanners can deliver a histogram without gaps because they can look back to the image and pick up extra shades of gray that would fill the gaps. These days, almost all scanners are 36-bit or higher. If your scanner is capable of delivering a 16-bit grayscale image to Photoshop, the only adjustment you need to make during scanning is to make sure the highlights and shadows still have detail. If the histogram in your scanner has spikes at the ends, lower the contrast setting and res-can until you don't get the spikes.

By moving the lower-left slider in the Levels dialog box, you will change black to the shade of gray the slider is pointing to (**Figure 4.24**. You want to move this slider until it points to the darkest shade of gray that will not plug up and become black (known as the maximum shadow dot).

At first glance this stuff might seem complicated, but it is really quite simple. All you do is use the numbers from the tables or ask your printing company for settings. If you always print on the same kind of paper, you'll always use the same numbers.

A Quick Levels Recap

There are several steps to using Levels to adjust grayscale images, but as I've said, they're all quick and easy once you get used to them. Here's a brief recap of the role of each of the sliders in the Levels dialog box:

1. Move the upper-left slider until it touches the first bar on the histogram to force the darkest area of the image to black. Use the hidden Threshold feature—hold Option/Alt—to go as far as possible without damaging the image (**Figures 4.25** and **4.26**).

2. Move the upper-right slider until it touches the last bar on the histogram to force the brightest area of the image to white. Again, use the hidden feature to go as far as possible without damaging the image (**Figure 4.27**).

3. Move the middle slider until the brightness of the image looks appropriate (**Figure 4.28**).

4. Move the lower-left slider to make sure the shadows won't plug up and become pure black on the printing press. Use the tables I've provided for settings, or ask your printer for more precise ones (**Figure 4.29**).

5. Move the lower-right slider to make sure you don't lose detail in the highlights when the smallest dots in your image disappear on the printing press. Use the tables for settings, or ask your printing company for more precise ones (**Figure 4.30**). I usually adjust all five sliders before clicking OK to apply them.

Figure 4.25 The original image.

Figure 4.26 Result of adjusting upper-left slider.

Figure 4.27 Result of adjusting upper-right slider.

Figure 4.28 Result of adjusting middle slider.

Figure 4.29 Result of adjusting lower-left slider.

Figure 4.30 Result of adjusting lower-right slider.

Postadjustment Analysis

Any time you adjust an image, you run the risk of introducing artifacts, so let's take a look at what can happen to your image after applying Levels. But don't worry—remember, there is usually at least one "fix" for every artifact.

Low Contrast Onscreen Appearance

If you've adjusted an image that will eventually be reproduced on a commercial printing press, your results will most likely look rather flat onscreen (lacking contrast). This problem is a temporary one since the image will gain contrast when it's printed on press (dark areas become darker and bright areas become brighter). You're welcome to adjust the top three sliders in Levels to get an acceptable image and then hold off on adjusting the bottom two sliders until you're done working on the image in Photoshop. That way, the image will have good contrast for the vast majority of the time you work on it and then the bottom two sliders can be adjusted right before saving the image so that it's ready to be reproduced on press.

To see an updated histogram after adjusting the image, you must first apply the adjustment, and then re-open the Levels dialog box. You can also choose Window > Histogram to see before and after histograms overlaid on each other.

I don't use this technique on every image, just on those that have extremely noticeable posterization.

If you don't have the time or patience to apply the Eliminating Posterization technique mentioned here, consider choosing Filter > Noise > Add Noise and use a setting of 3 or 4. That can help to reduce posterization, but will not be able to help in cases of extreme posterization.

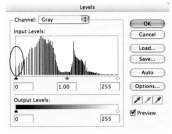

Figure 4.31 Gaps in a histogram indicate posterization.

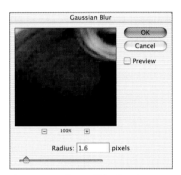

Figure 4.32 Turn off the Preview check box to see the edges of the posterized area.

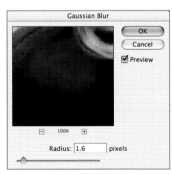

Figure 4.33 With the Preview check box turned on, increase the Radius setting until the posterized area appears smooth.

Recognizing Posterization

When you look at an updated histogram, you might see wide gaps in the histogram—this indicates posterization (**Figure 4.31**). Posterization is when you should have a smooth transition between areas and instead you see a drastic jump between a bright and dark area. Some call this banding or stair-stepping. As long as the gaps in the histogram are smaller than three pixels wide, you probably won't notice it at all in the image.

Adjusting the image usually causes these gaps. As you adjust the image, the bars on the histogram spread out and gaps start to appear (remember that Slinky). The more extreme the adjustment you make, the wider the gaps. And if you see those huge gaps in the histogram, it'll probably mean that the posterization is noticeable enough that you'll want to fix it (it usually shows up in the dark areas of the image).

Eliminating Posterization

Here's a trick that can minimize the posterization. I should warn you that you have to apply this technique manually to each area that is posterized. Although it might take you a little bit of time, the results will be worth it.

To begin, select the Magic Wand tool, set the Tolerance to 0, and click on an area that looks posterized. Next, choose Select > Modify > Border, and use a setting of 2 for slight posterization or 4 for a moderate amount of posterization. Now apply Filter > Blur > Gaussian Blur until the area looks smooth (**Figures 4.32** and **4.33**). Repeat this process on all of the posterized areas until you're satisfied with the results.

If you find that a large number of your images end up with post-scan posterization, you might want to look into getting a scanner that's capable of delivering 16-bit images to Photoshop. A typical grayscale image contains no more than 256 shades of gray, which is technically known as an 8-bit image. That's sufficient for most images, but extreme adjustments will cause posterization. One way to avoid posterization is to use a scanner that can produce images that contain thousands of shades of gray, which is technically known as a 16-bit image. Most scanners are capable of capturing more than 256 shades of gray from a photograph, but few are capable of actually delivering all those shades to Photoshop. So, the next time you shop for a scanner, be sure to ask if it is capable of delivering 16-bit images to Photoshop.

Closing Thoughts

Even though it's taken me a whole chapter to describe how to optimize your grayscale photos, keep in mind that the whole process takes about a minute once you're used to it. When you feel that you have mastered Levels, you will be ready to take on the ultimate adjustment tool—Curves. Curves is equipped to do the same basic corrections as Levels, but can also do much, much more. In general, with grayscale images I always start out using Levels and then move on to Curves to fix any problems that Levels can't handle; I also use Curves to work with color. It's like graduating from a Ford Taurus to a Ferrari. The Ferrari takes more skill and coordination to master, but you get one hell of a ride. But that's another chapter.

5
Understanding Curves

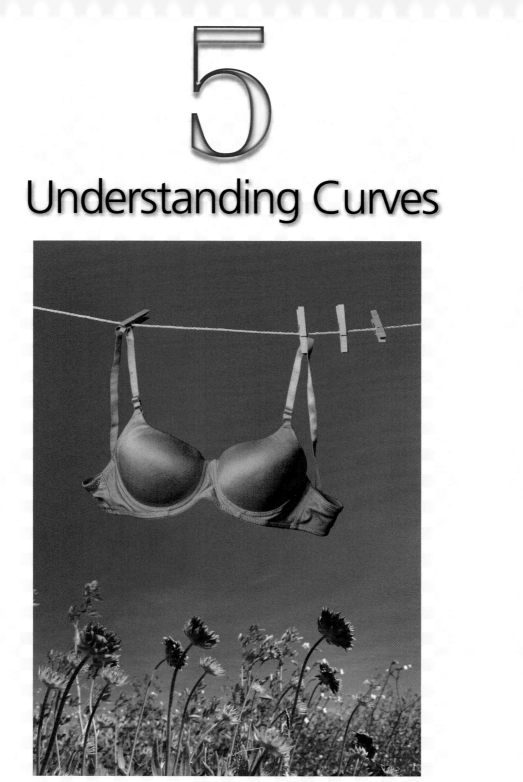

Have patience. All things are difficult before they become easy.

—Saadi

If I were going to be dropped on a deserted island and could bring only one thing with me, I might choose a Swiss Army knife. With that knife, I could cut firewood, spear fish, and clean my teeth (remember the toothpick?). Much like a Swiss Army knife, Curves (Image > Adjustments > Curves) can be used for just about anything. In fact, if I had to pick one adjustment tool to use all the time, it would definitely be Curves. By mastering the Curves dialog box, you have so much control over your images that you might wonder why you would ever need to use the Levels or Brightness/Contrast dialog box.

The Power of Curves

Let's take a look at some of the things you can do with the Curves dialog box. You can

▶ Pull out far more detail than is possible to see with the Sharpening filters (**Figures 5.1** to **5.3**).

▶ Lighten or darken areas without making selections (**Figures 5.4** and **5.5**).

▶ Turn ordinary text into extraordinary text (**Figures 5.6** and **5.7**).

▶ Enhance color and contrast in seconds (**Figures 5.8** and **5.9**).

Figure 5.1 The original image. (©2007 Ben Willmore)

Figure 5.2 After applying the Unsharp Mask filter.

Figure 5.3 After a simple Curves adjustment.

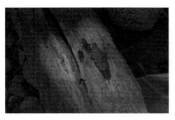

Figure 5.6 The original text effect.

Figure 5.4 The original image. (©2007 Ben Willmore)

Figure 5.5 After a simple Curves adjustment.

Figure 5.7 After a simple Curves adjustment.

Figure 5.8 The original image. (©2007 PhotoSpin, www.photospin.com)

Figure 5.9 After a simple Curves adjustment.

None of these changes could be made by using Levels or Brightness/Contrast (that is, not without making complicated selections or losing control over the result). Now you can see why you'll want to master Curves!

Using Curves, you can perform all the adjustments available in the Levels, Brightness/Contrast, and Threshold dialog boxes, and much, much more. In fact, you can independently adjust each of the 256 shades of gray in your image (**Figure 5.10**).

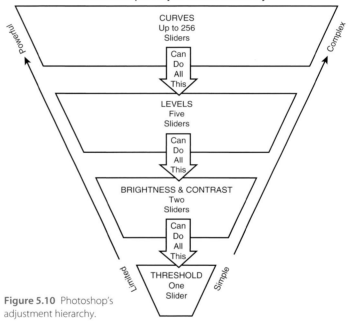

Figure 5.10 Photoshop's adjustment hierarchy.

But First, a Test!

Before we delve into Curves, I want to test your present knowledge of the Curves dialog box. Don't worry, though, because the lower your score, the more you should enjoy this chapter.

Look at the curve shown in **Figure 5.11** and see if you can answer the following questions:

▶ Which shades will lose detail from this adjustment?

▶ Which shades will become brighter?

▶ What happened to 62% gray?

▶ What happened to the image's contrast?

If you truly understand the Curves dialog box, you found these questions extremely easy to answer. However, if you hesitated before answering any of them or couldn't answer them at all, this chapter was designed for you.

The Idea Behind Curves

Because the Curves dialog box allows you to adjust every shade of gray in an image independently of the others (256 in all), it works quite a bit differently from the other adjustment tools. To get a clearer picture of what Curves does, let's construct our own Curves dialog box from scratch, using something you're already familiar with: the plain old vanilla bar chart. You know what I'm talking about—those wretched bar charts that can't be avoided in magazines, brochures, television, and pretty much everywhere you look. Now we can finally put one to good use by using it to help us understand Curves.

What if you create a bar chart that indicates how much light your monitor uses to display each color in an image? This bar chart would be just like any other that you've seen, where taller bars mean more light and shorter bars mean less. You could show the shade of gray you are using below each bar, and then draw a line from the top of each bar over to the left so you could label how much light is being used for each shade. I think you'd end up with something that looks like **Figure 5.12**. Or you could just as easily change the chart to indicate how much ink your inkjet printer would use to reproduce the image. Now that we're talking about ink, short bars would mean less ink, which would produce a light shade of gray, and tall bars would mean a lot of ink and would produce a dark shade of gray. To make the change, all we'd have to do is flip all the shades at the bottom of the graph so the dark ones are below the tall bars and the bright ones are below the short bars. The result would look like **Figure 5.13**, right?

Okay, now that you've got the concept, let's expand on that to accommodate the real world. Our basic bar chart might

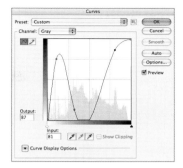

Figure 5.11 Can you figure out exactly what this curve will do to an image?

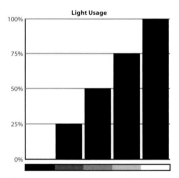

Figure 5.12 This bar chart indicates the amount of light used to display the shades of gray shown at the bottom.

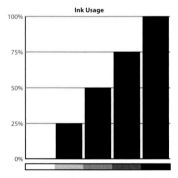

Figure 5.13 Flip the shades at the bottom, and you've got a graph that represents ink usage.

NOTES

All the techniques mentioned in this chapter apply equally to images prepared for Web pages and those prepared for print. You might notice that I concentrate on ink settings throughout this chapter. I find that most users are more comfortable thinking about how ink would affect their image instead of light. Ink is the exact opposite of light, so Photoshop can easily translate what you're attempting to do, even if your image will be displayed using light.

work for a simple logo with just a few shades of gray (one bar representing each shade), but most of your images will contain many more than that. So, we just increase the number of bars (**Figure 5.14**), right? Well, sort of. The fact is your image can contain up to 256 shades of gray. But if we jam 256 bars (one for each shade) into our chart, they won't look like bars anymore; they'll just turn into a big mass (**Figure 5.15**). You can't see the individual bars because there isn't any space between them.

All the same, our images contain up to 256 shades of gray, so we really need that many bars in our chart. Now that they're all smashed together, we don't have room to label each bar, so why don't we just overlay a grid (**Figure 5.16**) and label that instead? If that grid isn't detailed enough for you, we could add a more detailed grid, such as the one shown in **Figure 5.17**.

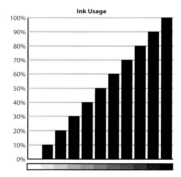

Figure 5.14 Add more bars for additional accuracy.

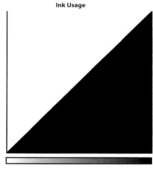

Figure 5.15 The 256 bars take up so much space that the chart no longer looks like a bar chart.

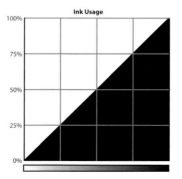

Figure 5.16 A grid can help you figure out how much ink is used.

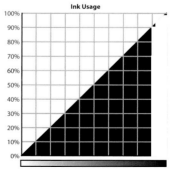

Figure 5.17 The more detailed grid allows you to be even more accurate.

The sample chart we've created isn't really all that useful—yet. It's not telling you anything you can't find in the Info or Color palettes. For example, if you really want to know how much ink (or light) you'd use to reproduce a shade of gray, you could just open the Info palette by choosing Window > Info (**Figure 5.18**), and then move your pointer over the image; the Info palette would indicate how much ink would be used in that area. The Color palette (Window > Color) is set up similarly and will tell you how much ink or light makes up a shade of gray (**Figure 5.19**). The main difference between the two methods is that the Info palette gives you information about your image—specifically, what's under the pointer. The Color palette isn't image-specific but gives you generic information about how much ink or light makes up a shade of gray.

NOTES

16-bit images in Photoshop can contain up to 32,738 shades of gray. When working with this type of image, Photoshop still presents you with a curve that represents only 256 shades of gray, even though it's accurately adjusting all the 32,738 shades that are in your image.

Figure 5.18 The Info palette indicates how much ink or light would be used to reproduce the color that is under the pointer.

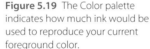

Figure 5.19 The Color palette indicates how much ink would be used to reproduce your current foreground color.

The Curves dialog box, meanwhile, is really just a simple bar chart—with a lot of bars that are very close together—that shows how much ink or light will be used in your image. The gradient at the bottom shows all the shades of gray you could possibly have, and the chart above shows how much ink or light will be used to create each shade. But the wonderful thing about the Curves dialog box is that it doesn't just sit there like a static bar chart that only gives you information. It's interactive—you can use it to change the amount of ink (or light) used to reproduce your image (**Figure 5.20**).

Think of our Ink Usage bar graph: As the shades of gray get steadily darker, each shade uses slightly more ink, resulting in a straight diagonal line. But in the Curves

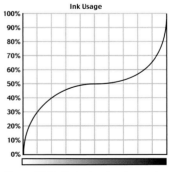

Figure 5.20 Changing the shape of the line in the Curves graph changes how much ink is used throughout the image.

graph, you can move points on the line. For example, you can flatten the line so that in your modified image, many shades of gray are represented by a single shade. Or you can make a dramatic change to the line, dragging a point up or down so that a shade changes to become much darker or lighter.

The Gradients Are Your Guide

Pick any shade of gray from the gradient, and then look above it to figure out how much ink would be used to create it (**Figure 5.21**). You can use the grid to help you calculate the exact amount of ink used (about 23% in this case). But wouldn't you rather see what 23% looks like? Suppose we replace those percentage numbers with another gradient that shows how bright each area would be (**Figure 5.22**). Just to make sure you don't get the two gradients confused, read the next two sentences twice: The bottom gradient represents the shades of gray you are changing. The side gradient indicates how bright or dark a shade will become if you move the line to a certain height (**Figure 5.23**).

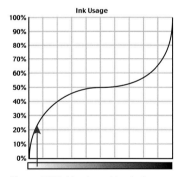

Figure 5.21 Use the grid to help determine how much ink is used in an area.

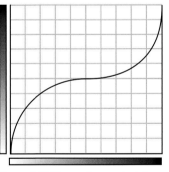

Figure 5.22 The gradient on the left indicates how dark an area will become if the curve is moved to a certain height.

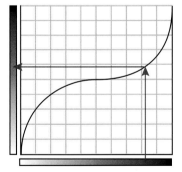

Figure 5.23 The bottom gradient scale is what you're changing. The left gradient scale is what you changed it to.

Congratulations. You've survived Ben's Bar Charts 101. Now you're ready to graduate from charts and take flight with the full-fledged Curves dialog box (**Figure 5.24**). Does it look familiar? It should. Along the bottom you see a grayscale ramp showing all of the original gray tones in your image, and running vertically along the side is a grayscale ramp showing what each point on the curve will become after you click OK.

The "curve" is the diagonal line that runs from the lower-left to the upper-right. When you first open the Curves dialog box, the curve is not curvy. As you saw, the curve indicates correspondence between the original gray tones on the bottom and the new gray tones on the side. When the curve is a straight diagonal, all output tones are identical to the input tones.

In Photoshop CS3, Adobe has added a grayed out histogram display behind the actual curve. This makes it easier to determine which part of the curve corresponds to specific tonal regions within your image. It also makes it easier to remember that you read the curve from black on the left to white on the right.

Finally, if you click the Curve Display Options button, you'll find some additional controls which we'll be looking at later (**Figure 5.25**).

Color Modes and Curves

If you go back to when we first started to create the bar chart, you'll remember that we started measuring how much light our monitor was using to display things. Then we flip-flopped and measured how much ink we'd use for printing. You can make the same change in the Curves dialog box. Remember how we accomplished that switch earlier in the chapter—didn't we just reverse the shades of gray at the bottom of the chart? Hold that thought, and click the Curve Display Options button to reveal some additional controls.

Where it says "Show Amount of" there are two radio buttons, one for Light and the other for Pigment/Ink %. You can click either of these to determine whether the curve reads from light to dark or dark to light. The grayscale ramps will reverse, just like we saw earlier with our bar charts. (**Figures 5.26** and **5.27**).

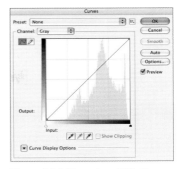

Figure 5.24 Photoshop CS3's Curves dialog box.

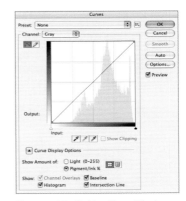

Figure 5.25 Clicking Curve Display Options provides you with some additional controls.

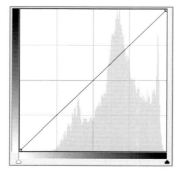 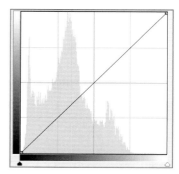

Figure 5.26 When black is at the top, you are using ink (remember, up means more).

Figure 5.27 When white is at the top, you are using light (again, up means more).

The *mode* of your image determines what you'll start with. Photoshop assumes that images in grayscale, CMYK, or Lab mode will be printed, and defaults to using the gradient that represents ink. Because your monitor displays everything using red, green, and blue light, images in RGB mode use the gradient that represents light.

Photoshop doesn't care which system you use. It can easily translate between the two, because light is the exact opposite of ink. When you switch from one scale to the other, not only do the light and dark ends of the gradients get swapped, but also the curve flips upside down. Be sure to look out for which mode I use throughout the examples in this chapter; otherwise, you could get the exact opposite result.

Remember, the side gradient indicates what you'll end up with if you move a point on the curve to a certain height. You can always glance at the side to find out how much light or ink you're using. Just remember that up means more of something, and that you can use either light or ink.

Next comes the grid. Remember how we ended up with one that is more detailed than the one we started with? Well, you can toggle between those two grids by Option/Alt-clicking anywhere within the grid area. It doesn't affect the result you'll get in Curves; it's just a personal preference (**Figure 5.28**). You can also change grids by clicking the grid icons that appear when you open the Curve Display Options.

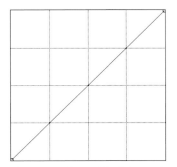 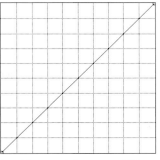

Figure 5.28 Option/Alt-click anywhere on the grid to toggle between a 25% increment grid (left) and a 10% increment grid (right).

Taking Curves for a Test Drive

Go ahead—open an image, choose Image > Adjustments > Curves, and start messing with the curve. Click anywhere on the curve to add a point, and then drag it around to change the shape of the curve. If you want to get rid of a point, drag it off the edge of the grid. You can also click a point and then use the arrow keys on your keyboard to nudge it around the grid. You can even add the Shift key to the arrow keys to nudge it in larger increments.

Note that when you drag, Photoshop displays a set of light gray crosshairs to help you see exactly how the bottom grayscale ramp corresponds to the left ramp (**Figure 5.29**). If you find these distracting, turn off the Intersection Line check box in the Curve Display Options. Personally, I find them very handy!

Photoshop also leaves a light gray "baseline"—a copy of the original flat curve, so that you can see exactly how much your new curve deviates from the original. As with the intersection lines, if you prefer working with a "clean" display, you can turn off the Baseline check box in the Curve Display Options.

You should quickly find that it's pretty easy to screw up your image! That's because we haven't talked about specific types of adjustments yet. So, let's explore the final piece of the Curves puzzle. To understand what you're doing, you must compare the curve you're making to the original line. Now let's see what we can do with all this.

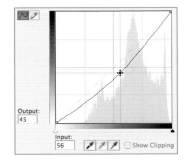

Figure 5.29 The light gray "baseline" represents the original line.

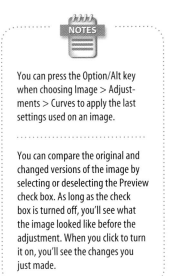

NOTES

You can press the Option/Alt key when choosing Image > Adjustments > Curves to apply the last settings used on an image.

You can compare the original and changed versions of the image by selecting or deselecting the Preview check box. As long as the check box is turned off, you'll see what the image looked like before the adjustment. When you click to turn it on, you'll see the changes you just made.

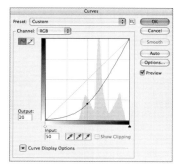

Figure 5.30 Start with a dark grayscale image. (©2007 PhotoSpin, www.photospin.com)

Figure 5.31 Move the curve down to reduce how much ink is used.

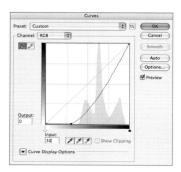

Figure 5.32 Comparing the curve with the gradients.

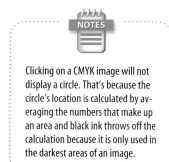

Figure 5.33 To figure out how much ink you've removed, look below where the line used to be.

NOTES

Clicking on a CMYK image will not display a circle. That's because the circle's location is calculated by averaging the numbers that make up an area and black ink throws off the calculation because it is only used in the darkest areas of an image.

Improving Dark Images

Try this: Open any grayscale image that you think is too dark (I'll show you how to work with color in a minute), like the one shown in **Figure 5.30**. Next, choose Image > Adjustments > Curves, and add a point by clicking the middle of the line. Pull the line straight down and see what happens to your image (**Figure 5.31**). Compare the curve with the gradient at the left of the Curves dialog box. The farther you move the curve down, the less ink you use and therefore the brighter the image becomes. If part of the curve bottoms out, the shade represented by that area becomes pure white because there will be no ink used when the image is printed. (Remember, because this is a grayscale image, the Curves dialog box is using the ink percentage scale, not light, so dragging down means lighter.)

Any part of a curve that's below the original line indicates an area that is using less ink, which means that it has been brightened. Look at the gradient directly below those areas to determine which shades of the image were brightened (**Figure 5.32**). The farther the line is moved down from its original position, the brighter the image will become (**Figure 5.33**).

Increasing Contrast and Detail

So far, we've learned that moving the curve up or down increases or decreases the amount of ink or light used to make the image. Now let's look at how changing the angle of the curve can help us. What if you had an image where the brightest area was white and the darkest area was only 25% gray? Would it be easy to see the detail in the image? I don't think so (**Figure 5.34**).

Now think about how that image would change if we applied the curve shown in **Figure 5.35**. If you look closely at this curve, you'll notice that areas that are white in the original image wouldn't change at all and areas that used to be 25% gray would end up being around 75% gray. Wouldn't that make it much easier to see the detail in the whole image? In an overexposed image like this one, you have to make the curve steeper in the lighter part of the curve. (We already learned that in an underexposed image—refer to Figure 5.30—you have to make the dark part of the curve steeper to bring out the detail.) You always have to compare the curve with the original line to determine how much of a change you've made. If you make the curve just a little steeper than the original, you'll add just a little contrast to that area. Anytime you add contrast, it becomes easier to see the detail in that area because the difference between the bright and dark parts becomes more pronounced (**Figure 5.36**). Remember to look at the gradient below to figure out which shades of gray you are changing.

Open any grayscale image, and choose Image > Adjustments > Curves. Move your pointer over the image, and then click and drag across the area where you want to exaggerate the detail. You'll notice that a circle appears in the Curves dialog box. Photoshop is simply looking at the bottom gradient to find the shade of gray under your pointer; it then puts a circle on the curve directly above that shade. This circle indicates the area of the curve that needs to be changed to affect the area you're dragging across. Add control points on either side of this area of the curve. Next, move the top point you just added up toward the top of the chart, and move the bottom point down toward the bottom of the chart. The area you dragged across should appear to have more contrast (**Figures 5.37** to **5.39**). As contrast improves in an image, you should be able to see more details.

Figure 5.34 You can't see much detail in this image because the brightness is limited to 0%–25%. (©2007 Andy Katz)

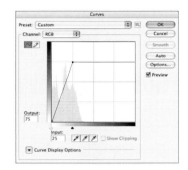

Figure 5.35 This curve adds more contrast, making it easier to see the detail in the whole image.

Figure 5.36 After making the curve steeper, it's easier to see the detail.

Figure 5.37 Original image. (©2007 Andy Katz)

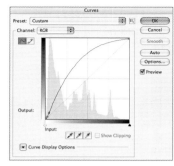

Figure 5.38 Find the range you'd like to change, and then make the curve steeper in that area.

Figure 5.39 After making the curve steeper.

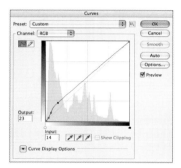

Figure 5.40 Fix the rest of the curve so you don't exaggerate the contrast in other areas.

You might also need to fix the rest of the curve to make sure that the contrast in those areas doesn't change radically. You can do this by adding another point and moving it so that the majority of the curve looks normal—that is, diagonal (**Figure 5.40**).

Decreasing Contrast and Detail

Any part of the curve that's flatter (more horizontal) than the original line indicates an area where the contrast has been reduced (shades of gray become more similar). Look at the gradient directly below these areas to determine which shades of the image were changed. The flatter the line becomes, the less contrast you'll see in that area of the image. When you lower the amount of contrast in an image, it becomes harder to see detail. This can be useful if you want detail to be less visible. If the curve becomes completely horizontal in an area, you've lost all detail there (**Figures 5.41** to **5.43**). Remember, the curve is a bar chart—the same height means the same brightness.

Figure 5.41 Original image. (©2007 Andy Katz)

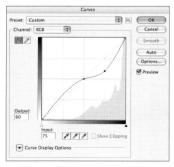

Figure 5.42 Curves used to reduce apparent detail in woodwork.

Figure 5.43 Result of applying Curves to reduce apparent detail.

Let's Analyze a Classic Tip

Have you ever heard the tip, "Make an S curve"? Well, let's explore exactly what an S curve does (**Figure 5.44**).

Remember, to find out what a curve is doing to your image, you should compare the curve with the original line. Look at the areas of the curve that are steeper than the original line—in this case, the middle of the curve. The shades represented by these steeper areas will appear to have more detail. Whenever you pull detail out of one part of an image, you'll also lose detail in another part. Therefore, look at either end of the curve, at the areas of the curve that are flatter than the original line (more horizontal). These areas appear to have less detail. Thus, an S curve attempts to exaggerate detail in the middle grays of the image. However, it also gives you less detail in the highlights and shadows.

Checking Ink Ranges

Look at **Figure 5.45**, paying particular attention to the gradient on the left side of the Curves dialog box. As you know, this gradient indicates how dark an area will become if you move the curve to a particular height. Pick a shade of gray from that gradient (such as 90%); then look directly to the right of it to determine if you'll have any areas that shade of gray. Pick another shade and do the same thing. If the curve starts in the lower-left corner and ends in the upper-right corner, each one of the shades should be used somewhere in the image. However, there might be a few shades that are used in more than one area of the curve. The adjustment shown in Figure 5.45 is analogous to using the Output sliders in the Levels dialog box.

NOTES

You can reset the Curves dialog box back to the default line by pressing and holding Option/Alt and then clicking the Reset button. The Cancel button turns into a Reset button when you hold down the proper key.

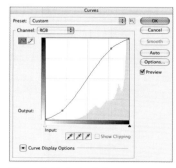

Figure 5.44 A classic S curve.

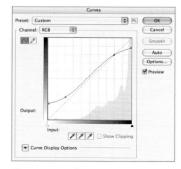

Figure 5.45 After this adjustment the image won't contain any areas darker than 90% or brighter than 18%.

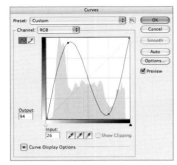

Figure 5.46 Areas between 25% and 75% have been inverted.

Inverting Your Image

You can think of Curves like a stock market graph. As long as the curve is rising, you're fine; however, if the curve starts to fall, you should expect unusual results. Look at **Figure 5.46** and try to figure out what's happening in the area that's going downhill. The dark areas of the image (around 75%) became bright, and the bright areas (around 25%) became dark. That means you've inverted that part of the image. You'll usually want to minimize or avoid this situation unless you're going for a special effect (**Figures 5.47** and **5.48**).

Figure 5.47 Original image. (©2007 PhotoSpin, www.photospin.com)

Figure 5.48 Result of applying the curve shown in Figure 5.46 and fading it using Luminosity mode.

Freeform Curves

To change the curve, you're not limited to adding and moving points. Another way to define a curve is to click the pencil icon at the bottom of the Curves dialog box and draw a freeform shape (**Figure 5.49**). However, the shape you draw has to resemble a line moving from left to right. Go ahead, just try to draw a circle. You can't do it. That's because the Curves dialog box is just like a bar chart, and you can't have two bars for a single shade. Just for giggles, draw a really wild-looking line across the grid area, and then look at your image. Drawing your own line with the Pencil tool is usually better for special effects than for simple image adjustments.

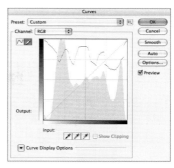

Figure 5.49 A curve created with the Pencil tool.

Let's take a quick look at some of the things you can do when working with a freeform curve:

▶ **Smoothing:** After creating a curve with the Pencil tool, you can click the Smooth button to smooth out the shape you drew (**Figure 5.50**). You can keep clicking the Smooth button to further smooth out the curve. .

▶ **Converting to points:** To convert any line drawn with the Pencil tool into a normal curve, click the curve icon (**Figure 5.51**).

▶ **Drawing straight lines:** You can also draw straight lines with the Pencil tool (**Figure 5.52**). Just Shift-click across the graph area, and Photoshop will connect the dots to create a straight line.

▶ **Posterizing:** By drawing a stair-step shape with the Pencil tool, you can accomplish the same effect as if you had used the Posterize command (**Figure 5.53**).

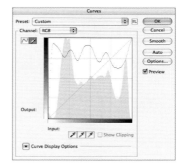

Figure 5.50 A freeform curve after Smooth is applied.

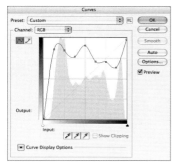

Figure 5.51 The result of converting a freeform curve into a normal curve.

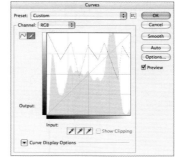

Figure 5.52 Straight lines drawn by Shift-clicking with the Pencil tool.

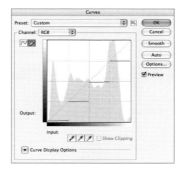

Figure 5.53 Drawing stair steps is the same as choosing Image > Adjust > Posterize.

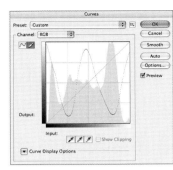

Figure 5.55 Image from the CD.

Figure 5.54 Freeform curve used to create chrome effect.

Figure 5.56 Result of applying the curve in Figure 5.54

If you want to create a chrome effect like the one shown in Figure 5.56, try this out: open the image called chrome.jpg from the CD, and then play around with the Pencil tool in the Curves dialog box. Try making a huge M or W, and experiment with different shapes. You should be able to transform the 3D type into some cool-looking chrome text if you experiment long enough (**Figures 5.54** to **5.56**).

Input and Output Numbers

The Input and Output numbers at the bottom of the Curves dialog box allow you to be very precise when adjusting an image. Input is the shade of gray being changed; Output is what it will become. When the points on the curve appear as hollow squares, the Input and Output numbers relate to your pointer. The Input number tells you which shade of gray is directly below your pointer. The Output number tells you what the shade of gray (height of the bar chart) would be if you moved the curve to the height of your pointer.

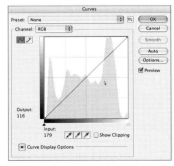

Figure 5.57 Input and Output numbers indicate the location of your pointer relative to the two gradients in the Curves dialog box.

Try it. Click the curve icon (not the pencil), and then make sure that none of the points on the curve are solid. Do this by moving your pointer around until it looks like a white arrow, and then click the mouse. Now move your pointer around the grid area. You'll notice the Input and Output numbers changing. All they're doing is telling you which shades of gray are directly below and to the left of your pointer (**Figure 5.57**). If you trace over the shape of a curve, the Input and Output numbers will show you exactly what the curve is doing to all the shades of gray in your image.

Two Numbering Systems

Two different numbering systems can be used in the Curves dialog box. When you change the "Show Amount of" radio buttons from Light to Pigment/Ink, Photoshop automatically changes the numbering system from the 0–255 system to percentages (**Figure 5.58**).

Figure 5.58 Click the arrow symbol to switch numbering systems.

If you're working on an image that's in RGB mode, Photoshop assumes you're going to use the image onscreen instead of printing it. Therefore, when you open Curves, it uses Input and Output numbers ranging from 0 to 255. These numbers represent the amount of light your monitor will use to display the image onscreen (0 = no light, or black; 255 = maximum light, or white). Using this numbering system allows you to have control over each shade.

If you're working on an image that's in grayscale or CMYK mode, Photoshop assumes you'll be printing the image. Therefore, when you open Curves, it uses numbers ranging from 0% to 100%. These numbers represent the amount of ink used to reproduce each level of gray in the image (0% = no ink; 100% = solid ink).

When you switch between the two numbering systems, Photoshop also reverses the gradients at the bottom and left of the graph. It does this to keep the zero point of each numbering system in the lower-left corner of the graph, which effectively changes between light and ink.

When you switch the numbering system, this also changes the gradient on the left side of the Curves dialog box. Therefore, if you're using the 0–255 numbering system, you have to move a curve up to brighten the image and down to darken it (the exact opposite of what you do in the 0–100% numbering system). I always look at the gradient on the left to remind me: If black is at the top (the 0–100% system), you're using ink, and moving a curve up will darken the image. If white is at the top of the gradient (the 0–255 system), you're using light, and moving a curve up will brighten the image.

NOTES

There are two main causes for undesirable results: making the curve flatten out (become horizontal) or making the curve go downhill (when moving from left to right). You can often fix these problems by adding a point in the middle of the problem area (the flat or downhill part of the curve) and then moving that point so that it appears next to the point that is farthest away from the area that was causing the problem. The idea is to finesse the position of the point so that it appears right next to one of the other points and is in a position that prevents the curve from becoming flat or going downhill.

When you're changing the Input and Output numbers, press the up or down arrow key to change a number by 1, or press Shift–up arrow or Shift–down arrow to change a number by 10.

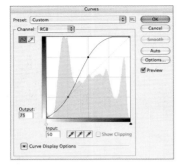

Figure 5.59 To alter the position of a point on the curve, just change one of the numbers.

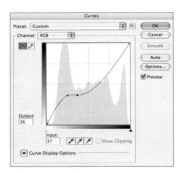

Figure 5.60 When two points are at the same height, those two areas will have the same brightness level.

Entering Numbers

After you've created a point, it appears as a solid square. This represents the point that's currently being edited. The Input and Output numbers at the bottom of the dialog box indicate the change this point will make to an image. The Input number represents the shade of gray that's being changed. The Output number indicates what's happening to that shade of gray—the value that you're changing it to. As long as the point appears as a solid square, you can type numbers into the Input and Output fields to change the location of the point (**Figure 5.59**).

Those numbers can be very useful. We'll end up depending on them once we get into the chapter on color correction (Chapter 7). But for now, let's see how they can be useful when attempting to change the brightness of an image. Remember that you can click on your image and a circle will appear in the Curves dialog box that indicates what part of the curve would affect the shade in that area? Well, you can also Command/Ctrl-click on your image and Photoshop will add a point where that circle would show up. So, what if you'd like two areas of your image to have the same brightness level? Command/Ctrl-click one of them to lock in its brightness level. Then, before you release the mouse button, glance at the numbers at the bottom of the Curves dialog box to see exactly how bright that area is. Command/Ctrl-click the second area, and change the Output number to match that of the first object (**Figure 5.60**). The bar chart will be the same height in both areas, which means that both areas will end up with the same brightness. But you have to be careful when doing this, because the bar chart will flatten out between those two points. When that happens, there won't be any detail in those shades, so other parts of your image might seem to disappear (**Figures 5.61** and **5.62**).

Figure 5.61 Original image. (©2007 PhotoSpin, www.photospin.com)

Figure 5.62 Result of making the far and close buildings the same brightness levels.

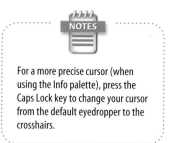

For a more precise cursor (when using the Info palette), press the Caps Lock key to change your cursor from the default eyedropper to the crosshairs.

The Info Palette

The Info palette can also show you how Curves affect your image (**Figure 5.63**). When you move your pointer over the image, the Info palette indicates what's happening to that area of the image. The left number in the Info palette tells you how dark the area is before using Curves. The right number tells you how dark it will be after Curves is applied.

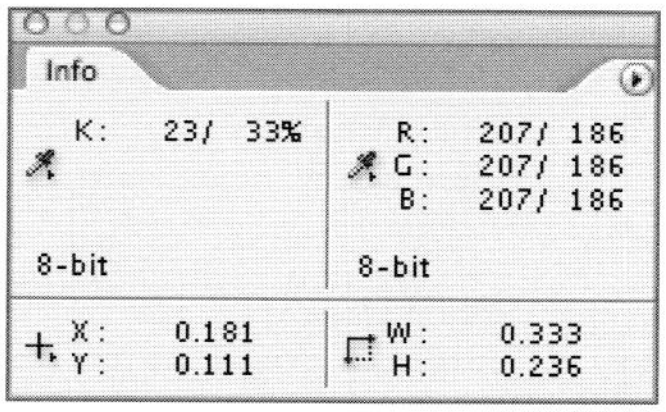

Color Is Different

The concepts and adjustments we talk about with Curves apply equally to grayscale and color images. But when you work on a color image, you have to be more careful; otherwise, you might end up shifting the colors rather than just the brightness of your image. There are two ways to apply Curves to your image, and therefore two methods for limiting its effect on the brightness of a color image. First, you can apply Curves to the currently active layer by choosing Image > Adjustments > Curves. Immediately after applying Curves, you can choose Edit > Fade Curves and set the Mode pop-up menu to Luminosity (**Figure 5.64**). The Fade command limits the last change you made (Curves, in our case) to changing only the brightness (luminosity is just another word for brightness) of the image—it will not be able to shift the colors or change how saturated they are.

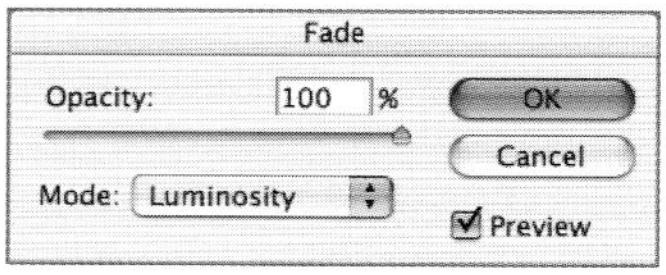

Your other choice would be to apply Curves to more than one layer by choosing Layer > New Adjustment Layer > Curves. Then, when prompted (**Figure 5.65**), you would set the Mode pop-up menu to Luminosity. An adjustment

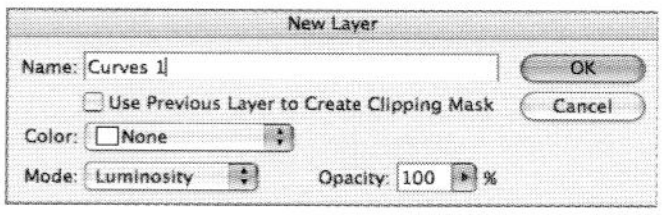

Figure 5.63 The left number is what you have before using Curves; the right number is what you get after using Curves.

Figure 5.64 Choose Edit > Fade Curves to limit your changes to the brightness of your image.

Figure 5.65 When creating an adjustment layer, change the Mode menu selection to Luminosity.

layer will affect all the layers below it but none of the layers above it. It's also a nonpermanent change, because you can double-click on the adjustment layer thumbnail in that layer to reopen the Curves dialog box and make changes. That means that any Curves techniques you use for adjusting grayscale images will work on color images if you use the Luminosity Blending mode (**Figures 5.66** to **5.68**).

Figure 5.66 Original image. (©2007 Stockbyte, www.stockbyte.com)

Figure 5.67 After adjusting contrast with Curves, the color and saturation change.

Figure 5.68 Using the Luminosity Blending mode prevents adjustments from shifting the colors in the image.

Color shifts aren't the only problems you'll encounter when adjusting color images with Curves. The mode your image is in might have an adverse effect on the adjustment. RGB color images are made from three components (red, green, and blue). A bright green color might be made out of 0 red, 255 green, and 128 blue. When you first open the Curves dialog box, the pop-up menu at the top of the dialog box will be set to RGB, which will cause any points to affect the exact same R, G, and B values. Clicking on that green color in your image will display a circle at 165 on the curve, which will affect all the areas that contain 165 red, 165 blue, and 165 green. Equal amounts of R, G, and B create gray. So, simply clicking on the curve of a color image will usually cause the colors to shift in an unsatisfactory way, because the circle that appears when clicking on your image will not accurately target the area you clicked on. While working in RGB mode, all color areas will shift because their

RGB mix will change as the Curves dialog box shifts the RGB values in equal amounts. Ideally it would affect only the exact mix of RGB that the color is made from, but it doesn't work that way in RGB mode. The solution to this problem is to convert your image to Lab mode by choosing Image > Mode > Lab Color. In Lab mode, your image is made from three components: Lightness, A, and B. When you adjust your image, the Curves dialog box will automatically set itself to work on the Lightness information, which will prevent your adjustment from shifting the color of your image and will also make it so that the circle will show up in the correct position to make accurate adjustments. When you're done with your adjustment, I'd suggest that you convert the image back to RGB mode because many of Photoshop's features are not available in Lab mode. I don't use Lab mode for every color image; I reserve it for those images that are troublesome in RGB mode.

A Quick Recap

Now, to verify that you're ready to move on, you should make sure you understand the general concepts. Take a look at the curve in **Figure 5.69** and see if you can answer the following questions:

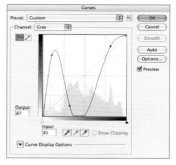

Figure 5.69 Can you figure out what this curve will do to an image?

▶ Which areas of the image will lose detail with this adjustment?

▶ Which areas of the image will become brighter?

▶ What happened to 62% gray?

▶ What happened to the image's contrast?

Just in case you couldn't answer all these questions, let's recap what we've covered:

▶ Flattening a curve reduces contrast and makes it more difficult to see detail.

▶ Making a curve steeper increases contrast and makes it easier to see detail.

▶ Up means darken in the 0–100% system.

▶ Down means darken in the 0–255 system.

▶ Up means brighten in the 0–255 system.

▶ Down means brighten in the 0–100% system.

Figure 5.70 The Histogram palette.

Figure 5.71 Imagine that there is a gradient below the histogram.

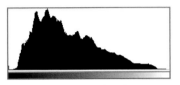

Figure 5.72 The gray histogram reflects the unadjusted image, whereas the black version reflects the adjusted image.

NOTES

The Histogram palette can be used in two different sizes—Compact or Expanded. I prefer to use the Expanded version because it is exactly 256 pixels wide and most images contain 256 shades of gray, which makes that version the most accurate histogram for your image. You can switch between the two different views on the side menu of the Histogram palette.

The Histogram Palette

The histogram that is displayed behind the curve in the Curves dialog is a really useful addition and, used properly, it can help you make sure that your adjustments don't get out of control and end up harming your images instead of improving them. In addition to the histogram displayed in the Curves dialog box, Photoshop's Histogram palette (**Figure 5.70**) can also help you ensure that you don't push your edits and adjustments too far. So, now that you have an idea of how to think about Curves, let's figure out how to use these two tools to help with our edits. To display the Histogram palette, choose Window > Histogram.

As you learned earlier, a histogram is a simple bar chart that shows you the range of brightness levels that make up your image and how prevalent each of these shades is. When you look at the histogram, imagine that there's a gradient stretched across the bottom of the bar chart that has black on the left and white on the right (just like it is in the Curves dialog box). (**Figure 5.71**). If the histogram shows a bar above a particular shade of gray, that shade is used somewhere in your image. If there's no bar, that brightness level is not used in your image. The height of the bar indicates how prevalent a particular brightness level is compared to the others that make up your image.

The Histogram palette shows the same histogram but with an added bonus. When you start to adjust an image, the Histogram palette will overlay a histogram that represents the current, adjusted state of the image (black) above the original histogram that shows what the image looked like before you started adjusting it (gray) (**Figure 5.72**).

Achieving Optimal Contrast

If the histogram doesn't extend all the way from black to white, your image has a limited brightness range (**Figures 5.73** and **5.74**). When that's the case, you can usually move the upper-right and lower-left points on a curve toward the middle, which will widen the histogram (**Figures 5.75** to **5.77**). As you do, keep an eye on the histogram. Most images will look their best when the histogram extends all the way across the area available, without producing any tall spikes on either end.

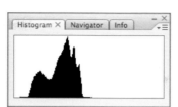

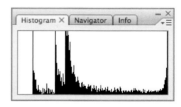

Figure 5.73 This image has a very limited brightness range. (©2007 Ben Willmore)

Figure 5.74 The histogram for the image in Figure 5.73.

Figure 5.75 The Curves adjustment used to add contrast to the image.

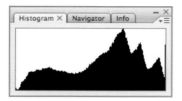

Figure 5.76 The result of applying the curve shown in Figure 5.75.

Figure 5.77 The histogram for the adjusted image.

With CS3, Adobe has added two new controls that make this edit a little simpler. Notice that below the grayscale ramp beneath the curve there's a black point and white point slider, just like the one that you have in the Levels dialog box. Moving these sliders is the same as adjusting the points on the end of the curve.

Preventing Blown-Out Highlights and Plugged-Up Shadows

Because the height of the bars indicates how prevalent each shade is within your image, tall spikes on the ends of the histogram indicate that the image contains large quantities of white or black (**Figure 5.78**). That is usually an indication that you don't have any detail in the brightest or darkest areas of the image (**Figure 5.79**). If your image contains shiny areas that reflect light directly into the camera (like shiny metal or glass), it's OK if those areas end up with no detail. But if that's not the case, part of your curve must have topped or bottomed out. You should think about moving that area of the curve away from the top or bottom so you can get back the detail that was originally in that part of your image (**Figures 5.80** and **5.81**).

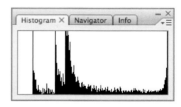

Figure 5.78 This histogram indicates that black and white take up a lot of space in the image.

Figure 5.79 This image does not contain detail in the highlights or shadow areas. (©2007 Andy Katz)

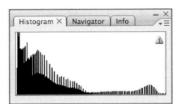

Figure 5.80 The histogram no longer has spikes on the ends after adjusting the curve to prevent topping or bottoming out.

Figure 5.81 The result of preventing the curve from bottoming or topping out.

Figure 5.82 This comb-like histogram indicates possible posterization.

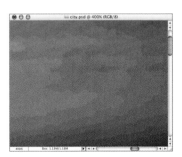

Figure 5.83 This stair-stepped area used to be smooth before a steep curve was applied to the image.

Avoiding Posterization

If you notice that the histogram in the Histogram palette is showing gaps that sort of look like a comb (**Figure 5.82**), you'll want to keep an eye on the brightness levels that are directly below that area of the histogram. Gaps in a histogram indicate that certain brightness levels are nowhere to be found in your image, which can indicate posterization (stair-stepped transitions where there would usually be a smooth transition—as in **Figure 5.83**). That usually happens when you make part of a curve rather steep. As long as the gaps are small (two to three pixels wide), it's not likely that you'll notice it in your image. If they start getting a lot wider than that, you might want to inspect your image and think about making your curve less steep. The histogram in the Curves dialog box does not show these gaps, because it only shows the original, unedited histogram.

To better understand posterization, try this: Create a new grayscale document, press D to reset the foreground and background colors to black and white, and then click and drag across the document with the Gradient tool. Now look at the Histogram palette. Then, choose Image > Adjustments > Posterize and experiment with different settings while you watch the histogram—the gaps don't have to be all that wide before you notice the posterization (**Figure 5.84**).

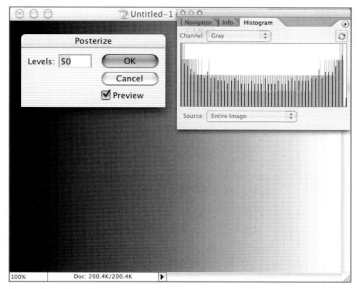

NOTES

If you notice slight posterization in your image, you might want to apply a little bit of noise to it (Filter > Noise > Add Noise, Amount: 3, Gaussian), which should make it less noticeable. If that doesn't do the trick, go back to the Grayscale chapter (Chapter 4, "Optimizing Grayscale Images") and check out the manual method for eliminating posterization.

Figure 5.84 Posterize a grayscale image to get a sense of how wide the gaps have to be to see the posterization in your image.

You can minimize posterization by working with 16-bit images. Unlike standard 8-bit images that are made from 256 shades of gray (or 256 shades each of red, green, and blue), 16-bit images contain up to 32,767 shades of gray. You can obtain 16-bit images from RAW format digital camera files when opening them in the Camera Raw dialog box (see Chapter 8, "Using Camera Raw," for more details), or from some newer flatbed or film scanners. You can tell if you're working with a 16-bit file by looking at the title bar for the image. After the filename, you should see something like (RGB/16). That would indicate that you have a 16-bit RGB-mode image.

The Histogram palette usually builds its histogram by analyzing an 8-bit cached image, just to make sure the palette display updates quickly. A cached image is a smaller version of your image that has 8 bits of information. If you notice the comb look when adjusting a 16-bit image (**Figure 5.85**), look for the warning triangle near the upper right of the histogram. That indicates that the histogram is being created from a lower-resolution 8-bit image. Clicking the triangle will cause the histogram to be redrawn directly from the high-resolution 16-bit file, which should eliminate the comb look and therefore indicate that your image isn't really posterized (**Figure 5.86**).

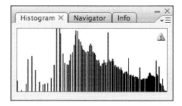

Figure 5.85 This histogram indicates that the image might be posterized.

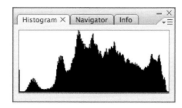

Figure 5.86 The uncached histogram is a more accurate view of your image.

Sneaky Contrast Adjustments

Flattening a curve is usually harmful to an image because the detail in the area you are adjusting will be very difficult to see. You can often cheat, however, by analyzing the histogram to determine which areas of your image won't be harmed by flattening the curve. Because short lines in a histogram indicate shades that are not very prevalent in the image, those areas can often be flattened in a curve without noticeable degradation to the image. Flattening one part of the curve allows you to make the rest of the curve steeper, which will increase the contrast of those areas and make the area appear to have more detail.

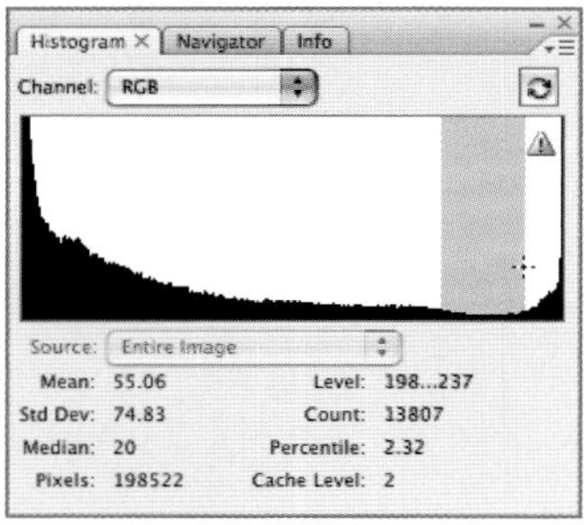

Figure 5.87 Drag across the extremely low areas of the histogram.

So, when you see a flat area of the histogram in the Curves dialog box, place two points on the curve, one at each end of the flat section of the histogram. Here's how it works: While you're in the Curves dialog box, glance over at the Histogram palette and look for short, flat areas. When you find a flat area (not all images have them), choose Show Statistics from the side menu of the Histogram palette, and then click and drag across that area in the Histogram palette, but don't release the mouse button (**Figure 5.87**). Now, look at the Level numbers that show up just below the histogram (if you don't see any numbers under the histogram, choose Expanded View from the side menu of the Histogram palette). Next, release the mouse button and move your cursor around the Curves dialog box to see whether the numbers at the bottom are 0–100% or 0–255 numbers. If they are ranging from 0–100%, click the Curve Display Options button and change the Show Amount of setting to switch to the 0–255 numbering system. Now click in the middle of the curve and change the numbers that appear in the Input and Output fields at the bottom of the Curves dialog box to the first number you saw in the Histogram palette (**Figure 5.88**). Add a second point and do the same for the second number you saw in the Histogram palette. Then, move the upper dot straight down and the lower dot straight up until the area between the two becomes almost horizontal (**Figure 5.89**). (Keep an eye on your image to see how flat you can get away with without screwing up the image.) That should increase the contrast across most of the image while reducing contrast in those brightness levels that are not very prevalent in the image (**Figures 5.90** and **5.91**).

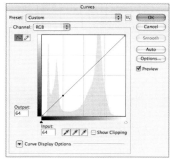

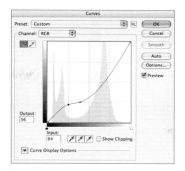

Figure 5.88 Add the first point and then enter the number from the Level area of the Histogram palette.

Figure 5.89 After adding the second point, move one point up and the other down to flatten part of the curve.

Figure 5.90 The original image. (©2007 Ben Willmore)

Figure 5.91 Result of applying the curve shown in Figure 5.89.

Just because I've decided to talk about the Histogram palette here in the Curves chapter, doesn't mean that I only use it when making Curves adjustments. The Histogram palette is useful for performing *any* type of adjustment and for analyzing your image to determine what types of adjustments you might need to consider.

In general, I don't adjust my images based solely on what the histogram is showing me. Instead, I adjust the image until I like its general appearance, and then I look at the Histogram palette to look for signs that I might have gone too far. If I notice spikes on the ends or a huge comb look, I'll take a closer look at my image to determine if it's worth backing off from my adjustment. Who cares what the histogram looks like in the end—it's the visual look of your image that is most important. The histogram is just like that seatbelt warning light in your car—you're welcome to ignore it, but there's a reason it's on.

Figure 5.92 The simple version of the Shadow/Highlight dialog box.

Shadow/Highlight

If you have an image that needs more pronounced shadows and/or highlight detail, the Shadow/Highlight command (Image > Adjustments > Shadow/Highlight) (**Figure 5.92**) is a good alternative to Curves. In its simplest form, you just move the Shadows slider to brighten the darker areas of your image (**Figures 5.93** and **5.94**) and/or move the Highlights slider to darken the brighter areas of your image (**Figures 5.95** and **5.96**).

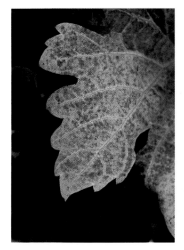 

Figure 5.93 Original image. (©2007 Andy Katz)

Figure 5.94 Result of moving the Shadows slider to the right.

Figure 5.95 Original image. (©2007 Andy Katz)

Figure 5.96 Result of moving the Highlights slider to the right.

If you need more control over the adjustment, click the Show More Options check box so you can see the full range of settings available (**Figure 5.97**). I suggest that you start by setting the Amount to 0%, the Tonal Width to 50%, and the Radius to 30px in both the Shadows and Highlights area. The Amount setting determines how radical a change you'll make to your image. Because you're starting with that setting at zero, these settings won't do a thing to your image—yet.

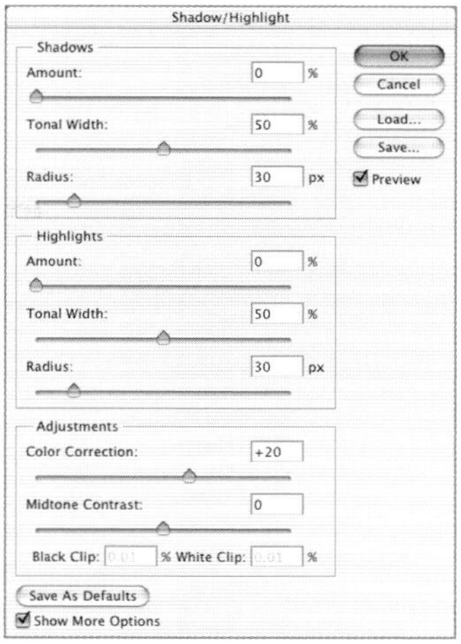

If you want to pull out some detail in the dark areas of your image, move the Amount slider in the Shadows area toward the right while you watch your image. Keep moving it until the dark areas of your image become the desired brightness. Now start messing with the Tonal Width setting. That will control the brightness range in your image. Extremely low settings will limit the adjustment to the darkest areas of your image; higher settings will allow the adjustment to creep into the brighter areas of your image (**Figures 5.98** through **5.100**). The Shadow/Highlight command adjusts areas based on the brightness level of the surrounding image. So, once you've defined the brightness range you'd like to work with (via the Tonal Width slider), you'll need to experiment with the Radius slider. That setting determines how much of the surrounding image you want Photoshop to look at when determining how to blend the changes you're making into the surrounding image. Just slide it around until the changes to the dark areas of the image look appropriate considering their surroundings. Moving it toward the right will cause the area you're adjusting to blend into the surrounding image more, whereas moving it to the left will

Figure 5.97 The expanded Shadow/Highlight dialog box.

Figure 5.98 Original image.

Figure 5.99 Tonal Width 0%.

Figure 5.100 Tonal Width 30%.

Figure 5.101 This image is divided into thirds—the left uses a Radius of 0px, the middle uses 50px, and the right uses 100px. (©2007 Ben Willmore)

cause a more pronounced difference between the shadows and midtones of your image (**Figure 5.101**). When you've finished your first round with the settings, you'll most likely want to go back to the Amount and Tonal Width settings to fine-tune the result.

The Highlights adjustments work just like the Shadows adjustments, but attempt to darken the brightest areas of your image to exaggerate the detail in that area.

When you brighten the shadows or darken the highlights, you'll often exaggerate any color that was lurking in those areas (**Figures 5.102** and **5.103**). If you find the color to be a little too distracting, try moving the Color Correction slider toward the left to make the areas you've adjusted less colorful (**Figure 5.104**). Or, on the other hand, if you'd like to make those areas even more colorful, move the slider toward the right. The default setting is +20, which is a good starting point.

Figure 5.102 Original image.

Figure 5.103 After adjusting the image with Shadow/Highlight, the color in those areas is exaggerated.

Figure 5.104 Moving the Color Correction slider toward the left reduces the amount of color that shows up in the brightest and darkest areas of the image.

NOTES

If you're having trouble seeing exactly what an adjustment is doing to your image, you should experiment with an extremely simple image until you get the hang of it. Try it on a new grayscale image that you've applied a gradient to.

Once you have the brightness and color looking good, you'll need to fine-tune the contrast in the areas of the image that you haven't changed. You can do that by moving the Midtone Contrast slider to the left (to lower contrast) or right (to increase contrast). There aren't any set rules for using these sliders. Your image is your guide (**Figures 5.105** through **5.107**).

Figure 5.105 Original image. (©2007 Andy Katz)

Figure 5.106 Adjusted with Shadow/Highlight, Midtone Contrast −40.

Figure 5.107 Adjusted with Shadow/Highlight, Midtone Contrast +40.

Darkening the highlights on some images can make them look rather dull, especially when working with something that contains bright shiny objects (**Figure 5.108**). In order for something to look truly shiny, the brightest areas of the image (usually direct reflections of light into the camera lens) need to be pure white. If it's not white, you get dullsville (**Figure 5.109**). If you notice those bright reflections becoming darker when you adjust the Highlights setting, you'll need to mess with the White Clip setting that's found at the bottom of the Shadow/Highlight dialog box. With it set to zero, Photoshop is capable of darkening all the bright areas of the image. As you raise that setting, Photoshop will force a narrow range of the brightest shades in your image to pure white. The higher the setting, the wider the range of shades that Shadow/Highlight will end up forcing to white. Just watch your image and increase the White Clip setting until those shiny reflections look nice and bright (**Figure 5.110**).

NOTES

The Shadow/Highlight command cannot be used as an adjustment layer because it is too complex an adjustment. Adjustment layers are limited to things that can take any input (any shade of gray or color) and know what to do with it without having to know what the rest of the image looks like. Because Shadow/Highlight compares the area you're adjusting to its surroundings, it's not simple enough to be implemented as an adjustment layer.

Figure 5.108 The original image. (©2007 Stockbyte, www.stockbyte.com)

Figure 5.109 After darkening the highlights, the image looks a little dull.

Figure 5.110 Increasing the White Clip setting produces a higher-contrast image.

The Black Clip setting forces the darkest areas of your image to black to make sure that they won't be lightened when you move the Shadows Amount setting. That can be useful if you want high-contrast shadow areas or if you have text or other line art that wouldn't look right if they were lightened.

I'm amazed at how many images can benefit from a quick visit to the Shadow/Highlight dialog box. I use it so often that I've defined a keyboard shortcut to it. If you'd like to figure out how to do the same, be sure to check out the section "Editing Keyboard Shortcuts" in Chapter 1, "Tools and Palette Primer."

Closing Thoughts

My hope is that after you've read this chapter you'll have come to the conclusion that the Curves feature really isn't such a brain twister. And if you come out of it thinking of ways you might use Curves in the future, even better. Learning to use the Curves dialog box is one of a handful of things that separate the experts from everyone else. But there's no reason why you can't propel yourself into the expert category. And don't forget to get in the habit of keeping an eye on the Histogram palette (and don't just use it with Curves) as well as spending some more time working with the Shadow/Highlight feature. All of these tools can give you that extra bit of versatility and control that can make a big difference with your next adjustment. So hang in there and stick with it. The initial learning curve might be somewhat daunting, but the fringe benefits are dynamite.

Color Management

Courtesy of Andy Katz, andykatzphotography.com

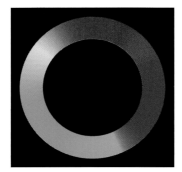

Figure 6.1 The color wheel.

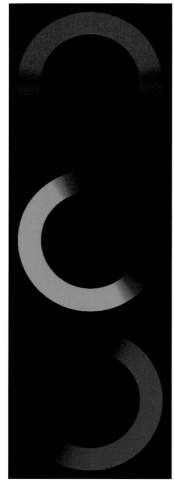

Figure 6.2 The RGB components of the color wheel.

This would be so much easier if I weren't color-blind.
— Donkey from the movie Shrek

This chapter should probably be named "Confessions of a Photoshop Expert," and it's the one that I wish I could have read myself a few years ago. My embarrassing secret? There was a time I found color management to be so painstakingly cumbersome and time-consuming that I found every reason to avoid it.

But color management is not rocket science. The truth is that all this stuff can really work if you can just get over a bunch of terms and figure out how to deal with a few simple settings. And once it's all set up, you don't have to do that much to maintain everything. Not only that, but with things working properly, you can do some amazing things. You can get your screen to match your printer, get your desktop printer to simulate a printing press, and much more. So, let's jump in and see what all the fuss is about.

For me to truly understand anything in Photoshop, I usually have to simplify it to such an extent that it becomes almost obvious. So, let's start out from the beginning and slowly work our way into the more technical bits. I promise this will all make sense and will be easy for you to set up for your situation. Stick with me, because once you've gotten this nailed, your Photoshop life will be infinitely easier. Here goes….

How Color Works

In figuring out color management, I read all about how our eyes work and that's when I learned that we could see only three colors of light—red, green, and blue. Everything we see is a combination of those colors. That's right, when you look at a rainbow, all your eyes see are red, green, and blue (**Figures 6.1** and **6.2**). When we see all three of those colors in a balanced amount (equal amounts of red, green, and blue), we see white light. The more light there is, the brighter it is; the less light there is, the darker it is. We often call a low level of white light gray, so that's what I'll call a

192

balanced amount of red, green, and blue. When they aren't balanced, we see color. Photoshop works the same way.

Go ahead and launch Photoshop, click on your foreground color, and pick any color you'd like. Now glance over at the RGB numbers that appear in the right side of that dialog box—they show you how that foreground color can be made out of a combination of red, green, and blue (**Figure 6.3**). That's also how your computer screen works (**Figure 6.4**). Each pixel that makes up your screen is made out of three tiny bars of color right next to each other—again RGB. A digital camera works on the same principle; it just measures how much RGB light travels through the lens. So, it really is an RGB world out there. But things change just a tiny bit when you print things.

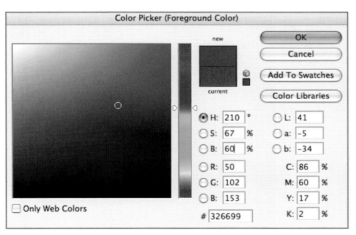

Figure 6.3 Photoshop's Color Picker.

Figure 6.4 A magnified view of your screen.

Remember that white light is made from a balanced amount of red, green, and blue light. So, for red ink to look red when you shine white light at a sheet of paper, it has to let only red light reflect off it and into your eyes; otherwise, it wouldn't look red (**Figure 6.5**). That means that red ink absorbs green and blue in order to just let the red light bounce off the sheet of paper. So if that's the case, then blue ink must absorb everything but blue, and green light must absorb everything but green. So, when you combine any two of those inks (let's say red ink printed on top of green ink), all you'd get is black because the inks end up absorbing all three colors of light (**Figure 6.6**).

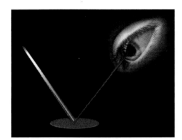

Figure 6.5 Red ink absorbs green and blue light.

Figure 6.6 Red and green ink create black.

That presents a problem that is easily solved. When we print, we don't need red, green, and blue inks; instead, we need three inks that control how much RGB bounces off a sheet of paper. We need one ink that controls how much red light enters our eye, another to control green light, and a third to control blue.

So, let's figure out what we need. Take a look at **Figure 6.7.** It represents three flashlights, one with a red filter, one with green, and one with blue. Now, check out the area where the blue and green flashlights overlap, but the red one does not; you should see cyan. That means that cyan ink simply absorbs red light while allowing the other two colors of light to bounce off the sheet of paper. If you analyze Figure 6.7 further, you might be able to figure out that magenta ink absorbs green light and yellow ink absorbs blue light. That's why the Info palette is arranged the way it is (**Figure 6.8**). One side looks at light and the other looks at ink. If you're wondering about the K in CMYK, it stands for key, which is really just a term used for black ink. It's used because a lot of people in the printing industry call cyan blue and they didn't want to confuse anyone by calling black B (and B is already used in RGB), so they came up with K instead to confuse the rest of us. Since black ink can't shift the color of anything, we'll talk about it later in this chapter. Now that we've got a basic idea of how color is reproduced, let's take a look at why your screen doesn't match your desktop printer and why your printer delivers a different result than your next-door neighbor's—in essence, why we need to bother with color management.

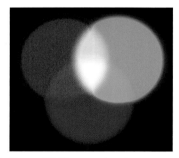

Figure 6.7 Three overlapping flashlight beams.

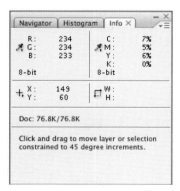

Figure 6.8 The Info palette.

The Problem with Color

Here are the problems we need to overcome: If you were to purchase a red felt-tip marker from three different manufacturers (maybe Crayola, Sharpie, and a generic brand), would you expect them to produce identical results? It's true that they are all red, but each one would, in fact, be a different shade of red. Maybe a Sharpie marker would produce a darker red and a Crayola a more vivid red. Not only that, but buying two red markers from the same company doesn't even guarantee consistent results; after all, they could be from different batches or one could be older than the other.

Well, the same thing goes for printing. Each printer will deliver a slightly different result when printing the same image because the inks are slightly different, so don't expect to send the same info to an Epson and a Canon printer and get the same results. The problems don't stop there.

Would you expect a Sony television set to look the same as a Panasonic? Just take a stroll through your local electronics superstore and look at all the TVs that are tuned to the same station. Even though they are being sent the exact same signal, they all look different. That's because they all use different shades of red, green, and blue. So why would you expect two different brands of monitors to look the same? They also use different shades of RGB.

Some inkjet printers use two shades of cyan ink, two shades of magenta, and two shades of black, but the general principles still apply.

Color Management to the Rescue

This is why color management is needed. It's designed to deal with all these variations among devices (monitors, scanners, printers, cameras, and so on). All we have to do is measure the exact color of red, green, and blue that your scanner and monitor use and also measure which shades of CMY that your printer uses (I'm ignoring the K in CMYK because black ink won't shift the color of things). Then Photoshop can use its wizardry to send different information to each device to compensate for its unique qualities in an attempt to get consistent results on all those devices.

But first, one more issue: Remember when I said that your eyes see white light when a balanced amount of red, green, and blue light enters your eye? Well, you don't end up with white when you use a balanced amount of RGB or CMY on your monitor, printer, or scanner, because the slightly different shades of RGB or CMY (just like those felt-tip pens), produce slightly different results on each device. So balanced RGB on one device might look a little greenish or bluish instead of looking gray. That can cause a lot of problems because many of Photoshop's features (such as color correction) make the assumption that equal amounts of R, G, and B produce no color at all.

The solution is to make your images out of idealized shades of red, green, and blue that have nothing to do with your monitor, scanner, or printer. We do that partially because the monitor you use to view your image isn't capable of accurately displaying what 100% cyan ink looks like and your printer isn't capable of reproducing the deepest blue that you can see on screen, so you don't want your images to have those same limitations. This special set of RGB colors is what all our images will be made from; then Photoshop will go to work to make sure it can print and display correctly using the less-than-ideal colors of RGB or CMY used by our monitor and printers (**Figure 6.9**).

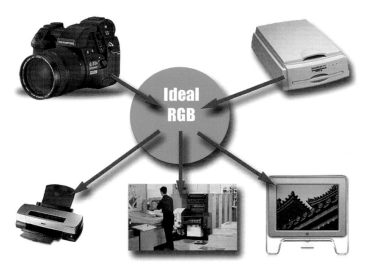

Figure 6.9 The overall concept of different RGBs being used.

Implementing Color Management

Let's see how all this relates to Photoshop's color-management features. When we measure the exact shade of RGB or CMY that a device uses, the end result will be an ICC profile. An ICC profile is just a small file that describes how something reproduces color. It's in a format that is approved by the International Color Consortium (ICC). That's the file you feed Photoshop so it can do the magic necessary to produce consistent color on each device. You'll end up with a profile for your monitor, your desktop printer, your scanner, and in rare cases your digital camera (the camera's white balance setting is often used as a substitute for having a custom camera profile), with each profile telling Photoshop which shades of RGB or CMY it uses to make color.

If you compare two printers and one has a more vivid set of CMY inks loaded, that printer will be capable of reproducing a more vivid range of colors than the other one (just like different brands of markers). Each set of RGB colors (or CMY, for that matter) will reproduce color in a unique way. The range of colors you can reproduce on any given device is known as its gamut. Let's say that you can reproduce a nice deep blue on your inkjet, but you can't on your friend's inkjet (maybe it comes out as a more muted blue). That just means the particular color was in gamut on your printer but was out of gamut on your friend's printer. And, as you might already know, more exotic colors like fluorescent orange are out of gamut on just about any desktop printer.

There's just one more term with which I want you to get familiar. Remember that idealized version of RGB out of which we're going to create our images? The one where a balanced amount of RGB makes gray? Well, that's known as our RGB working space. A working space indicates what color you'll use when you create a new document instead of opening an existing one.

So, now that we know some of the terms Photoshop will be throwing at us, we can get to the business of getting all this stuff set up properly. We'll figure out the details of picking that idealized version of RGB, measuring the shades of RGB and CMY that our devices use, and learn how to tell Photoshop how to deal with all that information.

Choosing an RGB Working Space

The first order of business is to pick that idealized version of RGB (known as your RGB working space) out of which we'll make our images. Picking a working space is just like picking which brand and type of film to use for a 35mm camera. If there was one best choice in that area, that would be all that's available. A lot of people just grab Kodak 400-speed film, but there are legions of photographers who will happily debate the merits of each film type. It's the same with RGB working spaces. One might be better for your specific situation than another, but they will all work. Let's see what's available: To see your choices, choose Edit > Color Settings and click on the RGB pop-up menu (**Figure 6.10**). Here's my general take on this menu: With most of the choices, equal amounts of R, G, and B make gray. The main difference is in the range of colors that you can create (also known as gamut). Don't stress about it. It's just like film for a camera—they all take OK photos, but there might be one that's better for your specific needs. Here's how I think about each of the RGB working spaces you can choose from.

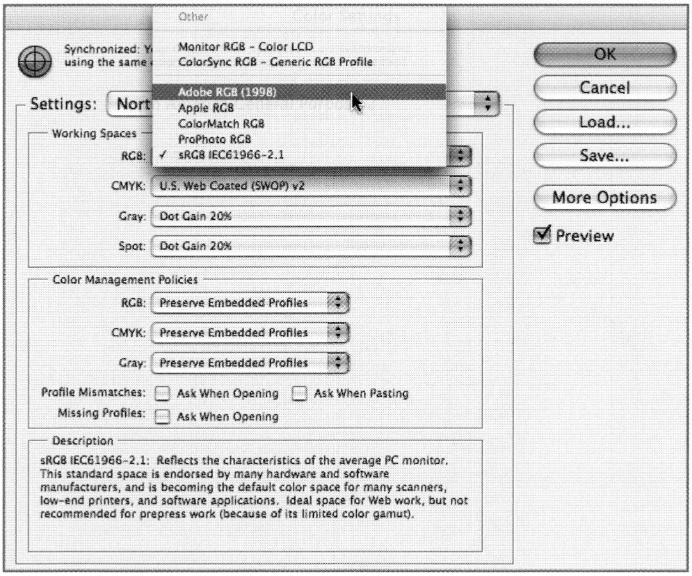

Figure 6.10 The RGB working spaces pop-up menu.

RGB Working Spaces

The RGB working spaces include the following:

▶ **Adobe RGB:** The best general choice for people who end up printing their images on desktop inkjet printers or sending them to commercial printing presses.

▶ **Apple RGB:** A less-than-ideal choice because adjustments won't affect the image evenly from light to dark. Useful if you have old images that didn't use color management, which will be talked about later.

▶ **ColorMatch RGB:** Not a bad choice for images that will end up on a commercial printing press, but not quite as ideal as Adobe RGB for that purpose.

▶ **ProPhotoRGB:** Ideal for photographs that are scanned in 16-bit mode from color transparencies, because it offers a very wide range of colors. Can cause posterization in 8-bit images.

▶ **Monitor RGB:** Use when you'd like your images to look identical in both Photoshop and your Web browser. An alternative to sRGB, but it does not take into consideration what other people will see when viewing your Web site.

▶ **sRGB:** Good for people who create Web graphics and would like to limit the colors used in their images to those that can be seen on an average user's screen. Less than ideal for anyone who will end up printing on a commercial printing press (but is okay for newsprint) or photographic process because it has such a limited range of colors available.

Now that we've gotten our RGB working space out of the way, let's make sure that our images will be friendly to others. We'll do that by including a profile of our working space with each image we create. That way when others open it, their copy of Photoshop will know what colors of RGB the image was made from, so it can display it properly. When you save an image, make sure the Embed Color Profile check box is turned on (**Figure 6.11**). That will "tag" the image with an ICC profile.

NOTES

Make sure the Color Management Policies pop-up menus are all set to Preserve Embedded Profiles; otherwise, you just might want Photoshop to warn you when opening an image or when pasting.

If you turn off all three checkboxes at the bottom of the Color Settings dialog box, you'll want to look for a "#" or "*" in the title bar of your image once you open it. A "*" indicates an image with a profile that does not match your RGB working space, and a "#" indicates an image that is untagged (missing profile).

If you want to see how the RGB working spaces relate to the range of colors that can be reproduced on different printers, visit www.digitalmastery.com/color.

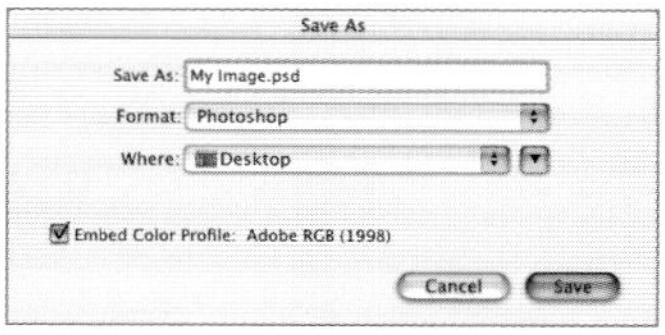

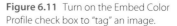

Figure 6.11 Turn on the Embed Color Profile check box to "tag" an image.

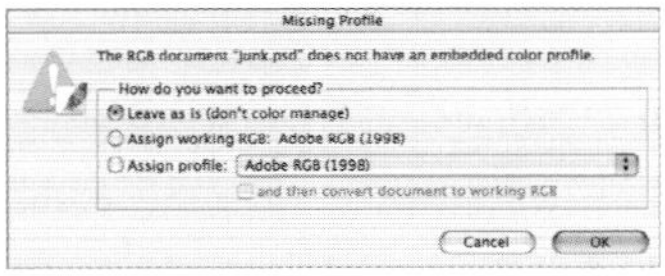

Figure 6.12 The Missing Profile dialog box.

NOTES

At this point in the chapter, I'm assuming that you haven't messed with any color-management settings except for the ones we've discussed. If you aren't seeing any mismatch warnings, turn on the three check boxes that appear at the bottom of the Color Settings dialog box.

If you don't tag your images, Photoshop will ask you to guess which colors of RGB the image was made from when you reopen the image (**Figure 6.12**). If you guess wrong, the image won't look like it's supposed to. I get a lot of untagged images, but I really don't like the way Photoshop makes you blindly choose a profile without seeing the consequences. If you get an untagged image, here's what I suggest you do: Just choose the Leave As Is option and then click OK. Then, immediately after opening it, choose Assign Profile from the Edit menu. Then try the top four choices listed under the profile pop-up menu (just make sure the Preview check box is on). Each time you change that setting, you should see your image change. Keep cycling through until you find one that makes your image look good. The person who sent you the image didn't include enough info for Photoshop to know what the colors should look like, so you're just guessing. And, no, it's not worth calling the person who sent it to you because he or she obviously doesn't know enough about color management to have it set up correctly, so you'll just end up confusing that person by asking which setting to use.

Profile Mismatch Warnings

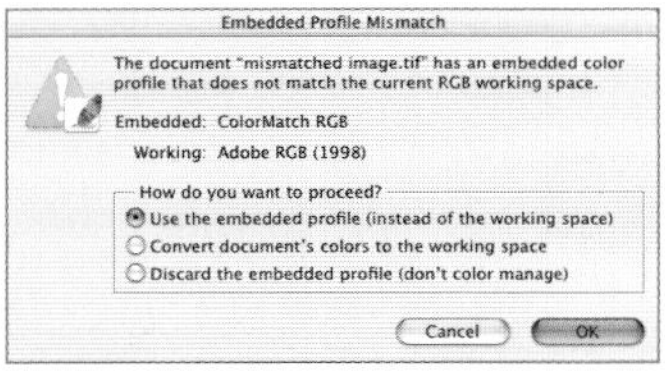

Now, just because your image has a proper profile assigned to it doesn't mean that Photoshop will stop bugging you about all this color business. If you open an image and the profile that is assigned to it is not the same as what you used when creating new documents (known as your RGB Working Space), Photoshop will warn you (**Figure 6.13**). Most of the time, you'll just want to choose the top option and click OK, which tells Photoshop not do anything special with the image. But if the embedded profile that's attached to the image is the name of a product (scanner, monitor, printer, and so on), equal amounts of red, green, and blue might not make a perfect gray. When that's the case, you should choose the Convert option if you plan on adjusting the image in Photoshop.

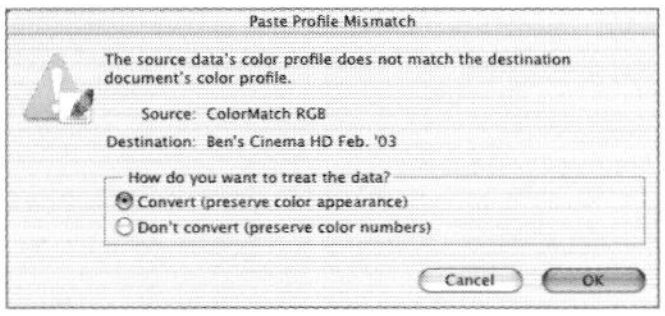

Figure 6.13 The Embedded Profile Mismatch dialog box.

Photoshop also warns you if you copy and paste between two documents that have different profiles attached to them (**Figure 6.14**). When that happens, you'll almost always want to choose the Convert option since it's the only choice that will not shift the colors in your image. But if

Figure 6.14 The Paste Profile Mismatch dialog box.

you happen to have an image that contains web-safe colors (if you don't know what this is, I can almost guarantee that you don't have them in your image) or scientific data (like information downloaded from a weather satellite), you might want to choose the bottom option.

The numbers that make up an image are usually more important than the actual look of the image when you have web-safe colors or scientific data, and the bottom choice is the only option that ensures that those numbers don't change.

I don't know about you, but I get sick of seeing all those color mismatch dialog boxes. There are so few times when it matters that the profile attached to an image is different than your RGB working space that I like to take measures to minimize how much Photoshop warns me about things like that. I suggest that you turn off the three check boxes that show up at the bottom of the Color Settings dialog box (**Figure 6.15**). That will prevent Photoshop from warning you about missing or mismatched profiles altogether. But after you've done that, you'll have to make sure you take the proper steps when you do run across an image that actually needs to use something other than the default settings.

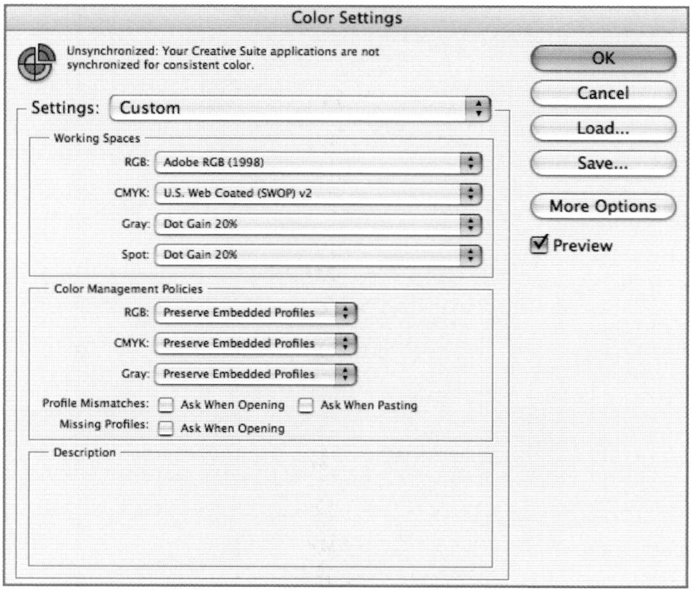

Figure 6.15 Turn off the three check boxes at the bottom of the Color Settings dialog box.

Figure 6.16 Assign Profile dialog box.

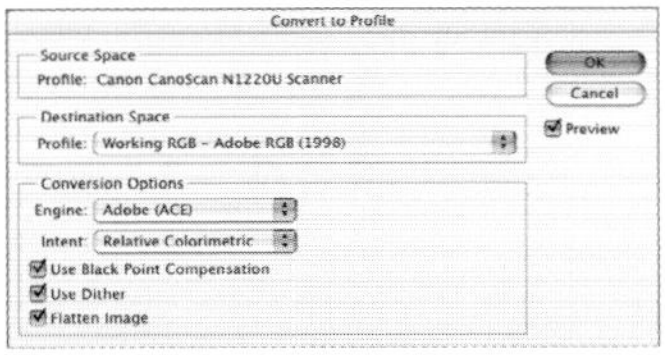

Figure 6.17 The Convert to Profile dialog box.

From now on, when you open an image, take a quick look at the bottom edge of the document. That's where you'll find a triangle that points to the right. Click on that triangle and choose Document Profile to find out what profile is attached to the image. If you ever see an image that says "Untagged RGB," it means that the image might not display properly. That's when you'll want to choose Assign Profile from the Edit menu and find which choice from the Profile drop-down makes your image look its best (**Figure 6.16**).

If, on the other hand, you see the name of a product (scanner, monitor, printer, and so on), that means that equal amounts of red, green, and blue might not produce gray, which means color correction and other features might not work as they were designed to. That's when you'll want to choose Convert to Profile from the Edit menu (**Figure 6.17**). In the Convert to Profile dialog box, choose Working RGB from the Profile pop-up menu and leave all the others settings at their default settings.

Device Profiles

Now that you have Photoshop set up for creating new images and opening preexisting ones, let's get all your devices set up. Remember, a profile tells Photoshop what color of RGB or CMY your device uses. This is also where you're going to need to start thinking about how accurate you need your images to be and therefore how much money you are willing to spend.

The more precise the profile, the more accurate your color will be. There are three ways to get a profile and they each come with their own level of cost and quality:

▶ **Canned profiles:** Just like canned spinach, it's nothing like the real thing, but better than going hungry. These profiles are typically free and are usually created at the factory, and do not take into account the variations among products and the specifics of your situation (paper lot and ink batch for printer, and so on). They can often be found on the CD that came with the device or on the manufacturer's Web site.

▶ **Visual adjustment:** Like 14-day-old carrots—better than frozen, but not by much. These profiles are created using low-cost or free software that depend on your eyes to be the measurement devices to create a profile. This method is mainly used for computer displays and usually involves much guesswork. Some people swear that they can get a good profile this way, whereas others believe that profiles created with visual tools are terrible. Nobody can agree, so use them at your own risk—risk of bad colors, that is.

▶ **Custom profiles:** Like fresh-picked garden vegetables, nothing compares to it. These profiles are the most accurate and are completely customized to your specific situation. They are created using sophisticated measurement devices and will deliver the most accurate color matching between devices.

If you're on a budget, you'll be working with one of the first two choices. But if you're really serious about color, you'll want to look into the last option.

Creating a Monitor Profile

Let's start by making sure Photoshop knows how to display images correctly on your screen. We'll do that by measuring the exact colors of RGB that your monitor uses and also measuring how bright your monitor is. I wouldn't even think about using a canned profile for a monitor unless it's an LCD screen. Unlike standard CRT monitors, LCDs are much more consistent among batches and over time. It would be most ideal to use a hardware measurement device to profile your monitor, but since they cost money, each one comes with different software, and most offer few options, I'll just show you how to profile your screen using your eyes and free software that comes with your machine. The method for creating visually measured profiles varies depending on which operating system you use. In Mac OS X, choose System Preferences from the Apple menu, click the displays icon, click the Color tab, and then click the Calibrate button. In Windows, choose Start > Settings > Control Panel and then double-click the Adobe Gamma icon. You'll get different choices depending on what type of monitor you have (LCDs have fewer settings). Let's take a look at what you might expect when creating a profile in Mac OS X. Not every option that you see here will be available when you try it—it depends on the type of monitor you own and how much information your monitor can share with the calibration software. Since you'll find similar settings in Adobe Gamma on Windows, this information should apply to everyone regardless of what type of computer you have.

Using Apple's Calibration Utility

When the calibration utility starts up, you'll be presented with an Introduction screen. Turning on the Expert Mode check box requires you to make more adjustments than the standard mode, so I suggest you turn it on because you'll end up with a more accurate profile (**Figure 6.18**).

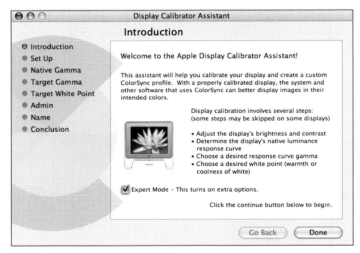

Figure 6.18 The Introduction screen.

Over the next five screens you will adjust the gamma of your monitor. It's really just trying to figure out what it takes to get all three colors (red, green, and blue) at the same brightness level, which will make it possible to display a true gray when it's requested. On each screen, the general idea is to squint your eyes as you move the slider until there's as little difference as possible between the Apple in the middle image and it's stripey background (**Figure 6.19**). After you've done that, it will ask you what gamma setting you'd like to use (**Figure 6.20**). Gamma is a

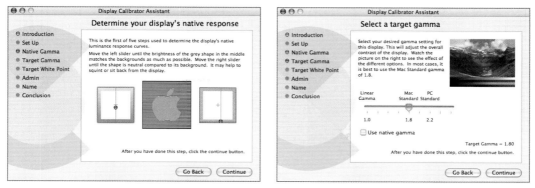

Figure 6.19 The Display Adjustments screen.

Figure 6.20 Adjusting the gamma.

technical term that describes how bright your monitor will be. The standard setting for a Mac is 1.8, so go ahead and choose that (use 2.2 for Windows).

Next you'll be asked to select a white point (**Figure 6.21**). That will determine what color you get when your screen is displaying the brightest white of which it is capable. I find that most of these settings darken your screen too much, so I'd use the Use Native White Point setting (previously this was called No White Point setting). It's more important that Photoshop knows the setting that you've chosen than to choose the one that makes the white look its best because Photoshop can compensate for whichever setting you decide to use.

NOTES

It's most ideal to perform this calibration while you are working under the same lighting conditions that you'll use throughout the day. So, make sure you don't have radically different lighting conditions between the time you calibrate and the time you want to use your monitor for critical color judgments. It's also a good idea to let your monitor warm up for at least a half hour before you proceed.

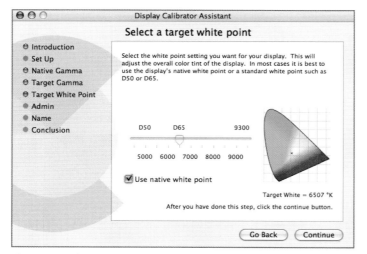

Figure 6.21 White point setting.

Figure 6.22 Sharing the profile.

Figure 6.23 Saving the profile.

Next you can choose whether you want your created profile to be available only to the current user account or to all accounts on the machine (**Figure 6.22**). There's really no need to be stingy, so you might as well turn on "Allow other users to use this calibration."

The last step is to give your newly created profile a name (**Figure 6.23**). I usually call it something like "Ben's display 10/15/2007" so I can remember how long it's been since I created it.

After you've saved your profile, the Calibration utility automatically saves it in the proper location so that Photoshop uses the proper information. Your monitor profile doesn't get loaded into Photoshop; instead, your operating system gets the profile so it can use the same profile with all applications that are designed to deal with color management. Then when Photoshop needs to display your image properly, it talks to your computer's operating system to figure out which profile should be used. You can always check which profile is being used and make sure Photoshop is aware of it by checking the RGB Working Space pop-up menu in the Color Settings dialog box (**Figure 6.24**). (It will be listed as the Monitor RGB setting.) Just be sure not to actually set your RGB working space to that setting because it's most ideal to have that setting be independent of your monitor or printer. The color and brightness of your screen changes over time, so you should create a new profile at least every three months.

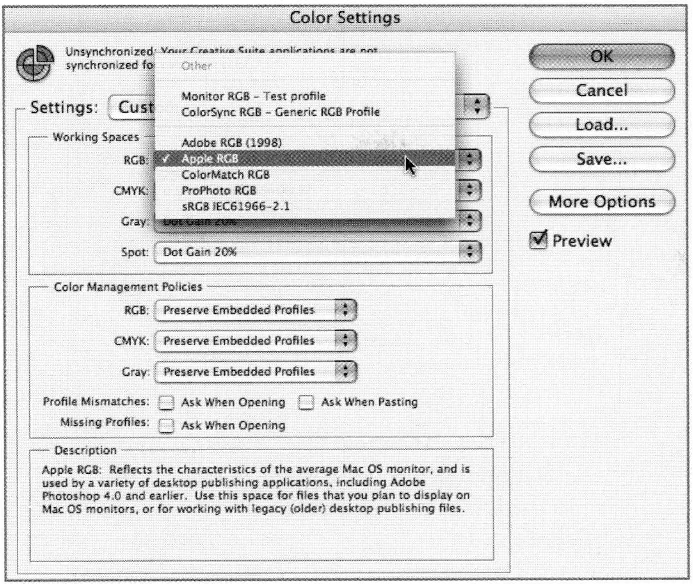

Figure 6.24 The RGB Working Space pop-up menu in the Color Settings dialog box.

Now, I don't know about you, but I didn't feel overly confident when I was creating that profile. After all, I had to guess at what colors of RGB my display uses, and it seemed overly easy to screw things up (such as choosing an unusual white point setting). Because of that, I don't suggest you rely on a visually measured profile if you do any serious color work in Photoshop. Instead, I'd invest in a color-measurement device that will do all the work for you and deliver a much more accurate profile.

Creating a Custom Profile

Shelling out some bucks for accurate color is well worth the money for anyone who is a true Photoshop professional. After all, you can easily end up paying just as much to fix a mistake that was made because of inaccurate color (such as reprinting a brochure). You'll need to purchase a colorimeter (**Figure 6.25**), which start at about $100, to get an accurate profile. You can purchase one from computer catalogs or Web sites such as www.rodsandcones.com or www.profilecity.com. When you open the box, you'll find three things: the colorimeter, a manual, and a

Figure 6.25 With a colorimeter you can make much more accurate profiles.

CD. So, plug the colorimeter in (it usually connects via a USB port), pop the CD into your computer, and install the software. When you run the software, it will ask you to put the colorimeter on the middle of your screen. Then it will flash a bunch of colors in front of it, and before you know it, you'll have a custom profile. In general, this hardware/software combo ends up measuring the exact shades of RGB that your specific display uses, and it measures how consistent it is across the range from bright to dark.

If you're going to drop the cash needed to purchase a colorimeter, you might as well profile your display once a week. After all, it takes only a few minutes.

Creating a Printer Profile

The next step is to create a printer profile so that the printer will accurately simulate what you see on that newly profiled display of yours. When profiling a printer, you have three choices: a canned profile, a scanner-based profile, and a custom profile. Let's see what's needed to get those set up.

Most desktop color printers come with an ICC profile on the CD that shipped with the unit. If you don't find it there, try visiting the manufacturer's Web site. It will often be part of the driver software you can download. This would be considered a canned profile because it was created using someone else's printer (same model though), using his or her batch of paper and ink. Canned profiles are usually perfectly acceptable for casual Photoshop users. You just have to be aware that they are specific to the ink and paper set used when the profile was made. That means that the profile might produce unsatisfactory results if you use a brand of paper or ink that is different from what the profile was designed for. Once you download that canned profile, you'll need to put it in a special place on your hard drive so that Photoshop knows where to find it. Here's where the profile belongs:

- ▶ **Windows Vista:** Windows/System32/Spool/Drivers/Color
- ▶ **Windows 2000:** WinNT/System/Spool/Drivers/Color
- ▶ **Windows NT:** WinNT/System32/Color
- ▶ **Windows XP:** Windows/System32/Spool/Drivers/Color
- ▶ **Mac OS X:** Users/CurrentUser/Library/ColorSync/Profiles

While you're playing around in that folder, you might as well throw away the profiles that are for devices that you'll never use (but only delete ones that you're absolutely sure you won't need; otherwise, you'll have to reinstall Photoshop to get them back). That way Photoshop's Profile pop-up menu won't be so cluttered with choices.

If you really want the most accurate color reproduction from your desktop color printer, you should think about having a custom profile made. Creating a profile isn't difficult. All you do is purchase a color-measurement device that's known as a spectrophotometer and install the software. Then you get the reference image that comes with the software and measure the result using the measurement device (**Figure 6.26**). The only problem is that the measurement device can easily set you back $1,000 or more! That's fine if you work for a large company that has dozens of printers or if you are a commercial printing company, but it's out of reach for most other users. But that's OK, because there is a way to get the benefit of a custom profile without parting with the money for that spiffy measurement device. You can visit a Web site such as www. profilecity.com and have one created one for you. Here's how it works: You pay the site just under $100 (don't quote me on that now) and it emails you a reference image. Then you print that image and snail mail it back to the Web site. The company uses one of those expensive measurement devices to create a profile and then it is emailed it to you. The only problem is that you really should have a profile for each ink and paper combination that you'll end up sending through your printer. That means one for the extra-glossy stuff that almost feels like plastic and works great for photos and another for the slightly shiny version you use for brochures and maybe a third for that dull cheap paper that you have loaded most of the time. As you can guess, the money can add up quite quickly. But that kind of money is pocket change if you work for a commercial printing company and you want to make sure that you can supply your customers with an accurate profile of a particular ink/paper/press combination.

Figure 6.26 A $1,000 device used to create a printer profile.

There are two more alternatives, and they will cost about as much as two or three of those custom profiles. You can buy a special scanner designed specifically for creating printer profiles (but not as accurate as the device I mentioned previously), or for a little less money, you can use your own scanner and a piece of software called Monaco EZ Color. Let's take a quick look at how each of those choices work.

Your first choice is Color Vision's PrintFIX. It's a small desktop scanner (**Figure 6.27**) that can be used to create printer profiles. It's pretty simple to use. After installing the hardware and software, you choose File > Automate > PrintFIX, choose the model of printer you'd like to profile (**Figure 6.28**), and click the OK button. That will open a special image (**Figure 6.29**) that you should print on the printer you'd like to profile.

Figure 6.27 Color Vision's PrintFIX scanner.

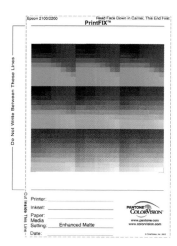

Figure 6.29 The PrintFIX target image that will be printed and then scanned.

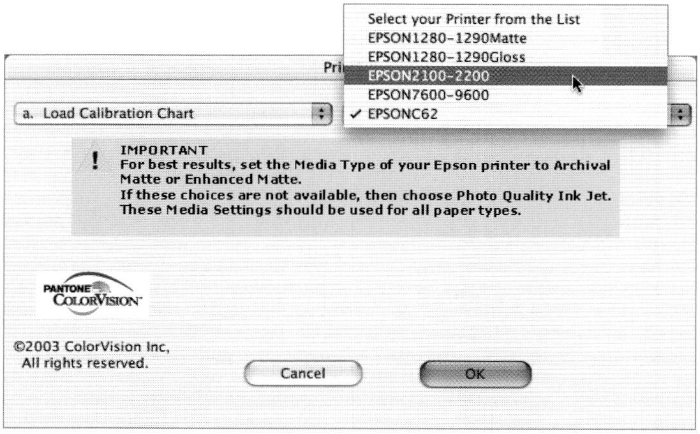

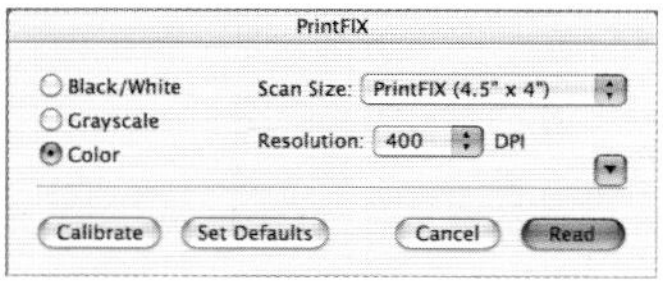

Figure 6.28 Choosing the name of the printer to be profiled.

The next step is to scan that printed image back into Photoshop. To access the scanner from Photoshop, choose File > Import > PrintFIX (**Figure 6.30**). That's where you specify the resolution of your printer and which type of image you're scanning (grayscale or color). But before you scan your printed image, you'll want to calibrate the scanner to ensure that you get an accurate scan. The PrintFIX scanner comes with a small sheet of paper that contains some black strips. All you have to do is insert that image into the slot on the PrintFIX scanner and then click the Calibrate button in the PrintFIX software. Then to actually scan your printed image, slip it into the little plastic sleeve that came with the printer, insert it into the slot on the

Figure 6.30 The PrintFIX scanning dialog box.

scanner, and then click the Read button to start the scan. Once the scan is complete, you'll have the resulting image open in Photoshop.

To turn that scanned image into a profile for your printer, choose File > Automate > PrintFIX, choose Build Profile from the pop-up menu (**Figure 6.31**), and then click OK. The PrintFIX software will prompt you for a name for your profile (**Figure 6.32**) and will save it in the proper location so that Photoshop will be able to see it.

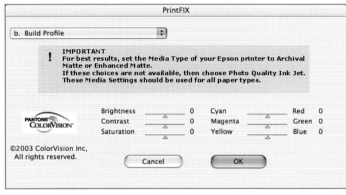

Figure 6.31 Building a profile in PrintFIX.

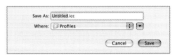

Figure 6.32 Once PrintFIX is done working on the image, it will prompt you to save the printer profile.

Once you have a profile made, you should print a few images to see just how accurately it reproduces your images. If you find that it's not 100% accurate, choose File > Automate > PrintFIX once again, tweak the settings that appear at the bottom of the dialog box (Brightness, Contrast, and so on), and do another test print to see if you've improved your profile.

If you don't want to spend the money on the PrintFIX solution, you might want to consider purchasing a special piece of software (such as Monaco EZ Color) that allows you to use your flatbed scanner as a measurement device to create a printer profile. Let's see how it works: You start by choosing what type of profile you'd like to create (**Figure 6.33**). The software is capable of creating display, printer, and scanner profiles, and can use a colorimeter for the display portion if you own one.

Figure 6.33 Choosing the profile type.

When you indicate that you'd like to create a printer profile, it walks you through a series of steps that include printing a reference image (**Figure 6.34**). Once that print has dried, you grab a special image that was supplied in the box for the product and put both the special image and the image you just printed onto your scanner and scan them. Then you indicate where the edges of the images are (**Figure 6.35**), and the software measures all the colors based on what your scanner captured. The end result is a set of profiles—one for your scanner and one for your printer. That way, you can create as many profiles as you'd like and you don't have to pay $100 a pop for each one. I've found that these profiles are good enough for most Photoshop users, although it can be hit or miss depending on how good of a scanner you use.

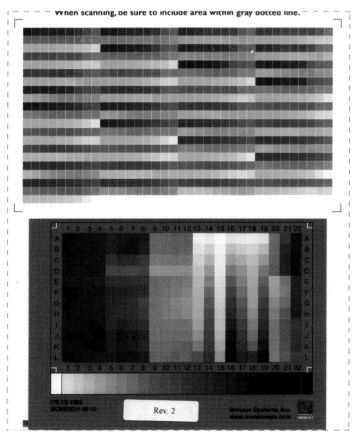

Figure 6.34 Printing a reference image.

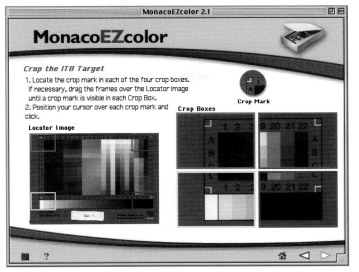

Figure 6.35 Defining the edges of the image.

Profiling a Printing Press

If you ever plan to reproduce your images on a commercial printing press, you'll have to convert your images to CMYK mode before you send them off. For Photoshop to correctly convert your image to CMYK mode, it needs a bunch of information about how the image will be reproduced (supplied by an ICC profile). When I'm creating an image that will be printed at a commercial printer, the first thing I do is call my sales rep and ask if he has an ICC profile for the press/paper combination that I'll be using. Most of the time he tells me that he doesn't. I don't blame him because commercial printers deal with hundreds of ink and paper combinations, so it would be very time consuming and expensive to profile each one. But sometimes I get lucky, and if so, I simply plop the profile in the proper folder, choose Edit > Color and set the CMYK Working Space pop-up menu to that choice. Most of the time, though, I have to take a different approach.

Adobe was nice enough to include a bunch of profiles that can be used for different printing conditions. They show up in the CMYK Working Space pop-up menu. You just have to make sure you have a profile selected

It turns out that the U.S. Sheetfed Uncoated and U.S. Web Uncoated profiles are identical. It's still a good idea to choose the one that is specific to your printing conditions, though; otherwise, people who open your files might assume that they are not set up properly.

that accurately reflects the printing conditions that will be used to reproduce your image before you convert to CMYK mode. I'll attempt to translate their names and then show you how to get better results.

Here's the rundown on choosing a profile for many standard publication types:

▶ Use U.S. Sheetfed Coated for glossy brochures.

▶ Use U.S. Sheetfed Uncoated for dull-finish brochures.

▶ Use U.S. Web Coated (SWOP) for magazines.

▶ Use U.S. Web Uncoated for dull-finish publications.

The profiles that come with Photoshop make huge assumptions about the paper and inks that you are using. That means it's possible to get a much better result if you happen to have a custom profile created specifically for the paper and press on which you'll be printing. If you find that your printing company doesn't have a custom profile available and you aren't getting acceptable results from the profiles I mentioned earlier, you might want to bypass profiles altogether and set up the CMYK conversion the traditional way. You'll find information about that on my Web site at www.digitalmastery.com/colormanagement.

Profiling Your Scanner

You don't have too many options when it comes to scanners. There aren't many manufacturers that provide canned profiles (some high-end ones do), and you can't visually create a profile. But the good news is that you don't have to buy any expensive hardware to get the job done. All you need is a piece of software (such as Monaco EZ Color). The software comes with a reference image that's known as an IT8 target (**Figure 6.36**). Scan the image and then feed it to the software, and out pops an ICC profile for your scanner. You'll want to place it in the same location I mentioned when I was talking about printer profiles.

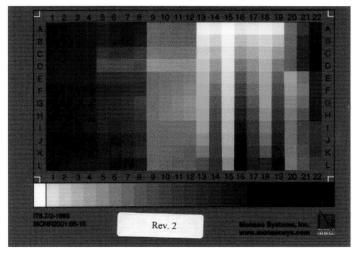

Figure 6.36 An IT8 target.

Color Management in Action

Now that we have everything set up and placed in the proper location, let's see what we can do with all this fancy stuff. Let's say you've used a colorimeter to profile your screen, and you used some software to create scanner and printer profiles (just don't forget to put those profiles in the proper location, as I mentioned previously). Now here comes the fun part.

Accurate Scans

From now on, when you scan an image, you won't have to worry about all the color settings that are in your scanner. You just turn off all that stuff and let color management take over. You simply specify the resolution and scaling settings you'd like to use and then press the Scan button. When the image is in Photoshop, choose Assign Profile from the Edit menu (**Figure 6.37**) and choose your scanner profile from the Profile pop-up menu. That's it! The profile supplies the information needed for Photoshop to know how your scanner captures color and therefore should produce an accurate scan (assuming your profile is accurate, that is).

NOTES

Some scanners will automatically assign the proper profile to your images. You can find out if your scanner does this by clicking on the black arrow that appears at the bottom of a Photoshop document and choosing Document Profile. Then scan an image and see if your scanner's profile is listed at the bottom of the document window. If it is, there is no reason to assign a profile because it already has the correct one assigned.

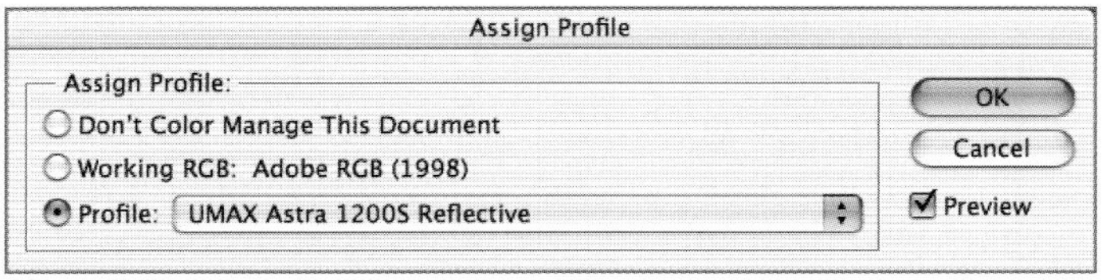

Figure 6.37 The Assign Profile dialog box.

Well, actually that's not quite it, after all. Remember when I talked about equal amounts of red, green, and blue creating gray and that that's not what you get when you use the less-than-ideal shades of RGB that your monitor, printer, and scanner use? Well, if you plan to manipulate your image, you'll most likely want to convert it into that idealized version of RGB that we call our RGB working space. To do that, choose Convert to Profile from the Edit menu (**Figure 6.38**). When that dialog box pops up, you might get a little scared because it's full of overly techie terms, but don't worry about it. At the top it simply lists the profile you assigned after you scanned the image. Next, it asks you for the profile you'd like to convert it to. That's where you want to choose Working RGB, which should be the top choice (the name will also have something like "Adobe RGB" attached to it to remind you of what you chose when you set up that part of Photoshop). Leave the Engine setting at its default. There aren't too many reasons to change that one, and if you knew about the reasons, you'd be writing this book instead of reading it—you'd have to be that color savvy. Then experiment with the choices that appear under the Intent pop-up menu.

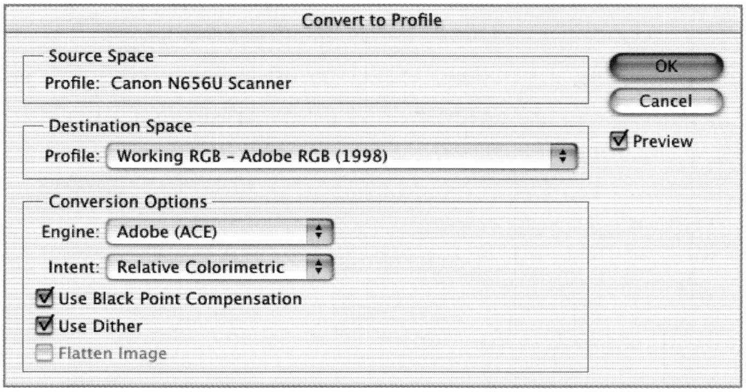

Figure 6.38 The Convert to Profile dialog box.

Now, there is an important difference between assigning a profile and converting to a profile. They might sound similar but so does being pulled over for speeding versus being arrested for speed. With one, you'd just be out a few bucks, but with the other you just might end up in jail! Assigning a profile is informing Photoshop what colors of RGB the image is made out of. That will make the colors shift in your image as Photoshop uses the same amount of red, green, and blue, but uses different shades of color (like different brands of markers). Or you could think of it like substituting ingredients in a recipe without adjusting the amount that's used to compensate for the new ingredient. Converting to a profile means to simulate the current look of the image (trying not to change the overall look of the image) but to make it out of different shades of RGB than the original. That's like replacing an ingredient in a recipe and adjusting the amount you use to compensate for the difference between what the recipe called for and what you ended up substituting. Read over those last few sentences three times to make sure you really understand the difference because it can sound rather subtle, but it's not.

Simulating a Printing Press Onscreen

I often create images that will end up being reproduced on a commercial printing press. Sometimes it's for a brochure and other times it's for a magazine article, but whatever it is for, I want to see what the printed result will look like onscreen in Photoshop. To accomplish that, I usually choose View > Proof Setup > Working CMYK. That should do two things: It will go to the Color Settings dialog box to see what type of printing conditions will be used (we talked about that earlier in this chapter) and it turns on the Proof Colors setting (View > Proof Colors). With Proof Colors turned on, Photoshop attempts to simulate what your image will look like when it's printed on a commercial printing press. I use this setting anytime I'm making an adjustment to the saturation of the image because the range of colors that can be reproduced on a printing press (known as its gamut) is much smaller than what you can see onscreen. Deep blues and vivid colors can shift wildly.

NOTES

Assign Profile will always change the appearance of an image because it's changing the red, green, and blue colors without adjusting the amounts of those colors used to produce the image. I only use that command when an image either has the wrong profile embedded or has no profile embedded. Convert to Profile, on the other hand, always tries to maintain the original appearance by adjusting the amounts of red, green, and blue that make up the image. I use the Convert command whenever I need to make the image out of a different set of RGB colors but want to maintain the original appearance (like when converting to sRGB for the Internet). Both commands change which version of RGB the image is made from, but only Convert will maintain the original look of the image.

That happens because those colors simply can't be reproduced using the CMYK inks that are used in commercial printing. To stop this simulation, turn off the Proof Colors setting from the View menu.

Accurate Prints

Now that you have a profile for your printer ready, Photoshop can give you much more accurate prints, but you'll have to make sure everything is set up correctly to deliver what you want. Choose File > Print and choose Color Management from the pop-up menu at the top of the dialog box. Photoshop will now prompt you to make some choices (**Figure 6.39**). Let's take a look at them one by one: For Photoshop to accurately simulate colors on your desktop printer, you have to feed it an ICC profile for that device. Do that by setting the Color Handling pop-up menu to Photoshop Manages Colors and choosing the appropriate profile from the Printer Profile pop-up menu.

Figure 6.39 The color management choices used when printing.

Now you'll need to choose between the two options under the Print heading to decide what you'd like to simulate. If you just want your printer to match what you saw on your screen, choose Document, set the Rendering Intent pop-up menu to Relative Colorimetric, and turn on the Black

Point Compensation checkbox. If, on the other hand, you want to simulate what your image would look like when printed on a commercial printing press, choose Proof and turn on the Simulate Paper Color checkbox if you would like to simulate the paper stock (which might be a lot darker than the sheet of paper you have loaded into your desktop printer). The only other thing you have to do is turn off any color-adjustment controls that your printer driver offers, since we're letting Photoshop do all the work instead (otherwise, it will double compensate, which will make your image look terrible).

Better CMYK Conversions

You'll want to convert your images to CMYK mode if they will be printed on a commercial printing press. The traditional way of doing that is to simply choose Image > Mode > CMYK. That's fine if you're in a hurry, but by doing that you are bypassing a bunch of settings that might make your image look better. Here's your alternative: Choose Convert to Profile from the Edit menu (**Figure 6.40**). It looks complicated, but it's not. The top just tells you the colors of RGB that your image is made from (that's known as your source space). Then, as long as you've set up the CMYK working space to what's right for your printing conditions, all you have to do is choose Working CMYK from the Destination Space pop-up menu. And now all that's left is to play with the Intent pop-up menu and those two check boxes to see which combination of settings will produce the best result. Let's take a look at the choices that are available in the Intent pop-up menu. Most images will start off with many colors that are just too vivid to be reproduced in CMYK mode (known as colors that are out of gamut for you techie folks). When you convert to CMYK mode, Photoshop has to do something with those colors to get them into the range of what can be reproduced on a printing press. The choices in the Intent pop-up menu determine how Photoshop will deal with those out-of-gamut colors.

NOTES

I suggest that you leave your image in RGB mode when printing to an ink jet printer. Even though the printer uses cyan, magenta, yellow, and black ink, Photoshop uses the same software that draws your screen image to send information to the printer. That software only handles RGB information, so there is no advantage to printing from CMYK. PostScript language printers can bypass that screen-drawing software and therefore can produce acceptable results from either RGB or CMYK mode.

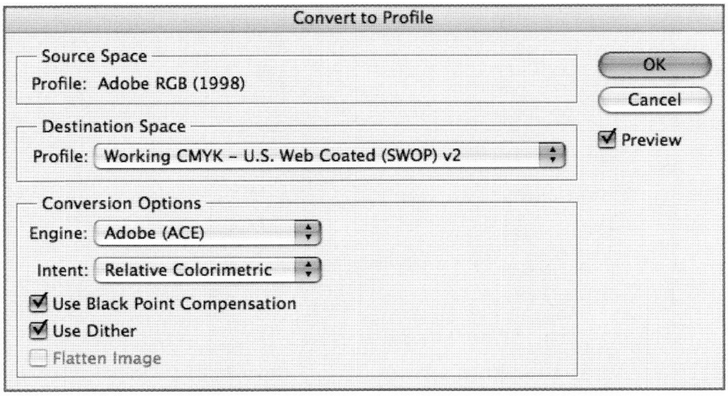

Figure 6.40 The Convert to Profile dialog box.

Perceptual

With the Perceptual option, Photoshop will alter not only those colors that are not printable, but also the ones that can be reproduced just to make sure the relationship between the colors remains consistent. That way you don't have to worry about one overly vivid color becoming the exact same shade of a less vivid color that's right next to it. The only problem with this feature is that it has no idea which colors are actually in your image, so it shifts colors around even if all the colors in your image are within the range of colors that can be reproduced in CMYK mode. That means that all of the colors in your image will become less saturated just to ensure that colors that can't be printed will get shifted to printable ones.

Saturation

Saturation will take the most saturated colors in your image and make sure they end up as the most saturated colors that are possible in CMYK mode. That might sound nice, but it doesn't take into account the brightness, color, and saturation differences between colors. That means that it is free to shift the colors in your image as long as saturated colors remain saturated, even if they don't end up looking anything like the color at which they started. That limits its usefulness to solid-colored graphics such as bar charts and business graphics where the relationship between colors isn't important and you just want to maintain vivid colors no matter what.

Relative and Absolute Colorimetric

Both Relative and Absolute Colorimetric shift only those colors that are not reproducible in CMYK, leaving the rest of the colors largely unchanged. The main difference between the two is that Relative Colorimetric makes sure that white in the original image ends up as white in CMYK mode. That's not overly important unless you're using an RGB working space that creates a white that is darker than what you can create in CMYK mode. This feature is mainly used in the Print dialog box when printing an image to a desktop color printer that can reproduce a brighter white than a printing press. In that situation the difference between relative and absolute is the difference between simulating the "whiteness" of the paper that will be used on the printing press (such as newsprint) or not. If your image doesn't contain too many overly vivid colors, you might find that Relative Colorimetric might not be a bad choice.

When I'm converting an image to CMYK, I'm not consciously thinking about what all these choices mean; instead, I'm just trying each one and looking at my image to see which choice produces the most pleasing result. Each choice has both advantages and disadvantages, and the only way to find the best setting is to experiment.

Closing Thoughts

If you worked up a sweat reading this chapter and thought to yourself, "This is truly a cesspool of unending terms and settings, and I'm never going to get through it all," you're not alone. That's what I thought at first. But after going through the motions a few times, and perhaps reading this chapter again, you'll get more comfortable with the concepts here and find some sanity in the chaos. In a perfect world we wouldn't have to deal with all this, but the truth is that, from the viewpoint of your hardware, you're really asking for a gargantuan thing when you want your screen to match your printout. All your devices are different, and Photoshop really needs all this information to manage everything gracefully. But if you spend the time, effort, and money it takes to get everything working properly, you will be generously rewarded with very consistent color across all your devices. And your life will become a lot easier when you can trust your screen and know that your $200 inkjet printer is doing a darn good job of both simulating what you saw onscreen and what will appear on a printing press.

7
Color Correction

Courtesy of Andy Katz, andykatzphotography.com

The camera, you know, will never capture you.
Photography, in my experience, has the miraculous
power of transferring wine into water.

—Oscar Wilde in *Lillie*

In the previous chapter, "Color Management," we learned how to make colors consistent among our various devices (monitor, scanner, printer, camera, and so on). In this chapter, we're going to tackle color correction, which is an entirely separate matter. This chapter is all about controlling the colors in your image and getting rid of color casts that might be having an adverse effect on the final result.

After presenting hundreds of seminars, I've learned that the majority of people perform color correction by picking their favorite adjustment tool (Color Balance, Hue/Saturation, Curves, or the like) and then using a somewhat hit-or-miss technique. They blindly move a few sliders back and forth in the hope that their onscreen image will improve. If that doesn't work, they simply repeat the process with a different adjustment option. Those same people often turn to me asking for "advanced color-correction techniques" because they're frustrated and don't feel like they're really in control of the color in their images. If this describes the way you're adjusting your colors, you'll be pleasantly surprised when you learn about the science of professional color correction, where 95% of all guesswork is removed and where you know exactly which tool and what settings to use to achieve great color. First, let's look at a general concept that will help us to color correct an image. Then I'll walk you through the step-by-step technique I use to get good-looking color in Photoshop.

Use Gray to Fix Color?!?

For the time being I want you to wipe out any thoughts of color. And, no, I'm not crazy. This approach really works, so stick with me. As we learned in the "Color Management" chapter, gray is made up of equal amounts of red, green, and blue. With that in mind, open an image and see if you can find an area that should be gray. Then, look in the Info palette to see if it really is gray in Photoshop—all without having to trust your monitor or your eyes! On the CD, open the image that's called *make gray.jpg*. The door on the right should be a shade of gray. If the RGB numbers in the Info palette aren't equal—no matter what it looks like on your monitor—it's not gray. If it's not gray, it must be contaminated with color (**Figure 7.1**). But could that color be contaminating more than the gray area? Most likely. Then why not use the door as an area to measure what's wrong with the entire image so we have the information we need to fix it? Let's give it a try.

Just because I mention RGB mode throughout this chapter doesn't mean that the techniques don't work just as well in CMYK mode. It's just that the initial concept I show you really needs to be performed in RGB mode. So, even though you'll end up dealing with RGB settings at the beginning, Photoshop can translate them into CMYK numbers once you start performing the steps listed under the "Professional Color Correction" section of this chapter. If you just look at the CMYK area of the Color Picker, you'll see what you'd end up with in CMYK mode.

Figure 7.1 If the RGB numbers are not equal, then that area is not gray. (©2007 Andy Katz)

Using the example image, you'll see that the RGB numbers are not equal, telling us that there is indeed color lurking somewhere in that gray. How could those contaminating colors get in there? Here are a few potential culprits: a mixed lighting situation that confused the auto white balance mechanism of your camera; choosing the wrong manual white balance setting; the temperature of the chemicals used to develop the film being too hot or too cool; inappropriate filters used in a photographic enlarger when your prints are being made; and aging bulbs in a scanner that might shift the colors during the scanning process. We're going to use the Curves dialog box to make our adjustment. But don't worry, you don't have to remember everything from Chapter 5, "Understanding Curves" to do this. For what we're trying to accomplish, here's what you need to know:

▶ Command/Ctrl-clicking on your image will add a point.

▶ The Input number indicates what you are changing.

▶ The Output number determines what you'll end up with in the area you are changing.

And don't worry, even if you skipped the chapter on Curves, you'll still be able to quickly color correct your images. At this stage, we're only going to manually adjust a curve. After that, I'll show you a much faster and easier method, so just stick with me knowing that it will end up being really easy.

Start by putting your cursor on the gray door. Now glance over at the Info palette and write down the RGB numbers (131R, 166G, and 161B in my case). To make that door area a real gray, we'll need to make those RGB numbers equal. But we don't want to change the brightness of the door. To make sure that doesn't happen, grab a calculator and add the three RGB numbers together to find out the total amount of light that is making up the door (131 + 166 + 161 = 458, for example). We don't want to change the brightness of the door, so we'll want to keep the total amount of light the same as what we started with, but using equal amounts of red, green, and blue. To figure out the exact numbers to use, just divide the total brightness of the door (458 in my case) by three (458 ÷ 3 = 152.6667), and then round off the result so you don't have any decimals (153 in my case). Now that we know what we're starting with (from the Info palette) and what we want to end up with (from the calculator), we can adjust our image.

If you choose Image > Adjustments > Curves and then Command-click on your image while the menu at the top of the dialog box is set to RGB, you'll place a point on the curve at that tone. If you move that point up or down, you end up changing red, green, and blue in equal amounts, which would just change the brightness of the image (which

> **NOTES**
>
> When performing RGB color correction, make sure that white appears at the top of the gradient that is on the left of the Curves dialog box; otherwise, the numbers will range from 0%–100% instead of 0–255. If black appears at the top of the gradient, open Curve Display Options (at the bottom of the dialog box) and choose Light (0-255) for the Show Amount of option.. That will flip the gradients and use the numbering system needed for RGB color correction.

is what we did in the Curves chapter). But for our purposes, we want to work on the individual colors separately. To have Photoshop add a point to each of the red, green, and blue curves, hold Shift-Command (Mac) or Shift-Ctrl (Windows) and click on the gray door. If you want to see what happened, open the Channel pop-up menu at the top of the Curves dialog box, and select either the Red, Green, or Blue channels. You should find a new point on each of those curves. The position of each one of those points is based on the numbers that showed up in the Info palette. All you need to do is switch between the red, green, and blue curves and change the output numbers for each one so that they match the numbers you came up with when you used a calculator to average the RGB numbers (153 in my case) in the Info palette (**Figure 7.2**). After you've done that, you can take a peek at your image to see what you've done (**Figure 7.3**). The door should be gray. If it's not, and you're quite sure you followed the steps correctly, your monitor is way out of whack and may need calibration (see Chapter 6, "Color Management," for details on how to do that).

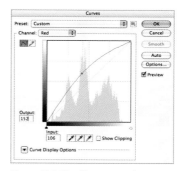

Figure 7.2 The Output number you enter for each curve will move the point to the correct position.

Figure 7.3 When you're done, the area should be gray. The left numbers indicate what was originally in the image; the right numbers indicate the result of our adjustment.

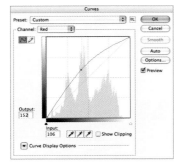

Figure 7.4 The red curve.

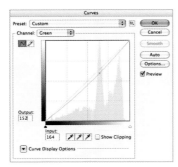

Figure 7.5 The green curve.

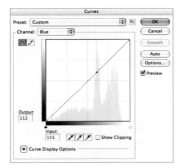

Figure 7.6 The blue curve.

But now, look back at the three curves we applied to this image (**Figures 7.4** to **7.6**). We measured what was wrong with the image in the gray areas, but our adjustment changed the entire image. That's logical enough, because whatever is wrong with the gray areas is also affecting the rest of the image. But when you look at those curves, does it look like we really changed the full length of the curve? Almost—but not quite. We didn't change the brightest and darkest areas. So, we really haven't accomplished our color correction, and we won't until we've taken some more steps. But from this exercise, we saw that our concept of measuring and adjusting gray works. Now let's see how we can make this process faster and easier, and then we'll move on to adjusting the brightest and darkest areas.

It might feel quite low tech to be scribbling a bunch of numbers on a sheet of paper and using a calculator when we have a multi-thousand-dollar computer in front of us. The folks at Adobe realized that and gave us a tool that will do 99% of the work for us, so let's see what they came up with. Choose File > Revert to return the image to its original state, and then choose Image > Adjustments > Curves. Click the middle eyedropper in the lower right of the dialog box, and then move your cursor out onto the image and click on that gray door again. With a single click, it should change to gray. Photoshop is using the same concept we used when we wrote down the RGB numbers and averaged them; it's just doing it in a fraction of a second and there is no paper involved. In fact, those eyedroppers will help us even more if we adjust the full range of shades from the brightest to the darkest. Let's see how it works.

Professional Color Correction

Okay, you can start thinking in color again. We will look at the process of professional color correction in three parts: balancing colors, adjusting skin tones, and adjusting saturation. You don't always have to perform all three parts, but the more you do, the better your result will be.

Balancing Your Colors

To eliminate any color casts that are in your image, you'll need to look for color contamination in the gray areas of your image, and then use that information to help correct the whole image. Three standard areas of your image will usually contain a shade of gray: the brightest area of the image, which is known as the highlight; the darkest area of the image, which is known as the shadow (on most photos, the highlight and shadow areas shouldn't contain color); and a gray object in the image.

Now that we know which areas need to be adjusted, let's make the actual adjustment. Start by choosing Image > Adjustments > Curves. We'll be working with all three of the Curves eyedroppers. All three droppers adjust the area you click on so that it ends up with a balanced combination of red, green, and blue, which effectively removes any color contamination for that area. The only difference between the eyedroppers is that the one full of black makes things really, really dark, the eyedropper full of white makes things really bright, and the middle eyedropper doesn't change the brightness of an area. We'll use those to adjust the shadow, highlight, and gray areas, respectively. But we first have to set up things correctly.

Double-click on the right most eyedropper to bring up the Color Picker. This eyedropper will be used to adjust the brightest part of the image (the highlight). You don't want the highlight to become pure white because it would look too bright. You want to reserve pure white for those areas that shine light directly into the camera lens (like lightbulbs and shiny reflections). That means you want the highlight to be just a bit darker than white.

If you remember the chapter on grayscale images (Chapter 4, "Optimizing Grayscale Images"), I mentioned that the lightest percentage of ink you can use on a printing press is usually 3% (5% for some newspapers). That means we don't want to use less than 3% of any ink in the brightest part of our image; otherwise, we might lose critical detail. But we're adjusting our image in RGB mode, and when you do that, you'll be using a numbering system that ranges from 0 to 255, not 0% to 100%. So let's figure out how to create a minimum of 3% ink in RGB mode.

After double-clicking the rightmost eyedropper, set the saturation setting (S) to 0 and the brightness setting (B) to 100%, and click on the number next to the letter B (brightness). Use the down arrow key to change that setting until the magenta (M) and yellow (Y) readouts indicate at least 3%. Cyan (C) will be higher, but don't worry about that. At this point, the numbers will show you exactly what RGB values are needed to produce that much ink—in my case, 240R, 240G, 240B (**Figure 7.7**).

> **NOTES**
>
> Black ink is usually limited to the darkest areas of the CMYK printing process, so no black will show up when you're looking for 3% ink values.

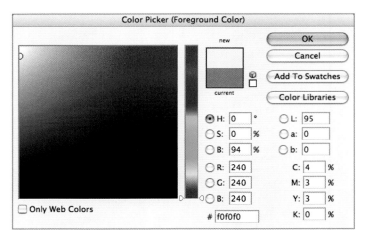

Figure 7.7 A good highlight value is 240R, 240G, 240B.

Now, on to the dark side. We're going to make the darkest area of your image pure black (0R, 0G, 0B) in order to use the full range your computer monitor is capable of displaying. Black wouldn't be a good choice if you are really outputting to a printing press (you'd lose a lot of detail), but we'll set it up so that Photoshop adjusts your image automatically if you have to convert to CMYK mode. That way we'll be guaranteed that no detail will be lost no matter what the output. So, double-click the leftmost eyedropper and make sure it's set to black. When you click

OK in the Curves dialog box, Photoshop asks you if you would like to "Save the new target colors as the defaults?". I suggest that you click the Yes button so that Photoshop remembers those settings and uses them every time you use the eyedroppers to color correct your images.

Now that we have everything set up properly, let's start adjusting images. Open any image that needs to be color corrected, and then choose Layer > New Adjustment Layer > Curves. Name your adjustment layer something like Color Correct and click OK to proceed to the curves dialog. Click the black eyedropper and then click on the shadow area. When I mention the shadow, I don't mean a traditional shadow like the kind cast from an object; instead, I'm talking about the darkest area of an image. Almost all images have a shadow area, but it can sometimes be hard to locate because there may be multiple candidates. (I'll show you how to find them before we're done with this chapter.)

Once you've done that, click the white eyedropper and then click on the brightest part of the image. That is the brightest area that should still contain detail. You'll often find it in a white shirt collar or button, a Styrofoam cup, the whites of someone's eyes, or a sheet of paper. In **Figure 7.8**, the brightest white falls on a fold in the sheer curtain material.

Figure 7.8 The brightest white falls on a fold in the curtain.

Finally, click the middle eyedropper and then click on any area that should be gray in the final image—not bluish gray or pinkish gray, but pure gray (also known as neutral gray). You might have to really hunt for a gray; it is not always obvious. It could be a sweatshirt, a white shirt, or the edge of a book. On the other hand, you might run across an image that has dozens of gray areas to choose from. In that case, try to pick one that is not overly bright or dark, because we are already adjusting the highlight and shadow of the image. The closer we get to a middle gray, the more effective your adjustment will be. If you have any doubt at all that the area you have chosen should be gray, just experiment by clicking on one area to see what happens; then press Command/ Ctrl-Z to undo the change, and then try another area. Repeat this process until you've found an area that really causes the image to improve, but don't try too hard—not every image contains a true gray. For example, you might not be able to find one in a photograph of a forest. If you can't find one, then (of course) don't adjust it.

Using Threshold to Locate Highlight and Shadow

Here's a way to find the highlight and shadow areas without guessing. Choose Image > Adjustments > Threshold and move the slider all the way to the right; then slowly move it toward the middle (**Figure 7.9**). The brightest area of the image will be the first area that shows up as white (you can use the up and down arrow keys to move the slider). You don't want to find the very brightest speck (that could be a scratch or a reflection on something shiny), so be sure to look for a general area at least five or six pixels in size (something that's easy enough to click on without having to be overly precise). Once you've found the correct area, you can hold down the Shift key and click on that part of your image to add a color sample to that area (**Figure 7.10**). (You have to hold Shift only if you're still in an adjustment dialog box like Threshold.) A color sampler is simply a visual reminder of where that area is.

You can use the up and down arrow keys to move the Threshold slider. That will allow you to concentrate on your image instead of having to concentrate on being precise with the mouse.

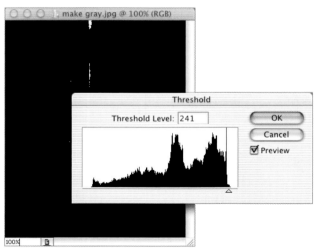

Figure 7.9 Use the Threshold command to find elusive highlights.

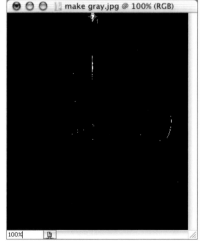

Figure 7.10 After using the Color Sampler tool, you should see a crosshair on the image.

Now let's use Threshold to find the darkest area of the image. This time, start with the slider all the way to the left, and then slowly move it toward the center. This shows you where the darkest area of the image is hiding. You don't want to find the darkest speck (that could be dust), so be sure to look for a general area at least five or six pixels in size. Once you've located the shadow, Shift-click on that area to place a sample point on top of it, and then click Cancel to get out of the Threshold dialog box. If you click OK instead of Cancel, your image will remain completely black and white. Now you should have two crosshairs on your image, one for the highlight and one for the shadow, as shown in **Figure 7.11**. When you use the eyedroppers in the Curves dialog box, you can press Caps Lock to turn your cursor into a crosshair, which will make it easy to tell when you're lined up with those color samplers. You can get rid of the color samplers by choosing the Color Sampler tool (it's hidden under the Eyedropper tool) and clicking the Clear button in the options bar.

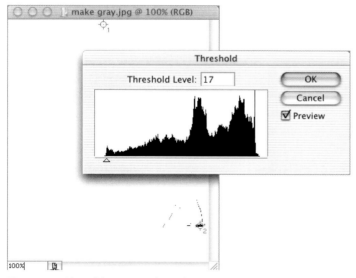

Figure 7.11 After adding a second sample point, you should see two crosshairs on your image.

Only use those eyedroppers that help to improve the look of your image. If one of them shifts the colors in an undesirable way, press Command/Ctrl-Z to undo that step and either try another area or don't use that eyedropper. Just because a single eyedropper harms your image doesn't mean that the other two eyedroppers won't help it, so always try all three, even if you think they might not help the image. You'll be surprised at how often all three can be used. You'll find that the white eyedropper doesn't help images that have desirable color casts. That's where you want the image to look warm or cool. Examples would be dinner by candlelight, a fireplace, and sunrise or sunset. And if you find that none of the eyedroppers seems to help, be sure to check out the techniques I mention in Chapter 9, "Color Manipulation."

Now let's explore two alternative methods for adjusting the highlight, shadow, and gray areas of an image.

Using a Grayscale to Correct Multiple Images

Here's an interesting trick I like to use when I know I'll be color correcting a large number of images that will be shot under the same lighting conditions, or when I photograph artwork. If you stop by a high-end camera store, you can ask for a grayscale (also known as a step wedge or a grayscale step wedge—**Figure 7.12**). Once you have one, you can place it in the scene where you are about to take a large number of photos (let's say for a yearbook or a product brochure) or when shooting any kind of art. Now, this is important—before you start shooting your actual scenes, you will want to take a photograph of the wedge under the exact same lighting conditions, using the same white balance setting that you'll use for the rest of the photos (if you're shooting film, you'll want to use the same film for all of your shots). As long as your settings and lighting don't change, you can use this first shot as a reference for correcting all of your other shots.

Figure 7.12 A grayscale from a high-end camera store.

After the images are transferred to your computer (or developed, scanned, and loaded into Photoshop) create a new Curves adjustment layer on the reference image. Click the white eyedropper and then click on the brightest gray rectangle on the grayscale. Next, click the black eyedropper and then click on the darkest rectangle; and finally, click the middle eyedropper and then click on the middle gray rectangle. That should remove any color cast that was present in the image.

You can apply that same adjustment to the other images by dragging the Curves adjustment layer from the grayscale image and dropping it onto another image that was photographed under the same lighting conditions. That way you can perform color correction with no guesswork and quickly apply the same adjustment to a large number of images.

You might find that this technique changes the contrast of your image too much. If that's the case, either use the middle eyedropper (skipping the other two) or use a Blending mode to control how the adjustment affects your image. If you applied your Curves adjustment directly (by choosing Image > Adjustments > Curves), choose Edit > Fade Curves right after applying the adjustment and change the pop-up menu to Color. Or, if you used an adjustment layer, change the Blending mode menu that's found at the top of the Layers palette to Color. That will prevent the adjustment from changing the brightness or contrast of your image but will still allow it to shift the colors.

Auto Color

Photoshop includes a great feature that attempts to automate the process of color correction: Auto Color (**Figure 7.13**). It uses the same general concepts we've been talking about in this chapter, and you'll find that it works well with a large variety of images. You can access Auto Color by creating a new Curves adjustment layer and then clicking the Options button. The Shadows, Midtones, and Highlights settings use the same setting that we specified when we double-clicked on the eyedroppers in the Curves dialog box. The only difference is that Photoshop attempts to locate the highlight, shadow, and gray areas automatically.

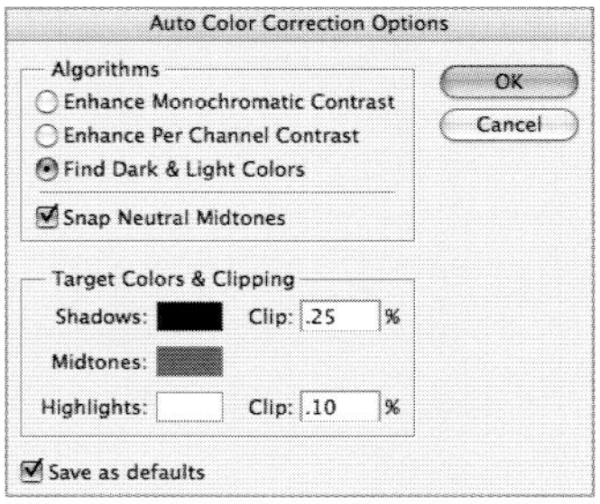

> **NOTES**
>
> The grayscale correction technique is appropriate only when you want to end up with an image that looks like it was shot under a white light source. It won't improve the look of images that contain desirable color casts like those shot under candlelight or during sunrise or sunset.

Figure 7.13 The Auto Color Correction Options dialog box.

235

This dialog box is interactive—changes will immediately affect the image. I'd set the Shadows Clip value to 0.25% and the Highlights Clip value to 0.10%, and then choose the Find Dark & Light Colors option at the top of the dialog box so that Photoshop uses Threshold to find the bright/dark areas and applies the eyedroppers to them. Then turn on the Snap Neutral Midtones check box so it uses the middle eyedropper on areas that are close to being gray. I find that this automated feature works on a surprising number of images. But as with most automated features, you'll find that you have to take over and use the old eyedroppers technique whenever Auto Color fails to deliver a satisfactory result.

If you find that the highlights in your image become blown out (no detail), you can click on the White Clip setting and press the down arrow key on your keyboard a few times until you see the detail return. You can do the same thing with the Black Clip setting to make sure you don't lose detail in the shadows of your image. I generally use the .10% setting that I mentioned earlier, and I only change it when I actually notice that I'm losing detail. If you're usually satisfied with the .10% values, be sure to turn on the Save As Defaults check box so Photoshop will remember those settings. Then, you can quickly apply the new default settings to any image by choosing Image > Adjustments > Auto Color. And if you notice the contrast of the image changing too much, choose Edit > Fade Auto Color right after applying that command and set the pop-up menu to Color. That will prevent any brightness or contrast shifts.

Adjusting the highlight, shadow, and gray areas of an image can dramatically improve the quality of an image. But even with those adjustments, you occasionally need to fine-tune any skin tones that might be in the image.

Adjusting Skin Tones

You might be thinking that I'm going to give you some kind of magic formula for creating great skin tones (kind of like what I did with grays), but if I give you just one formula, every skin tone in nature's vast diversity would look identical in your images! I'd much rather show you how to get a unique formula for each color of skin you might run across—Asian skin, olive skin, sun-burnt skin, fair skin, and all the different shades of black skin. Even better, we can do all that without trusting your monitor at all. (Of course, they will still look good on your screen, but unless you've calibrated your screen using a hardware device, you shouldn't make critical decisions based on your screen image.)

Any stock photo company will have a veritable treasure trove of flesh that you can transform into your own personal stockpile of skin tones. Simply go online to any stock provider—say, www.istockphoto.com—and download a low-resolution comp image of the person who has the skin tone that best matches your needs. Use the Eyedropper tool and click on an area of the skin that is a medium brightness (**Figure 7.14**). Now click on your foreground color to see the RGB formula needed to create that exact color.

Figure 7.14 Reference photo from a stock photo catalog. (©2007 Stockbyte, www.stockbyte.com)

Now let's figure out how to use that information to improve the skin tones in your own image. Open the image you need to correct and use the Color Sampler tool to click on the area that contains the troublesome skin. Be sure to click in an area with medium brightness, similar to the level in the other (stock photo) image. That should give you an extra readout in the Info palette (readout #1 if you just opened a fresh image, or readout #4 if you still have the three we used earlier in this chapter).

Next, click the eyedropper icon that shows up next to that new readout in the Info palette. Choose HSB from the menu (**Figure 7.15**), note the brightness (B) setting, and then set that menu back to RGB. Now, click on your foreground color to look at the color from the stock photo again. We want to use that basic color, but we don't want to change the brightness of our image much. To accomplish that, change the brightness (B) setting to what you saw in the photo you are attempting to color correct and then write down the RGB numbers that show up in the Color Picker (**Figure 7.16**). In just a moment, we're going to use those RGB numbers to tell Curves how to shift the skin color in the problem photo to match the skin color in the reference photo.

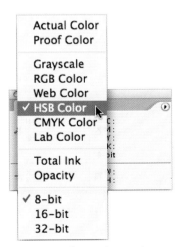

Figure 7.15 Change the sampler mode to HSB to determine the brightness of the area you are working on.

237

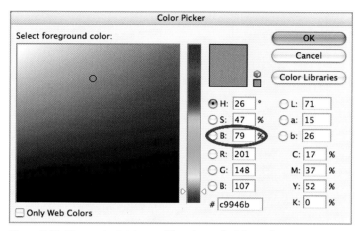

Figure 7.16 Change the brightness (B) setting to find the perfect skin-tone setting.

But first, it's time to isolate the skin tones in your problem image and then make your adjustment. I usually choose Select > Color Range to isolate the skin. If you've never used it before, be sure to read about it in Chapter 2, "Selection Primer." Once you have a general selection of the skin (don't worry if it's not perfect), it's time to make the adjustment.

If the file you're working on already contains one or more adjustment layers (like the one we used for adjusting the Shadow, Highlight and Gray area earlier in this chapter), make sure the topmost adjustment layer is active before continuing. Now, to start the adjustment, choose Layer > New Adjustment Layer > Curves. Then, to add a point to each of the red, green, and blue curves, hold Shift-Command (Mac) or Shift-Ctrl (Windows) and click on that same medium brightness area we sampled from earlier. Now, all you have to do is switch between the Red, Green, and Blue curves (use the menu at the top of the Curves dialog box) and type in the R, G, and B numbers you calculated and wrote down a few minutes ago (the ones you got from the Color Picker) in the Output of the Red, Green, and Blue curves. Once you've got the right numbers typed in, your skin tone should look much better (**Figure 7.17**).

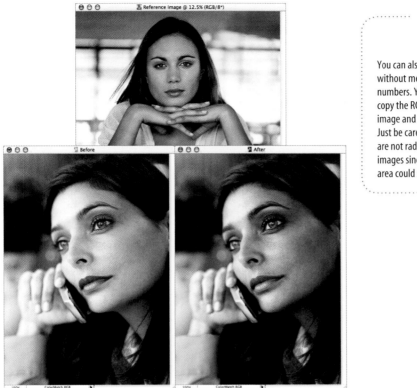

Figure 7.17 After adjusting for skin tones, the skin should look similar to the stock photo version. (original images ©2007 Stockbyte, www.stockbyte.com)

Now that you've performed the adjustment, you should take a look at your image to determine if the selection you made earlier accurately isolated the skin. If you need to fine-tune where the adjustment applies, you can go back and paint on the layer mask that is attached to the Curves adjustment layer to control which areas of the image are affected. If you're not familiar with layer masks, be sure to check out Chapter 13, "Advanced Masking," and Chapter 14, "Collage."

The more you get accustomed to using this technique, the less you'll have to rely on stock photos for reference photos. You'll get used to knowing that the more red you pull out of your image, the more tan someone looks, and that the balance between green and blue determines the fairness of someone's skin.

If the skin-tone adjustment was a little too much for you to handle, just start off by adjusting the highlight, shadow, and gray areas, and come back to this chapter after you've gotten comfortable with those. That might make it a little easier to understand and implement. The general concept is easy (and sneaky), but the execution isn't quite as simple as all that, because we have to make sure we don't mess up our earlier adjustments.

Closing Thoughts

The techniques described in this chapter are the very same ones used by the high-paid color maestros who are responsible for all of those ever-so-perfect glossy magazine ads. It will take you a while to really get the hang of these techniques, but once you do, it should take you less than two minutes to correct most images.

Here's one last bit of advice: Be sure to always correct your images separately before blending them together. That way, you will be able to maintain the color integrity of each component of your big picture.

Using Camera Raw

©2007 iStockphoto.com/bkindler

There is a building. Inside this building there is a level where no elevator can go, and no stair can reach. This level is filled with doors. These doors lead to many places. Hidden places. But one door is special. One door leads to the source.

— The Keymaker, The Matrix Reloaded

Previously the purview of only high-end photographers with high-end gear (read: "expensive"), raw-format photography is now a fairly common technique that is used by photographers of all skill levels to ensure maximum image quality and a higher level of editing latitude. Raw files are different from JPEG or TIFF images in that they contain all the data that was captured from the camera, but with minimal processing.

Your digital camera has to do quite a bit of processing to turn the raw data from your camera into a JPEG or TIFF file. It must interpolate color, adjust for white balance, gamma correct, convert to a color profile, sharpen, and finally perform saturation and other adjustments before finally compressing the file into a JPEG image. You can think of a raw file as the pure unadulterated data that came from the camera's sensor. Many image editors can't open raw images directly, but Photoshop can. Raw offers several advantages over shooting in JPEG:

▶ Because your files aren't compressed, you don't have to worry about the resulting image exhibiting unsightly JPEG artifacts.

▶ Most digital cameras capture 10 to 14 bits of color per pixel, but JPEG files only allow for 8 bits per pixel, meaning your camera must discard some of its color data when it converts to a JPEG file. With a raw image, you can keep *all* of the color data, which means you can push your edits farther before you run into posterization.

▶ With raw you don't have to worry about the White Balance setting on your camera because you can specify that setting when opening the image in Photoshop.

▶ Raw files often allow you to recover overexposed high-lights. You read that correctly: the details in highlight areas that have blown out to complete white can often be restored.

▶ When improved raw converters are released, you can go back to your raw images and reprocess them, possibly securing a higher-quality image. A raw file is truly like a digital negative.

▶ When working with raw files in Photoshop and Bridge, you have access to handy batch processing mechanisms that can greatly speed your raw-based workflow.

When you attempt to open a raw format image in Photoshop, you will be presented with the Camera Raw dialog box. This is where you can adjust everything from the overall color of the image to the brightness and contrast, as well as control how much sharpening will be applied.

Shortly after Photoshop CS3 released with Camera Raw 4.0, Adobe released Camera Raw 4.1 (4.2 as of this writing), which is a fairly significant update to its predecessor. If you notice that your version of Camera Raw isn't matching the screenshots or features shown in this chapter, it is probably because you are using a different version. To find out which version of Camera Raw you are using, open up a Raw image and go to Photoshop>About Camera Raw or look at the very top of the Camera Raw dialog box.

The Camera Raw Dialog Box

Let's start with a brief overview of the layout of the Camera Raw dialog box (**Figure 8.1**), and then we'll dive deeper and look at each specific setting.

Figure 8.1 The Camera Raw dialog box. (©2007 Ben Willmore)

Across the top of the dialog box, you'll find nine tools and two rotation icons.

Figure 8.2 The cropping rectangle indicates which areas of the image will appear when it is opened.

Figure 8.3 Click and hold the Crop tool icon to access this menu.

Figure 8.4 Clicking the Crop tool and choosing Custom allows you to enter a precise size.

Zoom and Hand tools. The Zoom and Hand tools allow you to navigate around your image (just like in Photoshop), but I find the following keyboard shortcuts to be a more efficient way to get around: Hold Command/Ctrl and press the plus or minus keys to zoom in or out on the image, and hold the spacebar to temporarily make the Hand tool active. The current magnification is indicated just below the image.

Eyedropper tools. Next to the navigation tools, you'll find two Eyedropper tools; the left one is known as the White Balance tool and works much like the middle eyedropper that is found in both the Levels and Curves dialog box, whereas the right one is known as the Color Sampler tool, which causes RGB readouts to appear above the image preview, much like what you'd get in the Info palette within Photoshop. (We talked about both the Info palette and the Eyedroppers back in Chapter 7, "Color Correction.") I'll show you how to use the White Balance tool when we start talking about the features that appear on the right side of the Camera Raw dialog box.

Crop and Straighten tools. Next to the Eyedropper tools, you'll find the Crop and Straighten tools. After choosing the Crop tool, you can click and drag across your image to determine how much of the image will appear when it's opened in Photoshop (**Figure 8.2**). Clicking and holding on the Crop tool presents you with a menu of preset width/height ratios and an option for a Custom size (**Figure 8.3**). Choosing Custom allows you to enter a precise width and height (like 8 x 10 Inches) (**Figure 8.4**). After choosing a preset or custom crop setting, the cropping rectangle becomes constrained when dragging over the image.

If you have a crooked image, click the Straighten tool and then click and drag across any straight line that should be horizontal or vertical in your image (such as the horizon line) (**Figure 8.5**). Once you release the mouse button, you'll be presented with a cropping rectangle that reflects how the image will be rotated when it's opened in Photoshop (**Figure 8.6**). Unfortunately, there is no Done button for Crop and Straighten tools, which means you'll only see the cropped and rotated version of the image after you open it within Photoshop (**Figure 8.7**).

Figure 8.5 A crooked image. (©2007 Ben Willmore)

Figure 8.6 Straightened in Camera Raw.

Figure 8.7 Result in Photoshop.

Retouch and Red Eye tools. Next to the Crop and Straighten tools are the Retouch and Red Eye tools. The Retouch tool lets you perform adjustments similar to what you can do in Photoshop using the Healing Brush and Clone Stamp tools. However, the Retouch tool isn't a brush like the Rubber Stamp. Instead you click and drag to define a circle that you want to clone from, and then click somewhere else to specify the area that you want the cloned information copied to (**Figure 8.8**). After you've defined both circles, you can click on them and drag them around to refine your adjustment, or change the size of the circles by using the Radius slider.

Photoshop's RAW format isn't the same as Camera Raw format. The names sound almost identical, but Camera Raw files can only originate from a digital camera, and Photoshop cannot change the file at all. Camera Raw files are locked because they are designed to contain only the information that came from your digital camera; therefore, they cannot be directly modified after the photo is taken. Think of it like the files on a CD. You can open them, but you can't save back to the CD because it's locked. That doesn't limit at all what you can do to the images; it just means that you have to save the changes under a different name. With Camera Raw files, it means that changes have to be saved in a different file format (like TIFF, Photoshop, or JPG). Photoshop's RAW file format, on the other hand, is mainly used to export images so they can be imported into unusual software that can't handle common file formats (it's something I doubt most of you will ever have to use).

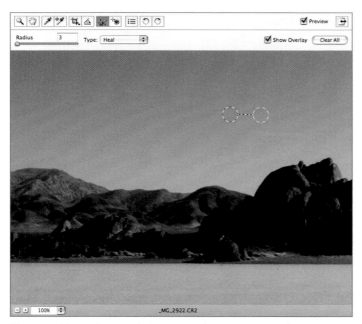

Figure 8.8 Here we're using the Retouch tool to remove sensor dust. (©2007 Ben Long)

245

Figure 8.9 The Heal pop-up menu lets you switch between healing and a regular clone operation.

If your camera was released after Photoshop CS3, you might have to download an update to the Camera Raw plug-in. You can find updates by visiting www.adobe.com, clicking on Support, then Downloads and then Photoshop. Once you've downloaded the update, double-click on it to decompress the file and place it in the following location on your hard drive: Mac: Library/Application Support/Adobe/Plug-ins/CS3/File Formats or Windows: C:/Program Files/Adobe/Plug-ins/File Formats.

Most raw files contain 12-bits of information. Photoshop, on the other hand, can deal with 8- or 16-bit files. That's like owning 12 cars and having to choose between an 8- or 16-car garage. The 8-car garage would cost half as much (in Photoshop, that means half the file size), but you'd have to give something up to use it. A 16-car garage might be more than you need, but since 8 or 16 are your only choices, it's the only choice that doesn't make you compromise. The choice might sound like a no-brainer until you consider that the average family in the United States contains only 3.14 people and would find 8 cars to be more than enough.

Finally, you can change the way the correction is made by changing the Heal pop-up menu (**Figure 8.9**). When set to Heal, the correction works just like the Heal tool in Photoshop: After copying the data from the source location to the destination, Photoshop blends the copied pixels in with the surrounding areas to make a cleaner patch. If you set the menu to Clone, the pixels are copied without any blending.

The Retouch tool is not intended for any complex retouching or fancy effects. Rather, these tools provide you with a simple way to handle sensor dust and scanning artifacts that need to be removed.

We've all seen red-eye, the demonic look that can show up in people's eyes when the light from your camera's flash bounces off their retinas. You can correct red-eye in Camera Raw by selecting the Red Eye tool and then clicking on the red part of a person's pupil. The Pupil Size and Darken sliders let you refine your correction.

Camera Raw Preferences. To the right of these adjustment tools is a button for opening the Camera Raw Preferences dialog box. There are a number of settings that you can customize from the Preferences dialog, and we'll be looking at a few of them later in this chapter.

Rotating tools. Finally, you'll find two tools used for rotating the image 90° to the right or left. I find it to be much more efficient to type L or R.

Management controls. Further to the right are two important window management controls. When the Preview checkbox is turned on, your image is displayed with all of your corrections applied. If you turn off the Preview checkbox, you'll see your original, unaltered image. This provides a simple before and after switch that you can also access by simply pressing P.

The button on the far right side is the Toggle full screen mode button, which expands the Camera Raw window to fill the full screen. In addition to affording you a larger image to work with, Full Screen mode hides any other distracting interface elements and controls. As in Photoshop itself, you can toggle in and out of Full Screen Mode by pressing F.

Workflow options. Beneath the image preview you'll find the workflow settings for your image—a line of text that tells color space, bit depth, pixel dimensions, and resolution setting (**Figure 8.10**). You might notice that these settings look kind of like a link on a Web page and, sure enough, if you click on them, the Workflow Options dialog box opens (**Figure 8.11**).

The workflow options let you specify how much information will be delivered to Photoshop when you open your image. The Space pop-up menu controls the range of colors your image is capable of using (also known as a color space). I recommend that you set it to the same RGB Working Space that you chose back in Chapter 6 "Color Management," but if you haven't read that chapter, just leave it set to Adobe RGB.

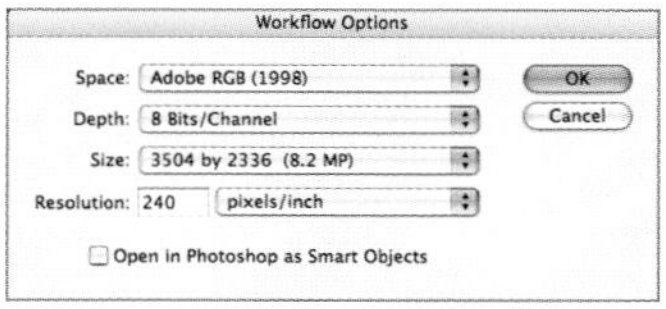

The Depth pop-up menu determines how many shades Photoshop can use between black and white. Choosing 8 Bits/Channel delivers an image that contains a maximum of 256 brightness levels, which makes for 16.7 million colors. Choosing 16 Bits/Channel delivers an image that contains a maximum of 4096 brightness levels, which makes for about 68 billion colors! The problem is that 16-bit files take up twice as much space as 8-bit files on your hard drive, and both your computer screen and your printer aren't capable of reproducing more than 8-bits of information.

There's a lot of hype out there about the advantages of 16-bit files, but when it comes down to the end result, the difference between 8 and 16 bit is barely detectable (except in some circumstances, which you can read about in the sidebar). There are folks out there who might try to shame you into using 16-bit mode by showing you a histogram (bar chart) that shows the difference between 8- and 16-bit results. If that ever happens to you, please ignore the bar chart and ask to see two prints side by side. If you actually see a noticeable difference between the prints, consider taking their advice and use 16-bit images. If, on the other hand, having reasonable file sizes and a relatively fast computer are your priorities, then use 8-bit images like I do and know that your results will still look great. I suggest only using 16 Bits/Channel when you plan on making major adjustments within Photoshop or when you really

Adobe RGB (1998): 8 bit; 3504 by 2336 (8.2MP); 240 ppi

Figure 8.10 Clicking on the Workflow Settings link at the bottom of the Camera Raw window opens the Workflow Options dialog box.

Figure 8.11 The Workflow Options dialog box lets you configure color space, bit depth, and other parameters for your final image.

NOTES

Computer monitors and desktop printers are not capable of reproducing more than 256 brightness levels (also known as 8 bits). So, are the 4096 brightness levels that come with a 12-bit image overkill or are they worth keeping? Well, what if you have a very dark image that only contains brightness levels from black to 90% gray and you end up adjusting the image in Photoshop to make the brightest area white while keeping the darkest area black. Since the original image contained only 10% of the shades available, an 8-bit version would contain a maximum of 26 brightness levels and the 12-bit version would have 410! Wouldn't the 12-bit image produce a smoother result? It's only in extreme cases that the extra information is helpful, so I only use them when I plan to make an extreme adjustment in Photoshop (all adjustments in the Camera Raw dialog box are applied to the full 12 bits of information).

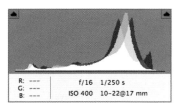

Figure 8.12 The Camera Raw histogram and EXIF readout, along with the RGB display.

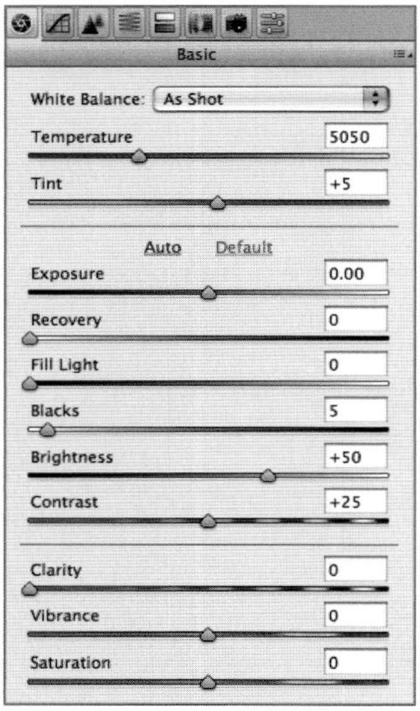

Figure 8.13 The Basic tab contains tools that you'll use on all of your raw images.

don't care how large your files become or how slow your computer runs while you're working on an image.

The Size and Resolution settings determine the physical size of your image when it's opened in Photoshop. The Size setting that doesn't have a plus or minus symbol next to it reflects the amount of information your camera captured, whereas the setting with the symbols reflects choices that will cause Photoshop to scale your image up or down. This is also known as interpolation and is discussed in "Resolution Solutions," a bonus chapter included on the CD.

Finally, there's that Open in Photoshop as Smart Objects checkbox. We'll discuss Smart Objects in detail in Chapter 14, "Collage."

Once you've configured your workflow settings, click OK to return to the Camera Raw dialog box.

In the upper right of the dialog box, you'll find a histogram that shows you how the sliders in the Camera Raw dialog box affect the overall tonality of the image. I'll cover the histogram and its uses when we get to the point where we're adjusting images.

Directly beneath the histogram, Adobe has conveniently placed a simple readout that shows the f-stop, shutter speed, ISO, and focal length that were used for the image (**Figure 8.12**). Right next to that is an RGB readout that shows you the component color values for any pixel that you move the mouse over, just like the Info palette in Photoshop.

Below these readouts, you'll find an array of sliders organized into tabs of different categories (Basic, Tone Curve, Detail, HSL/Grayscale, Split Toning, Lens Corrections, Camera Calibration, and Presets), each with its own set of controls. Let's look at these settings one at a time. I'll describe them in the same order in which I usually adjust my own images.

The Basic Tab

The Basic tab should be your mandatory first stop in the Camera Raw dialog box. I use it for every image I open with Camera Raw (**Figure 8.13**); all the other settings under the other tabs can be considered optional. The Basic tab is where you can change the overall tone and color of the image. I like to start with the White Balance settings.

White Balance

The White Balance setting allows you to shift the overall color of your image, making it feel warm, cool, or neutral. There are three ways to set the white balance of your image: the pop-up menu, the sliders, or the Eyedropper tool.

You might find yourself using the White Balance pop-up menu because it's simple and easy. That's where you'll find presets for different types of lighting conditions (Daylight, Cloudy, Tungsten, Fluorescent). If you know which type of light an image was shot under, choose that preset so Photoshop will correct for that particular light source. If you're not sure what the lighting conditions were when the image was shot, just click through them and watch your image change until you find the one that makes the colors in your image look their best (**Figures 8.14** and **8.15**). Or, if you're in a big hurry, just set the menu to Auto and Photoshop will use the setting that it thinks is appropriate for the lighting conditions of your image. All this pop-up menu is doing is moving the Temperature and Tint sliders to preset positions. But before you start fiddling with those sliders, I'd recommend beginning with the pop-up menu because that will easily get you to a good starting point, which you can then fine-tune with the sliders.

Moving the Temperature slider toward the left shifts the colors in your image toward blue; sliding it to the right shifts them toward yellow. The Tint slider shifts the color in your image toward green or magenta. The combination of these two sliders allows you to shift the image toward just about any color. For instance, if you move both the Temperature and Tint sliders toward the right, you'll be simultaneously shifting the image toward yellow and magenta. Those two colors combined produce red, so that's the color your image will shift toward. Moving them in the opposite direction shifts things toward both blue and green, which sends the colors toward cyan.

Figure 8.14 Result of using the Daylight White Balance setting on an image captured under daylight lighting conditions. (©2007 Ben Willmore)

Figure 8.15 Result of using Tungsten White Balance on an image captured under daylight conditions.

Figure 8.16 Image opened with random Temperature and Tint settings. (©2007 Ben Willmore)

Figure 8.17 Image opened by clicking with the Eyedropper tool on an area that should not contain color.

If you want your image to look completely neutral (not warm or cool), you might consider using the Eyedropper tool that is located in the upper left of the Camera Raw dialog box. With that tool active, you can click on your image and Photoshop will figure out the proper Temperature and Tint settings that would be needed to remove all the color from the area you clicked on. All you have to do is find an area that shouldn't contain color and then click on it (**Figures 8.16** and **8.17**). Just look for anything that appears to be a shade of gray in the image. It could be someone's gray sweatshirt, a wall that's painted white, a button on someone's shirt, or anything else that shouldn't contain a trace of color. Then, if you feel the image is just too sterile looking, you can adjust the Temperature and Tint sliders to make the image a little warmer (toward yellow and magenta) or cooler (toward green and blue).

It doesn't really matter which of the three methods you use (pop-up menu, sliders, or Eyedropper) because in the end, all of them are just manipulating the Temperature and Tint sliders to produce the final result. Your personal interpretation of what you'd like your image to look like will dictate what you end up with.

Exposure Slider

The Exposure slider controls the brightness of the brightest area of your image. It's a lot like the upper-right slider in the Levels dialog box (we talked about that one back in Chapter 4). As you move the Exposure slider farther to the right, more areas of your image become pure white. Because of that, you have to be very careful; otherwise, you'll end up trashing the detail in the brightest part of your image.

There are four ways to tell if you're losing detail. The least reliable of them is to simply watch your image to see if any areas are becoming solid white or black. You often can't tell the difference between a very bright area and one that has become solid white. An alternative is to watch the histogram while adjusting the Exposure slider (**Figure 8.18**). If a spike appears on the right end of the histogram, you're starting to lose highlight detail.

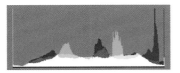

Figure 8.18 Camera Raw's histogram showing a clipped highlight.

As you know, your image is made out of red, green, and blue light (also known as channels). If the spike is in color, you're losing detail in one or two of the three colors that make up your image, but still have detail left in the highlights. If the spike is white on the other hand, your highlights are becoming solid white and have no detail. A spike only matters if it shows up on the absolute right end of the histogram. A spike in the middle or near the end does not indicate a loss of detail. (To learn more about histograms, check out Chapter 4, "Optimizing Grayscale Images," and Chapter 5, "Understanding Curves.") The problem with this approach is that light sources and reflections of shiny objects (like glass, water, or metal) look better when they don't contain detail, and the histogram can't distinguish between those areas and other important parts of your image.

In the upper corners of the Histogram are two small buttons, one above the right side and one above the left. Clicking the right one toggles the highlight clipping view. When it's turned on, any areas that are losing highlight detail turn red in the Camera Raw dialog box (**Figures 8.19** and **8.20**). That makes it much easier to know when and where you're starting to lose detail. The only snag is that the red overlay does not differentiate between losing detail in just one or two of the three colors that make up your image (in which case you still have some detail remaining), and losing detail in all three colors, which produces solid white. To get the most informative and useful indication of lost detail, hold down the Option/Alt key while you move the Exposure slider. That will cause Photoshop to change the way it displays your image (**Figure 8.21**). In this view, areas that show up as solid white have lost all detail and will end up solid white when the image is opened in Photoshop. Areas that show up in color indicate where you're losing detail in one or two of the colors that make up your image, but the areas have not become solid white yet. Finally, areas that appear solid black have detail in all three of the colors that make up your image and are therefore not at risk.

NOTES

Depending on how much you've zoomed in, the Eyedropper will look at different numbers of pixels in your image. If you view your image at 100%, it will look at the exact pixel that is under your cursor when you click the mouse button. Viewing your image at 50% will make the Eyedropper look at a 2×2 pixel area of your image. I find that I like the results better when I'm viewing my image at 25% or 50%, because I don't have to worry about clicking on an odd-colored pixel that would get averaged into the colors that are surrounding it.

Figure 8.19 This image contains very saturated colors, which will often cause detail to be lost in one or two of the colors that make up the image.

Figure 8.20 Using the Highlights check box indicated that a large area was losing detail, even though only a small area had become solid white.

Figure 8.21 Holding the Option/Alt key when dragging the Exposure slider indicated that only a small area was becoming solid white.

Figure 8.22 Hold Option/Alt and drag the Exposure slider until you see the first hints of white.

Figure 8.23 Back off on the Exposure setting until you don't see any white.

My approach to adjusting this slider is to move it toward the right (with Option/Alt held down) until I see the first hints of white showing up (**Figure 8.22**). Then I'll back off a tiny amount and think of that as the farthest I'd want to move it (**Figure 8.23**) (unless the area that's becoming white is a light source or reflection of the light source, in which case forcing it to white might actually improve the look of the image). Then I'll look at the colored areas that are showing up, and if there are areas that contain critical detail, I'll continue to move the slider back toward the left until I see only small areas of color. I don't mind having large areas of color if I want my image to look really saturated, because you have to max out at least one of the colors that make up your image (red, green, and blue) in order to get a truly saturated color. Once I've found the general range that I like, I'll let go of the Option/Alt key and see how this setting is affecting the brightest areas of my image, and then fine-tune it if necessary. The vast majority of the time I end up leaving it at the position that was just shy of seeing solid white when I had the Option/Alt key held down.

The Exposure setting is only used to control how bright the absolute brightest areas of your image should be. I don't suggest you try to control the overall brightness of your image with this slider. There are better ways to do that, which we'll get to in a few moments. Right now, let's talk about the Recovery slider and how it can come to the rescue when your image has clipped highlights.

Recovery Slider

One of the most important things to take away from the previous paragraph is the idea that highlights don't always clip in all three channels. Very often, a highlight will only clip in one or two channels, though it might appear to be completely blown out, or to have lost detail. When a highlight is only partially clipped, there's a chance that Camera Raw can use the remaining channels to *rebuild* the clipped channels, and thus restore detail to areas that appear to be blown out. The Recovery slider attempts to do just that.

If you have clipped highlights—as evidenced by a big spike on the right side of the histogram—try sliding the Recovery slider to the right. As you do, you might very well see the spike shrink and disappear, and in your image see detail appear in the blown-out highlight sections of your image (**Figure 8.24**).

Highlight recovery can often work wonders, turning seemingly unusable images into well-exposed shots full of detail. Note that you can also perform highlight recovery by moving the Exposure slider to the left. This will perform the exact same recovery operation as the Recovery slider, but it will also darken the midtones and shadows in your image. The Recovery slider constrains its effects to just the highlights in your image, which means you won't have to do as much work later to try to restore brightness.

NOTES

Most digital cameras also capture "headroom"—additional information above the brightest levels represented in the file. This data is necessary for some of the color and white balance calculations that must be performed to produce an image. This data is also stored in the file, and Camera Raw can reach into that data to bolster its highlight recovery efforts.

Figure 8.24 The left image has overexposed highlights as evidenced by the spike on the right side of the histogram and the lack of detail in the clouds. By using the Recovery slider, we can restore detail to the clouds. The rest of the image still needs work, but this is a great start. (©2007 Ben Long)

Figure 8.25 Above: Before using the Fill Light slider. Below: After using the Fill Light slider, which works just like the Shadow slider in the Shadow/Highlight adjustment that you learned about in Chapter 5. (©2007 Ben Long)

Fill Light Slider

In Chapter 5, you were introduced to Photoshop's Shadow/Highlight adjustment, which let you brighten only the shadow areas of an image (or only the highlights). The Fill Light slider works just like the Shadow slider in the Shadow/Highlight adjustment. Slide it to the right, and the shadow areas of your image will brighten. It's called Fill Light because the overall effect is very similar to what you'd see if you shined a fill light—or fired a fill flash—into your scene. Shadows under people's eyes and chins will lessen, and overall contrast will be reduced (**Figure 8.25**).

The Fill Light slider lacks the refined degree of control that the Shadow/Highlight dialog box provides, but having it in Camera Raw is a great convenience, because it just might save you an additional processing step later.

Blacks Slider

The Blacks slider controls how dark the absolute darkest areas of your image will be. It's very similar to the upper-left slider in the Levels dialog box (which we talked about in Chapter 4). It works just like the Exposure slider in that you can hold Option/Alt to see which areas are becoming solid black (they will look black), which areas are starting to have less detail (colored areas), and which areas haven't lost any detail (they will look white). You also have a Shadows button above the left side of the histogram, which makes areas that are losing detail appear in blue in Camera Raw. Unlike the Highlights button, the Shadows button only indicates where an area has become solid black. It doesn't indicate areas that are losing detail in just one or two of the colors that make up the image. I still prefer to use the Option/Alt key method because I often want to know where I'm losing detail in just one or two colors in the image. I usually hold Option/Alt and move the Blacks slider until I see the first hints of pure black showing up and then back off just slightly so I don't trash the detail anywhere (**Figure 8.26**).

Figure 8.26 When moving the Blacks slider, try not to force any areas to black.

Figure 8.27 Image opened using default Brightness setting of 50. (©2007 Ben Willmore)

If you decide not to use the Shadows checkbox feature when moving the Blacks slider, be sure to keep an eye on the histogram. If you see a spike on the left side, you know that you're losing shadow detail. If the spike is white instead of a color, you're starting to get some solid black areas in your image.

Brightness Slider

Now that we've determined how bright the brightest areas should be and how dark the darkest areas should be, it's time to adjust the brightness levels that fall between black and white.

Figure 8.28 Result of moving the Brightness slider all the way to the left to darken the image.

The Brightness slider is very similar to the middle slider in the Levels dialog box because it attempts to adjust the overall brightness of your image without screwing up the brightest or darkest areas. Move the slider to the left if your image needs to be darker (**Figures 8.27** and **8.28**), or move it to the right to brighten the image (**Figure 8.29**). If you're planning to make radical changes in brightness, I recommend that you use Curves (see Chapter 5) after you've opened the image in Photoshop. You'll simply have a lot more control over the process that way, but it won't hurt if you make a slight tweak using the Brightness slider.

Figure 8.29 Result of moving the Brightness slider all the way to the right to brighten the image.

Figure 8.30 Image opened with –40 contrast setting. (©2007 Ben Willmore)

Figure 8.31 Image opened with default contrast setting of +25.

Figure 8.32 Image opened with +70 contrast setting.

Contrast Slider

I consider the Contrast slider to be optional. Most of the time, I'd rather adjust the contrast of my images using Curves because they provide much more control than I'd ever get by moving a generic Contrast slider. But, when I'm in a hurry, I often limit my adjustments to what's available in the Camera Raw dialog box. In those instances, I'll settle for the generic Contrast adjustment instead of spending the time it would take to fine-tune it with Curves (**Figures 8.30** through **8.32**).

Clarity Slider

This is a great new addition that comes with the 4.1 update of Camera Raw and can be used with a large variety of photographs. It was devised to boost contrast at the micro level and even though it's a relatively subtle adjustment it can add noticeable punch and crispness to your images. It's a unique adjustment in that it can't be reproduced in Curves because it uses the image itself to make a mask on which to apply the mid tone contrast adjustment. Tread lightly with this slider as a heavy hand can make the image look too contrasty. (**Figures 8.33** and **8.34**).

Figure 8.33 Image opened with 0 Clarity setting. (©2007 Ben Willmore)

Figure 8.34 Image opened with +75 Clarity setting.

Vibrance Slider

The Vibrance slider is a variation on a Saturation adjustment. Rather than adjusting the saturation of the entire image, the Vibrance slider attempts to protect flesh tones. If you've ever performed a saturation boost on an image and found that skin tones ended up too red or had splotches in them, you'll appreciate the Vibrance slider (**Figure 8.35**).

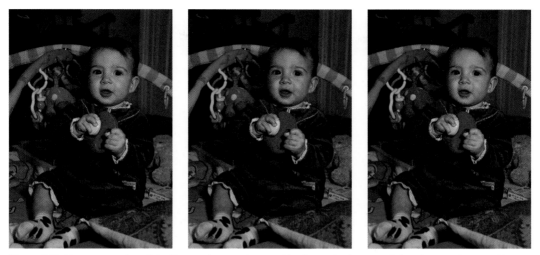

Figure 8.35 Here you see the original image, the same image with a Saturation boost, and then the same image with a boost in Vibrancy but no saturation. The Vibrancy increase makes some colors more saturated but does a good job of protecting the skin tones.

Saturation Slider

I think of the Saturation slider as optional. The truth is you'll have much more control over your image if you adjust it in Photoshop with the Hue/Saturation dialog box. But, if you're in a hurry, or if you're batch processing a large number of images using the same settings, you might decide to use this slider instead of taking the time to do it as two steps. If you have more time, you can test the waters with this slider and make the actual adjustments with the Hue/Saturation dialog box afterward (**Figures 8.36** through **8.38**).

If you want a better idea of how the White Balance setting is affecting the colors of your image, you can temporarily pump up the saturation of your image with this slider. Then, once you like the overall color of the image, bring the Saturation slider back to zero.

Figure 8.36 Image opened with −50 Saturation setting. (©2007 Ben Willmore)

Figure 8.37 Image opened with 0 Saturation setting.

Figure 8.38 Image opened with +50 Saturation setting.

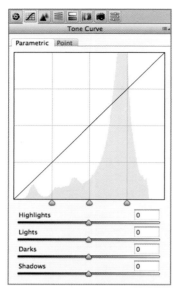

Figure 8.39 The Tone Curve tab lets you make tonal adjustments using a modified Curves interface.

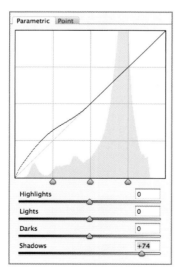

Figure 8.40 Sliding the Parametric sliders will automatically reshape the appropriate part of the curve.

The Tone Curve Tab

The Tone Curve tab (**Figure 8.39**) gives you a tool that works much like the Curves dialog box that we covered in Chapter 5. As you'll see, it's a little different than the regular Photoshop Curves dialog box.

The Tone Curve tab is divided into two sub-tabs: Parametric and Point. While the Parametric mode is the default, the Point mode is more like a normal Curves interface, so let's look at that one first.

Like the normal Curves dialog, the Tone Curve shows a histogram with an editable curve laid over it. By default, the curve already has some points on it that are intended to provide a medium contrast adjustment. The Tone Curve has four preset curves that you can select from using the Curve pop-up menu. If you choose Linear from the pop-up menu, you'll get a curve that is just like the default one found in Photoshop.

In Photoshop, you simply click on your image, which causes a circle to appear on the curve. The circle indicates the area of the curve that will affect the brightness level on which you're clicking. In the Camera Raw dialog box, you have to hold the Command/Ctrl key and hover over your image (without pressing the mouse button) to see the circle appear. If you click the mouse button while holding Command/Ctrl, a dot will be added right where the circle was showing up.

Two things to note about the Point curve: When you add a point to the curve and move it up or down, you won't see its effects until you release the mouse button; the tone curve is *much* more sensitive than the Photoshop Curves dialog box. You'll most likely find that your curve adjustments are *very* small.

The Parametric curve provides a very different way of working, one that combines the power of Curves with the ease of a Levels adjustment. In the Parametric tab, you'll see the same curve/histogram display, but beneath it you'll find four sliders, one each for Highlights, Lights, Darks, and Shadows. As you slide these sliders, the appropriate part of the curve will automatically bend and reshape to affect just the tonal range specified by the slider (**Figure 8.40**).

For further refinement, you can slide the three sliders at the bottom of the curve display. These change the midpoint of each of the slider ranges. So, you can use the bottom sliders to specify how much adjustment you want, and then use the sliders directly beneath the curve graph to fine-tune that adjustment to a very specific part of the curve (**Figure 8.41**).

After using the Tone Curve tab for quite some time, I've found it to be not as intuitive as the one built into Photoshop, and I miss the ability to use Curves combined with some of the more sophisticated features in Photoshop (Adjustment Layers, Blending modes, Layer Masks, etc.) which is what really makes Curves powerful and gives you the ability to make much more precise and effective adjustments (see Chapter 10 "Adjustment Layers" for information on these features). For those reasons, I find that I only use the Point Curve in Camera Raw when I plan on saving the image directly out of the Camera Raw dialog box or when images will be used with the automated features found under the Tools menu in Bridge. For all other purposes, I use the Curves dialog box within Photoshop.

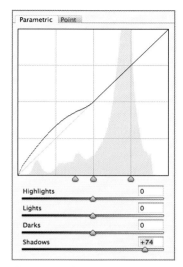

Figure 8.41 Sliding the sliders directly beneath the curve lets you adjust the midpoint of each Parametric slider.

The Detail Tab

Digital cameras often produce images that look a bit soft and can contain tiny specks of noise that can be distracting. The Detail tab is where you can deal with these problems and hopefully produce a sharp and noise-free image (**Figure 8.42**). These settings make rather subtle changes to your image, so it's best to work with them when you're viewing your image at 100% magnification.

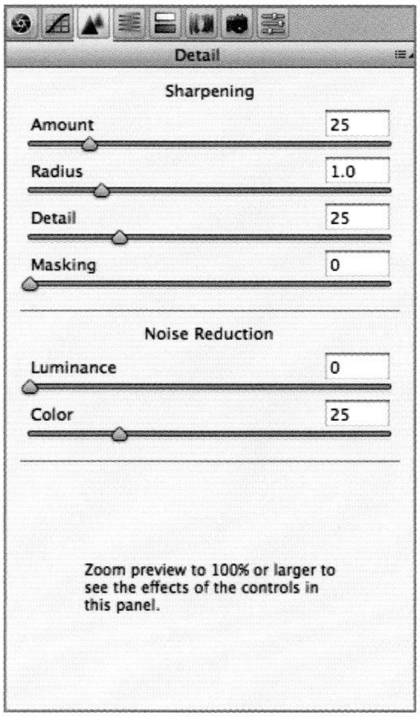

Sharpening

I must confess that I almost never use the Sharpening sliders because I prefer to sharpen my image as the final step right before I print. It's ideal if you sharpen an image after it has been scaled down to its final size. Whatever you do, don't ignore these sliders because the defaults are not set at 0.

But, again, if you're in a hurry or feeling just plain lazy, there are merits to the Sharpness sliders. The Camera Raw 4.1 update gave us three more sliders (Radius, Detail, and

Figure 8.42 The settings found under the Detail tab are designed to reduce noise and make an image look sharper.

Masking), allowing for a great deal more control over sharpening than with previous versions. With the added controls, it might now be useful to save combinations of these sliders as presets for specific image types such as portraits or landscapes (I'll talk about the Camera Raw Presets tab later in this chapter). In some cases, you might find that moving the sliders doesn't appear to do anything to your image. That usually happens when you're zoomed out so you can see the entire image. Before you start to sharpen your image, double-click the Zoom tool in the upper left of the Camera Raw dialog box. That will get you to 100% view, where you'll be able to see exactly what the Sharpness sliders are doing to your image. When you're done, you can always double-click the Hand tool to get back to the view that shows your entire image. I won't say much about sharpening here because there is an entire chapter (Chapter 11, "Sharpening") dedicated to the subject later in this book.

Noise Reduction

Digital image noise comes in two flavors: luminance and chrominance, or color. The Luminance slider is designed to reduce the noise that shows up when you use high ISO settings with your digital camera (**Figure 8.43**). It won't deal with those colorful specks you see on occasion (that's what Color Noise Reduction is for), but it should be able to handle the dark specks that you get when you try to brighten up an image that was shot in low lighting conditions. All you need to do is zoom in to 100% view (double-click the Zoom tool to get there), and then experiment with the slider until the noise is minimized (**Figure 8.44**). Just be sure to look at the fine detail in your image to make sure it hasn't removed important detail like freckles or skin texture.

Figure 8.43 Zooming in on this image reveals bright specks.

Figure 8.44 The specks are less obvious after adjusting the Luminance Smoothing setting.

Color Noise Reduction

The Color Noise Reduction slider attempts to blend in any colorful specks that appear on your image (**Figure 8.45**) by making them look similar to the colors that surround them (**Figure 8.46**). These colorful specks are often the result of shooting with high ISO settings on your digital camera. Just like with Luminance Smoothing, you'll want to be at 100% view and move the slider just high enough to blend the multicolored specks into your image.

You have to be careful with the Luminance Smoothing and Color Noise Reduction sliders because they will both soften your image. That's why they're grouped in this tab with the Sharpening slider. Be sure to toggle the Preview check box at the bottom of your image off and on to make sure it's worth applying these settings. Sometimes it's better to have a noisy image that still has detail and sharpness than one with no noise that looks overly soft. Also, remember that you can always sharpen your image after you open it in Photoshop, which means that it doesn't have to remain as soft as it might appear after you apply smoothing and noise reduction.

HSL / Grayscale Tab

There will be times when you may need to make color shifts and adjustments to specific parts of the color range, so Camera Raw now provides the HSL/Grayscale tab. Like many other additions to Camera Raw 4, the HSL/Grayscale control has been purloined from Photoshop Lightroom.

The HSL control is divided into three tabs: Hue, Saturation, and Luminance.

In each tab you'll find the same selection of color ranges: reds, oranges, yellows, greens, aquas, blues, purples, and magentas. One tab does not override another; you can make adjustments on each tab to create a cumulative correction. You'll probably find, however, that you need to switch from tab to tab to make your adjustments. If you increase luminance, for example, very often you'll have a different impression of the hue or saturation in your image.

Figure 8.45 With the Color Noise Reduction setting at zero, you can see specks of many different colors.

Figure 8.46 After adjusting the Color Noise Reduction slider, the colorful specks blend into the surrounding colors.

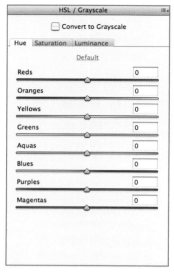

Figure 8.47 By using the sliders in the Hue tab, you can shift the hues of specific color ranges in your image.

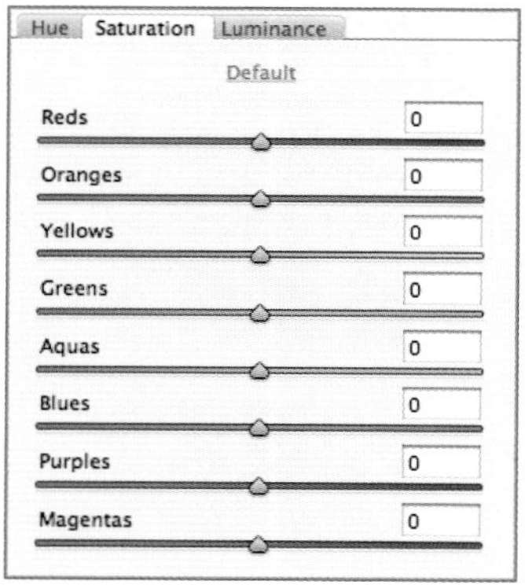

Figure 8.48 The Saturation tab's sliders let you increase or decrease the saturation of specific color ranges.

Hue

In the Hue tab, you can adjust the hue of each color range simply by dragging the slider to the left or right (**Figure 8.47**). The Hue tab doesn't let you make huge swings in hue; you can't turn reds into blues, for example. For those extreme shifts, you'll need to use the hue controls in Photoshop. The Hue tab is for making slight adjustments to remove casts or slight corrections to particular color ranges.

If the reds in your image are a little too orange, for example, slide the Reds slider to the left.

Saturation

The Saturation tab lets you adjust the saturation of each specific color range (**Figure 8.48**). You can adjust the saturation of just the red tones in the image, for example, by dragging the Reds slider back and forth. Slide to the left to desaturate a particular color range; slide right to increase the saturation.

Luminance

In the Luminance tab, you can adjust the luminance, or brightness, of each color range. Sliding to the right brightens a color range; sliding to the left darkens colors.

Convert to Grayscale

Above the three tabs in the HSL/Grayscale control you'll find a Convert to Grayscale check box. If you select it, the three tabs will disappear and change to a single Grayscale Mix tab (**Figure 8.49**). The image preview will show your new grayscale image, and the histogram will change to a single-channel histogram.

The color sliders now work the way they do in Hue/Saturation/Luminance mode, but instead of altering hue, they alter the shade of gray of those particular colors. So if you slide the Reds slider to the right, for example, any red tones in your image will get lighter.

By default, when you turn on the Convert to Grayscale check box, Camera Raw analyzes your images and calculates initial settings for the sliders. If you alter the sliders and want to go back to the initial conversion settings, click the Auto button. Clicking the Default button restores all sliders to their defaults position. If you haven't changed them manually, all the default positions will be zero.

There's no image-quality advantage to be had by performing your grayscale conversions in Camera Raw rather than in the new Black and White dialog box in Photoshop CS3. In fact, the Black and White dialog box (covered in Chapter 9 , "Color Correction,") has a little more flexibility. In that dialog box, for example, you can click and drag tones in your image to change them.

The advantage of grayscale conversion in Camera Raw is that like all other Camera Raw adjustments, grayscale conversion is nondestructive, and you can batch-process it by using any of the normal batch-processing operations.

Tone and Color Adjustments After Grayscale Conversion

Remember that Camera Raw is a nondestructive editor. As you adjust settings, it constantly reprocesses your original raw camera data to present a new image onscreen. When you turn on the Convert to Grayscale check box in the HSL/Grayscale control, the grayscale conversion you define is just another item added to the list of edits and adjustments that the software must make before it can show the final image onscreen. This means that even after you've told Camera Raw to convert your image to grayscale, you can continue to alter color and tone by using any of the program's controls (**Figure 8.50**).

Figure 8.49 The Grayscale Mix sliders let you create custom grayscale conversions directly within Camera Raw.

NOTES

Each HSL/Grayscale tab includes a Default button that resets the sliders for that particular tab. If you want to reset all three tabs, you'll need to click each Default button individually.

Figure 8.50 After converting the image in Figure 8.25 to grayscale, you can use the Grayscale Mix sliders to change the gray value of specific tones in the image. Shifting the Reds slider up and down, for example, yields these different results.

You're effectively changing the color of your image "underneath" the grayscale conversion. When you convert to grayscale, Camera Raw uses the original color values to determine a resulting grayscale value. So if you alter the color values by using any of Camera Raw's color editing tools, the resulting gray values will change. This is yet another way that you can alter the gray values in your final image.

Split Toning Tab

Split toning allows you to apply separate tonings to the shadows and highlights in your image. For each area, you can select different hue and saturation settings. Split toning will work with either grayscale or color images, but you'll probably use it most often on grayscale pictures.

It doesn't matter whether you tone highlights or shadows first. For this example, we started with the highlights. First, we slid the Highlights Saturation to around 50 (**Figure 8.51**). We goosed the saturation because it can be difficult to see the effects of a hue choice when the saturation is at zero.

Figure 8.51 Begin your split-toning operation by increasing the Saturation setting in either the Highlights or Shadows section. This will allow you to see your later hue choice more easily. (©2007 Ben Long)

Next, we used the Hue slider to choose the hue we wanted for toning, then we slid the Saturation slider down to something reasonable (**Figure 8.52**). We then performed the same steps using the Shadows slider to produce the image shown in **Figure 8.53**.

Figure 8.52 After setting the Hue slider, set the Saturation slider back to something more reasonable.

Figure 8.53 Perform the same operation on the shadow tones in your image to complete the split toning.

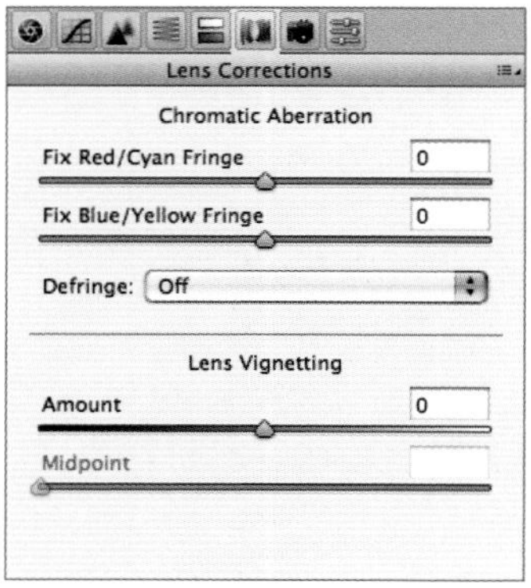

Figure 8.54 The Lens Correction tab provides some handy tools for correcting optical aberrations.

The Balance slider lets you shift the highlights toning more into the shadow areas, and vice versa. This allows you to have more or less of either type of tone.

Split toning can be applied to color images or images that you're performing a black-and-white conversion on. As explained earlier, when you're performing black-and-white conversion, changes to color affect the final gray tones that Camera Raw produces. So performing a split-toning operation on an image that has a grayscale conversion applied will alter the final gray tones that Camera Raw generates.

The Lens Corrections Tab

The Lens Corrections tab contains another collection of settings that are completely optional (**Figure 8.54**). I use them only when I notice specific problems with my images that have to do with the lens that I used to shoot them.

Some lenses—particularly wide-angle lenses—often have the problem of focusing different wavelengths of light at different points. When that happens, you can end up with a halo of color on the edges of high contrast lines in your image. I'm no expert on optics, but I've been told that this particular problem is called *chromatic aberration*. I just think of it as messed up color on the outer portions of images taken with wide-angle lenses, because that's where I've run into it. The higher the contrast between objects, the more obvious it will be. Also, note that it can happen with *any* lens, and chromatic aberrations are often what separate an inexpensive lens from a pricier one.

If you notice a halo of red on one side of an object and cyan on the opposite side, try moving the Fix Red/Cyan Fringe slider back and forth to see if you can reduce the halos (**Figures 8.55** through **8.57**). If, on the other hand, you see blue and yellow halos, then adjust the Fix Blue/Yellow Fringe slider instead. You might need to adjust both of the sliders depending on exactly what colors you're seeing on the edges of objects. Because these sliders are performing a very simple operation—scaling the colors that make up your image—they can't always get rid of this type of problem.

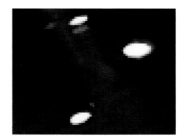

Figure 8.55 Original image. (Image courtesy of Tim Whitehouse)

Figure 8.56 The Chromatic Aberration settings used to correct the image shown in Figure 8.55.

Figure 8.57 After adjusting the Chromatic Aberration settings, the color halos are no longer obvious.

The two Vignetting sliders are designed to compensate for light falloff on the edge of your image. *Vignetting* is a term the photography folks like to throw around that generally refers to lighter centers with darker edges. So, if you ever notice that the outer edges of your image are darker than the middle, move the Vignetting Amount slider toward the right until the brightness of the edge looks more like the middle of your image. Once you've done that, you'll need to adjust the Vignetting Midpoint setting to control how far the brightening effect of the last slider encroaches on the center of your image. Just move it until the formerly dark edges blend into the rest of the image.

When you have images with specular highlights (such as the surface of a windy lake on a sunny day), you will often encounter some degree of fringing, which is purple, red or magenta color surrounding the hot specular highlights. The new Defringe drop down menu in the Lens Correction tab will help to reduce this negative effect. There are three options; Off, Highlight Edge and All Edges. Selecting the Highlight Edge option removes most of the color additions but there may still be a degree of fringing. Setting to All Edges removes the majority of the fringe effects, but it can negatively affect color saturation in areas where the defringing is occurring so you'll have to decide whether or not this adjustment is useful on an image by image basis. (**Figures 8.58** and **8.59**) As with Sharpening and noise reduction you really only see the effect at 100% zoom or higher.

Figure 8.58 Original image. (©2007 Ben Willmore)

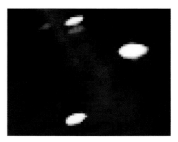

Figure 8.59 Setting the Defringe drop down menu to All Edges removes the color fringing around the highlights.

Figure 8.60 Original image. (©2007 Ben Willmore)

Figure 8.61 Moving the Vignetting slider all the way to the left darkened the corners of the image.

Figure 8.62 Lowering the Contrast and Saturation settings helps the image look more like an old faded photo.

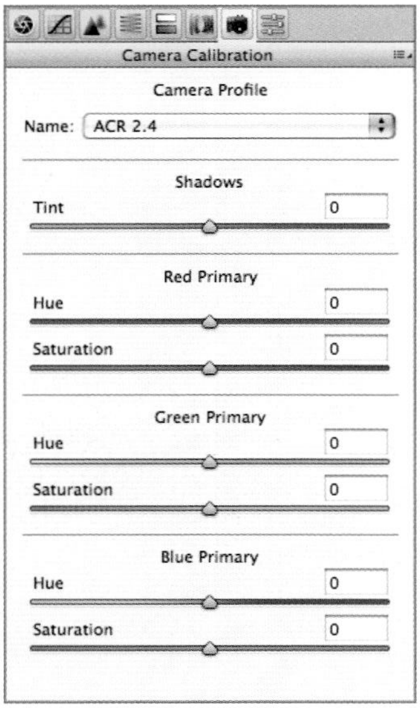

You can also use these sliders to add vignetting to your image (**Figures 8.60** and **8.61**), which will effectively darken the corners and edges of the image. Photographers often like that effect because it draws the viewer's attention toward the center of the image. I like to do that in combination with lowering the Saturation and Contrast sliders under the Adjust tab to simulate the look of an old faded photo (**Figure 8.62**).

The Camera Calibration Tab

The sliders under the Camera Calibration tab (**Figure 8.63**) allow you to change the way Photoshop interprets the color information that your camera delivers to Photoshop. You can use these settings to simulate different film types and to compensate for problems that come along with certain digital cameras.

You might find that certain models of digital cameras produce images that have an annoying color cast in the darkest areas of your image (**Figure 8.64**). If you have one of those cameras, just about every image you open will have a cast in the shadows of the image. The Tint slider

Figure 8.63 The settings found under the Calibrate tab allow you to change how Photoshop interprets the colors in your image.

in the Shadows section allows you to shift the color of the darkest areas of your image toward green or magenta (**Figure 8.65**).

Figure 8.64 Original image. (©2007 Ben Willmore)

Figure 8.65 Result of adjusting the Shadow Tint slider.

Figure 8.66 Original image.

If you find that you're simply not happy with the color that you get from your digital camera, you might want to experiment with the Red, Green, and Blue Hue and Saturation sliders. These sliders can also be used to simulate different film types (**Figures 8.66** and **8.67**). For instance, Fuji Velvia film delivers higher-contrast images with saturated colors, whereas Kodak Portra is fine-tuned to produce good-looking skin tones.

The red, green, and blue sliders will not change areas that are neutral gray. The red sliders will mainly affect the appearance of reds in your image and will affect yellow and magenta areas to a lesser extent. The green sliders will mainly affect the appearance of greens in your image and will affect cyan and yellow areas to a lesser extent. The blue sliders will mainly affect the appearance of blues in your image and will affect magenta and cyan areas to a lesser extent.

The Presets Tab

If you find yourself regularly making the same adjustments to your images—perhaps because your camera has certain characteristics that always need to be corrected in the same way—you might want to save your adjustments as a preset, so that you can easily apply it to images in the future.

A *preset* is simply a saved set of Camera Raw parameters that you can assign to any image.

Figure 8.67 Result of experimenting with the RGB settings.

Figure 8.68 You can create a new preset using this button at the bottom of the Presets tab.

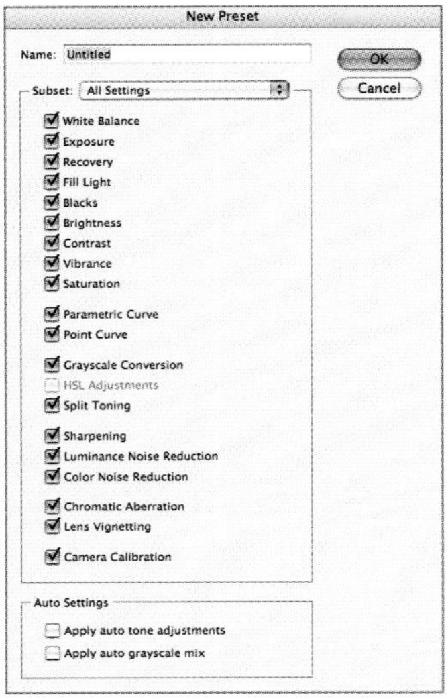

New Preset

Name: Untitled

Subset: All Settings

☑ White Balance
☑ Exposure
☑ Recovery
☑ Fill Light
☑ Blacks
☑ Brightness
☑ Contrast
☑ Vibrance
☑ Saturation

☑ Parametric Curve
☑ Point Curve

☑ Grayscale Conversion
☐ HSL Adjustments
☑ Split Toning

☑ Sharpening
☑ Luminance Noise Reduction
☑ Color Noise Reduction

☑ Chromatic Aberration
☑ Lens Vignetting

☑ Camera Calibration

Auto Settings
☐ Apply auto tone adjustments
☐ Apply auto grayscale mix

Figure 8.69 You can choose which parameters you want to store in a preset.

NOTES

The Camera Raw dialog box can be used as part of Photoshop or part of Bridge. When used within Bridge, Photoshop will be freed up for performing other tasks (like applying complex actions) while you adjust images within Bridge. Type Command/Ctrl-R to open raw files within Bridge instead of Photoshop.

To save a preset in Camera Raw, configure your parameters the way that you want them, then switch to the Presets tab and click the New Preset button at the bottom of the pane (**Figure 8.68**). Next, configure the New Preset dialog box (**Figure 8.69**) by selecting any items you want to save in your preset.

If you want your preset to use any of Camera Raw's auto-adjustment features, for example, turn on the Apply Auto Tone Adjustments check box. Then enter a name in the Name field and click OK.

To apply a preset to a raw file, open the image in Camera Raw, switch to the Presets tab and click the preset you'd like to apply.

Your image will be adjusted according to the settings saved in your selected preset.

Adjusting Multiple Images

To adjust multiple images in the Camera Raw dialog box, you'll first have to select more than one image in Adobe Bridge. Holding Command/Ctrl when clicking on images in Bridge adds those images to the ones that are currently selected. If you hold Shift, you'll end up selecting all the images that appear between the last one you clicked and the one you click next. When you have the images you'd like to adjust selected in Bridge, either double-click on one of the selected images (with no keys held) or type Command/Ctrl-O to open them in Camera Raw within Photoshop.

The images will appear as thumbnails down the left side of the Camera Raw dialog box (**Figure 8.70**). You can click between the thumbnails to view and adjust each image individually, or use the same keys used in Bridge to select multiple thumbnails. When multiple thumbnails are selected, a blue border appears around the thumbnail that is currently being viewed and any changes made to the sliders in Camera Raw will affect all the selected images. The Synchronize button above the thumbnail area presents you with a dialog box that allows you to copy some of the settings from the image you're currently viewing and apply them to all the selected images (**Figure 8.71**).

Figure 8.70 Multiple images appear as thumbnails in Camera Raw. (©2007 Ben Willmore)

Figure 8.71 Clicking the Synchronize button brings up this dialog box.

Finishing Touches

Camera Raw never makes any changes to your actual raw file. In fact, it's not possible to make changes to a raw file, because it doesn't contain any finished image data. So, the adjustments that you make in Camera Raw are stored separately from your image data. What's great about this scheme is that you can go back at any time and change your Camera Raw settings, and then reprocess your raw file. In this way, you can derive lots of different corrections from the same file.

By default, Camera Raw stores your changes in *Sidecar XMP files*. These are small text files that Camera Raw creates in the same directory as your original file. The advantage of sidecar files is that you can copy and move them along with the original raw file. The advantage of storing settings internally is that you don't have extra data to keep track of.

The next time you open a raw file that you've already edited, Camera Raw checks to see if there are any settings that have been assigned to that file. If there are, it automatically configures the Camera Raw controls to reflect those settings. You're then free to alter or change the settings.

271

After you're done adjusting your settings, you need to decide what you want Camera Raw to do. At the bottom of the dialog box you'll find four buttons:

▶ **Cancel:** This button discards any adjustments applied to the images and closes the Camera Raw dialog box.

▶ **Done:** This button saves your settings (in either the internal database or as a sidecar XMP file, depending on your settings) and then the raw file is closed.

▶ **Open Image:** This button does the same as the Done button, but also opens the image within Photoshop.

▶ **Save Image:** This button saves your settings, and then saves the selected images in one of four file formats without leaving the Camera Raw dialog box.

So, in general, click Cancel if you screw up and want to start over again, click Done if you want to keep the adjustments but don't need to open the image immediately, (if you're not planning on doing any more work in Photoshop at that point, you might just want to move on to your next raw file), and click Open if you want to work with the image right away in Photoshop. If you click the Save button in the Camera Raw dialog box, you'll be presented with another dialog box full of options (**Figure 8.72**). There are three main choices: where to save the images, what to name files, and which file format to use. When you click the Save button, you'll be returned to the Camera Raw dialog box and you'll see a progress report appear in the space above the Save button that indicates how many images have been saved and how many are still being processed.

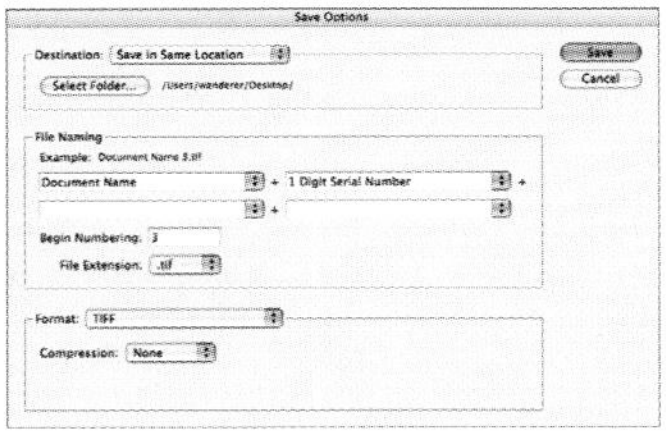

Figure 8.72 Clicking the Save button brings up this dialog box.

Closing Thoughts

At first glance, the Camera Raw dialog box may look like an unruly beast, and it may have taken me a couple dozen pages to describe all the settings available when working with raw files, but you should know that it usually only takes me about a minute to adjust most images. Once you've gone through the settings a few times, it should be the same for you.

Color Manipulation

Look at this chapter as a box chock-full of color manipulation tools and methods. There is no one all-purpose tool, because, as expected, Photoshop has provided an abundance of ways to shift the colors in your image. Which tool and method you use depends on what type of original image you have and what type of change you envision. This chapter is organized on a simple premise: I'll start with my personal favorites, and then progress into the less well-known methods that I don't use very often, but which, from time to time, can still be very effective.

Before we get to the fun stuff, you first need some basic knowledge about color because that is essential to understanding what's going on behind the scenes with Photoshop's color manipulation tools.

At the Core Is the Color Wheel

The vast majority of Photoshop's color controls are based on a classic color wheel (**Figure 9.1**). If you understand a few basic concepts about the color wheel, you'll be ahead of the game when it comes to controlling color in Photoshop.

Hue = Basic Color

Take another look at Figure 9.1 and you'll notice that only six basic colors are shown: cyan, blue, magenta, red, yellow, and green. That's because every color you could ever imagine is based on one of those colors or what you get in the transition between them. Take red, for example. Darken it and you get maroon, or make it less vivid and you'll have pink. But in the end both are just different versions of red.

Photoshop describes these basic colors, or hues, using numbers that it gets by figuring out how many degrees the color is from red going clockwise around a color wheel.

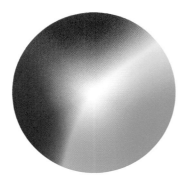

Figure 9.1 Most of Photoshop's color adjustment features are based on the color wheel.

If you divide the color wheel into sixths and start with red at 0, you'll find the other colors as follows: yellow at 60°, green at 120°, cyan at 180°, blue at 240°, and magenta at 300° (**Figure 9.2**). You don't have to remember any of those numbers, but it will be helpful to know that hue numbers in Photoshop are based on the color wheel. When you adjust the hue (using an adjustment like Hue/Saturation), you're effectively spinning the color wheel by moving each basic color in your image an equal amount (or angle) around the edge of the color wheel.

The other way you can shift the basic colors in your image is to push them toward one of the six primary colors that are found in the color wheel (using an adjustment like Color Balance). Red, green, and blue are the exact opposites of cyan, magenta, and yellow. Cyan ink's sole job in life is to absorb red light, magenta ink's job is to absorb green light, and yellow ink absorbs blue light. That's why you'll never find an adjustment that allows you to shift something toward cyan and red at the same time. They are opposites, so moving toward red automatically takes you away from cyan. When you push your image toward one of the primary colors, all the colors within the image shift in that direction and become more similar, whereas shifting the hue by spinning the color wheel leaves colors as different as they used to be and moves each one an equal distance around the color wheel.

Saturation = How Colorful

If you move from the outer ring of a color wheel toward the center, you'll notice that the colors mellow out and become much less colorful. In fact, the shades in the absolute center of the color wheel contain no color at all (they're gray). Photoshop describes how colorful something is by using percentages, and calls this property *saturation*. If something has no saturation at all (0%), then it has no color at all (no hint of any of the basic colors that show up around the outer edge of the color wheel), and therefore will only contain shades of gray. If, on the other hand, you have something that has 100% saturated colors, it will be as colorful as possible (just like the colors that appear on the outer rim of the color wheel).

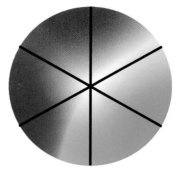

Figure 9.2 If you divide the color wheel into six equal parts, you'll find the primary colors that make up your image (RGB, CYM).

Figure 9.3 A three-dimensional color wheel would have dark colors at the bottom and bright colors at the top.

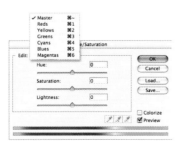

Figure 9.4 The Hue/Saturation dialog box.

Brightness/Lightness/Luminosity

The only things missing from our color wheel are the different brightness levels for all those colors. You could create a 3D color wheel in the shape of a cylinder with dark colors at its base and the brightest colors at the top (**Figure 9.3**). But because we'll probably never see anything that fancy in Photoshop, we'll just describe the brightness of a color using one of three words: brightness, lightness, and luminosity. Each of those words is just a slightly different way to describe how bright a color is, and as you become more traveled in Photoshop, you'll notice that Adobe can never seem to make up its mind on which one to use. So don't let all the terms confuse you, because they basically mean the same thing.

Every color you've ever seen in Photoshop can be described as a combination of hue, saturation, and brightness (HSB). You'll find me referring to that term every once in a while. The adjustments we'll be doing will end up shifting the colors in our image based on that color wheel. Most of what we do will result in either moving a color around the wheel to change its hue or shifting it toward another color by pushing it to the opposite side of the wheel. Now that you have a general idea of how to think about a color wheel, let's jump in and see how we can mess with the colors in our images.

The Hue/Saturation Dialog Box

Choose Hue/Saturation from the Adjustment Layer pop-up menu at the bottom of the Layers palette to get started. (The icon looks like a circle, half of which is filled with black.) That will create an adjustment layer and send you into the Hue/Saturation dialog box (**Figure 9.4**). You can make three types of changes with this type of an adjustment—changes to Hue, Saturation, and Lightness.

If you look at the bottom of the Hue/Saturation dialog box, you'll see two strips of color, which show you all the possible hues you can use in Photoshop. Those color strips are really just a standard color wheel that's been straightened out. The color on the far left is the same as the one

Figure 9.5 The original image.
(©2007 iStockphoto.com/ Terraxplorer)

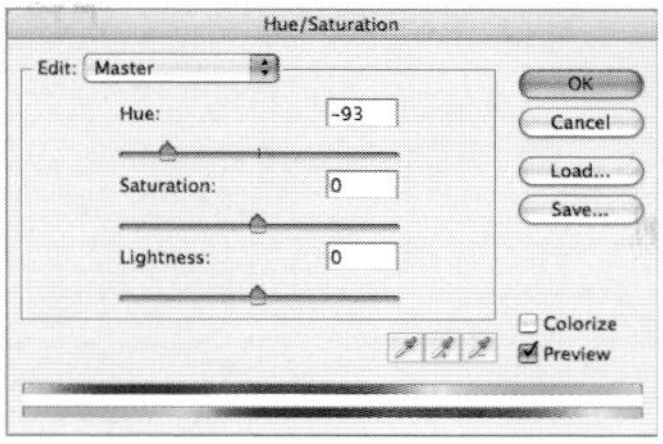

Figure 9.6 Moving the Hue slider
shifts all the hues in your image.

Figure 9.7 The result of applying the
adjustment shown in Figure 9.6.

on the far right, so you could easily bend it into a circle to make a color wheel. The Hue slider allows you to change the basic colors that make up your image. Go ahead and open any colorful image and move the Hue slider around to see what happens (**Figures 9.5** to **9.7**). The top strip of color indicates all the hues that you could possibly have in your image, whereas the bottom bar indicates what you've done to each of the hues. You can pick a color from the top strip and look straight down to the lower strip to figure out what Photoshop has done to it. For now, just remember that hue means basic color, and that the Hue slider changes the basic color of everything in your image. In a little while I'll show you how to get much more control over the specific colors in your image, but first we should look at the other two types of changes we can make with the Hue/Saturation dialog box.

Using the same photo, move the Saturation slider all the way to the left; your image should become completely black and white. Move the slider all the way to the right and all the colors in your image should become ridiculously vivid (**Figure 9.8**). Most images can use a modest saturation boost; for now that's all I'll say on the subject, but I'll get back to it in a little while.

The last control is a bit more straightforward than the other two, but you'll have to be very careful when you adjust the Lightness slider. Go ahead and slide it all the way

Figure 9.8 This image is divided in half; the left side shows the original image, and the right side shows what happens when you move the Saturation slider all the way to the right.
(©2007 iStockphoto.com/skodonnell)

to the left and then all the way to the right to see what happens to your image. You should end up with a solid black image at one extreme and a solid white one at the other. That's a pretty generic adjustment and can easily mess up your image (especially when applying it to the entire image). This slider becomes much more useful once we figure out how to isolate a range of color to adjust.

Isolating a Range of Colors

When the Edit pop-up menu at the top of the Hue/Saturation dialog box is set to Master, any change you make will affect all the colors in your image. If you'd rather have your changes affect only certain colors, choose a color from that pop-up menu before adjusting your image. Watch what happens to those two color strips at the bottom of the dialog box as you switch between the choices that are available from the Edit pop-up menu (**Figure 9.9**). The tiny sliders that show up indicate the range of colors that you'll be changing. The change will fully apply to the hues between the two vertical bars and then fade out near the hues that appear above the triangular sliders. The problem is that the Edit pop-up menu lists only six generic colors, and the color you need to isolate could be in between one of those colors.

Figure 9.9 Choosing a color from the Edit pop-up menu causes sliders to show up between the two strips of color.

To get around that limitation, all you have to do is move your mouse over the image and click on the color you would like to change. If you have changed the pop-up menu to a color other than Master, the sliders will center on the color you click on. The sliders should now be in the right position to work with that color. Go ahead and try it. Create a Hue/Saturation adjustment layer (by selecting Hue/Saturation from the Adjustment Layer pop-up menu at the bottom of the Layers palette), choose a color from the Edit pop-up menu, and then click on a color in your image before moving any of the sliders in that dialog box.

If you find that the sliders are wrapping around the ends of those color strips (which usually happens when working on cyan and green objects), you might want to "spin the color wheel." When that's the case, hold the Command/Ctrl key and move your mouse over the color strips until your cursor looks like a hand. Then drag left or right until the sliders end up near the middle of the Hue/Saturation dialog box.

If you really want to get precise control over the range of colors you're attempting to alter, you'll need to mess with those tiny sliders that appeared after you chose a color from the Edit pop-up menu. I like to start by smashing them together into one mass, which forces Photoshop to work on the narrowest range of colors possible. So go ahead and do that, and then, to make sure it's focusing on the right color, click on the color within your image that you want to change (remember that this centers the sliders on the color you click on). At this point, you probably can't tell if it's going to change a wide enough range of colors, so you can move the Saturation slider all the way to the left just to see what changes in your image. That will make parts of the image become black and white (**Figure 9.10**). If it's not working on a wide enough range of colors, hold down the Shift key and click on additional areas of the image (you can also click and drag across an area to get all the colors in an object). Shift-clicking spreads out the vertical sliders, causing Photoshop to work on a wider range of colors. If you accidentally click on a color that you don't want to shift, hold Option/Alt and click on that area again to remove it from the range of colors that are being adjusted (it will narrow the gap between the two vertical sliders). With the Saturation slider all the way to the left, you will have all the areas you want to shift showing up as black and white (**Figure 9.11**). Now move the Saturation slider back to the middle and mess with all three main sliders (Hue, Saturation, and Lightness) until you get the change you're looking for (**Figure 9.12**).

NOTES

I've found that it's much easier to isolate a range of colors when working in RGB mode instead of CMYK mode. In CMYK, I'll often Shift-click on an area and the sliders won't move the correct distance to affect the color I just clicked on. But, if I simply choose Image > Mode > RGB, I'll have no problem isolating the colors. If I really need to end up with a CMYK image, I'll just choose Image > Mode > CMYK after adjusting the image. If you used an adjustment layer to make the change, Photoshop prompts you to flatten the image when you convert it to CMYK mode. It does that because it cannot make the same change while the image is in CMYK, so it wants to permanently apply the change before converting. Just click Flatten when it prompts you; otherwise, your image will revert back to what it looked like before you adjusted it.

Figure 9.10 Clicking on the image and lowering the Saturation setting turns areas black and white. (©2007 Stockbyte, www.stockbyte.com)

Figure 9.11 Shift-click on additional colors until all the colors you'd like to shift become black and white.

Figure 9.12 Once you've isolated the range you'd like to change, move all three adjustment sliders to get to the color you desire.

Figure 9.13 You have to be careful working with colors that blend in with their surroundings. (©2007 Ben Willmore)

Figure 9.14 Moving the outer slider toward the color you need to blend into will fade the adjustment into those colors.

The eyedropper tools that show up near the lower right of the Hue/Saturation dialog box also control where the sliders appear. By default, the leftmost eyedropper will be active (as long as the Edit pop-up menu is set to a color, not Master). When you click on your image with that tool selected, you'll be centering the sliders on the color you clicked on. If you click on the plus eyedropper and then click on your image, it spreads out the vertical bar sliders to include the colors you click across (just like when we held Shift earlier). The minus eyedropper narrows the width between the vertical sliders and therefore narrows the range of colors that are being affected (just like when we Option/Alt-clicked earlier). I usually don't mess with those icons at all, preferring to use the keyboard commands I mentioned.

If the area you're trying to change is in motion, out of focus, or blends into the surrounding colors (**Figure 9.13**), you'll need to deal with the transition between it and its surroundings. To make the adjustment fade into the surrounding colors, move one or both of the triangular sliders away from the vertical bars and watch your image until the change smoothly blends into what's around the object you were attempting to adjust (**Figure 9.14**).

Now let's get to work and figure out specific uses for the Hue/Saturation dialog box.

Saturating Your World

Many images that come from a digital camera or flatbed scanner can benefit from a boost in saturation (**Figure 9.15**). For a general boost of color, I recommend making a Hue/Saturation adjustment layer and ratcheting up the Saturation slider until the colors in your image start to pop (**Figure 9.16**). When you do that, you'll probably notice that some colors become too vivid before others have reached their true potential. To avoid oversaturating, choose the color that's objectionable from the Edit pop-up menu, click on the color within your image to center the color isolation sliders, and then move the Saturation slider toward the left to mellow it out (**Figure 9.17**).

Figure 9.15 This image could use a saturation boost. (©2007 Andy Katz)

Figure 9.16 After saturating the image, the green areas are just too colorful.

Figure 9.17 After isolating the greens and lowering their saturation, the image looks great.

Enhancing Skies

If you've ever looked at a lot of photographs that contain blue skies, you might have noticed that many of those skies are actually closer to a light shade of cyan than a shade of true blue (**Figure 9.18**). If you like your skies to look as genuinely blue as possible, start by creating a Hue/Saturation adjustment layer and choose Blues from the Edit pop-up menu. Click somewhere within the sky to center the sliders and then make the following adjustment: Move the Lightness slider toward the left to darken the sky; move the Saturation slider toward the right to make the sky more colorful; and then experiment with the Hue slider until you get the best shade of blue (**Figures 9.19** and **9.20**).

Figure 9.18 This cyanish sky could use a tweak. (@2007 PhotoSpin, www.photospin.com)

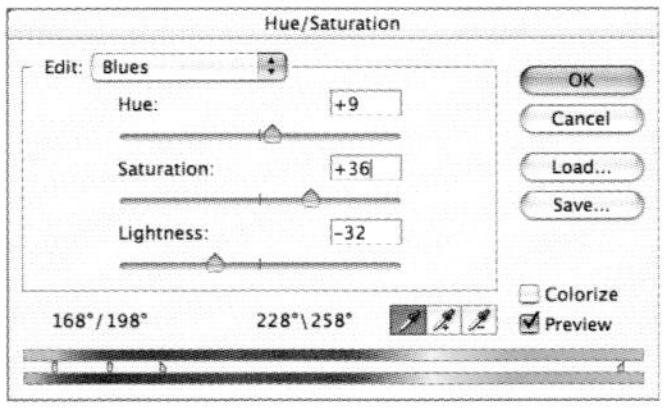

Figure 9.19 The Hue/Saturation adjustment used to produce Figure 9.20.

Figure 9.20 After adjusting the image with Hue/Saturation, the sky is true blue.

281

Figure 9.21 The original image. (©2007 PhotoSpin, www. photospin.com)

Figure 9.22 After adjusting the sky, areas of the foreground have shifted slightly.

The only problem with this technique is that you might run into an image that contains blue areas that are not part of the sky (**Figures 9.21** and **9.22**). If those are areas that you don't want to shift, you'll have to make changes after you're done creating the Hue/Saturation adjustment layer. If you look at an adjustment layer, you'll find that it contains a white rectangle just to the right of the adjustment layer icon for that layer. That rectangle is a layer mask, and it can be used to further limit the areas that your adjustment will apply to. All you have to do is grab the Paintbrush tool and paint with black at full opacity, and you'll prevent the adjustment from applying to the areas you paint over. As long as the Hue/Saturation adjustment layer is active in your Layers palette, the paint you apply will affect where the adjustment applies. Painting with black hides the adjustment; painting with white brings it back. So, after enhancing a sky, you might want to grab a large, soft-edged brush and paint with black over any areas that you want to preserve (**Figure 9.23**).

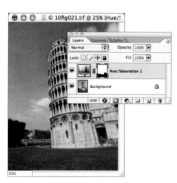

Figure 9.23 Painting with black on the layer mask of the adjustment layer prevents the adjustment from applying to the bottom of the image

Color to Grayscale

In Photoshop CS3, the best way to convert a color image to a grayscale image (what is traditionally known as "black and white") is to use the new Black and White adjustment (Image > Adjustments > Black and White). As you spend more time with Photoshop, you'll come across more and more methods for black and white conversion, from the Channel Mixer, to desaturations, and more. But the Black and White adjustment is such a powerful tool, and so easy to use, that there's really no reason to use any other technique.

Best of all, the Black and White adjustment can be applied as an adjustment layer, so you get all of the advantages of adjustment layers (which we'll learn more about in the next chapter) for your grayscale conversions.

The Black and White dialog box is really a souped-up Channel Mixer. The options here let you specify exactly how you want particular color ranges in your image to be converted to grayscale (**Figure 9.24**).

The sliders are very easy to use. If you move the Yellows slider to the right, for example, the yellow tones in your image will be represented by lighter shades of gray; move the slider to the left, and the yellow will darken. The same is true for all the other sliders (**Figure 9.25**).

Figure 9.24 Photoshop's Black and White conversion dialog box.

Figure 9.25 As you move the sliders in the Black and White dialog box, the corresponding colors in your grayscale image become lighter or darker. (©2007 Ben Long)

283

The Black and White dialog box functions very differently from the Channel Mixer. In the Channel Mixer, if you increase the percentage of the red channel, the red values of every pixel in your image increase, so colors that have red components brighten (**Figure 9.26**). The Black and White dialog box is much smarter than that. If you increase the Reds setting, only those tones in your image that are truly red increase.

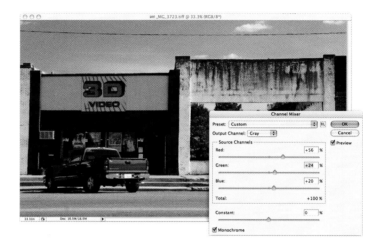

Figure 9.26 With the Channel Mixer, moving a slider changes that component of every color in the image.

Consequently, unlike the Channel Mixer, with the Black and White adjustment you don't have to worry about the total percentage values of your image. If the totals add up to more than 100 percent, you won't see a change in over-all exposure in your image.

Also note that the sliders aren't interrelated. If you want to increase blue, you don't need to decrease yellow too. The control is smart enough to know which pixels need to be affected by a particular edit.

If the total percentage value of all the sliders is greater than 100, your image will end up with a brighter exposure than when you started. A total value lower than 100 will result in a darker image.

The Auto button performs an automatic conversion and is well worth experimenting with. The Auto algorithm does a very good job of mapping different colors to different tones to produce a nice contrasty image.

Tinting

The Black and White dialog box also includes tinting con-trols, so you can perform black-and-white conversion and color toning in one step (**Figure 9.27**).

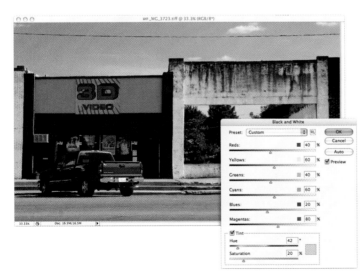

Figure 9.27 The tint controls in the Black and White adjustment let you perform grayscale conversion and tinting in one step.

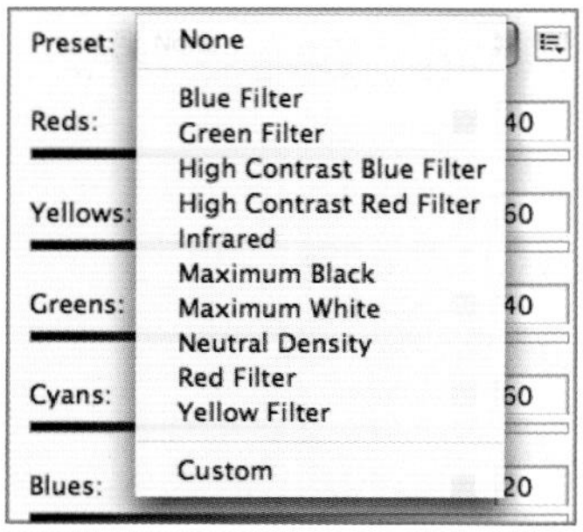

Figure 9.28 The Black and White dialog box is equipped with several Preset configurations.

Figure 9.29 When you first turn on the Colorize check box, the color you'll get is based on your foreground color. (©2007 Stockbyte, www.stockbyte.com)

Turn on the Tint check box to activate the tint controls; then select the hue that you want to tint with and adjust the Saturation slider to specify the strength of the tint.

Presets

The Black and White dialog box is equipped with several Preset configurations (**Figure 9.28**). In addition, you can save your own presets by using the Save and Load pop-up menu located to the immediate right of the Preset menu.

Colorizing Grayscale Photos

If you enjoy the look of hand-tinted photographs but don't want to deal with the chemicals and mess that are usually involved, you might get excited about colorizing your images with a mouse.

There are many ways to colorize a black and white image. You can use a Hue/Saturation adjustment layer to add color to a black and white image. I recommend starting out with this technique because it gives you lots of flexibility to tweak later. All you have to do is choose Image > Mode > RGB, select one of the areas you'd like to add color to, and create a Hue/Saturation adjustment layer. With this choice, you'll first need to turn on the Colorize check box, which should shift the selected area to a color similar to your foreground color (**Figure 9.29**). When the color has been applied, you can adjust the Hue setting to cycle through the full spectrum of colors. Once you've chosen the basic color, you can adjust the Saturation setting to control how vivid the color is, and change the Lightness setting to determine how dark the area should be (**Figure 9.30**).

With this select-and-adjust approach, you'll need to create a new adjustment layer for each color you'd like to use (**Figure 9.31**). After you've created an adjustment layer, you can fine-tune the result by painting on the adjustment layer's mask with black or white while the adjustment layer is active. Painting with white causes the adjustment to apply to a larger area of the image, whereas black limits which areas get adjusted. If you find that the color is too intense, simply paint with a shade of gray on the adjustment layer, which causes the adjustment to apply in differing amounts.

Figure 9.30 You can fine-tune the color by adjusting the Hue, Saturation, and Lightness sliders.

The darker the shade of gray, the less the adjustment will apply. You can also double-click the thumbnail icon for the adjustment layer (to the left of the name of the layer) to modify the settings that are being applied.

What you want to watch out for with this type of adjustment is that there will usually be way too much color in the darkest and brightest areas of your image (**Figure 9.32**). To limit the amount of color applied to these areas, you'll need to use the blending sliders by choosing Layer > Layer Style > Blending Options while the adjustment layer is active. Then pull in the lower-left slider in the Blend If area until you notice all the color disappearing from the darkest areas of your image. You don't want to completely remove the color, so hold the Option/Alt key and pull on the left edge of the slider that you just moved until you get a smooth transition in the shadow areas of your image. Then, before you click OK, move the right slider a short distance and then Option/Alt-drag its right edge until the color blends into the brightest parts of the image. With a little experimentation, you'll be able to find the setting that looks best for your image (**Figures 9.33** and **9.34**).

Figure 9.31 As you apply color to more and more areas, you'll end up with a lot of adjustment layers.

NOTES

I'll show you another method for colorizing grayscale images when we talk about the Color Replacement Brush and Match Color command later in this chapter.

Figure 9.32 There is too much color in the darkest areas of this image. (©2007 Stockbyte, www.stockbyte.com)

Figure 9.33 These are the blending slider settings used to create Figure 9.34.

Figure 9.34 After reducing the amount of color in the shadow areas, the image looks more realistic.

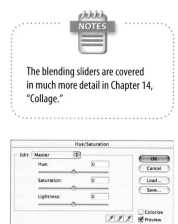

The blending sliders are covered in much more detail in Chapter 14, "Collage."

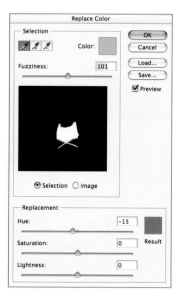

Figure 9.35 When returning to an adjustment layer, look at the color bars at the bottom and try to figure out which color you adjusted previously (yellow, in this case).

Figure 9.36 The Replace Color dialog box is a combination of the Color Range command and the Hue/Saturation dialog box.

Digging a Little Deeper

If you ever need to go back to re-edit a Hue/Saturation adjustment layer that you created earlier, you'll need to be extra careful. You can double-click the adjustment layer icon on the left side of the adjustment layer to change the adjustment. But, before you start to make changes, you'll need to choose the same color you originally chose from the Edit pop-up menu; otherwise, any changes you make will affect the entire image because the Edit pop-up menu will be set to Master. If you can't remember which color you worked on previously, glance at the color strips at the bottom of the dialog box to see if you can figure out which areas in the bottom strip are different than the top one (**Figure 9.35**). Then look at the top strip directly above that area to figure out which color to choose from the Edit pop-up menu. Once you choose the proper color from that pop-up menu, Photoshop will get you back to adjusting the specific color you isolated when you originally created the adjustment layer.

Moving the Saturation slider too far to the right can end up distorting the relationship between the colors in your image. As one color reaches its maximum saturation, it simply can't become more saturated, but the other colors in the image will continue to become more vivid as you move the Saturation slider farther toward the right. You can figure out the maximum saturation boost to give your image without distorting the relationship between the colors by paying attention to what happens in the Info Palette. Just choose Window > Info, and then click the eyedropper icon in that palette and choose HSB. Then, when you're increasing the saturation of your image, move your cursor over the most saturated areas of your image and make sure to stop increasing the saturation once you see that the "S" (Saturation) number in the HSB part of the Info Palette reaches 100%. If you go any further than that, you'll be distorting the relationship between colors in your image.

Replacing Color

If you like the general ideas we just worked with but didn't have complete success isolating areas based on hues, you might want to try choosing Image > Adjustments > Replace Color (**Figure 9.36**). In essence, Replace Color combines the Color Range command (Select > Color Range) that we talked about back in Chapter 2, "Selection Primer," with the same color shifting controls that are found in the Hue/Saturation dialog box. The one advantage of using the Replace Color command is that instead of having to figure out the exact Hue/Saturation/Lightness settings necessary to get the result you're looking for, you can define the color you'd like to end up with by clicking the color swatch that shows up in the lower right of the dialog box. But unfortunately, Replace Color is not available as an adjustment layer, so I don't use it all that often. I prefer to use the Color Range command (Select > Color Range) and then create a Hue/Saturation adjustment layer because I find it gives me much more flexibility if I ever need to fine-tune things after the initial adjustment.

Both Hue/Saturation and Replace Color effectively rotate the color wheel to shift the colors in your image. Now let's take a look at how we can shift the general color of an image toward one of the primary colors (red, yellow, green, cyan, blue, magenta).

Variations

If you like simple and easy features, you'll enjoy using the Variations command (Image > Adjustments > Variations) (**Figure 9.37**). It starts off with your original image in the middle of a seven-image cluster. When you click one of the surrounding images, it replaces the one in the middle and repopulates the surrounding views with new alternatives (**Figure 9.38**). You can control how different the alternatives are from the center image by adjusting the Fine/Coarse slider in the upper right of the dialog box. This type of adjustment will concentrate on either the brightest areas of the image (known as Highlights), the middle brightness levels (known as Midtones), or the dark areas of the image (known as Shadows). You can adjust all three areas in one adjustment, but you'll have to choose them one at a time and make an adjustment before clicking OK. After you've made a change to the image, you'll be able to compare the original to your current selection by comparing the two images that appear in the upper left of the dialog box.

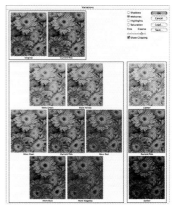

Figure 9.37 The Variations dialog box presents you with simple previews of multiple adjustments. (©2007 PhotoSpin, www.photospin.com)

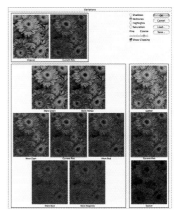

Figure 9.38 After you click on one of the choices, the surrounding views repopulate with new choices.

You can change the brightness and saturation of your image using Variations. However, I find that Levels and Curves are far superior for adjusting the brightness, and I prefer to use Hue/Saturation to adjust saturation because I can have much more control over which colors become saturated.

If you notice intense colors showing up in areas where they don't belong (**Figure 9.39**), that's most likely Photoshop stepping in to warn you that you might be losing detail in that area. If you'd rather not see those unusual colors, turn off the Show Clipping check box near the upper right of the dialog box.

I mainly use Variations for very basic chores where I prefer a simple visual interface, the most common of which would be to tint a grayscale photo. All I have to do is change the mode of the image to RGB (Image > Mode > RGB) and then I can go to Variations and click away until I get the color tinting I desire (**Figure 9.40**).

Figure 9.39 If you ever see very out of place colors, it's usually an indication that clipping has occurred, which is a sign that you might be losing detail in those areas. (©2007 Stockbyte, www.stockbyte.com)

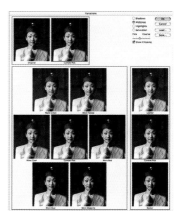

Figure 9.40 Adding color to a grayscale image is easy with Variations. (©2007 Stockbyte, www.stockbyte.com)

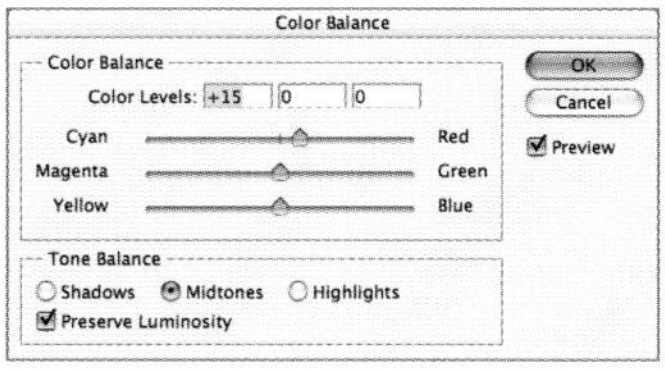

Figure 9.41 The Color Balance dialog box is a good alternative to Variations.

Color Balance

Most of the time, I pass over Variations in favor of the Color Balance command (**Figure 9.41**) because it's available as an adjustment layer, which makes future changes much easier. Just like in Variations, the Color Balance dialog box allows you to shift the color of the Highlights, Midtones, or Shadows toward one of the primary colors; the only difference is that you'll have to look at the main screen to get a preview. Moving a slider to +15 or −15 is approximately the same as making one click in the Variations dialog box with the default setting on the Fine/Coarse slider. But because you're not forced to make adjustments in preset increments, I feel that it's much easier to be precise with this feature than with Variations.

Both Variations and Color Balance effectively shift the colors of your image toward one side of the color wheel. It's almost as if you start at the center of the color wheel and then shift toward one of the primary colors (**Figure 9.42**). All the colors in the image move toward that color, whereas Hue/Saturation and Replace Color spin the color wheel, which shifts all the colors in unusual ways (not just toward one particular color). There are a bunch of other commands that allow you to shift toward cyan or red, magenta or green, and yellow or blue in a less obvious way. Let's take a look at a few of the adjustments that allow you to work with those primary colors.

Figure 9.42 Color Balance pushes the colors in your image toward one of the primary colors.

Levels/Curves

Choosing Image > Adjustments > Curves allows you to pick between red, green, and blue, or cyan, magenta, and yellow (depending on which mode your image is in) in the Channel pop-up menu (**Figure 9.43**). When you work on the Red channel, you'll be able to shift the overall color of your image toward either red or cyan by moving the curve up or down. If you work on the Green channel, you'll be able to shift toward green and magenta, and the Blue channel allows you to shift toward blue and yellow.

I find that it's most effective if you Command/Ctrl-click on the area of the image you'd like to concentrate your adjustment on. That will add a point to the curve in the specific location needed to accurately focus on the area you clicked. Once you've done that, you can use the up and down arrow keys to shift the colors toward one of the primary colors (which one will depend on the choice you made from the Channel pop-up menu) (**Figure 9.44**).

Figure 9.43 Move the curve up or down to push the colors in your image toward or away from the color you choose in the Channel pop-up menu. (©2007 PhotoSpin, www. photospin.com)

Figure 9.44 Command-click on your image to add a point to the curve, then use the up/down arrows to shift the color. (©2007 PhotoSpin, www. photospin.com)

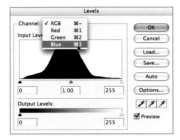

Figure 9.45 You can also use Levels to make adjustments similar to what we did with Curves.

Figure 9.46 The original image. (©2007 PhotoSpin, www.photospin.com)

Figure 9.47 Using Auto Color to shift the image toward warm tones.

Figure 9.48 Click No or you'll introduce a color cast to every image you adjust with Auto Color.

You can make similar changes using the Levels command (Image > Adjustments > Levels). It also allows you to choose from the channels that make up your image (RGB or CMYK) (**Figure 9.45**). With an image in RGB mode, moving any of the upper sliders toward the left will push the color of your image toward the color you have chosen from the Channel pop-up menu. Moving the sliders toward the right will shift the colors toward the opposite of that color.

Auto Color

I often get frustrated when attempting to make generic color shifts using Levels or Curves because the image can change in unexpected ways (due to the fact that you're not just controlling the highlight/midtones/shadows like many other adjustments). If I'm having trouble getting the overall look I was aiming for, I'll end up clicking the Options button in either Levels or Curves, which sends me into the Auto Color Correction Options dialog box. I like to set the Algorithms setting to Enhance Monochromatic Contrast so I don't get rid of color in the highlights or shadows of the image. Then, to shift the overall color of the image, I turn on the Snap Neutral Midtones check box and click on the color swatch that appears next to the word Midtones. It should start with gray, but if you shift that color toward another color, the general atmosphere of the photo should change as you introduce a color cast (**Figures 9.46** and **9.47**). That's great for changing the overall feeling of a photo to make it appear more warm (toward red/orange) or cool (toward blue/cyan).

When you click OK in both the Auto Color dialog box and Levels, you'll be asked if you'd like to use the new target colors as the default (**Figure 9.48**). I'd click No unless you plan on shifting the overall look of a large number of photos. Otherwise, when you use Auto Color for color correction (as mentioned in Chapter 7, "Color Correction"), it will introduce color casts instead of getting rid of them.

Figure 9.49 This image has a desirable color cast. (©2007 Stockbyte, www.stockbyte.com)

Figure 9.50 This image is more neutral than the one in Figure 10.49. (©2007 Stockbyte, www.stockbyte.com)

Figure 9.51 When the two images are combined, they don't look like they belong together.

I also like to use Auto Color when combining two images that differ in general color (**Figures 9.49** and **9.50**). If one image has what I like to call a desirable color cast (fireplace, sunset, and candlelight are examples) and the other does not, they will not look like they belong together (**Figure 9.51**). I want Photoshop to transfer the desirable color cast to the second image by analyzing what's going on in the brightest and darkest areas of the image (because a color cast contaminates those areas that otherwise would not contain any color). To accomplish that, I'll place each image side by side so I can see both documents at the same time. Then, with the image that doesn't have a color cast active, I'll choose Image > Adjustments > Curves, click the Options button, and then set the Algorithms setting to Find Dark & Light Colors and turn off the Snap Neutral Midtones check box (**Figure 9.52**). Now all we have to do is plug in the right colors in the Highlights and Shadows areas. Click on the Shadows color swatch to access the Color Picker, and then move your mouse over the image that contains the desirable color cast and click on the darkest area of the image (**Figure 9.53**). Next, click on the Highlights color swatch to access the Color Picker once again, and this time click on the brightest area of the image that contains the desirable color cast (**Figure 9.54**) (but avoid areas that are blown out to pure white) and then click OK. That should change the color of the active photo so that it will have a color cast similar to the second image (**Figure 9.55**).

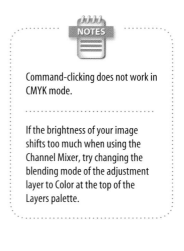

Figure 9.52 These are the Auto Settings I use for matching two images.

NOTES

Command-clicking does not work in CMYK mode.

If the brightness of your image shifts too much when using the Channel Mixer, try changing the blending mode of the adjustment layer to Color at the top of the Layers palette.

Figure 9.53 Click on the Shadows swatch and then click on the darkest part of the image that has the color cast.

Figure 9.54 Click on the Highlights swatch and then click on the brightest area of the image.

Figure 9.55 After adjusting the color, the two images have similar color qualities.

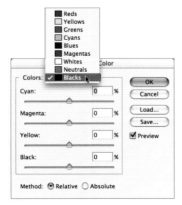

Figure 9.56 With Selective Color you can push certain colors toward any of the primary colors.

Selective Color

Auto Color isn't the only way to force colors into the brightest, darkest, and neutral gray areas of an image. If you choose Image > Adjustments > Selective Color, you can select which general colors you'd like to change from the Colors pop-up menu and then shift them toward a primary color (**Figure 9.56**). Moving the sliders toward the right shifts the selected color toward the color listed to the left of the slider. Moving the slider toward the left shifts it away from the color listed and toward its exact opposite. So, even though this dialog box only lists cyan, magenta, yellow, and black, you can still shift things toward red, green, and blue by moving the sliders toward the left. If the Relative radio button is turned on, you'll change areas relative to what they started at. That means that if you have 50% cyan and you move the Cyan slider to 10%, you'll end up with 55% cyan because 10% of 50% is 5%. If, on the other hand, you use the Absolute setting, you'll simply add the exact amount that you dial in. That means that if you have 50% cyan and you move the Cyan slider to 10%, you'll end up with 60% cyan because it added the exact amount of cyan that you dialed in.

One nice aspect of Selective Color is that you can shift the color of the blacks in your image. All you have to do is choose Blacks from the Colors pop-up menu, move the Black slider toward the left to lighten the area, and then move whichever color sliders you'd like to use toward the right to push color into those areas (**Figures 9.57** to **9.58**). Or, if you're working in CMYK mode, you can make the black areas of your image richer by moving the Cyan slider toward the right. This adjustment is commonly used when creating large areas of black in an image that will be printed on a commercial printing press. I often like to have at least 40% cyan in those areas.

You can also use Selective Color to brighten the highlights in your image by choosing Whites from the Colors menu and then moving the Cyan, Magenta, and Yellow sliders toward the left (**Figures 9.59** to **9.61**). This change can be useful for metallic objects where the brightest areas need to be pure white in order to make the object appear to be highly polished and therefore shiny.

Figure 9.57 The original image. (©2007 Stockbyte, www.stockbyte.com)

Figure 9.58 Using Selective Color you can shift the color of black areas.

Figure 9.59 The original image. (©2007 Stockbyte, www.stockbyte.com)

Figure 9.60 After adjusting the Whites, the highlights are much brighter, making the object look more polished.

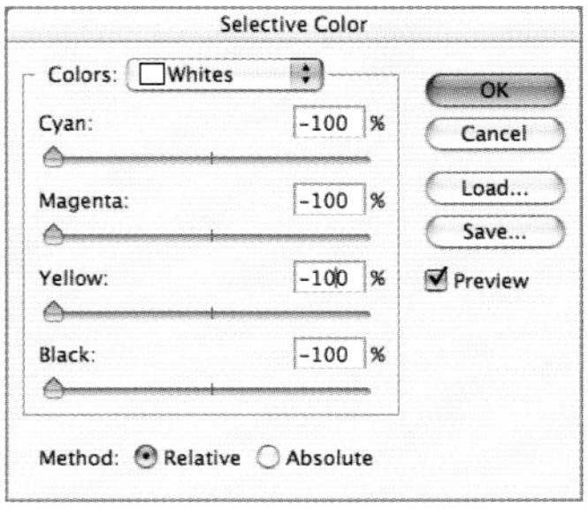

Figure 9.61 The Selective Color adjustment used to brighten the highlights.

Figure 9.62 This is the image that I'd like to match. (©2007 Andy Katz)

Figure 9.63 This is the image that needs adjusting. (©2007 Andy Katz)

Figure 9.64 The Match Color dialog box.

Match Color

Match Color attempts to match the general color and contrast of two images. Let's start off with simple examples and then progress into more complex and unusual solutions.

Let's say you have two images, one of which has a very warm feeling and the other of which is rather neutral. But both images have somewhat similar content color and contrast (**Figures 9.62** and **9.63**). In order to match the general feeling of the two images, you need to first open both images, then click on the image you'd like to change and choose Image > Adjustments > Match Color (**Figure 9.64**). At the bottom of the Match Color dialog box, change the Source pop-up menu to the name of the image to which you'd like to match the color. If the image contains adjustment layers, be sure to choose Merged from the Layer pop-up menu. That's all there is to it (**Figure 9.65**)!

Figure 9.65 The result of matching the color between the two images

If you find that the results are less than stellar, you'll need to give Photoshop a little help to better match the images. Go back to the image you like and select an area that contains the most important information that defines the general look of the image (**Figure 9.66**). Then switch back to the photo you'd like to change and make a selection of the areas that define the general look of that image (**Figure 9.67**). When you get to the Match Color dialog box, turn on the two check boxes near the bottom so Photoshop refers to only the selected area of each image when attempting to match the color. You will probably also want to turn on the Ignore Selection When Applying Adjustment check box so that Photoshop can adjust the entire image while comparing the selected areas in the two images (**Figures 9.68** and **9.69**).

Figure 9.66 Select the area of the reference photo you want to match. (©2007 Stockbyte, www.stockbyte.com)

After you've produced an acceptable match between the two images, you might want to adjust the Image Options to fine-tune the end result. The Luminance slider will change the brightness of the image, whereas the Color Intensity slider will control how saturated the colors are. If you don't want to precisely match the reference photo, but would like to instead head in that general direction, try increasing the Fade setting. If you set the Fade setting to 100, you'll see the original unchanged image (plus any Luminance and Color Intensity adjustments). By lowering the Fade setting, you can start to push the image toward the look of the reference image. Just move the Fade slider around until you like the amount of change you are getting.

Figure 9.67 Select the area of the image you want to adjust that should look like the reference photo. (©2007 Stockbyte, www.stockbyte.com)

Figure 9.68 The result of matching two images without a selection.

Figure 9.69 The result of matching two images using a selection.

Figure 9.70 The original image has a blue cast. (©2007 Stockbyte, www. stockbyte.com)

Figure 9.71 After neutralizing the cast, the image looks less blue.

Figure 9.72 Make a selection on the reference photograph to indicate the color you'd like to match. (©2007 Stockbyte, www.stockbyte.com)

On occasion, you might need to adjust a multitude of images to match a single source image. When that's the case, set the Source menu to the name of the image you want to match, then click the Save Statistics button and name that preset. Now, at any time in the future, you can click the Load button to use the general feeling of that photo again even though Photoshop won't need to open the file itself. I have a bunch of these files saved—one for warm sunset-like images, another for cool water-like images, and yet another for high contrast, less colorful images. That way I can quickly get a certain effect without having to remember which photo I originally matched.

Now the Match Color dialog box might be designed to match two photographs, but that doesn't mean that it's not useful on single images. Just set the Source pop-up menu to None and then mess with the Image Options settings. You might just find that you prefer the Color Intensity setting over the Saturation setting that is found in the Hue/Saturation dialog box.

If you have an image that has an obvious color cast, like one taken underwater, for example (**Figure 9.70**), you might want to try turning on the Neutralize check box. That will cause the Match Color dialog box to attempt to color correct the image. The results aren't always perfect, but it's often a good start for those images that have massive colorcasts (**Figure 9.71**).

I also like to use the Match Color command to colorize grayscale photographs. I'll open a full-color reference photo, select an area (like an area of skin that contains both bright and dark areas) so Photoshop knows what I'd like to match to (**Figure 9.72**). Then, I'll switch to the grayscale photo, and choose Image > Mode > RGB so that it's in a mode that can contain color. Now I make a very precise selection of the area I'd like to add color to (like all the skin in the image) and choose Image > Adjustments > Match Color. To make sure Photoshop thinks only about the selected areas, I'd turn on the two check boxes at the bottom of the dialog box and turn off the check box at the top. This often produces a result that is superior to what you'd get with other tools because instead of applying a generic color across the entire area, it will usually apply a slightly different color to the bright and dark areas of an object (**Figure 9.73**).

Red Eye Tool

Photoshop's Red Eye tool (which is grouped with the Healing brush and Path tool) is designed to quickly and easily remove red eye (**Figure 9.74**). All you have to do is click near the eye and Photoshop will search for the closest red circle, remove all the color, and then darken the area. This tool is only sensitive to red areas and therefore is not useful for the green or orange eyes that often result from animals being photographed using an on-camera flash (in those cases, use the Color Replacement tool, which is coming up next in this chapter).

Figure 9.73 Convert the grayscale image to RGB mode, make a precise selection, and then match the color.

Figure 9.74 The Red Eye Tool has only two settings available in the options bar.

The Darken Amount setting determines how dark the pupil will become (**Figure 9.75**). If you find your results are looking solid black, you might want to choose Edit > Undo, use a lower Darken Amount setting, and then try again.

Low Pupil Size settings usually produce more detail in the pupil of the eye, whereas higher settings leave little or no detail. I find that settings between 10 and 20 usually produce an acceptable amount of detail and settings of 50 or above produce an almost solid black pupil.

Figure 9.75 Darken Amount settings from left to right: 10%, 40%, 80% (note: I've increased the contrast of these images to make the differences more obvious since the onscreen difference is rather subtle and might be difficult to see in printed form).

Color Replacement Tool

The Color Replacement tool allows you to quickly paint across an area and change its color. What's really nice about this tool is that you don't have to be overly precise with your painting because you're only going to affect the area you paint across. That's because Photoshop will replace only the colors that you mouse over with the cross-hair that shows up in the center of your brush cursor.

When you paint, Photoshop uses your foreground color to change what's in the active layer based on the choice you've made in the Mode pop-up menu in the options bar at the top of your screen (**Figure 9.76**):

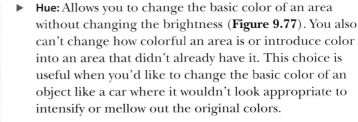

Figure 9.76 The options bar determines how the Color Replacement tool will interact with your image.

Figure 9.77 I created this two-tone car (the original was red) with five clicks of the mouse button and a soft-edged brush. (©2007 PhotoSpin, www.photospin.com)

▶ **Hue:** Allows you to change the basic color of an area without changing the brightness (**Figure 9.77**). You also can't change how colorful an area is or introduce color into an area that didn't already have it. This choice is useful when you'd like to change the basic color of an object like a car where it wouldn't look appropriate to intensify or mellow out the original colors.

▶ **Saturation:** Allows you to make an area as colorful as your foreground color. It does not allow you to change the basic color or brightness of an area. I love to use this option to remove the color from certain areas of a photo. I love that I don't have to be all that careful when I'm painting because it uses the same technology as the Background Eraser. To force areas to black and white, just paint with black, white, or any shade of gray. Your foreground color doesn't contain any color, so the area you end up painting over will have all its color removed (**Figures 9.78** and **9.79**).

Figure 9.78 The original image. (©2007 Ben Willmore)

Figure 9.79 I removed the color from the background using Saturation mode and painting with black.

▶ **Color:** Allows you to change both the basic color and the saturation of the color, but will not allow you to change the brightness. In essence, it applies the color you are painting with to the brightness of the original image. This choice is useful when you need to push a lot of color into an area that didn't have much color to begin with. An example would be a dark brown field that should look green. Just paint with a relatively vivid version of green so the field becomes much more colorful than it was in the original image (**Figure 9.80**).

Figure 9.80 The left side of this image was changed by painting with green in Color mode. (©2007 Andy Katz)

▶ **Luminosity:** Allows you to change the brightness of an area to match the brightness of the color you are painting with. This mode will not allow you to shift the colors at all. I don't use this option very often, but it can be helpful if you need to fix green or orange-eye that's common in animals. I just choose a very dark color that's almost black and then click in the center of the eye (**Figure 9.81**).

If you find that you're having trouble getting good results with this tool, you'll want to learn more about the setting that determines which areas are changed and which are ignored. This tool uses the same technology as the Background Eraser tool, which we'll cover in detail in Chapter 13, "Advanced Masking." So go check out that chapter and then come back and try these ideas again.

This tool applies your foreground color to the active layer, so you should know that you could change your foreground color by holding the Option/Alt key and clicking on your image.

Figure 9.81 A single click on one of the eyes reduced the orange-eye problem. (©2007 Kristine Evans)

Channel Mixer

So far, most of the adjustments we've talked about have been relatively straightforward. You usually tell Photoshop what you want to change (midtones, highlights, and so on) and then tell it what you'd like to shift them toward. But the Channel Mixer is a different beast (**Figure 9.82**). It forces you to think about how Photoshop works behind the scenes. The Channel Mixer lets you literally mix the contents of the channels that show up in the Channels palette (Window > Channels).

Figure 9.82 The Channel Mixer dialog box.

When you choose Image > Adjustments > Channel Mixer, you can choose the channel you'd like to affect from the Output Channel pop-up menu. Then you can move the Source Channels sliders to brighten or darken the output channel. Because RGB mode creates your image out of red, green, and blue light, moving sliders toward the right will add more light and therefore brighten the output channel based on the contents of the channel whose slider you moved. Moving the slider in the opposite direction will reduce the amount of light being applied to the output channel. CMYK mode creates your image out of four colors of ink, so moving a slider toward the right will add additional ink to the output channel, thereby darkening it. Moving a slider to the left in CMYK mode will lessen the amount of ink in the output channel, effectively brightening it. This might sound complicated at first, but once you see a few examples, you should start to see the simplicity behind it.

Let's say you have a CMYK mode image of a banana (**Figure 9.83**) and you'd like to reproduce it using only two colors of ink. That way you could save money and show off to your friends that you've really mastered Photoshop. Well, because most bananas are yellow, I think we'll end up using yellow ink for the banana, and then we'll use some black ink so we can get shadows that are darker than the yellow ink. I'd start by choosing Image > Adjustments > Channel Mixer, and then I'd choose Cyan from the Output Channel pop-up menu and move the Cyan Source Channels slider all the way to the left to indicate that you don't want to use any of what was originally in the Cyan channel (**Figure 9.84**). Then choose Magenta from the Output pop-up menu and move the Magenta slider all the way to the left to clear out the Magenta channel (**Figure 9.85**). Now the image should be made out of just yellow and black ink, but it most likely looks quite light because there's not enough black ink to compensate for not using any cyan or magenta ink. To fix that, choose Black from the Output Channel pop-up menu, and then slide the Cyan and Magenta sliders toward the right until the brightness looks as close to the original as you can get (**Figure 9.86**). (Turn the Preview check box off and back on again to compare the original

Figure 9.83 The original banana image is in CMYK mode. (©2007 PhotoSpin, www.photospin.com)

to the end result.) Once you have it as close as you can get to the look of the original, click OK and then drag the Cyan and Magenta channels to the trash at the bottom of the Channels palette. Finally, to get a more appropriate shade of yellow, double-click to the right of the name of the Yellow channel in the Channels palette so you can pick a new color and experiment until the image looks the best it can (**Figure 9.87**). If you'd like to know more about reproducing images using inks other than CMYK, be sure to check out the "Spot Color" section in the bonus chapter "Channels," on the CD at the back of the book.

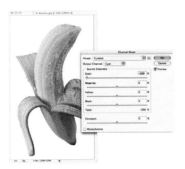

Figure 9.84 Moving the Cyan slider all the way to the left will remove all cyan from the image.

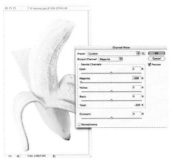

Figure 9.85 Moving the Magenta slider all the way to the left will remove all magenta from the image.

Figure 9.86 Adding what used to be in the Cyan and Magenta channels to the Black channel will compensate for using fewer inks.

Now that you've seen one example, let's use the Channel Mixer to convert a full-color image into a grayscale one. With CS3, you'll be better served using the new Black and White adjustment. However, if you're using an older version of Photoshop, the Channel Mixer is a good alternative to other grayscale conversion methods. While you might think that you could just choose Image > Mode > Grayscale and be done with it, you'll get better quality by experimenting with the Channel Mixer. But before you get started, go open the Channels palette and click through all the channels to get an idea of what you'll be working with (**Figure 9.88**). You'll need to start with one of those channels as the base of your grayscale conversion, so make note of which one displays the best grayscale version of the image. Now, choose Image > Adjustments > Channel Mixer, and turn on the

Figure 9.87 The final image is made out of only two colors of ink!

Monochrome check box at the bottom of the dialog box to remove all the color from your image. Then, to start with the channel you liked best, move the appropriate slider to the 100% position and move the other sliders to 0% (**Figure 9.89**). Now experiment with moving the other sliders to the right and left to see how they affect the image. As you move a slider toward the right, the image will get brighter, which will necessitate that you move another slider toward the left to compensate. By using different mixes of the channels, you'll get different grayscale results. There is no obvious formula for what will give you the best results; you'll just have to experiment until you like the detail, contrast, and brightness of the end result (**Figure 9.90**). A general rule of thumb is that getting the sliders to add up to 100% should deliver an image that is close to the same brightness as the original image. Once you like what you have, click OK and then choose Image > Mode > Grayscale.

Figure 9.88 Channels from left to right: red, green, blue. (©2007 Stockbyte, www.stockbyte.com)

Figure 9.89 Dial in the channel that looked the best.

Figure 9.90 This is just one of many end results you could get with a few minutes of experimentation.

Gradient Map

The Gradient Map (Image > Adjustments > Gradient Map) (**Figure 9.91**) does a rather simple and unusual thing: It first converts an image to grayscale, and then replaces the shades of gray in the image with different colors that show up in a gradient. When you first get into the dialog box, it defaults to a black and white gradient, which should just make your image look grayscale. Then, if you click on the down arrow to the right of the gradient preview, you'll be able to choose a preset gradient to replace the shades of gray that were in the original image (**Figures 9.92 and 9.93**). If you'd prefer to bypass the preset gradients and create your own gradient, you can click in the middle of the gradient preview to access the gradient editor. If you'd like to know how to create your own gradients, be sure to read the information about the Gradient tool in Chapter 1, "Tool and Palette Primer."

The main problem with using the Gradient Map command is that you can easily end up with bright colors across the full range of the image, which will trash the contrast of your image (**Figure 9.94**). To prevent that, choose Layer > New Adjustment Layer > Gradient Map. When prompted, set the Mode pop-up menu to Color, and then click OK to get to the Gradient Map dialog box. Because the adjustment layer you just created is using the Color blending mode, it will be able to change only the colors in your image and will not be able to mess with the brightness (**Figure 9.95**).

Figure 9.91 The Gradient Map dialog box.

Figure 9.92 The original image.(©2007 Stockbyte, www.stockbyte.com)

Figure 9.93 Gradient Map replaces brightness levels with different colors.

Figure 9.94 The contrast of the image has changed radically.

Figure 9.95 Using the Color blending mode prevents the Gradient Map from messing up the contrast of the image.

Figure 9.96 The original image. (©2007 Stockbyte, www.stockbyte.com)

Figure 9.97 The result of applying a black, orange, yellow gradient map.

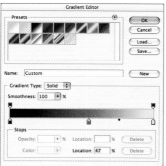

Figure 9.98 The three-color gradient used to create Figure 9.97.

Figure 9.99 The result of dragging the black slider toward the middle of the gradient.

I often use the Gradient Map command to transform a backlit image into one that looks like it was taken at sunset (**Figures 9.96** and **9.97**). All you have to do is create a gradient that starts with black and slowly fades to orange and then yellow (**Figure 9.98**). If you want to turn the image into more of a silhouetted image, just slide the black color swatch in the gradient editor toward the right until you no longer see much detail in the subject of the photo (**Figure 9.99**).

Closing Thoughts

As you've seen in this chapter, a boggling multitude of techniques exist for manipulating the colors in your images. You don't have to know or remember how to use every single one of them—just pick out the ones you're most comfortable with and stick with them for a while. Then, once you feel confident with them, come on back and read this chapter again and add a few more techniques to your adjustment arsenal. To be honest, I mainly use Hue/Saturation, Auto Color, and the Color Replacement brush for most of my color manipulation tasks. But don't use those three just because I do; instead, try them all and find your own favorites.

10
Adjustment Layers

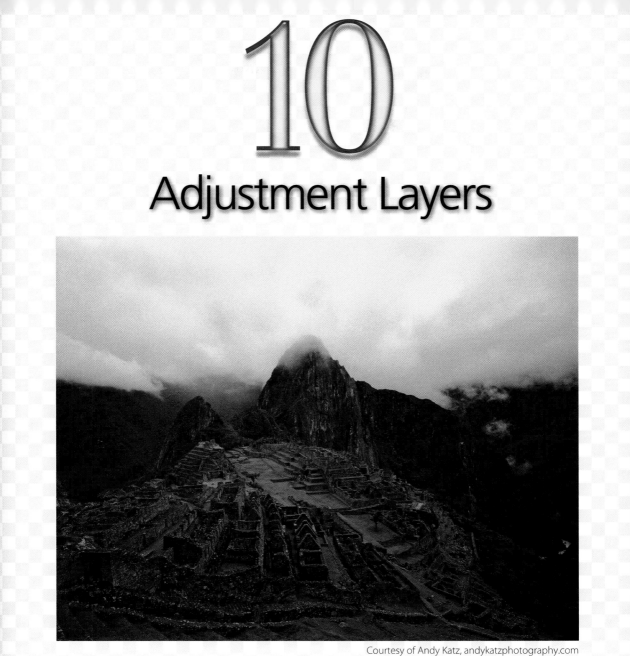

Courtesy of Andy Katz, andykatzphotography.com

[sitting atop a big gun, hands on controls]
I don't know what these levers do, but it's pointing in your direction!

—Adric, from *Doctor Who*

When it comes to making adjustments to your images, we've already covered a lot of territory. We've explored Levels, Curves, Hue/Saturation, and a vast number of techniques for color correcting and manipulating your images. You might have noticed that I often suggested you use an adjustment layer to implement the techniques; I use adjustment layers on the majority of images I work with and consider this feature to be the key to working quickly, having absolute flexibility, and obtaining the highest possible quality.

Imagine being able to make adjustments without damaging or altering the original image. You can also go back at any time and refine the adjustment or remove it altogether and start over with another adjustment. All of that is possible when using adjustment layers. Combine them with Layer Masks and blending modes, and you've got an unbeatable combination that is the cornerstone for working nondestructively.

Two Methods For Adjusting An Image

There are two methods for applying an adjustment: adjusting a layer directly or applying the adjustment through an adjustment layer. Let's look at the fundamental differences between the two approaches.

Direct Adjustments

When an adjustment is applied by choosing from the Adjustments menu (Image > Adjustments) (**Figure 10.1**), the adjustment will only affect the active layer, and the

Figure 10.1 Choosing Image > Adjustments applies an adjustment directly to the active layer.

original state of the layer will be permanently changed once you save and close the document. I like to think of this approach as my "in-a-hurry and not-too-worried about changing it later adjustment." The two major downsides to making a direct adjustment are:

▶ If you need to isolate an area, you have to create a selection before applying the adjustment or use the History Brush after the adjustment is applied, but nothing can be done after the image has been saved and closed.

▶ To alter the effects of a blending mode (more on this later in the chapter), you have to choose Edit > Fade (**Figure 10.2**) immediately after applying an adjustment and cannot change your mind after using any other tools.

Don't feel bad about adjusting an image directly. There's really nothing wrong with it as long as you know what the image needs, don't need to do a lot of experimenting, and don't make any mistakes. Your image will not suffer in any way whatsoever by adjusting it directly. Having said that, I must move along on my mission to convince you that adjustment layers are by far the most efficient and nondestructive way to adjust your images.

Adjustment Layers

To create an adjustment layer, choose Layer > New Adjustment Layer, and then select any of the available adjustments (Levels, Curves, Hue/Saturation, etc.) or click on the Adjustment Layer pop-up menu at the bottom of the Layers palette (**Figure 10.3**). Once you've completed your adjustment, it will appear as a separate layer in the Layers palette (**Figure 10.4**). You can think of it as if you are standing at the top of the Layers palette looking down and that the adjustment layers are like filters that you attach to the lens of a camera, or like a pair of sunglasses. Anything you see through that adjustment layer (filter) will be affected by the adjustment, whereas layers that appear above the adjustment layer will not be affected (**Figure 10.5** to **10.7**).

Figure 10.2 Choosing Edit > Fade immediately after adjusting a layer allows you to change the opacity and blending mode used to apply the adjustment.

Figure 10.3 The Adjustment Layer pop-up menu at the bottom of the Layers palette.

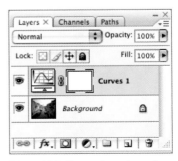

Figure 10.4 The top layer shown is an adjustment layer.

309

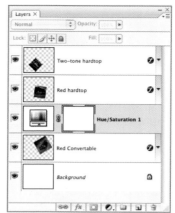

Figure 10.5 The original image is made from a total of four layers.

Figure 10.6 Adding an adjustment layer.

Figure 10.7 The layers under the adjustment layers are the only ones affected by the adjustment.

NOTES

If setting the Opacity to 100% doesn't produce a strong enough effect, try duplicating the adjustment layer, which will often double the effect of the adjustment (depending on the type of adjustment being applied).

A generic Adjustment Layer icon (which looks like a half black and half white circle) will appear when the thumbnails used in the Layers palette are too small to allow room for the full-sized versions. This can happen when the document is much wider than it is tall.

The adjustment is in its own layer; that means it is isolated from the underlying image, which allows you to retain the unmodified original. At any time you can simply turn off the eyeball icon on the adjustment layer and the image will return to its unmodified state. You can lessen the effect of the adjustment layer by lowering its Opacity setting. Since the adjustment has not been permanently applied to the image, you can also double-click the adjustment layer icon to modify the adjustment settings. There are also many features that can be added to the adjustment layer to limit which layers are affected by the adjustment, limit which areas of the document are affected, or change how the adjustment interacts with the underlying layers (that's what the rest of this chapter is all about).

What makes adjustment layers so much more useful than direct adjustments is that the image can be saved (in formats that support layers) and then reopened in the future for more editing of the adjustments. Adjustments made through adjustment layers only become permanent when you merge them into the underlying image or save the image in a file format that doesn't support layers.

Using Adjustment Layers

Let's take a look at the accessories that are attached to an adjustment layer (**Figure 10.8**). On the far left, you'll find an eyeball icon that determines if the adjustment layer is currently affecting the appearance of your image. To its right is another icon that represents the type of adjustment that is being applied (**Figure 10.9**). When you double-click the adjustment icon, you'll be sent back to the dialog box that was used when the adjustment layer was created, which allows you to modify the adjustment settings being applied to the image (for instance, if you have a Levels adjustment layer, you'll be sent back to the Levels dialog box). To the right of the adjustment icon is a link symbol, which really doesn't apply to adjustment layers. And to the right of that is a Layer Mask that allows you to limit where the adjustment will affect the underlying image.

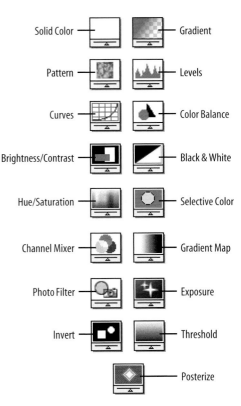

Figure 10.9 The Adjustment Layer icons represent the type of adjustment being applied.

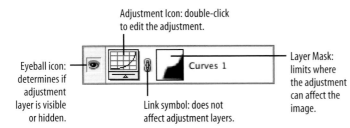

Figure 10.8 The anatomy of an adjustment layer.

Stacking Order

When you have more than one adjustment layer on an image, the stacking order of the layers determines the order in which the adjustments are applied. Adjustment layers are applied from bottom to top with the bottommost adjustment considered to be the first one that's applied. You should always have the topmost adjustment layer active when creating a new adjustment layer because new adjustment layers are always added directly above whichever layer is active. Try to maintain the stacking order that you started with, always adding new adjustments to the top of the stack because adding an adjustment layer in between two others, or changing the stacking order of the layers, can cause unpredictable changes to the overall look of your image.

Before and After Views

If your document contains multiple adjustment layers, and you want to view the original, unadjusted image, you'll have to hide all the adjustment layers by clicking their eyeball icons. To see the result of your adjustments, make the adjustment layers visible by clicking the eyeball icons again. All that eyeball clicking makes it difficult to get a quick before and after view of your image. To solve this problem, hold Option/Alt and click the eyeball icon for the Background layer (or whichever layer contains the original image). That will hide all the layers except the one you're clicking on. Just repeat the process to toggle all the hidden layers so they come back into view.

Dragging Between Documents

It's rather common to have more than one photograph that needs the same type of adjustment (they might have similar subject matters and similar lighting). When that's the case, you can adjust one of the documents using adjustment layers and then drag those adjustment layers on top of the second document (**Figure 10.10** and **10.11**). You can select as many adjustment layers as needed and drag from either the main document window or the Layers palette. Just be aware that those layers will be deposited above whichever layer is active in the destination document, which can cause some unexpected results if the destination document already contains adjustment layers and the topmost layer is not active.

Now that you have an idea of how adjustment layers operate and know about the icons that appear on an adjustment layer, let's explore a simple type of adjustment so you'll have something to play with as you move through this chapter.

Figure 10.10 Select the adjustment layers you'd like to copy and then drag them to another document. (©2007 Ben Willmore)

Figure 10.11 Once you release the mouse button, a copy of the adjustment layers will appear in the destination document.

Photo Filter Adjustments

We'll create a special type of adjustment that should give you enough ammunition to start applying adjustment layers to your own images. A Photo Filter adjustment layer allows you to quickly shift the overall color in your image. It has an effect that is much like placing a colored filter in front of a camera lens or putting on colored sunglasses. All you have to do is open an image and choose Photo Filter from the Adjustment Layer pop-up menu at the bottom of the Layers palette. When the Photo Filter dialog box appears (**Figure 10.12**), either choose a preset color from the Filter pop-up menu or click on the color swatch to choose your own custom color. Once you've chosen the color you desire, adjust the Density slider to control how radically the filter will affect the image (**Figures 10.13 to 10.15**). If you find that your image is getting too dark as you increase the Density setting, I'll bet the Preserve Luminosity check box is turned off. When that check box is turned off, adding a Photo Filter adjustment darkens your image, just as colored sunglasses allow less light to enter your eye. Turning on the Preserve Luminosity check box prevents Photoshop from changing the brightness of your image but still allows you to shift its colors. I leave the Preserve Luminosity check box on for the vast majority of images that I adjust. I'd much rather make a separate adjustment layer (Levels, Curves, or any other type) if I want to change the brightness of the image.

Just in case you skipped Chapter 9, "Color Manipulation," and ended up here without knowing how to think about color adjustments in Photoshop, I'll clue you in on a basic concept of color manipulation. When you use a Photo Filter layer, you'll be pushing all the colors in your image toward one side of the color wheel. If your image has an obvious color cast, all of the colors within the image will be shifted to one side of the color wheel (**Figures 10.16 and 10.17**). When that's the case, you can often remove the color cast by applying a Photo Filter that uses the color that's found directly across the color wheel from the color that is contaminating your image (blue in this case) (**Figures 10.18 and 10.19**).

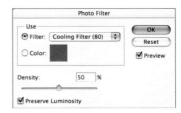

Figure 10.12 The Photo Filter dialog box.

Figure 10.13 The original image. (©2007 Ben Willmore)

Figure 10.14 Result of applying a blue Photo Filter with a Density of 20%.

Figure 10.15 Result of applying a blue Photo Filter with a Density of 50%.

Figure 10.16 This image was taken at sunrise, and therefore has a strong orange color cast. (©2007 Ben Willmore)

Figure 10.18 After applying a blue Photo Filter adjustment layer, the color cast is gone.

Figure 10.17 When an image has an orange color cast, all of the colors within the image will be shifted toward the orange side of the color wheel.

Figure 10.19 Applying a blue Photo Filter adjustment layer shifts the colors away from the orange side of the color wheel, bringing them closer to the blue side.

Now let's start to explore the more powerful aspects of adjustment layers.

Blending Modes

The Blending Mode pop-up menu found in the upper left of the Layers palette determines how the active layer will interact with the underlying image. This menu can be especially useful when applying adjustment layers since it allows you to limit how they can affect your image.

There are three main Blending modes that I find to be especially useful when using adjustment layers:

▶ The Hue Blending mode allows an adjustment to change the basic color of the underlying image while preventing it from changing the brightness or contrast of the underlying image (also known as tonality), or how colorful the image is (also known as saturation). I primarily use this mode when I want to adjust the overall color of an image without adding color to areas that are neutral gray (**Figures 10.20** to **10.22**). It can also be useful when you notice that a color adjustment is making your image too colorful or is mellowing out the color too much.

Figure 10.20 Original unadjusted image. (©2007 Andy Katz)

Figure 10.21 Color shifted using Normal mode.

Figure 10.22 Color shifted using Hue mode.

▶ The Color Blending mode allows an adjustment to affect both the hue (basic color) and saturation (how colorful) of the underlying image while preventing it from changing the tonality of the underlying image. I use this Blending mode anytime I'm attempting to change the color of an image without shifting the brightness in an undesirable way (**Figures 10.23** to **10.25**).

Figure 10.23 Original unadjusted image.

Figure 10.24 Color shifted using Normal mode.

Figure 10.25 Color shifted using Color mode.

▶ The Luminosity Blending mode limits an adjustment so that it can only affect the brightness and contrast of the underlying image while preventing it from changing the color of the image. This mode is useful when you want to adjust the brightness of the image without shifting the color or making the image too colorful (which is often a consequence of darkening the image) (**Figures 10.26** to **10.28**).

Figure 10.26 Original unadjusted image. (©2007 Andy Katz)

Figure 10.27 Darkened using Normal mode.

Figure 10.28 Darkened using Luminosity mode.

Figure 10.29 The New Layer dialog box.

Using the pop-up menu at the top of the Layers palette isn't always the most ideal method for changing the Blending mode of an adjustment layer because it's only available after an adjustment has been applied. If you'd like to choose a Blending mode before applying an adjustment, hold Option/Alt when choosing an adjustment type from the Adjustment Layer pop-up menu at the bottom of the Layers palette. That will cause the New Layer dialog box to appear, which includes a Mode pop-up menu where you can specify the Blending mode you'd like to use for the adjustment layer you are about to create (**Figure 10.29**).

Empty Adjustment Layers

Adjustment layers and Blending modes can be an effective combination when applying the enhancement techniques described in Chapter 12, "Enhancement." Adjustment layers can be used anytime that you would usually duplicate a layer and change its Blending mode. As an alternative, you can use a Blending mode that's often referred to as an "empty adjustment layer." To do this, create a new adjustment layer, but don't move any

Figure 10.30 Original single-layer image. (©2007 Andy Katz)

Figure 10.31 Result of using Multiply mode on a duplicate (either method).

Figure 10.32 Result of retouching the original layer when an empty adjustment layer is used.

of the sliders in the Adjustment dialog box (so it doesn't change the appearance of the image). This technique works because Photoshop acts as if the adjustment layer contains the result of the adjustment being applied. Since an empty adjustment doesn't change the image, it's considered to be identical to the underlying image.

The advantage of using an empty adjustment layer over duplicating a layer is that any future retouching that is applied to the underlying image will automatically be reflected in the empty version (**Figures 10.30** to **10.32**) but will not affect a duplicate layer (**Figure 10.33**).

Adjusting Isolated Areas

Adjustment layers wouldn't be so wonderful if they always affected your entire image. To get them to really strut their stuff, you must combine them with Layer Masks, which allows you to limit which areas of your image will be affected by each adjustment layer. Let's look at all the different ways we can work with Layer Masks and adjustment layers.

Figure 10.33 Result of performing the exact same retouching on the original layer when a duplicate layer is used.

Layer Masks

By default, each adjustment layer comes equipped with a Layer Mask. This mask appears to the right of the Adjustment icon. If no selection is present when the adjustment layer was created, the Layer Mask will be entirely white. In a Layer Mask, all white causes the adjustment to affect the entire image. Black, on the other hand, prevents the adjustment from affecting areas. To control where an adjustment layer can affect your image, paint with black or white while the adjustment layer is active (**Figures 10.34** to **10.36**). The black and white paint will appear within the Layer Mask thumbnail image in the Layers palette (**Figure 10.37**).

Figure 10.34 Original, unadjusted image. (©2007 Andy Katz)

Figure 10.35 Unmasked adjustment result

Figure 10.36 Result of painting on the Layer Mask to limit where the adjustment applies

Figure 10.37 Layers palette view shows the paint that's been applied to the Layer Mask.

Painting with black causes the image to revert back to its unadjusted state. Keep in mind that painting with black will not always cause drastic changes to your image. If the difference between the original and adjusted version of the image is subtle, painting with black will cause very subtle changes to the image.

If you get sloppy and paint with black over too large an area, you can switch to painting with white to effectively undo your painting (since the Layer Mask started out filled with white and white areas allow the adjustment to apply to the image).

You're not limited to using the painting tools to modify a Layer Mask. Any tool that is available to a grayscale image can be used to edit the Layer Mask. I like to use the Gradient tool to create very gradual transitions (**Figures 10.38** to **10.40**) and occasionally apply filters to a mask to generate an interesting transition.

Figure 10.38 Original, unadjusted image. (©2007 Ben Willmore)

Figure 10.39 Unmasked adjustment result.

Figure 10.40 Result of applying a gradient to the adjustment layer's Layer Mask.

Working with Selections

If a selection is active at the time an adjustment layer is created, the unselected areas will be filled with black in the resulting Layer Mask, thus preventing the adjustment from affecting those areas. This can confuse many users since the "marching ants" that indicate the edge of a selection will suddenly disappear when an adjustment layer is created. That is because that selection has been converted into a Layer Mask (**Figures 10.41** and **10.42**).

NOTES

I often use the masking techniques described in Chapter 13, "Advanced Masking," to create a selection, and then use that selection to limit which area of my image is affected by an adjustment layer.

Figure 10.41 Selection visible before creating an adjustment layer. (©2007 Ben Willmore)

Figure 10.42 The selection has been converted into a Layer Mask that's used to darken the sky.

Figure 10.43 Painting in Quick Mask mode. (©2007 Ben Willmore)

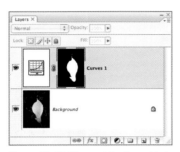

Figure 10.44 The resulting Layer Mask.

Figure 10.45 The red X indicates the Layer Mask is not currently affecting the adjustment.

Figure 10.46 Viewing the Layer Mask in the main image window.

Using Quick Mask Mode

If you find painting on a Layer Mask to be more convenient than creating selections, but would prefer to isolate an area before applying an adjustment, try this:

Before adjusting the image, type Q to enter Quick Mask mode (which will not change the look of your image unless you happen to have a selection active). Now, paint with black over the areas you don't want to be affected by the adjustment you plan to make. The areas you paint over with black will show up as a red overlay on the image (**Figure 10.43**). If you accidently cause the red overlay to appear on an area that should be adjusted, paint with white to remove the red overlay. Once the red overlay is covering all the areas that should not be adjusted, type Q to convert the Quick Mask into a selection and then, with that selection active, create an adjustment layer. The areas that appeared as red in Quick Mask mode will be black in the Layer Mask attached to the newly created adjustment layer, which will prevent the adjustment from affecting those areas (**Figure 10.44**).

Disabling the Layer Mask

If you'd like to see what an image would look like if the Layer Mask wasn't limiting where an adjustment was applying, hold Shift and click in the middle of the Layer Mask to disable the mask. That causes a red X to appear over the Layer Mask to indicate that it has been temporarily disabled (**Figure 10.45**). When you're done viewing your image in that way, you can Shift-click the mask a second time to turn it back on.

Viewing the Layer Mask Directly

When you paint on a Layer Mask, the resulting paint usually only appears in the tiny Layer Mask thumbnail image in the Layers palette. That can make it difficult to see what you're doing. To view the contents of the Layer Mask as a full-sized image, hold Option/Alt and click on the Layer Mask thumbnail in the Layers palette (**Figure 10.46**). You're welcome to modify the mask while viewing it directly. I use this view to inspect the results of painting on the Layer Mask and to clean up unexpected problems (like gaps between paint strokes). If you created a selection using an automated selection technique (like Color Range, the Background Eraser, or the Extract command), you might notice some noise in the Layer Mask (**Figure 10.47**). When that's the case, try using the noise reduction techniques covered in Chapter 11, "Sharpening" to rid the mask of the noise. When you're done editing the mask in this view, hold Option/Alt and click on the Layer Mask thumbnail image again to turn off this view.

Figure 10.47 A noisy mask.

Viewing the Layer Mask as a Color Overlay

You can view the contents of a Layer Mask as a color overlay on your image by typing \ when an adjustment layer is active (much like Quick Mask mode, which we talked about earlier). I use this view to see how closely my painting matches the subject of the photograph (**Figure 10.48**) and to touch up the results by painting with black or white. When you're done using this view, just type \ a second time to turn off the colored overlay. You can also modify the color being used by double-clicking on the Layer Mask thumbnail image in the Layers palette (**Figure 10.49**).

Figure 10.48 Viewing the Layer Mask as a color overlay. (©2007 Andy Katz)

Figure 10.49 Double-clicking the Layer Mask allows you to specify the color that will be used for the overlay.

Moving or Copying the Mask to Another Layer

You can drag a Layer Mask from one layer to another. All you have to do is click in the middle of the Layer Mask thumbnail image and release the mouse button after moving your mouse onto another layer. If you'd rather copy the Layer Mask instead of moving it, hold the Option/Alt key when dragging the mask.

Figure 10.50 Select the layers you'd like to group.

Masking Multiple Adjustment Layers

If you have multiple adjustment layers that you'd like to apply to a particular area of your image, select those adjustment layers, choose Layer > Group Layers, and then click the Layer Mask icon at the bottom of the Layers palette to add a Layer Mask to the group (**Figures 10.50** and **10.51**). Any changes made to the Layer Mask that is attached to the group will affect all the adjustment layers within the group. You can even paint on the Layer Mask attached to each adjustment layer to further limit where it can affect the image.

Figure 10.51 Add a Layer Mask to the group to mask all the layers within the group.

Limiting The Brightness Range That's Affected

You can limit the brightness range that an adjustment layer is able to affect by double-clicking to the right of the adjustment layer's name and adjusting the Blending sliders. The Blending sliders are found at the bottom of the Blending Options section of the Layer Style dialog box (**Figure 10.52**).

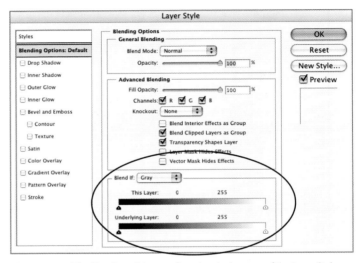

Figure 10.52 The Blending sliders are found at the bottom of the Layer Style dialog box.

The sliders found under the This Layer heading will analyze the result of the adjustment being applied and allow you to hide the dark (left slider) or light (right slider) portions of that result so that you can see the underlying image (which is usually the original photograph). The sliders found under the Underlying Layer slider will cause the dark (left slider) or bright (right slider) portions of the original image to show through and therefore prevent the adjustment from affecting those areas. You can hold Option/Alt and drag any one of the sliders to split it into two halves, which will produce a gradual transition between the area that is being hidden and the rest of the image (for a more detailed explanation of the Blending sliders, check out Chapter 14, "Collage.")

Blending sliders are particularly useful when darkening or adding contrast to part of an image using a Levels or Curves adjustment layer. Oftentimes, certain areas of the image change too much as you make the adjustment. But by simply letting parts of the underlying image show through (using the Blending sliders), the adjustment doesn't affect the entire image (**Figure 10.53**).

You can also use Blending sliders when colorizing an image. Create a Hue/Saturation Adjustment Layer, and turn on the Colorize check box to add some color. Then, double-click just to the right of the adjustment layer's name and allow the darkest areas of the underlying image to show through (lower-left slider). Make sure to split the sliders rather wide to ensure a smooth transition. This is what usually separates realistic-looking images from the fake ones, because not much color shows up in the darkest areas of most color photographs (**Figures 10.54** to **10.56**).

Figure 10.53 This image is divided into thirds. The middle is what the image looked like before it was adjusted, the left is what I got after tweaking the image with Curves, and the right is the result of limiting the changes so they don't affect the areas that contain a lot of blue light (the sky). (©2007 Ben Willmore)

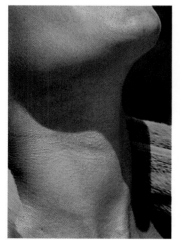

Figure 10.54 The original full-color image. (©Stockbyte, www.stockbyte.com)

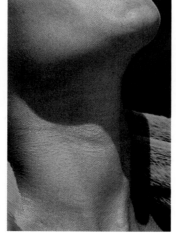

Figure 10.55 Result of converting to grayscale and then adding color.

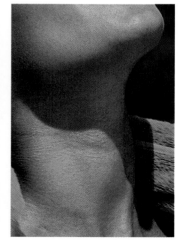

Figure 10.56 Result of using the Blending sliders to limit how much color is applied to the darkest areas of the image.

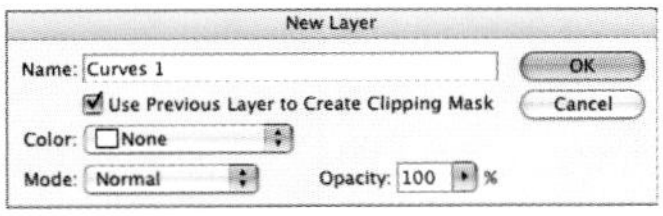

Figure 10.57 The New Layer dialog box.

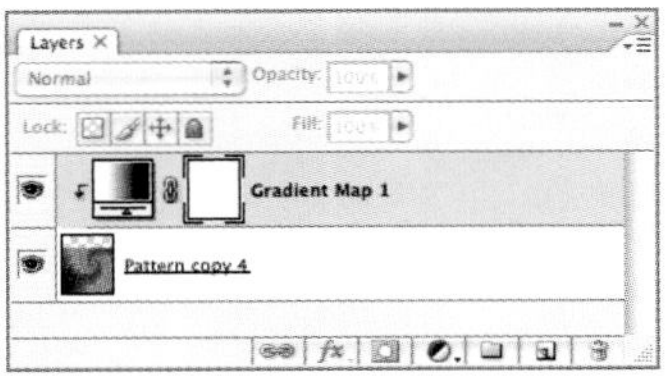

Figure 10.58 The down arrow indicates the adjustment will only affect the underlying image.

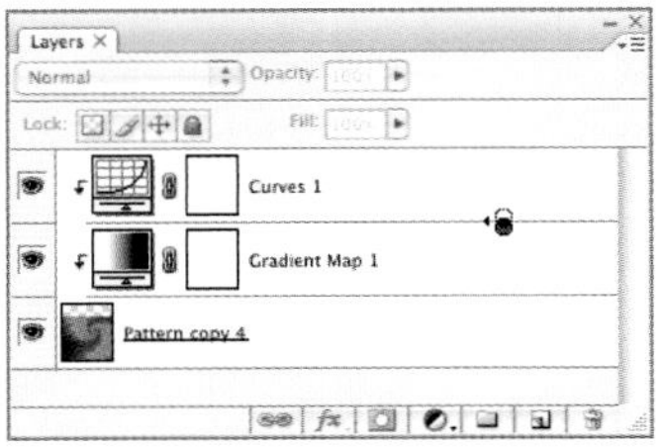

Figure 10.59 Option /Alt-clicking between two layers will also create a Clipping Mask.

Figure 10.60 Select the image and Adjustment Layers.

Limiting Which Layers Are Affected

The techniques we've talked about up until now work great when you're working with single image documents. When you graduate to more complex collages that contain a multitude of images and many layers, you'll have to supplement those techniques with ones that allow you to control the number of layers affected by an adjustment.

Adjusting a Single Layer

You can limit an adjustment layer to affect a single layer by creating a Clipping Mask. Create a new adjustment layer and hold the Option/Alt key (Windows) when choosing an adjustment from the adjustment layer pop-up menu at the bottom of the Layers palette. Then, when the New Layer dialog box appears, turn on the Use Previous Layer to Create Clipping Mask check box, which will cause a small down arrow to appear next to the adjustment layer, which indicates that it is only applying to the underlying layer (**Figures 10.57** and **10.58**). If the adjustment layer is preexisting, position it directly above the layer you'd like to affect, and with the adjustment layer active, choose Layer > Create Clipping Mask.

You can clip more than one adjustment layer to a single layer by holding the Option/Alt key and clicking on the horizontal line that separates the adjustment layers from the layer you'd like to adjust (**Figure 10.59**). When using this technique, start from the bottommost adjustment layer and work your way to the top adjustment layer that you want to apply to the image.

Adjusting a Limited Number of Layers

There are two methods for causing one or more adjustment layers to affect a limited number of layers:

The first method involves grouping the layers into a folder. Start by selecting the adjustment layers and all the layers they should affect (**Figure 10.60**). To place those layers into a group, hold Shift and click the Group icon (which looks like a folder) at the bottom of the Layers palette. Now, click on the newly created Group and change the Blending Mode menu at the top of the Layers palette from Pass Through (which allows the adjustments to affect layers that are outside of the group) to Normal (which will limit all adjustment layers and Blending modes used within the group to only affect the layers within the group) (**Figure 10.61**).

The second method is to group the layers into a Smart Object. Adjustment layers contained in a Smart Object cannot affect layers that appear outside of the Smart Object. As with the previous technique, start by selecting the adjustment layers and all the layers they should affect, but this time choose Layer > Smart Objects > Group Into New Smart Object. That will cause all the selected layers to be encapsulated into a single Smart Object Layer (**Figures 10.62** and **10.63**). To edit its contents, double-click on the Smart Object layer's thumbnail image in the Layers palette, which will cause the encapsulated layer to appear as a separate layer. This is the method I prefer to use when I plan to drag the affected layers into a more complex document because it simplifies the Layers palette view of the image (which usually reduces confusion when working with complex documents). For more information on working with Smart Objects, check out Chapter 14.

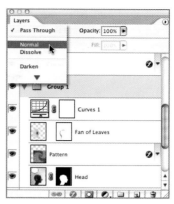

Figure 10.61 Setting the group to Normal mode.

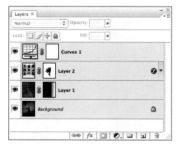

Figure 10.62 Selecting multiple layers.

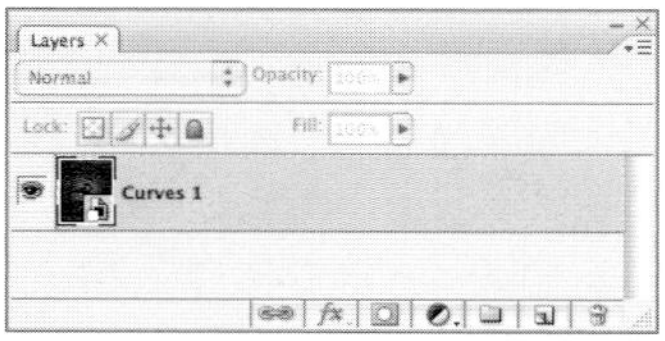

Figure 10.63 The result of grouping the selected layers into a Smart Object.

Figure 10.64 The original image contains bright and dark areas that are not part of the actual photograph. (©2007 Ben Willmore)

When a Layer Mask is active, resetting your foreground and background colors will change your foreground color to white and your background color to black, which is the opposite of what you'd get if the mask wasn't active.

Histograms and Automatic Adjustments

When you work with images that contain large areas of white/black (like ones with fancy borders—see **Figure 10.64**), the histogram can become less than useful because it will indicate that your image contains the full range of brightness levels (**Figure 10.65**) even though the image itself (minus the border) might be rather low contrast. To get around this, you'll need to take steps to limit what the histogram looks at when analyzing your image. That way you can optimize the contrast of the important areas of the image without having to look at the spikes at the ends of the histogram that would reflect the large areas of black or white that are in the border area. I also use this technique when I want to radically enhance the contrast of an image while retaining detail only in the most important areas.

To limit what the histogram looks at, select the important areas of your image and then create a Curves adjustment layer by choosing Layer > New Adjustment Layer > Curves. When a selection is active, the Histogram palette will analyze only the selected area (**Figure 10.66**), but the moment you create an adjustment layer, it will start thinking about the entire image again because the selection is converted into a Layer Mask. To get the histogram to think about only the area you had selected a moment ago, click OK in the Curves dialog box without adjusting the image. Now, look in the Layers palette (**Figure 10.67**) and Command/Ctrl-click on the Layer Mask that is on the adjustment layer you just created (it's the black and white rectangle near the right side). That will bring your selection back and limit the area of the image that the histogram looks at. Then, to adjust the image, double-click on the Adjustment Layer thumbnail that's just to the left of that Layer Mask and adjust away.

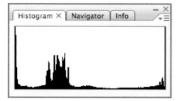

Figure 10.65 This histogram is analyzing the entire image, including its border and background.

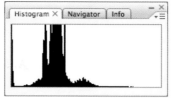

Figure 10.66 This histogram is analyzing only the selected area of the image.

Figure 10.67 The Layers palette includes an adjustment layer with a Layer Mask that is partially filled with black.

When you use this technique, the adjustment will apply only to that same selected area (**Figure 10.68**). But don't worry, as long as you used an adjustment layer, you'll be able to force the adjustment to apply to the entire image. When you've finished your adjustment, click OK in the Curves dialog box and look in the Layers palette. The Layer Mask that is attached to the adjustment layer should contain some black. That's what's limiting which areas of the image your adjustments are applying to. All you have to do to get the adjustment to apply to the entire image is Select > Deselect, type D to reset your foreground color, and then press Option-Delete (Mac) or Alt-Backspace (Windows) to fill the Layer Mask that's attached to that layer with white. By doing that, you will have adjusted the whole image (**Figure 10.69**) while the histogram only looked at the selected area of the image—but in the end, the adjustment applies to the entire image.

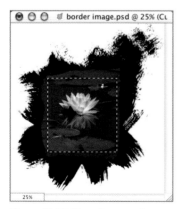

Figure 10.68 The adjustment is affecting only the selected areas.

Figure 10.69 After filling the Layer Mask with white, the adjustment affects the entire image.

Figure 10.70 Original unadjusted image. (©2007 iStockPhoto.com)

Figure 10.71 The result of applying a radical adjustment.

Figure 10.72 The result of healing the transition area.

Potential Problems

Working with adjustment layers is usually a trouble-free experience. Having said that, there are a few areas where adjustment layers can cause unexpected problems:

▶ If you drag an image along with its adjustment layers to another document, the adjustment layers will affect the entire destination document. To prevent this problem, use the techniques I mentioned earlier in this chapter (like Clipping Masks) to limit which layers are affected by the adjustment layers before you drag them to the destination document. (If the background image is the one being adjusted, you'll have to change its name before using it as part of a Clipping Mask.)

▶ Be careful when changing the color mode of your image (like RGB to CMYK). Certain adjustment layers will not make the transition, and others will produce different results. For that reason, it's best to flatten your image before changing the mode.

▶ If you've decided to work with 16-bit images in Photoshop, but need to end up with an 8-bit version, be sure to flatten the image before making the conversion. If you retain the layers, they will be recalculated using the 8-bit version of the image, which will cause you to lose any quality difference you would have had from working with a 16-bit image. Flattening the image will cause the adjustments to be applied to the full 16-bits of data, which will produce a higher quality 8-bit result.

▶ You have to be careful when retouching an image that contains adjustment layers; otherwise, you might cause the adjustments to apply to the image twice. For more information about how to avoid this problem, check out Chapter 16, "Workflow."

▶ It's often difficult to make radical adjustments to isolated areas without causing an obvious transition between the adjusted area and the surrounding image (**Figures 10.70** and **10.71**). This problem can often be remedied by placing an empty layer at the top of the layers stack and then retouching the transition area with the Healing brush. That will blend both sides of the transition to create a smooth blend (**Figure 10.72**).

Limitations of Adjustment Layers

There is one limitation of adjustment layers that prevent certain adjustments from being available as an adjustment layer. An adjustment layer must be able to be fed a single pixel and figure out how it should be modified without having to rely on the information contained in the surrounding image. The Match Color, Replace Color, Shadow/Highlight, Exposure, and Equalize adjustments must be able to compare the area being adjusted to the surrounding image (or a second image) to determine how to adjust the image, which prevents them from being used as adjustment layers.

There are five other adjustments that are not found in the Adjustment Layers pop-up menu at the bottom of the Layers palette: Auto Levels, Auto Contrast, Auto Color, Desaturate, and Variables. These are really shortcuts for using adjustments in certain ways. You can use the following equivalents to get the same functionality in an adjustment layer:

▶ Auto Levels is the same as clicking the Options button in the Levels or Curves dialog box and choosing the Enhance Per Channel Contrast while leaving the other settings at their defaults.

▶ Auto Contrast is the same as clicking the Options button in the Levels or Curves dialog box and choosing the Enhance Monochromatic Contrast while leaving the other settings at their defaults.

▶ Auto Color is the same as clicking the Options button in the Levels or Curves dialog box and choosing the Find Dark & Light Colors while leaving the other settings at their defaults.

▶ Desaturate is the same as moving the Saturation slider in the Hue/Saturation dialog box to -100.

▶ Variations is a visual interface for a combination of the Saturation slider in Hue/Saturation, the Brightness slider in Brightness/Contrast, and the choices available in the Color Balance dialog box.

Closing Thoughts

I hope this chapter has inspired you to go out and use adjustment layers. If you commit to using them, I expect you will soon be asking yourself, "How did I ever live without them?" Just know that you don't have to remember every detail covered in this chapter to start getting immediate benefits from this versatile feature. The most important points to keep in mind are:

▶ Adjustment layers are applied according to the stacking order of the Layers palette, with the bottommost adjustment layer being applied first and the topmost one last.

▶ Double-click the Adjustment Layer icon on the left side of the layer in the Layers palette to reedit the adjustment.

▶ Paint with black to prevent the adjustment from applying to an area, or paint with white to allow it to affect an area.

▶ The adjustment layers will remain in your image as long as you save in a file format that supports layers such as Photoshop or TIFF.

If you're planning to use adjustment layers for the vast majority of adjustments that you'll be applying, be sure to visit Chapter 1, "Tools and Palette Primer," and learn how to reassign the keyboard shortcuts assigned to the commands that are found under the Adjustments menu (Image > Adjustments). Change them so that they end up creating adjustment layers instead of going directly to the Adjustment's dialog box. (To assign a keyboard shortcut to a particular type of adjustment layer, assign a keyboard command to the choices found in the New Adjustment Layer menu [Layer > New Adjustment Layer]).

Sharpening

Obviously, you failed to detect the subtle diamond pattern in my tie.

—Niles from *Frasier*

This chapter is about those very subtle details that can make the difference between a so-so image and one that pops off the page. Almost all digital images start life looking slightly soft. It's just a fact of life that all of our capture devices (digital cameras, scanners, and so on) can't deliver as much detail as the original image contained. (High-end drum scans are the one exception because they get sharpened during the scanning process.) Only images that are created from scratch in Photoshop or another program (like a 3D rendering application) will be 100% sharp to begin with. And even those images can become soft if you attempt to make the image larger or smaller in Photoshop (known as interpolating the image). Finally, when you output your image to an inkjet printer, printing press, or other output device, you will lose additional detail because most output devices simply are not capable of reproducing the amount of detail you see onscreen. By exaggerating the differences between areas (sharpening), we can attempt to compensate for all the factors that can make an image look soft.

Figure 11.1 A raw scan looks rather dull compared to one that's been sharpened.

After you learn to properly sharpen your images, you'll find that they look much crisper when you print them and that they are an obvious improvement over unsharpened scans (**Figures 11.1** and **11.2**). But no matter how much sharpening we apply to an image, it won't compensate for an out-of-focus original, so try to stick with images that aren't overly blurry.

Removing Film Grain and Scanner/Camera Noise

Sharpening an image will exaggerate almost all the detail in the image, so any film grain or noise will also get exaggerated (**Figures 11.3** and **11.4**). That's fine if you want an image with pronounced grain, but if you prefer a smoother look, you might want to check out my techniques for removing grain/noise from your images.

Figure 11.2 A properly sharpened image. (©2007 Ben Willmore)

Figure 11.3 This original image contains a lot of film grain. (©Stockbyte, www.stockbyte.com)

Figure 11.4 Sharpening the image exaggerates the film grain.

Five main filters are used to remove noise from your images: Gaussian Blur, Despeckle, Median, Dust & Scratches, and Reduce Noise. (As I discuss this topic, I'll call film grain *noise* just to simplify matters.) Let's look at these filters one at a time, starting with the least sophisticated and moving to the most advanced. With each filter I describe, I'll show you the results on two images: a simple image that contains different sized black dots that represent noise (**Figure 11.5**) and a normal image (**Figure 11.6**) to show how much the filter trashes the real detail in the image. That way you'll be able to see how effective each filter is at removing noise while at the same time seeing how much of the detail in your images you'll lose in the process.

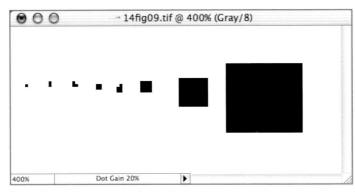

Figure 11.5 This image contains black dots that vary from one pixel to over 25 pixels wide

Figure 11.6 This image represents a normal photo that has slight noise. (©Stockbyte, www.stockbyte.com)

Gaussian Blur

The Gaussian Blur filter will do the opposite of what we are trying to accomplish when we sharpen an image—it makes the transitions in the image less distinct and therefore renders the image less sharp (**Figures 11.7** and **11.8**). This is a common method used to remove noise; however, just because it's common doesn't mean that I'm going to recommend it. There are much more sophisticated methods that won't trash the general detail in your image.

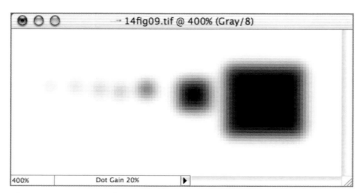

Figure 11.7 A setting of 2.0 pixels was necessary to blend the smallest dots into the surrounding image.

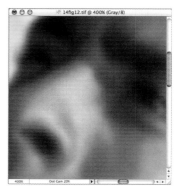

Figure 11.8 After blurring the image, it looks nowhere near as sharp as the original.

Despeckle

The next few filters we'll explore are found under the Noise menu (Filter > Noise). The first choice in that menu is Add Noise, which is designed for adding specks to your image; the rest of the filters listed in that menu are designed for getting rid of noise. The Despeckle filter blends the tiniest specks into the surrounding image while leaving the major detail in your image untouched (**Figures 11.9** and **11.10**). The only problem with this filter is that it isn't always strong enough to completely remove noise from your image. So, if you get an image with minimal noise, you might want to give this filter a try; but when the noise in your image is considerable, try the other options found in the Noise menu.

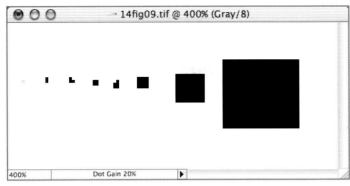

Figure 11.9 After applying the Despeckle filter, the single-pixel speck has changed to a light gray speck. (I doubt you can see it here.)

Figure 11.10 After applying the Despeckle filter to this image, the film grain has started to blend into the surrounding image.

Median

The Median filter uses an interesting approach to rid your image of unwanted noise—it rounds the corners of things, which causes tiny specks to literally implode. As you increase the Amount setting, the filter rounds the corners to a larger degree, which makes larger specks in the image blend into the surrounding image (**Figures 11.11** and **11.12**). What's really nice about this filter is that it doesn't make anything look blurry. I don't usually need to use settings above 2 when applying this filter.

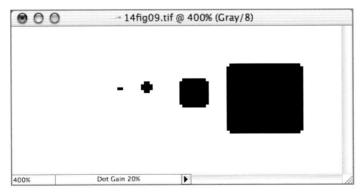

Figure 11.11 Using the Median filter with a Radius of 1 (its lowest setting) effectively removed the small specks.

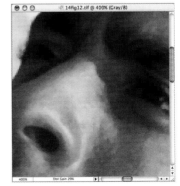

Figure 11.12 Applying Median to this image caused it to lose some detail, but it didn't get blurry.

Dust & Scratches

The Dust & Scratches filter uses the same technology as the Median filter, but it adds a Threshold setting to determine which shades in your image should be affected by the filter. A setting of zero allows the filter to apply to the entire image, and will therefore work exactly like the Median filter. Raising the Threshold setting limits the changes to areas that are similar in brightness. The general idea here is to start with a Threshold of zero so you work on the whole image, and then adjust the Radius setting until the noise in the image is gone. Then, to make sure you lose the absolute minimal amount of true detail, change the Threshold setting to 255 and use the down arrow key to slowly change that setting until you find the highest number that will rid your image of unwanted noise (**Figures 11.13** and **11.14**).

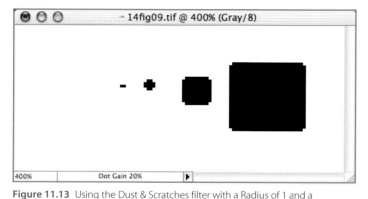

Figure 11.13 Using the Dust & Scratches filter with a Radius of 1 and a Threshold of 16 produced the same result on our specks.

Figure 11.14 Dust & Scratches results.

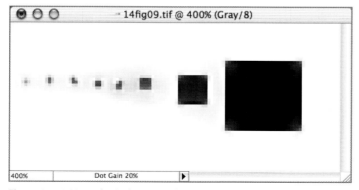

Figure 11.15 Using the Reduce Noise filter with a Strength of 10 and a Preserve Details setting of 1 produced minimal distortion in the largest specks while making the smaller specks fade into their surroundings.

Figure 11.16 Reduce Noise produced a somewhat smoother result than the Dust & Scratches filter while retaining more highlight detail in the eye.

Reduce Noise

The Reduce Noise filter is the most sophisticated method for reducing noise. It incorporates many of the tricks that we used to do piecemeal by using Blending modes or applying filters to individual channels. It often produces a result that looks smooth while retaining much of the detail from the original image (**Figures 11.15** and **11.16**). When applying the Reduce Noise filter, I suggest you start by moving all the sliders to the far left so they have no effect on the image.

If you notice any multicolored noise in your image (specks of yellow, blue, red, etc.), adjust the Reduce Color Noise slider until those colors blend into their surroundings (**Figures 11.17** and **11.18**). If you find that the noise is primarily a single color, consider applying the features found in Advanced mode (which we'll talk about next) before continuing with the techniques mentioned here.

After tackling any color noise problems, it's time to rid your image of luminance noise (specks that vary in brightness instead of color). Adjust the Strength slider until you've removed as much of the remaining noise as possible, move the Preserve Details slider all the way to the right, and then lower it until you find the highest setting that gives a good balance between noise reduction and image detail (**Figure 11.19**).

Figure 11.17 The original image contains specks of various colors. (©2007 Ben Willmore)

Figure 11.18 Result of adjusting the Reduce Color Noise slider.

Figure 11.19 The Reduce Noise filter.

Figure 11.20 The red channel.

Figure 11.21 The green channel.

Figure 11.22 The blue channel.

Images saved in the JPEG file format will exhibit artifacts that make the image look as if it has been divided up into 8 x 8 pixel squares. You can attempt to blend those squares into the surrounding image by turning on the Remove JPEG Artifact check box. Just remember to inspect the image to make sure it doesn't destroy too much important detail in the image.

Advanced Mode

If your image has very fine detail or considerable noise, you'll need to take additional steps to ensure that you don't trash too much detail in the image when you're attempting to remove noise. Color images are made out of three (RGB) or four (CMYK) color components, which are known as color channels. It's rather common to find more noise in one of those channels than the others (**Figures 11.20** to **11.22**). When that's the case, try applying the noise removal filters to the individual channels before attempting to reduce noise from the image as a whole; otherwise, you might end up trashing the detail in most of the channels just to rid one pesky channel of noise (usually the blue or yellow channel) (**Figures 11.23** to **11.25**). So the next time you need to be heavy-handed with the Strength slider, try setting it to zero, switch to Advanced mode at the top of the dialog box, and then click the Per Channel tab. After you've done that, you can cycle through the RGB or CMYK channels to see if the noise shows up more in one channel than another and adjust each channel accordingly (**Figures 11.26** to **11.28**). When you've done all you can to the individual channels, you can click the Overall tab and adjust the image further.

Figure 11.23 The full-color image after each channel is treated separately.

Figure 11.24 The red channel after adjusting all channels at once.

Figure 11.25 The green channel after adjusting all channels at once.

Figure 11.26 The red channel treated separately.

Figure 11.27 The green channel treated separately.

Figure 11.28 The blue channel treated separately.

Reclaiming Detail with the History Brush

You might find that after applying one of the noise reduction filters, the important detail in your image, such as eyes or freckles, has been lost. When that's the case, you can use the History brush right after applying the noise reduction filter to paint back the desired detail, effectively removing the effect of the filter from the areas you paint across. If the History brush presents you with a "no" symbol (circle with a diagonal line across it), it means that you've either changed the dimensions of your image or changed the color mode of your image since you've opened it. When that's the case, choose Window > History and click just to the left of the History State that is directly above the one that lists the noise reduction filter you just applied (**Figure 11.29**). After you've done that, the History brush should work on your image. Just paint across the areas that have lost important detail, and you should see them come back.

Now that we've figured out how to rid our images of unwanted noise and film grain, let's look at how sharpening is able to exaggerate detail, and then we'll explore the exact steps needed to sharpen any image.

Figure 11.29 Click just to the left of the History State that is directly above the one that lists a noise reduction filter.

NOTES

You can also use the History brush with its Blending mode set to Lighten or Darken to rid your image of sharpening-related halos. Use Darken mode to remove the bright halos and Lighten mode to remove the dark halos.

Figure 11.30 The Unsharp Mask dialog box.

Figure 11.31 This simple document contains only three shades of gray.

Figure 11.32 This will be our photographic reference image. (©2007 Andy Katz)

How Sharpening Works

To sharpen an image, choose Filter > Sharpen. Photoshop presents you with a submenu of choices. The top three might sound friendly (Sharpen, Sharpen More, Sharpen Edges), but ignore those because they are simply presets that enter different numbers into the bottom choice (Unsharp Mask). The bottom two filters in the list are the only ones that allow you to control exactly how much the image will be sharpened. We'll start by exploring the Unsharp Mask filter and then refine our knowledge by exploring Photoshop's Smart Sharpen filter.

The reason Unsharp Mask has its confusing name is because way back before people used desktop computers, they sharpened images in a photographic darkroom. They would have to go through a process that involved a blurry (unsharp) version of the image. This would take well over an hour (don't worry—in Photoshop it takes only seconds) and would not be much fun. The process they'd go through in the darkroom was known as making an unsharp mask, so Adobe just borrowed that term.

The Unsharp Mask filter increases the contrast where two colors (or shades of gray) touch in the image, making their edges more prominent and therefore easier to see. To easily view the effect of the Unsharp Mask filter (**Figure 11.30**), I'll demonstrate using two documents: one that contains only three shades of gray (20%, 30%, and 50%) (**Figure 11.31**), and one that is a normal photographic image (**Figure 11.32**). With the simple document, I'll show a normal-sized image as well as a portion of each image that has been magnified by 800%. When you choose Unsharp Mask, you'll be presented with three sliders: Amount, Radius, and Threshold.

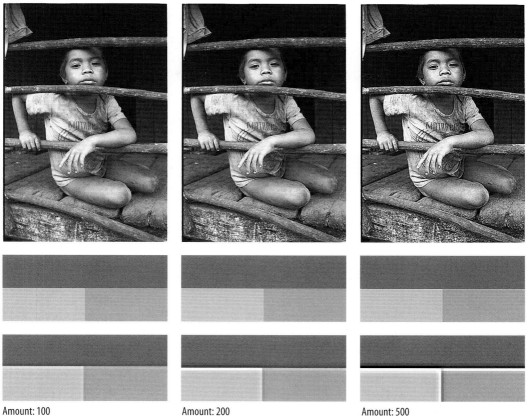

Amount: 100   Amount: 200   Amount: 500

Figure 11.33 The effect of the Amount setting.

▶ **Amount:** Determines how much contrast will be added to the edges of objects and, therefore, how obvious the sharpening will be (**Figure 11.33**).

▶ **Radius:** Determines how much space will be used for the contrast boost that the Amount setting creates. No matter which settings you use, sharpening will produce a bright halo on one side of the edge of an object and a dark halo on the opposite side of that same edge. If you use too much, you'll be adding a very noticeable glow around the edges of objects instead of a barely noticeable halo (**Figure 11.34**).

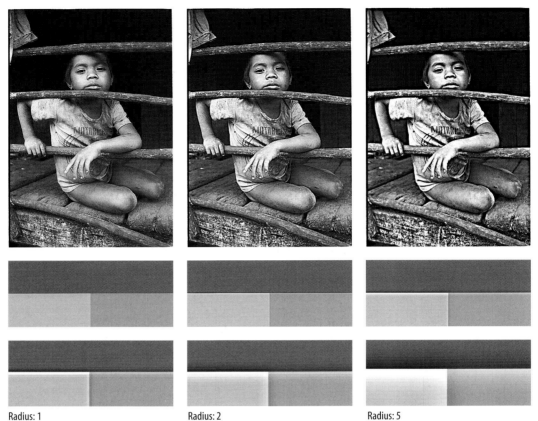

Radius: 1   Radius: 2   Radius: 5

Figure 11.34 The effect of the Radius setting.

▶ **Threshold:** Determines how different two touching colors have to be for sharpening to kick in. With Threshold set at 0, everything will get sharpened. As you increase this setting, only the areas that are drastically different will be sharpened (**Figure 11.35**). If the setting is too low, unwanted artifacts like noise and film grain will be exaggerated and relatively smooth areas might start to show texture. If the setting is too high, the sharpening will apply to very few areas in the image, which will look too obvious because those areas will not fit in with their surroundings (which didn't get sharpened).

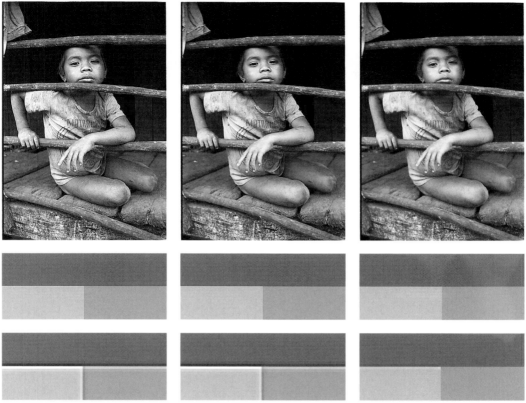

Threshold: 0   Threshold: 10   Threshold: 50

Figure 11.35 The effect of the Threshold setting.

Now that we've explored all the options that are available
with the Unsharp Mask filter, let's get down to business
and find out how to apply them to an image. But before
you start applying the Unsharp Mask filter, double-click the
Zoom tool to view your image at 100% view; otherwise, you
won't be able to see the full effect of the sharpening you
apply to the image.

Figure 11.36 Start with the generic settings of 500, 1, and 0. (©2007 Andy Katz)

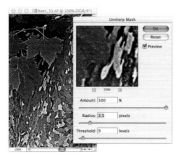

Figure 11.37 Adjust the Threshold setting until smooth areas look smooth.

Sharpening an Image

To sharpen an image, choose Filter > Sharpen > Unsharp Mask and type in the generic numbers of Amount = 500, Radius = 1, and Threshold = 0, just to make sure you can easily see the effect of sharpening the image (**Figure 11.36**). Now, adjust the Threshold setting. With it set to 0, everything in the image will be sharpened. That can cause areas that used to have fine detail (like a brick wall) or areas that used to look relatively smooth (like a skin tone or a shadow) to suddenly have overly exaggerated detail. That will make those bricks look noisy and will add years to anyone's face because you've exaggerated every imperfection. To avoid that, slowly increase the Threshold setting until those areas smooth out (**Figure 11.37**). You'll usually end up using settings in the single digits. Next, experiment with the Radius setting and try to find the highest setting that makes the image look like it's been sharpened without making it look like everything is glowing (**Figures 11.38** and **11.39**) (usually in the range of .5 to 2). Images with very fine detail look best with lower Radius settings, whereas images that contain little detail or that will be printed large and viewed from a distance look best with higher Radius settings. Then adjust the Amount setting until the image looks naturally sharp instead of artificial (**Figure 11.40**) (usually in the range of 15 to 200, depending on the Radius setting you used). Let your eyes be your guide. There are two common indicators that the Amount setting is too high.

▶ Obvious bright halos appear around the edge of objects. (There will always be halos; you just want to make sure they aren't very noticeable.)

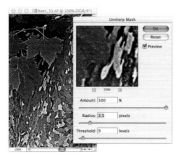

Figure 11.38 Too high of a Radius setting makes everything look as if it's glowing.

Figure 11.39 Try to find the highest Radius setting that doesn't make objects look like they're glowing.

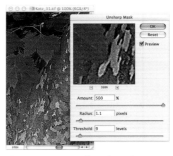

Figure 11.40 Finally, adjust the Amount setting until the image looks realistically sharp.

▶ Very fine detail (like hair, or texture in bricks) will become overly contrasty—almost pure black and pure white.

That's how I approach sharpening most images, but sometimes you'll need to take a different approach. The Radius setting can have a radical effect on sharpening. You'll need to achieve a balance between Amount and Radius. High Amount settings (90–250ish) will require low Radius settings (.5–1.5), and low Amount settings (10–30) will require higher Radius settings (5–20). High Amount settings work for most images, and that's why we took the initial approach I just talked about. But if you have a grainy image and you want to maintain but not exaggerate the grain (**Figure 11.41**), you'll need to take a slightly different approach. A grainy image will start to look unusual when you get an Amount setting anywhere near 100 (**Figure 11.42**); you might even need to bring the Amount setting down to near 20 before the grain stops being exaggerated too much. At that point, you'll barely be able to tell that the image has been sharpened (**Figure 11.43**), so to compensate for that, you'll need to get the Radius setting up until the image starts to look sharp (**Figure 11.44**) (maybe up to 15 or so) (**Figures 11.45** and **11.46**). But on most images, you'll find that you'll be able to get away with much higher Amount settings without causing grain problems. In that case, you might end up with an Amount setting around 120, and then you'll need to experiment with the Radius setting to see what looks best (probably between .5 and 1.5).

Figure 11.41 This is a grainy image. (©2007 Andy Katz)

Figure 11.42 With the Amount setting at 150, the grain is becoming too obvious. (Look very closely to see the difference.)

Figure 11.43 With the Amount setting at 20, you can barely tell the image has been sharpened.

Figure 11.44 Bringing the Radius setting up to 20 makes the sharpening more prominent.

Figure 11.45 This image was sharpened using settings of 150, 1.2, and 3.

Figure 11.46 This image was sharpened using settings of 20, 20, and 3.

Figure 11.47 Smart Sharpen options.

Figure 11.48 Gaussian setting.

Figure 11.49 Lens Blur setting.

Figure 11.50 Lens Blur setting with More Accurate check box on.

Using Smart Sharpen

The Smart Sharpen filter (**Figure 11.47**) expands on the concepts of Unsharp Mask to deliver a more sophisticated method for sharpening images. However, there are many instances where I still prefer the Unsharp Mask for reasons I'll explain in just a bit.

The Amount and Radius settings in the Smart Sharpen filter work just like the ones found in the Unsharp Mask filter. In fact, the results are identical when the Remove pop-up menu is set to Gaussian Blur (**Figure 11.48**). Setting the Remove menu to Lens Blur causes the halos that come along with sharpening to be less pronounced, which allows you to get away with higher Amount and Radius settings before the sharpening halos become overly obvious (**Figure 11.49**). I use this setting whenever quality is more important than speed (which is 98% of the time for me). You can also set the Remove pop-up menu to Motion Blur and then experiment with the Angle setting to reduce the blurring effect of lens shake. It's not a miracle worker though, so it will only be effective when the camera shake was almost unnoticeable.

Turning on the More Accurate check box causes the image to be sharpened in two passes (just like applying the Unsharp Mask filter twice). This can make edges much more prominent (**Figure 11.50**), but you have to be very careful because it also has a tendency to over exaggerate grain and noise in images.

I find that I still use the Unsharp Mask filter for images that contain fine texture, such as skin or brick, because the Smart Sharpen filter does not offer the Threshold setting that allows you to limit the sharpening effect to areas of more pronounced detail.

Advanced Mode

The Smart Sharpen filter also offers an Advanced mode, which allows you to control the strength of the sharpening that will be applied to the shadows and highlights of the image (**Figure 11.51**). This can be useful in instances when a considerable amount of noise is present in the dark portion of an image. In Advanced mode, you'll be presented with a Fade Amount slider, which determines the strength of the sharpening effect, a Tonal Width setting, which determines the brightness range that will be affected by the sharpening, and a Radius setting, which determines how the sharpening effect will blend into the surrounding image. I usually start with the Fade setting at 100% and the Radius at 3 so that I can see the full effect of the sharpening. Then I adjust the Tonal Width until the sharpening no longer affects any overly noisy areas. Finally, I'll adjust the Fade Amount slider to see just how much sharpening I can get away with without exaggerating the noise in the image.

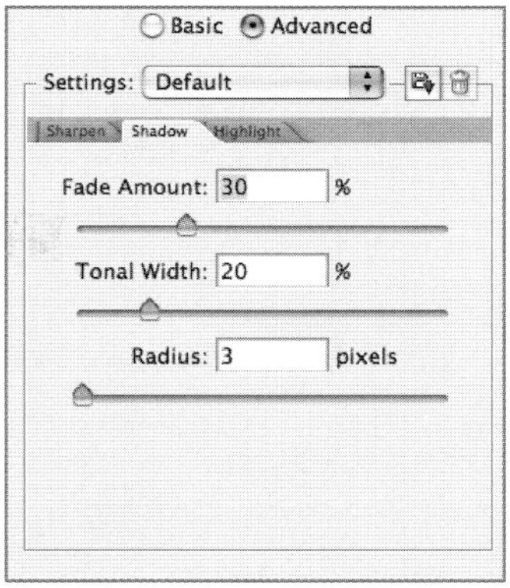

The process of sharpening an image is more of an art than a science, so it will take a good bit of practice before you start feeling confident in this area. Everyone has a different idea of how sharp an image should look, and most output devices aren't capable of reproducing the amount of detail you see onscreen. If you sharpen the image so it looks great onscreen, when you print the image it might still look rather soft. The following are some general thoughts on how to approach sharpening for different types of output:

▶ **Web/Multimedia:** When the final image will be displayed onscreen, you can completely trust your screen when sharpening the image. Most of the time you'll end up with Radius settings between .5 and 1 and Amount settings below 100%. Just be aware that sharpening increases the file size of JPEG file format images (**Figures 11.52** to **11.54**). So, if you're planning on saving your image as a JPEG file, use the absolute minimum amount of sharpening that makes the image not look soft.

▶ **Photographic output devices:** These devices include film recorders, LightJets, and other devices that use photographic film or paper to reproduce an image. They can reproduce the majority of the detail you see onscreen. With these devices you have to be very careful to make sure the Radius setting you use is quite low (.25 to .7 for most images) so that the halos that come from sharpening aren't obvious on the end result.

▶ **Desktop printer:** This would include inkjet and laser printers as well as any other printer that you have immediate access to. I like to experiment with an image that is representative of the type of image you use the most.

Figure 11.51 Advanced options.

Figure 11.52 Original unsharpened image (file size: 25.51 Kbytes). (©2007 Andy Katz)

Figure 11.53 Sharpened with settings of 70, .5, and 4 (file size: 28.63 Kbytes).

Figure 11.54 Sharpened with settings of 175, .7, and 4 (file size: 37.51 Kbytes).

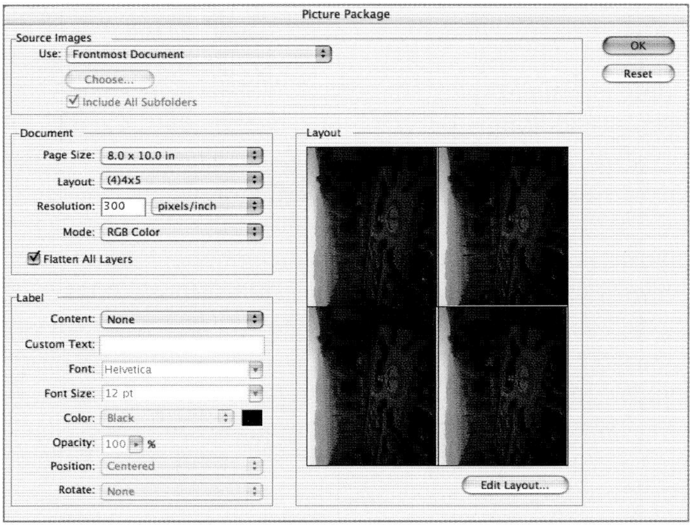

Figure 11.55 Use Picture Package to create multiple copies of an image on a single page.

With your experimental image open, choose File > Automate > Picture Package (**Figure 11.55**). Set the Page Size pop-up menu to the choice that is closest to the size of paper you typically use, and set the Resolution to what is best for your particular printer. (See Bonus Chapter 5, "Resolution Solutions," on the CD at the back of this book, if you're not sure which resolution is best for your device.) Now choose a Layout setting that gives you at least four images, and click OK. That will produce a document that contains multiple copies of your experimental image. Select one of the images with the Marquee tool and sharpen it until it looks great onscreen, and make note of the settings you used. Then move to the second image and be a little more aggressive with the Amount or Radius setting. Continue experimenting with more aggressive settings until you've sharpened each image a different amount, and write down the setting you used for each. Now print that image at 100% scale and compare the resulting print to what you see onscreen at 100% view. Look over the printed images and find the one that has the most realistic looking sharpness, and then look at that same image onscreen to see how much you'll need to exaggerate your sharpening to achieve that amount of sharpening in the print.

▶ **Commercial printing press:** Start by sharpening your images until they look very sharp onscreen, and then analyze the printed result when you get a job back from the printing company. If the printed result doesn't look too sharp, slowly ratchet up the Amount and Radius settings on subsequent images until you find that the printed images look very sharp, but still natural. Each time compare the printed result to the original digital file, viewing the image at 100% magnification. As you work on more and more jobs, you'll start to get a feeling for how much you need to overdo the sharpening onscreen to get a nice sharp end result. You'll find that different types of printing will reproduce differing amounts of detail. (Newspaper images need to be sharpened much more than images that will be printed in a glossy brochure.)

If thinking about all the different settings needed for different output devices drives you crazy, you might want to think about adding a commercial plug-in filter to Photoshop. Nik Multimedia (www.nikmultimedia.com) makes a set of plug-in filters known as Nik Sharpener Pro (**Figure 11.56**), which takes a lot of the guesswork out of sharpening your images.

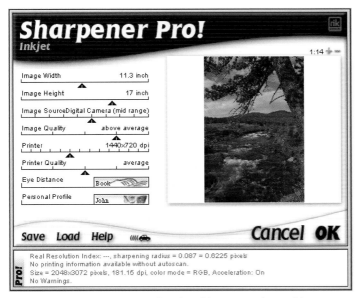

Figure 11.56 Nik Sharpener Pro takes a lot of the guesswork out of sharpening.

The package comes with separate filters for different types of output (including ink jet, color laser, offset printing, and Internet) and compensates for different viewing distances and image sizes, all without having to think about Amount, Radius, and Threshold settings. I find that the results are just a little bit too aggressive, so I choose Edit > Fade right after applying the filter and lower the Opacity setting a bit. It's a personal preference as to what you consider to be a naturally sharp result, so the Opacity setting you'll end up using will be unique to you.

If you plan on using an image for more than one purpose, it would be ideal if you were to create a unique image for each use. You can choose Image > Duplicate to create an exact copy of an image. Then, be sure to choose Image > Image Size (**Figure 11.57**) to set the size and resolution that is proper for the output device for which this particular image is destined. Finally, sharpen the image based on your experience with that particular device and repeat the process, always going back to the full-sized master image and repeating those steps for each device you plan on using.

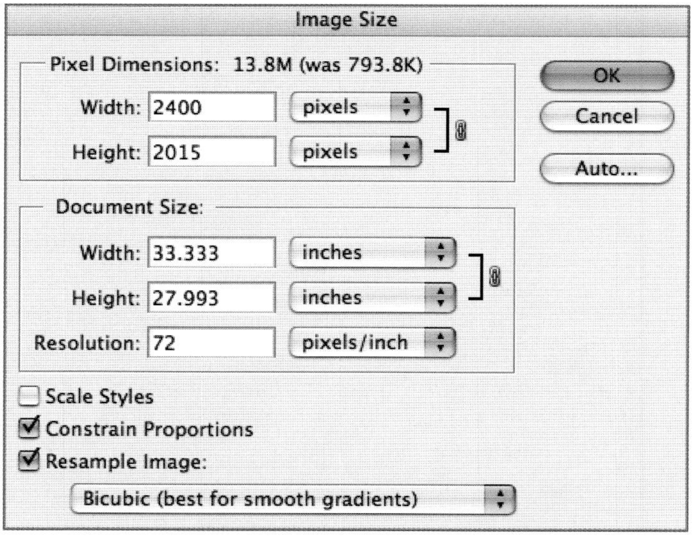

Figure 11.57 Use the Image Size dialog box to specify the size and resolution of your image.

Or, if you simply can't deal with one image for each device, work with a single image and do the following: Set the resolution to what's needed for your most demanding output device (needing the highest resolution image) and sharpen it for the device that looks the closest to your screen (the one that needs the least radical sharpening). Then use that one image for all output devices. That's kind of like buying one size of shoe for an entire basketball team. As long as it's large enough for the biggest person, everyone should be able to fit in it, but it won't be ideal for everyone.

Tricks of the Trade

Now that we've talked about the general process of sharpening an image, let's start to explore some more advanced ideas that will allow you to get more control over your sharpening.

Sharpen Luminosity

If you look closely at a color image after it's been sharpened, you might notice bright-colored halos around objects that were not all that colorful in the original photo (**Figure 11.58**) (like a red halo around a pink dress). To prevent that type of unwanted sharpening artifact, choose Edit > Fade immediately after sharpening an image. When the Fade dialog box appears, set the Mode pop-up menu to Luminosity and then click the OK button (**Figure 11.59**). That will force the sharpening you just applied to affect only the brightness of the image and will prevent it from shifting or intensifying the colors in your image (**Figure 11.60**). If you read a lot of books and magazine articles about Photoshop, you might discover that many people attempt to get the same result by converting their image to LAB mode and then sharpening the image. The only problem with that approach is that any time you change the mode of your image, you lose a little quality. So, I only switch modes when I have a good reason to do so. Fade gives us the same benefits as converting to LAB mode, so I prefer to leave my image in the mode it started in when I sharpen it.

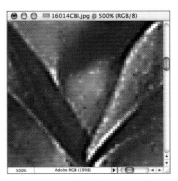

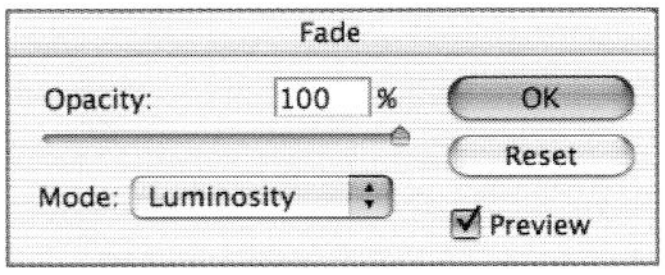

Figure 11.58 After sharpening this image, the color became more intense in the transition areas. (©Stockbyte, www.stockbyte.com)

Figure 11.59 Choose Edit > Fade and set the Mode pop-up menu to Luminosity.

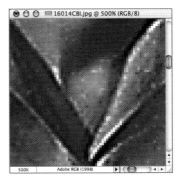

Figure 11.60 After fading with Luminosity, the color went back to normal. This might be hard to see in printed form; look closely at the edge of the collar where it touches her skin.

Sharpen the Black Channel

If your image is destined for CMYK mode, be sure to make an extra sharpening pass on the black channel. Just open the Channels palette (Window > Channels), click on the Black channel, and sharpen away. Because black ink is mainly used in the darker areas of the image, you can get away with some rather aggressive settings. (Try these: Amount = 350, Radius = 1, Threshold = 2.) Perform this sharpening pass after you've already sharpened the full color image (**Figures 11.61** to **11.63**).

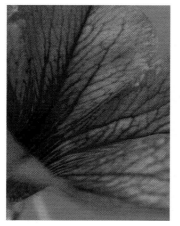

Figure 11.61
Original unsharpened image.
(©Stockbyte, www.stockbyte.com)

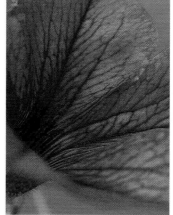

Figure 11.62 Result of sharpening the image while in RGB mode.

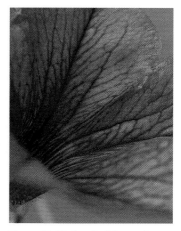

Figure 11.63 Result of sharpening the black channel. Look in the darkest part of the image to see the difference.

Sharpen Channels Separately

Certain images don't look all that good after being sharpened. For instance, when you sharpen a face, it sometimes seems to just fall apart, making the person look years older. Another example would be scanned images where color noise is exaggerated. In those cases, you should consider clicking through the channels that appear in the Channels palette and sharpening only the channels that would help the image. When it comes to skin, that would be the channel that is the lightest (red in RGB mode or cyan in CMYK mode) (**Figure 11.64**). For noisy images, you should avoid sharpening the channel that contains the most noise (usually blue in RGB mode or yellow in CMYK mode) (**Figure 11.65**). I don't use this technique every time I'm sharpening, but I'll think about it when sharpening the full color image makes it look worse than the original.

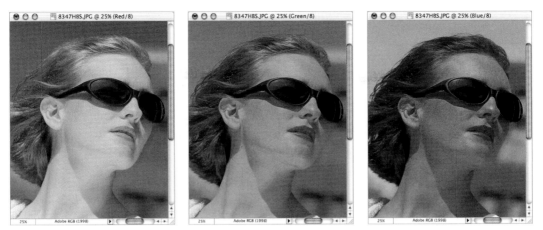

Figure 11.64 From left to right: red channel, green channel, blue channel. (©Stockbyte, www.stockbyte.com)

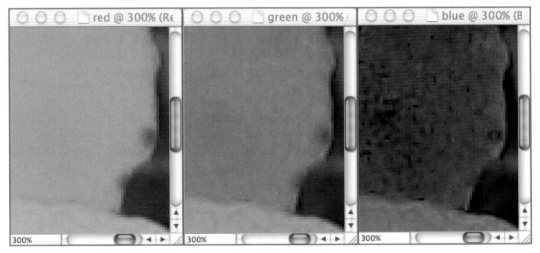

Figure 11.65 From left to right: red channel, green channel, blue channel.

Control Highlight and Shadow Separately

When you sharpen an image, Photoshop adds a dark halo on one side of an edge and a bright halo on the opposite side of the edge. When you're working with dark backgrounds (like a deep blue sky), the bright halos can be rather easy to see (**Figure 11.66**). That's when you might want to try controlling the bright and dark halos separately so that you can minimize the bright halo while maintaining the dark one. You can accomplish that by making two duplicates of the layer you want to sharpen. Then, click on each of those duplicate layers and set the Blending mode at the top of the Layers palette to Lighten for one and

353

Darken for the other (**Figure 11.67**). Now you can sharpen the two layers separately; the setting you apply to the layer that is set to Lighten will control the bright halos while the setting used on the layer set to Darken will control the dark halo (**Figure 11.68**).

Figure 11.66 The bright halos in this image are getting obvious. (©2007 Ben Willmore)

Figure 11.67 Duplicate the layer twice and set one layer to Lighten mode and the other to Darken mode.

Figure 11.68 When you separate the dark and bright halos, you have more control over them.

Closing Thoughts

If you read this chapter and felt like you were drowning in details, try a few of the techniques, then come back and read it again, and things will start to gel. It may take you a while to become truly comfortable with sharpening your images, but it's well worth the time because you can transform your flat and lifeless images into ones that are lively and ready to pop off the page. I'll leave you with one very important piece of sharpening advice: Oversharpened images never look good, so if you are ever unsure of how much sharpening to apply, always err on the side of conservatism.

PART III

Creative Explorations

 Enhancement

I'm trying to free your mind, Neo. But I can only show you the door. You're the one that has to walk through it.
— Morpheus, from *The Matrix*

In this chapter we're going to explore a tantalizing variety of enhancement techniques. The truth is that you can't put a measuring stick on the many ways there are to enhance your image. The possibilities in Photoshop are beyond the horizon and limited only by your willingness to experiment. But I think I can get you off to a good start so that you can feel comfortable tackling most jobs.

In an effort to impose some order on this somewhat random collection of techniques, I've structured this chapter around Photoshop's Blending modes. They are what you find at the top of the Layers palette and in many other areas. Blending modes comprise one of the most powerful features in Photoshop—and one of my personal favorites.

The Battalion of Blending Modes

The Blending Modes menu draws the map for this chapter, so let's just start at the top and work our way down the list. We'll take a detour or two on our way, but at least we'll know where we're headed. Let's start by taking a look at how the modes are organized; then we can jump in and start using them. The Blending modes are divided into six categories (**Figure 12.1**).

Dissolve Mode

The first Blending mode is called Dissolve, and although it might be useful to some people, it's the one that I use the least out of the whole collection. It only affects areas that are partially transparent. All it does is take areas that are partially transparent and transform them into a scattered

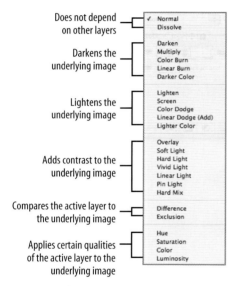

Does not depend on other layers

Darkens the underlying image

Lightens the underlying image

Adds contrast to the underlying image

Compares the active layer to the underlying image

Applies certain qualities of the active layer to the underlying image

Figure 12.1 The Blending Modes menu is organized into six sections.

spray of solid pixels. As a result, those areas end up looking noisy (**Figures 12.2** and **12.3**). I do see the Dissolve Blending mode used on occasion for product packaging, usually to create a noisy-looking shadow or glow around some text. You can accomplish this quite easily by adding a Drop Shadow or an Outer Glow layer style to a layer and setting its Blending mode (in the Layer Style dialog box) to Dissolve (**Figure 12.4**). It's not very often that I need this kind of a look, so let's move on and see what the other Blending modes can do.

Figure 12.2 A drop shadow created in Photoshop's default Blending mode.

Figure 12.3 The same drop shadow created in Dissolve mode.

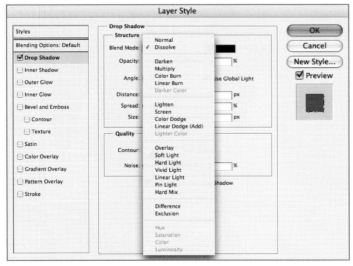

Figure 12.4 Choosing Dissolve from the Blend Mode menu in the Layer Style dialog box.

Behind Mode

Most of the Blending modes available in Photoshop show up in the pop-up menu at the top of the Layers palette, but the Behind Blending mode shows up in only a few areas of Photoshop (painting tools and the Edit > Fill dialog box). Behind mode limits the changes you make to a layer so that they only affect the transparent areas of the active layer. Using Behind mode is similar to working on a layer directly below the one that is active. Painting on a layer in Behind mode gives the impression that you're painting underneath the active layer (**Figures 12.5** to **12.7**).

I mainly use this mode with the Fill dialog box (Edit > Fill) as a quick-and-dirty way to fill the empty parts of a layer. I use it when I'm creating a slide show and don't want to see the checkerboard background anywhere. Choosing Edit > Fill, setting the Use pop-up menu to White, and changing the Mode pop-up menu to Behind, for example, fills all transparent pixels with white.

If you find that the Behind mode isn't working as you expected, glance at the top of the Layers palette to see if the Lock Transparency icon is turned on. When that icon is turned on, you can't change the transparent areas of the active layer, which makes the Behind mode useless.

Figure 12.5 A layer that contains transparent areas. (©2007 PhotoSpin, www.photospin.com)

Figure 12.6 Painting in Behind mode.

Figure 12.7 The brush strokes appear to be underneath the active layer.

Clear Mode

Clear mode is another Blending mode that shows up only in certain areas of Photoshop (like in the painting tools and Edit > Fill command). Clear mode is basically the same as using the Eraser tool, or selecting an area and then pressing Delete (Mac) or Backspace (Windows).

I generally use this mode to lower the opacity of a large area. Choosing Edit > Fill in Clear mode at 40% opacity, for example, reduces the opacity of the layer by 40%, leaving it 60% opaque (**Figures 12.8** and **12.9**).

When you use Clear mode, Photoshop completely ignores the color you are attempting to fill or paint with. It only pays attention to the Opacity setting and uses the paint or selection that is active to determine which areas should be deleted.

You'll find Clear mode in only a few areas of Photoshop, including the Line tool (using the Fill setting on the far left of the options bar), the Paint Bucket tool, the Brush tool, the Pencil tool, the Fill command, and the Stroke command.

NOTES

If you'd rather not permanently lower the opacity of an area, you might want to think about using a Layer Mask instead (see the next chapter for general info on Layer Masks). Clear mode is like putting gray in a Layer Mask. Filling with 40% opacity in Clear mode is the same as filling part of a Layer Mask with 40% gray.

The Lock Transparency icon at the top of the Layers palette prevents you from changing how transparent an area is. When that check box is turned on, the Behind and Clear modes will be grayed out.

Figure 12.8 The original foreground image with a white background.

Figure 12.9 The foreground image filled using Clear mode at 50% opacity.

Darken Blending Modes

The Blending modes on the second section of the menu are grouped together because they can only darken the underlying image. In all of these modes, white simply disappears, and in most of them, anything darker than white will darken the underlying image. Each mode has its own personality, so let's look at them one at a time.

Darken Mode

Darken compares the active layer to the underlying image and allows only those areas that are darker than that image to show up (**Figures 12.10** to **12.12**). It's that simple when you're working on grayscale images, but if you try the same mode out on a color image, you might be surprised by the result.

Figure 12.10 The top layer. (©2007 PhotoSpin, www.photospin.com)

Figure 12.11 The bottom layer. (© 2007 Stockbyte, www.stockbyte.com)

Figure 12.12 Result of using Darken mode on the top layer.

Color images are usually made up of three components: red, green, and blue. Darken mode compares two layers by looking at red, green, and blue individually. So, let's say you have a layer with some red in it that's made out of 230 Red, 50 Green, and 30 Blue, and you have a layer above it that contains a blue color made from 50 Red, 55 Green, and 200 Blue. The blue in the top layer would usually completely cover up the color below (**Figure 12.13**), but when you set the top layer to Darken mode, Photoshop compares the red, green, and blue components of each layer and uses the darkest of each. In this case, it would see that the red information on the top layer is darker (50 versus 230; lower numbers mean less light). When comparing the green components, it would see that the bottom layer is darker, and it would see that the blue component is darkest on the bottom layer. So, once it picked the darkest of each, it would end up with 50 Red, 50 Green, and 30 Blue, which would result in a dark yellow color (**Figure 12.14**). I don't usually think about the red, green, and blue components of each layer when I'm using Darken mode, but I occasionally blame them when I don't get the result I am looking for.

I mainly use Darken mode when I'm retouching an image, which we'll talk about in the next chapter, but for now, let's see how we might use it with Photoshop's filters. Let's say you've chosen Filter > Pixelate > Pointillize, but you don't like all the white areas that show up (**Figure 12.15**). If that's the case, you can choose Edit > Fade Pointillize immediately after applying the filter, and then you can tell Photoshop how to apply that filter to the original. If you choose Darken, Photoshop compares the filtered result with the original and only allows the filter to darken the original, which should in effect get rid of the white areas (unless the original contained white) (**Figure 12.16**). I often use this technique after applying the Sharpen filter, because the bright halos it produces are often distracting. By using Darken mode, I can limit that filter so that it creates only dark halos.

Figure 12.13 In Normal mode, the top layer obstructs your view of the underlying image.

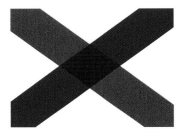

Figure 12.14 In Darken mode, Photoshop uses the darkest of the red, green, and blue components.

Figure 12.15 Result of applying the Pointillize filter. (©iStockphoto.com/redapplefalls)

Figure 12.16 Result of fading the Pointillize filter in Darken mode.

Figure 12.17 The first image to be printed. (©iStockphoto.com/texasmary)

Figure 12.18 Image with white background to be printed on the second pass. (©iStockphoto.com/ziggymaj)

Figure 12.19 Result of combining

Multiply Mode

Of all the Darken Blending modes, the one I use the most is Multiply. Multiply acts just like ink. To see what I mean, just imagine taking **Figure 12.17** and printing it on an inkjet printer. Then, imagine sending the sheet back through the printer and printing a second image on top of the first (**Figure 12.18**). All the second printing can do is darken the first because all an inkjet printer can do is add ink to the page (**Figure 12.19**). Or, if you're a photographer, think about what happens when you sandwich two 35mm slides together. The second can only darken the first, right? Well, it's the same concept. In this mode, white simply disappears. After all, how do you print white with an inkjet printer? You don't. Instead you just leave the paper alone. It's the same way in Multiply mode; white simply disappears. But anything darker than white will darken the underlying image.

This is a simple way to make text or graphics "overprint" on the underlying image instead of just covering it up (**Figures 12.20** and **12.21**). In essence, using Multiply mode causes one layer to act like a Magic Marker on the layer below. I find this mode to be extremely useful when working with images that contain natural shadows. I demonstrate how to print an existing shadow on top of a new background in Bonus Chapter 3 "Shadows," which can

Figure 12.20 Top layer set to Normal mode. (©Stockbyte, www.stockbyte.com)

Figure 12.21 Top layer set to Multiply mode.

Figure 12.22 Image that contains two layers: subject and shadow. (©iStockphoto.com/busypix)

Figure 12.23 Image to overlay the shadow onto. (©iStockphoto.com/4x6)

Figure 12.24 Result of combining two images and setting the shadow layer to Multiply.

be found on the CD at the back of this book (**Figures 12.22** to **12.24**). You can also use it anytime you have scanned text or other graphics that you'd like to print on something else. The main problem you'll have to look out for is areas that are not completely white. Any area that is darker than white will darken the underlying image. This means that you'll occasionally need to choose Image > Adjustments > Levels and move the upper-right slider to make sure the background is pure white. As an example, let's say that I'd like to take the tattoo from **Figure 12.25** and make it look as if it were on **Figure 12.26** instead. I'd go about that by placing the tattoo on a layer above the second image, setting the Blending mode of that layer to Multiply (**Figure 12.27**), choosing Image > Adjustments > Desaturate, and then adjusting the image using Levels until only the tattoo appeared and the background surrounding it disappeared (**Figure 12.28**). If there ended up being a few areas that simply didn't disappear, I'd switch to the Eraser tool to eradicate those trouble areas.

Figure 12.25 Tattoo to be transplanted to another image. (©Stockbyte, www.stockbyte.com)

Figure 12.26 Image to which the tattoo will be applied. (©Stockbyte, www.stockbyte.com)

Figure 12.27 Result of setting the tattoo layer to Multiply mode.

Figure 12.28 Result of desaturating and then adjusting the image with Levels.

Figure 12.29 In Normal mode, the three circles don't interact with each other.

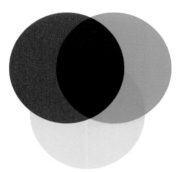

Figure 12.30 Result of setting each layer to Multiply mode.

During my seminars, I usually end up talking about how both your screen and printer simulate a wide range of colors using just red, green, and blue light, or cyan, magenta, and yellow ink. To demonstrate this, I usually create an image that contains three circles, one per layer: one cyan, one magenta, and the third yellow. The problem is that they don't act like ink when they overlap (**Figure 12.29**). So I simply set the Blending mode for each layer to Multiply, and then everything works the way I want it to (**Figure 12.30**).

Now let's see how we might be able to use Multiply in a project where you need to create a contour drawing out of a photograph (**Figure 12.31**). To start out, open any image. (Faces work rather well.) Because we're going to end up with black lines and no color information, let's choose Image > Mode > Grayscale. Now let's start playing with Photoshop's filters to get our contours. Choose Filter > Stylize > Trace Contour, and move the slider around a bit just to see what happens (**Figure 12.32**). You'll see that Trace Contour puts a black line around the edge of a particular shade of gray. There are just two problems: First, the contours aren't usually smooth, and second, there's only one contour for the entire image. To fix the first problem, just smooth out your image by applying either the Gaussian Blur or the Median filter. The latter requires a little more

Figure 12.31 Left: The original image. Right: Result of conversion to a contour drawing. (©Stockbyte, www.stockbyte.com)

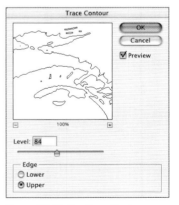

Figure 12.32 The Trace Contour dialog box.

effort, and that's where we can start putting the Multiply Blending mode to work. Duplicate the layer enough times so that you have one layer for each contour that you'd like to end up with. (I want to end up with six, so I'll press Command/Ctrl-J five times to end up with six layers total.) Then apply the Trace Contour filter to each layer, using a different level setting each time. The level setting can be found in the Trace Contour dialog box. You'll end up with six layers, each containing a different contour (**Figure 12.33**). Now to combine those images into one, set the Blending mode of each layer to Multiply so they print on top of each other, which will make the white areas disappear (**Figure 12.34**).

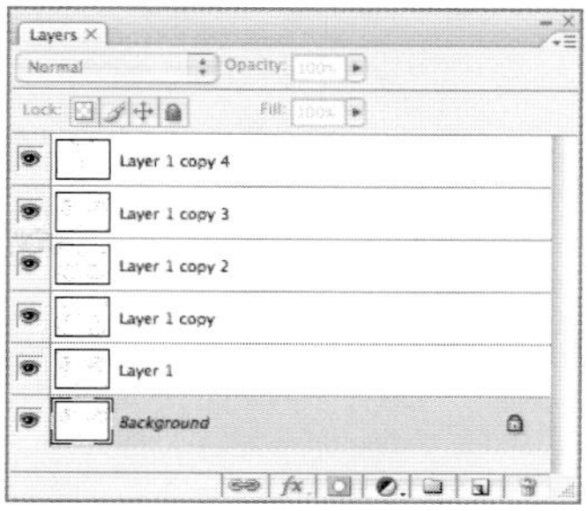

Here's another way of using Blending modes with filters. Let's say you've opened an image and then chosen Filter > Stylize > Find Edges. After doing that, you'd end up with a bunch of black lines that represent the edges of all the objects that were in your photo (**Figure 12.35**). But what if you wanted those black lines to print on top of the original image? Well, immediately after applying the filter, you could choose Edit > Fade Fine Edges and set the Blending Mode menu to Multiply. Photoshop would then apply the filtered image to the original as if you had printed on top of it (**Figure 12.36**).

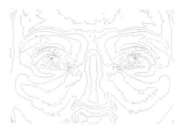

Figure 12.33 All the layers that are needed to create the drawing.

Figure 12.34 Result of combining all the layers in Multiply mode.

Figure 12.35 Result of applying the Find Edges filter. (original image: iStockphoto.com/suemack)

Figure 12.36 Result of fading the edges in Multiply mode.

You'll find that Multiply mode is used quite a bit in Photoshop's Layer Styles. This occasionally messes me up when I'm trying to do something unusual. Here's an

Figure 12.37 The black drop shadow does not contribute to the legibility of the text. (©iStockphoto.com/hologram)

Figure 12.38 A white shadow isn't possible in Multiply mode, so the mode has been changed to Normal.

example. Let's say I have some black text on a deep blue background, and I'd like to add a drop shadow. So, with the text layer active, I choose Layer > Layer Style > Drop Shadow. But a black drop shadow with black text makes the text hard to see (**Figure 12.37**), so I decide to change the shadow color to white. When I do this, however, the shadow simply disappears! That's because its mode is automatically set to Multiply (in the Layer Style dialog box), and white disappears in Multiply mode. To get things to work the way I want them to, I simply change the mode from Multiply to Normal, and everything works fine (**Figure 12.38**).

Color Burn Mode

The Color Burn mode is not easy to describe or understand but can be very useful nonetheless. Just as with all the Darken Blending modes, white doesn't do anything in Color Burn mode. Black will leave any red, green, or blue numbers that are 255 alone and force all others to zero. When you paint with a primary color (pure red, green, or blue), you'll end up with the amount of that primary color that was in the underlying image and nothing else. When you paint with a color that's made out of two primaries, Photoshop strips the third primary color out of the underlying image. Here's where the goodies come in. Paint with shades of gray to darken and intensify the colors that are in the underlying image. This can work wonders for darkening bland-looking skies, making them more colorful while at the same time maintaining the bright white clouds (**Figures 12.39** and **12.40**). I sometimes like the way

Figure 12.39 The original image. (© 2007 Stockbyte, www.stockbyte.com)

Figure 12.40 Result of painting with gray across the sky in Color Burn mode.

shadows look when I use Color Burn. If a shadow is falling on a textured background, more of the texture will come through because it will maintain more of the highlights (**Figures 12.41** and **12.42**). I also use this mode to colorize grayscale images. If you're going to try it, just make sure to change the mode of your image from grayscale to RGB or CMYK. You'll most likely want to lower the opacity of the painting tool you use; otherwise, you'll end up with a rather dark result. I'll talk more about using the mode for colorizing once we've had a chance to cover some of the other modes that are also used for that purpose.

Figure 12.41 Shadow applied in the default Blending mode: Multiply mode.

Linear Burn Mode

The Linear Burn mode acts much like Multiply mode but has a greater tendency to make areas pure black. It also seems to maintain more of the color from the underlying image. Use it anytime you'd think about using Multiply mode but would like a higher-contrast result. If you ever find that standard shadows (which usually use Multiply mode) look a little too gray, try Linear Burn; you might like the result better (**Figures 12.43** and **12.44**), although you will need to lower the Opacity setting to avoid getting an overly dark result. So, anytime you'd normally use Multiply mode, be sure to also try Linear Burn mode—especially if you're looking for a darker, more saturated result (**Figures 12.45** and **12.46**).

Figure 12.42 Shadow applied in Color Burn mode.

Figure 12.43 Shadow applied in Multiply mode.

Figure 12.44 Shadow applied in Linear Burn mode.

Figure 12.45 Two images combined in Multiply mode.

Figure 12.46 Two images combined in Linear Burn mode.

Lighten Blending Modes

For each of the darken Blending modes (Darken, Multiply, Color Burn, and Linear Burn), there is an equally useful opposite mode. With all the lighten Blending modes, black simply disappears, and anything brighter than black has the potential to brighten the underlying image.

Lighten Mode

Figure 12.47 Image with bulbs visible. (courtesy Nik Willmore, www.e-dot.com)

The Lighten mode compares the active layer to the underlying image and allows the areas of the active layer to show up that are brighter than the underlying image. But again, it looks at the red, green, and blue components of the image separately, which makes for some unpredictable results. Lighten mode was a lifesaver the last time I visited my brother in New York. He's an artist who has no sense for normal sleeping hours. Right when I was getting ready to call it a night, my brother decided to work on a computer project. The problem was that his computer was in the guest room, so I knew he was going to keep me up until he finished his project. Knowing that, I took a keen interest in the project. It turned out that he was attempting to create a photorealistic 3D rendering of a lamp that he was thinking of making. The only problem was that he could either get the glass part of the bulb to show up or the glowing filament, but he couldn't get both (**Figures 12.47** and **12.48**). It looked as if it was going to take him hours to figure it out, so in the interest of a good night's sleep, I volunteered to help. After looking at the two images he had created, I thought that if Photoshop could only compare them and let one image lighten the other, then I could get to sleep. So I loaded both images into Photoshop, one atop the other, set the Blending mode of the top layer to Lighten, and—bingo, I could call it a night (**Figure 12.49**).

Figure 12.48 Image with filament visible.

I use Lighten mode a lot when I'm experimenting with filters. For instance, choosing Filter > Stylize > Glowing Edges creates bright lines where the edges of an object were in your image (**Figure 12.50**). I sometimes use this filter to add extra interest to an image by choosing Edit > Fade Glowing Edges, and then setting the Blending Mode menu to Lighten immediately after applying the filter

Figure 12.49 Result of combining two images in Lighten mode.

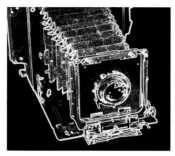

Figure 12.50 The colors shift when the Glowing Edges filter is applied. (original image ©Stockbyte, www.stockbyte.com)

Figure 12.51 More of the original image is visible after Lighten mode is used.

Figure 12.52 The original image. (© 2007 Stockbyte, www.stockbyte.com)

Figure 12.53 The Lighting Effects filter brightens and darkens the image.

Figure 12.54 Result of fading the Lighting Effects filter in Lighten mode.

(**Figure 12.51**). That way I can get the bright edge effect while maintaining the overall look of the original image. The same concept works great when you're using the Lighting Effects filter, which usually brightens or darkens an image. In Lighten mode, you can force that filter to only brighten the image (**Figures 12.52** to **12.54**). I like to use it after applying the Blur filter to add a soft-focus look (**Figure 12.55**). It can also be wonderful when sharpening an image. You can duplicate the layer twice, set the top layer to Lighten and the middle layer to Darken, and then sharpen the top two layers. Then you can control the dark and bright halos separately by lowering the opacity of each of those two layers. (This mode will be helpful in Chapter 15 when we talk about retouching.)

Figure 12.55 Top: The original image. Bottom: Blur filter and Lighten Blending mode used to create a soft-focus look. (©Stockbyte, www.stockbyte.com)

373

Screen Mode

If Multiply mode acts like ink, then Screen mode is its opposite, acting like light instead. In this mode, black simply disappears, whereas anything brighter than black brightens the underlying image. Screen mode is useful when you have an image that has a black background with anything that resembles light within it. I like to use it with things like sparklers and lightning. I just put the sparkler on a layer above another image, set the layer mode to Screen, choose Image > Adjust > Levels, and pull the upper-left slider in until the background of the sparkler disappears (**Figures 12.56** and **12.57**).

Figure 12.56 Result of using Screen mode to combine images. (©Stockbyte, www.stockbyte.com)

Screen mode is used in many of Photoshop's Layer Styles. Let's say you have some text and you add a glow around it by choosing Layer > Layer Style > Outer Glow. That will work fine as long as you choose a color that is bright like white or yellow, but it won't look so good if you use a dark color like navy blue (**Figure 12.58**). This is because Photoshop uses Screen mode as the default method for applying the glow to the underlying image, and shining a dark blue light at something isn't going to change it much. To remedy the situation, just change the Blending mode (in the Layer Style dialog box) to either Normal or Multiply (**Figure 12.59**).

Figure 12.57 Result of applying Levels to darken the background of the sparkler to black (black disappears in Screen mode).

Figure 12.58 A deep blue outer glow created in the default Blending mode: Screen mode.

Figure 12.59 Result of switching from Screen mode to Normal mode.

In my Photoshop seminars, I usually talk about how red, green, and blue light interact to create all the colors that a computer monitor can display. To demonstrate this, I start with a document that has a black background layer. Then I create three layers: one with a red circle, one with a blue one, and the third using green. But when I move these circles so they overlap, they don't interact as they would if they were made by shining a flashlight at a wall (**Figure**

12.60). By setting each of the layers to Screen mode, I can get the circles to interact with each other as if they were circles of light (**Figure 12.61**).

Color Dodge Mode

The Color Dodge mode usually brightens the underlying image while at the same time making the colors more saturated. It's very useful because it doesn't change the darkest part of your image much, which allows you to brighten an area while still maintaining good contrast. I usually just use the Paintbrush tool and paint with a dark shade of gray on a layer set to Color Dodge mode (**Figures 12.62** and **12.63**). It's sometimes useful for adding more interest to otherwise dull-looking hair. (Photographers often use a separate light source just to add highlights to hair.) I often use Color Dodge mode as a replacement for Screen mode when I'm adding an outer glow Layer Style to text (see **Figures 12.64** and **12.65**).

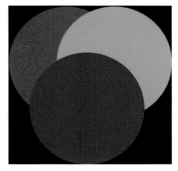

Figure 12.60 In Normal mode, the three circles don't interact with each other.

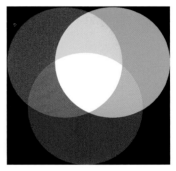

Figure 12.61 Result of switching each layer to Screen mode.

Figure 12.62 The original image. (©Stockbyte, www.stockbyte.com)

Figure 12.63 The water was brightened with gray paint in Color Dodge mode.

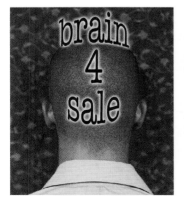

Figure 12.64 Yellow glow created in Screen mode. (original image ©Stockbyte, www.stockbyte.com)

Figure 12.65 The same yellow glow created in Color Dodge mode.

Figure 12.66 A simple glow created in Screen mode. (original image ©iStockphoto.com/benoitb)

Figure 12.67 The same glow created in Linear Dodge mode.

Linear Dodge

The Linear Dodge mode works much like Screen mode, but it has a greater tendency to make areas pure white. Use it any time you're considering Screen mode but would like a higher-contrast result (**Figures 12.66** and **12.67**).

Contrast Blending Modes

The majority of Blending modes available on the next section of the menu combines the ideas we've used in the Darken and Lighten Blending modes. In all of these modes, 50% gray simply disappears, and anything darker than 50% has the potential of darkening the underlying image, whereas areas brighter than 50% have the potential to brighten the underlying image. In essence, these modes increase the contrast of the underlying image by brightening one area while darkening another.

Overlay Mode

In Overlay mode, the information on the underlying image is used to brighten or darken the active layer. Any areas darker than 50% gray will act like ink (or Multiply mode), whereas any areas brighter than 50% gray will act like light (or Screen mode). Overlay mode is useful when you want to add color to the underlying image while maintaining its highlights and shadows (**Figures 12.68** and **12.69**). I also use this mode a lot when I'm working with Layer Styles. If I use both a pattern fill and a color overlay, the color overlay always completely covers up the pattern that is underneath it. But if I apply the color using the Overlay Blending mode

Figure 12.68 The original image. (©iStockphoto.com/constantgardener)

Figure 12.69 Result of placing solid red on a layer set to Overlay mode.

(in the Layer Style dialog box), it allows the highlights and shadows from the texture to brighten and darken the color that I'm applying (**Figures 12.70** and **12.71**). This allows me to create many grayscale patterns and then colorize them with the Color Overlay layer style.

Soft Light Mode

As with the other modes in this category, Soft Light mode makes 50% gray disappear while making brighter areas brighten and darker areas darken the underlying image. It usually does this with more subtle results than those you get in either Overlay or Hard Light mode. I primarily use this mode for applying textures to photographs. I cover a bunch of texture techniques in Bonus Chapter 4, "Type and Background Effects," but for now let's create just one. Open any photographic image and create a new, empty layer above that image. Next, type D to reset your fore-ground and background colors, and then choose Filter > Render Clouds. Now choose Filter > Stylize > Find Edges, and then Filter > Stylize > Emboss. Set the angle to 45°, the height to 1, and the amount as high as it can go. If you've done everything right, you should end up with a texture that resembles most refrigerators. To apply that texture to the underlying image, set its Blending mode to Soft Light at the top of the Layers palette (**Figure 12.72**).

Figure 12.70 When you use color overlay and a pattern fill, the color obstructs your view of the pattern.

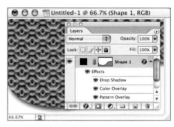

Figure 12.71 Applying the color overlay in Overlay mode allows it to combine with the underlying pattern.

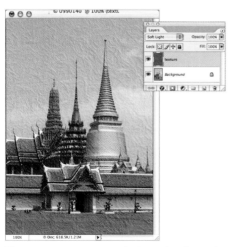

Figure 12.72 A texture applied in Soft Light mode. (©2007 PhotoSpin, www.photospin.com)

Figure 12.73 Two layers, both set to Normal mode. (©Stockbyte, www.stockbyte.com)

Figure 12.74 Result of switching the top layer to Soft Light mode.

Soft Light mode is also useful when you're attempting to add a reflection to a metallic image. Just place the image you want to reflect on a layer above the metallic object, and set its Blending mode to Soft Light (**Figures 12.73** and **12.74**).

Hard Light Mode

The Hard Light mode has got to be one of my absolute favorite Blending modes. In essence, it's a combination of Multiply mode (which acts like ink) and Screen mode (which acts like light). In Hard Light mode, any areas that are 50% gray will disappear, areas darker than 50% will darken the underlying image, and areas brighter than 50% will brighten the underlying image. You'll find me using this mode anytime I use the Emboss filter. When I choose Filter > Stylize > Emboss, I end up with a gray image that has almost no hint of the colors from the original image (**Figures 12.75** and **12.76**). But the gray gunk I do end up with happens to be exactly 50% gray (in RGB mode), which means that I can choose Edit > Fade Emboss and set the mode to Hard Light, and bingo…the gray is gone (**Figure 12.77**)! So Hard Light mode allows me to emboss an image while maintaining its color qualities. You can go one better by duplicating the layer before you emboss it. Then, choose Image > Adjustments > Desaturate to ensure there won't be any color shifts (**Figures 12.78** and **12.79**).

Figure 12.75 The original image. (©2007 Andy Katz)

Figure 12.76 The Emboss filter delivers a gray result.

Figure 12.77 Result of applying the Emboss filter in Hard Light mode.

Figure 12.78 Embossing a color image produces color residue.

Figure 12.79 Desaturating the image prevents color residue.

Next, set the duplicate layer to Hard Light mode, and then apply the Emboss filter. This way you'll get a real-time preview instead of staring at a bunch of gray stuff while you're applying the filter.

Vivid Light

The Vivid Light mode is a combination of Color Dodge and Color Burn. In Vivid Light mode, areas darker than 50% darken and the colors become more saturated; areas brighter than 50% brighten and the colors become more saturated. This mode is great when an image really needs some kick. Just duplicate the layer and set it to Vivid Light mode. You'll most likely need to turn down the Opacity setting to get an acceptable result (**Figures 12.80** and **12.81**). I also use Vivid Light when I want to apply a texture to an image and I'm concerned that Overlay, Soft Light, or Hard Light mode will make the colors look a little too dull. For example, you can create a new layer above the image you want to texturize. Next, choose Filter > Render > Clouds, then apply Filter > Sharpen > Unsharp Mask with settings of 500, 1.5, and 0, and finish by applying Filter > Stylize > Emboss with settings of 145, 1, and 500. Now if you set the texture layer to Vivid Light mode, you'll be adding texture and enhancing the colors in the image (**Figures 12.82** and **12.83**).

Figure 12.80 The original image could use a little contrast and saturation.
(©2007 PhotoSpin, www.photospin.com)

Figure 12.81 Result of duplicating the layer and setting it to Vivid Light mode.

Figure 12.82 The original image. (©iStockphoto.com/aldra)

Figure 12.83 Texture applied in Vivid Light mode.

Linear Light

The Linear Light mode is a combination of Linear Dodge and Linear Burn. I try this mode anytime I'm considering using Hard Light mode. It produces a higher-contrast result where more areas will become pure black and pure white. This is another mode that is great with textures. I mainly use it when I want the highlights and shadow areas of a texture to become pure white and pure black, which usually makes the texture look extra crisp. If you'd like to give it a try, just create a new layer above the image you want to enhance, and then fill that layer with white. Now, to make the texture, choose Filter > Artistic > Sponge, and use settings of 2, 12, and 5 to pull out some contrast; then choose Image > Adjustments > Auto Levels and finish it off with Filter > Stylize > Emboss with settings of 135, 1, and 65. Once you set the Blending mode to Linear Light,

Figure 12.84 The texture that will be applied to a photo.

Figure 12.85 Applying the texture in Linear Light mode produces more saturated colors. (©2007 Andy Katz)

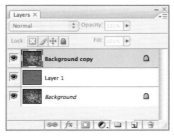

Figure 12.86 Place a duplicate of the original image on top, and set the mode to Color.

Figure 12.87 Result of applying a duplicate of the original in Color mode.

Figure 12.88 The original image. (©Stockbyte, www.stockbyte.com)

Figure 12.89 Blurring a duplicate layer set to Linear Light mode produces saturated colors.

Figure 12.90 Result of applying the original image in Color mode.

you should see what I'm talking about (**Figures 12.84 and 12.85**). If you find that the colors become too vivid, duplicate the original image, place it on top of the layers stack, and set its Blending mode to Color (**Figures 12.86 and 12.87**). (We'll talk about Color mode in a bit.) I often use this technique to create a high-contrast, soft-focus look. I'll end up with three versions of the original image, the bottom one being normal, the middle one being blurred and set to Linear Light mode, and the top one being set to Color mode and not blurred (**Figures 12.88 to 12.90**).

Pin Light

The Pin Light mode is a combination of Lighten and Darken modes. I find that I use this mode mainly when I'm experimenting with filters. I'll end up trying all the contrast modes, and on occasion Pin Light will be the most effective. But it's not very often that I think of a technique that is created specifically with Pin Light in mind. Here's an example of a situation where I ended up liking what Pin Light gave me. I duplicated the original layer, set the top layer to Pin Light, and left the bottom layer set to Normal. Then, with the top layer active, I chose Filter > Sketch > Note Paper and used settings of 25, 5, and 2. That created 3D highlights, but too much of the gray background was showing up (**Figure 12.91**). To finish it off, I chose Image > Adjustments > Levels and moved the middle slider until the background disappeared (**Figure 12.92**).

Figure 12.91 The Note Paper filter delivers a result that contains large areas of gray.

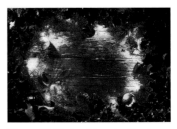

Figure 12.92 Applying the filter in Pin Light mode and adjusting the image with Levels. (©Stockbyte, www.stockbyte.com)

Figure 12.93 The original image.

Figure 12.94 Result of duplicating the layer and setting the Blending mode to Hard Mix.

Figure 12.95 Result of lowering the Fill Opacity of the duplicate layer to 70%.

Hard Mix

The Hard Mix mode posterizes the underlying layers based on the Fill Opacity setting of the layer that is using the Hard Mix Blending mode. A high Fill Opacity delivers extreme posterization, whereas lower Fill Opacity settings deliver a smoother-looking image (**Figures 12.93** to **12.95**). If the brightness of the layer is near 50% gray, the brightness of the underlying image will not change. Anything brighter than 50% gray will brighten the underlying image, whereas anything darker will darken it (**Figures 12.96** to **12.99**). A layer filled with 50% gray (RGB = 128, 128, 128) will neither brighten nor darken the underlying image, although varying the Fill Opacity will still control its posterization.

I like to use Hard Mix to create a "clipping display" just like what you'd get when you Option/Alt-drag one of the sliders in Levels (Image > Adjustments > Levels) or the Camera Raw dialog box. All you have to do is choose Layer > New Fill Layer > Solid Color, set the Mode pop-up menu to Hard Mix, and then work with a shade of gray. Using black shows you all the areas that are being blown out to white, whereas using white shows you all the areas that are plugged up to black. I just create two layers at the top of the Layers palette and turn them on whenever I need to check to see if I've lost detail in the highlights or shadows. This technique will be useful to you only if you're knowledgeable about clipping displays, so be sure to read Chapter 8, "Using Camera Raw," if you need a refresher.

Using Hard Mix mode with a 50% Fill Opacity often looks identical to the results you get using the Vivid Light Blending mode at 100% Fill Opacity. For that reason, I try Hard Mix and experiment with the Fill Opacity setting anytime I'm experimenting with the Vivid Light Blending mode.

How to Tell Them Apart

Here's my general thinking when using the contrast Blending modes. Overlay mode makes the underlying image more prominent than the active layer. Hard Light mode does the opposite, making the active layer more prominent. Soft Light mode usually makes both layers equally prominent. Vivid Light acts a lot like Hard Light but increases the saturation of the colors while preserving

Figure 12.96 The original image.

Figure 12.97 Using 50% gray leaves the brightness of the underlying image unchanged.

Figure 12.98 Using a shade brighter than 50% gray brightens the underlying image.

Figure 12.99 Using a shade darker than 50% gray darkens the underlying image.

more of the highlights and shadows from the underlying image. Linear Light is also like Hard Light, but it has a greater tendency to make areas pure black and pure white. Finally, Pin Light and Hard Mix are the loners in this group. Hard Mix mode increases the saturation of the colors and posterizes the image while lightening the underlying image in the highlight areas of the active layer and darkening the underlying image in the shadow areas. Pin Light compares the two layers, brightens the underlying image in the highlight areas of the active layer, and darkens the underlying image where there are shadows in the active layer (in a rather unpredictable way).

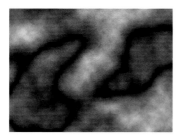

Figure 12.100 Painting on a layer below some clouds that are set to Difference mode.

Figure 12.101 Adding an Invert adjustment layer above the clouds.

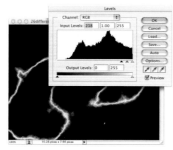

Figure 12.102 Pulling in the upper-left slider in Levels isolates the "lightning."

Comparative Blending Modes

The next two modes are very similar to each other. In general, they compare the active layer to the underlying image, looking for areas that are identical in both. Those areas appear as black, and all nonmatching areas show up as shades of gray or color. The closer the nonmatching areas are to being black in the end result, the more similar the areas are to the underlying image. In these modes, white on the active layer will invert whatever appears on the underlying image, but black on the active layer will not change the underlying image.

Difference Mode

The Difference mode works exactly as just described. Let's use it to create some homemade lightning. Start with a new document that contains a white background. Next, create a new layer, and reset your foreground and background colors by typing D; then choose Filter > Render Clouds, and set the layer containing the clouds to Difference mode. Now choose a large, soft-edged brush, and paint with black on the bottom layer. You should end up with a cloudy-looking image that has black areas around the edges of the area where you've painted (**Figure 12.100**). Now it's time to transform those black areas into lightning. We'll start the process by inverting the image to make black areas white. Do this by clicking on the topmost layer and then choosing Layer > New Adjustment Layer > Invert (**Figure 12.101**). Finally, choose Layer > New Adjustment Layer > Levels and move the upper-left slider until all you can see is the white "lightning" (**Figure 12.102**). Now you can continue painting on the bottommost layer to create more and more lightning. When you're all done, choose Layer > Merge Visible to combine the layers. You can apply the lightning to another image at any time by placing your lightning on a layer above and then setting the Blending mode of the layer to Screen, so it acts like light. There are a number of other neat things to do with the Difference mode, which we'll explore again in Bonus Chapter 4, "Type and Background Effects," which is on the CD at the back of this book.

Exclusion Mode

I'm sorry to say that this mode, along with Diffuse mode, usually just sits around collecting dust. It's just not very often that I have an image that will benefit from Exclusion mode, unless I'm going for a psychedelic, tripped-out '60s look. Let's see what I came up with when randomly experimenting with filters. I started by typing D to reset my foreground and background colors; then I chose Filter > Render Clouds (**Figure 12.103**). Next, I chose Filter > Noise > Median and used a setting somewhere around 10 (**Figure 12.104**). Then, to spice things up, I chose Filter > Sketch > Chrome with settings of 4 and 7. I chose Edit > Fade Chrome and tried both Difference and Exclusion modes (**Figure 12.105**). I preferred the look of Exclusion mode, so I clicked OK. I then chose Layer > New Adjustment Layer > Gradient Map and used the Color Burn Blending mode. I created a gradient that went from orange to yellow, experimenting until I liked what I ended up with (**Figure 12.106**).

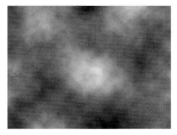
Figure 12.103 Result of applying the Clouds filter.

Figure 12.104 Smoothing out the clouds by using the Median filter.

Hue/Saturation/Brightness Blending Modes

The next set of modes divides the colors of your image into three components: hue, saturation, and brightness. Photoshop applies only one or two of these qualities to the underlying image. These are wonderfully helpful modes, and the ones that I feel have the most practical and obvious uses.

Figure 12.105 Fading the Chrome filter in Exclusion mode.

Hue Mode

The Hue mode looks at the basic colors contained on the active layer and applies them to the brightness and saturation information on the underlying layers. You can think of hue as the pure form of a color. In order to get to the pure form of a color, you have to ignore how dark the color is and how vivid it is, so you can concentrate just on its basic color. It's kind of like when you were a kid and only knew about a dozen words to describe color. Back then, you might have thought of a maroon car, or a pink dress, as being red.

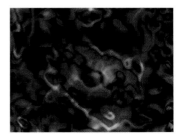
Figure 12.106 The end result after application of a gradient map.

Figure 12.107 Changing the color of an image in Hue mode. (©iStockphoto.com/SilentWolf)

Figure 12.108 A car with two-tone coloring created by applying the Gradient tool in Hue mode. (©2007 PhotoSpin, www.photospin.com)

That's because you were limited to describing things by their hue. This mode is great for changing the colors of objects that are already in color. All you have to do is create a new layer above the image, set it to Hue mode, and then paint away (**Figure 12.107**). I like to use the Gradient tool to create a two-tone look (**Figure 12.108**). You can even set the Gradient tool to Foreground to Transparent in order to shift one area and have it slowly fade out to the original color of the image (**Figures 12.109** and **12.110**). And then, after painting on the layer, you can really refine things by using the Eraser tool to bring areas back to normal (**Figure 12.111**).

Be careful, though, because there are a few things that might mess you up when you're using Hue mode. First, this mode cannot introduce color into an area that does not already contain color. (In order to do this, it would need to change the saturation of the area.) Second, it will not change the saturation of the underlying image. This means that if an area has just a hint of color in it, it will still have just as much color when you're done, because you will have only shifted that color to a different hue. Third, it also can't change how bright areas are. This means that painting across a white area will not change the image, because there is no way to introduce color into a white area without darkening it. You should use this mode when you need to shift the color of something that already contains color.

Figure 12.109 Adding a gradient set to Foreground to Transparent.

Figure 12.110 Result of applying the gradient in Hue mode.

Figure 12.111 Final result after the Eraser tool was used to remove the color change from a few spots.

Saturation Mode

As a seminar speaker, I often find myself in a room filled with Photoshop users, and I'm fond of getting them to think in new ways that will help them understand what's really going on with their pixels. When I talk about Saturation mode, I usually ask the participants to close their eyes and visualize what fluorescent…gray looks like! That usually sends them for a spin, because there is no such thing as fluorescent gray. However, the attempt to visualize it forces their brains to think completely about saturation and nothing else. Saturation determines how much color shows up in your image. If there is no saturation, there is no color at all, which just leaves brightness (grays). As things become more saturated, the color in that area becomes more vivid. When you get everything completely saturated, you end up with almost fluorescent colors.

Now, with that in mind, let's see how Photoshop's Saturation mode works. First off, it completely ignores what colors (red, green, yellow, orange, etc.) are on a layer. It also ignores how bright those colors are and just concentrates on how vivid they are. Then it changes the colors in the underlying image until they become just as saturated as those on the active layer. If you paint with the most vivid green you can find, the colors in the underlying image will become just as vivid—*but* bear in mind that the only areas that will end up as green will be those areas that were green to begin with (**Figures 12.112** and **12.113**). Saturation mode simply can't shift any of the basic colors; reds stay red, blues stay blue, and so on. They just become more or less vivid to match the quality of the active layer.

One of the most common uses for this mode is to force areas of an image to appear in black and white. All you have to do is create a new layer, set its Blending mode to Saturation, and then paint with any shade of gray. Because grays don't contain any color (they are pure brightness information), they will change the underlying image to grayscale (**Figure 12.114**). If you don't want to take the image all the way to grayscale, just lower the Opacity setting of the painting tool you are using (**Figures 12.115** and **12.116**). You can even

Figure 12.112 The original image. (© Stockbyte, www.stockbyte.com)

Figure 12.113 Applying a vivid green color to half the image in Saturation mode.

Figure 12.114 Painting with black on a layer set to Saturation mode changes the painted areas to grayscale. (©Stockbyte, www.stockbyte.com)

use the Gradient tool to make the transition fade out. Just set it to Foreground to Transparent, and drag across the layer that is set to Saturation mode (**Figure 12.117**).

Figure 12.115 The original image. (©2007 Andy Katz)

Figure 12.116 The area surrounding the bottle was painted in Saturation mode with gray at a medium Opacity setting.

Figure 12.117 Applying a gradient causes the color to slowly fade out. (©Stockbyte, www.stockbyte.com)

Color Mode

The Color mode applies both the hue (basic color) and saturation (vividness) of the active layer to the underlying image, leaving its brightness intact. In essence, it applies the color of the active layer to the brightness information of the underlying image. It's almost the same as Hue mode, with the exception that it can change the saturation of an area and therefore introduce color into an area that did not have it to begin with.

The most common (and most fun) use for this mode is to colorize grayscale photographs. All you have to do is change the mode of the image from grayscale to RGB or CMYK, create a new layer, set it to Color, and then paint away (**Figure 12.118**). If you feel the color you're adding is just too vivid, lower the opacity of your brush (**Figure 12.119**). Or, if you just can't get enough color into an area, you might want to try using Color Burn mode instead (**Figure 12.120**). If the highlights and shadows of the underlying image don't quite look right, try using Overlay mode (**Figure 12.121**).

Figure 12.118 Color applied in Color mode at 100% opacity.

Figure 12.119 Lowering the opacity reduces the amount of color applied.

Figure 12.120 Color applied in Color Burn mode with a medium Opacity setting.

Figure 12.121 Color applied in Overlay mode. (©2007 Stockbyte, www.stockbyte.com)

Figure 12.122 The Unsharp Mask filter produces vividly colored halos. (©Stockbyte, www.stockbyte.com)

Luminosity Mode

The Luminosity mode applies the brightness information of the active layer to the color in the underlying image. It can't shift colors or change how saturated those colors are. All it can do is change how bright they are.

I'm connected at the hip to Luminosity mode, because it seems that no matter what I'm doing, this mode is equipped to help out. Here are a few examples: Immediately after sharpening an image, I choose Edit > Fade Unsharp Mask and set the mode to Luminosity. This prevents the sharpening from adding odd colors to the edges of objects (**Figures 12.122** and **12.123**). A lot of people sharpen their images after converting them to Lab mode, but you can achieve the same result using the technique I just mentioned. Any time I adjust the brightness or contrast of an image using levels, Curves, or anything else, I'll end up choosing Edit > Fade and setting the mode to Luminosity; otherwise, the colors might become too vivid (**Figure 12.124**). If you're using an adjustment layer instead of applying the adjustment directly to the image, just set the Blending mode of the adjustment layer to Luminosity instead of using the Fade feature. If you apply a filter and you notice it shifting the color of the image (**Figures 12.125** to **12.127**), choose Edit > Fade, and then use Luminosity mode to limit the filter so that it changes only the brightness of the image.

Figure 12.123 Fading the filter in Luminosity mode prevents the overly saturated halos.

Figure 12.124 Left: The original image. Middle: A Curves adjustment designed to darken the image. Right: Result of fading the Curves adjustment in Luminosity mode. (©2007 Ben Willmore)

Figure 12.125 The original image. (©Stockbyte, www.stockbyte.com)

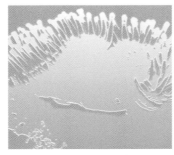

Figure 12.126 The Plaster filter.

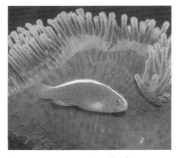

Figure 12.127 Fading the filter in Luminosity mode prevents the filter from shifting colors.

Closing Thoughts

If someone were to actually publish all of the great enhancement techniques out there, you'd be wading through a book 10 times the size of *War and Peace*. With this chapter, I've tried to give you some nice, tasty samples that will inspire you to go forth and try some more on your own. I hope you've enjoyed it. This part of Photoshop is always a pure pleasure for me—I could do this stuff every day. (Wait a minute—I do!) The more you work with Photoshop, the more you'll be able to add to your own personal cookbook of enhancement recipes. The trick is to find the time to experiment. I used to stay at work until rush-hour traffic died down just so I could have more time to play with Photoshop. When I went to college, there weren't any Photoshop classes, so I'm self-taught, thanks to a lot of midnight jam sessions with the tunes cranked up and Photoshop glowing on my computer screen. And look at me…I got to write this book!

13
Advanced Masking

©2007 Nick Koudis, www.koudis.com

Society is a masked ball, where every one hides his real character, and reveals it by hiding.

—Ralph Waldo Emerson

As I trot around the planet spreading the Photoshop gospel, I am besieged by users who really struggle when they try to isolate a complex object from its background. In almost every case, the problem is caused by using the wrong tool for the particular task or by not knowing how to properly use the right tool. Imagine giving a brain surgeon a pair of schoolroom safety scissors for his next operation. He would fling them on the floor in disdain and banish you from the operating room. Well, using advanced masking tools is like throwing away your school scissors (the basic selection tools) and trading them in for some finely tuned instruments that allow you to precisely isolate a complex object from its background and place that object on a different background.

This chapter will take you far beyond the basic selection tools I describe in Chapter 2, "Selection Primer," and will help you develop the advanced masking skills you need to tackle those less than simple images. You know the ones I'm talking about; they make most people wail in protest when they think about having to extract them from their backgrounds: people with frizzy semitransparent hair, trees with a thousand leaves, objects in motion, or something that is so similar to its background you can barely see where one ends and the other begins. By the end of this chapter, you should no longer be wailing. Instead, you should be able to easily evaluate the situation, quickly pick out the best tools for the job, and like a finely trained surgeon, understand how to go about executing the extraction in the most efficient, refined way possible. If you are someone who regularly faces this particular challenge (folks who do catalog, magazine, or newspaper work immediately come to mind), this chapter is a must read. But even if you don't get paid to use Photoshop and just want to torture your girlfriend by placing her head on the body of a sumo wrestler, this chapter has something for you, too.

The Key Is to Choose the Right Tool

In Photoshop, there is almost always more than one way of getting the job done. In the area of masking, however, certain tools were designed for specific types of images, and it's all too common to find someone becoming frustrated with a tool because it's the only one they know, and they're trying to force it to do something it's not really meant for. The key to getting good at masking is to be familiar with as many masking tools as possible and to have a good grasp of what each tool was designed for so you can choose the right tool for the job at hand. Let's take a brief look at what's available, and then we'll dig deeper and explore each feature in depth:

▶ **The Background Eraser:** This tool is best for crisp-edged objects that have a noticeable difference in color or brightness from the background that surrounds them. With this tool, you have to manually paint around the edges of objects to tell Photoshop which areas should be deleted, and Photoshop will try to figure out what should be kept or deleted.

▶ **The Extract command:** This command is best for images that have soft or fuzzy edges, like hair or objects in motion. With this command, you need to define three areas on your image: areas that should be left alone, areas that should be deleted, and areas that have a mix of both. Then, by comparing the first two areas, Photoshop figures out what to do with the third.

▶ **The Blending sliders:** These are a quick and dirty way to isolate objects that are radically different in brightness from what surrounds them. The most obvious uses for these would be things like fireworks, lightning, and text on a plain background.

▶ **Channels:** These are the old-fashioned way to remove the background on images. They used to be essential before the more sophisticated masking tools (Background Eraser and the Extract command) came along, but they are still useful when using those other tools would be too time-consuming. Channels are useful in a multitude of situations, but I most often use them on simple images.

▶ **The Pen tool:** This tool is best with crisp-edged objects that have mainly straight lines and very smooth curves. That means that it's ideal for images that are in focus and contain man-made objects like cars and computers. I would never think of using the Pen tool on overly complex images like trees or hair.

▶ **Layer Masks:** These are mainly used to refine the results you get from the other masking tools. Used all by themselves, they are no different than manually erasing the background with the standard Eraser tool; combined with other tools, however, they become a powerhouse that can often make the difference between a mediocre result and one that you'd be proud of.

Now that you have a general idea of what differentiates the various masking tools, let's jump in and explore each one in depth.

The Background Eraser

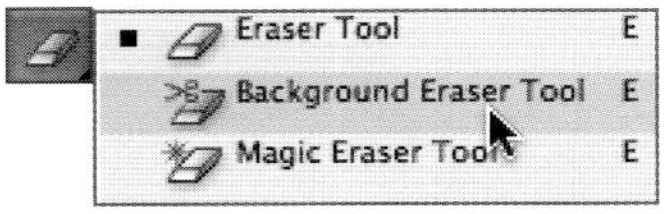

Figure 13.1 The Background Eraser tool is positioned in the same slot as the Eraser tool in Photoshop's tool palette.

Hiding under the normal Eraser tool is a special version known as the Background Eraser. Click and hold on the Eraser tool until you see a drop-down menu—the Background Eraser is the middle tool shown in that menu (**Figure 13.1**). When you move your cursor over an image, you'll notice that the Background Eraser gives you a round brush with a crosshair in the middle (**Figure 13.2**). When you click and drag on an image, Photoshop keeps a constant eye on what color is under the crosshair and deletes everything within the circle that is similar to that color (**Figure 13.3**). Your job is to trace near the edge of the object you want to keep. It's okay to have the circular part of your cursor overlap the subject. Just never let the crosshair hit the subject; otherwise, it will start to delete that area as well (**Figure 13.4**). The settings in the options bar at the top of your screen determine what should be kept or thrown away (**Figure 13.5**).

Figure 13.2 The Background Eraser presents you with a circle and a crosshair cursor. (©Stockbyte, www.stockbyte.com)

Figure 13.3 Clicking will delete the color that's under the crosshair from within the circle.

Figure 13.4 Be careful not to let the crosshair hit the subject of the photo; otherwise, it will be deleted.

Figure 13.5 The options bar settings for the Background Eraser tool.

Tolerance

Getting the right Tolerance setting is essential to using the Background Eraser tool successfully. This setting determines how much Photoshop will be able to stray from the color under the crosshair (**Figure 13.6**). If the background you are attempting to remove is very similar to the subject in brightness or color, you'll need to use a low Tolerance setting. Or, if the background is quite different from the subject, try a much higher Tolerance setting so that you can quickly remove the background without being overly careful about what you're dragging over.

I don't have any hard and fast guidelines to give you because this setting really depends on the image you're working with. I suggest that you start with the default setting of 50%, and then if you notice that some of the subject of the photo is being deleted along with the background, try a lower setting. If, on the other hand, not enough of the background is being deleted, you'll need to ramp up the Tolerance to allow Photoshop to delete a wider range of colors. You can change the Tolerance using the number keys on your keyboard (1 = 10%, 3 = 30%, 23 = 23%,

Figure 13.6 Tolerance settings used, from top to bottom: Original image, 1%, 5%, 10%, 20%, 30%, 40%, 50%, 60%.

and so on), and you can change the setting each time you release the mouse button. I usually work in sections using different Tolerance settings as the background changes. If you mess up, just press Command/Ctrl-Z to undo the last step and then try again.

Protect Foreground Color

On occasion, you'll find that the Tolerance setting alone isn't enough to isolate the subject from the background (**Figure 13.7**). That's when you'll want to start using the Protect Foreground Color check box. With that check box turned on, Photoshop will start thinking about two colors: the one under the crosshair, which will tell it what to delete, and the foreground color, which will tell it what to save (**Figure 13.8**). While the Background Eraser tool is active, you can hold Option/Alt and click on the part of your image you want to save—that will change your foreground color and therefore prevent the color you click on from being deleted. The only problem is that you might forget that you're protecting your foreground color, which can mess you up once you start working on a different part of the image where the color you are protecting is similar to the background you are attempting to delete. So be sure to keep one eye on this check box, and turn it off and on as you think necessary.

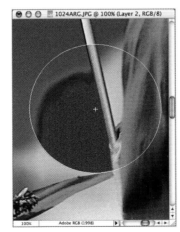

Figure 13.7 The green area was too similar to the background for the Background Eraser to successfully isolate it.

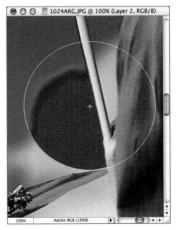

Figure 13.8 Result of sampling a color from the brightest area of the green area and turning on the Protect Foreground Color check box.

Sampling

If you find yourself getting frustrated because Photoshop is forcing you to be overly precise with your mousing, and you can see yourself going gray and toothless before you're done, you'll want to mess with the Sampling icons (from left to right: Continuous, Once, Background Swatch). Using the Continuous setting causes Photoshop to constantly keep an eye on the color that appears under the crosshair as you're moving your mouse (**Figures 13.9** and **13.10**). That's the default setting, and it works great with images that have multicolored backgrounds. If you have a background that doesn't vary in color much, however, you might want to try using the Once setting. With that setting, Photoshop pays attention to only the color under the crosshair at the exact moment that you click the mouse button. It won't stray from that color. That allows you to click on the background and then paint back and forth across your image without having to constantly pay attention to what's under the crosshair (**Figure 13.11**). Just make sure that you don't drag across any areas of the subject that are very similar to the background color. I mainly use this option on simple images that have a pretty big difference between the subject and background (like a dark tree against an almost solid blue sky). The Background Swatch setting is useful on those rare occasions when you can't find an easily clickable area of background color. I use that option after I've attempted to remove the background on an image using other tools, and then I

Figure 13.9 Original image. (©Stockbyte, www.stockbyte.com)

Figure 13.10 Result of using the Continuous option.

Figure 13.11 Result of using the Once option.

Figure 13.12 This image is divided into two halves. The left side shows what the image looked like after attempting to remove the background; the right side shows what it looked like after using the Background Swatch setting with a cyanish-blue background color.

notice a slight halo around the edge of my object (**Figure 13.12**). The halo is often too thin to target with this tool. Instead, you can click on the background color in the Color Picker, choose a color that is visually similar to the halo you are trying to remove, and then experiment with the Tolerance setting until you're able to remove it.

Limits

With default settings, the Background Eraser tool will delete only those areas that actually touch the crosshair. It won't be able to jump across one area that shouldn't be deleted to find another area similar to the one being deleted. That can cause problems when you're working with images of trees, fences, or other objects that break the background into multiple disconnected regions (**Figure 13.13**). You can change that behavior by changing the Limits menu from Contiguous (meaning only touching the crosshair) to Discontiguous, which will allow it to delete the color that's under the crosshair from the entire circle, even if something like a tree branch isolates an area so it doesn't touch the crosshair (**Figure 13.14**).

Figure 13.13 Result of using the Contiguous option. (©Stockbyte, www.stockbyte.com)

Figure 13.14 Result of using the Discontiguous option.

You'll also find an option in the Limits menu called Find Edges, which works similarly to the Contiguous setting but tries to prevent the subject from fading out into the background and becoming semitransparent. So, if you ever notice that part of the subject is becoming semitransparent (**Figure 13.15**), choose Undo and try working on that area a second time using the Find Edges setting (**Figure 13.16**).

Figure 13.15 Result of using the Contiguous option. (©Stockbyte, www.stockbyte.com)

Figure 13.16 Result of using the Find Edges option.

Tips and Tweaks

Now that you've seen all the options that go along with the Background Eraser, let's look at a few things that can help you get better results. When I first started to use this tool, I was very impressed with the results; later, however, I discovered that I wasn't really seeing the whole story. You see, the checkerboard that shows up under your image to indicate an area has been deleted makes it difficult to find the more finely detailed problem areas—the checkerboard can actually hide flaws in your erasure. (**Figure 13.17**).

To really see what you're getting, Command/Ctrl-click on the New Layer icon at the bottom of the Layers palette to create a new layer below the currently active layer. Next, change your foreground color to something that contrasts with your image (like a vivid orange color), and then press Option-Delete (Mac) or Alt-Backspace (Windows) to fill the active layer with your foreground color (**Figure 13.18**). After doing that, you should be able to see any residue that the Background Eraser tool left behind (**Figure 13.19**). Just remember to click on the layer that contains the image you were working with so you don't start deleting this solid-colored layer when you get back to using the Background Eraser.

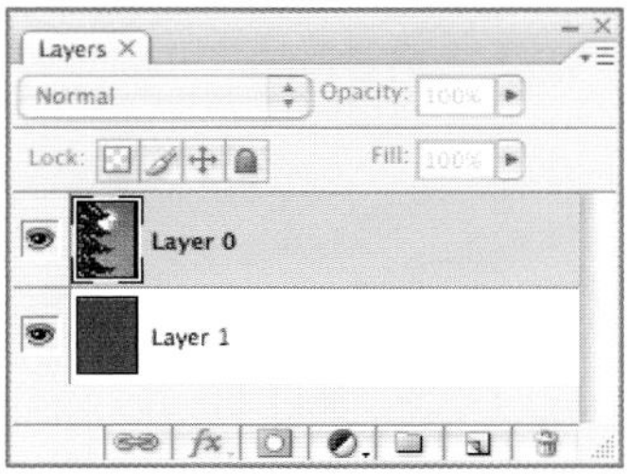

Figure 13.17 The checkerboard background disguises most problems. (©Stockbyte, www.stockbyte.com)

Figure 13.18 Fill a layer with a solid color and place it below your image to reveal any problem areas.

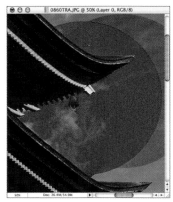

Figure 13.19 Adding a layer full of a solid color reveals problem areas.

You'll want to stay away from hard-edged brushes when you're working with an object that has a slightly soft edge. Hard-edged brushes often produce a series of circles that can make the edge of your image resemble a pearl necklace (**Figure 13.20**). When you switch to a soft-edged brush, the edge of the area you are working on should be nice and smooth (**Figure 13.21**).

Figure 13.20 Using a hard-edged brush produces abrupt transitions in soft-edged objects. (©Stockbyte, www.stockbyte.com)

Figure 13.21 Using a soft-edged brush produces an acceptable transition on soft-edged objects.

Figure 13.22 A Wacom pressure-sensitive graphics tablet makes the Background Eraser tool much more versatile.

For the ultimate in control, consider getting a Wacom pressure-sensitive graphics tablet (**Figure 13.22**). When using a tablet, you can click on the brush preview that shows up in the options bar at the top of your screen and set the Size or Tolerance setting to Pen Pressure. That will vary either the size of your brush or the Tolerance setting (or both) based on how hard you press with the pen. I like to use the Tolerance setting because then I can press lightly where there is a slight difference between the subject and background and press harder where there is a more pronounced difference. That allows me to trace around the entire edge of an object in a single stroke, which can save quite a bit of time.

The Extract Filter

When you choose Filter > Extract, a huge dialog box will pretty much take over your screen (**Figure 13.23**). This is command central for removing the backgrounds on complex objects like hair, soft-edged objects and objects

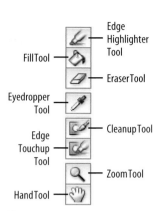

Figure 13.23 The Extract dialog box offers a multitude of features designed for removing the background on complex images. (©Stockbyte, www.stockbyte.com)

Figure 13.24
The Extract command's tools.

in motion. Before we start working with the tools in the Extract dialog box, let me give you an overview of what's needed to successfully extract an image from its background. Extract needs three pieces of information: which areas should be thrown away, which areas should be kept, and which areas contain the transition between the first two areas (including semitransparent areas).

The general idea is to use the Edge Highlighter tool (**Figure 13.24**) to define the boundary between subject and background (it shows up as a green overlay) (**Figure 13.25**), and then to click with the Fill tool (which looks like a paint bucket) to fill whichever side of that boundary you'd like to keep (it shows up as a blue overlay) (**Figure 13.26**). The only thing that prevents the Fill tool from filling the entire image is the green highlighting. That makes it important to create a continuous outline around the subject of the photo with no breaks in it. When you preview the extraction, Photoshop will throw away the areas that don't have any color on top of them and keep the areas that are covered with blue. It will also figure out what

Figure 13.25 The green highlighting defines the transition from subject to background.

Figure 13.26 The blue fill defines the area you'd like to keep.

Figure 13.27 Previewing the extraction shows you what Photoshop is planning on keeping and throwing away.

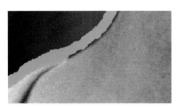

Figure 13.28 Try not to leave a gap between the highlighting and the subject, like I did on the top portion of this image. It's better to have a slight overlap on the subject of the photo, like I did at the bottom of this image.

Figure 13.29 The bottom portion of this image was highlighted using the Smart Highlighting option, whereas the top portion was not.

to do in the transition areas that are covered with green by comparing that area to the keep and throw-away areas (**Figure 13.27**).

Start with the Highlighter

Go ahead and grab an image of someone with flyaway hair; if you don't have one, you're welcome to grab the image I'm working on from the CD at the back of the book. You'll find it in the folder called Practice Images. Just go to the Chapter 13 folder and look for a file called Flyaway Hair.tif. Now with your image open, choose Filter > Extract. Next, take a glance at the tools in the upper left of the dialog box; the Highlighter tool is active by default, and that's where we need to start.

Before you start tracing around the edge of your image, you should know that any areas that you cover with the Highlighter have the potential of being deleted. All other areas will either be kept or thrown away. This means that your highlighting needs to overlap both the subject and the background; otherwise, you won't get a good transition. It also means that if you're going to be sloppy, it's best to overspray onto the background because that area will be deleted anyway. In fact, it's good to have a little overspray on the subject; otherwise, you'll end up leaving a tiny one-pixel rim of the background between your highlighting and the subject of the image (**Figure 13.28**). That tiny rim will confuse the Extract command, making it think that things similar to that rim should be kept instead of deleted.

Change the size of your brush based on how far the edge of the subject fades. Areas that gradually fade out (like blurry edges) will need a wider highlight than crisp-edged areas. If you run across an area that has a very crisp edge with no fuzzy or partially transparent areas, you'll want to turn on the Smart Highlighting check box. With that option turned on, Photoshop attempts to find the edge within your cursor and puts minimal highlighting on it (**Figure 13.29**). That prevents the area having a soft edge. Just be sure that option is turned off when working on areas that have very soft or complex edges. So, go forth and highlight the entire edge of the subject to show Photoshop which areas of the image contain a combination of background and subject.

After you've defined the boundary between subject and background, you'll need to check for parts of the subject that extend beyond the edge of the highlighted area. Anything beyond the edge of the highlighting will be deleted, so if you find any of the subject (like wisps of hair) out there, go cover it up with highlighting (**Figure 13.30**). Then you'll need to make one last highlighting pass, this time looking on the other side of the highlighting for any hint of the background (**Figure 13.31**). Because that side will eventually be filled (defining it as an area that should be kept), hints of the background in that area will cause remnants of the background to remain after the extraction. Remember: The highlighting should overlap the subject of the photo—you just don't want huge amounts of highlighting on the areas you want to keep.

Figure 13.30 These wisps of hair need to be covered with highlighting; otherwise, they will be deleted and might confuse Photoshop as to what should be deleted in the rest of the image.

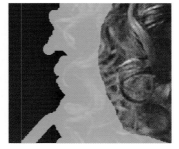

Figure 13.31 The small black areas within the hair are actually parts of the background, so they should be covered by highlighting; otherwise, they will be kept.

When you're painting with the highlighter, you can change the Brush Size setting by pressing the bracket keys (][). If it's taking you too long to highlight the entire edge of the object, try holding the Shift key and clicking in multiple areas (don't drag). Photoshop will connect the "dots" with straight lines, which can really speed things up. You can also hold the Option/Alt key to temporarily transform the Highlighter into an eraser so you can remove overspray from your image. Also, if you're working on a green object and you find that the green highlighting is too hard to see, you can choose a different color from the Highlight pop-up menu in the upper right of your screen.

Fill with the Paint Bucket Tool

When you've finished highlighting the edge of the image (**Figure 13.32**), choose the Fill tool and click in the middle of the subject of your photo. When you do that, the Fill tool will completely ignore the photograph you are working on and instead use the highlighting to determine which area should be filled (**Figure 13.33**). If, after clicking once with the Fill tool, the entire subject is not covered in blue, click on additional areas of the subject that aren't yet covered. If you find that the entire image (minus the highlighting) is covered with blue, that means that your highlighting didn't make it all the way around the subject of the photograph, so go touch up the highlighting and then try to fill the subject again.

Figure 13.32 Make sure your highlighting makes a continuous line around the edge of the subject with no breaks.

Keeping in mind that all areas that are covered with the blue fill will not be deleted, take a quick look to make sure no part of the background you are looking to delete is covered in blue. If you've messed up, then fine-tune your highlighting and refill the subject. If you find the blue fill is too difficult to see, you are welcome to choose another color from the Fill pop-up menu in the upper right of the dialog box. If you think that you have everything set up correctly, click the Preview button to see what your extraction will look like.

Figure 13.33 Click on the area of the image you'd like to keep with the Fill tool.

If the subject of the photo is quite similar to the background, but they differ in texture, try turning on the Textured Image check box. With that option turned on, Photoshop will look for differences in both color and texture between the subject and background areas, which can produce a much better result (**Figures 13.34** to **13.36**).

Most of the time, the preview will look rather promising, but that can be deceptive because the checkerboard

Figure 13.34 The original image. (© 2007 Stockbyte, www.stockbyte.com)

Figure 13.35 The result of extracting an image with the Textured Image check box turned off.

Figure 13.36 The Textured Image check box can help to differentiate between textured and nontextured areas.

behind your image can hide a lot of problems. I find it much more effective to replace the checkerboard with a solid color that contrasts with the subject. You can do this by choosing Other from the Display pop-up menu in the lower right of the dialog box.

Zoom In and Fine Tune

Now it's time to use the Zoom tool to check things up close. Just remember that any area that's covered with the blue fill will not be deleted. So, scroll around your image and look for remnants of the old background (**Figure 13.37**). If you find any, turn on the Show Fill check box and see if they become covered with blue. If they are, grab the Highlighter tool and cover up those areas.

Figure 13.37 Replacing the checkerboard with a solid color will often reveal problem areas.

If the area is not covered with blue fill, you most likely have an area with way too much highlighting (**Figure 13.38**). When that happens, Photoshop gets confused because it doesn't have enough information about what should be kept or thrown away. You're simply giving it too large of an area to do a good job with. When that's the case, grab the Eraser tool and use a tiny brush to poke holes in the highlighting in areas where you see hints of the background (**Figures 13.39** and **13.40**). Anytime you use the Highlighter tool, the fill will disappear, so you'll need to use the Fill tool to refill the subject area and then preview the extraction again.

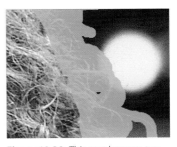

Figure 13.38 This area has way too much highlighting for Photoshop to know the difference between the hair and the bright area of the background.

Figure 13.39 Use the Eraser tool and a small brush to poke holes in the highlighting to uncover parts of the background.

Figure 13.40 After modifying the highlighting, Photoshop is able to do a much better job of isolating the subject, but we'll need to refine the result later.

Figure 13.41 This image was extracted using a Smooth setting of 0.

Figure 13.42 This image was extracted using a Smooth setting of 100. The difference is subtle and more noticeable onscreen.

After you've made sure that none of the background is visible, switch gears and look for areas of the subject that might have been unintentionally deleted. You can do that by toggling back and forth between the Extracted and Original choices in the Show pop-up menu. If it looks like areas of the subject were deleted, choose Original from the Show pop-up menu. Turn on the Show Highlight and Show Fill check boxes, and then search around your image for areas that contain the hints of the subject that aren't covered with highlight or fill. Remember: Areas that do not have any color on them (either highlight or fill) will be deleted. So grab the Highlighter tool and cover up all those areas of the subject that don't have color on top of them. Now you'll need to refill the subject and preview the image again.

If just a tiny bit of the background is visible after previewing, and most of the subject is intact, start experimenting with the Smooth setting. As you raise the Smooth setting, the transition between the subject and the area that's been extracted should become softer (**Figures 13.41** and **13.42**). To see the effect of changing the Smooth setting, you'll need to preview the image once more.

Clean It Up

At this point, you can still refine the result, but let's get away from the Highlighter and Fill tools and take a look at the Cleanup and Edge Touchup tools. You can drag across your image using the Cleanup tool to slowly lower the opacity of an area. This can be useful when attempting to rid your image of specks that don't quite touch the subject of the photograph. Or, if you hold down the Option/Alt key, the Cleanup tool will increase the opacity of an area, which allows you to bring back areas that should not have been deleted (**Figures 13.43** and **13.44**). Then, to make the edge crisper, use the Edge Touchup tool. If you hold the Command/Ctrl key, a crosshair appears in the center of your cursor. Move the crosshair to the place where the subject of the photo should end, and Photoshop will create a crisp edge in that position. That can be useful when Photoshop leaves too much leftover information near the edge of your image.

When you're playing with the highlight and fill, you might be tempted to click OK to see how the image would look with the rest of the layers in your image—don't do it! If you click OK and then try to return to the Extract dialog box, you'll have to start over from scratch because the feature will not remember where your highlight was. So, make sure the edge of the object looks right before clicking OK.

Figure 13.43 Areas of the hair have been deleted.

Figure 13.44 Areas were brought back by painting across the image with the Cleanup tool while the Option/Alt key was held.

Use Force Foreground for Intricate Images

If the subject of your photo is too small or intricate to trace around and leave space for the fill in the middle (**Figure 13.45**), cover the entire subject with the Highlighter tool (**Figure 13.46**). When it comes time to define the fill, turn on the Force Foreground check box and click on the color of the subject using the Eyedropper tool. (The Fill tool will become grayed out.) That will make Photoshop look through the entire highlight area and attempt to keep things that are similar to the color you clicked on with the Eyedropper (**Figure 13.47**).

I like to use the Force Foreground option to remove the background from translucent objects like glass or plastic bottles (**Figure 13.48**). The main thing that makes a bottle

Figure 13.45 Thin objects are too small to leave room for a fill. (©Stockbyte, www.stockbyte.com)

Figure 13.46 Cover the entire subject with the Highlighter tool.

Figure 13.47 Result of using the Force Foreground check box after clicking on the darkest area of the highlighted area with the Eyedropper tool.

show up is its highlights. So, to remove the background from a bottle, cover the translucent areas of the bottle with the Highlighter tool (**Figure 13.49**), turn on the Force Foreground check box, and then use the Eyedropper tool to click on the brightest highlight on the bottle. That will get Photoshop to look for the brightest areas within the highlighted area, which should deliver the bottle without the background (**Figure 13.50**).

Figure 13.48 A translucent object is mainly defined by its highlights. (©Stockbyte, www.stockbyte.com)

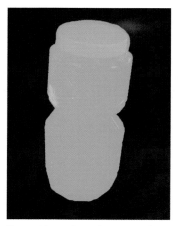

Figure 13.49 Cover the entire subject with highlighting. In this case, I also covered the lid of the jar because it was the same color as the subject, which can confuse Photoshop about what should be kept and deleted.

Figure 13.50 Result of extracting the jar using the Force Foreground setting.

After you click OK and exit the Extract dialog box, Photoshop will truly delete the background—as opposed to just selecting it—and will clean up any hint of the old background from the edge.

Using Extract to Make a Selection

If you'd rather get a selection out of the Extract command, Command/Ctrl-click on the layer thumbnail image in the Layers palette (after extracting it from its background), and choose Select > Save Selection. Next, choose Select > Deselect, and then View > History, and click in the indent to the left of the step listed before the Extract command (**Figure 13.51**). Finally, choose Edit > Fill and choose History from the Use pop-up menu. Now you should have the original image back, as well as a saved selection that you can retrieve at any time by choosing Select > Load Selection.

Figure 13.51 In the History palette, click to the left of the step listed before the Extract command.

The Blending Sliders

Don't let this ho-hum name fool you. When it comes to advanced masking, this feature is like the sleepy-eyed pitcher with the secret curve ball that can win the game. You'll definitely want to give this baby a test drive. The Blending sliders are found by choosing Layer > Layer Style > Blending Options, or by double-clicking in the empty area on a layer in the Layers palette to the right of its name. We'll talk about these sliders in more detail in Chapter 14, "Collage," so for now we're going to limit our discussion to the top set of sliders, the ones labeled "This Layer" (**Figure 13.52**). These sliders allow you to show or hide part of a layer based on its brightness. I find them to be very useful when the subject of a photograph is radically brighter (such as lightning or fireworks) or darker (such as text) than the background. The Blending sliders are available on any layer other than the background image. If you need to apply them to the background, double-click on the background and change its name first.

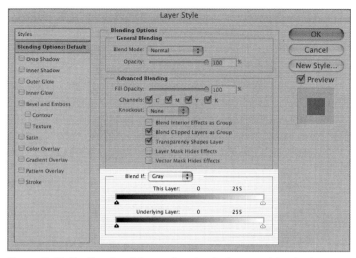

Figure 13.52 The Blending sliders are found at the bottom of the Blending Options dialog box.

If you have a subject that is brighter than the background (**Figure 13.53**), you'll want to slide the upper-left slider toward the middle until every hint of the background disappears from view (**Figure 13.54**). Then, to control the edge quality (how soft or hard it is), hold the Option/Alt key and pull on the left edge of the slider you adjusted a minute ago (**Figure 13.55**). That will cause the brightness levels that are just a little darker than the subject to start to

Figure 13.53 The subject of this photo is much brighter than the background, which makes it an ideal candidate for the Blending sliders. (©Stockbyte, www.stockbyte.com)

Figure 13.54 Hiding the dark areas has caused the background to disappear.

show up as partially transparent areas, which should produce a softer edge (**Figure 13.56**). If the subject is darker than the background, you'll want to move the upper-right slider toward the middle to hide the background. Then Option/Alt-drag the right edge of the slider to control the transition from visible areas to hidden areas.

Figure 13.55 Option/Alt-drag the edge of a slider to split it into two halves and create a more gradual transition between visible and hidden areas.

Figure 13.56 This is the end result of splitting the sliders. You'll have to look very closely, but you should notice more partially transparent areas.

If you have an image in which the background or subject happens to be predominantly a single color that is not found in the surrounding area (**Figure 13.57**), you might be able to use the Blending If pop-up menu to help isolate it from its surroundings. You'll first need to open the Channels palette (Window > Channels), and then click through all the channels (they show up as grayscale images) to find which one shows the most contrast between

Figure 13.57 The Blending sliders can be very useful when the subject of a photo is a color that is not contained in the rest of the image. (©Stockbyte, www.stockbyte.com)

the subject and background (**Figure 13.58**). Once you've found the right channel, take note of it, and then click on the topmost channel to get back to your full-color image. Now go to the Blending sliders, choose the name of that channel from the Blend If pop-up menu, and pull in the left or right slider (depending on whether the background in that channel was dark or bright) until the background disappears (**Figures 13.59** and **13.60**).

Figure 13.58 Click through the channels to figure out which choice to make in the Blending Options dialog box.

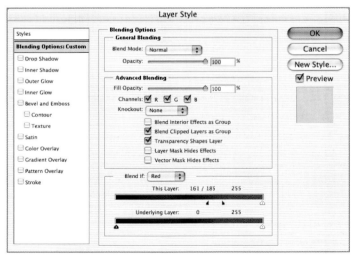

Figure 13.59 Choose the name of the channel that had the most contrast between subject and background from the Blend If pop-up menu.

Figure 13.60 The end result of applying the sliders shown in Figure 13.59.

Unlike the Extract command and the Background Eraser, which truly delete the background of your image, the Blending sliders temporarily hide areas. You can go back to the sliders and move them to their default locations to bring back the areas that were being hidden by the sliders. To permanently delete the hidden areas, do the following: Command/Ctrl-click the New Layer icon at the bottom of the Layers palette to create a new layer below the one that has the sliders applied. Click on the layer above the one you just created to make the slider-applied layer active. Finally, choose Layer > Merge Down, and the slider-applied layer will combine with the empty layer. Because the underlying layer didn't have the sliders applied, Photoshop will be forced to retain the look of the slider-applied layer without actually using the sliders.

Channels

In the ancient days of Photoshop (that would be nine or ten years ago), you were almost forced to use channels to isolate complex images from their backgrounds. These days, I mainly use them with simpler images, especially when I'm working with an illustration instead of a photographic image. When that's the case, I often convert the image into spot colors so that each color in the image prints with a different color of ink (instead of printing with standard CMYK inks). Channels are the subject of one of the bonus chapters that are found on the CD at the back of this book, but in this chapter, because we're learning how to isolate objects, it's useful to look at channels from a different angle and see how to use the Channels palette to isolate each color within an image. This might seem cumbersome at first, but stick with me and I think you'll see the value of this approach. If you want to follow along with my example (**Figure 13.61**), grab the image called potato chips.tif from the CD at the back of the book. You'll find it in Chapter 13 of the folder called Practice Images.

Let's say you have a logo or graphic that you'd like to reproduce on a commercial printing press using red, blue, and yellow ink. I'd look at the original and decide which areas will use each ink and if any areas need a combination

Figure 13.61 I'll be working with this image of a bag of potato chips. (©2007 PhotoSpin, www.photospin.com)

If you followed the techniques we talked about in Chapter 7, "Color Correction," the eyedroppers will need to be reset to their default settings. To do that, double-click on the white eyedropper and change the RGB numbers to 255, 255, 255. Then double-click on the black eyedropper and change the RGB numbers to 0, 0, 0.

of more than one ink. In the example we're using here, it's rather obvious which areas should use red and blue ink, but I'd like to use a combination of yellow and red to make up the potato chips. Then, to determine which channels we'll need to work with, click through all the channels in the Channels palette and look for good contrast between the color we're attempting to isolate and whatever surrounds it (**Figure 13.62**). In our example, we'll use the red channel to isolate the blue areas, the blue channel to isolate the red areas, and a combination of the red and blue channels for the potato chips.

Figure 13.62 From left to right: the red channel, the green channel, the blue channel.

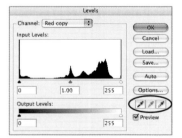

Figure 13.63 Use the eyedroppers that show up in the lower right of the Levels dialog box.

To isolate the blues in this image, drag the red channel to the New Channel icon at the bottom of the Channels palette. (It looks like a sheet of paper with the corner folded over.) Then, isolate the area that should print with blue ink by making it black; the surrounding areas should end up white to indicate that no blue ink should be used. To accomplish that, choose Image > Adjustments > Levels, and then work with the eyedroppers that show up in the lower right of the dialog box (**Figure 13.63**).

Now click on the black eyedropper, and then click on the darkest area that should print with blue ink. That will force the area you click on to black. Then, before you click OK in the Levels dialog box, click on the white eyedropper and then click on the darkest area of the image that should not print with blue ink to force it to white (**Figure 13.64**). That should do most of the work needed to isolate the blues in the image. If you find any residue left over, just use the Eraser tool to clean it up. Set up this channel to print with blue ink by double-clicking just to the right of the channel's name in the Channels palette (which will bring up the Channel Options dialog box). Click Spot Color and choose the color you'd like to use (**Figure 13.65**), just like I detail in the bonus chapter, "Channels," on the CD (I used PMS 2748, which is 8R, 32G, 120B).

Duplicate the blue channel and use the Levels dialog box once again to isolate the reds in the image. This will force the areas that should print with red ink to black and the areas that shouldn't be red to become white (**Figure 13.66**). You don't have to get every non-red area to become white; just get as much of those areas to be white as you can without sacrificing how dark the red areas look. In this case, you might need to manually select a few areas and fill them with white to get rid of the potato chips in the image (**Figure 13.67**). Once you have all the red areas isolated, double-click on the channel and choose the spot color you'd like to use in that area. (I used PMS 1805, which is 151R, 40G, 46B.)

Figure 13.64 Result of forcing areas to white.

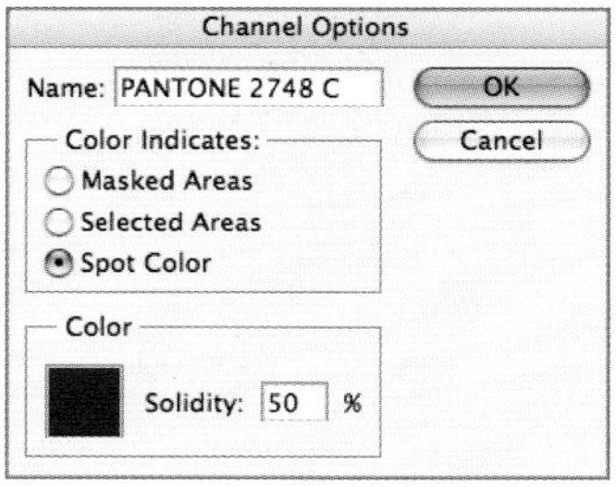

Figure 13.65 Double-click to the right of the channel name to change its options.

Figure 13.66 Result of forcing areas to white.

Figure 13.67 Result of cleaning up the remaining areas.

Figure 13.68 Result of duplicating the blue channel and removing everything but the potato chips.

Figure 13.69 Result of adjusting the chips area with Levels.

The potato chips blend in with the surrounding image in each channel (no good isolation possible), so you'll have to manually select those areas with the Lasso tool. Then, to get that information into a channel that prints with yellow ink, duplicate the blue channel, choose Select > Inverse, and then press Delete (Mac) or Backspace (Windows) (assuming your background color is white) (**Figure 13.68**). Double-click on the channel, set it to Spot Color, and choose a yellow color. (I used PMS 141, which is 228R, 199G, 109B.) Because you'll need to use a lot of yellow ink in the chips, you might need to choose Select > Deselect, and then Image > Adjustments > Levels, and bring in the upper-left slider until a good portion of the chips becomes black (**Figure 13.69**). Now you can view your red, blue, and yellow ink image by turning on the eyeballs next to those three channels and turning off the eyeball on the topmost (RGB) channel.

You can fine-tune the image some more by reselecting the chips (by choosing Select > Reselect from the menu), clicking on the cyan channel, choosing Edit > Copy, pasting the chips into the red channel, and then adjusting the result with Levels (**Figure 13.70**). That will put a hint of red in the chips, giving them a warmer feeling. You could also select the white parts of the bag and paste them into the blue ink channel to add some shading to the bag (**Figures 13.71** and **13.72**).

Figure 13.70 Result of adding the chips to the red channel.

Figure 13.71 Result of adding the white and gray areas of the bag to the blue channel.

Figure 13.72 Completed image.

The Pen Tool

The Pen tool, which can be found on the toolbar and looks like the tip of an old-fashioned ink pen, gives you a result that more closely resembles the work of a pair of scissors than anything else we've covered in this chapter. If you're sloppy with it, the result will look very crude. If you take enough time with it, you can end up with a nice, crisp result, but you definitely wouldn't want to use this tool with an object that has a soft or blurry edge.

The Pen tool can be a bit tricky to learn because it doesn't work like anything else in Photoshop. Instead of creating shapes out of a grid of solid-colored squares (pixels), the Pen tool creates shapes from a collection of points and directional handles (**Figure 13.73**). If you've used Adobe Illustrator, you might be familiar with paths, but just in case you're not, let's take a look at how they work. Before we get started creating paths, take a look in the options bar at the top of your screen (**Figure 13.74**) and make sure the Paths icon is active so you end up making a path instead of a shape layer. The Paths icon is the second from the left of the icons that appear just to the right of the Pen tool icon.

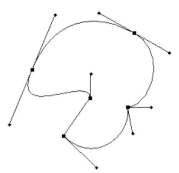

Figure 13.73 A path is made from many points and directional handles.

Figure 13.74 The options bar for the Pen tool.

First off, you'll need to think of the shape that you'd like to create as being made of a series of curves and straight lines that connect to one another. Visualize tracing around the shape and looking for transitions where one curve connects with another. That might be in an area where a very tight curve starts to become more gradual, like on some coffee cup handles (**Figure 13.75**). At each of these transitions, you'll want to click with the Pen tool to add a point.

When adding a point, you'll need to click and drag if you want to create a smooth curve. If you don't drag, you'll end up with a sharp corner instead of a curve. When you click and drag, you'll add a point and pull a set of directional handles out of that point. The angle of the directional handles determines what direction the path will go in

Figure 13.75 The curve of the handle changes from a tight curve to a more gradual one right where a point would be needed. (©Stockbyte, www.stockbyte.com)

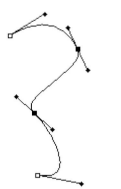

Figure 13.76 Click and drag to create a smooth curve.

Figure 13.77 The length of the directional handles determines the overall shape of the curve.

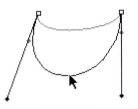

Figure 13.78 Hold Command/Ctrl and drag the curve to adjust the length of the directional handles.

when it leaves that handle, so make sure it points in the direction in which you want the curve to go (**Figure 13.76**). Think of it as if you were walking around the edge of the shape using baby steps. What direction would you take for your first step? That's the same direction the directional handle should point in when entering and exiting a point. When you first pull out a set of handles, they will both move at the same time and act a bit like a seesaw in that their angles will create a straight line that goes all the way through the point.

The lengths of the directional handles determine the overall shape of the curve (**Figure 13.77**). Getting the length of the handles to be just right is difficult because the curve won't show up until the next handle is made, and its handles will also influence the shape of the curve—so for now, keep your handles short.

Once you've added the next point and have gotten the angle of the handle that points toward the last point positioned correctly, it'll be time to adjust the length of the handles. I find it easiest to adjust the handle lengths by holding the Command/Ctrl key and dragging the middle of the curve that appears between the two points you just created (**Figure 13.78**). It's a little troublesome at first, but by pulling on the middle of the curve, you should be able to get the curve to fit the shape you were attempting to create. If you find that you just can't get it to the shape you want, then one of the directional handles must be pointing in the wrong direction. If you continue to hold down the Command/Ctrl key, you will be able to reposition the directional handles as well.

On occasion, you'll find that you need one curve to abruptly change direction instead of smoothly flowing into another curve. When that happens, remember that the directional handles determine which direction your path will go in when it leaves a point. That means you'll need the two handles that come out of a point to be at radically different angles. You can accomplish that by holding the Option/Alt key and dragging one of the handles that protrude from the point you just created (**Figure 13.79**).

Sometimes you will need to have a curve end at an abrupt corner, where the next portion of the shape will be a straight line. In that case, you'll need a handle on the side of the point that points toward the curve, and no handle on the side of the straight line. To accomplish that, right after adding the point and pulling out the handles, Option/Alt-click the point, and Photoshop will retract the handle on the open end of the path (**Figure 13.80**).

By combining these ideas, you should be able to create just about any smooth shape you can think of. But because it's not an overly natural process, it might take you a while to master using the Pen tool. Once you've got a path, you can drag it to the selection icon (third icon from the left) at the bottom of the Paths palette (Window > Paths) to turn it into a selection.

Layer Masks

Now that you've seen how Photoshop's masking features work, let's take a look at how we can refine the results using a Layer Mask. A Layer Mask will hide areas of the image instead of permanently deleting them. That allows us to fix areas that didn't quite look right and to modify the edge quality of the image. But before we can play with a Layer Mask, we'll need to convert the results we got with the masking tools into a Layer Mask so that the areas that have been deleted will instead be hidden in such a way that you can easily bring them back into view.

So, with the image that you've already isolated using one of the other masking tools, you'll first need to Command/Ctrl-click in the Layers palette on the layer thumbnail image for the layer you removed the background from. That will give you a selection of the visible areas of the layer (**Figure 13.81**). To use that selection as the basis for a Layer Mask, click the Layer Mask icon at the bottom of the Layers palette. (It's the second icon from the left.) Now take a look at the currently active layer in the Layers palette (**Figure 13.82**). You should see two thumbnail preview images for that layer: one of the actual layer contents and

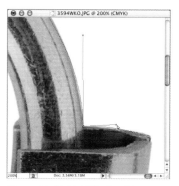

Figure 13.79 Hold Option/Alt to change the angle of one directional handle without affecting the other handle connected to that point. (©Stockbyte, www.stockbyte.com)

Figure 13.80 A curve ending in an abrupt corner.

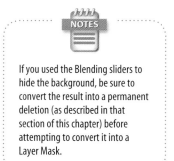

NOTES

If you used the Blending sliders to hide the background, be sure to convert the result into a permanent deletion (as described in that section of this chapter) before attempting to convert it into a Layer Mask.

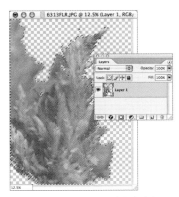

Figure 13.81 Command/Ctrl-click on the layer to get a selection based on its contents.

Figure 13.82 After adding a Layer Mask, you'll find two thumbnail preview images for that layer.

Now that you know how to use the Pen tool, be sure to read Chapter 14, "Collage," to find out how to turn a path into a Vector Mask.

If you'd like to know more about the general concept of working with Layer Masks, be sure to check out Chapter 14, "Collage."

a second that's full of black wherever the layer is transparent and white where the layer contains information. That second thumbnail is the Layer Mask. Black hides layers in a Layer Mask, whereas white lets an area show up.

Now all we have to do is bring back the areas of the image that have been deleted, and then the Layer Mask will be the only thing preventing those areas from being visible. In the Layers palette, click the left thumbnail preview icon to make the image active instead of the Layer Mask (brackets around the corners indicate what's active), and then choose Edit > Fill. In the Fill dialog box, set the Use pop-up menu to History, set the Opacity to 100% and the Mode menu to Normal, and then click OK. Now, to double-check that everything worked as planned, hold down the Shift key and click in the middle of the Layer Mask thumbnail preview image in the Layers palette. That should cause the background of your image to become visible again. If that's the case, Shift-click it again; if the background doesn't become visible, choose Window > History, click in the empty space to the left of the step just above the one that references the masking technique you used to remove the background, and then try using Edit > Fill again. Bear in mind that the "history" feature works only while you are in the same session of Photoshop. If you close out your file and reopen it, the history (that is, the old background) will no longer be available.

Now that the Layer Mask is the only thing causing the background to be hidden, we can refine the result in a multitude of ways. But before we start, be sure to click in the middle of the Layer Mask thumbnail preview image in the Layers palette to make it active. (Brackets should appear on its corners in the Layers palette.) If you'd like to hide additional parts of your image, choose the Paintbrush tool and paint with black. To bring areas back into view, paint with white instead.

You can Option/Alt-click the Layer Mask preview thumbnail image in the Layers palette to view the Layer Mask on the main screen (**Figure 13.83**). Look for black areas that contain specks of white or gray (**Figure 13.84**). That's where the image hasn't been completely hidden. You might need to paint over those areas with black to force those parts of the image to become hidden. If you see a bunch of gray areas that shouldn't be visible, try choosing Image > Adjustments > Levels, and move the upper-left slider until those gray areas turn solid black (**Figure 13.85**). Or, if you see a bunch of tiny white specks, choose Filter > Noise > Despeckle. If that doesn't get rid of them, try Filter > Noise > Median, and use the lowest setting that rids your image of the specks. After cleaning up the obvious problem areas, Option/Alt-click on the Layer Mask preview thumbnail image in the Layers palette to hide the Layer Mask and show the image.

Figure 13.83 Option/Alt-click on the Layer Mask thumbnail preview image in the Layers palette to view the mask within the document window.

Figure 13.84 The background of this image is full of gray specks.

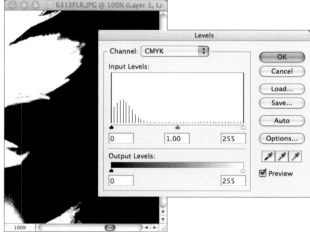

Figure 13.85 After adjusting the layer mask with Levels, the gray specks are gone.

Next, look at areas that have soft edges and make sure that they don't look too noisy (**Figure 13.86**). You can smooth out a noisy transition by painting across an area with the Blur tool. (It looks like a drop of water in the Tools palette [**Figure 13.87**].) You can also use the Blur tool if you notice a crisp edge that looks a little jaggy. The Blur tool will soften that edge without making the image itself blurry.

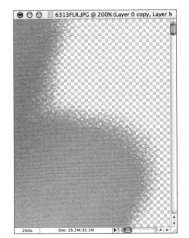

Figure 13.86 This soft-edged transition looks rather noisy.

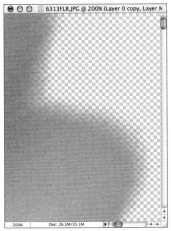

Figure 13.87 After blurring the Layer Mask, the transition looks much smoother.

NOTES

If the Minimum and Maximum filters seem a little backwards to you, consider that they are working on the white areas of the mask instead of the black areas.

If you find a tiny halo of the old background showing up around the edge of an object (**Figure 13.88**), make a general selection that includes that area and then choose Filter > Other > Minimum (**Figure 13.89**). You can also use the Filter > Other > Maximum selection to cause more of the image to show up. (It's the opposite of the Minimum filter.)

Once you think the image looks good, make one last check by Shift-clicking on the Layer Mask thumbnail preview image in the Layers palette to view the entire image, and then press the \ key to view the mask as a color overlay (**Figure 13.90**). That allows you to zoom in on the image and look for areas where the color overlay doesn't quite match the edge of the original image. That's when I'd paint or blur the Layer Mask until it matches the edge of the original image. To get back to normal, press \ again to turn off the color overlay, and then Shift-click the Layer Mask preview again to hide the background of the image.

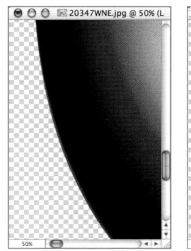

Figure 13.88 If you look closely at the edge of this object, you should be able to see a rim of the old background showing up. (© 2007 Stockbyte, www.stockbyte.com)

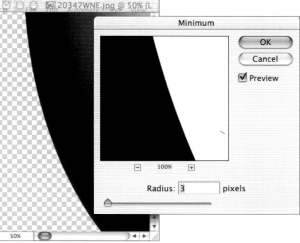

Figure 13.89 Applying the Minimum filter can eliminate the rim.

I also occasionally copy and paste areas of a Layer Mask to fill in other areas that need the right texture. I'll even resort to using Photoshop's funky brushes to produce the right transition on images where none of the masking tools were able to produce the correct edge—like where a white goat's hair was blown out against a backdrop of the sun. (I'd just use the brush that produces something similar to grass.)

Figure 13.90 Double-check your work by disabling the Layer Mask, and then view it as a red overlay by pressing \.

If you ever want to permanently delete the background, just drag the Layer Mask thumbnail to the Trash icon at the bottom of the Layers palette. When prompted, choose Apply and you will have permanently deleted the background on the image. To remove the empty space around your image, you can choose Image > Trim and use the Transparent Pixels option. If you later notice a tiny halo around the edge of objects (and don't feel like going back to edit the Layer Mask to remove it), choose Layer > Matting > Defringe, and use a setting of 1, which should remove the halo.

Closing Thoughts

When trying to mask out the background of an image, try to make the process as easy as possible by thinking about the following concepts. Consider making a general selection of the background area and pressing Delete or Backspace before using any of the masking tools. That way you won't waste your time using the finer, surgical tools to delete the big obvious areas that don't require that kind of precision. Then you can let the masking tools concentrate on the difficult edge areas between the subject and background.

Perform color correction on your image before attempting to isolate the subject from the background. Any unwanted color casts in the image will cause the subject and background to be more similar in color and contrast, making it more difficult to remove the background.

If the subject and background are rather similar, consider using a temporary adjustment layer to exaggerate the difference between subject and background before attempting to remove the background.

Don't limit yourself to a single technique when removing a background. Instead, think about the strengths of each technique and use it wherever it's appropriate (Extract on hair, Pen on crisp curves, and so on).

If you have any control over the photography, be sure to use a simple background that contrasts with the subject of the photo so it's easy to extract.

Finally, no tool is perfect, and sometimes you have to fall back on manual techniques like painting on Layer Masks or tracing objects with the Lasso tool. We all need to do that on occasion, but the more you know about Photoshop's masking tools, the less you'll have to rely on those cruder selection tools that usually produce less than elegant results.

14

Collage

Digital Artist: Regina Cleveland, Photo elements: iStockphoto.com

What you see on these screens up here is a fantasy, a computer-enhanced hallucination!

—Stephen Falken in WarGames

No matter how many times I see them, I'm always in awe of the amazing special effects you see in big-budget Hollywood flicks. I know it's all man-made digital voodoo, but I still get a thrill when the effects are done so well. Consider *Jurassic Park*, where they blended the computer-generated dinos with actors and live-action backgrounds—so incredibly lifelike that you wouldn't be surprised to find yourself standing behind a velociraptor in the popcorn line.

In Photoshop, you can create your own kind of movie magic by blending diverse visual elements into one big picture. (The only difference is the picture doesn't move.) Some people call this compositing or image blending. This is where Photoshop really gets to strut its stuff, and where you can put your creative agility to the test. The possibilities with compositing are truly boundless. Where else could you create a passionate embrace between an ugly, smelly, wrinkly bulldog and his archrival, a prim and proper kittycat? (Robert Bowen did it, and the piece won the Golden Lion Award in Cannes! See **Figure 14.1**.) With Photoshop, all you need is your imagination and a bag full of good collage techniques.

Four Techniques to Choose From

See Chapter 13, "Advanced Masking," for ideas on how to isolate objects from their backgrounds.

In this chapter, we'll explore the features that allow you to combine multiple images into one seamless composite. We'll cover Clipping Masks, Blending sliders, Layer Masks, and Vector Masks. Once you've mastered all four, you'll be able to combine your images together like magic. But before we start to create collages, let's take an introductory look at how these features work.

Figure 14.1 Robert Bowen, working with Howard Berman, created this image for Sony using Photoshop and won a Golden Lion Award. (Courtesy of Robert Bowen Studio, Sony Electronics, Inc., and Lowe & Partners/SMS. Photography by Howard Berman. Art Director: Maria Kostyk-Petro)

Clipping Masks

When you create a Clipping Mask, the layer you're working on will show up only in those places where there is information on the layer directly below it. This can be useful for simple effects like controlling where shadows fall or placing a photo inside of some text.

Sample Use: You've spent hours creating a big retro headline that could have come from the movie poster of *Creature from the Black Lagoon.* Your client—not exactly the king of good taste—calls and says he wants you to put flames inside the headline. You put aside your better judgment and agree to the flames, but only because he pays on time. Then he calls back; he's got some unresolved issues. He doesn't know whether he wants flames or hot lava inside the text, and he's also thinking about changing the headline altogether. He wonders out loud if it will take long or cost much more to do this. "Well," you say, "I think I could wrap this up in about three hours." Greatly relieved, he tells you you're a miracle worker and hangs up. Then you pop open the Layers palette, where you've used a Clipping Mask to get the flames to show up in inside the shape of the headline, and faster than you can say "hocus pocus" you've tweaked the text, swapped out some lava for the flames, and are off to the beach for a three-hour (paid) vacation.

Blending Sliders

The Blending sliders allow you to make certain areas of a layer disappear or show up based on how bright or dark they are. For example, it's very easy to make all of the dark parts of an object disappear.

Sample Use: A "big fish" prospect that you've been trying to snag for months finally throws you a bone. She's desperate because the super-swanky design studio she usually uses can't meet her deadline. You know she's just using you, but what the hey, it's a shot at a new client. She's given you some images that you've loaded into Photoshop. One is a photograph of some big, fat, billowy clouds; the other is of a bunch of whales. She wants you to make it look like the whales are swimming around in the clouds. In some places, she wants the whales to replace the sky that is behind the clouds, but in other places, she wants the whales to actually blend in with the clouds. Very surreal. She impatiently bites her nails and wants to know how many hours it will take to get the effect. You know you can nail this job in a jiffy with the Blending sliders, so while your hands are busy with the mouse, you give her a fearless look and reply, "I'll do it while you wait." She frowns, "I can't just sit around here for hours!" You smile, "No problem, it's already done." The look on her face delivers the good news—you've got a client for life.

Layer Masks

I consider Layer Masks to be the most powerful feature for creating collages in Photoshop. With Layer Masks you can make any part of a layer disappear, and you can control exactly how much you'd like its edge to fade out. What you can do with Layer Masks is infinite.

Sample Use: You're waiting for your biggest client, a 20-year-old creative genius with a ring in his nose. Although this is just a planning meeting, you know from experience that The Genius will want to see some action. Armed with your fastest computer and with Photoshop at the ready, you're not fazed when the kid comes in and starts throwing around madcap ideas like they're going out of style. Blending seems to be the theme of the day. First he wants something that looks like a skyscraper growing out of a pencil. Then he changes his mind and decides he wants to fuse together a hippopotamus and a ballerina. But then he gets a funny look on his face and says, "I know! Let's put Godzilla in an Elvis suit!" Ahhh, you think, a perfect day for Layer Masks. Without batting an eyelash, you go about the business of giving 'Zilla' his new look. Six months later, you almost choke on your coffee when you find out that your Elvis-Zilla ad got an award.

Vector Masks

Vector Masks allow you to attach a crisp-edged path to a layer; anything outside of the path will be hidden both onscreen and when printed. This feature is special because the edge remains smooth when printed to a PostScript printer, even if the pixels in the image are so large that the rest of the image appears jaggy.

Sample Use: You're doing a freebie brochure for your non-profit client, Defenders of the Naked Mole Rat. They want the rat to be the most noticeable image on the cover, so you make their logo small and place it in the corner so it doesn't distract from the lovely rat. But at the last minute (of course!), your penniless client does an about-face and wants you to enlarge the logo to make it almost fill the page. You're tired of doing things for free and fed up with her endless requests, so you tell the client that scaling up the logo that large is a big request when it comes to Photoshop. You even demonstrate your point by scaling one of the photographic elements of the brochure up to a huge size, and of course it looks terrible—very blurry and jaggy. She squeezes out a few tears and gives you her song and dance about the plight of this dear little creature, and how crucial it is to have this brochure just right. You tell her that you'll work on it through the night, and send her on her way. The minute she's out the door, you scale up the logo in a millisecond, and because you used a Vector Mask, the edge remains perfectly crisp and will print that way as well. The job is done. The Naked Mole Rat lives on; unfortunately, since you're so good, the client will never go away.

Now that you have a feeling for the blending options that are available, let's get into the specifics of how this all works.

Figure 14.2 Result of creating a Clipping Mask to clip the photo so that it shows up only within the text. (©2007 Stockbyte, www.stockbyte.com)

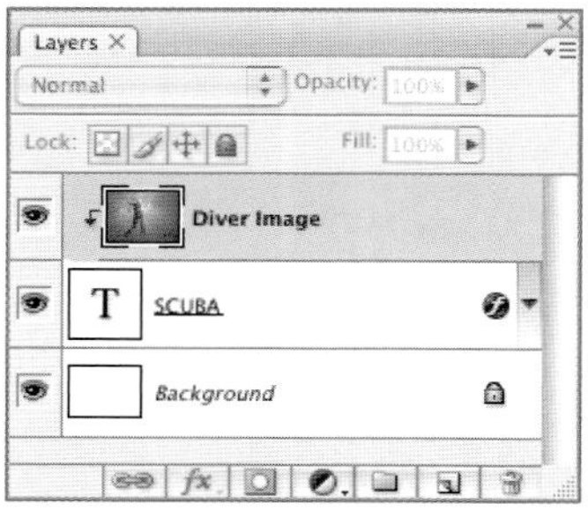

Figure 14.3 Layers palette view.

Clipping Masks

When you create a Clipping Mask, Photoshop changes the active layer so that it shows up only where there is information on the layer directly below it. Then, to show you that something special is going on with the layer you were working on, it indents the layer preview thumbnail in the Layers palette and adds a small down arrow to indicate that this layer now relates to the layer directly below it (**Figures 14.2 and 14.3**). The underlying layer is the Clipping Mask, and the layer with the arrow next to it is the one being clipped by that mask. You can have a Clipping Mask apply to multiple layers, effectively making multiple layers show up only where there is information on one layer. The arrows indicate which layer is the Clipping Mask—it's the layer that all those arrows point to (the first layer that isn't indented below the layers that have the arrows). You can create a Clipping Mask by using any of the following techniques:

► Option/Alt-click between two layers in the Layers palette.

► Choose Layer > Create Clipping Mask.

► Press Option-Command-G (Mac) or Alt-Ctrl-G (Windows).

Changing the Stacking Order

Changing the stacking order of the layers may accidentally deactivate the Clipping Mask on some layers, so you'll want to be careful. If you have a bunch of layers with a Clipping Mask applied, and you move one of them above a layer that doesn't have a Clipping Mask applied, you'll be deactivating the Clipping Mask on that layer. Or if you move a layer with no Clipping Mask between two layers that do have Clipping Masks, it will suddenly have the same Clipping Mask applied to it. If you move the Clipping Mask layer (the one that's not indented and has all those arrows pointing to it) above or below a layer that isn't part of that Clipping Mask, all the layers that are affected by the Clipping Mask will move with it.

Now that you know how to use Clipping Masks, let's take a look at what they can help you with.

Limiting Shadows

I use Clipping Masks all the time when I'm creating shadows. Let's say you have a lizard, and underneath the lizard is a leaf, and you want the lizard to cast a shadow on the leaf. Once you create a layer that contains a shadow, all you need to do is create a Clipping Mask (make sure the leaf layer is directly below it), and then the shadow will show up only where the leaf is (**Figures 14.4** to **14.6**).

If you've created your shadow using a Layer Style, choose Layer > Layer Style > Create Layer to isolate the shadow onto its own layer. Then you can mask it with any layer you'd like.

The Magnifying Glass Trick

I travel all over the country presenting seminars and speaking at conferences, and I know I can always get people to ask questions by showing them my magnifying glass trick. I start by opening what looks like a simple image of an ampersand (&). Then, as I move my cursor, a magnifying glass passes over the ampersand and it appears as if it's really magnifying the image! That's not really possible in Photoshop, of course, but I can still trick people into thinking that it's happening for a few seconds. Let's see how the magnifying glass trick works.

Start off by opening any image you'd like to work with. I use a simple one of a black ampersand on a white background. Next, you'll need an image of a magnifying glass or loupe that you can place on a layer above the ampersand. (I've included two on the CD at the back of this book.) Now select the background and the glass portion of the magnifying glass and press Delete (Mac) or Backspace (Windows) to remove those areas (**Figure 14.7**).

The magnifying glass trick images shown here are a little special. The glass area is partially transparent instead of being completely removed. If you're feeling a little adventuresome and want to work with a similar image, you'll need to follow a quick but complex series of steps that are related to a discussion in the bonus chapter, "Shadows," on the CD. I don't want to take too big a side trip here, so it's going to feel like rapid-fire keyboard commands. If you want to know a little more about how this technique works,

Figure 14.4 Original image. (©2007 iStockphoto.com/Elerium/ jamesbenet)

Figure 14.5 Creating a Clipping Mask between the shadow and the leaf layer.

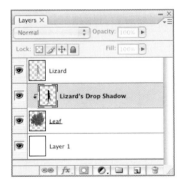

Figure 14.6 Layers palette view.

Figure 14.7 Remove the background of the magnifying glass and place it on top of the image.

refer to the chapter on Shadows. Here are the steps you should follow instead of deleting the glass area.

Start by selecting the glass portion of the magnifying glass and then press Shift-Command-J (Mac) or Shift-Ctrl-J (Windows) to move it to its own layer. Next Option/Alt-click on the eyeball icon next to the layer that was just created (the one that contains the glass area) to hide all the other layers. Now comes the weird part: With only that one layer visible, press Option-Command-~ (Mac) or Alt-Ctrl-~ (Windows), which should produce a selection, then type Shift-Command-I (Mac) or Shift-Ctrl-I (Windows) to invert the selection. With that selection still active, press Shift-Command-N (Mac) or Shift-Ctrl-N (Windows) to create a new layer, press D to reset the foreground/background colors, press Option-Delete (Mac) or Alt-Backspace (Windows) to fill the selection with black, and then press Command/Ctrl-D to get rid of the selection. Then to finish the effect, drag the layer that is directly below the active one (which should contain the nontransparent version of the glass) to the trash, click on the layer that contains that transparent glass, and then press Command/Ctrl-E to merge it into the main magnifying glass image. If you followed those keyboard shortcuts to the letter, you should end up with a magnifying glass image that contains a partially transparent glass area. Now, with that little detour out of the way, let's continue on with the steps needed to make the magnifying glass trick work.

Next, drag the name of the image you are using (not the magnifying glass) to the New Layer icon to duplicate it. Use a simple filter like Mosaic (choose Filter > Pixelate > Mosaic) to make an obvious change to the duplicate image (**Figure 14.8**).

Now let's get that modified image to show up only within the glass area of the magnifying glass. Grab the Elliptical Marquee tool and make a selection where the glass should be in the magnifying glass image. Make sure it lines up perfectly on all sides. Next, create a new empty layer, press Option/Alt-Delete to fill that area with your foreground

Figure 14.8 Make a drastic change to the duplicate layer using a filter.

color (it doesn't matter which color you use), and then choose Select > Deselect. Move the layer you just created so that it's positioned directly between the original image and the filtered version in the stacking order of the Layers palette (**Figure 14.9**).

Now, let's get the whole trick to work. Click on the layer directly above the one that contains the circle you just made, and then choose Layer > Create Clipping Mask. Now click on the magnifying glass layer and link it to the circle layer by clicking just to the left of the circle layer's thumbnail image in the Layers palette. That'll make both layers move at the same time (**Figure 14.10**). To see if the trick is working, use the Move tool to drag around your screen. That should make it so the filtered image shows up only in the "magnified" area (**Figure 14.11**).

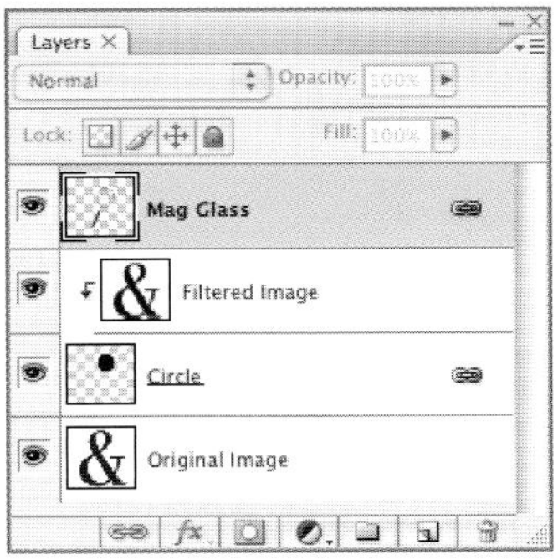

The concept of Clipping Masks is rather simple—they make one layer show up only when there is information on the layer directly below it. But when you incorporate them into a complex image (like the magnifying glass trick), they can become the centerpiece of a mind-bending technique. Clipping Masks aren't the only way to make multiple layers interact, so let's move on and explore the Blending sliders.

Blending Sliders

The Blending sliders allow you to quickly make areas of a layer transparent, based on how bright or dark the image appears. You'll find the Blending sliders by double-clicking in the empty space to the right of the name of a layer. (This opens the Layer Style dialog box.) The Blending sliders are at the bottom of the Layer Style dialog box (**Figure 14.12**). The first thing you'll notice is that there are two sets of sliders. One is labeled "This Layer" and the other is labeled "Underlying Layer." The slider called This Layer makes areas of the active layer disappear. The slider labeled Underlying Layer deals with all the layers underneath the layer that was double-clicked. This slider makes parts of the underlying image show up as if a hole has been punched through the active layer.

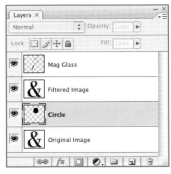

Figure 14.9 The new layer should be placed between the two image layers.

Figure 14.10 The final setup in the Layers palette.

Figure 14.11 The magnifying glass trick in action.

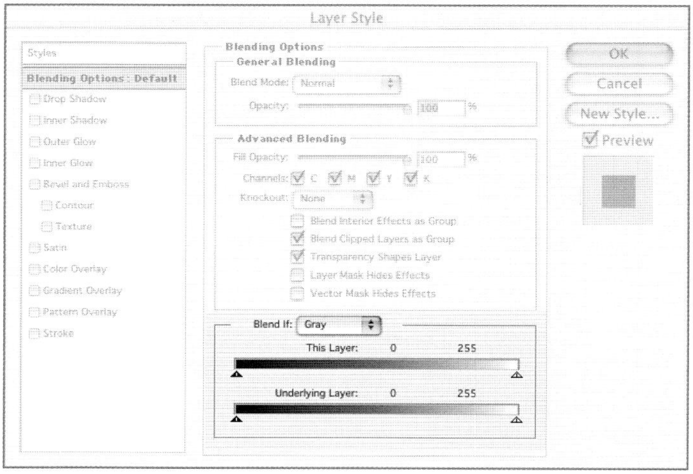

Figure 14.12 The Blending sliders.

"This Layer" Sliders

Figure 14.13 Original unblended images. (© 2007 iStockphoto.com/ titaniumdoughnut/ironrodart)

First, let's take a look at the topmost sliders. If you move the left slider toward the middle, the dark areas of the image (that is, all the shades that are to the left of the slider) start to disappear. This slider can be a great help when you're trying to remove the background from fireworks or lightning. The only problem is, once you get the background to disappear, the edges of the lightning will have hard, jagged edges (**Figures 14.13** to **14.15**).

Figure 14.14 Removing the dark sky from the lightning image.

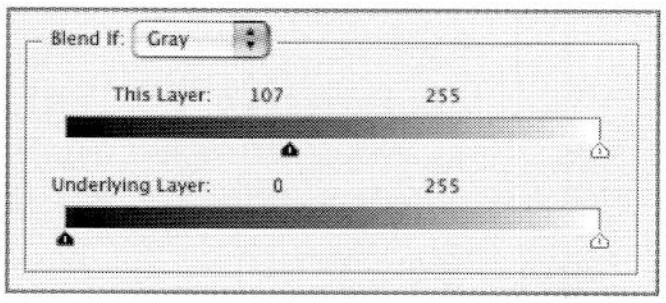

Figure 14.15 Moving the upper-left slider makes the dark areas of the current layer disappear.

To remedy this situation, all you have to do is split the slider into two pieces by Option/Alt-dragging on its right edge. When this slider is split into two parts, the shades of gray that are between the halves become partially transparent and blend into the underlying image (**Figures 14.16** and **14.17**). The shades close to the left half of the slider will be almost completely transparent, and the shades near the right half will be almost completely opaque.

When you move the right slider, you will be making the bright areas of the image (all the shades of gray to the right of the slider) disappear. This slider can be useful when you come across a multicolored logo that needs to be removed from its white background. Just like with the upper-left slider, you can split this slider into two halves by Option/Alt-dragging its left edge (**Figures 14.18** to **14.20**).

"Underlying" Sliders

By moving the two sliders on the Underlying bar, you'll be able to make areas of the underlying image show up as if they were creating a hole in the layer you double-clicked. These sliders are useful when you don't want a layer to completely obstruct the view of the underlying image. I might use this to reveal some of the texture in the underlying image. And, just like the top sliders, you can Option/Alt-click to separate the sliders into two parts (**Figures 14.21** to **14.23**).

Figure 14.16 The edges of the lightning blend into the underlying image.

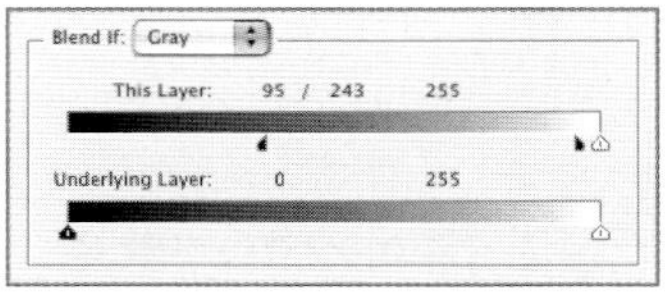

Figure 14.17 Splitting a triangle into halves allows the image to smoothly blend into the underlying image.

Figure 14.18 Original image. (©iStockphoto.com/meltonmedia)

Figure 14.19 Result of removing all white areas by using the Blending sliders.

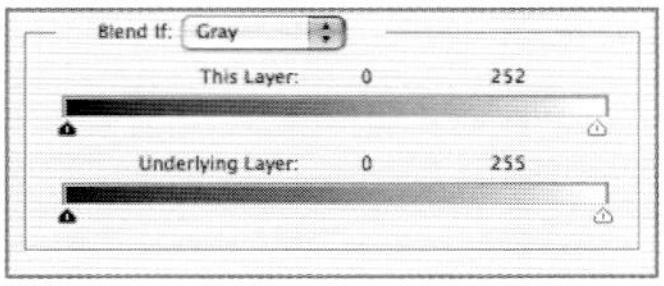

Figure 14.20 Moving the upper-right sliders makes the bright areas of this layer disappear.

Figure 14.21 Original image. (Swirl: ©iStockphoto.com/ziggymaj, Hand: ©iStockphoto.com/Hanis)

Figure 14.22 Result of blending in the dark parts of the underlying image.

Figure 14.23 Moving the lower-left slider makes the dark areas of the underlying image show up as if they are poking a hole in the active layer.

NOTES

If you've chosen a color from the pop-up menu before applying the Blending sliders, be sure to flatten your image when converting it to another color mode (RGB to CMYK, for example). The appearance of unflattened layers will change because the Blending settings will no longer affect the same color channels. If you apply the sliders to the Red channel (first choice in the menu) and then convert the image to CMYK mode, the same slider settings will now be applied to the Cyan channel (because it's the first choice in the menu). The image will not look the same because the Cyan channel doesn't contain the same information as the Red channel.

Understanding the Numbers

The numbers that appear above the sliders indicate the exact location of each slider. If you haven't split any of the sliders, you should see a total of four numbers (one for each slider). When you split one of the sliders into two parts, you'll see one number for each half of the slider. These numbers use the same numbering system as the Levels dialog box.

If you move the upper-left slider until its number changes to 166, for example, you'll have made all the shades darker than 35% gray on that layer disappear. It would be much easier if Adobe would allow us to switch between percentages and the 0–255 numbering system like you can when using the Curves dialog box.

Using Color Channels

If you leave the pop-up menu at the top of the Blending slider area set to gray, Photoshop will ignore the colors in your document and just analyze the brightness of the image (as if the image were in Grayscale mode). By changing this menu, you will be telling Photoshop to look at the information in the individual color channels to determine which areas should be visible (**Figure 14.24**). For example, if you have a document that is in CMYK mode and you change the pop-up menu to cyan and move the upper-right slider to 26, you'll make all areas of the layer that contain 10% or less cyan disappear. This can be useful when you want to remove a background that contains one dominant color.

Choosing the best channel from this pop-up menu usually involves a lot of trial and error. I'll show you how I usually figure out which color would be most effective for different images.

First of all, if the color you would like to work with matches one of the components of your image (red, green, or blue in RGB mode), the choice is pretty straightforward. For example, to work on someone's blue eyes, just work on the blue channel. But what if you want to work on an area that is yellow and your image is in RGB mode? Well, to find out what to do, I usually hold down the Command/Ctrl key and press the number keys on my keyboard (1–3 for RGB mode, 1–4 for CMYK mode, ~ to return to the full-color image); this will display the different color channels. You'll want to look for the channel that separates the area you're interested in from the areas surrounding it (**Figures 14.25** to **14.27**). When you find the one that looks best, choose its name from the Blend If pop-up menu in the Layer Style dialog box. Once you've found the best channel, glance up at the top of your document and you'll see the name of the channel you are viewing right next to the name of the document.

Now that you have a general feeling for how the Blending sliders work, let's take a look at some of the things we can do with them.

Enhancing Clouds

It's not hard to get a photo of some great-looking clouds, but there is one problem—when you're combining clouds with another image, you can't see through the sky! Here's what you can do in this situation: Double-click in the empty area to the right of the name of the layer your clouds are on. By moving the upper-left slider toward the center, you're going to make the sky disappear so you can see the underlying image. To make the edges of the clouds blend into the

Figure 14.24 The Blend If pop-up menu in the Layer Style dialog box determines which channels will be analyzed.

Figure 14.25 Red channel. (©2007 Stockbyte, www.stockbyte.com)

Figure 14.26 Green channel.

Figure 14.27 Blue channel.

Figure 14.28 Original image. (©2007 iStockphoto.com/lisegagne)

Figure 14.29 Clouds image. (©2007 iStockphoto.com/duckycards)

Figure 14.30 Result of discarding the dark area of the clouds by using the Blending sliders.

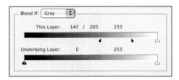

Figure 14.31 Settings used on the preceding image.

underlying image, hold down the Option/Alt key and split the upper-left slider into two parts. By experimenting with both halves of the slider, you'll be able to create the look of fog, faint clouds, or dense clouds (**Figures 14.28** to **14.31**). This technique also works with Photoshop's Clouds filter (found under the Filter > Render menu).

Making the Changes Permanent

The problem with the Blending sliders is that they are just settings attached to a layer, and Photoshop doesn't provide an obvious way to permanently apply their effects. Well, if you've used only the top sliders, there is an easy way to get Photoshop to permanently delete the hidden areas. To do this, create a brand-new empty layer, and then move that empty layer underneath the layer that is using the Blending sliders. Merge those two layers by clicking on the layer that is using the Blending sliders, going to the side menu on the Layers palette, and choosing Merge Down. Photoshop will then permanently delete the areas that were transparent. This can be nice if your client requested the layered file, but you don't want your client to know how you did it (**Figures 14.32** and **14.33**)!

Figure 14.32 Merging the layer with an empty one.

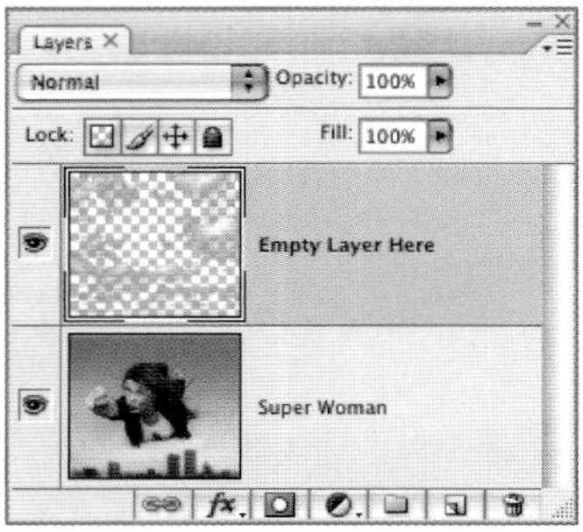

We've only scratched the surface of what you can do with Blending sliders. Use them anytime you want to make something show up or disappear based on how bright it is. Now let's move on to my favorite method for creating collages—Layer Masks.

Figure 14.33 The result.

Layer Masks

By adding a Layer Mask to a layer, you can control exactly where that layer is transparent and where it's opaque. You'll find that Layer Masks are used to create most high-end images—this feature really separates the beginners from the pros. But there's no reason why you can't be as adept at Layer Masks as the most seasoned veteran. It just takes a little time and sweat.

Creating a Layer Mask

You can add a Layer Mask to the active layer by clicking on the icon third from the left at the bottom of the Layers palette. (It looks like a rectangle with a circle inside it.) When you click this icon, you'll notice that the layer you're working on contains two thumbnail images in the palette. The one on the left is its normal preview thumbnail; the one on the right is the Layer Mask thumbnail. The Layer Mask is not empty (empty looks like a checkerboard); instead, it's full of white. After adding a Layer Mask, you can edit it by painting across the image window with any painting tool. Even though this would usually change the image, you're really just editing the Layer Mask; it just isn't visible on the main screen. The color you paint with (which is really a shade of gray) determines what happens to the image. Painting with black will make areas disappear, and painting with white will bring back the areas again. And remember, because you are using a painting tool, you can choose a hard- or soft-edged brush to control what the edge looks like (**Figures 14.34** and **14.35**).

What's nice about a Layer Mask is that it doesn't permanently delete areas; it just makes them temporarily disappear. If you paint with white, you'll be able to bring back areas that are transparent. This can be helpful if you're doing a very quick job for a client who wants to see a general concept. You can do just a very crude job of getting rid of the backgrounds of images, and then later on go back in and refine that Layer Mask to get it to look just right.

The only layer that you can't add a Layer Mask to is the Background image. But you can change its name to make it become a regular layer (double-click to do this), and then add a Layer Mask.

Add Layer Mask icon

Figure 14.34 Layers palette view.

Figure 14.35 The softness of your brush determines how soft the edge of the image will appear. (©iStockphoto.com/BirdImages)

Switching Between the Layer Mask and the Image

Now that you have two thumbnails attached to a layer, you have to be able to determine if you are working on the Layer Mask or the main image. If you look at the Layer Mask thumbnail right after you've created one, you'll notice a frame around the corners of the mask (**Figures 14.36** and **14.37**). That frame indicates what you're working on. If you want to work on the main image instead of the Layer Mask, click the image thumbnail in the Layers palette. The frame will appear around the image thumbnail, indicating that you are editing the main image instead of the Layer Mask. To work on the Layer Mask again, just click its thumbnail and the outline will move.

Figure 14.36 Editing the main image. **Figure 14.37** Editing the Layer Mask.

Hiding Selected Areas

If a selection is present when adding a Layer Mask, Photoshop automatically fills the nonselected areas of the Layer Mask with black so the image is visible in the selected area only (**Figures 14.38** and **14.39**). Or, if you'd like to hide the selected area and show the rest of the image, hold the Option/Alt key when you click the Layer Mask icon. You can see exactly what Photoshop has done by glancing at the Layer Mask thumbnail in the Layers palette (**Figure 14.40**).

Figure 14.38 Make a selection before adding a Layer Mask. (©iStockphoto.com/Mlenny)

Figure 14.39 Result of adding a Layer Mask.

Figure 14.40 Layers palette view.

If you choose Add Layer Mask from the Layer menu instead of just using the icon in the palette, you will be offered some choices:

▶ **Reveal Selection:** Hides the nonselected areas, giving you the same result as using the Layer Mask icon in the Layers palette.

▶ **Hide Selection:** Hides only the areas that are currently selected, leaving the nonselected areas visible.

▶ **Reveal All:** Does not hide any areas of the layer.

▶ **Hide All:** Hides the entire layer.

Paste Into

If there is a selection present when you're pasting an image into your document, you can choose Edit > Paste Into (instead of Edit > Paste) to automatically create a Layer Mask. This Layer Mask will make the image show up only in the area that was selected. You can also hold down the Option/Alt key and choose Edit > Paste Into to hide the selected areas. If you choose Select > All before choosing Paste Into, Photoshop will create a Layer Mask and reveal the entire image. You can also hold down the Option/Alt key and choose Paste Into to hide the entire image.

Disabling a Layer Mask

After you've created a Layer Mask, you can temporarily disable it by Shift-clicking its thumbnail in the Layers palette (**Figures 14.41** to **14.43**). With each click, you will toggle the Layer Mask on or off. This is a great help when you want to see what the layer would look like if you didn't have a Layer Mask restricting where it shows up.

Viewing a Layer Mask

The thumbnails that show up in the Layers palette are just miniature versions of the images that show up in the main document window. That's true for not only the Layer thumbnail image, but also the Layer Mask thumbnail. You can view the Layer Mask in the main image window by holding down the Option/Alt key and clicking on the

Figure 14.41 Layer Mask active.

Figure 14.42 Layer Mask disabled.

Figure 14.43 Layers palette view.

Figure 14.44 Viewing the Layer Mask in the main image window.

You can view a Layer Mask as a color overlay (just like Quick Mask mode) by Shift-Option-clicking (Mac) or Shift-Alt-clicking (Windows) on the Layer Mask icon, or by just pressing \ (backslash).

Layer Mask thumbnail (**Figure 14.44**). You'll see it looks just like a grayscale image, and you can actually paint right on this image. I use this a lot when I get someone else's document, or when I open an old document I worked on months ago and can't remember exactly what I did in the Layer Mask. To stop viewing the Layer Mask, just Option/Alt-click its thumbnail a second time.

Shades of Gray

Photoshop treats a Layer Mask as if it were a grayscale document. That means that you can use any editing tool that is available to a grayscale image. Areas that are full of pure black will become transparent, pure white areas will become completely opaque, and areas that contain shades of gray will become partially transparent. Painting with 20% gray in a Layer Mask will hide 20% of the layer's opacity, leaving 80% of the layer visible. So using a painting tool with an Opacity setting of 80% will produce the same result as painting with 100% opacity and then adding a Layer Mask that is full of 20% gray.

Filling Areas

Because Photoshop treats Layer Masks as if they are grayscale documents, you can create selections and fill those areas with black or white to hide or show the contents of a layer. To fill a selected area with the current foreground color (which is black by default), press Option-Delete (Mac) or Alt-Backspace (Windows). To fill a selected area with the current background color (white by default), press Command-Delete (Mac) or Ctrl-Backspace (Windows). This is nice because it frees you from having to use the painting tools.

Using Gradients

The most common way to make one image fade into another is to add a Layer Mask and then use the Gradient tool. In a Layer Mask, areas that are pure black become completely transparent, and areas that are pure white become completely opaque. Shades of gray in a Layer Mask will make the image become partially transparent. So, if you would like one image to fade into another, apply a gradient to a Layer Mask with the Gradient tool set to Black, White (**Figures 14.45** to **14.47**).

Figure 14.45 Images before adding Layer Masks.
(Bottle: ©iStockphoto.com/Difydave, Rolling Pin: ©iStockphoto.com/dlewis33)

Figure 14.46 Result of applying a gradient to each Layer Mask.

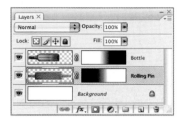

Figure 14.47 Layers palette view.

If you try to apply the gradient a second time, you might run into a few problems. If you apply the gradient from right to left one time, and then immediately after that you apply a second gradient in the other direction, the second gradient will completely obstruct the first one. To combine two gradients, set the Gradient tool to Foreground to Transparent, and make sure the foreground color is set to black. Then you should be able to apply the Gradient tool as many times as you want within a Layer Mask, and it simply adds to what was already in the Layer Mask (**Figures 14.48** to **14.51**).

Figure 14.48 First gradient.

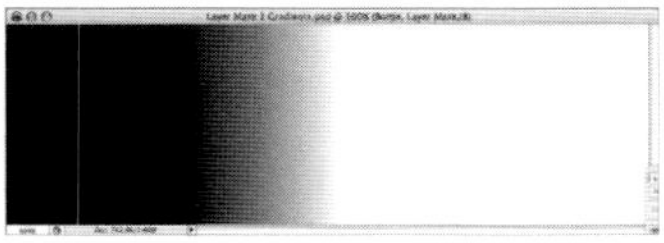

Figure 14.49 Second gradient using Foreground to Background setting.

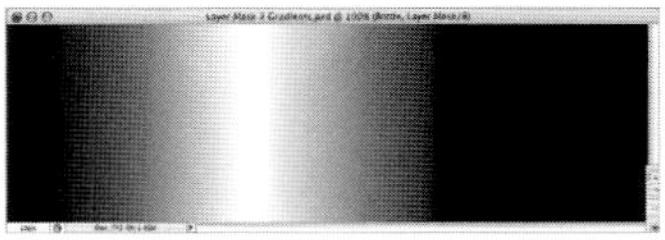

Figure 14.50 Second gradient using Foreground to Transparent setting.

Figure 14.51 Both ends of the rolling pin image blend into the underlying image (the wine bottle) because two gradients were used.

Applying Filters

After painting in a Layer Mask, you can enhance the result by applying filters to it (**Figures 14.52** to **14.55**). Choose Filter > Distort, and then select something like Ripple. Then, instead of having a really smooth transition, there will be some texture in it.

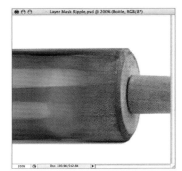

Figure 14.52 Original image.

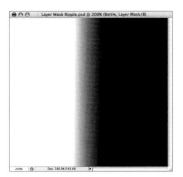

Figure 14.53 Original Layer Mask.

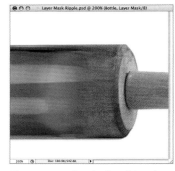

Figure 14.54 Result of applying the Ripple filter to the Layer Mask.

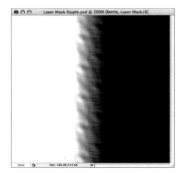

Figure 14.55 Modified Layer Mask.

If you want the edge of an image to fade out slowly, you can choose Filter > Blur > Gaussian Blur. You can blur a Layer Mask as many times as you'd like; each time you blur it, the edge will become softer (**Figures 14.56** to **14.58**).

Figure 14.56 Lime image contains a pure black and pure white Layer Mask. (©2007 iStockphoto.com/photoport)

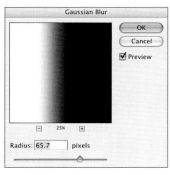

Figure 14.57 Apply the Gaussian Blur filter to a Layer Mask to give it softer edges.

Figure 14.58 Result of blurring the Layer Mask.

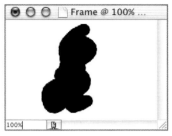

Figure 14.59 Original image.

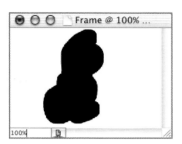

Figure 14.60 Minimum filter results.

Figure 14.61 Maximum filter results.

You can also expand or contract the areas that are transparent by choosing Minimum or Maximum from the Other menu (Filter > Other) (**Figures 14.59** to **14.61**). The Minimum filter will make more areas transparent, whereas the Maximum filter will make fewer areas transparent.

Interesting Edges

To create a rippled-edge effect on your mask, try this out: Open the photograph you want to apply the effect to, and make a selection with the Marquee tool. Make sure your selection is a little inside the edge of the photograph (so there's room for our effect). To get the photograph to show up only where the rectangular selection is, click the Layer Mask icon at the bottom of the Layers palette.

Now you can distort the edge of the photo by using any filter you'd like (**Figures 14.62** to **14.64**). For now, just use

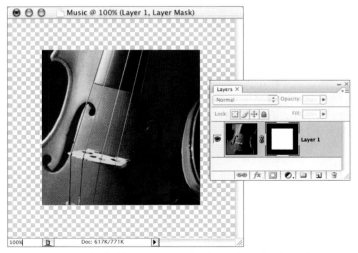

Figure 14.62 Result of adding a Layer Mask to limit where the photo shows up. (©2007 Stockbyte, www.stockbyte.com)

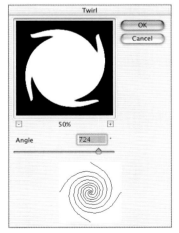

Figure 14.63 First apply the Twirl filter.

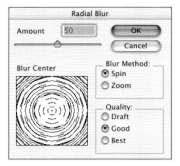

Figure 14.64 Then apply the Radial Blur filter.

Figure 14.65 Result of adding an Inner Glow layer effect.

one of the filters under the Distort menu (Filter > Distort), such as Ripple, Twirl, or Polar Coordinates. (This only works on 8-bit images.)

When you're happy with how the edge looks, you might want to add some other effects, such as a glowing border around our shape. There's a trick for that, too. Choose Layer > Layer Style > Inner Glow (**Figures 14.65** and **14.66**). Now click on the color swatch to pick the color you would like to use and set the Blend Mode pop-up menu to Normal. To get the color to appear around the edge of the image only, be sure to click Edge in the Elements section of the dialog box. Now you can experiment with the Opacity, Size, and Choke settings to fine-tune the result. If you are having trouble getting the edge to completely show up, try increasing the Opacity and Choke settings. You don't have to restrict yourself to the Inner Glow effect, so experiment with the other Layer Styles until you find your favorite.

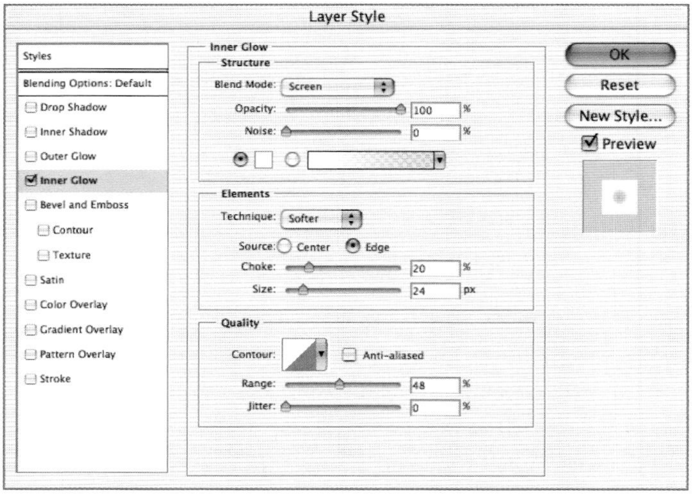

Figure 14.66 Inner Glow settings used to create the border.

Adjusting with Levels

You can also adjust the appearance of a Layer Mask (as long as it contains shades of gray) by choosing Image > Adjustments > Levels. The sliders in the Levels dialog box (**Figure 14.67**) will do the following to your image:

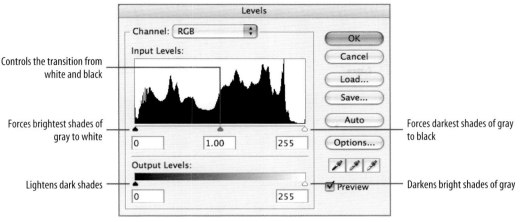

Figure 14.67 The Levels dialog box.

▶ **Upper-left slider:** Forces the darkest shades of gray to black, which will make more areas transparent.

▶ **Upper-right slider:** Forces the brightest shades of gray to white, which will make more areas opaque.

▶ **Middle slider:** Changes the transition from black to white and therefore changes the transition from opaque to transparent.

▶ **Lower-left slider:** Lightens the dark shades of gray, which will make transparent areas appear more opaque.

▶ **Lower-right slider:** Darkens the bright shades of gray, which will make opaque areas appear more transparent.

Image as Layer Mask

You can achieve interesting transition effects by pasting scanned images into a Layer Mask (**Figures 14.68** and **14.69**). I like to run off to the art supply store, purchase interesting handmade papers, and spatter a bunch of ink on them using paintbrushes. Then, to get the image into a Layer Mask, I scan the paper, select the entire image by choosing Select > Select All, and then copy the image by choosing Edit > Copy. After I've done that, I close the scanned image and switch over to the image I would like to use it in. Next, I click on the layer I would like to work on and add a Layer Mask. In order to paste something into a Layer Mask, you must be viewing the Layer Mask. That means you must Option/Alt-click the Layer Mask before pasting something into it. To stop viewing the Layer Mask, just Option/Alt-click its thumbnail again.

Figure 14.68 Left: Original Image. Right: Scanned image to be used as a Layer Mask. (Paper: ©istockphoto.com/Bastar, Splatter: ©iStockphoto.com/sx70)

Figure 14.69 The images blended together using the scanned image as a Layer Mask.

Using the Move Tool

After you have created the perfect Layer Mask, you might want to start rearranging your document by using the Move tool. You have three choices: You can move just the layer, just the Layer Mask, or both at the same time. The link symbol between the Layer Mask and image thumbnails determines what the Move tool will actually move. If the link symbol is present (that's the default), the layer and Layer Mask will move together (**Figures 14.70** to **14.72**).

Figure 14.70 Original images. (Ballerina: ©iStockphoto.com/Piepereit, Frame: ©istockphoto.com/blackred)

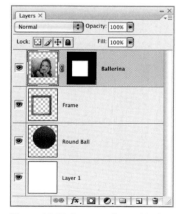

Figure 14.71 Layer and Layer Mask thumbnails linked together.

Figure 14.72 Main image layer and Layer Mask moved together.

If you turn off the link symbol (by clicking it), you'll only be moving whatever has the frame around it. That means if the Layer Mask has it, you'll just be moving that around the screen. If the main image has it, you'll move just the main image around the screen, leaving the Layer Mask in its original position (**Figures 14.73** and **14.74**). If part of the Layer Mask lines up with another part of the image, you'll want to move just the layer and not the Layer Mask (**Figures 14.75** and **14.76**).

To quickly paste something into a Layer Mask, press the \ key to view the Layer Mask, press Command/Ctrl-V to paste the image, and finally press \ again to stop viewing the Layer Mask. This technique does not view the Layer Mask as it would normally appear; it shows up as a color overlay.

On occasion, it can be useful to have two Layer Masks masking a single layer. To accomplish that, add the first Layer Mask directly to the layer, then group the layers (clicking the icon, which looks like a folder), and add a Layer Mask to the group. That way you can remove the background on the image using the Layer Mask that is attached directly to the layer, and make further refinements using the Layer Mask that is attached to the group. That allows you to experiment with the Layer Mask that is attached to the group without any chance of messing up the mask that is applied directly to the layer.

Figure 14.73 Moving just the Layer Mask, leaving the main image stationary.

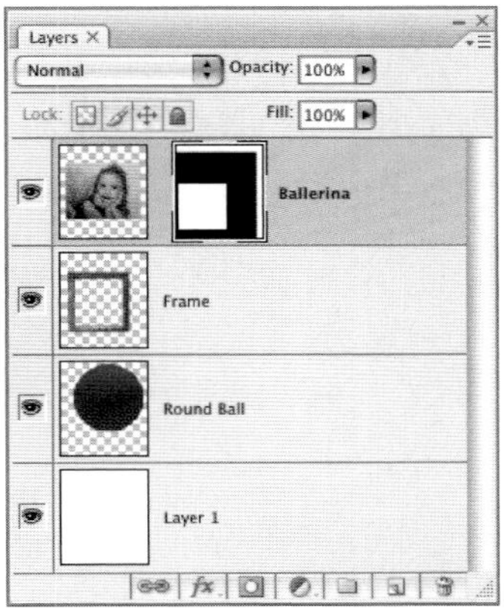

Figure 14.74 When the link symbol is missing, the frame (Layer Mask) determines what will get moved.

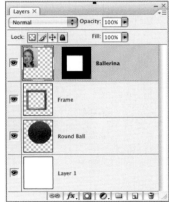

Figure 14.75 Moving the main image, leaving the Layer Mask stationary.

Figure 14.76 The link symbol is missing and the frame is indicating that the main image is active, so only the main image will be moved.

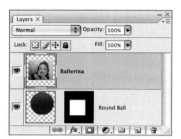

Figure 14.77 Drag the Layer Mask to the layer you'd like to move it to.

Copying to Another Layer

If you'd like to move a Layer Mask from one layer to another, click in the middle of the Layer Mask and drag it on top of another layer in the Layers palette. If the destination layer already has a Layer Mask attached to it, Photoshop will ask you if you'd like to replace the mask with the one you are dragging. If you'd rather copy the mask instead of moving it, hold the Option/Alt key (**Figures 14.77** and **14.78**).

Load as Selection

Once you have perfected a Layer Mask, you might need to select the areas that are visible in order to add a border or perform another effect. You can do this in many ways. The fastest method is to Command/Ctrl-click the Layer Mask thumbnail (**Figures 14.79** and **14.80**). If there is already a selection present, you can Shift-Command-click (Mac) or Shift-Ctrl-click (Windows) to add to the selection; Option-Command-click (Mac) or Alt-Ctrl-click (Windows) to subtract from it; or Shift-Option-Command-click (Mac) or Shift-Alt-Ctrl-click (Windows) to intersect the selection. Or, if you are not very good at remembering a bunch of keyboard commands, you can Control-click/right-click the Layer Mask thumbnail to get a menu of options.

Figure 14.78 Result of moving the Layer Mask between layers.

Figure 14.79 Command/Ctrl-click the Layer Mask thumbnail to select the areas that are visible.

Figure 14.80 Result of Command-clicking (Mac) or Ctrl-clicking (Windows) on the "x" layer's Layer Mask thumbnail. (Notice the marching ants.)

Figure 14.81 The original image included a Layer Style. (©istockphoto.com/spxChrome)

Figure 14.82 Applying a Layer Mask changes where the style appears.

Figure 14.83 Using the Layer Mask Hides Effects check box causes the Layer Mask to hide the Layer Style.

Masking Layer Styles

If you have a Layer Style (like Bevel and Emboss) applied to a layer that contains a Layer Mask, you'll find that the mask changes where the style shows up (**Figures 14.81** and **14.82**). If you'd rather have the Layer Mask hide the style instead of changing where it shows up, double-click on the layer to access the Layer Style dialog box. Turning on the Layer Mask Hides Effects check box causes the Layer Mask to hide the original style position instead of changing where it shows up (**Figures 14.83** and **14.84**).

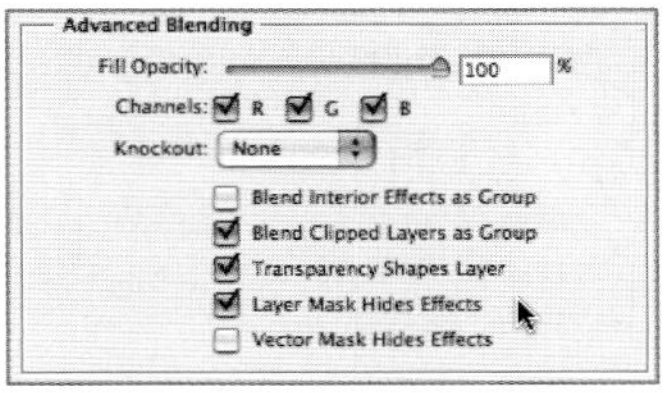

Figure 14.84 The Advanced Blending section of the Layer Style dialog box.

Converting the Blending Sliders into a Layer Mask

Earlier in this chapter, we talked about making areas of a layer transparent using the Blending sliders in the Layer Style dialog box. Occasionally, you might need to turn off the sliders and create a Layer Mask that produces the same result. (Why? Well, you might want to be able to edit the Layer Mask using painting tools and filters instead of just the Blending sliders.) To accomplish this, you'll need to go through a multi-step process.

First, create a new empty layer below the layer that is using the Blending sliders. Next, click the layer above it (the one that uses the Blending sliders) and press Option-Command-E (Mac) or Alt-Ctrl-E (Windows). This deposits information into the layer that does not use the Blending sliders but produces the same results (permanently deleting the transparent areas).

Figure 14.85 Result of typing Option-Command-E (Mac) or Alt-Ctrl-E (Windows) with an empty layer.

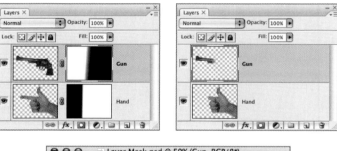

Figure 14.86 Layer Mask added after Command/Ctrl-clicking the merged layer.

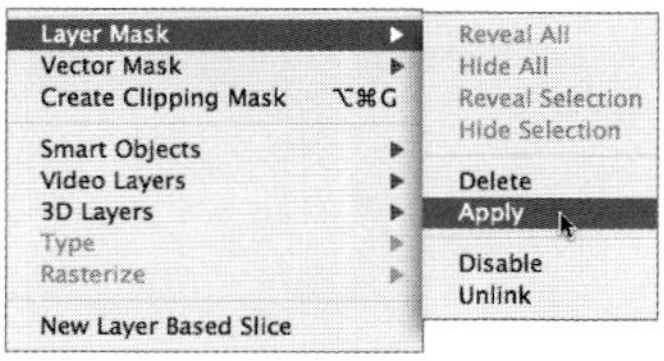

Figure 14.87 The Layer>Layer Mask menu.

Now you can double-click to the right of the name of the layer that uses the Blending sliders, and then set all the sliders back to their default positions so they are no longer affecting the layer. Then, to add a Layer Mask that produces the same result, Command/Ctrl-click the layer thumbnail on the layer directly below the one that was using the sliders (to select the nontransparent areas of the layer). Finally, click the Layer Mask icon on the layer that used the sliders to add a Layer Mask based on that selection, and then trash the middle layer (**Figures 14.85** and **14.86**).

Removing a Layer Mask

If you know you will no longer need to edit a Layer Mask and would like to permanently delete the areas that are transparent, make sure the Layer Mask thumbnail is active and choose one of the options from the Remove Layer Mask menu (Layer > Remove Layer Mask) (**Figures 14.87** and **14.88**). When you do this, you will be presented with two choices:

Figure 14.88 Bottom: Main image window.
Top Left: Layers palette view before "applying" the layer masks.
Top Right: Layers palette view after "applying" the layer masks.
(Gun: ©iStockphoto.com/bpalmer, Hand: ©istockphoto.com/Sveta)

▶ **Apply:** Removes the Layer Mask and deletes all transparent areas.

▶ **Delete:** Removes the Layer Mask and brings the image back into full view.

Now that we've covered the mechanics of using Layer Masks, let's take a look at how Photoshop can help automate the process of combining multiple images into one seamless panoramic image.

A quick way to remove a Layer Mask is to drag its thumbnail to the Trash icon that is located at the bottom of the Layers palette.

For instant access to the Layer Mask menu, control/right-click the Layer Mask thumbnail.

Creating a Panoramic Image with Photomerge

The Photomerge feature automates the process of combining images into a seamless panoramic. To start creating your own panoramic images, open the images in Photoshop and then choose File > Automate > Photomerge. The initial Photomerge dialog box will prompt you to specify which images you'd like to use to create a panoramic. Because you've already opened the images you want to use, just set the Use pop-up menu to Open Files. Alternately, you can use the Browse button to choose files that you want to merge (**Figure 14.89**). Next, check the Blend Images Together check box. This will create a seamless final image. However, if you want, you can leave this option turned off to make an old-fashioned, David Hockney-like photo collage of overlapping images. If you didn't shoot your panorama well enough to create a seamless image, this can be a way to salvage the shot.

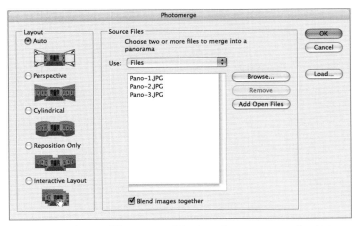

Figure 14.89 The initial Photomerge dialog box allows you to specify which images you'd like to merge into a panoramic.

On the left side of the dialog, you'll find a selection of Layout options. These are designed to facilitate the different ways that you might have shot the panorama. In almost all cases, the Auto option will be the best choice. However, if your final stitchings don't look right, you may want to try a different layout option.

Once you've chosen your files, click OK to start the merging process. Merging can take a while, depending on the speed of your machine, but it can be fun to watch. If the Layers and History palettes are open, you can get a good idea of what Photoshop is up to. Basically, it's copying each image into its own layer in one document. It then uses Photoshop's new Auto Align and Auto Blend features (which we'll learn about later) to perform the actual merge.

When you're finished, you'll have a single document with a separate layer for each image (**Figure 14.90**). Right off the bat, you'll notice that Photoshop does not automatically crop your image, you'll have to do this by hand. While manual crop may seem an extra hassle, it's actually nice to have the control, because it means you can choose to preserve as much image detail as you want. For example, in Figure 14.90, I might choose to clone in some of the missing sky in order to get a larger image.

The next thing you should notice is that the Layers palette includes Layer Masks for each layer (**Figure 14.91**). These Layer Masks control exactly which part of each layer is visible and are the mechanism that Photoshop uses to create the seams in your image. Since the Photomerge feature leaves the Layer Masks intact rather than flattening the final image, you can easily adjust a bad seam by simply painting into that layer's Layer Mask.

Figure 14.90 After merging, you'll have a layered document, complete with Layer Masks.

Figure 14.91 The Layer Masks define the seams that are used to create the final merge.

Panoramic stitching was much more complicated in previous versions of Photoshop, mostly because the program wasn't capable of doing a very good job of aligning images. This meant that you usually had to do some manual aligning, as well as a lot of retouching of seams. With CS3's Photomerge, these troubles are, more often than not, a thing of the past. If you do run into trouble, either because you have a particularly complex set of images or because you're going for a particular look, you'll want to choose Manual Layout in the initial Photomerge dialog. This will bring up the Manual Layout dialog, which lets you position your images by hand (**Figure 14.92**).

From the small toolbox in the upper-left corner, you can choose between Select and Rotate tools. With the Select tool, you can simply click on an image and drag to reposition it. If the Snap to Image box is turned on, Photoshop will automatically position the image where it thinks is best. If you'd prefer completely manual control, turn off Snap to Image.

You can use the Rotate tool to apply rotations to an image to make it fit better, and you can remove an image altogether by dragging it to the bar at the top of the window (**Figure 14.93**).

Figure 14.92 Using Manual Layout you can arrange your source images by hand.

Figure 14.93 You can remove an image from a panorama by dragging it to the well at the top of the window.

The Set Vanishing Point tool, located just below the Rotate tool lets you change the overall perspective in your image by defining a new vanishing point. The vanishing point is simply the point at which all perspective lines in the image recede to, and altering the vanishing point can create a very different sense of space in your final panorama (**Figure 14.94**).

Figure 14.94 The Set Vanishing Point tool lets you change the overall perspective in your final panorama. (©2007 Ben Long)

When you're done, click the Save Composition button and give this arrangement of images a name. Saving this document allows you to come back to Photomerge and reload your composition instead of having to start from scratch.

While the new Photomerge feature does an excellent job of stitching panoramas, you'll still find that your images will sometimes need some minor corrections and retouchings using the tools that we'll cover in Chapter 15 , "Retouching."

Vector Masks

Vector Masks allow you to control which area of a layer will be visible by using an easily editable, smooth-shaped, crisp-edged path. By the time they make it to your computer screen, all photographs are made out of pixels, and the resolution of the file determines how large the pixels will be when printed. If those pixels are large enough, the image will appear jaggy when printed. But with Vector Masks, you can create a very low-resolution (read: jaggy) image and still get a smooth-shaped, crisp-edged transition between the content of a layer and the underlying image.

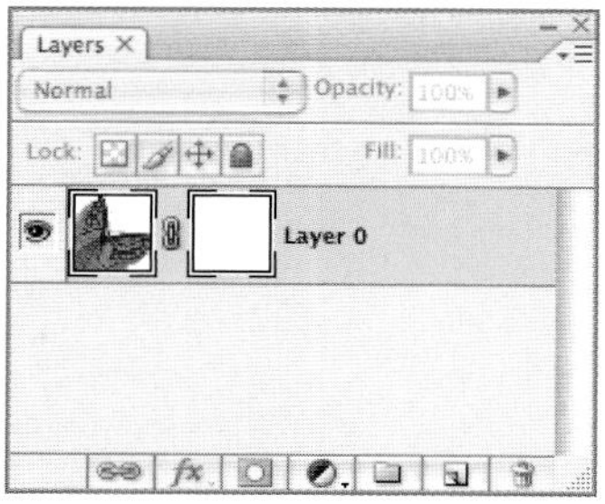

Adding a Vector Mask

The simplest way to add a Vector Mask is to choose Layer > Vector Mask > Reveal All. After you choose that option, the layer that is active will have two thumbnail images in the Layers palette (**Figure 14.95**). It should look like you just

Figure 14.95 After adding a Vector Mask, you will see two thumbnail images in the Layers palette.

added a Layer Mask. The only difference is that with a Layer Mask, you paint with shades of gray to control which areas of a layer will be hidden or visible, whereas with a Vector Mask, you define the area that will be visible using a path.

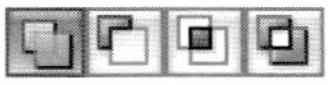

The easiest way to define where the image should be visible is to use one of the Shape tools. Before you start creating shapes, be sure to take a peek at the settings in the options bar. You should find four options available on the left side of the options bar when a layer that contains a Vector Mask is active. The leftmost choice allows you to create a shape to define where the image should be visible (**Figure 14.96**). The second choice allows you to define a shape where the image should be hidden (**Figure 14.97**). The third choice limits the areas that are already visible, so they show up only within the shape you draw (**Figure 14.98**). The last choice inverts the visibility of the area inside the shape you draw, making visible areas hidden and hidden areas visible (**Figure 14.99**).

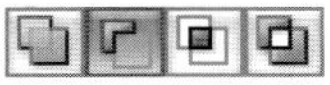

You can also use any of the Pen tools to create and modify a Vector Mask. If you're not already familiar with the Pen tools, start out with the Freeform Pen tool because it allows you to create a path by drawing a freeform shape, much like the Lasso tool allows you to create a selection. If you'd like to learn how to use the Pen tool, check out Chapter 13, "Advanced Masking."

If you already have a path saved in your file (it will show up in the Paths palette), you can use it as a Vector Mask. Just make sure the layer you'd like to apply it to is active (you can't add one to the background layer), click on the name of the path in the Paths palette, and then choose Layer > Add Vector Mask > Current Path. That will allow you to use any paths that are included with stock photos you have purchased.

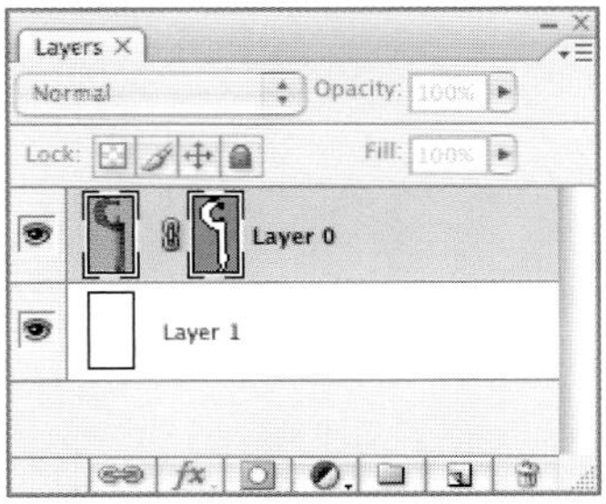

Disabling the Vector Mask

After you have created a Vector Mask, you can temporarily disable it by Shift-clicking its thumbnail in the Layers palette (**Figures 14.100** and **14.101**). With each click, you will toggle the Vector Mask on and off. This is a great help when you want to see what a layer would look like if you didn't have a Vector Mask restricting where it shows up.

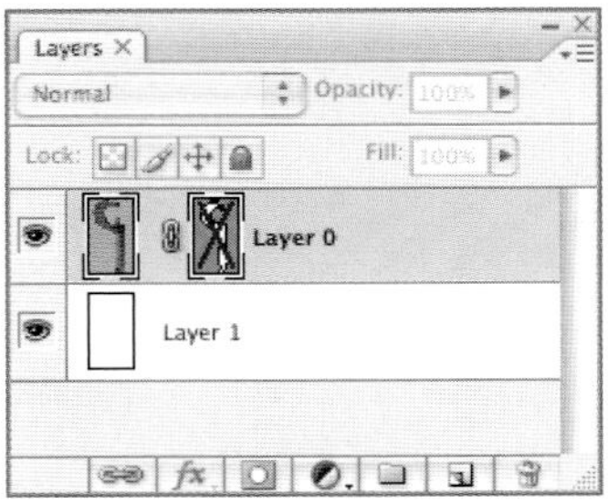

Figure 14.96 This shape defines where the image is visible.

Figure 14.97 The shape that was added is being used to hide part of the image.

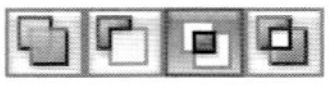

Figure 14.98 The shape that was added is being used to limit where the image is visible.

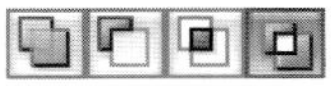

Figure 14.99 The shape that was added is being used to invert the visibility of the image.

Figure 14.100 Vector Mask active.

Figure 14.101 Vector Mask disabled.

Figure 14.102 Layer and Vector Mask linked together.

NOTES

To change the options for a shape, click on the shape with the Solid Arrow tool and then change the settings that appear in the options bar.

Using the Move Tool

When you use the Move tool to reposition a layer, you'll notice that the layer and the Vector Mask move together (**Figures 14.102** to **14.104**). If you turn off the link symbol (by clicking it), you'll leave the Vector Mask alone and just move the image (**Figure 14.105**).

If you'd like to move the Vector Mask and leave the image stationary, use the Solid Arrow tool that appears directly above the Pen tools (**Figure 14.106**).

Figure 14.103 Original image. (©2007 Stockbyte, www.stockbyte.com)

Figure 14.104 Layer and Vector Mask moved together.

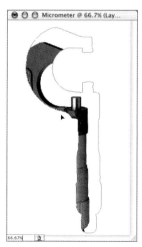

Figure 14.105 Vector Mask left stationary while the layer is repositioned.

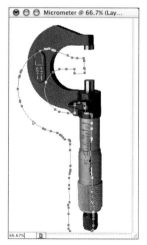

Figure 14.106 Use the Solid Arrow tool to reposition a Vector Mask.

Transforming the Vector Mask

The Edit > Transform commands are very useful when working on a Vector Mask. Because the path is made from a collection of points and directional handles (instead of pixels), scaling, rotating, and other transformations will not degrade the quality of the shape. All you have to do is make sure the path is visible before you choose Transform Path from the Edit menu. You can toggle the visibility of a Vector Mask by shift-clicking its thumbnail in the Layers palette.

Using Vector Masks with Layer Masks

You can have both a Layer Mask and a Vector Mask attached to a single layer. (Just click the Layer Mask icon twice.) When that's the case, you'll end up with your image visible only where both the Layer Mask and Vector Mask allow things to be visible (**Figure 14.107**). If you have multiple layers that have Layer Masks applied to them, you can mask the cumulative effect of those layers with a Vector Mask by doing the following: Select the layers to which you'd like to apply a Vector Mask and then Shift-click the Create a New Group icon at the bottom of the Layers palette (it's the one that looks like a folder) (**Figure 14.108** and **14.109**). Next, click on the newly created group to make it active, and then add a Vector Mask. Any shapes that you add to the Vector Mask will limit where all the layers that are contained in that group show up (**Figure 14.110**). That's how I'd create the feather images Adobe used for the Photoshop CS packaging (**Figure 14.111**).

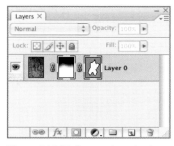

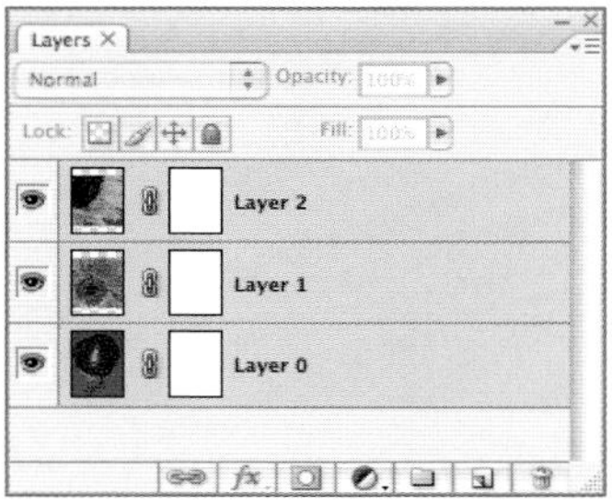

Figure 14.107 You can have both a Layer Mask and a Vector Mask attached to the same layer.

Figure 14.108 Select the layers you'd like to have in a group.

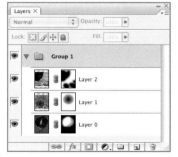

Figure 14.109 After clicking the Create a New Group icon, the layers will appear inside a folder in the Layers palette.

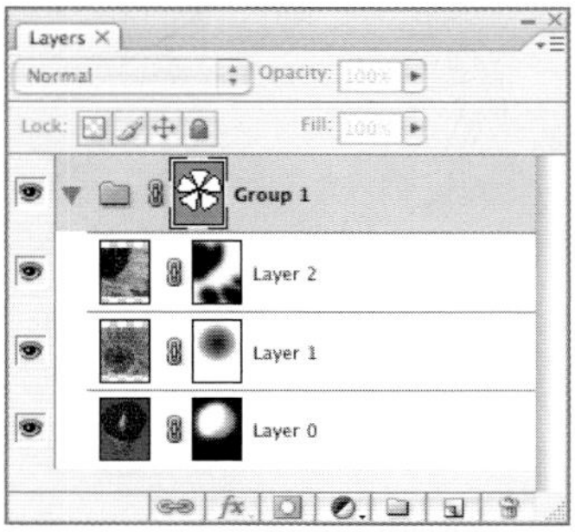

Figure 14.110 Add a Vector Mask to the set to limit where all the layers within the set show up.

Figure 14.111 The result is something that resembles Photoshop CS's product identity campaign. (©2007 Stockbyte, www.stockbyte.com)

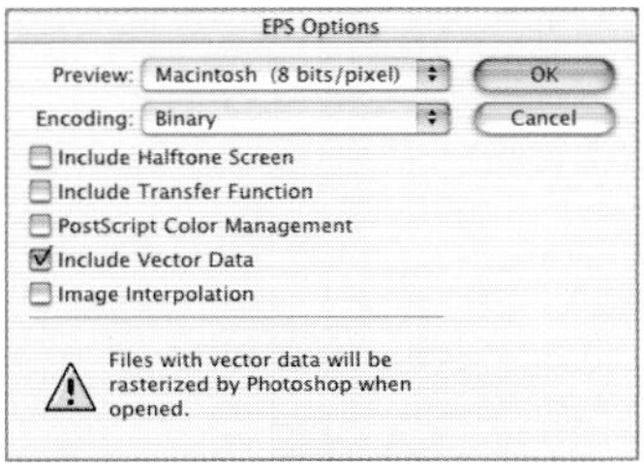

Figure 14.112 Saving an EPS file.

Figure 14.113 Image imported into a page layout program without a clipping path. (©2007 www.PeterHoey.com)

Removing the Vector Mask

If you find that you'd like to remove the Vector Mask from your image, just choose Layer > Delete Vector Mask, or drag its thumbnail to the trash can that appears at the bottom of the Layers palette. You can also convert a Vector Mask into a Layer Mask by choosing Layer > Rasterize > Vector Mask. But be aware that you'll lose the crisp-edged, smooth look of the path, and any transformations applied to the Layer Mask will cause it to appear blurry.

Saving Vector Data

If you plan on saving your image and using it in a page layout program (instead of using it for a Web site), you'll need to be careful about how you save it; otherwise, the crisp edge of your path may be lost. Remember when I said that a path is different from pixels in that it's made out of points and directional handles? Well, technically, that's known as vector information, whereas images made from pixels are known as raster information. In order to maintain the crisp edges of your paths, you'll need to save your image in the EPS or PDF file formats (which support vector data). Not only that, but you'll have to turn on the Include Vector Data check box (**Figure 14.112**) when saving your file. (This option shows up only after you click the Save button.) There's one last thing: Your paths will only print with crisp edges if you print to a PostScript output device like a $500+ laser printer. Most inkjet printers don't understand PostScript, so your image has the potential of appearing jaggy on those.

Clipping Paths

You can also assign a path to a document, as opposed to a single layer. A clipping path will limit which areas of an image will show up and print in a page layout program (**Figures 14.113** and **14.114**). To create one, use the Pen or a Shape tool to create a path, and then choose Window > Paths to open the Paths palette. Next, double-click the name of the path and assign it a name. Then choose Clipping Path from the side menu of the Paths palette (**Figure 14.115**). When prompted, be sure to enter a Flatness setting. When the image is printed, it will be converted into a polygon made out of straight lines of identical length.

Figure 14.114 Image imported into a page layout program with a clipping path.

The Flatness setting will determine the length of those lines. Low settings produce short lines, which require more memory and processing time to output. If you use too low of a setting, your printer might run out of memory when attempting to output your image. The more complex your path is (lots of points and directional handles), the higher the Flatness setting needs to be to avoid printing problems. In general, I use a setting between 3 and 10, depending on the complexity of the path I'm using. After you've assigned a clipping path to an image, you'll need to save it in the TIFF or EPS file format in order for it to be understood by a page layout program.

Smart Objects

Introduced in Photoshop CS2, Smart Objects provide a completely different way of working in Photoshop. Instead of the good old one-element-per-layer tradition, images are dealt with in a way that is similar to how page-layout programs link to external image files. If you're not familiar with that concept, it basically means that when you place an image on a page, you're actually just viewing a preview of the image that is stored on your hard drive. You're free to scale, rotate, and crop the image, but you cannot edit it directly in the page-layout program. Instead, you must open the linked image in Photoshop, make your changes, resave it, and then update the link to the image in the page-layout program. Adobe took this idea and applied it to Photoshop. You can now place an external image file, or encapsulate multiple layers into a Photoshop document, as a Smart Object. But instead of "linking" to external files, the images are "embedded" in the Photoshop document. The Smart Object acts much like a linked file in that you are limited to scaling, transforming, and masking its contents, but if you want to make edits, you must do so in a separate document. There are many advantages to working with Smart Objects:

▶ They allow you to create a complex document without having to show all the layers that make up the image.

▶ You can scale a layer to a small size while retaining the ability to later enlarge the layer using the full-sized layers that were originally used to create the Smart Object.

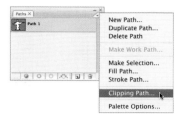

Figure 14.115 Choose Clipping Path from the side menu of the Paths palette.

You can print an image that contains vector data on a non-PostScript printer and maintain the crisp edges by saving it as a PDF file and printing it from Adobe Acrobat.

► You can duplicate a Smart Object multiple times and make edits to the original, and all the duplicates will automatically update to match the original.

► You can embed an Adobe Illustrator or Camera Raw file into a Photoshop file and later make changes in Illustrator or the Camera Raw dialog box. You can also extract the original file at any time.

► You can apply some filters nondestructively thanks to the new Smart Filters feature.

► You can work nondestructively with Camera Raw files, allowing you to go back and adjust your camera raw conversion settings at any time.

There are also limitations to what can be done to a Smart Object. The Smart Object layer cannot be edited directly, which means you will not be able to paint or directly adjust the Smart Object without using a few special tricks, or editing the layers that make up the Smart Object.

Creating Smart Objects

There are several methods for creating a Smart Object. The easiest way is to simply choose File > Open as Smart Object, and then pick the image that you want to open (you can select more than one by Shift-clicking multiple file names). The image will open as normal and, at first glance, you won't see anything conspicuously different. But, if you look at the title bar of the image, you'll see "<<image name>> as Smart Object" and then the usual color mode and zoom percentage stats.

Figure 14.116 The icon in the lower right of the layer thumbnail indicates this is a Smart Object layer.

The other indication that you're working with a different kind of image is in the Layers palette. There is no "Background" layer like there is in a normal document. Instead, your image sits as a Smart Object in its own layer with a special badge superimposed over its thumbnail (**Figure 14.116**).

Finally, select the Brush tool and hold it over your image. You'll get a very stubborn "no" icon that indicates that that tool will *not* work on this image. Remember, Smart Objects don't contain normal pixel data, and so can't be edited on a pixel-by-pixel basis using the normal Photoshop procedures.

There are other ways to create Smart Objects. If the layers you'd like to use are contained in the currently active document, just select them and choose Layer > Smart Objects >

Convert to Smart Object. If, on the other hand, the layer or layers are part of an external file, choose File > Place instead. The external file can be in any file format that Photoshop can open. That includes Adobe Illustrator and Camera Raw files. Once you've created a Smart Object, it will appear as a single layer in the Layers palette, and it will display the special icon to indicate that it's a Smart Object.

Grouping layers into a Smart Object will prevent the individual layers within the Smart Object from interacting with layers outside of the Smart Object. That means that the general appearance of your document might change depending on which features were used to create it:

▸ The Underlying Layer sliders in the Layer Style dialog box will not affect layers outside of the Smart Object.

▸ The layers will become adjacent to each other in the Layers palette and no longer be intermixed with other layers.

▸ Adjustment layers used within the Smart Object cannot affect layers outside of the Smart Object.

▸ Blending modes used on individual layers will be limited to interacting with the other layers that are found within the Smart Object.

Multiple Instances

Once you've created a Smart Object, you can drag it to the New Layer icon at the bottom of the Layers palette to duplicate the layer and create another instance of the same Smart Object. Each instance of the Smart Object will refer to the same set of layers that were used to create the Smart Object. Layer Styles, Masks, and warping can be used to modify individual instances of the Smart Object. Editing the layers that make up the Smart Object causes all the instances of that Smart Object to update to reflect the changes. In the example here, a single leaf was used to create a Smart Object, then that Smart Object layer was duplicated nine times to create the other leaves, which were rotated (**Figure 14.117**) and styled (**Figure 14.118**) to create the composition shown. Since all ten leaves that appeared in the final image were instances of the same leaf, editing the leaf caused all ten leaves to update to reflect the change (**Figure 14.119**). In this case, a subtle change was made to a Vector Mask, which changed how much of the leaf was visible.

NOTES

You can use any of the following methods to create a second instance of a Smart Object:

▸ Choose Layer > New > Layer Via Copy, or press Command/Ctrl-J.

▸ Hold Option/Alt and drag when the Move tool is active.

▸ Choose Layer > Duplicate Layer.

▸ Drag the Smart Object to the New Layer icon at the bottom of the Layers palette.

Figure 14.117 Ten instances of the same Smart Object have been rotated to create this complex image.

Figure 14.118 Layer Styles were used to add color to each instance of the Smart Object.

Figure 14.119 Editing the Smart Object caused all instances of the Smart Object to be updated.

Figure 14.120 Left: Ten Smart Objects are used to create a complex document, Right: The same document viewed after nesting the ten Smart Object layers into a single Smart Object.

Nested Smart Objects

You can nest one Smart Object within another by choosing Layer > Smart Objects > Group Into New Smart Object (when at least one Smart Object is selected). Nested Smart Objects are useful when you want to simplify the Layers palette view of your image (**Figure 14.120**) or cause Layer Styles to think of multiple layers as a single object instead of applying to each individual element that makes up the image (**Figures 14.121** and **14.122**). This will also allow you to apply warping to all the layers at once (we'll talk about warping later in this chapter).

When you nest one Smart Object inside another, you cause that nested Smart Object to become independent of any other instances that are used outside of the Smart Object it is nested within. Therefore, editing the nested Smart Object will only affect other instances of that Smart Object that appear within the Smart Object it is nested within, and will leave other Smart Objects unchanged. It might sound confusing just reading about it, but once you've driven this thing around the block a few times, it will make sense.

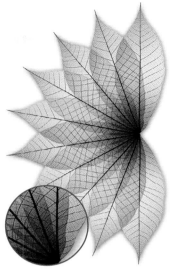

NOTES

Choosing Layer > Smart Objects > New Smart Object Via Copy will create an Smart Object that is independent of the other Smart Objects in the document. That will allow you to edit the newly created Smart Object without affecting other Smart Objects in the document.

Figure 14.121 A Drop Shadow Layer Style was applied to each of the individual leaf Smart Object Layers.

Figure 14.122 A Drop Shadow Layer Style applied after nesting the leaf layers into a single Smart Object.

Editing Smart Objects

To edit the layers that make up a Smart Object, either choose Layer > Smart Objects > Edit Contents, or double-click on the Smart Object's thumbnail image in the Layers palette. The contents of the Smart Object will appear in a separate document window where you can edit the individual layers within the Smart Object using any of Photoshop's tools. When you've finished modifying the Smart Object, type Command/Ctrl-S to save the changes and update the parent document that contains the Smart Object.

If your Smart Object contains a Camera Raw file, editing the contents will take you back to the Camera Raw dialog box, where you'll be able to adjust your raw conversion parameters.

Choosing Layer > Smart Objects > Replace Contents allows you to replace the entire contents of a Smart Object with the contents of a file on your hard drive. This is useful when working with Camera Raw files since it allows you to start a design with placeholder images that you can later replace with alternative images.

Figure 14.123 When you add a filter to a Smart Layer, it appears in a special Smart Filters effect in the Layers palette.

Figure 14.124 Painting into the layer mask of a Smart Filter allows you to constrain the effects of the filter to specific areas of your image.

NOTES

The new Filter > Convert for Smart Object command does the exact same thing as the Layer > Smart Objects > Convert to Smart Objects command. It's just there because you have to convert a layer to a Smart Object before you can apply a filter as a Smart Filter, so Adobe has added this extra option for making Smart Objects.

Smart Filters

In previous versions of Photoshop there was no way to apply a filter to a Smart Object without first rasterizing that object into a normal layer. But with CS3's Smart Filters, you can now apply filters to a Smart Object, just as you would to any other type of layer. Just select the filter you want to apply from the Filter menu. The filter's dialog box (if it has one) will appear as it always does, and your image will be processed.

Not all filters are available as Smart Filters, but you should find that all of the crucial filters—sharpening, blurring, and so on—are available in CS3.

After the filter is added, a Smart Filters effect is added to your layer in the Layers palette (**Figure 14.123**). As you can see, this is exactly the same way that CS3 displays layer styles. As you add filters, they are added to the Smart Filter entry for that layer.

If you want to change the parameters of any filter you've added, simply double-click its entry in the Layers palette. The filter's dialog box will appear, allowing you to adjust its settings.

You can re-order the filters by simply dragging them up and down the list. Applying filters in different orders will sometimes produce different results. Finally, you can delete a filter by selecting it in the Layers palette and pressing the Delete key.

The Smart Filters collection that is attached to a layer has a built-in masking function that works just like a Layer Mask or the mask that's attached to an adjustment layer. To use the Smart Filter mask, just click on it in the Layers palette to select it, and then use any Photoshop painting tools to paint into the mask (**Figure 14.124**).

Note that the Layer Mask applies to *all* of the filters that you've added to that Smart Object. You can't create separate masks for each effect.

Smart Filters differ from Adjustment Layers in that they affect only the image that they're attached to. You can't use an Unsharp Mask filter to sharpen all of the layers in an image, for example. Instead, you'll need to apply separate Unsharp Mask filters to each layer in your document; each configured with the same settings.

Smart Objects Tips & Tricks

Let's look at a few interesting ways to use Smart Objects. These ideas just scratch the surface of what you can do. The more you experiment, the more you'll come up with useful ways to use Smart Objects.

Camera Raw

You can blend two different interpretations of the same RAW format image using Smart Objects. All you have to do is embed a Camera Raw file into an existing document by choosing File > Place. When you place a raw file, you'll be presented with the Camera Raw dialog box where you can interpret the tonality and color of your image. The problem is that you might not be able to find a single interpretation that does justice to the entire image (**Figure 14.125**). When that's the case, choose Layer > Smart Objects > New Smart Object via Copy to create a second Smart Object that is independent of the first. You can then double-click on the thumbnail image for the Smart Object, causing the Camera Raw dialog box to appear, where you can choose different settings to be applied to the second Smart Object. Once you have two different interpretations of the raw file (**Figures 14.126** and **14.127**), you can add a Layer Mask to the top Smart Object and use it to control where each version of the raw file contributes to the final image (**Figure 14.128**).

Figure 14.125 Using a single set of Camera Raw settings produces a less than desirable result. (©2007 Ben Willmore)

Figure 14.126 The sky was ignored and the bottom was optimized in this Camera Raw interpretation.

Figure 14.127 The bottom was ignored and the sky was optimized in this Camera Raw interpretation.

Figure 14.128 The two interpretations of the same raw file were combined using a Layer Mask.

Painting and Adjustments

Many of Photoshop's tools will be disabled when a Smart Object is active in the Layers palette. Here are a few tricks you can use to get around that limitation:

▶ To apply paint to a Smart Object, create a new layer directly above the Smart Object and choose Layer > Create Clipping Mask so that any paint applied to the layer will only show up where the Smart Object appears.

▶ To adjust a Smart Object without affecting the rest of the image (with the Smart Object layer selected), hold Option/Alt, click on the Adjustment Layer pop-up menu at the bottom of the Layers palette, and choose the adjustment you'd like to apply. When the New Layer dialog box appears, turn on the Use Previous Layer to Create Clipping Mask check box to limit the adjustment to the Smart Object layer.

▶ If you want to apply a filter that's not available as a Smart Filter, try this: Duplicate the Smart Object layer by typing Command/Ctrl-J, hide the original (by clicking the eyeball icon), and then apply the filter. When you apply the filter, Photoshop will merge the layers that make up the Smart Object (also known as rasterizing), which will turn it into a normal layer. But since you duplicated the Smart Object, you'll still have a copy that you can later edit and then re-filter.

▶ Be careful when adding layers to a Smart Object. If the original Smart Object was created after opening a flat JPG file that contained no layers, then adding layers will cause problems. Photoshop will act as if the Smart Object is actually a JPG file, and since JPG files can't contain layers, Photoshop will present you with a Save As dialog box, forcing you to save the document in a file format that supports layers. That means that adding a layer will cause your edited Smart Object to be saved on your hard drive instead of being embedded in the parent document in which you used the Smart Object. To update the parent document, choose Layer > Smart Object > Replace Contents and point Photoshop to the newly saved layered file.

Warping

Photoshop's warping features allow you to bend and distort your images in interesting ways. Choosing Edit > Transform > Warp causes various warp settings to appear in the options bar at the top of your screen (**Figure 14.129**) and places a grid over the active layer (**Figure 14.130**). There are 15 preset warp shapes available (**Figures 14.131** and **14.132**). After choosing a preset from the Warp pop-up menu in the options bar, you can adjust the Bend and H (Horizontal) and V (Vertical) fields in the options bar to control the extent of the warp that's applied to the active layer. If you need to warp an image to match an element in a photograph, set the Warp pop-up menu to Custom.

Figure 14.130 Choosing Edit > Transform > Warp causes a warp grid to appear over your image. (©2007 iStockphoto.com)

Figure 14.129 The options bar settings available when warping a layer.

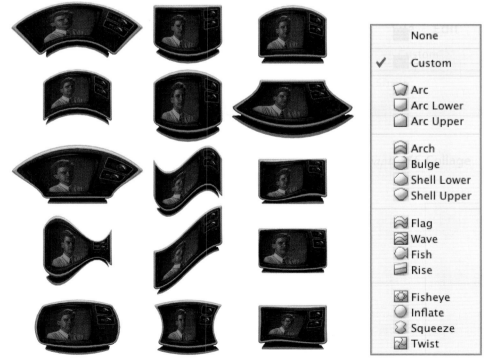

Figure 14.131 The 15 default warp presets shown in the same order they appear in the Warp pop-up menu (from left to right and top to bottom).

Figure 14.132 The Warp pop-up menu contains 15 preset shapes.

When applying a Custom warp, you can drag the corner points, handles, or grid lines to distort the image. To match the contours of an object, start by positioning the corner handles to meet up with the underlying image (**Figure 14.133**). Next, adjust the corner handles to specify the angle at which the edge of the image should be to match the underlying image (**Figures 14.134** and **14.135**). Then, to fine-tune the results, drag the grid lines until the image is distorted to match the underlying object (**Figure 14.136**). If you warp a Smart Object layer, you can choose Layer > Smart Object > Replace Contents to swap out a different image while retaining the warping last applied to the layer (**Figures 14.137** and **14.138**).

Figure 14.133 Choosing Custom from the Warp pop-up menu presents you with a grid.

Figure 14.134 Drag the four corners of the grid so they line up with the object you are trying to match.

Figure 14.135 Adjust the corner handles to match the area you are attempting to match.

Figure 14.136 Fine-tune the results by dragging on the grid lines.

Figure 14.137 End result of warping the image to match the page. (©2007 iStockphoto.com and Ben Willmore)

Figure 14.138 If a Smart Object was used, you can choose Layer > Smart Objects > Replace Contents to swap out the image while retaining the warping applied.

Creating Complex Collages

We've covered a lot of features in this chapter. Now we're ready to put them all together, combine them with the Blending modes we learned about in Chapter 12 "Enhancement," and throw in a few other techniques to create a complex collage (**Figure 14.139**). If you haven't read through all of this chapter, and haven't read Chapter 13, it might be difficult to keep up, so make sure you've covered that material before you dive into this project.

The collage used here was originally created by Regina Cleveland. She challenged me to re-create it and gave me a total of four photos, which she snagged from www.istock-photo.com (**Figures 14.140** to **14.143**), along with a shot of yours truly taken by my friend Andy Katz (**Figure 14.144**).

Figure 14.139 The collage used on the cover of this book was created by Regina Cleveland.

Figure 14.140 This leaf image started out as a black and white shot. (©2007 iStockphoto.com/BritishBeefUK)

Figure 14.1141 This pattern was used on both the head and background. (©2007 iStockphoto.com/LindaMarieB)

Figure 14.142 The head was isolated from its background. (©2007 iStockphoto.com/puentes)

Figure 14.143 The lens from this camera was used in the center of the image. (©2007 iStockphoto.com/avarkisp)

Figure 14.144 This shot of me goofing off was used as a reflection in the lens. (©2007 Andy Katz)

NOTES

Regina created the original collage image, but I'm re-creating it here using the features and techniques that I'd use, which are a little different than Regina's methods. That's why my results might look slightly different than the collage used on the original book cover (the one here is a mock-up).

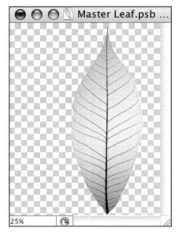

Figure 14.145 The leaf was isolated from its background using a Vector Mask.

Figure 14.146 Layers palette view of isolated leaf.

NOTES

Allowing images to extend beyond the edge of the final page size is known as using bleed. Bleed is necessary because high-speed page trimmers are not 100% accurate and could leave a sliver of white on the edge of a page if the image ended precisely where the edge is expected to be.

As I outline the steps I took to re-create this collage, I'd like to invite you to follow along with the same images I used. To get the photos, as well as the final layered Photoshop file, go to the folder on the CD called Practice Images; you'll find them (as well as the Photoshop file called Book Cover.psd) in the subfolder called Ch 14, "Collage."

Creating the Fan of Leaves

The first element I started with was the single leaf image, which, when later multiplied, would provide a headdress for the face. I double-clicked on the Background image to turn it into a normal layer and then used a Vector Mask to isolate the leaf from its background (**Figures 14.145** and **14.146**). I knew this element was going to be scaled and rotated many times, and I wanted to retain as much of the original detail as I possibly could, so I converted the layer into a Smart Object by Control-clicking on the layer (that's the same as right-clicking in Windows) and choosing Group into New Smart Object.

The original leaf document didn't have enough space to create the fan of leaves, so I created a new document that was the exact size of the book cover, plus nine points (that's just over 1/8 of an inch) of extra space on three sides to allow for bleed (the forth side would merge with the spine of the book and therefore didn't need any bleed). Once the document was open, I positioned three guides (using the View > New Guide command) to indicate the trimmed page size. Then, before doing any more work, I dragged the leaf Smart Object to the newly created document using the Move tool and scaled it to an appropriate size using the Edit > Free Transform command.

The fan was going to need a total of ten leaves spanning across a 180 degree arc. To evenly space the leaves I divided the total degrees of rotation (180) by the number of leaves that would be used (9, since two of the leaves were going to end up at the exact same angle and therefore shouldn't be counted twice). Since dividing 180 by 9 produces 20, that meant that each leaf needed to be rotated by 20 degrees compared to the one adjacent to it.

With those calculations in hand, I duplicated the original Smart Object layer by pressing Command/Ctrl-J to create a second instance of the Smart Object. I then rotated the duplicate by pressing Command/Ctrl-T to access the Free Transform command, and dragged the pivot point (which looks like a crosshair and appears in the center of the layer that's being transformed) straight down, and positioned it on the bottom center transformation point (**Figure 14.147**). To get the proper amount of rotation, I entered 20 into the Angle field in the options bar, which ended up rotating the image to the right—the wrong direction—so I added a minus sign before the percentage to rotate it in the opposite direction. After pressing Return/Enter twice (the first time to have Photoshop accept the number and the second time to complete the rotation), I repeated the process (duplicate, move pivot point, rotate) until a total of ten leaves were in place (**Figure 14.148**).

When you attempt to rotate a Smart Object that has already been rotated, the Angle field in the options bar will indicate how many degrees the Smart Object has been rotated from its original position. So, to rotate each leaf by -20 degrees from the one adjacent to it, we used the following numbers: -20, -40, -60, -80, -100, -120, -140, -160, and -180.

Figure 14.147 Drag the pivot point to the point that appears at the tip of the leaf.

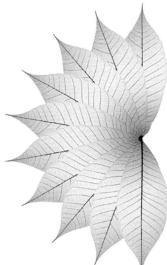

Figure 14.148 Result of duplicating and rotating the leaf Smart Object nine times.

Figure 14.149 The leaves looked more integrated after setting each Smart Object layer to Multiply mode.

Next, I needed to get the leaves to interact with each other instead of obscuring the underlying leaves. I cycled through the layers and changed the Blending Mode menu at the top of the Layers palette to Multiply, which if you remember from Chapter 12, "Enhancement," causes each layer to act as if it's being printed on top of the underlying layers using ink (**Figure 14.149**). At this point the fan of leaves was starting to look interesting, but it lacked any hint of color.

I added color by applying a Gradient Overlay Layer Style to each layer using the Color Blending mode. If you recall from Chapter 12, "Enhancement," Color mode applies the color of the active layer to the brightness information from the underlying image (I don't really expect you to remember all this stuff; that's why you have the book to refer back to, after all). In this case, Color mode will cause the Gradient Overlay to apply color to the brightness values that are in the leaf. To accomplish that, I clicked on the Layer Style pop-up menu at the bottom of the Layers palette (it's that little doohickey that looks like a circle with an "f" inside), chose Gradient Overlay, then set the Blending Mode pop-up menu to Color, clicked on the Gradient Preview, and changed the color used on one end of the gradient. I then adjusted the Opacity and Angle settings until I liked how the color was affecting the leaf (**Figure 14.150**).

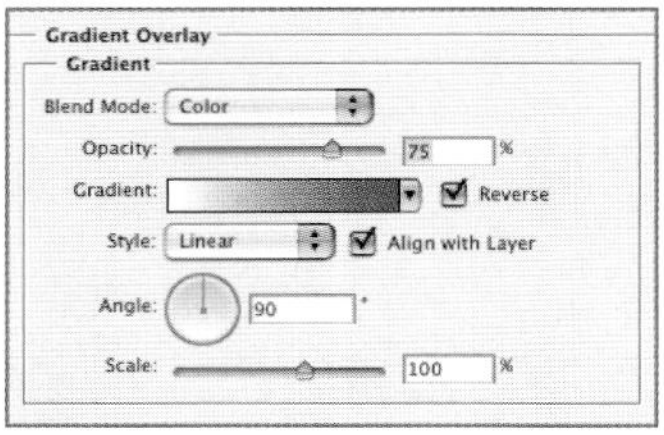

Then, to apply similar settings to the other leaf Smart Objects, I Control-clicked/right-clicked on the style-laden layer in the Layers palette and chose Copy Layer Style. I then selected all the other Smart Object layers, Control-clicked/right-clicked on one of the layers and chose Paste Layer Style, which made all the leaves take on the same color (**Figures 14.151** and **14.152**). To get each leaf to be a different color, I double-clicked on the Layer Style icon on each layer, changed the color used in each gradient and adjusted the Angle setting to cause the color to be concentrated near the outer tip of each leaf (**Figure 14.153**).

Figure 14.150 One of the Gradient Overlays that was applied to the leaves.

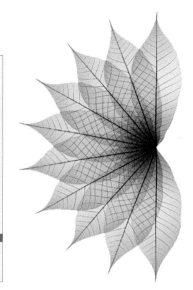

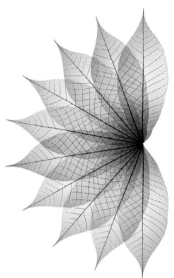

Figure 14.151 Copying and pasting the Layer Style caused it to apply to each of the selected layers.

Figure 14.152 The leaves appeared as a single color since the same Layer Style was being applied to each leaf.

Figure 14.153 The leaves took on different colors after modifying the Layer Style applied to each layer.

Adding The Head

At this stage, the fan of leaves was feeling rather done, but lacked a background. A stylistic head was the next element to tackle. I opened it in Photoshop and dragged it into the book cover document using the Move tool. A problem developed after scaling the head layer to an appropriate size and moving it to the bottom of the Layers stack. All the leaf Smart Object layers ended up looking like they were printed on top of the head because they were all set to use the Multiply Blending mode (**Figure 14.154**). Since the Multiply mode was needed to cause the leaves to print on top of each other instead of obscuring each other, I selected all the leaf Smart Object layers and chose Layer > Smart Objects > Group into New Smart Object to nest them into a new Smart Object. That solved the problem because the individual layers that make up a Smart Object cannot interact with layers that are found outside the Smart Object. A Smart Object can only interact with the underlying image as a whole and the Blending mode for the newly created Smart Object was set to Normal, which prevented it from interacting with the rest of the image (**Figure 14.155**). Grouping the leaf layers into a Smart Object also had the added benefit of greatly simplifying the Layers palette.

Figure 14.154 Set to Multiply mode, the leaves looked like they were printed on top of the head.

Figure 14.155 Grouping the leaf layers into a Smart Object and setting the Smart Object's Blending mode to Normal.

Figure 14.156 The background was removed from the head with the Magic Wand tool and a Layer Mask.

A quick method to check the accuracy of a Layer Mask is to Shift-click on the Layer Mask thumbnail in the Layers palette (to prevent it from hiding parts of the layer) and then press the \ key to view the mask as a color overlay. If the color overlay doesn't closely match the edge of the subject, paint with black or white to change the mask. When you're done refining the mask, type \ again to turn off the color overlay, and then Shift-click the Layer Mask thumbnail once more to turn it back on.

The cover of this book traditionally features a white background, which meant that the background of the head image needed to be removed. I started by hiding the fan of leaves Smart Object so it wouldn't obstruct my view of the head layer. Removing the background on the head layer was an easy process because the background was quite different from the subject in both color and brightness. I employed the Magic Wand tool to do this job. I made a single click on the background, but that wasn't enough to select the whole area, so I held the Shift key as I clicked on unselected portions of the background. It took me less than a dozen clicks with the Magic Wand tool to get a decent selection of the background. Then, to hide the background on the head, I held the Option/Alt key and clicked the Layer Mask icon at the bottom of the Layers palette (it's the circle inside the square icon). Holding Option/Alt caused the selected areas to become hidden when the mask was created (**Figure 14.156**). I had to touch up a few spots near the mouth and nose since the original selection wasn't perfect.

The head was now ready for her beauty treatment. I placed the paisley/fractal pattern image on the layer directly above the head. I then chose Layer > Create Clipping Mask to make the pattern only show up where the head was (**Figure 14.157**). Then, to make the pattern interact with the head, I switched to the Move tool, held Shift and pressed the plus key on my keyboard quite a few times to cycle through all the Blending modes in the pop-up menu at the top of the Layers palette. After going through the whole list a few times, I settled on the Overlay Blending mode (**Figure 14.158**). I think that improved the look of the head quite a bit, but I noticed that the colors weren't popping the way they were in the original collage done by Regina. With the pattern layer still active, I chose Gradient Overlay from the Layer Style pop-up menu at the bottom of the Layers palette, created a colorful gradient, and then experimented with the Blending Mode pop-up menu until I liked the results (**Figures 14.159** and **14.160**).

Figure 14.157 A Clipping Mask was used to make the pattern only show up where the head was.

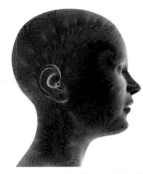

Figure 14.158 The Overlay Blending mode was used to cause the pattern to overlay onto the head.

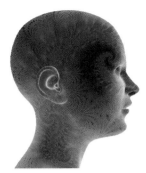

Figure 14.159 Additional color was added by adding a Gradient Overlay Layer Style to the pattern layer.

Adding the Camera Lens

At this point, I made the fan of leaves Smart Object visible again and repositioned it so that the center of the fan was close to being centered on the round part of the head (**Figure 14.161**). It was time to add the camera lens to the middle of the fan so I opened the photo of a 35mm camera, extracted the camera body from the lens using a Vector Mask, and then dragged it into position within the collage. To add a little accent to the lens, I chose Drop Shadow from the Layer Style pop-up menu at the bottom of the Layers palette, set the Blending mode to Screen and chose a cyan color (**Figure 14.162**).

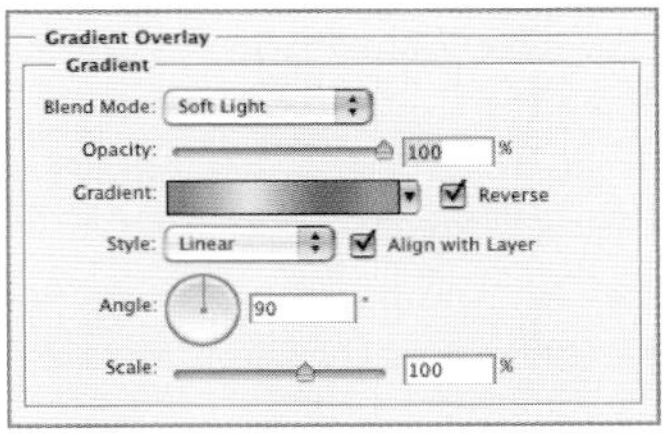

Figure 14.160 This Gradient Overlay was applied to the pattern layer.

Figure 14.161 Result of repositioning the fan of leaves.

Figure 14.162 A camera lens was added, along with a Drop Shadow Layer Style.

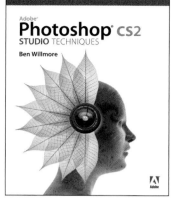

Figure 14.163 Text and logo treatments were added to the cover.

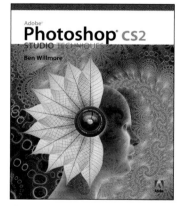

Figure 14.164 The pattern from the head was duplicated and used as the base of the background.

Adding Type and Logo Treatments

To make sure the collage had sufficient room for all the elements that would appear on the cover, I decided it was time to add the cover text. The text entry was pretty straight-forward; I ended up with four Type layers. (For more about working with text, check out the bonus chapter, "Type and Background Effects," on the CD at the back of this book.) The logo that appears in the lower right of the cover was supplied by my publisher as an EPS file. To add that element, I chose File > Place and pointed Photoshop to the logo file. That embedded the EPS file into my collage as a Smart Object layer, which allowed me to scale it to any size without losing quality. To complete the graphic elements on the cover, I added a red bar across the top of the document using the Rectangular Shape tool (**Figure 14.163**).

Creating the Background Texture

Now I was ready to tackle the background behind the head. The pattern applied to the head was the same used for the background, so I duplicated the pattern layer, dragged it to the bottom of the Layers palette and scaled and positioned it to fill most of the white space at the bottom of the image (**Figure 14.164**). At this stage, the head and the background contained similar colors, and I needed to completely shift the color of the background. I did this by holding Option/ Alt, choosing Gradient Map from the Adjustment Layer pop-up menu at the bottom of the Layers Palette (for more information about Gradient Map adjustments, check out Chapter 9, "Color Manipulation"), and turning on the Use Previous Layer to Create Clipping Mask check box so the adjustment would only affect the background pattern. I edited the gradient to force the colors in the background toward red and orange (**Figures 14.165** and **14.166**). Then, to make the background fade into the white found at the top of the cover, I added a Layer Mask and applied a gradient to the mask (**Figure 14.167**).

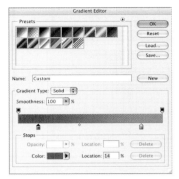

Figure 14.165 A Gradient Map adjustment layer was used to shift the background colors toward red and orange.

Figure 14.166 Result of shifting the colors in the background.

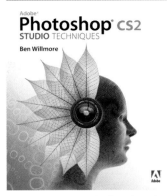

Figure 14.167 Result of masking the background with a gradient.

Final Tweaks

Finally, the cover contained all of the major pieces found in the original version given to me by Regina, and now it just needed a few tweaks to refine the results. For the background pattern, I duplicated the fan of leaves Smart Object, set its Blending mode to Screen, lowered the opacity and scaled it up to lighten the background, using the same shape as the leaves. To make the fan of leaves partially transparent, I added a Layer Mask and painted with a soft-edged brush at a low opacity, which let the shape of the head show through. For the lens reflection effect, I added a photo above the lens (yes, that would be yours truly) and used the Overlay Blending mode. And last, to make it look like a beam of light was emanating from the lens, I created a new layer, made a triangular selection, filled it with white and lowered its opacity to connect the lens to the eye (**Figure 14.168**). With a big "Whew!" I considered myself done with the collage, and now only needed to put it into a 3-D mock-up of the book's cover.

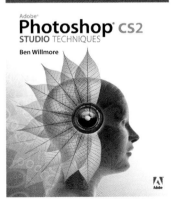

Figure 14.168 The finished cover complete with lens reflection.

Creating a 3-D Cover Mock-Up

To create the 3-D cover mock-up shown here, I took a photograph of a similarly sized book. I flattened the newly created collage and moved it into the book photograph. I then distorted the cover to match the shape of photographic cover by using the Distort command (Edit > Transform > Distort)

Figure 14.169 After transforming the cover image, it matched the perspective of the photograph.

Figure 14.170 Adding shading with the Gradient tool helped to make the end result look more realistic.

(**Figure 14.169**). Finally, I used the Gradient tool in Multiply mode to add subtle shading to the cover, which added realism to the end result (**Figure 14.170**).

Closing Thoughts

I hope that you get as much of a kick out of creating collages as I do. It's one of those things that never gets old; I can always count on another surprise waiting for me around the corner. If you want to create truly realistic-looking collages, you should keep the following ideas in mind:

▶ When combining images that were shot under different lighting conditions, be sure to color correct the images individually before turning them into a collage; otherwise, each one will have a different color cast.

▶ If you're basing a collage on an image that has a desirable color cast (such as candlelight, fireplace, sunrise, sunset), use the techniques mentioned in Chapter 9, "Color Manipulation," to infuse all the images with the same desirable color cast.

▶ When combining images, make sure that the direction the light is coming from in each image is consistent; otherwise, your viewers' eyes will pick up on the fact that the image is a fake, although they might not be able to pinpoint exactly why they think that.

▶ The direction the light is coming from in your image should also dictate the direction in which shadows fall. Shadows should fall directly opposite of where the light is coming from.

▶ When placing objects in a scene, think about where each object appears in 3D space and make sure it has the appropriate focus compared to its surroundings.

▶ The film grain that shows up in an image is usually consistent across the image, so either use the noise removal techniques covered in Chapter 11, "Sharpening," on each image, or apply the Add Noise filter (Filter > Noise > Add Noise) to images to make sure each one has the same amount of grain.

If you keep these ideas in mind, then with a little practice and a lot of perspiration, you should be able to create collages that fool even a trained eye.

Retouching

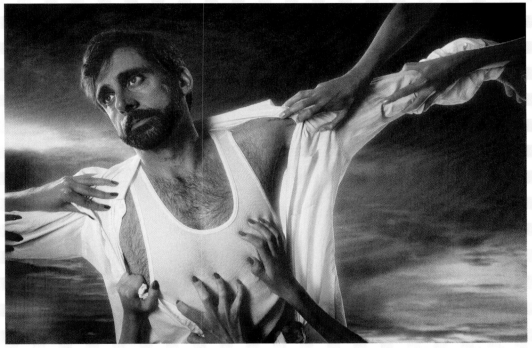

©2007 Nick Koudis, www.koudis.com

A doctor can bury his mistakes, but an architect can only advise his clients to plant vines.

—Frank Lloyd Wright

The doctoring of photographs didn't begin with the advent of computers in magazine production departments. One of history's most notorious photograph "doctors" was Joseph Stalin, who used photo retouching as a way to manipulate the masses. People who vanished in real life, whether banished to the farthest reaches of the Soviet Union or eliminated by the secret police, vanished from photos as well, and even from paintings. In many cases, they were airbrushed out completely; in others, their faces were clumsily blacked out with ink.

And then there were the Hollywood photo doctors. They didn't want to get rid of anyone; they just wanted to make them look better. I think they actually coined the term "too good to be true." Think about it—have you ever seen a photograph of a starlet with a blemish, or a wart, or bags under her eyes, or even the slightest indication that her skin actually had pores? Of course not!

If you look at it from these two extremes, you can appreciate why the subject of retouching is something of a, well, touchy subject. If you're brave enough to bring it up at a photographer's convention, you're likely to spark a pretty lively debate. A purist might tell you that every aspect of a photograph (including the flaws) is a perfect reflection of reality and should never be tampered with. Then again, a graphic artist, who makes a living from altering images, might tell you that an original photograph is just the foundation of an image, and that the so-called tampering is, in fact, a means of enhancing and improving upon it. Either way you look at it, you can't deny the fact that some degree of retouching photographs has become an everyday necessity for almost anyone who deals with graphic images. And when it comes to retouching, hands down, nothing does it better than Photoshop.

Photoshop packs an awesome arsenal of retouching tools. These include the Patch tool, Healing brush tool, Spot Healing brush, Red Eye tool, Clone Stamp tool, Dodge and Burn tools, and Blur and Sharpen tools, among others. The incredible Vanishing Point filter allows us to edit and retouch in near 3-D perspective, and CS3's awesome new Clone Source palette is home to a multitude of new features that make the Healing brush and Clone Stamp tools much more versatile. We'll play with all of the retouching toys (except for Red Eye, which is covered in Chapter 9, "Color Manipulation"), and for each one I'll also give you a little bag of tricks. You'll learn how to do all sorts of neat things, including retouching old ripped photos, getting rid of those shiny spots on foreheads, and adjusting the saturation of small areas. Or, you can give someone instant plastic surgery. Remove a few wrinkles, perform an eye lift, reduce those dark rings around the eyes, and poof!—you've taken off 10 years. So let's look at these tools one at a time, starting with what I consider to be the most important one.

Patch Tool

The Patch tool (which is hidden under the Healing brush, and looks like a scrap of cloth with stitching in the Tools palette) is one of the most innovative yet simple tools ever. The general concept is simple. You select an area of your image that needs to be touched up (maybe a blemish or tattoo) (**Figure 15.1**), and then you click in the middle of the selection and drag it to an area of your image that has similar texture but with no blemishes. As you move your mouse, Photoshop previews the area you're going to copy from in the area you initially selected (**Figure 15.2**). Then, when you release the mouse button, Photoshop does an amazing job of blending the second area into the first (**Figure 15.3**). It makes sure that the brightness and color is consistent with what was on the edge of the original selection, and it blends the texture from the second area with that color. You simply have to try it to see what I mean.

You can even sample from an area that is radically different in brightness and color (**Figure 15.4**), because the Patch tool will pick up only the texture from the area that is sampled (**Figure 15.5**). The main thing you should look for is an area that has the proper texture for the area you are attempting to retouch.

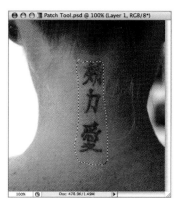

Figure 15.1 Original image. (©iStockphoto.com/dystortia)

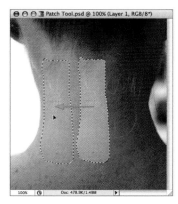

Figure 15.2 Drag the selection to an area of clean texture.

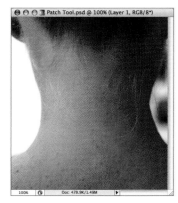

Figure 15.3 The result of using the Patch tool.

Figure 15.4 Drag the selection to an area that contains radically different colors and brightness. (©Stockbyte, www.stockbyte.com)

Just because this tool is rather sophisticated in the way it blends with the image, that doesn't mean you shouldn't be careful when making the selection. I always try to make the smallest selection that will completely encompass the defect I'm trying to retouch (**Figure 15.6**). The larger the area being patched, the less likely it will look good (**Figure 15.7**).

Figure 15.6 A small selection produces a nice blend. (©Stockbyte, www.stockbyte.com)

Figure 15.7 A large selection makes the image look artificial. (Notice her neck.)

Figure 15.5 Only the texture gets copied from the area you drag the selection to.

This tool doesn't have many options to deal with (**Figure 15.8**). The main choice is whether to patch the source or the destination. With the Patch option set to Source (which I use 95% of the time), Photoshop replaces the area that was originally selected with a combination of the brightness and color values from its edge, along with the texture from the area you drag the selection to (**Figures 15.9** and **15.10**). Using the Destination setting does the opposite, letting you pick from a clean area of the original and then dragging it over the area that needs to be patched (**Figures 15.11** and **15.12**).

Figure 15.8 The options bar for the Patch tool.

Figure 15.9 Using the source setting while dragging an area under the eye to an area of clean texture. (©iStockphoto.com/Soubrette)

Figure 15.10 After releasing the mouse button, the clean texture is copied to the area under the eye and blended in automatically.

Figure 15.11 Using the destination setting while dragging a clean area of the skin to an area that needs retouching.

Figure 15.12 After releasing the mouse button, the area that was moved gets blended into the surrounding image.

If you can't find a clean area from which to steal texture, you can select a pattern by clicking on the down arrow in the options bar (**Figure 15.13**) and then clicking the Use Pattern button. You'll find that patching with a pattern isn't all that effective unless you've created a custom pattern for this specific purpose. Be sure to check out the bonus chapter, "Type and Background Effects," on the CD for details on how to create your own patterns.

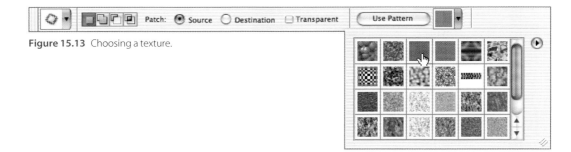

Figure 15.13 Choosing a texture.

I find that the Patch tool is best for those situations where you have scratches, blemishes, or other defects in an area that should otherwise be relatively consistent in color (such as skin). It can even maintain some of the three-dimensionality of the surface with its blending capabilities (**Figures 15.14** and **15.15**). But you'll find that it's not very useful when you have an area that has multiple colors bordering it that shouldn't blend together. That's because Photoshop attempts to blend the patched area into all the surrounding colors. In that case, you should switch to the Clone Stamp tool.

Figure 15.14 The original image. (©Stockbyte, www.stockbyte.com)

Figure 15.15 Result of using the Patch tool (three passes were used to cover such a large area).

If you use the Patch tool to remove all wrinkles and blemishes from someone's face, you might find that the person is no longer recognizable. When I retouch facial features, I like to choose Edit > Fade immediately after applying a patch (**Figure 15.16**). That allows me to change how the patch applies to the original image. I like to move the Opacity slider all the way to the left and then slowly move it toward the right until I find the lowest Opacity setting that will lessen the look of the undesirable feature without completely removing it (**Figures 15.17** to **15.19**). This technique is essential when working with shiny skin. If you use the Patch tool at full strength, you'll lose the dimensionality of the forehead, but fading it back will make the area look less shiny, without completely evening out the lighting on the person's skin.

I find that the Patch tool is most useful when working on large areas. It's just too cumbersome when you have to retouch dozens of small blemishes. When that's the case, I usually switch to the Healing brush, which can make those small retouching jobs a breeze.

Figure 15.16 The Edit > Fade dialog box.

An alternative to using the Fade command is to duplicate the original image layer before performing retouching, and then adjust the Opacity setting at the top of the Layers palette to blend the retouched layer with the underlying image.

Figure 15.17 The original image. (©Stockbyte, www.stockbyte.com)

Figure 15.18 Result of using the Patch tool at full strength to reduce shiny skin on chin.

Figure 15.19 Result of fading each application of the Patch tool to approximately 50% opacity.

Healing Brush Tool

The Healing brush works using the same general concepts as the Patch tool. It attempts to patch a defect in your image using the texture from another area while blending all the edges with the surrounding colors. The main difference is that the Patch tool works by moving a selection, whereas the Healing brush allows you to paint over the area that needs to be repaired. To use it, you'll first have to Option/Alt-click on the area you would like to use to fix an area (**Figure 15.20**), and then click and drag across the area that needs fixing (**Figure 15.21**). When you do that, be sure to cover the entire area without releasing the mouse button. Once you let go, Photoshop will check out the edges of the area you covered to make sure your "patch" blends with the color and brightness that is in the surrounding area (**Figure 15.22**). You might need to use a soft-edged brush to get a good blend (**Figures 15.23** and **15.24**). Just make sure that you choose your brush from the Brush drop-down menu in the options bar. This tool ignores the stand-alone Brushes palette because it doesn't use the advanced settings available in that palette. I prefer to use a brush with a Hardness setting of 75%.

Figure 15.20 Option/Alt-clicking on the original image to choose the area to sample from. (©iStockphoto.com/jtyler)

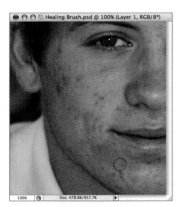

Figure 15.21 Painting across the area that needs to be retouched. Look closely at his chin.

Figure 15.22 When you release the mouse button, Photoshop blends the retouched area into the surrounding image.

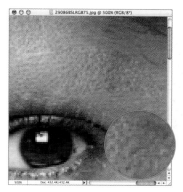 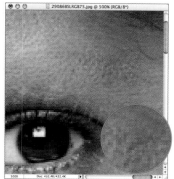

Figure 15.23 Result of using a hard-edged brush. (©Stockbyte, www.stockbyte.com)

Figure 15.24 The difference is very subtle, but a soft-edged brush blends with the surrounding image more than the hard-edged version.

Layers

If you are using layers in your document, the Healing brush tool will work on one layer at a time, unless you turn on the Sample All Layers check box located on the options bar. With this option turned on, Photoshop acts as if your document has no layers at all. In other words, it will be able to take from any layer that is below your cursor, as if they were all combined. However, it will apply, or deposit, the information you are healing only onto the currently active layer. That way, you can create a new empty layer, turn on the Sample All Layers check box, and retouch your image (**Figure 15.25**). Don't worry if you mess up, because the information is sitting on its own layer, with the unretouched image directly below it (**Figures 15.26** and **15.27**). This allows you to switch over to the Eraser tool and erase small areas of that layer, or do other things such as lower the opacity of the layer.

A few Blending modes, such as Multiply, are available in the options bar, but you'll find that they work a little differently from what you might be used to. Most tools would apply their general effect, and then once everything is done, they would apply the Blending mode. But in this tool, the Blending mode is applied before Photoshop does the work needed to blend the patched area with the surrounding image (**Figures 15.28** and **15.29**).

Figure 15.25 You can place your retouching on a new layer so it is isolated from the underlying image.

Figure 15.26 The underlying image will be untouched under the retouching layer. (©Stockbyte, www.stockbyte.com)

Figure 15.29 How Multiply mode looks when using the Healing Brush.

Figure 15.28 How Multiply mode would usually look. Look at the bridge of her nose. (©Stockbyte, www.stockbyte.com)

Figure 15.29 How Multiply mode looks when using the Healing Brush.

Spot Healing Brush Tool

The Spot Healing brush makes quick work of removing tiny defects in most images. It uses the same concepts as the Healing brush and Patch tool. The only difference is that it does not require you to choose an area of clean texture to copy from. Instead, it analyzes the surrounding area and attempts to find appropriate texture. All you have to do is click and drag over a defect that needs to be removed and Photoshop does the rest. When you click and drag, the area that will be retouched will first become covered in black. When you release the mouse button, you'll see the results of the retouching (**Figures 15.30** to **15.32**). If the results don't look good, try dragging over the defect a second time and Photoshop will use a different area to pull texture from. If there are no clean areas of texture surrounding the defect you're attempting to retouch, try using the Create Texture setting in the options bar (**Figure 15.33**), which will cause Photoshop to create its own texture based on the surrounding image. This setting is especially useful on images that are scratched or have a lot of detail in the surrounding area (**Figure 15.34**).

Figure 15.30 Original image.

Figure 15.31 Painting with the Spot Healing brush over the scratch.

Figure 15.32 Result.

Figure 15.33 The Spot Healing brush settings found in the options bar.

Figure 15.34 This image has small specks and scratches. (©2007 Andy Katz)

If you really need to use a soft-edged brush (0% hardness), consider using the Healing brush with its Blending mode set to Replace. That will make it act just like the Clone Stamp tool, but it will not produce blurry results with soft-edged brushes.

If you've messed with the settings in the Preferences > Displays & Cursors area, the second cursor might also look like a crosshair. When that's the case, you can set the Painting Cursors setting to Brush Size to get it back to the default setting. If you find that you're still getting a crosshair cursor after changing your preferences, make sure your Caps Lock key is not turned on. When it's turned on, your painting cursors turn into a crosshair.

When you've reached the point where you think you're done working on an image, zoom in to 100% magnification (by double-clicking the Zoom tool) and look for any tiny defects in the image (such as dust, scratches, or pin holes), and fix them with the Spot Healing brush. To make sure that you inspect the entire image, press the Home key (available on most extended keyboards) to get to the upper-left corner of the image. Then use the Page Up and Page Down keys to move one full screen up or down (add Shift to move less than one full screen). Adding Command/Ctrl to the Page Up and Page Down keys will move you one full screen to the right or left.

The Patch tool, Healing brush, and Spot Healing brush are useful only when the area that needs to be retouched should match the color and brightness of the areas that surround it. When you run across an area that shouldn't blend into its surroundings, you'll have to switch over to the trusty old standby—the Clone Stamp tool (**Figures 15.35** and **15.36**).

Figure 15.35 The areas that need to be retouched shouldn't simply blend in with the colors that surround them. (©iStockphoto.com/RedBarnStudio)

Figure 15.36 The Clone Stamp tool was used to retouch this image.

Clone Stamp Tool

The Clone Stamp tool copies information from one area of your image and applies it somewhere else. Before applying the Clone Stamp tool, there is one thing you should know: All retouching tools use the Brush Presets palette, shown in **Figure 15.37**. The brush that you use with the Healing Brush isn't all that important because it will end up blending your retouching into the surrounding image, but the brush you choose is critical when using the Clone Stamp tool because it doesn't have those blending capabilities. So you have to decide if you want what you're about to apply to fade into the image or to have a distinct edge. For most applications it helps to have a soft edge on your brush so you can't see the exact edge of where you've stopped.

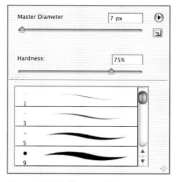

Figure 15.37 The brush that you choose determines how much your retouching work will blend into the underlying image.

I find that the default soft-edged brushes are often too soft, which can cause the area you retouch to look blurry compared with the rest of the image. To prevent that from happening, hold Shift and press the right bracket key (]) while you keep an eye on the brush preview in the options bar. Each time you press that key combination you'll be changing your brush's hardness setting in increments of 25%. The default brushes have a hardness of either 100% (for hard-edged brushes) or 0% (for soft ones). I find that 25% and 50% are better for retouching with soft-edged brushes.

Cloning Around

After you've chosen your brush, you'll need to tell Photoshop exactly where you'd like to copy from. Do this by holding down the Option/Alt key and clicking the mouse button (**Figure 15.38**). Then move to a different part of the image and click and drag the mouse (with no key held). When you do, you'll notice two cursors (**Figure 15.39**). The first one is in the shape of a crosshair; it shows you the source of Photoshop's cloning. When you apply the Clone Stamp tool, there will be a second cursor—a circle showing you exactly where it's being applied. When you move your mouse around, you'll notice both of the cursors moving in the same direction. As you drag, Photoshop is constantly copying from the crosshair and pasting into the circle.

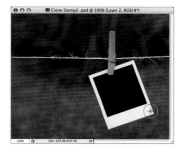

Figure 15.38 Option/Alt-click to define the spot you'd like to start cloning from. (©iStockphoto.com/laartist)

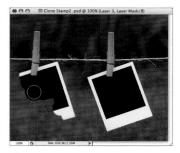

Figure 15.39 The Clone Stamp tool copies from under the crosshair and pastes into the circle.

Clone Aligned

The Clone Stamp tool operates in two different modes: Aligned and Non-aligned (it's just a simple check box in the options bar). In Aligned mode, when you apply the Clone Stamp tool, it doesn't matter if you let go of the mouse button and click again. Each time you let go and click again, the pieces that you're applying line up (**Figure 15.40**). It's as if you're putting together a puzzle: Once you have all of the pieces together, it looks like a complete image (**Figure 15.41**).

Figure 15.40 You can release the mouse button as many times as you want with the Aligned check box turned on because the pieces of the cloned image will line up like puzzle pieces.

Figure 15.41 Once you put all the pieces together, you'll end up with a complete image. (©iStockphoto.com/vasiliki)

Clone Non-Aligned

If you turn off the Aligned check box, it's a different story. Apply the tool and let go of the mouse button. The next time you click the mouse button it will reset itself, starting back at the original point from where it was cloning (**Figure 15.42**). If you click in the middle of someone's nose, go up to the forehead, and click and drag, you'll be planting a nose in the middle of the forehead. Then if you let go, move over a little bit, and click again, you'll add a second nose. But this will happen only if you have the Aligned check box off. For most retouching, leave the check box on. That way you don't have to be careful with letting go of

Figure 15.42 When the Aligned check box is turned off, the Clone Stamp tool resets itself to the original starting point each time you release the mouse button. (©iStockphoto.com/mammamaart)

the mouse button. Assume you'll need to have it turned on to follow the techniques I cover here, unless I specifically tell you to turn it off.

Opacity Settings

Sometimes you don't want to completely cover something up; you may just want to lessen its impact (**Figure 15.43**). For example, you might not want to completely wipe out a recognizable feature (such as Gorbachev's birthmark) for fear that it'll be obvious the image was enhanced. To do this, lower the opacity on the Clone Stamp tool (**Figure 15.44**). You can also press the number keys on your keyboard; pressing 1 will give you 10%, 2 will give you 20%, and so on. To get it all the way up to 100%, just press 0 (zero). This allows you to paint over an area and partially replace it, so that the area you're applying blends with what used to be in that area.

Straight Lines

Have you ever seen a carpenter "snap a chalk line" to get a straight line over an area? There are occasions when I've been grateful to know how to do something similar in Photoshop. Let's say you have an image of a woman that you need to remove from a background that contains a straight line (a wall in my case). That means that you're going to have to replace the woman with a new section of wall. For that to look realistic, the section of wall you use to replace the woman will have to perfectly line up with the sections of wall on either side of her head. When you get into this kind of situation, try this: Move your cursor until it's touching the original line (or edge of the wall, in this case). When it's perfectly touching it, Option/Alt-click, as shown in **Figure 15.45**. Then go to the area where you want the new piece of wall to appear and click where you think it would naturally line up with the other part of the wall. Then when you drag, your two cursors will line up just right, making the line look continuous and straight, as in **Figure 15.46**. You can even Shift-click in two spots, and Photoshop will trace a straight line with the Clone Stamp between those two areas. Other examples of when to use this tool would be for stairs, a lamppost, or any object with straight lines that has been obstructed by another object.

Figure 15.43 You might want to play down some recognizable feature. (©Stockbyte, www.stockbyte.com)

Figure 15.44 By lowering the opacity of the Clone Stamp tool, you can reduce the impact of undesirable features.

Figure 15.45 On straight lines, Option/Alt-click when your cursor touches the line; then click in another area that also touches the line.

Figure 15.46 If the cursors align, lines will remain nice and straight. (©Stockbyte, www.stockbyte.com)

Patchwork

Sampling from one area and applying it all over the place will make it look pretty obvious that you've cloned something. You'll start seeing repeated shapes. For instance, if there happens to be a little dark area in the image you were cloning from, you will see that same dark area in the image you've applied it to. And if you look at it closely enough, you will see the shape repeat itself, which can start to look like a pattern. (You've just been busted cloning!) If you want to do this to fill in an area, you can go back and fix up the places that appear patterned by Option/Alt-clicking a random area around the place you've retouched, and then applying it on top of one of the patterned areas. But watch out—Photoshop's round brushes can be a dead giveaway, because you can easily pick out the areas that you're trying to disguise. This is a great time to use one of the odd-shaped brushes that appear at the bottom of the Brushes palette (**Figure 15.47**). These will provide better cover for areas that look obviously cloned. Another trick is to apply some noise to the entire image, which will make any retouching you've performed blend right into the image. To accomplish that, choose Filter > Noise > Add Noise, use an amount somewhere around 3, set the Distribution to Uniform, and turn off the Monochromatic check box.

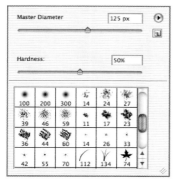

Figure 15.47 To eliminate repeated patterns, use the unusual brushes found at the bottom of the Brushes palette.

Lighten/Darken

Anyone who does retouching will invariably find themselves needing to retouch the wrinkles that show up under people's eyes. In most cases, the Healing brush does an excellent job because it automatically blends into the surrounding image, but it does have one weakness: It sometimes tries to blend into the eyelashes, which causes the area under the eyes to become too dark. When that's the case, you can use the Clone Stamp tool and sample the area directly below the wrinkles to clone over the wrinkles. But before you start retouching that area, I suggest that you mess with the Blending Mode settings from the options bar. (We talked about Blending modes in Chapter 12, "Enhancement," so here we'll just look at what we need for the Clone Stamp tool.) The Blending Mode pop-up menu in the options bar is labeled Mode. The Lighten and Darken options are both very useful when retouching. If you set that menu to Darken, it will compare what you're about to apply to what the image looks like underneath, and it will only allow you to darken things. So let's say you had a light-colored scratch in the background of your image (**Figure 15.48**). You could clone from an area directly around it that is the correct brightness. But before you apply the cloned material to the scratch, you might want to set the Blending mode to Darken (**Figure 15.49**). In Darken, all Photoshop can do is darken your picture. Under no circumstances will it be able to lighten it. When working with the wrinkles under eyes, I use the Lighten Blending mode and lower the Opacity setting of the Clone Stamp tool to somewhere around 40%.

Figure 15.48 Original image.

Figure 15.49 Scratch retouched by using the Clone Stamp tool set to Darken.

Automatic Sharpening

The automatic sharpening function that's built into some scanners makes retouching much more difficult. If possible, turn off any sharpening settings in your scanning software (**Figures 15.50** and **15.51**).

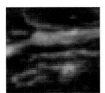

Figure 15.50 Unsharpened image.

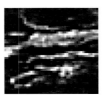

Figure 15.51 Image sharpened during a scan.

To clone between two documents, both documents need to be in the same color mode. If one of the documents is in RGB and the other is in CMYK, Photoshop won't allow you to cross-clone.

Cloning Between Documents

With the Clone Stamp tool, you're not limited to cloning from what's in the active document. You can open a second image and clone from that image as well (**Figure 15.52**). Make the second image (the source for your cloning) active, and then Option/Alt-click on it. Return to your first image to clone from the point you clicked in the second image.

Figure 15.52 Cloning between two documents. (©Stockbyte, www.stockbyte.com)

Unlike with the Patch tool and Healing brush, the Clone Stamp tool forces you to take full control over how your retouched image matches the surrounding image. You have to think about how the brightness, color, and texture of the cloned area will affect the area you plan on retouching as well as how the softness of the brush you choose will cause that information to blend into the surrounding image. That makes the Clone Stamp tool essential in those instances when the area you are retouching shouldn't completely blend into the surrounding areas.

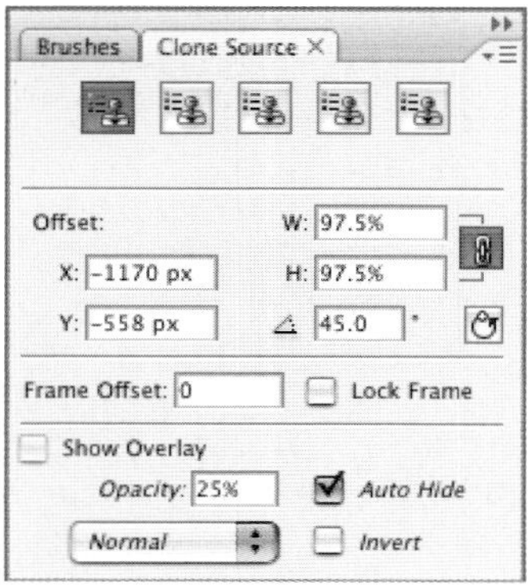

Clone Source

Photoshop CS3 adds a new, handy add-on for the Clone tool. The new Clone Source palette, which sits in the new palette dock (**Figure 15.53**).

The five buttons at the top of the palette let you store as many as five different source points, which makes it easy to switch from one source point to another when making complex clone operations. This saves you the hassle of having to manually reset your clone source point.

Figure 15.53 The new Clone Source palette provides powerful cloning features.

Using the Offset fields, you can adjust any source point numerically, making it easy to adjust a point that's off by just a pixel or two.

The Rotate field to the immediate right of the Y field lets you rotate your cloned pixels automatically. If you enter 45, for example, the resulting cloned strokes will be rotated 45 degrees.

Above the Rotate field are width and height fields, which let you scale your source while cloning. If you unlock the lock box between those two fields, each axis will be scaled independently, allowing you to create a geometric distortion in your result.

The Show Overlay check box provides you with a handy visual reference while cloning. When this box is turned on, a semiopaque copy of your source will be superimposed over your image, giving you a preview of what your strokes will look like given the current offset (**Figure 15.54**). If you don't like the results, you can easily adjust the offset numerically until the overlay shows your cloned results in the desired position.

The Opacity field controls the opacity of the overlaid image—not the opacity of your cloned strokes—and the Blending Mode pop-up menu and Invert check box provide options for improving the visibility of the overlaid source image.

The Auto Hide option causes the overlay to disappear automatically when you start painting. Any time you release the mouse button, the overlay reappears.

Option/Alt-Shift-left bracket ([ ) and Option/Alt-Shift-right bracket ( ]) changes the width and height of your clone source. Option/Alt-Shift-< and Option/Alt-Shift-> changes the rotation value.

Vanishing Point

All the retouching tools we've talked about until now have had one major shortcoming—they think the world is flat! That's right, they have no idea that your image might contain objects that appear to change proportion as they recede from the camera. The solution is to use the

You can adjust any of the parameters by clicking and dragging left or right in the field that you want to adjust.

The Clone Source icons are especially useful when you're using multiple clone sources to reconstruct a complex area (such as removing a tree from in front of a building) because you can quickly switch back and forth between clone sources which makes it easier to produce a complex result that is created from multiple sources.

Figure 15.54 If you turn on Show Overlay in the Clone Source palette, you can see exactly where your cloned image will appear. (©2007 Ben Long)

Figure 15.55 Original image.
(©2007 iStockphoto.com/wolv)

Figure 15.56 Painting in Photoshop.

Figure 15.57 Done in Vanishing Point.

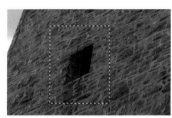

Figure 15.58 Selection made in Photoshop.
(© 2007 iStockphoto.com/Lobsterclaws)

Figure 15.59 Selection made in Vanishing Point.

Vanishing Point filter, which allows you to create different perspective planes in your image, thus allowing you to paint, retouch, scale, and distort in the perspectives you've just established.

Just take a look at **Figure 15.55** to see what I mean. Most people's brains would recognize that the dock has a consistent width but that it looks smaller in the distance due to the effects of perspective. Photoshop on the other hand, has no clue what your image looks like and simply thinks of it as a flat surface. If you were to use the Paintbrush tool in Photoshop and paint an outline of the dock, you'd end up with what's shown in **Figure 15.56**. But if you were to get into Vanishing Point, establish the dock's perspective, and then paint on the image, your results would be quite different (**Figure 15.57**). Selections made in Vanishing Point will also conform to the perspective planes that make up your image (**Figures 15.58** and **15.59**).

Defining Planes

Before you can get all this magic to work properly, you have to educate Vanishing Point about your image by defining the perspective planes that make up your image. When you first open the filter (Filter > Vanishing Point), you'll be presented with a large dialog box and a small tool palette. Choose the Create Plane tool (which looks like a tiny grid) and click on the four corners of a flat surface in your image so Vanishing Point is aware of how the perspective affects that surface. The rectangle you are defining will change color to indicate if Vanishing Point is having trouble with the plane you're attempting to define. If the grid turns red, Vanishing Point can't figure out how

NOTES

There are many filters that are not available when working in CMYK mode. You'll have to convert CMYK image to RGB mode (Image > Mode menu) to use the Vanishing Point and Lens Correction filters.

Figure 15.60 A red outline is a sign of problems.

Figure 15.61 A yellow grid is usable, but not ideal.

Figure 15.62 A blue grid indicates everything is okay.

that shape could possibly be a flat rectangular surface as it relates to the perspective you are defining (**Figure 15.60**). If it turns yellow (**Figure 15.61**), you have a grid that could be used, but the results will be less than ideal. When the grid becomes blue (**Figure 15.62**), Vanishing Point is saying "all systems go" and you're ready to start painting or retouching your image. If you define a plane by clicking on the four corners of a small object, you may need to extend the side handles so the grid covers the entire surface (or at least the area you plan to modify). If you plan to work with more than one surface in your image, you'll have to define each plane so Vanishing Point knows how those surfaces relate (**Figure 15.63**).

Duplicating Areas

Once you have the planes defined, you can use the other tools from Vanishing Point's tool palette. If you use the Marquee tool to make selections, you can hold Option/Alt and drag within the selected area to move a duplicate of the selected area. As you move the selected area, Vanishing Point scales the image based on the perspective plane on which you drag (**Figures 15.64** and **15.65**). But since this chapter is all about retouching, let's check out what can be done with the main retouching tool in Vanishing Point— the Clone Stamp tool.

> **NOTES**
>
> While using Vanishing Point, you can press the X key at any time to temporarily zoom in on your image. That can help you to be more precise when defining a perspective plane or performing retouching.

Figure 15.63 Define planes for each surface you intend to modify.

501

Figure 15.64 Moving areas in Photoshop produces unrealistic results.

Figure 15.65 Moving areas in Vanishing Point looks realistic.

Cloning in Perspective

Figure 15.66 This wall is distorted due to perspective. (©2007 iStockphoto.com/belterz)

Figure 15.67 Photoshop's retouching tools aren't aware of the effects of perspective, so cloned areas are not scaled to the proper size and therefore don't match the surrounding image.

Before Vanishing Point came along, Photoshop's Clone stamp tool could not recognize distortions caused by perspective (**Figure 15.66**). Consequently, it created unacceptable results when used on an image that contained noticeable perspective (**Figure 15.67**). The main problem is that the Clone Stamp tool is not capable of scaling the cloned area to make it match the perspective of the surface you are attempting to retouch. In the example shown here, the area being covered by the sign is primarily a row of larger bricks. If you look closely at the results obtained in Photoshop, you might notice that the row of large bricks ends up being patched with bricks that are much too small to look appropriate. The Clone Stamp tool in Vanishing Point, however, can do a much better job. To start, you would use the Create Plane tool and click on the two corners that make up the left edge of a brick and then click on the two corners that make up the right edge of another brick in the same row so that Photoshop is aware of how the bricks are distorted by perspective (**Figure 15.68**). Then, you would drag the size handles of the resulting grid to define the overall area that needs to be retouched (**Figure 15.69**). Once the plane has been defined, the Clone Stamp tool can be used to retouch areas, and its results will be scaled to conform to the perspective of the image (**Figure 15.70**).

Figure 15.68 The initial plane lines up with a row of bricks.

Figure 15.69 Expanding the plane to cover the area that needs to be edited.

Figure 15.70 The results show that the bricks on the right were scaled so they are the appropriate size for the areas on the left

Figure 15.71 The Vanishing Point dialog box with the Clone Stamp options visible. (©2007 iStockphoto.com/urbancow)

Figure 15.72 Heal set to Off.

Figure 15.73 Heal set to Luminance.

Figure 15.74 Heal set to On.

The Clone Stamp tool incorporates many of the options that are available in Photoshop's Healing brush, along with a few that are unique to Vanishing Point (**Figure 15.71**). Setting the Heal pop-up menu to Off causes the Clone Stamp tool to work just like its namesake in Photoshop, in that the Hardness setting of your brush will be the only thing that causes your retouching to blend into the surrounding image (**Figure 15.72**). Setting the Heal pop-up menu to Luminance causes the Clone Stamp tool to copy both color and texture from the area that is being cloned and to determine the brightness of the retouched area based on the surrounding image (**Figure 15.73**). Setting the menu to On causes the Clone Stamp tool to work like the Healing brush in Photoshop by only copying texture from the cloned area and picking up the brightness and color from the area that surrounds the retouching (**Figure 15.74**). The Off setting is useful when the area being retouched is not similar to its surroundings. The Luminance setting is useful when the surface being retouched is unevenly lit since it will match the brightness of the surrounding area. The On setting is best for those times when the area being retouched should have the same texture and color as the surrounding image.

The Dodge and Burn Tools

The words *dodge* and *burn* are taken from a traditional photographic darkroom. In a darkroom, an enlarger projects an image onto a sheet of photographic paper. While the image is being projected, you could put something in the way of the light source, which would obstruct the light in such a way that it would hit certain areas less than others—a technique known as dodging. Or you could add light by cupping your hands together, creating just a small hole in between them, and allowing the light to concentrate on a certain area more than others—a technique known as burning. Using a combination of these two methods, you can brighten or darken your image. Photoshop reproduces these techniques with two tools: Dodge and Burn. If you look at the icons for these tools, you'll see that one of them looks like a hand; that would be for burning, allowing the light to go through the opening of your hand. The other one looks like (at least I think it looks like) a lollipop, which you can use for obstructing, or dodging, the light.

The Dodge Tool

Let's take a closer look at the Dodge tool. Because it can lighten your image, the Dodge tool comes in handy when you are working on people with dark shadows under their eyes. But before we get into cosmetic surgery, I'll introduce you to a very important pop-up menu, called the Range menu, which is associated with this tool. You'll find it in the

NOTES

The Spacing setting of your brush will affect how much the image is changed when using the Dodge and Burn tools. Higher Spacing settings will affect the image less.

Figure 15.75 Dodge tool options bar.

options bar at the top of your screen (**Figure 15.75**). The pop-up menu has three choices: Shadows, Midtones, and Highlights. This menu tells Photoshop which shades of gray it should concentrate on when you paint across your image.

If you use the Shadows setting, you will change mainly the dark part of your image. As you paint across your image, your brush will brighten the areas it touches. But as you get into the midtones of the image, it will apply less and less paint. And if you paint over the light parts of the image, it won't change them much, if at all. The second choice is Midtones. If you use this setting, you will affect mainly the middle shades of gray in your image, or those areas that are about 25% to 75% gray. It shouldn't change the shadows or highlights very much. They may change a little bit, but only so they can blend into the midtones. The third choice is Highlights. Highlights will mainly affect the lightest parts of your image and slowly blend into the middle tones of your image.

Obviously, you'll need to decide exactly which setting would work best for your situation. If you don't do this before using the Dodge tool, you might cause yourself some grief. Let's say you're trying to fix dark areas around someone's eyes, but the Dodge tool doesn't seem to be doing the job (**Figure 15.76**). Then, after dozens of tries, you finally realize that the Range pop-up menu is set to Highlights instead of Midtones (look at the eyes in **Figures 15.77** and **15.78**).

You also have an Exposure setting on the options bar that controls how much brighter the image will become. You can use the number keys on your keyboard to change this setting.

Figure 15.76 Original image. (©Stockbyte, www.stockbyte.com)

Figure 15.77 Dodge tool set to Highlights. (Look at his eyes.)

Figure 15.78 Dodge tool set to Midtones.

505

Color Images

The Dodge tool works exceptionally well on grayscale images. All you have to do is choose which part of the image you want to work on—Shadows, Midtones, or Highlights—and paint across an area. Unfortunately, it's not as slick with color images. If you use the Dodge tool on color, you'll find that it tends to wash out some of the colors, and in some cases even change them (**Figures 15.79** and **15.80**).

One good solution is to duplicate the layer you're working on and set the Blending mode of the duplicate to Luminosity before using the Dodge tool. That should maintain the original colors and limit your changes to the brightness of the image. Or, you can forgo the Dodge tool and just use the Paintbrush tool. You can set your Paintbrush tool's Blending mode to Color Dodge and choose a bright shade of gray to paint with. But just going ahead and painting across an image will look rather ridiculous, because all it's doing is blowing out the detail (**Figure 15.81**).

To get the Color Dodge technique to work correctly, just choose a medium to light shade of gray to paint with (**Figure 15.82**). This allows you to create highlights or to brighten areas. Sometimes this works a little bit better than the Dodge tool.

Figure 15.79 Original image. (©2007 Andy Katz)

Figure 15.80 Large area lightened by using the Dodge tool.

Figure 15.81 Painting with a light shade of gray by using the Color Dodge mode.

Figure 15.82 Area lightened by painting with a medium shade of gray by using the Color Dodge Blending mode.

The Burn Tool

The Burn tool is designed for darkening areas of an image. Like the Dodge tool, it has Range options in its palette for Highlights, Midtones, and Shadows, as well as an Exposure setting. It, too, works great with gray-scale images. If you are ever dealing with a shiny spot on someone's forehead or nose because the light is reflecting off it, you can go ahead and try to fix it with the Burn tool (compare **Figures 15.83** and **15.84**).

Color Fixes

Just as with the Dodge tool, you'll start having problems when you use the Burn tool with a color image (**Figures 15.85** and **15.86**). When that happens, you're welcome to try painting with a shade of gray (with the Paintbrush tool) and setting the Blending mode to Color Burn, which will darken the image, making the colors more vivid while leaving the highlights largely untouched (**Figure 15.87**).

Another technique is to Option/Alt-click the New Layer icon at the bottom of the Layers palette. When you get the New Layer dialog box, change the Mode menu from Normal to Overlay, turn on the Fill with Overlay-Neutral Color check box, and then click OK (**Figure 15.88**). Now, with that new layer active, use the Dodge and Burn tools with the Range setting in the options bar set to Midtones (**Figures 15.89** and **15.90**). That allows you to perform

Figure 15.83 The original image. (©iStockphoto.com/iconogenic)

Figure 15.84 Cheek and area between eyebrows darkened by using the Burn tool.

Figure 15.85 Original image. (©iStockphoto.com/blaneyphoto)

Figure 15.86 Image darkened using the Burn tool.

Figure 15.87 Image darkened by painting with a shade of gray in Color Burn mode.

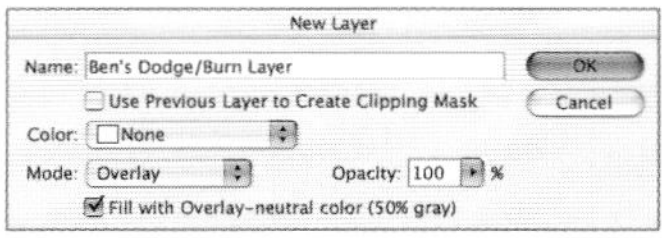

Figure 15.88 Creating a new layer in Overlay mode.

Figure 15.89 Original image. (©2007 Andy Katz)

Figure 15.90 Dodge and Burn used on a layer set to Overlay mode.

your dodging and burning on a separate layer and gives you fewer color problems. When I'm using this technique, I prefer to hold the Option/Alt key to temporarily switch between the Dodge and Burn tools. That way I don't have to go back to the Tools palette each time I want to switch from brightening to darkening my photo.

Now that you've learned how to brighten and darken your images with the Dodge and Burn tools, it's time to move on and learn how to adjust how colorful your images are with the Sponge tool.

The Sponge Tool

Hiding in with the Dodge and Burn tools is the Sponge tool. It works as if you have a sponge full of bleach, allowing you to paint across your image and soak up the color. Or you can do the opposite and intensify the colors—it's all determined by what you choose from the Mode menu in the options bar.

If you choose Desaturate, the Sponge tool will tone down the colors in the area you are painting. The more you paint across an area, the closer it will become to being grayscale. This can be useful when you'd like to make a product stand out from an otherwise distracting background (**Figure 15.91**). I also use it (with a very low Pressure setting) to minimize the yellow/orange color cast that usually shows up in the teeth of people who smoke or drink coffee a lot.

The Saturate setting will intensify the colors as you paint over them, which is great for giving people rosy cheeks (**Figure 15.92**). This can also be great for adding a bit more color to people's lips.

The Blur and Sharpen Tools

When you need to blur or sharpen an area, you have two choices: Select an area and apply a filter, or use the Blur and Sharpen tools. Using filters to blur and sharpen your image has a few advantages over using the tools, including getting a preview of the image before you commit to the settings being used and having the ability to apply the filter effect evenly to the area you are changing. But occasionally the Blur and Sharpen tools can really help when working on small areas, so let's take a look at how they work and when to use them.

The Blur Tool

The Blur tool is pretty straightforward. You can paint across any part of your image and blur everything that your cursor passes over. In the Blur tool options bar, you will find a Pressure setting that determines how much you will blur the image; higher settings blur the image more. This can be useful if there are little, itty-bitty areas of detail obstructing your image. I generally prefer to use the Gaussian Blur filter instead of this Blur tool because it does a better job of evenly blurring an area.

I like to use the Blur tool for reducing—not removing—wrinkles (**Figure 15.93**). If you turn the pressure way up on this tool and paint across a wrinkle a few times, you'll see it begin to disappear. But you'll also notice that it doesn't look very realistic. It might look as if you had smeared some Vaseline on the face. To really do a wrinkle justice, you have to take a closer look. Wrinkles are made out of two parts, a highlight and a shadow (light part and dark

Figure 15.91 Front and rear apples were desaturated to make the central one stand out. (©Stockbyte, www.stockbyte.com)

Figure 15.92 The cheek on the right was enhanced using the Sponge tool set to Saturate. (©Stockbyte, www.stockbyte.com)

part). If you paint across that with the Blur tool, the darker part of the wrinkle will be lightened, whereas the lightest part will be darkened, so that they become more similar in shade (**Figure 15.94**).

To reduce the impact of a wrinkle without completely getting rid of it (if I wanted to get rid of it, I would use the Healing brush tool), turn the Pressure setting all the way up. Then change the Blending mode to either Darken or Lighten. If the part that makes that wrinkle most prominent is the dark area, set the Blending Mode menu to Lighten (**Figure 15.95**). Then when you paint across the area, the only thing it will be able to do is lighten that wrinkle. But because you are using the Blur tool, it's not going to completely lighten it and make it disappear. Instead, it will reduce the impact of it. You really have to try this to see how it looks.

Figure 15.93 Original image. (©Stockbyte, www.stockbyte.com)

Figure 15.94 Wrinkles around her right eye have been blurred.

Figure 15.95 Wrinkles around the eye lessened by using the Blur tool with a Blending mode of Lighten.

Figure 15.96 By creating a new layer before using the Blur tool, you can isolate the unretouched image.

Layers

When I'm retouching wrinkles, I usually create a brand-new, empty layer (**Figure 15.96**). Then, in order to be able to use the Blur tool, I have to turn on the Sample All Layers check box in the options bar (**Figure 15.97**). Otherwise, Photoshop can look at only one layer at a time, and it won't have any information to blur. With these steps, Photoshop will copy the information from the underlying layers, blur it, and then paste it onto the layer you just created, leaving the underlying layers untouched.

By using this technique, I can easily delete areas or redo them without having to worry about permanently changing the original image. If you're attempting the wrinkle technique I mentioned earlier, you'll need to set the Blending mode of the layer to Lighten, and you might need to lower the Pressure setting of the Blur tool.

Figure 15.97 The Blur tool will not be able to use information on other layers unless you turn on the Sample All Layers check box.

The Lens Blur Filter

If you'd like to make a large area of your image blurry, you should try out the Lens Blur filter. Unlike the standard blur filters (Blur, Blur More, and Gaussian Blur), which blur your entire image the same amount, the Lens Blur filter will vary the amount of blurring that occurs (**Figures 15.98** and **15.99**), based on the contents of a grayscale image (**Figure 15.100**) (which you can create by using the Paintbrush tool). You can specify which shade of gray should represent an area that you want to keep in focus. Photoshop will then make all the other areas of the image progressively out of focus based on how different the surrounding shades of gray are compared to the one you specified as the in-focus shade. But it's really much easier to see it in action than to try to understand the concept. So, here's what you need to do:

Start by creating a new empty layer on top of the image you'd like to blur. Next, type D to reset your foreground color to black, and then use the Paintbrush tool to paint across the areas you'd like to keep in focus (**Figure 15.101**). The softness of your brush will determine how quickly the focus falls off, so use a really soft-edged brush if you want a smooth transition from the in-focus areas to the ones that should be blurred. You can also choose Filter > Blur > Gaussian Blur after you paint to create a much softer edge (**Figure 15.102**). When you're done painting, choose Edit > Fill, set the Use pop-up menu to White, set the Mode pop-up menu to Behind, and then click the OK button (**Figure 15.103**). That should fill the empty areas of the active layer with white. Now we need to get the contents of the active layer to

Figure 15.98 Original image. (©2007 PhotoSpin, www.photospin.com)

Figure 15.99 Result of applying the Lens Blur filter using the grayscale image shown in Figure 15.74.

Figure 15.100 Grayscale image used to blur Figure 15.99.

Figure 15.101 Paint with black on a new layer to define the areas that should remain in focus.

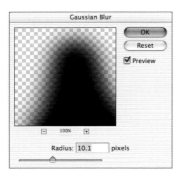

Figure 15.102 The Gaussian Blur filter

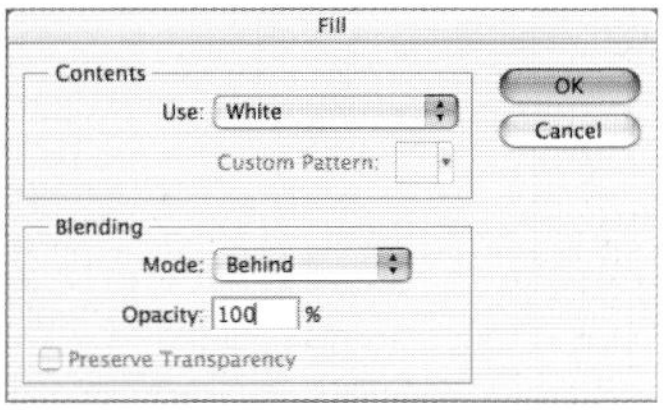

Figure 15.103 Use the Fill dialog box to fill the empty parts of the layer with white..

show up in an alpha channel. To accomplish that, open the Channels palette (Window > Channels), Command/Ctrl-click on the topmost channel (it will be called Gray, RGB, or CMYK depending on which mode your image is in) to get a selection, and then click the second icon from the left at the bottom of the Channels palette. To get back to working on the original image, switch back to the Layers palette (Window > Layers), drag the layer you painted onto the trash, choose Select > Deselect, click on the layer you'd like to blur, and then choose Filter > Blur > Lens Blur.

When the Lens Blur filter dialog box appears (**Figure 15.104**), turn on the Preview check box and choose Faster for the Preview method. (I find that the More Accurate setting is just too darn slow.) Next, choose the name of the alpha channel you created from the Source pop-up menu (it will usually be called Alpha 1, unless you renamed it), and then move your mouse over the preview image and click on the area you wanted to keep in focus. Clicking on your image will set the Blur Focal Distance setting, which determines which shade of gray in the alpha channel will be used to represent an area that should be in focus (0 = black). If you'd rather have that area become blurry instead, turn on the Invert check box. If you'd like to compare the blurred version of the image to the original, toggle the Preview check box off and on again.

Now that you have the filter thinking about the proper information, it's time to figure out what you'd like the blurry areas of the image to look like. The Radius slider determines just how blurry areas should become. When you purposefully throw an area out of focus using a camera (by using a low aperture setting), you will often see the shape of the aperture in the highlights of the image (**Figure 15.105**). The Shape, Blade Curvature, and Rotation settings attempt to simulate the shape of an aperture in the brightest areas of the image.

When you blur an image, the brightest areas of the image will often start to look a bit dull (**Figures 15.106** and **15.107**). That happens because blurring blends those

Figure 15.104 The Lens Blur dialog box.

Figure 15.105 The shape of the camera aperture often shows up in the brightest areas of the image.

bright areas into their surroundings, which makes them become darker. To compensate for that, you can increase the Brightness setting until the highlights in your image become bright again (**Figure 15.108**). The Threshold setting determines which shades will be brightened. Moving the slider toward the left causes Photoshop to brighten more shades, whereas moving it toward the right makes Photoshop brighten only the brightest shades in the image.

Figure 15.106 Original image.

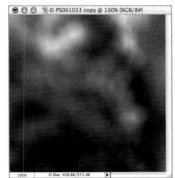

Figure 15.107 The highlights look dull after blurring the image.

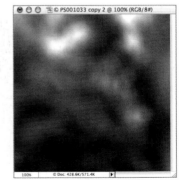

Figure 15.108 Adjusting the Brightness and Threshold settings brings back the brightness in the highlights.

Blurring an image usually removes any grain or noise that was in the image (**Figure 15.109**). Because the Lens Blur filter doesn't blur the entire image, you might end up with a lot of grain in the in-focus areas of the image and no grain in the areas you have blurred. That will make the image look very unnatural because the original image contained consistent grain across the entire image. To add grain into the areas you've blurred, experiment with the Noise setting found at the bottom of the Lens Blur dialog box. Just move the Amount slider up until the blurry areas have as much grain as the in-focus areas (**Figure 15.110**); then switch between the Uniform and Gaussian options until you determine which one delivers the best match to the grain of the original photo. Turn on the Monochromatic check box if the blurred areas look too colorful compared to the areas that haven't been blurred.

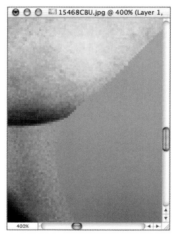 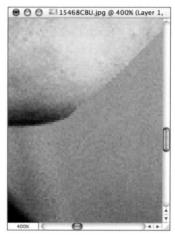

Figure 15.109 All the grain was removed when the right side of this image was blurred. (©Stockbyte, www.stockbyte.com)

Figure 15.110 Adjusting the Noise settings added grain back into the blurred area.

The Sharpen Tool

The Sharpen tool works in a fashion similar to that of its relative, the Sharpen filter. But with this tool you have to adjust the Pressure setting in the options bar to determine how much you want to sharpen the image. And you have to be careful: If you turn the Pressure setting up too high or paint across an area too many times, you're going to get some really weird effects (**Figures 15.111** to **15.113**).

Figure 15.111 Original image. (©Stockbyte, www.stockbyte.com)

Figure 15.112 Sharpened using the Sharpen tool with a medium Pressure setting.

Figure 15.113 Sharpened using the Sharpen tool with a high Pressure setting.

Reflected Highlights

When you run across an image that contains glass, metal, or other shiny objects, it usually contains extremely bright highlights (known as specular highlights). This usually happens when light reflects directly off one of those very shiny areas, such as the edge of a glass. These extra-bright highlights often look rather flat and lifeless after being adjusted (**Figure 15.114**). This happens because whenever we adjust an image to perform color correction, or prepare it for printing or multimedia, the brightest areas of the image usually become 3% or 4% gray (instead of white). But if you sharpen those areas, you're going to brighten them and make them pure white. This will make them stand out and look more realistic. So any time you have jewelry, glassware, or reflected light in people's eyes, you'll want to use the Sharpen tool, bring down the Strength to about 30%, and go over those areas once (**Figures 15.115** and **15.116**). That will make them almost pure white; when you print them, they will almost jump off the page, as they should (**Figure 15.117**).

I use the Blur and Sharpen tools to make subtle changes to my images. When I want a bit more radical of a change, I often use the Blur and Sharpen filters instead. The Lens Blur filter gives you the most control over blurring your image, but at the same time it's usually the slowest method for blurring your image. Now let's get away from traditional retouching techniques and see how we can correct distorted images.

Figure 15.114 Metallic highlights often look a bit dull after performing color correction.
(©Stockbyte, www.stockbyte.com)

Figure 15.115 The areas covered in red were sharpened to make them pop.

Figure 15.116 Metallic highlights sharpened.

Figure 15.117 The Sharpen tool setting to use on reflections.

Lens Correction Filter

The Lens Correction filter (which is found under the Filter > Distort menu) is designed to correct for distortion that is caused by either the camera lens itself, or by the angle the lens was pointed relative to the subject of the photo.

Let's start off with a quick tour and then we'll get busy fixing some images (**Figure 15.118**). Since this filter is often used on subjects that contain a lot of vertical and horizontal lines (like buildings), there is a grid that can help you see when you've removed all the distortion from an image. You can toggle the grid on and off with the Show Grid check box, control how much space there is between grid lines with the Size setting, and reposition the grid using the Move Grid tool (which looks like a hand on top of a grid). You can zoom in and scroll around your image using the Zoom and Hand tools, but I prefer to use the standard keyboard shortcuts of holding down Command/Ctrl and pressing the plus or minus keys and using the spacebar to temporarily access the Hand tool.

After you've experimented with some of the sliders on the right, you can toggle the Preview check box to see what the image looks like before and after the lens correction has been applied. Now that you know your way around the dialog box, let's see what all those sliders can actually accomplish.

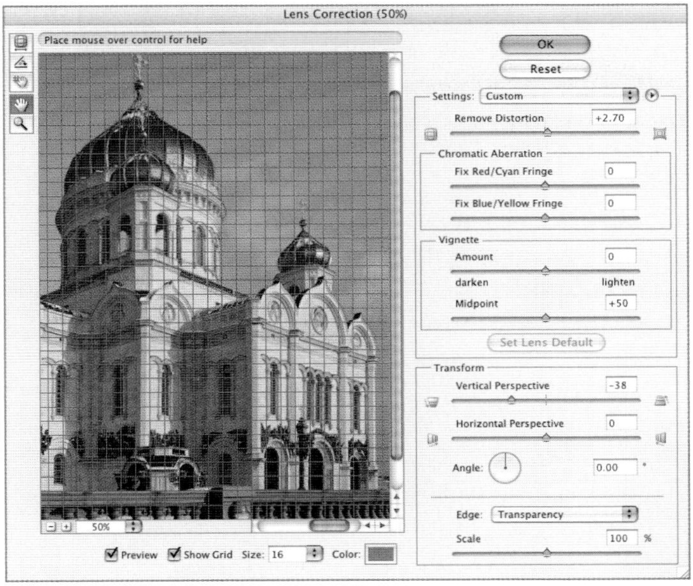

Figure 15.118 The Lens Correction dialog box. (©2007 iStockphoto.com/PhilSigin)

Remove Distortion

The Remove Distortion slider is designed to correct for barrel or pincushion distortion. That's when your image ends up either bent out away from the center or bent in toward the center. This causes vertical lines to become curved (**Figures 15.119** and **15.120**). You can either move the Remove Distortion slider, or drag on your image using the Remove Distortion tool (it's the top tool in the upper left of the dialog box). The grid is quite useful when adjusting this slider since it's often hard to tell if something is perfectly straight.

Figure 15.119 Original Image.

Figure 15.120 Result of adjusting the Remove Distortion slider.

Figure 15.121 Original Image (©2007 Ben Willmore)

Figure 15.122 Result of correcting for Chromatic Aberration.

Figure 15.123 Original Image. (©2007 Ben Willmore)

Figure 15.124 Result of darkening the corners with Vignetting.

Chromatic Aberration

These sliders are designed to get rid of color fringing that often appears on the edge of high contrast objects (**Figures 15.121** and **15.122**). This fringing is caused by light being bent as it passes through the elements that make up a camera lens, which causes the light to bend and separate much like white light turns into a rainbow of color when its sent through a prism. You won't see this fringing on every image, and you'll only be able to notice it when you zoom in to 100% view. These same two sliders are also available in the Camera Raw dialog box as is the next feature—Vignetting.

Vignette

Moving the Vignette slider toward the right causes the corners of your image to become brighter, whereas moving it to the left darkens the corners. The midpoint slider determines how far this brightness change will intrude toward the middle of the document. I don't run into too many images that have corners that are darker than the center of the image (although I see some older scanned images with that problem), but I like to use this feature because the darkened corners will usually direct the viewer's attention toward the middle of the image (**Figures 15.123** and **15.124**).

Transform

The Angle setting that's found under the Transform heading will simply rotate your image, which can be useful if the horizon line isn't level. All you have to do is choose the tool (it's right below the Remove Distortion tool) and then click and drag across an area that should be horizontal or vertical and Photoshop will calculate the proper rotation setting needed to straighten your image. (I should mention here that I prefer to use the Measure tool to precisely rotate and straighten an image. Read about the Measure tool in Chapter 1, "Tools and Palette Primer.")

The Vertical and Horizontal Perspective sliders are designed to make converging horizontal or vertical lines parallel (**Figures 15.125** and **15.126**). This is useful when you take a shot of a building by pointing your camera up toward the top, which usually causes the top of the building to appear smaller than the bottom in the resulting photograph.

Finally, at the bottom of the dialog box is an Edge setting, which determines what should be placed in any transparent areas of the image that are caused by the distortion correction you've applied. I usually leave the setting set to Transparency because I prefer to work on the transparent areas back in Photoshop.

Now that you have an idea of how to fix distorted images, let's shift gears and start applying creative distortion to your images.

Figure 15.125 Original Image. (©2007 iStockphoto.com/belterz)

The Liquify Filter

The Liquify filter allows you to pull and push on your image as if it were printed on Silly Putty. The results you will get out of this filter will either be overly obvious (looking like a reflection in a fun house mirror) or not noticeable to the untrained eye. It all depends on your intentions. When you choose Filter > Liquify, you'll see a dialog box that dominates your screen (**Figure 15.127**). Later you can play with the more extreme uses of the Liquify tools and conjure up special effects to your heart's content, but for now let's use a more real-world approach. The incremental changes will be subtle, so pay close attention to the captions for each figure.

Figure 15.126 Result of adjusting Vertical Perspective.

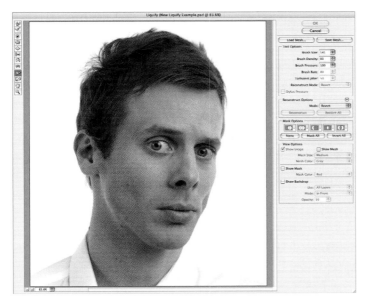

Figure 15.127 The Liquify dialog box. (©iStockphoto.com/bsilvia)

The first tool you'll find in the upper left of the Liquify dialog box is the Forward Warp tool. With that tool active, you can paint on your image to push the image in the direction that you're dragging (**Figure 15.128**). When you're done manipulating your image, you might find that you've gone a little too far in a few areas. If that's the case, grab the Reconstruct tool (second from the top tool) and paint across the area that you'd like to take back to normal (**Figure 15.129**). The more you paint across an area, the closer it will become to what the image looked like before you applied the Liquify command. Next is the Twirl Clockwise tool, which will slowly rotate the area inside your cursor clockwise (hold Option/Alt to rotate areas counterclockwise) (**Figure 15.130**). Under that you'll find the Pucker tool, which allows you to pull the image in toward the center of your brush (**Figure 15.131**). Or, you can do the opposite of that by using the Bloat tool (**Figure 15.132**). (Hold Option/Alt to temporarily switch between the Pucker and Bloat tools.) Below the Bloat tool is the Push Left tool, which acts as though the line you draw is a bulldozer and pushes the image away from it on the left side (**Figure 15.133**). (Press Option/Alt in Windows to move the image on the right side instead.) After that you'll find the Mirror tool, which will flip a portion of the image horizontally or vertically, depending on the direction you drag. If you drag downward, you'll be reflecting the area to the left of the cursor. Drag up and you'll reflect what's to the right (**Figure 15.134**). Drag right and you'll reflect the area below the cursor, and drag left to reflect the area above. Finally, the last general tool is the Turbulence tool, which allows you to push and pull on your image, much like the Warp tool, but it will add more of a wavy look, which can be useful when you're attempting to create water ripples and smoke (**Figure 15.135**).

Now that you have an idea of what each tool does, let's explore the options that show up in the upper right of the Liquify dialog box.

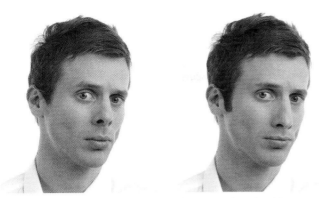

Figure 15.128 Left: the original image. Right: Warp tool used on his eyes, nose, mouth and hair.

Figure 15.129 Reconstruct tool used on right side of face (his right).

Figure 15.130 Twirl tool used on corner of his mouth.

Figure 15.131 Pucker tool used on his nostril, nose, eyes, and cheek.

Figure 15.132 Bloat tool used on his jaw and chin.

Figure 15.133 Push Left tool used on his lips.

Figure 15.134 Mirror tool used on area between eyebrows.

Figure 15.135 Turbulence tool used on his hair.

▶ **Brush Size:** There is no Brushes palette available to change the size of your brush in the Liquify dialog box. The size of the brush is determined by the number entered in the Brush Size field in the upper right of the dialog box. You can use the bracket keys (][) to change this setting in small increments, or press Shift with them to change the size in larger increments.

▶ **Brush Density:** This setting determines how thick the center of your brush is before it starts to fade out and affect your image less. Just imagine you're warping the image with your finger. You could think of this setting as how pointy of a finger you are using to warp your image (**Figures 15.136** to **15.138**). Low settings cause a radical change in a small area and then fade out to the edge of your brush, whereas higher settings spread the radical change into a wider area before it fades out to the edge of your brush.

▶ **Brush Pressure:** For all of these tools, the Brush Pressure setting will determine how radical a change you'll make when you paint across the image. You can think of the Brush Pressure setting as determining how hard you'd be pushing with your finger. The harder you push, the more of the image you'll move with each paint stroke (**Figures 15.139** to **15.141**). If you have a pressure-sensitive graphics tablet, you can turn on the Stylus Pressure check box to make Photoshop pay attention to how much pressure you're using with the pen. With this option turned on, the Brush Pressure setting will be determined by how hard you press down on your graphics tablet.

Figure 15.136 Original image. (©Stockbyte, www.stockbyte.com)

Figure 15.137 Image warped using a low Brush Density setting.

Figure 15.138 Image warped using a high Brush Density setting.

Figure 15.139 Original image. (© 2007 Stockbyte, www.stockbyte.com)

Figure 15.140 Warped using a medium Brush Pressure setting.

Figure 15.141 Warped using a high Brush Pressure setting.

▶ **Brush Rate:** This setting is available only with the Reconstruct, Twirl, Pucker, Bloat, and Turbulence tools. It determines how much of a change you'll make when you are stationary with the mouse button held down. The higher the setting, the more quickly the image will change when you pause on top of an area (**Figures 15.142** to **15.144**). This setting has no affect on what happens when the mouse is in motion.

Figure 15.142 Original image. (© 2007 Stockbyte, www.stockbyte.com)

Figure 15.143 Bloated for three seconds using a low Brush Rate setting.

Figure 15.144 Bloated for three seconds using a high Brush Rate setting.

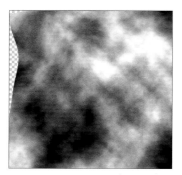

Figure 15.145 Turbulence tool applied (left side) for 10 seconds with a low Turbulent Jitter setting.

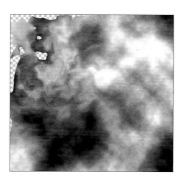

Figure 15.146 Turbulence tool applied (left side) for 10 seconds with a high Turbulent Jitter setting.

Figure 15.147 When creating an image like this one, I often experiment with the Reconstruction modes. (©2007 Andy Katz)

▶ **Turbulent Jitter:** This setting determines how smooth of a result you'll get with the Turbulence tool (it doesn't affect the other tools). Low settings produce a smoother distortion, whereas higher settings produce a more random distortion (**Figures 15.145** and **15.146**).

▶ **Reconstruction Mode:** This pop-up menu determines how the Reconstruct tool will attempt to bring the image back to its original state. You'll get radically different results depending on which setting you choose. The vast majority of the time I use the Revert setting; I generally only change the setting when I'm looking to create a creative image (**Figure 15.147**).

Before we move on, I want to make sure you know how to navigate around your image and how to undo changes. You can use standard keyboard shortcuts to zoom in or out on your image: Command-+ or Command- – (Mac) or Ctrl-+, Ctrl- – (Windows), or use the Zoom tool at the bottom of the tool list. To scroll around your image, either choose the Hand tool or hold the spacebar while you're in any other tool to temporarily access the Hand tool. You can perform multiple undo's by pressing Command/Ctrl-Z multiple times (add Shift to redo what you've just undone). Now that you know how to get around your image, let's look at how you can limit which areas of the image you can change.

If you find that you end up changing too much of the image, you can mask an area to prevent it from changing. The Freeze Mask tool (found along with the distortion tools on the left side of the dialog box) will apply a red overlay on your image to indicate which areas have been masked (**Figure 15.148**). The Freeze Mask tool also uses the Brush Density and Brush Pressure settings, which means that you can partially mask an area to make it change less than the nonmasked areas. (For example, 50% masked areas will change half as much as unmasked areas when they're painted over.) Areas that are partially masked will appear with a more transparent red overlay. If you'd rather not see the overlay, click to turn off the Show Mask check box. If you'd like to unmask an area, use the Thaw Mask tool to remove some of the red overlay, or click the None check box in the Mask Options area to unmask the entire image.

The Freeze Mask and Thaw Mask options are great when used with the Backdrop setting, which allows you to see through the transparent areas of a layer to the underlying layers. This way you can see exactly how your image lines up with the rest of the document (**Figure 15.149**).

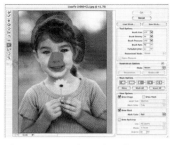

Figure 15.148 The red overlay indicates an area that has been masked. (©Stockbyte, www.stockbyte.com)

After you play around in this dialog box, it's often difficult to determine the exact areas in your image that have changed. You can see a different view of the changes you've made by selecting the Show Mesh check box (**Figure 15.150**). You might also want to turn off the Show Image check box so you can get a clear view of the mesh (**Figure 15.151**). You can also control the size and color of the mesh, which can help make the changes more noticeable when viewed at the same time as the image. You can still use all the Liquify tools while the mesh is visible.

Real-World Retouching with Liquify

Now that you know how to think about these tools, let's explore how you might use them when retouching an image. When you're trying each of these techniques, be extra careful not to go too far with your distortions; otherwise, the changes will become overly obvious. The idea is to change the image so that it looks better than the original without changing it so much that anyone would notice that it's been tampered with.

Figure 15.149 The left side indicates what you see when the Backdrop check box is turned off. The right side shows what you see when an underlying layer is visible. (©Stockbyte, www.stockbyte.com)

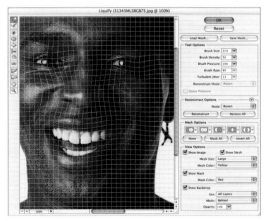

Figure 15.150 An image with the mesh visible. (©Stockbyte, www.stockbyte.com)

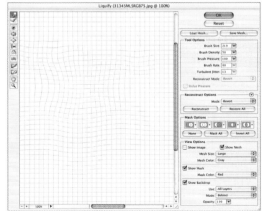

Figure 15.151 Viewing the mesh with the image hidden.

Retouching Eyes

In the world of fashion, it is not unusual to enlarge a model's eyes so that your attention is drawn to that part of his or her face (**Figures 15.152** and **15.153**). Even if you're not a fashion photographer, if you want to give it a whirl, here's what you need to do. (If you want to work on the same image I'm using, open the retouching eyes.jpg image in the Practice Images > Retouching folder on the CD.) First, use the Freeze Mask tool to mask off the surrounding areas of the eye that would probably not look right if they were distorted. That usually includes the eyebrows, nose, and sometimes the sides of the head (**Figure 15.154**). Next, switch to the Bloat tool, move your mouse over one of the eyes, placing the crosshair that shows up in the middle of the cursor in the pupil of the eye, and then adjust the Brush Size setting (by pressing the] or [keys) until your brush is just larger than the perimeter of the eye (**Figure 15.155**). You'll need to set the Brush Density setting to 100; otherwise, you'll end up enlarging the center of the eye more than the rest of the eye. While you're at it, you might as well change the Brush Rate setting to a low setting like 20 so that you don't have to be overly careful thinking about how long to hold down the mouse button to get the proper change in the image. Now that you have everything set up properly, center your cursor on the blacks of

Figure 15.152 Original image.
(©Stockbyte, www.stockbyte.com)

Figure 15.153 The eyes have been enlarged slightly.

Figure 15.154 Mask off the areas that you don't want to distort.

Figure 15.155 Use a brush slightly wider than the eye.

Figure 15.156 His right eye has been enlarged, but the left one hasn't.

the eye, and then press the mouse button until the eyes look slightly larger (about a second should do it) **(Figure 15.156)**. Then repeat the process on the second eye, making sure that you hold the mouse button for the same amount of time; otherwise, you'll have one eye larger than the other, and we want to avoid anything that would make our subject look like the Bride of Frankenstein.

You can also use Liquify to open eyes that are partially shut **(Figure 15.157)**. Liquify isn't my personal preference for this kind of work, however; I'd much rather have multiple photos to work with so that I can copy an open eye from one photo, paste it onto a closed eye in another image, and use the Healing brush to blend in the edges. But for those times when you have only one shot to work with, you'll want to use the Bloat and Warp tools to help pry an eye open **(Figure 15.158)**. Start by choosing the Bloat tool. Set the Brush Size setting so that your brush is about 3/4 of the width of the eye; set the Brush Density to a low setting (somewhere around 20 should work) so that you mainly scale the center of the eye; and set the Brush Rate to 20. Now, click on the center of the eye four or five times so that it starts to enlarge **(Figure 15.159)**. Then, to get the rest of the eye to look natural, make a few single

Figure 15.157 Original image. (©iStockphoto.com/theboone)

Figure 15.158 First try at opening an eye.

527

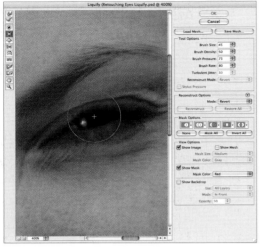

Figure 15.159 Click in the center of the eye a few times to pry it open.

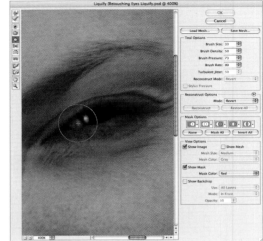

Figure 15.160 Click on the sides to even out the eye.

Figure 15.161 Reshape the eyelid with the Warp tool if necessary.

NOTES

The Liquify settings you choose will vary based on the image you're using and the amount of precision required to complete each task. The settings I've suggested are a good starting point.

clicks just to the right and left of the center of the eye (**Figure 15.160**). Finally, switch to the Warp tool, bring up the Brush Density setting to around 50, and set the Brush Pressure to around 60. Place the crosshair in the center of the brush onto the eyelid and drag up or down to reshape it (**Figure 15.161**). Keep tweaking the image until each eye has the proper shape. If you mess up and create a ghoulish rendition of an eye, switch to the Reconstruct tool, bring down the Brush Pressure and Brush Rate settings to around 20, and then click or paint across the eye to see if you can smooth it out.

Retouching Mouths

Remember Jack Nicholson when he played the Joker in the *Batman* movie? How he always had that maniacal smile frozen on his face? Well, we're not going to go that far, but we are going to use the Warp tool to transform a straight mouth into a smiling one (**Figures 15.162** and **15.163**). Start by choosing the Warp tool. Change the Brush Size setting until you get a brush about half the width of the mouth, set the Brush Density to 50, and set the Brush Pressure to 50 or more. Next, move your mouse so that the crosshair is just below the right edge of the mouth, and

Figure 15.162 Original image. (©iStockphoto.com/canadian)

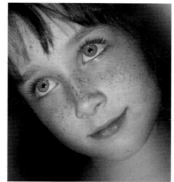

Figure 15.163 Result of forcing a smile with Liquify.

drag upward and to the side slightly to move the corner of the mouth up and out (**Figure 15.164**). Repeat this process on the left side of the mouth. Then, change the Brush Size setting to get a brush slightly smaller than the one you just used and place the crosshair on the top edge of the lips centered horizontally and drag down a small distance (**Figure 15.165**). If your mouth is looking too much like the Joker or it's just plain weird, don't worry, it just takes some practice to get an acceptable result. If you mess up, either paint across the area with the Reconstruct tool to get it closer to the original or click the Restore All button to start over.

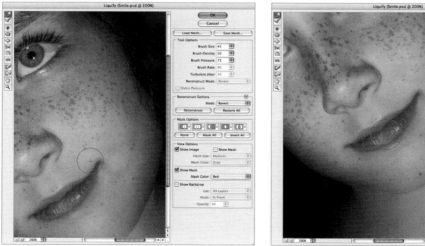

Figure 15.164 Use the Warp tool to push the side up and out.

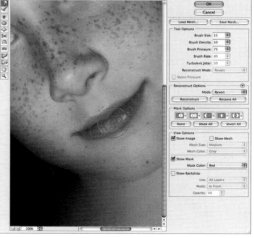

Figure 15.165 Pull the middle of the lip down slightly.

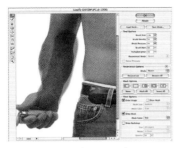

Figure 15.166 The original image with the arm masked so it won't shift. (©Stockbyte, www.stockbyte.com)

Figure 15.167 Result of warping the waist with a large brush.

Digital Liposuction

Forget the plastic surgeon! Forget handing over your life savings to some personal trainer to help you get rid of a few lousy pounds of cellulite. You've got Photoshop! If you need to nip or tuck some bulging flesh, you can do it by mastering the Warp, Pucker, and Push Left tools. When working on waistlines, you can use the Warp tool with a largish brush, a medium Brush Density setting (50ish), and a high Brush Pressure (80ish), and drag the background toward the waist (**Figures 15.166** and **15.167**). If you need to move a large area, you might want to consider using the Push tool. You'll want to choose a large brush, set the Brush Density to 100, and use a very low Brush Pressure (around 10). Then move your cursor so that the crosshair just touches the edge you need to move, and drag to push the flesh in one direction (**Figures 15.168** and **15.169**). Drag straight down if you need to push the skin toward the right of your cursor; hold Option/Alt if you need to move the skin in the opposite direction. But after doing that, you might find that the background gets distorted too much. When that happens, click OK in the Liquify dialog box and use the Clone Stamp tool to replace the distorted background with something that looks more appropriate.

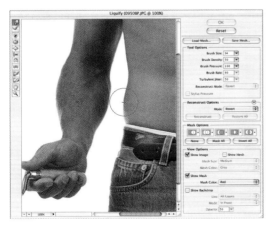

Figure 15.168 There is no need to mask when using the Push Left tool; just use a downward stroke with the crosshair on the edge you want to push.

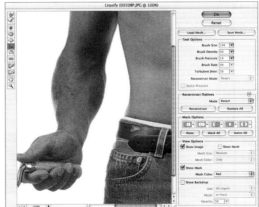

Figure 15.169 Result of pushing quite a bit of flesh using the Push Left tool.

Retouching and Restoring Real-World Photos

Now let's combine the ideas we've covered in this chapter with some of the features from other chapters to retouch and restore some real-world examples.

Fixing a Faded Image

The following image was exposed to sunlight while it was framed and hung on the wall (**Figure 15.170**). To restore it, we're going to use some color correction techniques from Chapter 7, "Color Correction"; some color manipulation ideas from Chapter 9, "Color Manipulation"; and a few tricks we talked about in this chapter. You're welcome to follow along by opening the wedding.jpg image in the Practice Images > Retouching folder on the CD.

Figure 15.170 The original image was faded from exposure to the sun. (©2007 Conner Huff, www.conman.net)

Let's start by fixing the faded area in the center of the image. To isolate that area, choose the Elliptical Marquee tool and click and drag across the center area. If you need to reposition the selection before you release the mouse button, hold the spacebar and drag around your image. If you need to continue changing the size of the selection, release the spacebar, but keep the mouse button pressed. Only release the mouse button when your selection closely matches the boundary of the faded area (**Figure 15.171**). Once you have that area isolated, choose Curves from the Adjustment Layer icon at the bottom of the Layers palette (fourth from the right). Now click the Options button to access the Auto Color dialog box and use the settings shown in **Figure 15.172**. Then click OK in both the Auto Color and Curves dialog boxes. That should transform the faded center of the image into a much better looking image (**Figure 15.173**), but the adjustment doesn't yet blend into the surrounding image. With the newly created adjustment layer active, choose Filter > Blur > Gaussian Blur, and experiment with the Amount setting until the adjustment blends with the surrounding image (I used 4) (**Figure 15.174**).

Figure 15.171 Select the center faded area with the Elliptical Marquee tool.

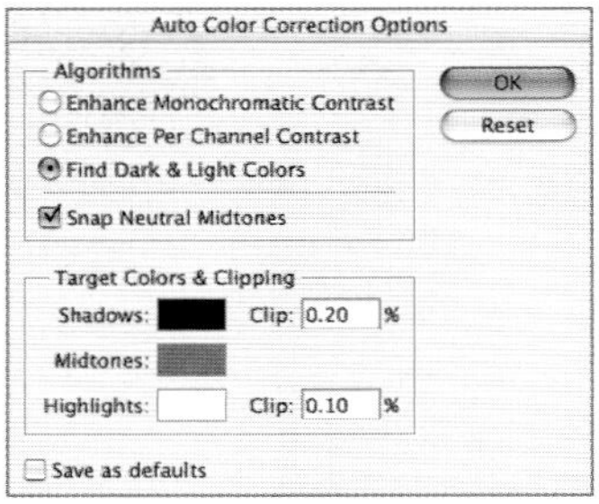

Figure 15.172 Apply the Auto Color settings shown here.

Now that the center of the image has more contrast, the outer area is looking a little faded in comparison. To target that area, hold the Command/Ctrl key and click on the Layer Mask that is attached to the adjustment layer created a few minutes ago (**Figure 15.175**). That should produce a selection of the central area of the image. To get the outer

Figure 15.173 After applying Auto Color, the center of the image should no longer be faded.

Figure 15.174 Blur the Layer Mask attached to the adjustment layer to blend in the adjustment blend.

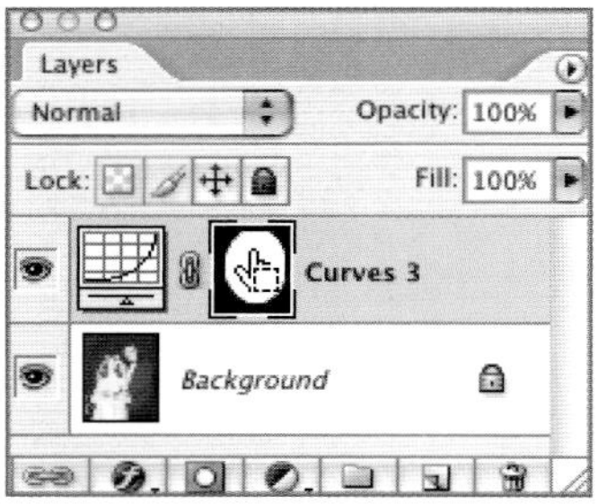

Figure 15.175 Command/Ctrl-click on the Layer Mask that's attached to the adjustment layer.

area, choose Select > Inverse. Now create another Curves adjustment layer, click the Auto button to apply the same Auto Color settings that we used on the middle of the image, and then click OK. That should add a bit of contrast to the outer area of the image (**Figure 15.176**).

Now I notice that the color in the wood wall behind the newlyweds doesn't quite match the surrounding image. To remedy the situation, create a new empty layer and place it at the top of the layers stack. Change the Blending Mode pop-up menu at the top of the Layers palette to Hue so that any paint that we apply to this layer will change the basic color of what's underneath without changing its brightness (**Figure 15.177**). Next, choose the Paintbrush tool and Option/Alt-click on the wood area where you think the color looks appropriate (**Figure 15.178**). Then release the Option/Alt key and paint over the areas that have discolored wood (**Figure 15.179**). You might also need to sample a color in his suit and paint across the lower-right corner to get consistent color there.

Now that the contrast and color look about right, I think the lower-right of the suit needs to be fixed so you no longer see the shape of the oval frame (**Figure 15.180**). I think the Healing brush will be great for this. But before we start playing with it, create a new layer at the top of the layers stack, choose the Healing brush, and turn on the Use All Layers check box in the options bar at the top of your screen. Then, to fix that transition, choose a brush wide enough to

Figure 15.176 After applying Auto Color to the surrounding image, the contrast on both sides should be similar.

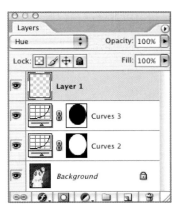

Figure 15.177 Add an empty layer to the top of the layers stack and set its Blending Mode to Hue.

Figure 15.178 Option/Alt-click on an area where the color looks good.

Figure 15.179 After painting over the wood areas, the colors look much better.

cover the transition we're attempting to fix and Option/Alt-click in the dark area just below the transition we need to fix. Now center your cursor on the transition just above the area you clicked on and drag across a small area of that transition. When you release the mouse button, Photoshop should blend that transition into the image (**Figure 15.181**). You'll need to work on small areas and make sure you don't hit too much of the pocket or fabric edges; otherwise, they will end up being blended into the surrounding image.

Once you get used to the techniques we used to fix this image, you'll be able to tackle similar images in about five minutes.

Figure 15.180 The outline of the old frame is still visible in the dark areas of his suit.

Figure 15.181 After healing, the transition where the old frame used to be is no longer visible.

Figure 15.182 The author, awaiting a nose job. (©2007 Gary Isaacs)

Figure 15.183 After a little surgery, my nose is much slimmer.

Plastic Surgery

Now let's combine the ideas from Chapter 14, "Collage," with the Healing brush to perform some surgery on yours truly (**Figure 15.182**). We'll attempt to transform my every-man nose into a Hollywood masterpiece, worthy of the best Beverly Hills doctor that money can buy (**Figure 15.183**). The general concept for performing plastic surgery is to isolate areas, rotate/transform them into a new position, and then blend in the seams so that nobody can tell that we messed with the image. Here's the play by play:

If you'd like to follow along, open the Ben.jpg image in the Practice Images > Retouching folder on the CD (no heckling from you readers allowed in this section). Start by making a generic selection around my nose using the Lasso tool (**Figure 15.184**). To make sure the edge blends into its surroundings, choose Select > Feather, and use a medium setting (it will depend on the size and resolution of your image—I used 5 for this image). Now let's copy that area onto its own layer so that we can work on it independently from the rest of the image. Do that by either choosing Layer > New > Layer Via Copy or typing Command/Ctrl-J. With that new layer active, choose Image > Transform > Distort, and then move the bottom two corners until my nose starts to look a bit slimmer (**Figure 15.185**).

Figure 15.184 Make a generic selection around the nose.

Figure 15.185 Slim down my nose by adjusting the four corners.

We'll need to transform a few other areas in order to cover up my old nose, which is peeking out from behind my new slim nose. So, click on the bottom layer in the image and then make a loose selection of the crease that runs between one side of my nose and the edge of my mouth/goatee (**Figure 15.186**). Then feather the selection and copy it to another layer, just like we did with my nose. Once it's on its own layer, move that layer up in the Layers palette so it appears above the slim version of my nose. To transform that area, type Command/Ctrl-T, and then move your mouse just outside the upper-right corner and drag to rotate the crease so that it matches up with the new slimmer nose (use the arrow keys if you need to reposition the transformed layer) (**Figure 15.187**). Don't worry if the edges don't blend in; we'll fix that later. Before we move on, repeat the steps that we did with the crease and apply them to the crease that appears on the other side of my nose/mouth (**Figure 15.188**).

Now that we have all the proper pieces transformed into new positions, we need to blend in all the transitions. That's where the Healing brush comes in. Create a new layer and place it at the top of the Layers palette. Switch to the Healing brush and turn on the Use All Layers check box in the options bar at the top of your screen.

Figure 15.186 Select one of the creases to the side of my nose.

Figure 15.187 Transform the crease so it matches up with my new nose.

Figure 15.188 Transform the other side as well.

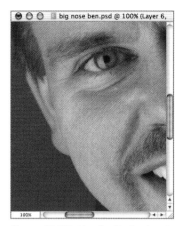

Figure 15.189 Use the Healing brush to fix any transition areas.

Now, Option/Alt-click in the general cheek area just outside one of the creases that we transformed. Then, with a brush big enough to cover the transition between the crease and the cheek, paint across the entire transition to blend it into the surrounding image (do it as one paint stroke so it blends properly) (**Figure 15.189**). If you're not comfortable using the Healing brush, make sure you review the beginning of this chapter and practice on a few images first.

If you'd like to compare the original image to the retouched version, just Option/Alt-click on the eyeball icon for the bottom layer in the Layers palette. That should toggle the visibility of all the layers we just created, effectively showing you before (new layers hidden) and after (new layers visible).

This jump-to-a-new-layer, transform, heal technique is a great way to resculpt faces. A perfect model is hard to find (and expensive), but a 10-minute visit to Photoshop can easily transform a less-than-perfect face into one that looks like a million bucks.

Closing Thoughts

We've covered all the tools you'll need to become a bona fide "photo doctor." Bear in mind that you don't need to limit yourself to just photographs; the tools and techniques we've covered in this chapter can be used for nonphotographic images as well. And, as with everything else in Photoshop, once you've gone around the block with these tools a few times, you'll probably think of a dozen other things you can do with them.

You'll be able to give someone a face-lift, remove your former boy- or girlfriend from a photograph, or clear-cut telephone poles from an otherwise perfect Kodak moment; but just promise me that you won't do anything underhanded for some ethically challenged dictator.

Workflow

©2007 Brian Kelsey, bpkelsey.com

Those are my principles, and if you don't like them...
well, I have others.

—Groucho Marx

If you've been reading this book from front to back, you should have picked up some great techniques for improving the quality of your images. That's good, but even the best techniques can fizzle if they are not performed in the proper order. The term "workflow" might not sound very exhilarating, but don't be tempted to skip this chapter because the order in which you perform each task can play a critical role in the quality of your images. And now that you are bursting at the seams with all of this newfound knowledge of Photoshop, you are ready to learn an effective start-to-finish workflow.

This chapter will provide you with the step-by-step workflow I use everyday. I've thought through this workflow long and hard and have refined it from working in Photoshop for well over a decade. Don't worry, it won't take you a decade to adopt these principles because like many aspects of Photoshop, once you've been through it a few times, the actual time you end up spending on workflow will be minimal.

I'll explain why each step appears in its order, and then you can make an educated decision as to whether you want to follow my workflow or create one of your own. In some instances you might not need to perform every single step; it will depend on the importance of the particular image. Just know that the more steps you perform, the higher the quality of your results.

In addition to the workflow steps, I'll take a few side trips to share with you some other tricks and tidbits that will be helpful to you as you build a workflow that will be best suited for your particular situation.

538

Step 1—Image Capture

We'll start at the beginning by looking at how you get an image into your computer. Higher quality input will make it easier to get a good result at the end of the workflow. Most images are digitized using either a scanner or digital camera. Let's look at how the digitizing can affect your Photoshop workflow. If you don't shoot your own photos, you can skip the "Digital Cameras" section and go right on to the "Scanners" section.

A megapixel is simply one million pixels. That means that a 6.3 mega-pixel digital camera will deliver approximately 6.3 million pixels total or a 3072 x 2048 image (3072 x 2048=6,291,456 pixels).

Digital Cameras

Quality starts with the choices you make when purchasing and setting up your digital camera. There are many books dedicated to how to use a camera effectively, but for our purposes I just want to cover three concepts: resolution, file formats, and histograms.

Resolution

The resolution of a camera determines how much detail it is capable of capturing and is measured in megapixels. A megapixel is an approximate measurement of how many millions of pixels the camera will deliver. If the camera doesn't capture enough information for the type of output you plan to use (onscreen, inkjet, printing press, etc.), you're doomed from the start (quality-wise, that is). **Table 16.1** indicates how large you can print an image based on

TABLE 16.1 Camera Megapixels and Corresponding Sizes in Inches (Pixels Per Inch setting is image resolution)

CAMERA MEGAPIXELS	TOTAL PIXELS	INKJET @250PPI	LASER @150PPI	NEWSPAPER @130PPI	MAGAZINE @200PPI	HIGH-END @300PPI
1	1152x864	4.6 x 3.5	7.7 x 5.8	8.9 x 6.6	5.8 x 4.3	3.8 x 2.9
2	1600x1200	6.4 x 4.8	10.7 x 8.0	12.3 x 9.2	8.0 x 6.0	5.3 x 4.0
3	2048x1536	8.2 x 6.1	13.7 x 10.2	15.8 x 11.8	10.2 x 7.7	6.8 x 5.1
4	2304x1728	9.2 x 6.9	15.4 x 11.5	16.7 x 13.3	11.5 x 8.6	7.7 x 5.8
5	2592x1944	10.4 x 7.8	16.3 x 13.0	19.9 x 15.0	13.0 x 9.7	8.6 x 6.5
6	2816x2112	11.3 x 8.4	18.8 x 14.1	21.7 x 16.2	14.1 x 10.6	9.4 x 7.0
7	3072x2304	12.3 x 9.2	20.5 x 15.4	23.6 x 16.7	15.4 x 11.5	10.2 x 7.7
8	3456x2304	13.8 x 9.2	23.0 x 15.4	26.6 x 16.7	16.3 x 11.5	11.5 x 7.7
12	4256x2848	16.0 x 11.4	28.4 x 19.0	32.7 x 21.9	21.3 x 14.2	14.2 x 9.5
16	4992x3328	19.7 x 13.3	32.8 x 22.2	37.9 x 25.6	24.6 x 16.6	16.4 x 11.1

how many megapixels it contains. Camera resolution isn't a critical factor when using an image onscreen because even the cheapest modern digital camera captures enough information to fill most computer screens. The largest screen I see high-end imaging professionals using is a 30" widescreen display, which can display 2560 x 1600 pixels, which is just over 4 megapixels. Use the table when shopping for a camera or to determine the limitations of your hardware.

File Formats

Figure 16.1 The artifacts in the unadjusted image are difficult to see. (@2007 iStockphoto.com/kevdog818)

Figure 16.2 After making a large adjustment to the image, the JPEG compression artifacts are easier to see.

Low-end digital cameras usually capture images in JPEG file format. That's an acceptable format when file size is more important than image quality, but it's less than ideal if you're trying to get the highest quality possible. The JPEG format applies what's known as lossy compression to your images in an effort to reduce the file size. It usually ends up with a file that is just under 1/4 the size of a RAW format image (which is a format used by high-end digital cameras). You probably won't notice the effects of this compression if you make very small prints and don't plan to make radical changes in Photoshop. But if you make larger-sized prints and make big adjustments to the color and contrast of the image, you will likely expose the compression artifacts that are hidden in your images (**Figures 16.1** and **16.2**). In digital photography, the JPEG file format is used mainly for personal use, or for low-end reproduction (like newspapers), or by people who, perhaps, don't understand the pros and cons of the different file formats. There's nothing wrong with using the JPEG file format as long as you've made an educated decision about the quality vs. size tradeoffs.

If you move up to a modern medium or high-end digital camera, you'll usually have the choice of shooting in JPEG or RAW file format. RAW files have the potential to produce much higher quality results than an image captured in the JPEG file format. Why? Because a raw file usually contains 16 times as many brightness levels as a JPEG file (4096 versus only 256). Also, the raw files don't have any lossy compression applied, so there are no compression related artifacts to be exposed when adjusting the image.

What's more, there are many settings that are only available when shooting in this file format (see Chapter 8, "Using Camera Raw," for more info about those settings), and one of those settings —White Balance—allows for quick and easy color correction that is capable of producing much higher quality results than anything that can be performed on a JPEG image (without manually setting the white balance in your camera).

I leave my camera set to use RAW file format about 90% of the time because quality is usually my first concern. The remaining 10% of the time I'm more concerned with file size (because my storage card is too full to fit another RAW format image), or I don't want to spend time in Photoshop before handing the files over to a friend or client (because JPEG files can be opened by any imaging software and raw files require special software like Photoshop).

Histograms

We covered the general concepts behind histograms back in Chapter 4, "Optimizing Grayscale Images," and Chapter 5, "Understanding Curves," so here I'm only going to cover what's unique about using the histogram on a digital camera.

Most digital cameras that are capable of shooting in the RAW file format also have the ability to display a histogram. When shooting, I use the histogram to help me insure that my image has sufficient shadow and highlight detail. The histogram indicates which brightness levels are used to make up your image and how prevalent each shade is within the image. If a spike appears on the left end of the histogram, that's an indication that a large area in the image has become solid black and lacks shadow detail (**Figure 16.3**). If a spike appears on the right end of the histogram, a large part of the image has become solid white, which means it lacks highlight detail (**Figure 16.4**). Highlight and shadow detail is important for multiple reasons:

▶ Photoshop can't magically create detail where an area is solid black or solid white. Images that lack shadow and highlight detail will prevent many adjustments from producing acceptable results.

NOTES

When looking for spikes on a histogram, it's only the first and last pixels (that make up the histogram) that are important, because those are the only areas that indicate if black or white is taking up a lot a space. Unlike spikes on the extreme ends of the histogram, spikes near the end or in the middle of the histogram do not indicate lost detail.

Figure 16.3 The spike on the left end of the histogram indicates a lack of shadow detail.

Figure 16.4 The spike on the right end of the histogram indicates a lack of highlight detail.

NOTES

The Exposure Compensation setting on your camera has no effect when shooting in Manual mode (where you pick both the Aperture and Shutter Speed being used). When shooting manually, you'll have to adjust the exposure by changing the Aperture or Shutter Speed setting, which will change the amount of light being captured (to help prevent spikes on the ends of the histogram).

▶ Most color correction techniques rely on being able to measure the color that appears in the brightest and darkest areas of an image. If those areas are black or white to begin with, the color correction techniques will be largely ineffective.

▶ The eye is drawn to solid white areas, which should usually be reserved for light sources and reflections of those light sources on shiny objects.

Let's look at an example of how I use the histogram to ensure that I don't lose detail in the brightest or darkest areas of an image. After taking an initial exposure of a scene, I'll review the in-camera histogram to see if a spike appears on either end. If a spike appears on the right edge of the histogram (**Figures 16.5** and **16.6**), that means the image is so bright that the highlights are solid white. In an attempt to avoid losing detail, I'd adjust the Exposure Compensation setting to -1 to capture one stop less light and take a second shot. If the histogram for the second image still has a spike (**Figures 16.7** and **16.8**), I'll adjust the Exposure Compensation setting to -2 to capture even less light and take a third shot. I'd continue to adjust the exposure and take more shots until I end up with an image that does not have a spike on the end of the histogram (**Figures 16.9** and **16.10**). If the spike were on the left side of the histogram, I would have used a positive Exposure Compensation setting on the camera to correct the problem.

If you run into a situation where you end up with a spike on one end of the histogram regardless of which Exposure Compensation setting is used, the scene you are attempting to photograph has a brightness range that is beyond that which your camera is capable of capturing in a single shot (**Figure 16.11**). When that's the case, you'll have to either choose between losing highlight or losing shadow detail, or take two exposures and combine them in Photoshop to create a hybrid image that has both shadow and highlight detail.

Figure 16.5 Using the default exposure caused the highlights to have no detail. (©2007 Ben Willmore)

Figure 16.7 Using a -1 exposure compensation setting was not enough to regain highlight detail.

Figure 16.9 Using a -2 exposure compensation setting produced an image with full highlight detail.

Figure 16.6 The spike on the right side indicates lost highlight detail.

Figure 16.8 The second exposure also lacks highlight detail.

Figure 16.10 The third exposure has full highlight and shadow detail.

Scanners

When using a scanner to digitize an image, it is equally important that you maintain shadow and highlight detail. Many scanners offer a histogram that will indicate if shadow or highlight detail has been lost. The features used to adjust the scan will vary from manufacturer to manufacturer, so you'll have to experiment with the features offered in the software that came with your scanner to determine which one will affect shadow and highlight detail. Some scanners are better than others at capturing shadow detail. The darkest shade the scanner can capture detail in without forcing an area to black is known as its D-Max. The higher the D-Max of your scanner, the deeper it can peer into the shadows of an image and still retain detail. So, if you notice that your scanner has trouble capturing shadow detail, you might want to shop for a new scanner that features a higher D-Max specification.

Figure 16.11 This histogram indicates a lack in both shadow and highlight detail.

When scanning an image, consider the following:

▶ Enlarging an image will require more information than reproducing it at its original size. When scanning a small original (like a 35mm slide), be sure to enter a percentage in the Scale field of your scanning software to indicate how much larger you plan to reproduce the image. If your scanning software doesn't offer a scale setting, just multiply the desired resolution by the percentage you want to enlarge the image and use the result as your scanning resolution. I always scan images for the largest size at which I'd ever consider reproducing them because I can always scale them down in Photoshop. No matter how many tricks you try to pull, scaling up an image in Photoshop always makes it look soft, so try to avoid that.

▶ If there's a possibility that the image will be cropped, I'll scan it at a size larger than it might be reproduced to make sure I have enough detail after the image is cropped.

▶ If the image will be used for multiple purposes (the Web, newspaper, and my desktop printer for instance), I'll scan it for the largest size and the output device that demands the highest image resolution.

▶ If the original image is color, but it will be reproduced as a grayscale image, I'll still scan it in color because then I can use the techniques from Chapter 9, "Color Manipulation," to achieve the highest quality grayscale conversion possible.

▶ Some scanners offer the choice of loading an 8- or 16-bit image into Photoshop (also known as 24- or 48-bit color). I talked about the differences between 8- and 16-bit images back in Chapter 8, "Using Camera Raw," and as with the Camera Raw dialog box, the controls in your scanner software operate on the full 16-bits of information. If you've decided to work with 8-bit images as I do, you'll get the highest quality if you adjust your images within the scanning software to get the best looking image before opening it in Photoshop (because all the scanner controls operate on 16-bits of data).

Step 2—Initial Rough Crop & Straighten

The first thing I do after opening an image is to crop, rotate, and straighten it. If the image was captured sideways, I'll rotate it while viewing the thumbnail image in Bridge since it has Rotate Right and Rotate Left icons that make rotation a breeze. Once the image is sitting upright in Photoshop, I'll make sure that any horizontal or vertical lines are perfectly level. To accomplish that, I click and hold on the Eyedropper tool in the Tools palette and choose the Measure tool (which looks like a ruler). With that tool active, I'll click and drag across any straight edge that should be perfectly horizontal or vertical (like a horizon or the side of a building) and then choose Image > Rotate Canvas > Arbitrary and use the default setting (which will be based on the angle of the line you drew with the Measure tool) (**Figures 16.12** and **16.13**). Next, I'll do an initial crop to discard any areas that I'm sure I won't need in the final image. Everything at this stage of the workflow was done for the following reasons:

Figure 16.12 Draw a line with the Measure tool to indicate a feature that should be horizontal. (©2007 Ben Willmore)

Figure 16.13 Result of rotating the image based on the Measurement tool's line drawn in Figure 16.12.

► There is no need to retouch or adjust areas that will not appear in your final image, so it's best to get rid of those areas now so you don't waste time making them look their best.

► It's ideal to have a straight image before text and other elements are added because straightening the image later might make those elements crooked, unless you're particularly careful with the methods you use.

► Color correction and other techniques optimize the contrast of an image by making the brightest area of the image close to white and the darkest area close to black. If the image is optimized before it is cropped, areas that might be discarded (through later cropping) will influence how much contrast is added to the whole image, even though they won't be seen in the end result. It's also important to remove any black or white borders from your image if you plan to apply any automated color correction or contrast adjustments since they can also throw off your results.

► Cropping the image now will allow Photoshop to run faster since it will have less information to process, which is more noticeable when you're working with very large file sizes.

At this stage, the idea is to get rid of elements that you are absolutely sure you don't need. At a later stage, you can perform a more precise crop.

This is also the stage at which you can attempt to correct distortion in the image by applying the Lens Correction filter. Just make sure you duplicate the original image layer first so you're never stuck with the end result of your lens correction.

Step 3—Spotting

At this point, I take a quick tour of my image and remove tiny scratches, specks, dust or other small defects that might cause problems down the road (this is commonly known as spotting) (**Figure 16.14**). This step does not have to be performed at this stage, but it should be complete before localized adjustments are made for the same reason that you should remove noise before that stage, which I'll talk about a little later in this chapter.

Figure 16.14 This image has small specks and scratches. (©2007 Andy Katz)

To perform spotting, zoom in to 100% magnification (by double-clicking the Zoom tool) and look for any tiny defects in the image, and fix them with the Spot Healing brush (which you can read about in Chapter 15, "Retouching"). To make sure that you inspect the entire image, press the Home key (available on most extended keyboards) to get to the upper-left corner of the image. Then use the Page Up and Page Down keys to move one full screen up or down (add Shift to move less than one full screen). Adding Command/Ctrl to the Page Up and Page Down keys will move you one full screen to the right or left.

Step 4—Color Correction

Color correction is the first adjustment I apply because it relies on being able to measure the color from the original, unadulterated image. (Learn how to color correct in Chapter 7, "Color Correction.") Any color or tonal adjustments that are applied before color correction is performed can only make the results of the correction less effective. Performing color correction will also change the contrast of the image, so it makes sense to do it before trying to adjust the overall contrast of the image (**Figures 16.15** and **16.16**).

I find that many people only color correct images that have an obvious need for it (images that look overly orange, blue, or yellow, for example). I perform color correction on 90% of the images I work with because you never know how much of an improvement is possible until you adjust the image. There have been many instances when I thought an image looked fine when it was first opened, but when I ran it through color correction, I was amazed at how much the image improved. Also, when performing color correction using the Eyedropper tools in Levels or Curves, always try all three eyedroppers instead of guessing at which ones you think the image might benefit from. I see far too many people relying on the middle eyedropper alone when their images could be vastly improved if they were to use all three eyedroppers.

I almost always use an adjustment layer (see Chapter 10 for more on adjustment layers) for my color correction so that I can preserve the original image. When I'm done with the correction, I'll click the eyeball icon for the adjustment layer in the Layers palette to compare the original image to the color corrected version. If I notice an undesirable contrast change (which might cause important shadow detail to become more difficult to see, for example), I'll set the Blending Mode pop-up menu at the top of the Layers palette to Color, which will prevent the adjustment from altering the brightness or contrast of the original image (**Figures 16.17** through **16.19**).

Figure 16.15 Images often look acceptable when you first open them. (©2007 Ben Willmore)

Figure 16.16 Color correction can improve the vast majority of images.

Figure 16.17 Original noncorrected image. (©2007 Ben Willmore)

Figure 16.18 Color correction using Normal Blending mode.

Figure 16.19 Color correction using Color Blending mode.

If I plan to use a color original as a grayscale image, then this is the stage at which I would convert the image to grayscale (using the techniques from Chapter 9, "Color Manipulation"), because a color corrected image produces more brightness separation between areas of differing color.

Step 5—Global Tonal Adjustments

Figure 16.20 This color corrected image is a bit dark. (©2007 Ben Willmore)

Figure 16.21 A Curves adjustment layer was used to adjust the tonality of this image.

Once the image has been color corrected, I can start thinking about the overall brightness and contrast (also known as tonality) (**Figures 16.20** and **16.21**). Before doing additional color adjustments, I adjust the tonality of the image with Curves (see Chapter 5) because darkening the image will often make the image more colorful, and adding contrast or brightening the image will often expose color problems that I might not have noticed before adjusting the tonality. At this point I work on the entire image because many problems that first appear to need a localized adjustment can often be fixed using a global adjustment, which saves me from having to spend the time to isolate areas of the image with a selection or mask.

I use a Curves adjustment layer to adjust the tonality of the image and once I'm done, I'll toggle the visibility of that adjustment layer to see how it affects the color of the image. If that the image is becoming too colorful or is shifting in an undesirable way, I'll change the Blending Mode pop-up menu at the top of the Layers palette to Luminosity to prevent the adjustment from affecting the colors in the image (**Figures 16.22** through **16.24**).

Figure 16.22 Image before tonal adjustment. (©2007 Ben Willmore)

Figure 16.23 Tonal adjustment using Normal Blending mode.

Figure 16.24 Tonal adjustment using Luminosity Blending mode.

Step 6—Global Color Adjustment

At this point, any color casts that plagued the image should be gone and the overall brightness and contrast should look okay, which will make it much easier to evaluate the color in the image. The colors in an image will often look rather flat and lifeless at this stage, so I'll add a Hue/Saturation adjustment layer and boost the Saturation until the colors come alive (**Figures 16.25** and **16.26**). If you intend to print the image, you'll have to be careful that the colors in the image don't become more colorful than what your printer is capable of reproducing. When that happens, your printed results will look less vibrant than what was seen onscreen and some color might shift (such as vivid blues becoming dark purple). If your final output will be a print of some sort, I'd review Chapter 6, "Color Management," to figure out how to set up the Proof Colors command (View > Proof Colors) so that you can preview what the image will look like when it's printed and turn on that command anytime you're adjusting the color of the image (especially when increasing saturation). This is also when I'd consider changing the overall feeling of the image to make it appear a little warmer (by shifting the colors toward red, orange, or yellow) or cooler (by shifting the colors toward blue or green). That is occasionally needed to prevent an image from appearing

Figure 16.25 Image before adjusting saturuation. (©2007 Ben Willmore)

Figure 16.26 Image after increasing saturation.

Figure 16.27 Color corrected image. (©2007 Ben Willmore)

Figure 16.28 The overall color has been shifted toward blue and red.

too sterile or to add a little personality to the image (**Figures 16.27** and **16.28**). Shifting the color feeling of the image can be done using a Curves adjustment layer and adjusting the individual color channels using the pop-up menu at the top of the Curves dialog box (as described in Chapter 9, "Color Manipulation").

This step (and the two other color related steps) can obviously be skipped if you end up converting your image to grayscale after performing color correction.

Step 7—Reduce or Remove Noise/Grain

This step might seem a little out of place in the middle of a bunch of adjustments, but the next few steps that come after this one involve isolating and adjusting specific areas of the image. I often rely on the tools from Chapter 13, "Advanced Masking" to isolate areas, and if you use those techniques on an overly noisy/grainy image, the grain has the potential of becoming incorporated into the mask that's used to isolate an area (**Figure 16.29**). If you attempt to reduce or eliminate the noise at a later stage, you might remove it from the image itself (Background layer), but it might also be ingrained (nice pun, huh) in the masks that are attached to some of the adjustment layers (used to isolate and adjust particular areas of the image), all of which makes it more difficult to deal with later. So why not work on the noise issue earlier in the workflow? Because many images are overly dark and lack contrast, which not only makes it difficult to evaluate how much noise is infecting your image, but hard to tell when the noise has been completely removed. If there is little or no noticeable noise, skip this step because noise removal techniques (as described in Chapter 11 "Sharpening") will soften your image.

Figure 16.29 This Layer Mask picked up grain from the image when an automated selection technique was used.

Step 8—Local Tonal Adjustments

With the image relatively noise-free, we can start to isolate particular areas and fine-tune the brightness and contrast of objects (**Figures 16.30** and **16.31**). This is when I'll isolate an area by making a selection and use Curves to do its magic on any areas that I was unable to fix when I performed the global tonal adjustment. It might be to brighten someone's face that was in the shade or to darken a background to make it less distracting. The range of possibilities is truly endless, and each person will have a different vision for what the image should look like, so there is no pre-set method for choosing areas that should be adjusted.

Step 9—Fine-Tune Localized Colors

It's always easier to evaluate color once the brightness of an area has been adjusted. So, at this stage, I'll start to isolate and adjust the individual colors in the image. The most common use for this type of an adjustment is to fine-tune skin tones since they don't always look perfect after performing color correction. To learn more about this type of adjustment, check out Chapter 9, "Color Manipulation."

Step 10—Interpret Colors

This step and the previous one might sound very similar, but the approach used and the potential results are quite different. In this case we'll apply a Hue/Saturation adjustment layer and isolate different colors by choosing a color from the Edit pop-up menu at the top of the dialog box (as described in Chapter 9, "Color Manipulation"). This is performed after the last step because this one has the potential to really mess with the colors in unusual ways, and it would make straightforward color adjustments (like the ones in the previous step) more difficult. This is when you can quickly isolate particular colors (no selection or mask needed for most areas) and quickly interpret the colors (like making a blue sky darker and more intensely blue, or making grass and trees more green) (**Figures 16.32** and **16.33**). It's only after making an adjustment with Hue/Saturation that I'd think about painting on the mask that's attached to the adjustment layer because most of the

Figure 16.30 Before localized tonal adjustments. (©2007 Ben Willmore)

Figure 16.31 The rocks were darkened and the goats were brightened with localized tonal adjustments.

Figure 16.32 Unadjusted color. (©2007 Ben Willmore)

Figure 16.33 After interpreting the colors using a Hue/Saturation adjustment layer.

isolating can be done right in the Hue/Saturation dialog box, so taking the time to select colors ahead of time might be a waste of time.

Step 11—Double & Triple Check Masks

If you've used any Layer Masks to isolate and adjust areas, it's time to double-check your work before you start retouching your image; otherwise, you might try to retouch defects caused by problems in the masks.

Figure 16.34 Viewing the mask as a color overlay.

First, check that the mask on each layer is really isolating the area or object you intend to work on. You can do that by clicking on one of the adjustment layers and pressing the backslash key (\) to view the mask as a color overlay (**Figure 16.34**). Your job is to then evaluate how closely the color overlay matches up with the object or area you were attempting to adjust. If you find any areas that don't match up, paint with black or white to modify the mask until it closely matches the area you were attempting to isolate.

Figure 16.35 Viewing the mask directly.

Then, before moving on, type backslash again to turn off the color overlay because this time we're going to view the mask directly by holding Option/Alt and clicking directly on the Layer Mask that is attached to the active adjustment layer (**Figure 16.35**). That will cause the contents of the mask to fill the main image window where you should be able to easily spot problems such as gaps between paint strokes, jaggy edges (where crude tools were used, such as the Magic Wand), or noise, if you deviated from this work-flow. To fix the defects, paint with black or white on the mask until no obvious problems are present. When you're done, Option/Alt-click on the Layer Mask a second time to get back to viewing your image.

Step 12—Retouching

Now that the image is in pristine shape color and tone-wise, it's time to start fixing problems with the Background image on which all of our adjustments are based. At this stage, those adjustment layers are both a blessing and a curse. On the one hand, they make the colors look good and produce a nice bright image that makes it easy to find any defects that are candidates for retouching (which is why we waited until now to think about retouching). On the other hand, if we're not careful, those adjustments are going to end up being applied twice, which would really mess up our image. Let's explore why this happens and how we can work around it.

These days many people are practicing what's known as nondestructive imaging (including me), which calls for preserving the original image at all costs and keeping all changes isolated on separate layers. That makes future changes very easy to manage. For tasks that involve retouching, that usually means creating a new, empty layer and using retouching tools that offer the Sample All Layers check box in the options bar. That check box causes the retouching tools to copy from a merged version of all the layers (in other words, it's like flattening all the layers together and using that as the source) and depositing the retouching onto whichever layer is active. That works fine as long as you don't have any adjustment layers in your document, but at the stage we're at now, it's going to give us trouble. Here's why.

Placing the empty, retouching layer on top of the layers stack will cause a problem if you later want to modify one of the adjustment layers that are in your image. Modifying an adjustment layer will not affect the layer that contains the retouching because it is positioned above all the adjustment layers and adjustment layers only affect the layers that appear below them in the Layers palette. That will cause the retouched area to no longer match the brightness or color of the rest of the image (**Figures 16.36** through **16.38**). If you place the retouching layer just above the original image near the bottom of the Layers palette, the retouching tools will copy from a merged version of the image (due to the Sample All Layers setting), which will include the adjustments, and the result will be applied to a layer that is near the bottom of the layers stack. That puts it below all the adjustment layers, which will cause those adjustments to be applied twice.

Figure 16.36 This image has been adjusted using multiple adjustment layers. (©2007 Ben Willmore)

Figure 16.37 Small areas have been retouched using the Sample All Layers check box on an empty layer at the top of the layers stack.

Figure 16.38 Turning off an adjustment layer causes the retouched areas to no longer match the surrounding areas.

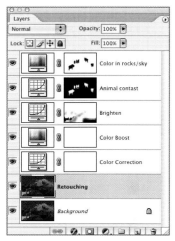

Figure 16.39 Retouching on a duplicate of the original Background image with the Sample All Layers check box turned off.

There are three possible solutions to this problem: Your first choice is to turn off the eyeball icons for all adjustment layers to prevent them from affecting the retouching, then turn them back on once retouching is complete. The problem with this approach is that those adjustment layers often help to reveal problems in your image and make it easier to determine if your retouching is really blending into the surrounding image. The second solution is to duplicate the original image layer (most likely the Background image), turn off the Sample All Layers check box (so the retouching tools only pay attention to the active layer), and then retouch the duplicate layer (**Figure 16.39**). This approach works fine regardless of the state of the adjustment layers (they can be turned on or off), but it does increase your file size since you have a complete duplicate of the original image layer. The third and best solution (in CS3) is to make a new blank layer—for retouching—above the background layer. Two of the retouching tools, the Healing Brush and Clone Stamp tool, have a new sample option called Current and Below. Using this sample option prevents the dreaded double adjustment from adjustment layers above, yet provides the benefits of having all the retouching on its own layer.

Retouching is essential at this point because the next step is going to be to really mess with the image by applying creative effects. Those effects have the potential to blend any unretouched defects into the image, which can make it much more difficult to correct the defects.

Step 13—Creative Effects

Now that we have an immaculate, perfectly adjusted image, the sky is the limit as far as where you can take it with creative techniques. You can combine images into an interesting collage, use Blending modes to create special effects, and apply filters to distort or stylize the image. Since we covered those ideas in the last few chapters, I'm not going to talk about any specific techniques but will instead talk about some of the challenges you might encounter.

If you have been working with a 16-bit image, you'll find that there are a large number of filters that are not available to your image. When that's the case, you should keep in mind that 8-bits is all that's needed to display or print an image at the highest quality possible on most output devices, and that the extra information that comes from a 16-bit image is mainly useful when performing adjustments. At this stage in our workflow, we're done applying adjustments, and we no longer need to be working with a 16-bit file, so you can convert to 8-bit mode (via the Image > Mode menu) before applying a filter. But, before you convert any images to 8-bit mode, you should always flatten your image. Why? Because if you don't, the adjustment layers in your image will be recalculated on the 8-bit image and you'll lose all benefits of working with a 16-bit file in the first place. However, if you flatten the image, all those adjustments will be applied while the image is still in 16-bit mode and you will therefore maintain the highest quality results. I don't usually work with 16-bit images because I don't like to flatten my image at this point and find that 8-bit files produce quite satisfactory results.

Step 14—Save Master File

At this stage, I consider the image to be just about done. The only thing that is left is to organize and clean up the Layers palette view of the image and then save the image. This is when I'll start to look through the Layers palette and throw away any layers that don't contribute to the end result I've obtained. If there are any hidden layers that I don't want to trash, I'll apply color coding to them so I can easily tell which layers should be visible (so I don't accidently turn on a layer that shouldn't be seen in the end result). I'll also go through and name each of the layers so I can tell how they contribute to the image. You never know when you might have to return to the document and make changes (possibly years later when you've forgotten all about how the image was made). I also try to simplify the Layers palette view by grouping layers into folders or Smart Objects (**Figures 16.40** and **16.41**). I'll also reevaluate the initial cropping I applied near the beginning of this workflow to see if I need to crop out additional areas.

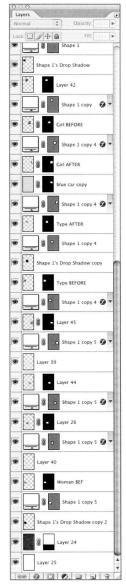

Figure 16.40 Returning to work on a complex document months later can be quite a headache if you don't name and organize your layers.

Figure 16.41 After organizing the layers, it's easy to tell where each element is located.

Figure 16.42 This image was sharpened using the Unsharp Mask filter (©2007 iStockphoto.com/mevans).

Figure 16.43 The Fade command was used to prevent color shifts.

Now that all essential work is done on the image, I'll save the layered image in Photoshop file format so it will retain all the layers, channels, styles, and other effects that were used to create the image, which makes for easy editing at a later date. I use Photoshop file format (also known as a .PSD file) so I can easily tell which files on my hard drive contain layers and which ones don't by just looking at the file extension. This is also the file that I archive for this project because it contains everything that was needed to create the final image. I consider this .PSD file my master file.

Step 15—Create Output-Specific Files

Now that the image is completely finished, I'll think about creating derivatives of the image to be used for specific purposes. Regardless of how the image will be used, I choose Layer > Flatten at this point since the layers are saved in the master file and I don't plan on making any more changes to the image. If the image will be reproduced on a printing press, the next step would be to convert the image to CMYK mode by choosing Image > Mode > CMYK Color. Next, I'd scale the image to the final size at which it will be printed and set the resolution by choosing Image > Image Size. Only after scaling it would I sharpen the image. The reason I wait until now to sharpen the image is because each output device requires a different amount of sharpening to produce the best results, so I don't want to apply generic sharpening to the master file since it might be used for multiple purposes. If I notice color shifts on the edge of objects due to the sharpening setting used, I'll choose Edit > Fade and set the Mode pop-up menu to Luminosity to prevent any color shifts (**Figures 16.42** and **16.43**).

At this point I can either save or print the image. The settings found in the Print with Preview dialog box were covered back in Chapter 6, "Color Management," so I'm not going to cover them here. If the image will be sent to someone else, I'll save the flattened, scaled, and sharpened image as a TIFF file. TIFF is a pretty universal file format that is used for high-quality printing.

If the image will be emailed, or displayed on the Internet, I'll have to be careful; otherwise, the colors could look quite different than what I'm seeing on my screen. Web browsers and other simple programs usually make the assumption that your images are in sRGB color space. If they aren't, the colors will shift when they image is displayed. To avoid that problem, choose Edit > Convert to Profile, set the Destination pop-up menu to sRGB and click OK before saving the image using the File > Save for Web command (**Figure 16.44**).

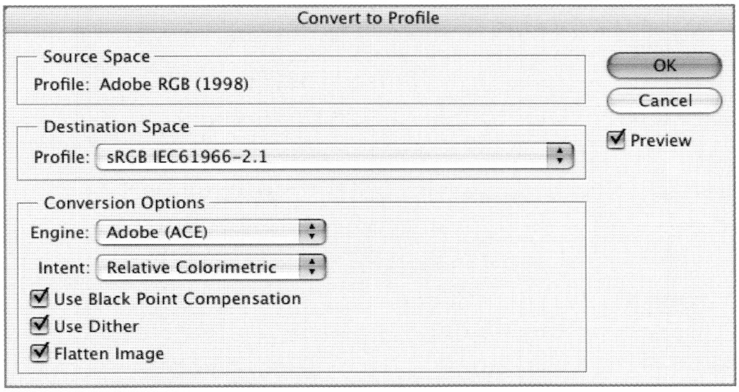

Figure 16.44 Images bound for the Internet should be converted to sRGB.

By using these file-specific formats, I can easily discern which images have been prepared for printing (TIFF files), which are for the Internet or email (JPEG files), and which are the master Photoshop files that contain all the layers used to create the image (PSD files). The master PSD file is the only file that I'm overly careful with because I can always use the PSD file to create a new JPEG or TIFF file. In fact, I usually throw away the TIFF and JPEG files once I've sent them to their desired recipient unless I'm pretty sure I'll need to use the image for the same purpose again.

Closing Thoughts

It might have taken a bit of time to work through this chapter, but once you've adopted your own personal workflow strategy, it really doesn't take any extra time to incorporate it into your Photoshop projects. In fact, it will ultimately save you time because good workflow is really the best prevention against problem images. What I've given you here is my personal workflow, which I like to think of as a 15-step program to healthier Photoshop files. It is based on the work that I do. You're welcome to deviate from it, but make sure you're doing so for the right reasons. Here is a snapshot of the steps:

Ben's 15-Step Program to Healthier Photoshop Files

Step 1—Image Capture

Step 2—Initial Rough Crop & Straighten

Step 3—Spotting

Step 4—Color Correction

Step 5—Global Tonal Adjustments

Step 6—Global Color Adjustment

Step 7—Reduce or Remove Noise/Grain

Step 8—Local Tonal Adjustments

Step 9—Fine-Tune Localized Color

Step 10—Interpret Colors

Step 11—Double & Triple Check Masks

Step 12—Retouching

Step 13—Creative Effects

Step 14—Save Master File

Step 15—Create Output-Specific Files

Just remember, you don't have to go through all the steps, but the more you do, the better your images will look. By reading this chapter, I hope you can see how all the features you've learned about in this book can really complement each other, and that when they are working together in harmony, the results can not only be awesome, but dependable!

Keep in Touch

I'd like to invite you to stay in touch with me by visiting my blog or my website:

At **DigitalMastery.com** (**Figure 16.45**) you'll find my seminar/conference schedule, books and DVDs, as well a bunch of free resources including my magazine articles, tips and tutorials.

At **WhereisBen.com** (**Figure 16.46**) you'll find my travel diary (destinations range from Dubai, Russia, and Iceland to places as obscure as Kerrville, Texas), my latest photos, more magazine articles, radio interviews, favorite websites and gadgets, and just about anything I find interesting.

I encourage you to visit my sites, and I'd love to see you at one my events, or hear from you if you have something to say that you feel would make this a better book. Just write to me at book@digitalmastery.com, or throw something (preferably soft) at me when you see me at Photoshop-World or at one of my seminars to get my attention.

My hope is that this book will help you feel like you're in control of Photoshop, instead of the other way around, and that you are able to spend more time enjoying and savoring your work, instead of feeling like you're struggling against the great unknown. Anyone can learn Photoshop; whether you're a fledging hobbyist working on your family album, or a seasoned professional sweating the next deadline, all it takes is some patience, a little bit of faith, and a true desire to learn this amazing program. And never forget the words of the great Gordon MacKenzie, "Orville Wright did not have a pilot's license."

Figure 16.45 Go to DigitalMastery. com for Ben's seminar schedule, magazine articles, and more.

Figure 16.46 Go to WhereIsBen.com to see Ben's photos and read about his latest adventures on the road.

Numbers

CD-ROM Licensing Agreement:

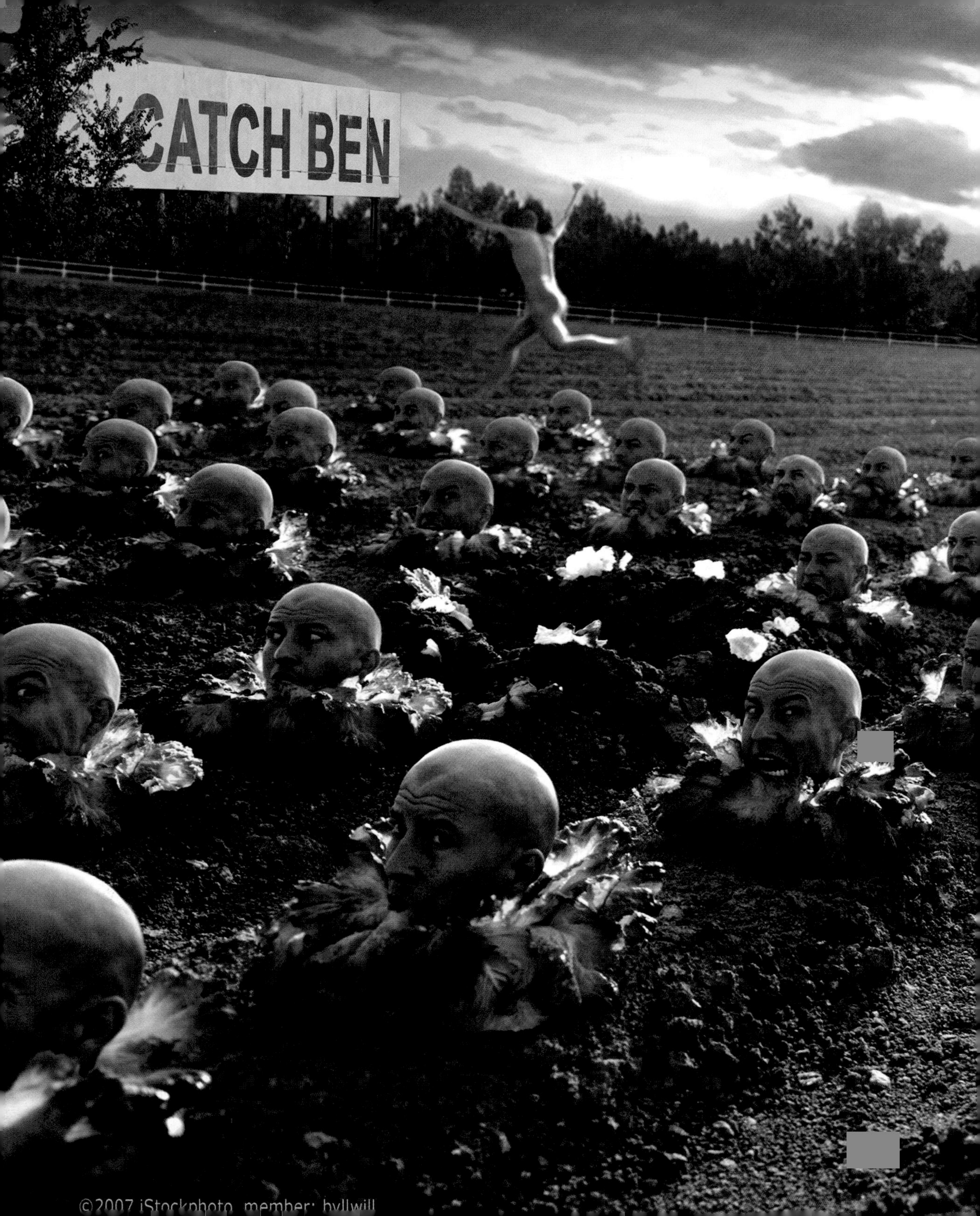
CATCH BEN

AT

DIGITALMASTERY.COM

and get ready to say, "Aha! I finally GET Photoshop!"

iStockphoto®

Our image. Your story.

Royalty-free stock photos,
illustrations and video
starting as low as $1.

Join for free and see.
iStockphoto.com

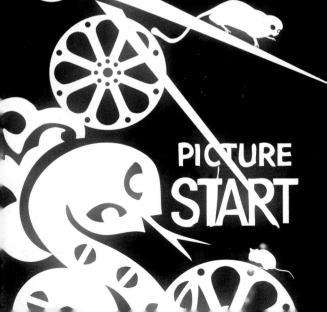

PICTURE
START